NEFESH HACHAIM

NEFESH HACHAIM

First printing — September 2009
Second printing — November 2010

ISBN: 978-1-60763-021-0

Editor: Rabbi R. Shahar
Proofreader: H. Goldsmith
Designer: J. Elliott

THE JUDAICA PRESS, INC.
123 Ditmas Avenue / Brooklyn, NY 11218
718-972-6200 / 800-972-6201
info@judaicapress.com
www.judaicapress.com

Manufactured in the United States of America

נפש החיים

Nefesh Hachaim

Rav Chaim of Volozhin's
classic exploration of the
fundamentals of Jewish belief

TRANSLATED BY
RABBI AVRAHAM YAAKOV FINKEL

קהל נחלת יצחק ד'הומנא

K'HAL NACHLAS YITZCHOK

141-43 73RD AVENUE
KEW GARDENS HILLS, NY 11367

בס"ד

NOACH ISAAC OELBAUM
RABBI
AUTHOR OF SEFORIM
MINCHAS CHEN

י"ד חשון תשס"ז
November 5, 2006

It gives me great pleasure to reiterate, Rabbi Avraham Yaakov Finkel has offered up yet another indispensable literary offering at the table of the Jewish world.

This latest undertaking of translating the "Nefesh Hachaim" of the legendary Reb Chaim Volozhiner, which has been a classic in Jewish literature for many generations spelling out his hashkafos on fundamental Jewish beliefs is a great contribution to the world of Jewish learning.

May the prolific author continue to enrich the Jewish world with his faithful rendition of our illustrious heritage.

With Torah Blessings,

Rabbi Noach Isaac Oelbaum

Rabbi Shmuel Blech

Congregation Anshei Sfard
13th & Madison Ave.
Lakewood, N.J. 08701

Rabbi Avraham Yaakov Finkel, well-known for his talented work, is not in need of my הסכמה. It would be rather presumptuous of me to assume the role of an expert — both in the full and clear understanding of an original work, and the accurate translation thereof in attempting to capture the flavor of its full breadth, depth and broader nuances.

It is, nevertheless, an opportunity to offer humble words of recognition and encouragement — something we all are in need of and benefit from. Rabbi Finkel practices his art with great care and sensitivity, reflective of the noble and well-versed person that he is. The materials that pass through his capable hands carry the indelible mark of a labor of love.

May he be rewarded that his work find favor in the eyes of those who thirst for guidance in the pursuit of Torah *chinuch* and ideals.

בידידות and warmest wishes for success,

Shmuel Blech

אגודת הרבנים דארצות הברית וקנדה

THE UNION OF ORTHODOX RABBIS
OF THE UNITED STATES AND CANADA
235 EAST BROADWAY
NEW YORK, N.Y. 10002

212-964-6337
212-964-6338

ב״ה ד׳ תשרי תשס״ז לפ״ק

הנה בא לפנינו הרב ר׳ אברהם יעקב פינקעל שליט״א והראה לנו שתירגם את הספר ״נפש החיים ״ מהגאון ר׳ חיים זצ״ל אב״ד ור״מ מוולאזין, לשפת אנגלית, דבר השוה לכל. כבר איתמחי גברא הרב פינקעל הנ״ל שתירגם הרבה ספרים כדי שכל אחד יכול ללמוד בספרים אלה.

ידוע שהגאון ר׳ חיים זצ״ל צוה לפני מותו לבנו להזדרז בהדפסת ספר נפש החיים לפני יתר חיבוריו מצד השתוקקתו הגדולה לזכות את הרבים בדבר המועיל ליראת שמים ולאהבת התורה.

תחזקנה ידיו להפיץ מעיינותיו חוצה ולהגדיל תורה ולהאדירה

הכו״ח לכבוד התורה בברכת התורה,

אגודת הרבנים דארצות הברית וקנדה

נאום ________

הרב צבי מאיר גינזבערג

ראש בית דין

Rabbi Avraham Yaakov Finkel today showed me his English translation of the *sefer Nefesh Hachaim* written by the *gaon* Rav Chaim of Volozhin, *zt"l*. This translation is of great benefit for everyone. Rabbi Finkel has gained a reputation by the numerous classic *sefarim* he has translated, making these important works accessible to the English-speaking public.

It is a well-known fact that the *gaon* Rav Chaim Volozhiner, *zt"l*, before his passing, urged his son to do his utmost to have his *sefer Nefesh Hachaim* published before any of his other *sefarim*, since he passionately wished to influence the people with this *sefer* to greater *yiras Shamayim* and intense love of Torah.

I wish Rabbi Finkel success in "spreading his springs outward" and "making the Torah great and glorious."

Signed in honor of the Torah and with blessings of the Torah.
Agudas HaRabbanim of the United States and Canada.

Rabbi Tzvi Meir Ginsberg
Rosh Beis Din

Acknowledgments

I wish to express my profound gratitude to **Hagaon Rav Yisrael Eliyahu Weintraub,** ***shlit"a,*** of B'nei B'rak, author of *Hagahos on Nefesh Hachaim.* After reviewing portions of this translation, Rav Weintraub wrote that he was "pleased with it" and wished me much success.

I also want to extend my heartfelt gratitude to **Rav Aharon Dovid Goldberg,** ***shlit"a,*** of Yeshivas Telshe (Wickliffe, Ohio), author of *Uvacharta Bachaim,* a commentary on *Nefesh Hachaim,* for graciously allowing me—"with great joy"—to translate selections of his highly acclaimed commentary.

I wish to express my sincere thanks to **Aryeh Mezei,** Publisher of Judaica Press, for undertaking and overseeing the publication of this important work.

I am grateful to **Nachum Shapiro**, Managing Editor, for his dedication in piloting this project, turning the manuscript into a beautifully polished book.

Finally, I wish to thank **Rabbi Ravi Shahar** for skillfully editing the manuscript.

Avraham Yaakov Finkel

Contents

Translator's Introduction 19
Biographical Notes 19
Rav Chaim and the Vilna Gaon 20
The Yeshivah of Volozhin 20
Nefesh Hachaim 22
Other works by Rav Chaim Volozhiner 23

GATE ONE 27

Chapter 1
The Image of G-d 29
Chapter 2
Continual Renewal 30
Chapter 3
Man's Actions Have an Impact on the Higher Worlds 31
Chapter 4
Why Did Nevuchadnetzar and Titus Succeed? 33
The Heart Corresponds to the Holy of Holies 35
Man, the Soul of the Universe 36
Chapter 5
The Soul of the Higher Worlds 37
Chapter 6
Virtuous Deeds Affect the Higher Worlds 38
Chapter 7
Hashem Is Your Shadow 39
Chapter 8
The *Keruvim* 40
Combining Torah Study and Worldly Pursuits 41
See How Hashem Loves You! 43
Chapter 9
Faith Can Bring About Miracles 43
Chapter 10
Does Man Outshine the Angels? 45
Chapter 11
The Angels Wait 47

Chapter 12
Repercussions of Man's Actions . . . 48
Reward of the World to Come . . . 49
All Your Actions Are Recorded . . . 49
Sin Is Its Own Punishment . . . 50
Chapter 13
The Impact of Words on the Higher Worlds . . . 51
Consequences of Evil Speech . . . 52
Chapter 14
The Significance of Intention . . . 53
An Apt Analogy . . . 54
Improper Thoughts Cause Damage to the Higher Worlds . . . 55
Action, Speech, Thought . . . 55
Chapter 15
The *Neshamah* . . . 56
Chapter 16
The Sparks of the *Neshamah* . . . 58
Chapter 17
Teshuvah . . . 60
Chapter 18
Kareis . . . 61
Chapter 19
Yaakov's Dream . . . 63
A Parable . . . 64
Chapter 20
Removing a Stain on *Nefesh* . . . 65
Removing Damage to *Ruach* . . . 66
Torah Study Removes the Stain on the *Neshamah* . . . 66
Chapter 21
Torah Study Elevates the Higher Worlds . . . 67
Why the Torah Was Not Given to the Patriarchs . . . 68
Chapter 22
A Word of Warning . . . 69
The Prophet Yeshayah Confronts King Chizkiah . . . 70
Man Cannot Fathom the Rationale of the Mitzvos . . 71
A One-Time Temporary Ruling . . . 71
We Must Observe All the Laws . . . 72

GATE TWO 75

Chapter 1
Praying With Heart and Soul 77

Chapter 2
The Meaning of *Berachah* 78

Chapter 3
The Names of G-d 80
The Formula of the *Berachos* 80

Chapter 4
G-d's Involvement With the World 81

Chapter 5
The Soul Is a Reflection of G-d 82

Chapter 6
Feeding the Universe 84

Chapter 7
Harmful Food 85

Chapter 8
Cause and Effect 86

Chapter 9
Tefillah – Prayer 87

Chapter 10
A Partner of the Creator 87
The Words of Prayer 88
G-d Yearns for the Prayers of *Tzaddikim* 88

Chapter 11
Kavanah – Intention 89
Personal Pleas 90
Praying for Relief of Pain 91

Chapter 12
Agonizing Over the Pain of the *Shechinah* 92
An Analogy 92
Channah's Plea 93
Tefillah In These Times 94

Chapter 13
How to Pray 94
Written with *Ruach Hakodesh* 95
Visualizing the Words 95

Chapter 14
With All Your Soul 96
Spoken Prayer 96
The Next Level of Tefillah 97
Connecting With the Higher World 98
Chapter 15
Each According to His Ability 98
Channah's Tefillah: the Epitome of Prayer 98
Chapter 16
The Three Parts of the Soul 99
Letters - Action - Nefesh 99
Vowel Signs - Speech - Ruach 100
Cantillation Marks - Thought - Neshamah 100
The Highest Level of Tefillah 100
Chapter 17
The Root of the Neshamah 101
Chapter 18
The Ultimate Level 102

GATE THREE **105**

Chapter 1
HaMakom, G-d Is the Place of the World 107
Chapter 2
The World Endures By the Will of Hashem 109
Chapter 3
A Word of Caution 110
Chapter 4
Hashem Fills and Surrounds All Worlds 112
Chapter 5
Hashem Is the Soul of the World 113
Chapter 6
Do Not Delve Into Hidden Things 114

PROLOGUE TO GATE FOUR **117**

Chapter 1
The Bane of Pride 119

Chapter 2
Do Not Disparage Your Fellow 120
Torah Study Equivalent to all Mitzvos 121
Chapter 3
Shelo Lishmah Leads to *Lishmah* 122
A Reassuring Thought 124
Chapter 4
The *Yetzer Hara*'s Deception 124
Doing Mitzvos at the Proper Time 125
Chapter 5
Performing the Mitzvah Is What Counts 127
Prayer Must Be Enunciated 127
Chapter 6
Kavanah Is Not Decisive 128
Chapter 7
Other Deceptions of the Yetzer Hara 128
Chapter 8
Another False Line of Reasoning 130
Summation 131
Conclusion 132

GATE FOUR 133

THE STUDY OF TORAH *LISHMAH*
– FOR ITS OWN SAKE

Chapter 1
Studying *Mussar* at the Expense of Torah 135
An Inversion of Values 136
A Misconception 136
Chapter 2
Torah *Lishmah* Is Not Fervent Devotion 137
Another Proof 138
Chapter 3
Torah for Torah's Sake 139
Chapter 4
Yiras Shamayim, Fear of G-d 140
Chapter 5
The Storehouse of *Yirah* 141

Chapter 6
Connecting With G-d 142
Chapter 7
Fear of G-d Is a Preservative 144
Chapter 8
Storehouse for Torah 145
Chapter 9
The Torah Brings on Yirah 146
Chapter 10
Blueprint of the World 147
Chapter 11
G-d, the Torah, and Yisrael Are One 149
The World Before the Giving of the Torah 150
The Fruits of Torah Study 150
Upholding the World 151
G-d's Friend and Partner 152
Chapter 12
Creating New Torah Insights 152
Chapter 13
G-d's Joy and Delight 153
Chapter 14
As if Standing at Sinai 154
Bringing Goodness to the World 155
Chapter 15
The Power of Torah Learning 156
The Torah Protects From Harm 157
Chapter 16
Relief From Anxieties 158
Exempt from Paying Taxes 158
Chapter 17
Torah Study Saves From Gehinnom 160
Everlasting Life 161
Chapter 18
Untouched by the Forces of Nature 163
He Controls the Forces of Nature 164
Chapter 19
The Torah Comprises the Names of G-d 165

G-d and the Torah Is One . . . 167
G-d Loves Torah Scholars . . . 167

Chapter 20
The Secrets of the Torah Are Revealed to Him . . . 168

Chapter 21
Tzaddikim Are More Powerful After Death . . . 170
The Original Light of Creation . . . 171

Chapter 22
Decline in Torah Study Leads to Disaster . . . 173
"A Time to Act for G-d" . . . 174
When One Becomes Lax in Torah Learning . . . 174
The Book and the Sword . . . 175

Chapter 23
After Death . . . 176
The Fate of One Who Refuses to Learn Torah . . . 177
Abandoned the Torah . . . 178

Chapter 24
The Gravity of His Punishment . . . 179

Chapter 25
Torah Learning Protects the World from Destruction . . . 181
One Man Can Save the World . . . 182

Chapter 26
The Exalted Root of the Torah . . . 183
Prayer Depends on Torah Study . . . 183

Chapter 27
The Gradual Descent of *Kedushah* . . . 184
The Torah Retained Its Heavenly *Kedushah* . . . 185

Chapter 28
Profound Secrets Hidden in the Torah Text . . . 186

Chapter 29
Study And Practice . . . 188
Healing For the Whole Body . . . 189
Like the Fish of the Sea . . . 190

Chapter 30
Superiority of Torah Study . . . 191
Torah Study Without Doing Mitzvos Is Worthless . . . 192

The Torah Confers Everlasting Life 193
Chapter 31
Torah Study Is Like Offering a Sacrifice 194
Torah Learning Brings Forgiveness. 195
Torah Learning is Like a Mikveh. 196
The Torah Makes the Sinner Turn Back 197
Like a Fountain 198
Chapter 32
Torah Learning Brings Joy to All the Worlds 198
Immune to the Blandishments of the *Yetzer Hara* . . 200
A Perfect Remedy. 201
The Torah Guards the Torah Scholar. 201
Like Fish In Water 202
The Torah Is Your Life. 203
Chapter 33
Studying Torah Without Letup. 204
Grasping the Tree of Life. 204
Words of Admonition 205
Chapter 34
A Small-Scale Sanctuary. 206
Torah Study Is Spiritual Food 207
A Concluding Thought 208

INDEX 209
GLOSSARY 217
HEBREW TEXT
OF THE NEFESH HACHAIM . . . . א-קמח

Translator's Introduction

It is with a sense of awe and trepidation that I present this translation of the *Nefesh Hachaim,* for in this work Rav Chaim Volozhiner touches on the most exalted concepts of Torah teachings. His timeless expositions on essential Torah principles reflect his saintly purity and towering greatness. His lofty thoughts open a window on man's relationship with Hashem, focusing on such fundamental Jewish values as Torah study, *tefillah* (prayer), *yiras Shamayim* (fear of G-d) and *kiyum hamitzvos* (fulfilling the mitzvos). As you engross yourself in his words, you sense that he is addressing you directly, speaking to you personally. His innovative insights make your spirit soar, catapulting you to a higher world, stirring you to reach for closer attachment to G-d through intensive Torah study *lishmah,* purely for its own sake.

BIOGRAPHICAL NOTES

Rav Chaim of Volozhin, popularly known as Rav Chaim Volozhiner, was born in 1749 in Volozhin, near Vilna, where his father, a noted Torah scholar, was a prominent communal leader. It was a trying time for the Jewish people. The Jews of eastern Europe, reeling from the twin disasters of the Chmelnicki massacres and the debacle of the false messiah Shabsai Tzvi, were disheartened and bewildered. The prevailing atmosphere of apathy and ignorance caused a sharp decline in Torah scholarship.

RAV CHAIM AND THE VILNA GAON

Rav Chaim Volozhiner was a beacon of light illuminating this dismal scene. As a young man, he studied under Rav Refael Cohen and the eminent Rav Aryeh Leib Ginsburg, better known as the *Shaagas Aryeh*. But the teacher who had the most profound influence on Rav Chaim's character and outlook was the legendary Gaon of Vilna, the greatest Torah scholar of the past two centuries. In the eyes of many Torah authorities, the Vilna Gaon ranks as an equal to the *Rishonim*, early authorities like the *Rambam*, the *Rosh* and the *Rashba*. Deeply awed by the Vilna Gaon's prodigious wisdom and piety, Rav Chaim eagerly absorbed his teachings and emulated his ways. For twenty years he was the Vilna Gaon's faithful and devoted *talmid muvhak* (primary student).

THE YESHIVAH OF VOLOZHIN

On the recommendation of Rav Refael Cohen, Rav Chaim was chosen as *rav* of Volozhin. With wisdom, humility and deep compassion, he led the community, and he soon became the leading Torah authority of Lithuanian and Russian Jewry. After the Vilna Gaon's passing, Rav Chaim was universally recognized as the successor of his great master. But his most enduring contribution to the Jewish people was the restoration of the Torah scholar to his traditional respected status in Jewish life.

To revitalize the lagging state of Torah learning, Rav Chaim Volozhiner founded the Yeshivah of Volozhin in 1802. It was an achievement of historic proportions. Beginning with ten students, the Yeshivah soon flourished, attracting a large number of eager young Torah scholars from far and wide. The Volozhin community and the Jews of the entire region welcomed and supported the Yeshivah, holding it in high esteem and regarding the students as the elite of Klal Yisrael (the Jewish people).

Maintaining a demanding schedule, Rav Chaim introduced his students to the Vilna Gaon's method of penetrating analysis of the Talmudic text with emphasis on the expositions of the *Rishonim,* and above all, insistence on intellectual honesty. This approach to Talmudic study became the model for the present-day major yeshivos, such as Beth Medrash Govoha of Lakewood, New Jersey, the yeshivos of Mir, Telshe, Slobodka, Brisk, Ponevezh, Pressburg, Torah Vodaath, Chaim Berlin, Ner Yisrael, Gateshead and many others. Today the *derech halimmud* (learning style) of the Yeshivah of Volozhin is followed by a mighty legion of tens of thousands of dedicated Torah students in Israel and America, and throughout the world. Thus, Rav Chaim Volozhiner rightfully has earned the title of "father of the yeshivah movement." His fruitful life ended on the 14th of Sivan, 1821.

He was succeeded by his son, Rav Yitzchak Volozhiner. Later, Rav Yitzchak's son-in-law, Rav Naftali Tzvi Yehudah Berlin (the *Netziv*), and Rav Chaim's grandson, Rav Yosef Dov Ber Soloveitchik (the *Beis Halevi*), served as *rashei yeshivah* (heads of the yeshivah). In 1865, Rav Yosef Dov Ber left the Yeshivah to serve as *rav* of Slutzk and later of Brisk. Subsequently, the post of *rosh yeshivah* was held by the famous Rav Chaim Soloveitchik, son of Rav Yosef Dov Ber and grandson of the *Netziv.* In spite of continual harassment by the Russian government, the Yeshivah continued to function. However, in 1892, the *Netziv* closed the Yeshivah rather than bow to government demands to introduce secular studies. Nevertheless, the seed planted by the Volozhin Yeshivah bore abundant fruit in the numerous yeshivos that proceeded from it.

NEFESH HACHAIM

In *Nefesh Hachaim,* Rav Chaim Volozhiner spells out his *hashkafah* (outlook) on fundamental Jewish beliefs, beginning with a discussion of the meaning of *tzelem Elokim* (the image of G-d). Since man is created in the image of G-d, each of his acts — good or evil — has a corresponding effect on the higher spiritual worlds. Thus, every deed has cosmic significance, which certainly is an electrifying idea. In Rav Chaim's words: "This means that the destiny of the countless higher and lower worlds is determined by man's actions."

The ensuing chapters deal with a variety of themes, including *tefillah, berachos,* the nature of the soul, *Olam Haba* (the World to Come), whether or not one should combine Torah study with earning a livelihood, and whether or not man is greater than the angels, to name just a few.

An important segment of *Nefesh Hachaim* is devoted to the overriding importance of studying Torah *lishmah,* solely for its own sake. Rav Chaim repeatedly emphasizes that the existence of the entire universe depends on the uninterrupted study of the Torah by Klal Yisrael, stating, "Should there be a moment when no one in the world is studying Torah, the entire universe and all the higher worlds instantly would revert to primordial nothingness." Torah study is the fulfillment of Hashem's purpose of creating the world, lighting up all the worlds with spiritual joy. Only when learning Torah is a Jew truly alive.

Rav Chaim sums up this idea in a beautiful analogy: "It says, '*[The Torah] is a tree of life to those who grasp her*' (Mishlei 3:18). Imagine that you were swept away in a raging river, and suddenly you see in front of you an overhanging tree. You would surely strain with all your might to grab hold of it, and not let go of it even for second, for releasing your grip means certain death! In the same way, the Torah is called the 'tree of life.' By holding on to it lovingly and learning it continually, you truly live a higher form of life. You are bound and tied, as it were, to G-d, because G-d and the Torah are One."

OTHER WORKS BY RAV CHAIM VOLOZHINER

In addition to the *Nefesh Hachaim,* Rav Chaim wrote a commentary on *Pirkei Avos* entitled *Ruach Chaim.* He also authored an introduction to the Vilna Gaon's commentary on *Sifra Ditzniusa,* one of the most esoteric parts of the Zohar, and he wrote a large number of responsa. Most of these were destroyed in the fire that ravaged Volozhin in 1815; only 251 responsa survived and were published under the title *Chut Hameshulash.*

I used the new edition of *Nefesh Hachaim* with the illuminating commentary *Uvacharta Bachaim* by Rav Aharon Dovid Goldberg (Yeshivas Telz, Wickliffe, Ohio, 5757/1997), with the express permission of the author. The commentary *Uvacharta Bachaim* bears the *haskamah* (approbation) of the eminent *gaon* Rav Yisrael Eliyahu Weintraub of B'nei B'rak, and includes a number of textual notes by Rav Weintraub.

Please note: The sections of *Nefesh Hachaim* dealing with Kabbalistic subjects have been omitted, as the subject matter is not suitable for translation.

It is my hope that the words of *Nefesh Hachaim* will bring about a deeper commitment to Torah study and the observance of mitzvos, so that we may merit to see the fulfillment of the verse, *"All your children will be students of Hashem, and your children's peace will be abundant"* (Yeshayah 54:13).

Avraham Yaakov Finkel
ELUL 5769

נפש החיים

NEFESH HACHAIM

שער א׳

GATE ONE

THE IMAGE OF G-D

The Torah says, *"G-d created man in His image, in the image of G-d did He create him"* (Bereishis 1:27). It says also, *"For in the image of G-d He made man"* (ibid. 9:6).

While the meaning of "the image of G-d" is one of the loftiest concepts imaginable, we will look at the word "image" the way the early commentators explain it in the verse, *"Let us make man with Our image, after Our likeness"* (ibid. 1:26).

The commentators say that the terms "image [of G-d]" and "likeness [of G-d]" cannot be taken literally, because it says explicitly, *"What likeness can you attribute to Him?"* (Yeshayah 40:18). The phrase "image [of G-d]" means "a semblance of certain aspects [of G-d]," the way [the psalmist compares himself to an owl] when he says, *"I am like a desert owl"* (Tehillim 102:7). He surely did not sprout wings, grow a beak and turn into an owl. He meant to say that his condition was as unstable and precarious as that of a lonely desert owl fluttering from place to place. That is how the early commentators[1] explain the term *demus,* "likeness." Similarly, the word *tzelem,* "image," should not be taken literally, either, for the terms *tzelem* and *demus* are similar in meaning.

---

1 A reference to the *Rambam, Moreh Nevuchim,* chapter 1, "The Meaning of *Demus.*"

CONTINUAL RENEWAL

Why did the Torah choose the name *Elokim,* in the phrase *b'tzelem Elokim,* "in the image of G-d," as opposed to a different Divine Name [like *E-l* or *Sha-ddai*]? Because the name *Elokim* signifies "the All-Powerful G-d," which correctly expresses the difference between the norms of mortal man and the norms of the Holy One, blessed be He. For example: One who builds a wooden house does not create the wood. He buys ready-made beams and boards and uses them to put up the house. When the house is finished, he puts it out of his mind and moves on to the next job. Of course, the house he built remains standing. Not so, Hashem *Yisbarach.* With His infinite power, He created the universe out of nothing. And ever since Creation, the universe exists only by virtue of the fact that He continually bestows an abundant flow of new [Divine] light on it. If this flow of light were to cease for an instant, the entire universe would revert to nothingness.

The Men of the Great Assembly[2] had this in mind when they formulated the passage [in the Shacharis prayer], *"In His goodness He renews daily, perpetually, the work of creation,"* which is to be understood literally as a renewal at each and every moment. In the same vein it says, "[*Give praise*] *to Him Who makes great lights*" (Tehillim 136:7). Note that it does not say, "Who *made* great lights," but "Who *makes* great lights," [because He does so continually.]

For this reason, G-d is called *Elokim,* "the All-Powerful."

2 The group of 120 Sages who led the Jewish people at the beginning of the Second Beis Hamikdash. They composed the text of the prayers.

For He is the Master of all that exists in that He constantly infuses the forces of nature with the power to function. [They do not act by themselves;] rather, He has the capacity to change or direct nature in accordance with His will.

Chapter 3 | פרק ג'

MAN'S ACTIONS HAVE AN IMPACT ON THE HIGHER WORLDS

Likewise, when G-d created man, He empowered him to control countless forces and worlds, handing them over to him so that he should direct them according to his actions, words or thoughts whether for good or, G-d forbid, for the opposite. With his good deeds, words and thoughts, man sustains and gives energy to countless forces and holy celestial worlds, increasing their holiness and light,[3] as it says, "*I have placed My words in your mouth ... to implant the heavens and to set a foundation for the earth*" (Yeshayah 51:16).[4]

The Sages [express this idea in their commentary on the verse, "*And all your children will be students of Hashem, and your children* (banayich) *will have abundant peace*" (Yeshayah 54:13). They] expound: Do not read *banayich*, "your children,"

3 An analogy: Shaking one end of a long rope causes the other end to move. So, too, man's every action — good or bad — has a corresponding effect in Heaven.

4 By performing mitzvos ("G-d's word"), one makes a salutary impact on the heavenly realm.

but *bonayich*, "your builders."[5] They are builders in the sense that [by doing mitzvos] they exert influence on the Higher Worlds, like a builder who designs a structure and brings it to completion.

Conversely, through man's wrongful actions, words and thoughts, he causes incalculable destruction in the higher worlds, darkening and diminishing the radiance and holiness [of these worlds], reinforcing the source of spiritual impurity, as it says, "*Those who ruin you and destroy you will emerge from your midst*" (Yeshayah 49:17).

This is the underlying sense of the verses, "*G-d created man with His image, in the image of G-d He created him,*" and "*For G-d made man with His own image.*" Just as G-d is *Elokim*, "Master of all Forces" everywhere, guiding and directing them each moment, so it was His will to grant man sovereignty over countless forces and worlds through the way he conducts himself in his actions, words and thoughts at every moment in time.[6] Thus, it is as though man influences the higher worlds, so to speak.

In this connection, the Midrash[7] says: "When Yisrael does the will of G-d they add strength to the Power Above, as it says: '*With G-d we shall succeed*' (Tehillim 60:14). But when

---

5 *Berachos* 64a. As in all cases where the Rabbis use the expression *al tikrei*, "do not read," they do not mean to alter the Masoretic text, but to suggest an additional meaning. Since the word *banayich* already appears in the verse, the repetition of the same word can only be intended to introduce a new idea — that children are also builders.

6 Not only does the Torah one studies and the mitzvos one performs exert an influence on the higher worlds, but every seemingly trivial act has either a positive or negative impact on the higher worlds, because in essence, every action is either a mitzvah or a transgression (*Uvacharta Bachaim*).

7 *Eichah Rabbasi* 1:33.

Yisrael disobeys G-d's will they undermine the Power Above, as it says, '*You weakened* (teshi) *the Rock Who gave birth to you*' (Devarim 32:18)."

The Zohar[8] reiterates this idea, commenting on the verse, "*It happened one day: The angels came to stand before Hashem*" (Iyov 1:6). Says the Zohar: When the accusing angels want to lodge complaints against Yisrael for their improper acts, they have solid grounds, for when Yisrael transgresses, they weaken G-d's strength, but when they act morally, they give strength and power to G-d. With regard to this it says, "*Give might to G-d.*" How so? By behaving virtuously.

Chapter 4 | פרק ד'

WHY DID NEVUCHADNETZAR AND TITUS SUCCEED?

You should never think: "What am I? How can my insignificant actions make a difference to the world?" You should realize and internalize that the things you say or do are not irrelevant, G-d forbid. On the contrary, your actions carry great weight. Every deed you perform has repercussions in the loftiest heights and affects the brilliance of the spiritual lights Above.

By the same token, you should realize with a trembling heart that your missteps cause a devastation [in the higher worlds] that is far greater than the destruction [of the Beis Hamikdash] at the hands of Nevuchadnetzar and Titus.[9] This is because the actions of Nevuchadnetzar and Titus did not cause any

8 At the beginning of *Parashas Bo*.

9 Nevuchadnetzar laid waste the first Beis Hamikdash in 423 BCE; Titus destroyed the second Beis Hamikdash in 69 CE.

damage in Heaven. Since the souls of these fiends were not rooted in the higher worlds, their actions did not affect those worlds at all. [The amount of damage that is caused above is dependent on the soul of the sinner. A small misdeed of a person with a lofty soul causes great damage in Heaven; a serious crime by an inferior soul makes no impact at all above.][10]

Due to our sins, G-d's strength was diminished [so that His attribute of Strict Justice prevailed over His attribute of Forbearance], and that is what gave Nevuchadnetzar and Titus the power to destroy the Beis Hamikdash here on earth. And the earthly Beis Hamikdash is the counterpart of the Beis Hamikdash in Heaven, or, as the Sages put it, "Titus ground up fine flour."[11] [Just as grinding fine flour is a pointless effort, so, too, Titus' destruction of the Beis Hamikdash was a hollow achievement, because G-d wanted the Beis Hamikdash to be destroyed.] So, you see, it was [not Titus, but] our sins that demolished the Beis Hamikdash above. Nevuchadnetzar and Titus destroyed only the Temple on earth [which was already destined to be destroyed because of our sins].

David Hamelech had this in mind when he said, "*[Attacking the gates of the Beis Hamikdash, the enemy] knew that it was as if he were assaulting G-d's Dwelling on High, because the wood [of the gates] swallowed up the axes*" (Tehillim 74:5). David prayed that the enemy would be punished as if he had caused damage Above, although in reality he did not harm [the Dwelling on High] at all.

---

10 *Ramchal, Daas Tevunos* 126.

11 *Sanhedrin* 96b.

THE HEART CORRESPONDS TO THE HOLY OF HOLIES

There is also something else here, which should make one tremble [with awe]. For one's body is a small-scale counterpart of all the forces and worlds in existence, [and which are concentrated in] the heavenly Beis Hamikdash. The heart — the center of the body — corresponds to the [heavenly] Holy of Holies, the seat of the *Shesiah* stone,[12] which is the source of all *kedushah* (holiness). The Sages alluded to this, stating: "If one cannot turn his face toward Yerushalayim [when reciting the Shemoneh Esrei], he should concentrate his thoughts on the Holy of Holies.[13]

The Zohar[14] summarizes this idea, saying: When G-d created man, He fashioned him according to the heavenly model and placed the source of his strength in the center of his body, namely in his heart. The heart directs all parts of the body, and all [limbs and organs] depend on it. [In that respect, the heart parallels] the Sanctuary, which includes the Holy of Holies where the Ark, the Cover and the *Keruvim* rest, and where the *Shechinah* resides. [For the Sanctuary] is the heart of the universe, and from it everything is nurtured.

Therefore, when an indecent thought enters one's mind, he is in effect bringing a harlot into the Holy of Holies of the celestial worlds. He releases forces of impurity that pollute the spiritual worlds; these forces are more corrupt and defiling than the impure demons created by Titus when he brought

12 The Foundation Stone. On this stone, situated in the Holy of Holies, rested the Ark and the Tablets; see *Yoma* 5a. It is the stone on which Yaakov slept when he had the dream of the ladder reaching toward Heaven.

13 *Berachos* 28b.

14 *Parashas Shelach* 161a

a harlot into the Holy of Holies.[15] Similarly, with every sin a person commits, whether out of anger or lust, he is bringing an alien fire[16] into his heart. This is accurately described in the verses, "*The Temple of our holiness and our splendor … has become a fiery conflagration*" (Yeshayah 64:10), and, "*My throne and the place of My footstool, where I will dwell amidst the children of Yisrael forever. The House of Yisrael will no longer defile My holy name with the abominations they committed … Now they will distance their promiscuity … that I may dwell among them forever*" (Yechezkel 43:7).[17]

MAN, THE SOUL OF THE UNIVERSE

In light of this, we can understand the verse, "*G-d formed man out of the dust of the ground and breathed into his nostrils the soul of life. Man [thus] became a living being* (literally, "a living soul") (Bereishis 2:7). Onkelos renders it, "*Man [thus] became a speaking spirit.*" The implication is that before man received his soul, his body was a lifeless mass of dust. When the living soul was breathed into him, he became a living being, with the power to move and to speak.

But note that it does not say, "There came into man (*vayehi ba'adam*) a living soul," but, "Man became (*vayehi ha'adam*) a living soul" [implying that man acts as a soul]. This explains what we stated above, that man, with the soul that was already in him, became the living soul of countless higher spiritual

15 *Gittin* 56b.

16 See Vayikra 10:1.

17 The *Mesillas Yesharim*, ch. 26, explaining the trait of saintliness, writes: A very saintly person like this is considered to be a tabernacle, sanctuary and altar. The Sages said: The righteous are a vehicle of Hashem. What they meant was that the *Shechinah* dwells upon them as it did in the Beis Hamikdash.

worlds. Just as all actions and movements of the body are made possible by the soul within it, so is man the soul and driving force of the countless higher and lower worlds, so that the [destiny of] all the worlds is determined by his [actions].

Chapter 5 | פרק ה'

THE SOUL OF THE HIGHER WORLDS

Regarding G-d's intention for mortal man to have an impact on the higher worlds, we must consider the following:

The Zohar[18] and the writings of the *Arizal* explain the process [of the ten "worlds" that form the channel by which G-d's infinite spiritual light is conveyed to the physical world]. In this chain of ten "worlds," a higher world constitutes the soul of the "body" of the world below it. This higher world, in turn, is the "body" that receives its soul from the world above it, and so on in an upward progression that reaches higher and higher, all the way to Hashem *Yisbarach,* Who is the soul of all the worlds.[19]

Man's station in this process is explained in the Zohar's[20] commentary on the verse, *"Behind and before, You have*

---

18 *Parashas Bereishis* 20a.

19 G-d bestows His spiritual light and life on the world through a series of ten spiritual worlds (also called the ten *sefiros,* emanations, spheres, attributes or vessels), reaching from the Divine Throne down to the physical universe. Beginning at the highest level, each world bestows the Divine light on the world below it, the lower world receiving the flow of spiritual light from the one above it. The Divine light flowing down through the sequence of ten worlds gradually becomes weaker, until it reaches its lowest point in the physical world where the spiritual light is totally obscured. *(Uvacharta Bachaim)*

20 *Parashas Yisro* 70b.

restricted me" (Tehillim 139:5). Man is described as being "*behind,*" because his body was the last to be created during the six days of Creation, but he is also characterized as being "*before,*" because his soul, which is the "breath of G-d's mouth," is rooted in the highest spiritual world, which existed before Creation. For this reason, all the higher worlds are governed by the conduct of man, because when G-d blew the soul of life into man's nostrils, "*Man became a living soul,*" the soul of the higher worlds.

[The remainder of this chapter is omitted, as it deals with profound Kabbalistic concepts.]

Chapter 6 | פרק ו'

VIRTUOUS DEEDS AFFECT THE HIGHER WORLDS

The above needs to be clarified. It is wrong to think that man is literally the soul of the higher worlds in the sense of the soul inhabiting the human body. Whereas the body instantly carries out the commands of its soul (mind), the higher worlds do not instantly react to a deed—good or bad—performed by man.

The matter can be explained as follows: After creating all the spiritual worlds and the entire physical universe, G-d created a marvelous being, namely man, whose physical organs correspond to all the spiritual lights and sublime palaces above that together make up the *shiur komah,* the totality of all spiritual powers and mystical worlds that are figuratively arranged in the form of man.

As the Zohar[21] explains, just as all spiritual powers above have their counterparts in man, so does each mitzvah correspond to a part of the human body. When a person fulfills a mitzvah with one of his limbs, he causes a spiritual reaction in the higher world that corresponds to that limb, either raising it toward its ultimate destiny or increasing its *kedushah*. This *kedushah* then flows back to the limb with which he performed the mitzvah. But the potency of this *kedushah* depends on the mental intent and the purity of thought with which the mitzvah was performed. By fulfilling all mitzvos perfectly, with all their details and with the purest of motives, one rectifies all the higher worlds, and Hashem's glory constantly hovers over him.

On the other hand, abusing a limb through sin causes damage to the higher world that corresponds to that limb. Depending on the gravity of the sin and the status of the corresponding higher world, that world is either totally destroyed or lowered, or its spiritual light dimmed, or, if it is in a very lofty realm, its *kedushah* is slightly diminished. This is what the Sages refer to when they say that each sin blemishes the image of the King.

Chapter 7 | פרק ז'

HASHEM IS YOUR SHADOW

To summarize: Man is the soul of a myriad worlds. How is this to be understood? Just as every motion of one's limbs is activated by his soul, so are the destinies of the spiritual worlds — their continuance or destruction — determined by the actions of man [in observing or transgressing the mitzvos].

21 *Parashas Yisro* 75b; *Tazria* 48a.

Man was given the choice to direct himself and the spiritual worlds on high toward good or evil, and, even if he already sinned and brought destruction to the higher worlds, he has the power to rectify his lapses and repair the ruin he caused, because his soul is the core of all the spiritual worlds and forces.

David Hamelech put it like this, *"G-d is your shadow at your right hand"* (Tehillim 121:5). Just as one's shadow mimics every motion one makes, so does G-d guide the higher worlds according to one's actions.[22] The Zohar[23] explains: If a person smiles, Heaven smiles at him; if he is sad and depressed, Heaven judges him with strictness. And so it says, *'Serve Hashem with gladness'* (Tehillim 100:2), for a joyful person draws down joy from above. Indeed, whatever one does down in this world evokes a similar response from above.

Chapter 8 | פרק ח׳

THE *KERUVIM*

The Gemara in *Bava Basra* 99a asks: How did the *Keruvim*[24] [in the Holy of Holies] stand? R. Yochanan and R. Elazar [disagree on the matter]. One says they faced each other. The other says they faced [forward, toward] the Beis Hamikdash. But according to the one who says that they faced each other, [the Gemara asks]: Doesn't it say [about the *Keruvim* in the

22 For example, if you open your hand to give *tzedakah*, G-d will open His hand and bestow abundance on you (*Uvacharta Bachaim*).

23 *Parashas Tetzaveh* 184b.

24 The *keruvim* (cherubs) had large wings and faces of young children. They were not made separately and then attached to the Cover. Instead, the entire Cover, including the *Keruvim*, were hammered out of one large ingot of gold (*Rashi* to Shemos 25:18).

Beis Hamikdash built by Shlomo that] *"They were facing the Beis Hamikdash"* (II Divrei Hayamim 3:13)? [The Gemara answers:] This is no difficulty: [When they were facing each other,][25] it was a sign that Yisrael was obeying the will of G-d; [when they turned toward the Beis Hamikdash,][26] it was a sign that Yisrael was not obeying the will of Hashem. [The Gemara asks:] According to the one who says that they faced forward toward the Beis Hamikdash, doesn't it say, *"The Keruvim shall face each other"* (Shemos 25:20)? [The Gemara answers:] They were standing at an angle; partially turned toward the Beis Hamikdash and partially facing each other.

[The question arises:] Why did the builders of Shlomo's Beis Hamikdash position the *Keruvim* to partially face the Beis Hamikdash [instead of facing each other directly]?

COMBINING TORAH STUDY AND WORLDLY PURSUITS

For an answer, let us turn to the Gemara in *Berachos* 35b:

It says, *"You will gather in your grain"* (Devarim 11:14). What does the Torah want to teach us [by mentioning the gathering of grain]? Since it says, *"Let not this Book of the Torah cease from your lips"* (Yehoshua 1:8), I might think that this is to be taken literally [and a person is not allowed to do anything but learn Torah]. Thus, it says, *"You will gather in your grain,"* which implies: Combine them (the words of Torah) with a worldly occupation, so says R. Yishmael. R. Shimon bar Yochai disagrees and says: If a person plows in the plowing season, sows

25 As a sign of affection, symbolic of the relationship between G-d and His people.

26 Away from each other, symbolic of the dampened love of G-d for Yisrael.

in the sowing season ... what is to become of the Torah (when will he find time to learn Torah)? Rather, when the Jewish people are doing G-d's will, their work will be done by others. And when the Jewish people are not doing G-d's will, they will have to do their work themselves, as it says, "*And* you *will gather your grain.*"

It is surprising that R. Shimon bar Yochai applies the phrase, "*And you will gather your grain,*" to the time when the Jewish people are not doing G-d's will, when the Torah says expressly that "*You will gather your grain*" applies "*if you are careful to heed My commandments ... and if you love Hashem your G-d and serve Him with all your heart and soul*" (Devarim 11:13).

R. Yishmael [who says that you should combine Torah study with earning a living] surely does not mean that one is allowed to totally give up Torah study for a short time to earn a livelihood, and that during that time he can be oblivious to Torah concepts. What he actually means is that even when one is busy making a living, his mind should be focused on Torah thoughts. He alludes to this when he says [in literal translation], "Conduct yourself *with them* [the words of Torah, while engaged] in a worldly occupation."

Said Abbaye: There were many who did as R. Yishmael [combining Torah study with a worldly occupation] and were successful, and many who tried to emulate R. Shimon bar Yochai [devoting themselves to Torah study exclusively] and were not successful.

The Gemara pointedly says "*many* did like R. Shimon bar Yochai," because surely the masses cannot possibly devote *all* their time to Torah study without doing at least a little work to earn a living. As the Mishnah in *Avos* 2:2 says: "Any Torah study that is not combined with work will ultimately fail."

But according to R. Shimon bar Yochai, anyone who has the means to dedicate himself to Torah and prayer full-time may not lay aside his Torah studies even briefly to engage in business. [Thus, according to him, combining Torah study with work is not the ideal. Therefore, he associates *"gather your grain"* with the time that the Jewish people are going against Hashem's will].

SEE HOW HASHEM LOVES YOU!

We know that one of the *Keruvim* symbolized G-d, and the other symbolized Yisrael. The direction in which the *Keruvim* were facing changed miraculously, reflecting either the love or the estrangement between G-d and Yisrael. When the Jews were totally devoted to G-d, the *Keruvim* were facing each other. If the Jews became somewhat lax, the *Keruvim* turned away slightly from each other. If they veered away from G-d, the *Keruvim* abruptly turned away from each other completely.

The Gemara in *Yoma* 54a says about this: Whenever the people came up to Yerushalayim on the *Yamim Tovim*, the Curtain [in front of the Holy of Holies] would be removed for them, and the *Keruvim* were revealed embracing each other, and they would be told: "See how Hashem loves you!"

Chapter 9 | פרק ט'

FAITH CAN BRING ABOUT MIRACLES

The generation that wandered in the wilderness was nourished by the *manna*, the "bread from Heaven," and the clothing they wore did not wear out, so they did not have to do any work at all to sustain themselves. All agree that a person of that generation could not be considered to be doing G-d's will unless he devoted himself completely to spiritual pursuits, learning Torah day and night without diverting his efforts to making a livelihood. As the Midrash puts it:[27] "The Torah was given to be expounded only by the generation that ate the *manna*." That is why the *Keruvim* in the Mishkan (Tabernacle) were positioned facing each other,[28] indicating that Yisrael was doing *only* G-d's will, without diverting their attention to worldly pursuits.

But in Shlomo's days, the Jewish masses were forced to shift from full-time Torah study to devoting some of their time to earning a livelihood. In R. Yishmael's view, they thereby fulfilled G-d's will, as it says in *Avos* 2:2: "Torah study is good together with an occupation ... Any Torah study that is not combined with work will ultimately fail" — that is, while working, one's thoughts should be focused on Torah themes. Thus, they positioned the *Keruvim* to face each other at a slight angle, in line with their oblique way of doing Hashem's will. Nevertheless, the *Keruvim* displayed love for each other, reflecting G-d's love for us, for the people were really doing His will [in the view of R. Yishmael].

But this still leaves us with the following question: Why was it necessary to position the *Keruvim* at an angle? The *Keruv* symbolizing G-d could have been placed directly face to face.

To understand this we must realize that the way G-d deals with the universe and with us conforms to our conduct. The better we do G-d's will, the more favorably He is inclined toward us. That's why the *Keruv* representing G-d had to be positioned at the same angle as the *Keruv* symbolizing Yisrael.

---

27 *Mechilta, Parashas Beshalach* 17.

28 See Shemos 25:20.

For this reason, at the Parting of the Reed Sea, G-d said to Moshe, *"Why are you crying out to Me? Speak to the children of Yisrael and let them begin to move!"* (Shemos 14:15). In effect, G-d was saying: "[It's not up to Me;] it depends on them! If their faith is strong, and they march fearlessly into the sea in the firm belief that the sea will split, their faith will cause an arousal above to make the miracle happen, and the sea will indeed split."

This idea is alluded to in the verse, *"I have likened you, My beloved [Yisrael], to a horse in Pharaoh's chariots"* (Shir Hashirim 1:9). Normally, the rider of a chariot leads the horse, but in Pharaoh's army, the horses pointed the way to the riders.[29] [G-d is saying:] That is exactly the way I compare you [Yisrael, to a horse of Pharaoh's chariots]. For even though I am a "Rider," namely, *"He who rides upon the highest Heaven"* (Tehillim 68:5), you (Yisrael) lead Me through your actions, for your actions determine the way I deal with the worlds. The same idea is expressed in the verse, *"He (G-d) rides across Heaven with your (Yisrael's) help"* (Devarim 33:26).

Chapter 10 | פרק י׳

DOES MAN OUTSHINE THE ANGELS?

The above will help us understand the difference of opinion among the early authorities as to whether man surpasses the angels, or the angels outrank man. Each of the proponents offers proof from texts in support of his thesis.

In light of our discussion, it is clear that both opinions

29 *Shemos Rabbah* 23; *Shir Hashirim Rabbah* 1:50.

are correct. No doubt, angels rank higher than man, both in essence, holiness and understanding.[30] However, in one aspect, man stands above the angels. Man can influence the higher worlds through his actions, because he is a microcosm of all the worlds. [Through man's virtuous deeds,] the angels, too, are exalted and attain greater *kedushah*. But an angel cannot affect the other worlds, for, unlike man, who is a microcosm of all the other worlds, an angel is only part of his own world. That is why angels are described as "standing" as in, "*Seraphim were standing*" (Yeshayah 6:2) and, "*I will grant you strides among these [angels] who are standing here*" (Zechariah 3:7).

Even within man himself, the three elements of his soul — *nefesh, ruach, neshamah*[31] — attain the power to elevate themselves and the higher worlds only when they descend to this material world and enter the physical body of man. For it says, "*G-d breathed into his nostrils the soul of life,*" and only then, "*man became a living being*" (Bereishis 2:7) — of all the worlds. The descent of the soul into this world is exemplified[32] by the ladder of Yaakov's dream, "*He had a vision in a dream. A ladder was standing …*" (Bereishis 28:2). The ladder clearly represents the soul of life. And, "*G-d's angels were going up and down on it,*" signifying that by standing on the ground, the soul's lower end becomes "clothed" in the garment of man's body.

30 Even Moshe attained only forty-nine of the fifty gates of understanding, as it says, "*You have made him a little less than G-d*" (Tehillim 12:10) (*Rosh Hashanah* 21b). R. Chananel and other commentators explain that "G-d" in this context refers to angels, for angels possess the fifty gates of understanding. (*Uvacharta Bachaim*)

31 *Nefesh* is the animalistic element of the soul, *ruach* is the element above *nefesh*, and *neshamah* is its most lofty component.

32 *Raya Mehemna, Parashas Naso* 123.

THE ANGELS WAIT

[As was mentioned above, through their good deeds, Yisrael has the ability to elevate the higher worlds.] For this reason, although the angels who sanctify Hashem's name in Heaven are holier than us, they wait to recite their *Kedushah*[33] until we have recited our *Kedushah* here on earth. This is not to say that they wait out of deference to Yisrael, but that they are simply not capable of sanctifying their Creator until the sound of Yisrael's *Kedushah* down on earth rises to Heaven. For by reciting the *Kedushah* we elevate the spiritual worlds and connect each world to the one above it, thereby increasing their holiness and splendor. (Perhaps this is the reason for the custom of rising up on our toes when we say the verses of the *Kedushah.*) And — G-d forbid — if all the Jews throughout the world were to cease reciting the *Kedushah,* the angels, too, would stop saying their *Kedushah.* The prophet had this in mind when he said, "*When they (Yisrael) would halt, [the angels] would let their wings droop*" (Yechezkel 1:24). Meaning, when Yisrael down on earth would halt saying the *Kedushah,* inevitably, the angels would let their wings droop [i.e., stop reciting the *Kedushah*].

This is also the significance of reciting Perek Shirah, of which our Sages said, "Whoever recites Perek Shirah daily [merits the World to Come]." For when one recites it, he encompasses all of the powers [in the universe, which took part in the creation of man]. He gives strength to the angels and celestial ministers

33 *Kedushah,* Sanctification, is recited in the *chazzan*'s repetition of the Shemoneh Esrei. It expresses the idea that G-d is exalted above material existence.

of the entire creation so that they can recite all these songs, and through this [strength provided by man, the heavenly angels and ministers] draw their life, and the influence that flows from them upon all the lower creatures.

Chapter 12 | פרק י"ב

REPERCUSSIONS OF MAN'S ACTIONS

As we mentioned in Chapter 10, the three levels of man's soul—*nefesh, ruach, neshamah*—must come down to this world and enter a man's body before they can connect and elevate the higher worlds. This is so, because in order to rectify the "World of Action,"[34] the soul must enter a human body down in the physical world.

The idea of our deeds having an impact on the higher worlds is referred to in the verse, "*He fashions their hearts all together, He comprehends all their deeds*" (Tehillim 33:15). Literally, it says, "*He comprehends* toward *all their deeds.*" This means that Hashem discerns the momentous effect man's deeds are having on rectifying the higher worlds, or—G-d forbid—the opposite.

This is also implied by the verse, "*For G-d will judge every deed—even everything hidden—whether good or evil*" (Koheles 12:14). The verse can be translated as: "*For each of his far-*

34 According to the Zohar, there are four worlds:
1. The World of the Emanations (*Atzilus*)—This is "the world of the Divine."
2. The World of Creation (*Beriyah*)—This is the world of the Divine Throne or the Chariot (*Merkavah*) of G-d, as described in Yechezkel 1.
3. The World of Creation (*Yetzirah*)—This is the world of the angels.
4. The World of Action (*Asiyah*)—This is the physical world.

reaching powerful deeds man will be judged." This means that when a person stands before the Heavenly Tribunal, G-d, Who is the Master of all powers, will judge him not only for each of his actions as such, but also for the impact his actions had on the higher worlds and powers — for good or for evil.

REWARD OF THE WORLD TO COME

The moment a person thinks of doing a mitzvah, his intention has a constructive and beneficial effect on the higher worlds. As a result, a holy celestial light is reflected on him, which helps him carry out the mitzvah. When he completes the mitzvah, the holy light returns to its source. This is what is meant by the "reward of the World to Come": The reward is the mitzvah itself. For when the soul leaves a man's body, it ascends to Gan Eden where it delights in the spiritual joys of the higher worlds that grew and increased through that person's good deeds.

Don't think that at Creation, the World to Come came into being as a separate entity, and when a person is upright he will be granted a portion of it. The truth is that every person creates his own *Olam Haba*. He prepares his own portion and adds to it through his good deeds.

ALL YOUR ACTIONS ARE RECORDED

Similarly, when it comes to Gehinnom, the sinner's punishment is the sin itself, as it says, "*The iniquities of the wicked one will trap him*" (Mishlei 5:22). For when a person transgresses, the blemish to his soul's heavenly root is instantaneous, and the legions of impurity are sustained and strengthened by his sin.

When committing a sin, the sinner draws to himself a

spirit of impurity that wraps itself around him.[35] As a result, throughout his life, the sinner is truly in Gehinnom; he just does not feel it until after his death. He is trapped in the snare he set for himself, caught by the impure spirits and demons he created with his wrongdoing. As the Sages put it: "Gehinnom is made deep for the evildoers."[36] Meaning, with their sins they dig their own Gehinnom, widen it and stoke its fires. As it says, "*But you are all igniters of fire, kindlers of sparks. Walk by the blaze of your fire, and in the sparks you have lit; from My hand has this decree come upon you, that you shall die in sorrow*" (Yeshayah 50:11).

This concept is alluded to in the verse, "*For He repays the deeds of man, and causes man to find according to his conduct*" (Iyov 34:11). This implies that each deed — good or bad — carries within itself the seeds of its reward or punishment. And this is what the Sages mean when they say (*Avos* 4:2): "The reward of a mitzvah is another mitzvah and the recompense for a transgression is another transgression."

SIN IS ITS OWN PUNISHMENT

However, adversity is not inflicted as punishment or revenge [for a sin]. Rather, sin is its own punishment, as it says, "*Evil*

35 Note: When it comes to sinning, the spirit of *tumah* (spiritual impurity) encircles the sinner only when he actually commits the sin, as opposed to when one does a mitzvah, the beneficial impact is made on the higher worlds the moment he intends doing the mitzvah. This is in line with the Gemara in *Kiddushin* 40a, "A good intention [even if it is not carried out,] the Holy One, blessed is He, combines it with the good deed, [and both the intention and the good deed are rewarded"]. However, if someone had the intention to transgress but was unable to carry it out, the Holy One, blessed is He, does not consider it as if he had actually transgressed. (*Uvacharta Bachaim*)

36 *Eruvin* 19a.

pursues sinners" (Mishlei 13:21). G-d designed the order of Creation in a way that whatever happens in the higher worlds is determined by the actions of man — whether good or bad. Man's actions are recorded automatically, and he is punished according to the damage his evil deeds brought about. The imperfection inflicted on the higher worlds and on his soul is rectified through punishment or through *teshuvah*. The Sages summed it up, saying: "All your deeds are recorded in a book" (*Avos* 2:1), which means that they are inscribed and filed by the deeds themselves.

Chapter 13 | פרק י״ג

THE IMPACT OF WORDS ON THE HIGHER WORLDS

In the same way, every word one speaks has an effect on the higher world, as it says, *"For behold, He forms mountains and creates winds; He recounts to a person what were the words [he spoke]"* (Amos 4:13). The prophet warns man: "Since you live in the lowly physical world, you cannot fathom how each single word you utter has either a constructive or destructive effect on the upper worlds. You may even think: What difference can my insignificant small talk make in the higher worlds? Let me assure you that every trivial word or conversation is stored away and never lost."

The Zohar[37] says: "Even the breath of one's speech is preserved." Every word one speaks, even the sound of his voice, is not discarded. And the Zohar[38] says furthermore: "Every

37 *Saba* 100b.
38 *Parashas Metzora* 55a.

word a man utters rises upward, splitting heavens to reach its destined place." Every utterance makes an impact on high and activates heavenly forces. Beneficial speech enhances the forces of *kedushah*, as it says, *"I have placed My words in your mouth ... to implant the heavens and to set a foundation for the earth"* (Yeshayah 51:16).

The Zohar[39] says: "When you discuss Torah thoughts, your words soar on high ... giving rise to joy in Heaven and on earth. From every word of Torah or prayer many angels are created. Conversely, harmful talk creates worlds of falsehood and brings about destruction in the higher worlds."

And the Zohar[40] says: "Woe to those who see but do not understand what they see. For every word reaches its destiny, as it says, '*For the birds of the sky carry the utterance*' (Koheles 10:20). And thousands of winged angels take hold of the utterance and carry it up to the Heavenly Tribunal to be judged—either favorably or the opposite, G-d forbid."

CONSEQUENCES OF EVIL SPEECH

And the Zohar says also:[41] "Large numbers of destructive angels attach themselves to the voice [that speaks evil] and take it to the Great Deep where many charges are lodged against it. Woe to the person who speaks evil."

[Concerning the gravity of the sin of speaking evil it says,] *"Why should G-d be angered by your speech and destroy the work of your hands?"* (Koheles 5:5). Comments the Gemara in *Arachin* 15a: We find that a person who maligns [a girl]

---

39 *Parashas Emor* 105a.

40 *Parashas Tzav* 31b.

41 *Parashas Lech Lecha* 92a.

is punished more severely than one who commits the act [of seducing a girl].[42] And the Gemara in *Sanhedrin* 92a says: Whoever does not keep his word is considered as if he worshipped idols.

And the prophet says, *"He recounts to a person the words he spoke"* (Amos 4:13). This means that when a person is brought before the Heavenly Court, G-d reveals to him the impact his words had on the higher worlds.

Chapter 14 | פרק י"ד

THE SIGNIFICANCE OF INTENTION

[Not only deeds and words,] but intentions, too, have an effect on the higher worlds. Indeed, it says, *"He Who fashions their hearts together, Who comprehends all their deeds"* (Tehillim 33:15). Literally translated it says: *"Who comprehends* toward *all their deeds."* The word "toward" implies the effect intentions are having on the higher worlds. (In Chapter 12, this verse was applied to the impact a person's actions have on the higher worlds.)

It is quite possible that two people will commit the same transgression yet receive different punishments. The reason may be that one possesses greater understanding than the other because his soul is rooted in a higher place [in the realm of souls]. We must remember that a person is punished according to the damage his sins caused in the higher worlds. As it says in *Tikkunim* 470: When a person transgresses in this world, his

42 He has to pay a hundred *sela* (coins) for maligning a girl, whereas for seducing a girl, he would have to pay only fifty *sela*.

sin goes up to the place from which his soul is taken, and he is punished according to his status.

AN APT ANALOGY

The Arizal explains it with an analogy: You cannot compare a person who sullies the king's courtyard to one who soils the king's palace, not to mention the king's throne, his royal garments or his crown. Although the higher the spiritual world, the less it is affected by sin, still, if the butler who is in charge of polishing the royal crown misses a tiny spot, his punishment is infinitely greater than that of the custodian who left a pile of filth in the palace courtyard. For this reason, G-d's punishments vary depending on the exaltedness of the root of the sinner's soul.

Another reason why two people committing the same transgression will receive different punishments is that they did not have the same mental intention. The extent of the damage to the higher worlds done by a sin depends on the motive for the sin. The person who has a stronger urge to sin deserves a greater punishment, because his sin brought damage to worlds that are loftier. For that reason, the punishment for an inadvertent sin is lighter than that for an intentional sin. Hence, the Gemara in *Yoma* 29a says: Immoral thoughts are more harmful than the immoral act itself.[43]

[The major significance of intentions may be seen in the verse,] *"He who fashions their hearts together, who discerns all their deeds"* (Tehillim 33:15). The Gemara in *Rosh Hashanah* 18a explains this to mean: The Creator understands people's

43 The *Rambam* explains: Thoughts stem from man's intellect, which is man's most sublime attribute, and when he sins with his thoughts, he abuses his most magnificent gift (*Moreh Nevuchim* 3:8).

intentions and attaches them to their deeds, judging each person according to the intention he had for doing the sin. The same thought is expressed in the passage, *"G-d will judge every deed — even everything hidden — whether good or evil"* (Koheles 12:14). This means that a person will be judged not only for the act of committing the sin itself, but also for the hidden intention that prompted him to do the sin.

IMPROPER THOUGHTS CAUSE DAMAGE TO THE HIGHER WORLDS

Indeed, it says, *"Hashem founded the earth with wisdom; He established the heavens with understanding; through His knowledge the depths were cleaved"* (Mishlei 3:19). Figuratively speaking, the verse encompasses all the worlds: "The earth" is the center, "heaven" takes in all the higher spiritual worlds, and "the depths" points to the lower worlds. The next verse reads, *"My child, do not let them stray from your eyes."* The term "eyes" frequently is a metaphor for thought, as in, *The wise man has his eyes* [i.e., his thoughts] *in his head* (Koheles 2:14). The term *yilazu*, "stray" in Mishnaic Hebrew, suggests damage and impairment. Thus, our verse implies: "My child, please have pity and compassion on the precious higher worlds, which were created with wisdom, understanding and knowledge. Be careful not to impair any of them through an improper thought."

ACTION, SPEECH, THOUGHT

The three concepts — action, speech and thought — correspond to the three levels of the soul: *nefesh, ruach* and *neshamah.*

Action corresponds to *nefesh,* the animal level of the soul [i.e., basic biological functions], as it says, *"For the blood is the life* — hanefesh" (Devarim 12:23). For the *nefesh* resides in man's blood. Concentrated in the liver, blood flows to all his limbs, with which he acts and moves. Without the constant flow of blood, a limb shrivels, is immobilized and dies.

Speech parallels the *ruach* level of the soul, as it says, "*With the breath* — ruach — *of his lips*" (Yeshayah 11:4). This is quite obvious, for with every word you speak, you exhale a whiff of breath — *ruach*. The *ruach* is seated in the heart. And Onkelos renders the verse, "*And man became a living spirit*" (Bereishis 2:7) as "man was imbued with a speaking spirit."

Thought conforms to the *neshamah* level of the soul. It is the element that gives man the ability to know and understand the holy Torah. For this reason, the *neshamah* resides in man's brain, the organ of thought, the *neshamah* being the highest of the three levels.

Chapter 15 | פרק ט"ו

THE *NESHAMAH*

One may ask: How can the *neshamah* be the highest level of the soul when the word *neshamah* is related to *neshimah*, which means "breath," and breathing is a bodily function and a physical thing?

We have to understand that *neshamah* does not refer to human breath. It denotes the "breath of G-d," as it says, "*He blew into his nostrils the spirit of life* (nishmas chaim)" (Bereishis 2:7).

The Gemara in *Sanhedrin* 91a compares G-d blowing the soul into man to a glass blower producing glassware. A glass blower does his work in three stages: First, he holds his breath before blowing into the tube. Second, his breath enters the tube. Third, his breath goes from the tube into the lump of heated glass at the end of the tube, which expands until it takes on the shape the glass blower envisions, at which point he stops blowing.

The three phases of glass blowing match the three levels of the soul: *nefesh, ruach, neshamah. Nefesh,* the lowest level, is lodged completely inside man's body.[44] *Ruach* is "poured" into him from above, and the highest point of *ruach* is connected to the lowest part of *neshamah,* as it says, *"Until a spirit from on high will be poured out upon us"* (Yeshayah 32:15).

But the essence of the *neshamah* itself is completely hidden. Its source is the breath of G-d Himself, and no part of it enters man's body. Only Adam before he sinned merited to have the essence of the *neshamah* dwell inside his body. In the wake of his sin, the *neshamah* left him, but it remained hovering over him.[45]

Moshe was the only one to merit having the essence of the *neshamah* residing within his body. Therefore, he was called *"a man of G-d"* (Devarim 33:1). No one else was worthy of this. All man can hope to attain is that *neshamah* "sparks" will glow over his head, in line with his stature and eminence. These *neshamah* "sparks" give him the extraordinary perception needed to understand the mystical concepts hidden in our holy Torah.[46]

Iyov expressed this idea, saying, *"But in truth it is a spirit*

44 *Nefesh* is the life force that man shares with the animals. Man differs from animals in the two other levels of the soul: *ruach,* which gives him the power of speech, and *neshamah,* which gives him knowledge and understanding. *(Uvacharta Bachaim)*

45 After the *neshamah* left Adam's body, a desire for the physical was aroused in him (*Uvacharta Bachaim*).

46 This is the level of *ruach hakodesh* (inspiration of holiness), through which things that cannot be comprehended by the human intellect are revealed to him (*Uvacharta Bachaim*).

(ruach) *in man, and it is the soul from the Almighty that gives them understanding*" (Iyov 32:9). This means that the spirit [i.e., the *ruach* element of the soul] is lowered into man. But the essence of the *neshamah* — the breath of G-d's Mouth — dwells in the exalted heights of the nearness of G-d; it is not present inside man. [It is the "sparks" of the *neshamah*] that impart to man the insight needed to grasp the profound mysteries of the holy Torah.

When the Zohar and the Kabbalists speak in terms of the *neshamah* residing in man's brain, they are referring to the radiant sparks of the *neshamah* that transmit wisdom and understanding to man's brain and intellect.[47]

Chapter 16 | פרק ט״ז

THE SPARKS OF THE *NESHAMAH*

[This paragraph contains profound mystical thoughts that cannot be translated. Paraphrased by *Uvacharta Bachaim,* it reads as follows:]

The three levels of the soul — *nefesh, ruach* and *neshamah* in man — are matched by corresponding levels in the higher world. The heavenly counterpart of *neshamah* is called *Eim Habanim,* "Mother of Children." Just as the condition of man on earth was changed by Adam's sin, and man's *ruach* level receives only sparks of the *neshamah,* so, too, in the higher realm, only the lowest part of the *Eim Habanim* enters that world, while its main part remains in its source above, giving off its light only from a distance.

47 They do not mean the *neshamah* itself, because since Adam's sin, no one has merited to have the essence of the *neshamah* reside within him (*Uvacharta Bachaim*).

This will help us understand the Midrash on the verse, *"Hashem grants wisdom; from His mouth [comes] knowledge and understanding"* (Mishlei 2:6). Comments the Midrash: "This may be compared to a king who had a son. Coming home from yeshivah, the son noticed that on the table there was a dish prepared for his father. When the father offered a portion to his son, the son said: 'Father, I want to eat only from the food that is in your mouth.' So the father gave him a bite from the food in his mouth."

The son's request exemplifies the desire to partake of the sparks of the light of the *neshamah* whose source is hidden in the breath of G-d's mouth. The Midrash pointedly says that the son was coming home from yeshivah, indicating that the only way to attain the sparks of the *neshamah* is by exerting oneself by delving deeply into the holy Torah,[48] and learning Torah for Torah's sake. [The sparks of the *neshamah* and the Torah] both emanate from the same source.

This is also the underlying idea of the following Midrash: When the children of Yisrael were assembled at the foot of Mount Sinai to receive the Torah, they asked to hear the commandments from the mouth of G-d Himself, as implied in, *"Let Him give me from the kisses of His mouth"* (Shir Hashirim 1:2). Standing at Sinai, all Yisrael merited to have hovering over them and shining on them the sparks of *neshamah* emanating

48 The Vilna Gaon often was visited by *maggidim* (heavenly messengers) who offered to reveal to him the mysteries of the Torah without any exertion on his part. The Gaon turned down all offers, saying: "I don't want to use shortcuts to acquire Torah knowledge. I want to gain Torah knowledge through toil and exertion. G-d will grant me wisdom, and when I understand a concept, I know that I have found favor in G-d's eyes. I want only [knowledge] that comes from His mouth. Insights coming from *maggidim* (heavenly messengers), knowledge for which I did not toil, I do not desire." (*Uvacharta Bachaim*)

from G-d's mouth.[49] This is alluded to in the Gemara in *Shabbos* 88a where it says that at Sinai the ministering angels placed two [spiritual] crowns [of Divine radiance] on the head of every single Jew. These crowns enabled them to discern the inner mysteries of the holy Torah.

Chapter 17 | פרק י"ז

TESHUVAH

We will now discuss the way *nefesh, ruach* and *neshamah* are linked to each other, because this forms the basis of the concept of *teshuvah* by means of which a person can remove sin from his soul, cleansing it from its stain of impurity.

One should strive to make his service to the Creator perfect and pure. To that end, one should constantly examine his deeds, words and thoughts to see whether he has lived up to Hashem's wishes, because his deeds, words and thoughts are the counterparts of the three facets of his soul: *nefesh, ruach* and *neshamah*. Seeing how G-d in His kindness wants to bestow more and more goodness on him, he should always earnestly engage in Torah study, doing mitzvos and correcting his shortcomings. He should remember that even if he has sunk to the very depths of the swamp of evil, everything can be turned around, for no one is permanently banished from G-d.[50]

---

49 Unlike B'nei Yisrael, who merited only the sparks of *neshamah*, Moshe was worthy of having the essence of his *neshamah* dwell inside his body, as mentioned in Chapter 15. Hence, Moshe was able to hear all the commandments from G-d Himself without being overawed, whereas B'nei Yisrael were frightened to the point that their souls left them, and they had to be revived, as told in *Shabbos* 88b. (*Uvacharta Bachaim*)

50 See I Shmuel 14:14.

[Paraphrased:] We know that the spiritual worlds are linked to each other in a chain-like progression, whereby the highest aspect of the lower world is connected to the lowest aspect of the world above it. The same holds true for the three elements of the soul. When a person decides to fulfill Hashem's will with his deeds, words and thoughts, the *nefesh, ruach* and *neshamah* elements of his soul [listed in ascending order] reach an ever higher spiritual plane. This happens in the following manner: The highest aspect of *nefesh* is linked to the lowest aspect of *ruach;* the highest aspect of *ruach* connects with the lowest aspect of *neshamah,* and the *neshamah* element is joined with its spiritual root in the nearness of Hashem.

This is what Avigail had in mind when she said to David, *"May my lord's soul* (nefesh) *be bound up in the bond of life, with Hashem your G-d"* (I Shmuel 25:29), meaning that also the *nefesh*-element [i.e., the animal aspect] of David's soul should become connected to G-d.

In the same vein, the Zohar[51] comments on the verse, *"For G-d's portion is His people, Yaakov is the cord of His inheritance"* (Devarim 32:9): The Jewish people are connected to G-d through the three elements of the soul like a rope that is moored in Heaven above and is lowered down to the physical world.

Chapter 18 | פרק י״ח

KAREIS

In His infinite goodness, G-d has made it possible for the three elements of the soul, *nefesh, ruach* and *neshamah,* to be linked

51 *Parashas Acharei* 71b.

to each other, thereby enabling man to rise gradually to ever loftier spiritual heights. Depending on the degree to which one immerses himself in Torah study and prayer with love and fear of G-d, he can reach the point of clinging to the bond of life, to G-d Himself, so to speak.

But there is more. There are a number of sins that are punishable by *kareis* [i.e., spiritual excision or destruction of the soul]. *Kareis* means that the soul is cut off from its root in the higher world, and the cord with which it was tied to the heavenly realm is severed. But in order that no one should remain permanently banished from G-d, He ordained that in the case of *kareis*, only the lower nine of the ten spiritual stages of the soul are cut off, whereas the tenth and highest stage is never disconnected from its heavenly root. By verbally confessing his sins, the transgressor can reconnect the nine stages of his soul that were cut off.

And so, if a person sinned through speech, for instance, by slandering or committing other sins that taint the *ruach* element of his soul, he can restore the *ruach* element by doing *teshuvah*. But the *neshamah* element of his soul is not affected at all by his sin, because it is rooted in a higher world, a realm that is immune to sinful influences. Man's actions have no effect on it at all. And if a person sins by thinking immoral thoughts, he hurts only himself, in that the sparks of the *neshamah* disappear, but the *neshamah* element itself is not tarnished by his immoral thoughts.[52]

52 Rabbi Yisrael Eliyahu Weintraub remarks that this is the reason why at the destruction of the first Beis Hamikdash, the Holy Ark was hidden away and was not captured by the enemies. The Holy Ark corresponds to the *neshamah* element of the soul; it can never be damaged or destroyed by sin. *(Uvacharta Bachaim)*

YAAKOV'S DREAM

The above concept is reflected in the verse, "*A man's spirit* (ruach) *will sustain him in his sickness, but who* (mi) *can support a broken spirit* (ruach)? (Mishlei 18:14). When the *nefesh* element is afflicted by a person's sins — and most sins are prompted by the *nefesh,* the lowest of the three elements — [and he does *teshuvah,*] it can be healed and elevated by the *ruach* element. And when the *ruach* element is marred by the sins that affect the *ruach,* it can be rectified by "*mi,*" i.e., the *neshamah* element, since "*mi*" is a byname for *neshamah.*[53]

[The next segment, which deals with Kabbalistic concepts, is omitted.]

[The Sages tell us that man is a microcosm, a miniature replica of the higher world.] This is borne out in Yaakov's vision of the ladder, which was standing on the ground and whose top reached upward to Heaven (Bereishis 28:12). It says that the ladder was "*mutzav artzah,*" which translated literally means "*standing toward the ground.*" The verse continues, "*and its top reached up toward Heaven,*" implying that it originated in Heaven above and was lowered down to earth.

The top of the ladder symbolizes the *neshamah* element of man's soul, which emanates from Heaven, from "the breath of Hashem's mouth." From there it is lowered like a ladder or chain to connect with the *ruach,* and the *ruach* connects with

53 This may be applied to the verse, "*Your ruin is as vast as the sea, who [mi] can heal you?*" (Eichah 2:13). Although our ruin is as vast as the sea because of our sins that tainted the *nefesh* and *ruach* elements of our souls, "*mi,*" the *neshamah* element, will heal us. *(Uvacharta Bachaim, Miluim)*

the *nefesh*, which is lowered into man down on earth. The vision of angels going up and down the ladder signifies that the status of the angels at any given moment is determined by man's actions, speech and thoughts. (The fact that the angels *"are going up and down"* indicates that man's mission is to elevate the physical world to the level of the spiritual, and in response, spiritual light descends from Heaven.)

A PARABLE

A beautiful parable illustrates this idea:[54] Resh Lakish says: The Holy One, blessed be He, connected His name to the Jewish people. It may be compared to a king who pondered about what to do with the key to his palace. "If I leave it lying around, it will get lost," he reasoned. "Let me attach a chain to it. If the key gets lost, I will pull the chain to retrieve it."

In the same way, G-d said: "If I leave Yisrael unattended, they will be swallowed up by the nations of the world. To prevent this from happening, I will attach My great Name to them." The Sages applied this parable to the Jewish nation as a whole, but they also had in mind the soul of the individual. Man is the key that opens and closes the doors to the higher and lower palaces of Heaven. They all are governed by the actions man performs with the *nefesh* element of his soul. Man's *nefesh* has its counterpart and root in the *nefesh* of the spiritual realm.

G-d in His abundant mercy and intense concern for man's well-being said: If I allow man's *nefesh* to go at will, the connection between *nefesh, ruach* and *neshamah* will be lost. *Nefesh* will descend to the lowest depths of depravity, and since *ruach*

54 *Yerushalmi, Taanis*, ch. 2.

will not be there to raise it up, *nefesh* will be lost forever, as it says [about someone who does not fast on Yom Kippur], *"I will destroy that soul from among its people"* (Vayikra 23:30). And how will a soul that sinned gain atonement?

G-d devised a wondrous process whereby the three elements of the soul, *nefesh, ruach* and *neshamah,* connect with each other, the top of the lower one fastened to the bottom of the one above it, like links of a chain. That way, even if the *nefesh* falls prey to evil forces, it can be extricated by *ruach,* which is above *nefesh.* This is the underlying meaning of the above parable where G-d says, "I will attach My great Name to them," i.e., to *nefesh, ruach* and *neshamah,* so that they remain forever connected to their root in the great Four-Letter Name of Hashem.[55]

Chapter 20 | פרק כ׳

REMOVING A STAIN ON *NEFESH*

When a person sinned and stained the *nefesh* element of his soul, or if, as a result of his sin, he sank to the bottom of the swamp of evil, his sincere verbal confession coming from the depth of his heart will reach the loftiest spiritual heights above. The power of his *teshuvah* causes a flow of additional *kedushah* to emanate from G-d Himself and to flow to the root of his *neshamah,* and from there to his *neshamah* itself, on to his *ruach.* His *ruach* then conveys this great light to the *nefesh* element of his soul, whereby the last traces of the forces of evil

55 The Vilna Gaon says that this is the greatest kindness G-d has bestowed on Yisrael, because it ensures the eternal survival of the Jewish people (*Uvacharta Bachaim*).

and impurity are erased. His *nefesh* is released from the grip of the shells of evil that encased and smothered it, and its previous bond with *ruach* is restored.

REPAIRING DAMAGE TO *RUACH*

If a person tainted the *ruach* element of his soul by slandering or other sins that blemish his *ruach* — the worst of which is the neglect of Torah study — then even his *nefesh* is no longer perfect, for it receives its vitality from his *ruach*. But with genuine remorse and *teshuvah*, he can bring an increased *kedushah* to flow to his *neshamah*, and from it down to his *ruach*. The spiritual pollution brought about by his sin onto his *ruach* is shattered, and his cleansed *ruach* is reattached to his *neshamah* in perfect union as before.

TORAH STUDY REMOVES THE STAIN ON THE *NESHAMAH*

If a person sins by having impure thoughts, he causes the radiant sparks of the *neshamah* element that hovered over his head to depart.[56] However, by totally immersing himself in Torah study, he brings back the holy sparks of the *neshamah*, which enable him to understand mysteries of the Torah [that he did not understand before]. The light of these sparks will radiate down to his *ruach* and *nefesh*, restoring them to perfection.[57]

56 In Chapter 15, we learned that Moshe was the only person to have the *neshamah* dwell within him; everyone else can only attain having *neshamah* "sparks" hover above his head.

57 Women who have immoral thoughts cannot cleanse their soul through intensive Torah study as men can, since they are not obligated to learn Torah. The Gemara in *Sotah* 21a explains that they can repair the damage to their soul by making sure that their sons study Torah and by waiting for their husbands until they come home from learning at the *beis midrash*. Since they are instrumental in increasing Torah learning, the light of Torah created through them helps them as if they themselves had learned. (*Uvacharta Bachaim*)

Thus, our Sages said (*Shabbos* 119b): "Whoever responds to the Kaddish by saying Amen; may His great Name be blessed ... with all his might, the evil decree [made] in judgment against him is torn .... Even if there is a trace of idolatry in him, he is forgiven." For when one extols Hashem's Name, He causes a flow of holiness and blessing to be added to the essence of his soul, and from thence to his *neshamah, ruach* and *nefesh*. The resulting effect is that any sin that had tainted these three elements of his soul is totally eradicated. Thus, [as a result of his response in Kaddish,] all his sins are forgiven.

This idea is reflected in the Gemara in *Avodah Zarah* 8a where it says: "Adam offered an ox whose horns preceded his hoofs." With the purest and holiest intentions, Adam meant to rectify his sin and mend the destruction his transgression had brought about. He wanted to rekindle the radiance that before his sin had illuminated his *neshamah*, the highest element of his soul, symbolized by the horns of the ox. This radiance would then shine on his *ruach* and *nefesh*, purifying his entire body from his head to his feet, exemplified by the horns and the hoofs of the ox.

Chapter 21 | פרק כ"א

TORAH STUDY ELEVATES THE HIGHER WORLDS

When a person learns Torah for Torah's sake in order to keep all that is written in it, his body — from head to toe — is purified. The Gemara in *Berachos* 16a derives this from the verse, *"How good are your tents, Yaakov ... They stretch out like streams"* (Bamidbar 24:5). Asks the Gemara: Why are "tents" mentioned alongside "streams"? To tell you, that just as streams bring a person up from a state of ritual impurity to one of purity, so do tents [where Torah is studied] elevate a person from a state of guilt to a state of merit. And just as a person's entire body is uplifted and cleansed when he is engrossed in Torah study, so are all the higher worlds elevated and purified through man's Torah study, for they are the heavenly counterparts of man on earth.

When a truly upright person serves G-d, he does not have in mind to elevate and cleanse his own body and soul; his sole intention is to exalt and ennoble the holy higher worlds. That was the way the Patriarchs and the early *tzaddikim* served G-d and observed the laws of the Torah, as it says in *Yoma* 28b: Our father Avraham kept the entire Torah [even before it was given]. The Patriarchs were not commanded to do this. However, with their lucid perception they saw how greatly the higher worlds would benefit if they fulfilled the mitzvos. Conversely, they recognized how much harm and devastation would come to the heavenly realm if they did not.

For the same reason, when Noach brought an offering after the Flood, he took only pure (kosher) animals and birds (Bereishis 8:20). [How did he know the distinguishing marks of pure (kosher) and impure (non-kosher) animals before the Torah was given?] Discerning the higher root of each animal, and sensing which were and which were not acceptable, he offered those rooted in holiness and rejected those rooted in pollution and evil.

WHY THE TORAH WAS NOT GIVEN TO THE PATRIARCHS

One may ask: If the Patriarchs kept the entire Torah, how could Yaakov marry two sisters, and how could Amram marry his aunt,[58] joining in unions that are forbidden by Torah law?

Yaakov discerned that according to the root of his *neshamah*, the higher worlds would benefit greatly if he married Rachel and Leah. He understood that the two sisters were destined to be the mothers of the House of Yisrael. For this reason, he was willing to suffer the hardship of slaving for the devious Lavan day and night for twenty years to be able to marry them. Similarly, Amram married his aunt Yocheved because he knew that she was destined to be the mother of Moshe, Aharon and Miriam, the future leaders of Yisrael.

This is also one of the reasons why the Torah was not given to the Patriarchs. If they had received the Torah, Yaakov would not have been allowed to marry two sisters, nor could Amram have married his aunt, even if they understood that — judging by the root of their *neshamah* — this would be highly beneficial to the higher worlds. Indeed, the marriages of Yaakov and Amram were the foundations of the House of Yisrael and the factors that set right all the upper and lower worlds. As to the fact that Kayin married his sister, [the answer is,] "*The world is built on kindness*" (Tehillim 89:30).[59]

Chapter 22 | פרק כ"ב

A WORD OF WARNING

Ever since the day Moshe brought the Torah down to earth, it is no longer in Heaven. Therefore, no man, no matter how

58 See Shemos 6:20.

59 Kayin was permitted to violate one of the seven Noachide commandments for the sake of building the world, and eventually the Jewish people (*Uvacharta Bachaim*).

great his understanding, may permit himself to say: According to my understanding of the root of my *neshamah,* I may violate a certain mitzvah or neglect a detail of one of the Rabbinic ordinances, or change the time of its performance. To prevent such thoughts from occurring, the Torah ends with the words, *"No other prophet like Moshe has arisen in Yisrael"* (Devarim 34:10), to tell us that after Moshe, no prophet or sage could add anything new. And the Gemara in *Shabbos* 104a comments on the passage, *"These are the commandments that Hashem gave Moshe at Mount Sinai"* — this teaches us that, from then on, no prophet was authorized to make innovations.

THE PROPHET YESHAYAH CONFRONTS KING CHIZKIYAH

The Gemara in *Berachos* 10a proves the point. We are told there that the prophet Yeshayah admonished King Chizkiyah, saying: "Why did you never get married?" Explained Chizkiyah: "The reason I did not get married was that I saw by Divine inspiration that I will have evil offspring." Thus, he refrained from marrying for the sake of Heaven, for he did not want to bring evildoers into the world. Nevertheless, Yeshayah, conveying G-d's message, told him, *"You will die, and you will not live"* (II Melachim 20:1). The redundant phrase implies: You will die in this world, and you will not live in the World to Come, because you did not try to have children. All of Chizkiyah's countless righteous deeds could not help to bring him to the World to Come, because he decided to exempt himself from one of the mitzvos of the Torah,[60] even though he

60 Chizkiyah did not make a mistake, for his son was the evil king Menasheh whose sins caused the destruction of the Beis Hamikdash (II Melachim 23:26, 27). The lesson to be learned is this: One must fulfill the mitzvos without considering the consequences, even if as great a disaster as the destruction of the Beis Hamikdash will result from it. *(Uvacharta Bachaim, Miluim)*

foresaw by Divine inspiration that he would have an evil son.

MAN CANNOT FATHOM THE RATIONALE OF THE MITZVOS

The deeper reasons for the mitzvos were not revealed to anyone in the world, not even to Moshe Rabbeinu. Only Adam before he sinned was privy to this hidden knowledge. The mysteries of the Torah are "the wine that has been preserved in its grapes from the six days of Creation."[61] The mysteries are "the light that shone on the first day of Creation, which enabled Adam to see from one end of the universe to the other,"[62] the implication being that the Torah is beyond all human comprehension. In light of that, how can man presume to make changes on the strength of his limited knowledge and insight? And so Yeshayah said to Chizkiyah: "What have you to do with G-d's secrets! You have to do what you were commanded, and let the Holy One, blessed be He, do whatever pleases Him" (*Berachos* 10a).

A ONE-TIME TEMPORARY RULING

In the days when prophecy flourished in Yisrael, a prophet was allowed to introduce a change in a law, but only as a temporary, stopgap ruling. He could do this, even if it meant violating one of the mitzvos. Eliyahu did this on Mount Carmel [when he brought a sacrifice outside the Beis Hamikdash to prove the falsehood of the prophets of Baal].[63] In an emergency, a prophet is authorized by the Torah to make temporary changes, as it

---

61 This wine has a spiritual quality since it was created out of nothing (*Maharsha, Berachos* 34b).

62 *Chagigah* 12a.

63 See I Melachim 18:20-39.

says, *To him (to the prophet) you must listen* (Devarim 18:15). His rulings must be obeyed even if, forced by circumstances, he orders a given mitzvah to be violated, the only exception being if he tells people to worship idols.[64]

But under no circumstances is a prophet allowed to enact a permanent change in the law. In the case of the mitzvos of reading the Megillah on Purim and that of kindling the Chanukah lights,[65] the Sages found verses in the Torah on which they based these mitzvos.[66]

In our time, when lamentably we have no prophets, even if the most illustrious sages convene and with profound insight and pure intent would decide to change a small detail of a given mitzvah or adjust the time of its performance, we may not listen to or obey them. And even if a heavenly voice verified their ruling, we would insist, "*[The Torah] is not in Heaven!*" (Devarim 30:12).[67]

WE MUST OBSERVE ALL THE LAWS

In Talmudic times, the Sages were permitted to establish Rabbinic mitzvos for which they found a basis in the Torah, such as the mitzvah of kindling Chanukah lights and the like, or to enact preventive measures. But since the completion of the Talmud, we must keep and observe all the laws and statutes that are recorded in the Written and Oral Torah, at their prescribed

64 *Yevamos* 90b.

65 The events commemorated with these mitzvos happened long after the closing of Tanach.

66 *Megillah* 14a.

67 The underlying thought is that since the Torah was given to us, the rules of Halachah (Torah law) are immutable, and no one, be he ever so great, stands above the rules of halachic decision-making laid down by the Torah and the Sages.

times, with all their minutiae, without deviating from them in the least.

And when a Jew observes the mitzvos properly, the mitzvos have a beneficial effect on the higher worlds, even if he does not understand their mystical meanings. Each mitzvah generates an upsurge of *kedushah* and spiritual light, and gives power to G-d. For G-d ordained the nature of the worlds that they should be governed by the deeds of man, and that each mitzvah that is performed on earth should ascend on high, where it accomplishes its designated goal.

G-d granted insight to the illustrious Kabbalists, enabling them to comprehend the hidden matters of our holy Torah. Counted among the Kabbalists are such luminaries as Rabbi Shimon bar Yochai,[68] his colleagues and disciples, and the Kabbalists of later generations like the holy Ari.[69] They taught us a little about the hidden reasons and intents of the mitzvos, so that each person — according to his intellectual capacity — can have an inkling of the effect his actions, words and thoughts are having on the spiritual worlds above. This should motivate him to serve G-d and fulfill the mitzvos with the utmost care, awe, love, *kedushah* and a pure heart. That way he will bring about great *tikkunim* (rectifications) in the higher worlds. Still, the most important aspect of all mitzvos is the actual performance of the mitzvah.

---

68 The author of the holy Zohar.

69 Rabbi Yitzchak Ashkenazi Luria, known as the Ari Hakadosh (1534-1572), was one of the most influential teachers of Kabbalah. His most distinguished student was Rabbi Chaim Vital (1543-1620).

שער ב׳

GATE TWO

PRAYING WITH HEART AND SOUL

It says, *"to love Hashem your G-d and to serve Him with all your heart and soul"* (Devarim 11:13). The Gemara in *Taanis* 2a asks: What does "serving G-d with all your heart" mean? The Gemara answers: It means serving Him through prayer. Now it is quite obvious that you should love G-d *"with all your heart,"* because love flows from the heart. We can understand also that we should love G-d with our soul, for this means that one should be willing to give his life for the sake of G-d. But this verse introduces a novel idea, namely, that our service of G-d — that is, our prayers — should involve both our heart and our soul.

Praying with all your heart implies two things:

First — Expelling from your mind all irrelevant thoughts, and fully concentrating on the words of prayer. As the Sages say:[1] One who prays must direct his thoughts toward Heaven, as we learn from the verses of Channah's prayer: *"Channah was speaking in her heart"* (I Shmuel 1:13) — from here [we learn] that one who prays must direct his thoughts [toward G-d]. And it also says, *"With all my heart I sought You"* (Tehillim 119:10).

Thus, the Sages further said[2] that one who prays should wait until he is in a supplicating frame of mind, as implied by the phrase, *to serve Him with all your heart*. For if an extraneous thought enters your heart, your heart is divided.

Second — Shutting out all pleasurable feelings while

1 *Berachos* 31a.

2 Ibid. 30b.

praying, focusing only on the exaltedness of G-d, taking delight in G-d through the words of prayer to the point that one's heart is drawn upward. As the Sages said:[3] One who prays should concentrate his mind heavenward. And as they said in *Shemos Rabbah* 22: You should purify your heart before beginning to pray.

It should be pointed out, however, that the concept of purifying one's heart before praying is only an enhancement of the mitzvah. When it comes to prayer, the important thing is the act of praying itself.

Before we discuss the concept of prayer as the way of serving G-d *"with all your heart,"* we must explain the meaning of *berachah,* and what is meant by "blessing G-d." For we find the term *berachah* mentioned in verses like, *"You will bless Hashem your G-d"* (Devarim 8:10), or in, *"Blessed is Hashem forever"* (Tehillim 89:53). Also, the Gemara in *Berachos* 7a relates that G-d said to R. Yishmael [the *Kohen Gadol*], "Yishmael, my son, bless Me!" Furthermore, all the *berachos* formulated by the Men of the Great Assembly[4] begin and end with *"Baruch ata* (Blessed are You)."

Chapter 2 | פרק ב'

THE MEANING OF *BERACHAH*

The word *baruch* does not mean "blessed" or "praised" [as an adjective], as most people think. Proof of this is that when G-d

3 *Yevamos* 105b.

4 This group of 120 Sages led the Jewish people at the beginning of the second Beis Hamikdash era. They laid the foundation of the prayers and enacted many ordinances designed to strengthen Torah observance.

said,[5] "Yishmael, my son, bless Me," R. Yishmael, the *Kohen Gadol*, did not praise G-d at all. Instead, he said: "May it be Your will that Your mercy should suppress Your anger ..." Thus, he responded by praying for Divine mercy.

The true meaning of *berachah* is asking G-d to increase that which is being blessed, as in, *"He will bless your bread and your water"* (Shemos 23:25) and *"He will bless the fruit of your womb"* (Devarim 7:13), and there are many more verses like these. These passages clearly denote increase; they certainly cannot be interpreted as expressions of praise and glorification.

But when we recite a *berachah* and "bless G-d" [as in most *berachos* where we say, "Blessed are You, Hashem, our G-d ..."], we are not speaking about G-d Himself. After all, G-d is perfect and lacks nothing; thus, "increasing" anything about Him is ridiculous.

The essence of G-d is completely beyond human comprehension. When we speak of G-d, we are referring to His attributes as they become apparent to us by the way He sustains and guides the world and His creations — with justice, kindness or mercy. That's why we describe Him as Almighty Judge, Merciful One and Compassionate One. And even the ineffable Name Y-H-V-H does not refer to G-d's essence but to His relationship with the worlds, since Y-H-V-H means: He was, He is and He will be, and He grants existence to all. In other words: It is His will to sustain and keep in existence all the worlds, every instant.

And so, the purpose of reciting a *berachah* is to increase our awareness of G-d in creation [first in our own mind, and then, in the minds and lives of as many people as we can reach].

5 *Berachos* 7a.

Therefore, when we bless G-d, we are really saying, "Please increase Your Presence in creation."

Chapter 3 | פרק ג׳

THE NAMES OF G-D

The Sages deal with this concept in expounding the verse, *"Moshe said to G-d, 'So I will go to the B'nei Yisrael and say, "Your fathers' G-d sent me to you." They will immediately ask me what His name is. What shall I say to them?'"* (Shemos 3:13). G-d replied: "So you want to know My name? I have many names, each of which represents a way I reveal Myself through My behavior toward the world. Depending on My actions, I may be called *E-l Sha-ddai, Tzeva-os* or *Elo-him*. When I exercise strict judgment, I am called *Elo-him* (Divine Judge). When I contend with evildoers, I am called *Tzeva-os* (Lord of Hosts). When I keep a person's sins pending, I am called *E-l Sha-ddai,* and when I am merciful, I am called Hashem, the Name that represents compassion. *"Eh-yeh Asher Eh-yeh — I Will Be Who I Will Be"* (Shemos 3:14) means that G-d's being is timeless, but His Name varies according to His actions.

THE FORMULA OF THE *BERACHOS*

For this reason, the Men of the Great Assembly formulated all *berachos* we say over a mitzvah to begin with *"Blessed are You, Hashem, our G-d, King of the world,"* whereby we refer to G-d in the second person (You), and to close the *berachah* with *"Who has sanctified us with His commandments ...,"* where we speak of G-d in the third person (He). The use of the second person acknowledges G-d's involvement in the world as "King of the world." Hence, we say *"Blessed are You,"* in the second person. But G-d Who commands us and sanctifies us is G-d the Infinite, Who is hidden and completely beyond human comprehension. Therefore, we refer to Him in the third person, saying, "Who has sanctified us ... and commanded us."

Chapter 4 | פרק ד׳

G-D'S INVOLVEMENT WITH THE WORLD

The underlying idea of all our *berachos* and prayers is that we direct our prayers to the One, Infinite and Absolute G-d. But we are unable, and even forbidden, to address the unknowable and transcendent Essence of G-d as He existed before the world was created. However, since G-d [by creating the world] has shown that He wants to relate to the world, is concerned with it and wants to rule over it, we pray to Him from the point of view of His relatedness to the universe. And for this reason, a *berachah* consists of two parts. We start a *berachah* in the second person, addressing G-d with the words: "You, Hashem, King of the world." But we continue in the third person: G-d who commanded and sanctified us is the Unknowable, Infinite, Hidden Divine Essence. We are implying: Since You wish the world to exist and You are involved with it and rule over it, therefore, our plea is that You may reign forever [and may Your kingship over us be revealed and become visible].

If G-d were not involved with the world, there would be no point in studying the Torah and doing the mitzvos. Indeed, it says, *"If you have sinned, how have you affected Him? If you were righteous, what would you have given Him, or what has He taken from your hands?"* (Iyov 35:5,6). And it says, *"If you have become wise, you have become wise for your own good"* (Mishlei 9:12), for the Essence of G-d is not affected by man's actions, whether good or bad.

This idea is expressed in the Midrash on the verse, *"The word of G-d is pure"* (Tehillim 18:31). Rav expounds: The mitzvos were given for the sole purpose of purifying the Jewish people. After all, what difference does it make to G-d if one slaughters an animal by cutting the throat or the neck? And in the same vein it says in *Tikkunim* 70: The Primary Cause is exalted above all. He blesses everyone and does not need anyone's blessing, for He is exalted above every blessing and praise.

Every time one makes a *berachah,* he increases blessing in the higher worlds. As the Zohar Chadash says, the power of *Birchas Hamazon* (Grace after Meals) is great, for it adds strength to the blessing of the heavenly retinue. For this reason, the Sages said[6] that anyone who eats without reciting a *berachah* is called a thief ... for he is stealing by preventing the flow of blessing and holiness [from that *berachah*] from reaching the upper worlds.

Chapter 5 | פרק ה'

THE SOUL IS A REFLECTION OF G-D

For a better understanding of how man's actions bring about an increase of blessing in the higher worlds, let us turn to the Gemara in *Berachos* 10a: David mentions the words, *"Bless G-d,*

6 *Berachos* 35b.

O my soul," in five verses.[7] What do these five verses correspond to? They correspond to the Holy One, blessed be He, and the soul. [This is manifest in the following analogy:] Just as the Holy One, blessed be He, fills the whole world, so does the soul fill the body .... Our awareness of G-d is the result of His relatedness and involvement with the world. And the arrangement of the higher and lower worlds in all their details is patterned after man in the order of his limbs and organs and in the way they are attached to each other. G-d's true Being extends throughout and fills all the worlds but is concealed in them. He is their soul, so to speak, like the soul of man that suffuses and is concealed in his body.

Expressing the same thought, the *Rambam* says in *Moreh Nevuchim* 72:1: The entire universe is nothing but one single being. The variety of its substances is like the various limbs and organs of a human being. After a lengthy explanation, he concludes that the source of the existence of the universe is G-d, blessed be His name. Because of this comparison, G-d is called "the life of the universe," as in, "*He swore by the life of the universe*" (Daniel 12:7).

The Sages, too, often make this comparison. For example, commenting on the verse, "*You may not allow the body* [of a man who was legally executed] *to remain on the gallows overnight ... since a person who has been hanged is a curse to Hashem*" (Devarim 21:23), Rabbi Meir says: This can be compared to two twin brothers [who lived in the same city]; one was appointed king, and the other became a highway robber. At the king's command, they hanged him. But all who saw him exclaimed, "The king is hanged!" [Being twins, they

7 Tehillim 103:1; 103:2; 103:22; 104:1; 104:35.

looked alike. So, too, man has some resemblance to G-d, having been created in His image.]

Chapter 6 | פרק ו׳

FEEDING THE UNIVERSE

Our physical body and our spiritual soul are held together by the food and drink we take in; without nourishment the soul leaves the body. The same is true for the mystical bond between G-d and the universe. It is G-d's will that this bond be kept intact by the spiritual food of Torah study, the observance of mitzvos and the prayers of Yisrael, the chosen people. Without Torah study, mitzvos and prayers, G-d removes His Presence from the world, and instantly it would revert to nothingness. The Sages expressed this idea in the Gemara in *Taanis* 3b: What is the meaning of, *"I have scattered you like the four winds of the heavens"* (Zechariah 3:7)? Just as it is impossible for the world to exist without winds, so, too, the world cannot exist without the Jewish people.

Expounding on the verse, *"Bless G-d, O my soul"* (Tehillim 104:1), the Midrash[8] says: Why did David praise G-d with his soul? He said: The soul does not eat, and neither does the Holy One, blessed be He. David implied: Although the soul itself does not eat or drink, its connection to the body depends on the physical food man eats. The same way, although the Infinite G-d is not affected at all by the performance of a mitzvah, Torah study or prayer, He willed that His involvement with the world should be determined by the good deeds of His holy

8 *Vayikra Rabbah* 4.

people. Their good deeds represent the "nourishment" that sustains the higher worlds and broadens their *kedushah* through G-d's involvement with them. Just as food lends strength to the body, so do the good deeds of the Jewish people invigorate the higher worlds, enabling them to receive a greater flow of *kedushah* from G-d.

This idea is implied in the verse, "*Come and partake of My food and drink*" (Mishlei 9:5), which the Sages explain to refer to the Torah, which in reality is G-d's food.

Chapter 7 | פרק ז'

HARMFUL FOOD

Conversely, sinful deeds are as damaging to the higher worlds as spoiled food is to the body. And just as bad food saps the body's strength, causes sickness and is expelled, so too, in the upper worlds, bad deeds are transformed into filth and cause the forces of pollution to gain the upper hand.

Shameful deeds bring about spiritual defect, ruin and deficiency in the higher worlds, because the Divine Presence does not extend into the worlds that are affected by evil deeds. And since all the higher worlds are linked to each other, they all suffer to some extent from this flaw.

The upper worlds do not recover until the forces of pollution are eliminated when the sinners receive the punishment they deserve. When that happens, the worlds are healed from the blight and regain their original purity. Another way for the worlds to regain their wholeness is through the sincere *teshuvah* of the sinner, for *teshuvah* washes away the stains of spiritual pollution, as it says, "*I will sprinkle pure water upon you, that you may become cleansed*" (Yechezkel 36:25).

CAUSE AND EFFECT

[With regard to the punishment of sinners,] the Gemara in *Bava Kamma* 50a makes a surprising statement: If anyone says that the Holy One, blessed be He, "overlooks" [when it comes to dealing out justice for sins], his life shall be overlooked [because with this attitude he incites people to sin]. [But isn't G-d merciful and compassionate?]

We must understand that the punishment of the sinner is not an act of G-d taking revenge. Punishment is a natural consequence of transgression; sin leads to punishment as a reaction of cause and effect. Just as eating harmful food causes sickness, and swallowing a poisonous substance results in death, so is punishment the natural outcome of transgression, and G-d's complacency and compassion has nothing to do with it. The stain of *tumah* (spiritual impurity) the sinner has brought on the higher worlds must be removed, either through punishment or *teshuvah*.

Clearly, our prayers for greater relatedness of G-d to man and the worlds are of enormous importance for the continued existence of the worlds, because prayer "feeds" the bond between G-d and all of creation. Why G-d desired to come out of His concealment and relate to something outside of Him will remain forever a mystery. But it is this thought that should be uppermost in one's mind when learning Torah or performing mitzvos. This should especially be one's *kavanah* (intention) during prayer, because in prayer man most openly appeals for greater connection with G-d, and for an increased flow of *kedushah* to the higher worlds.

Chapter 9 | פרק ט׳

TEFILLAH—PRAYER

Prayer to G-d at the proper time is the essential "food" for the upper worlds and for one's own soul. As the Zohar[9] says: G-d's food is *tefillah*; it takes the place of a sacrifice [in the Beis Hamikdash].

Raya Mehemna[10] says in the name of Rabbi Shimon: It is forbidden to eat anything before the Exalted King has eaten. What is His food? *Tefillah*. The function of *tefillah* is to intensify the involvement of G-d with man and the worlds, and to increase the flow of blessing and holiness to the worlds. This is what one should reflect on when praying.

Chapter 10 | פרק י׳

A PARTNER OF THE CREATOR

One should reflect on this not only when reciting a *berachah*, but with every single word of *tefillah*. For every word of *tefillah* or *berachah* rises on high to carry out the specific task it was assigned. The one who prays thereby becomes a partner of the Creator in building and establishing a multitude of worlds. And so it says in the *Tikkunim* 18:35b: When a person utters words of prayer, the birds spread their wings and open their beaks to receive them, as it says, "*A bird of the skies carries the utterance, and a winged creature reports the word*" (Koheles 10:20). G-d then takes these words and uses them to build new worlds, as

9 *Parashas Bereishis* 24:1
10 Part of the Zohar.

it says, *"For just as the new heavens and the new earth that I will make will endure"* (Yeshayah 66:22).

The mystery [of man's partnership with G-d] is revealed in the words, *"I have placed My words in your mouth ... to implant the heavens and to set a foundation for the earth, and to say to Zion,* 'Ammi atta' *(You are My people)"* (Yeshayah 51:16). Do not read[11] *ammi atta,* but *immi atta,* "You are with Me as My partners."

THE WORDS OF PRAYER

[Note: The text of the Shemoneh Esrei was composed by the Men of the Great Assembly, which led the Jewish people at the start of the Second Temple era and consisted of 120 great sages, among them many prophets.]

The reason the Shemoneh Esrei had to be written by the 120 sages is that only these illustrious sages had the prophetic insight to formulate each word and each syllable to have the desired mystical effect on the higher worlds. They perceived which particular word or phrase was needed for the *tikkun* (rectification) of the multitude of worlds.

G-D YEARNS FOR THE PRAYERS OF *TZADDIKIM*

This concept is expressed in *Yevamos* 64b: "The Holy One, blessed be He, yearns for the prayers of the righteous." In the same vein it says in *Midrash Tanchuma, Toldos*: "Why were the Matriarchs incapable of bearing children? Because the Holy One, blessed be He, longed for their prayers." And the

11 The Sages do not seek to change the traditional text. They imply that the verse contains an allusion in addition to its literal meaning, as if it were pronounced differently.

Zohar[12] says: Behold, Yitzchak lived with his wife for twenty years without having children, the reason being that G-d delights in the prayer of the righteous. He therefore withholds from them their needs until they offer their supplications. Why is this so? In order that there be an abundance of *kedushah* for whoever is in need. In fact, there is a verse that says it plainly, "*The prayer of the upright pleases Him*" (Mishlei 15:8).

For this reason, the Sages describe prayer as "things (words) that stand at the pinnacle of the world,"[13] implying that it is the individual words of prayer that rise to the highest heavens.[14] In the same vein, the Zohar[15] says: People don't realize that prayer splits the heavens, opens the gates and rises on high.

Chapter 11 | פרק י״א

KAVANAH—INTENTION

The primary purpose of prayer is to increase the presence of *kedushah* in the world. Just as a soldier sets aside his personal needs and concerns and willingly gives his life for the honor of king and country, so should an upright Jew forget his private trials and troubles and concentrate in his prayers on enhancing the strength of the higher holy worlds, on drawing down blessings and Divine light to the world, on removing the spirit

12 *Parashas Toldos* 137:1

13 *Berachos* 6b.

14 While the words of the prayers themselves rise to celestial heights, it is clear that one's private thoughts amplify the potency of the words. But even without *kavanah*, the words achieve the *tikkun* in the worlds above. (*Uvacharta Bachaim*)

15 *Parashas Vayikra* 201:1.

of impurity and on perfecting the universe through G-d's sovereignty.

This idea is the predominant theme of the prayers of Rosh Hashanah in which we pray for recognition of G-d's majesty by all mankind. Even our daily liturgy, which on the surface seems to consist of personal petitions, is actually replete with disguised pleas for an increased awareness of G-d's glory by all mankind. It is obvious that the Men of the Great Assembly — the authors of the Shemoneh Esrei — did not have in mind only the plain meaning of its words. For the Gemara in *Berachos* 26b says that they instituted the Shemoneh Esrei to replace the daily sacrifices, namely the *olah* offerings, which were completely consumed by the fire on the altar, and no part of which was used for human consumption. By the same token, prayer should be devoted wholly to furthering the greater glory of G-d.[16]

PERSONAL PLEAS

The Gemara in *Sanhedrin* 8a says: One is allowed to insert a petition about his personal needs or suffering into the appropriate *berachah* of the Shemoneh Esrei. However, one's own needs should not be his primary concern. He should bear in mind that all human suffering gives rise to a corresponding anguish of the *Shechinah*, and G-d's pain rather than his own discomfort should be his overriding consideration.

When you come to think of it, you must wonder how it is possible to pray for relief of suffering in the first place. Take the case of a sick person. The doctor will prescribe foul-tasting

16 Rav Chaim Volozhiner is referring only to the Shemoneh Esrei, which takes the place of the *olah* (burnt) offering. But one may offer personal *tefillos* for relief of one's individual hardship (*Uvacharta Bachaim*).

medicine or, if need be, amputate an entire limb to prevent the disease from spreading. Does the patient beg the doctor not to dispense the bitter medicine or to forgo the amputation? Certainly not. After all, the patient himself summoned the doctor! Then how can we appeal to G-d to take away our pain, knowing that our afflictions are the remedy that atones for our sins? As it says: Suffering is caused only by willful transgression (*Shabbos* 55a).

PRAYING FOR RELIEF OF PAIN

When praying for relief of suffering, one should focus on the anguish of the *Shechinah*. For example, when Jews suffer from oppression, we should grieve in our prayers over the desecration of G-d's name. [By oppressing the Jews, the tormentors show their contempt of G-d.] The same goes for an individual who suffers pain. Although his suffering does not involve a desecration of G-d's name, he can pray for the relief of the pain of the *Shechinah*, for every human pain produces a corresponding anguish in the *Shechinah*. As it says in *Sanhedrin* 46a: Rabbi Meir said: When man suffers, what does the *Shechinah* say? "My head feels heavy! My arms feel heavy!"

The Midrash[17] comments on the word *tammasi*, "My twin" (Shir Hashirim 5:2), stating:[18] In the case of twins, if one of them has a headache, the other feels it, too. The same way, the Holy One, blessed be He, says, "*I am with him in distress*" (Tehillim 91:15), meaning: G-d shares our distress. And when one feels sympathy for G-d to the point that he is

17 *Shemos Rabbah, Bo.*

18 *Tammasi* usually is translated as "My perfect one."

oblivious to his own troubles,[19] his sins are forgiven.[20] To the other extreme, any salvation that comes for Yisrael is salvation for G-d, too, as the next verse continues, *"and I will show him My salvation."*

Chapter 12 | פרק י"ב

AGONIZING OVER THE PAIN OF THE *SHECHINAH*

Rabbi Elazar Hakkapar had this in mind when he said: "Whoever includes G-d's name with his suffering, will find that his reward doubled" (*Berachos* 63a). [Why is his reward doubled?] We should understand that the *Shechinah* feels pain over his sin and also over his punishment, but the pain of the higher worlds caused by his sin is far greater than the pain that is felt there over his suffering.

AN ANALOGY

An analogy will explain it: In a drunken spree, a young man stumbled, breaking his neck. Unconscious, the fellow was oblivious to his life-threatening condition, but his father ate his heart out seeing his son slipping away. When the surgeon administered painful therapy and put him in a hard cast, the

19 This does not mean that he is unaware of his own pain. Rather, overwhelmed by the anguish of the *Shechinah*, he disregards his own pain. It is analogous to a man who has a toothache and watches helplessly how his son is falling down from the roof. His mental anguish over his son's mishap causes him to forget his toothache. (*Uvacharta Bachaim*)

20 The suffering that was the punishment for sins caused him to feel for the pain of the *Shechinah*. Thus, in a roundabout way, it was his sins that prompted his sorrow for G-d's honor, which explains why his sins are forgiven. (*Uvacharta bachaim*, quoting Rabbi Yisrael Eliyahu Weintraub)

son cried bitterly, and the father felt sorry for him. Of course, the father's grief at the time of the accident was immeasurably greater than his distress over the son's present discomfort.

The same applies to sin. When committing a transgression, the sinner causes dreadful pain in the higher worlds, while he himself—like a drunkard on a binge—is unaware of any wrongdoing. But G-d, in His mercy, sends the sinner afflictions as medications to purge his sin. The sinner suffers pain, and his pain causes corresponding discomfort on high, but this discomfort is much milder than the anguish triggered by the sin.

Therefore, when praying for a cure to an affliction, if one elevates his prayer by selflessly appealing for the relief of the Divine anguish his sin has caused and does *teshuvah* for the sin, then his own suffering is lifted. What's more, his reward is doubled to make up for the double pain he caused in the higher worlds [by his sin, and by the pain of his punishment]. Since he now regrets having caused the double pain, his willful transgressions are turned into merits.

CHANNAH'S PLEA

The same idea is expounded in the Gemara in *Berachos* 31b in connection with Channah: It says, "*She was feeling bitter, and she prayed to* (al) *Hashem*" (I Shmuel 1:10). [Literally, the word *al* means "upon." Thus, she prayed upon Hashem, meaning:] Even though she was feeling bitter about being childless, she brushed off her personal tragedy and did not pray about it at all, but directed her *tefillah* "upon Hashem," praying for relief of the anguish her barrenness caused in the higher worlds. The Gemara there expounds similar episodes in reference to Moshe and Eliyahu the prophet.

And so, when reciting the Shemoneh Esrei, one should not

concentrate on the personal pleas implied by the literal meaning of the *berachos*. Rather, one should direct his attention toward intensifying G-d's involvement with man and the world.

TEFILLAH IN THESE TIMES

In these times of economic hardship when everyone is preoccupied with his own troubles and difficulties, and people cannot fix their thoughts on G-d and the higher worlds, it is all the more important for everyone, according to his ability, to escape from the tidal wave of impure thoughts swirling around us. One should make an effort to pray properly, because prayer takes the place of the *korbanos* (sacrifices) that were brought in the Beis Hamikdash. The *korbanos* were dependent on the thoughts of the *kohen* (priest) who offered them. An improper *kavanah* of the *kohen* might cause the *korban* to become *pigul* (unacceptable). And through the *kohen*'s holy thoughts, the *korban* was exalted and elevated to become a pleasing aroma to G-d.

Chapter 13 | פרק י״ג

HOW TO PRAY

How are we to develop this attitude in out *tefillah*? It is best to follow the recommendation the *maggid* made to the *Beis Yosef*:[21] "When praying, one should banish all external thoughts, even

21 Rabbi Yosef Karo (1488-1575), better known as the Beis Yosef, is the author of the *Shulchan Aruch*. A heavenly spirit, called a *maggid*, made himself known to him only by his voice. The *maggid* taught him Kabbalistic interpretations and encouraged him to follow a righteous way of life. The interpretations on verses of the Torah were written down by Rabbi Yosef Karo in his *Maggid Meisharim* (Lublin, 1646).

those of Torah and mitzvos, concentrating on and visualizing the words themselves."

Notice, the *maggid* (preacher) did not say that one should concentrate on the meaning of the words, for the deeper sense of the *tefillah* is beyond our grasp. Even the little on the subject of intentions during prayer that was revealed to us by the saintly early Rabbis through to the revered Arizal[22] is like a drop in the ocean compared with the profound *kavanos* included in the Shemoneh Esrei by those who composed it, the 120 Men of the Great Assembly, among them many prophets.

WRITTEN WITH *RUACH HAKODESH*

It is obvious that no human being could have written such an awesome prayer, endowing its words with the power to rectify all the higher worlds until the coming of *Mashiach,* unless he had Divine inspiration. G-d Himself placed into the mouths of the Men of the Great Assembly the specific words that contain the hidden mystical meanings to rectify the heavenly realm. Therefore, how can anyone fathom the profound intention of the Holy One, blessed be He, whose light is inherent in every single word of the Shemoneh Esrei?[23]

VISUALIZING THE WORDS

Therefore, when praying, the most important thing is to enunciate each word, to visualize the letters of the words, having in mind thereby to increase the flow of holiness that comes with

22 Rabbi Yitzchak Luria, foremost Kabbalist, 1534-1572. His teachings were recorded by his disciple Rabbi Chaim Vital in his work *Etz Hachaim.*

23 The Chasam Sofer says: I have no doubt that even the composers of the Shemoneh Esrei themselves could not fathom the profundity of G-d's *kavanah* (*Chasam Sofer, Derashah for Shabbos Shuvah,* vol.1, p. 26).

the increased relatedness of G-d with the world. This is a tried and proven method of banishing all alien, trivial and improper thoughts. The more one trains himself in that, the better he achieves *kavanah pashtis*, pure and simple *kavanah*.[24]

Chapter 14 | פרק י"ד

WITH ALL YOUR SOUL

[In the previous chapter, Rav Chaim Volozhiner described the minimal way of praying to qualify for fulfilling the obligation. He now moves on to the next level.]

The passage, *"to serve Him with all your heart and all your soul"* (Devarim 11:13), implies that for prayer to be perfect it must involve the soul. By praying "with the soul," one attains a higher degree of purity, as we will explain later.

We find in many places in Tanach that prayer is called *nefesh*, "soul." For example, Channah said, *"I have poured out my soul before Hashem"* (I Shmuel 1:15), [explaining to Eli that she was praying,] and it says, [in reference to prayer,] *"Bless Hashem, O my soul"* (Tehillim 103:1) and *"Praise Hashem, O my soul"* (Tehillim 146:1).

SPOKEN PRAYER

The Gemara in *Berachos* 26b says that the prayers were instituted to replace the daily offerings in the Beis Hamikdash [through which one's sins are atoned]. On the Altar, the *nefesh* (life force) of the animal is elevated on High. And the Torah

---

24 Although the Halachah rules that prayers may be said in any language (*Berachos* 13a), the preferred way of doing the mitzvah is to pray in *lashon hakodesh*, the holy tongue.

says, "*The blood is the* nefesh" (Devarim 12:23). Therefore, through the sprinkling of the [offered animal's] blood on the Altar, one's sins were atoned. Since prayer takes the place of the offerings, it follows that prayer elevates the *nefesh* of the worshipper, bringing him closer to G-d.

Taking this one step further, we note that the Torah says that at Creation, G-d breathed life into Adam so that "*man became a living being* (nefesh chayah)" (Bereishis 2:7). Onkelos renders *nefesh chayah* as *ruach memallela,* "a speaking spirit." Onkelos seems to equate speech with *nefesh,* being that with every word one speaks, one exhales a breath of air. And the foremost attribute of the soul is the power of speech, since it sets apart man from beast. Thus, the breath one exhales when speaking is a manifestation of one's *nefesh,* and every word one utters is a facet of his *nefesh.*

THE NEXT LEVEL OF *TEFILLAH*

It says that you are "*to serve Him with all your soul*" (Devarim 11:13). Therefore, when one stands in prayer [reciting the Shemoneh Esrei] one feels as though his soul has been lifted from his body. He removes from his mind all worldly thoughts that have infiltrated his soul so that his prayer emanates from the very depth of his soul.[25] Before beginning to pray, he should banish all thoughts of physicality, to the point that he loathes his body, so that his prayer emanates only from his soul. With every word uttered — and words are facets of the soul — one unites with the mystery of mysteries inherent in that word.

25 Since the soul is inextricably fused with the body, when a person sins with his body he leaves a mark on his soul. But deep in every soul there is one place that is not affected by sin [i.e., "the very depth of his soul"]. (*Uvacharta Bachaim,* quoting Rabbi Yisrael Eliyahu Weintraub)

CONNECTING WITH THE HIGHER WORLD

When praying, one is in a higher world, so much so that at the end of the Shemoneh Esrei, one feels as if he is plummeting down from a higher realm and has trouble turning his mind to worldly things. Overcome with a burning love of G-d, he realizes that with every word of prayer, his soul rises from his body to attach itself to G-d, so to speak. In this vein, it says in the Gemara in *Taanis* 8a: A person's prayer is answered only if he puts his whole soul into it. This means that when praying, he uplifts his soul and attaches it to its heavenly root.

Chapter 15 | פרק ט״ו

EACH ACCORDING TO HIS ABILITY

The phrase *"to serve Him with all your soul"* (Devarim 11:13) can be interpreted two ways: either "with your entire soul" or "with all that you are capable of, even if it is only a little."[26] Both interpretations are true. Each person should serve Hashem to the best of his ability. If he is able to reach great spiritual heights of love and yearning for G-d, he can serve Him with his entire soul. However, not everyone can attain such a state of utter devotion. But at least one should try to have the proper *kavanah*, having in mind with each word one says to love Hashem, if not with "all his soul," then at least with "a fraction of his soul."

CHANNAH'S *TEFILLAH*: THE EPITOME OF PRAYER

The best way to prepare for serving G-d "with all of one's soul"

26 *Sanhedrin* 78a.

is by engaging in Torah study and doing mitzvos day and night. Channah, whose prayer was the outstanding example of *tefillah,* poured out her entire soul when praying to G-d, as she said, *"I have been pouring out my soul to G-d"* (I Shmuel 1:15).[27] "Pouring out" denotes "emptying the soul completely," draining the soul of any trace of desire for worldly concerns. The following chapter speaks about an even loftier level of prayer.

Chapter 16 | פרק ט"ז

THE THREE PARTS OF THE SOUL

The Kabbalists tell us that the soul comprises three separate entities, namely: *nefesh, ruach* and *neshamah* [of which *nefesh* is the lowest level], which in turn correspond to the three concepts that make up man: action, speech and thought. The same gradation exists in every word [in the Torah], namely: letters, vowel marks and cantillation marks (*trop*). And so it says in the Introduction to the *Tikkunim* 7b: The cantillation marks correspond to the *neshamah,* the vowel marks parallel the *ruach* and the letters conform to the *nefesh.*

LETTERS—ACTION—*NEFESH*

Accordingly, the letters correspond to action, because letters (consonants) without vowel marks represent nothing but the action of the scribe who wrote them in the *sefer Torah.* Without

27 Rabbi Yehudah Hachassid says in *Sefer Chassidim* 131: If a person prays for something that will bring glory to the Creator—for example, if he prays for success in his Torah studies or any other religious pursuit—and he pours out his soul for it, the Holy One, blessed be He, will answer his prayer even though he has not done many good deeds.

the vowel marks, the letters cannot be pronounced. Hence, letters without vowel marks are characterized as *nefesh* [the lowest of the three forms of soul].

VOWEL SIGNS—SPEECH—*RUACH*

The vowel marks correspond to the *ruach* level of the soul, because the combination of letters and vowels enables man to speak the words, and speech is equated with *ruach*. And as man lives by dint of his *ruach*, so do the vowels give life to the letters.

CANTILLATION MARKS—THOUGHT—*NESHAMAH*

The cantillation marks parallel thought and intention (*kavanah*), the aspect of the *neshamah* [because the cantillation marks are the punctuation marks that tell us how to group the words together, where a sentence ends and the next sentence begins. Without these marks, the Torah would be a meaningless sequence of letters and words]. Thus, cantillation marks bring out the thoughts contained in the letters and vowels, to parallel the *neshamah*.

THE HIGHEST LEVEL OF *TEFILLAH*

The loftiest level of prayer is reached by pouring out to G-d one's *nefesh, ruach* and *neshamah*. With every word of prayer — with its letters, vowels and cantillation marks representing *nefesh, ruach* and *neshamah* — one expresses his fervent longing to link his *nefesh, ruach* and *neshamah* to the words he utters in order to connect those words to the higher worlds.

THE ROOT OF THE *NESHAMAH*

There is, however, yet another soul above *neshamah,* called *shoresh haneshamah,* "root of the *neshamah.*" The Zohar calls it *chayah* or *yechidah,*[28] a spiritual level that was reached only by Adam before his transgression. But when he sinned, this soul was taken from him.[29] Ever since Adam, no one in this world has attained this lofty state. When Chanoch reached this level, inheriting the quality of Adam, the world could not cope with his *kedushah,* and he was forced to depart this world [as it says, "*Chanoch walked with G-d; then he was no more, because G-d had taken him*" (Bereishis 5:24), i.e., he entered Gan Eden without dying].

Eliyahu, too, departed this world when he attained a small portion of this heavenly splendor, as it says:[30] "G-d said: 'The world cannot cope having you among the living.'" This high level of *kedushah* will remain beyond man's reach until the resurrection.

As mentioned above, this aspect of the soul is called "*shoresh haneshamah,* root of the soul." [What does this mean?] When one thinks a certain thought [for example, he thinks a down-to-earth thought like: "I enjoy reading this book"], he does his thinking with his *neshamah,* as it says, "*It is the* neshamah *from*

---

28 *Chayah* is man's power of thinking, which is the root of life, as it says, "*Wisdom gives life to him who possesses it*" (Koheles 7:12) (*Uvacharta Bachaim*).

29 Although Adam did *teshuvah,* the *chayah/yechidah* element of his soul was not returned to him (*Uvacharta bachaim,* quoting Rabbi Yisrael Eliyahu Weintraub).

30 Zohar, *Parashas Vayigash* 209b.

the Almighty that gives them understanding" (Iyov 32:8). The thought is grasped by the person who thinks. But the root of the thinking process is completely hidden and unfathomable. In so doing, he has touched the *shoresh haneshamah,* the "root of the *neshamah,*" [the ultimate "I,"] which is completely concealed and unfathomable.

Chapter 18 | פרק י״ח

THE ULTIMATE LEVEL

When one has become used to praying with the intention of connecting his *nefesh, ruach* and *neshamah* to the letters, vowel marks and cantillation sign of each word, as set forth in Chapter 16, he will try to attach the three levels of his soul to the root of his *neshamah,* the *shoresh haneshamah.* When he achieves this, he feels as being completely detached from this world. He is totally indifferent to mundane concerns, because he has risen above his physicality.[31] Through his *shoresh haneshamah,* he unites with the heavenly root of the souls of all Yisrael.

For this reason the Men of the Great Assembly instituted that the verse, "*My Lord, open my lips, that my mouth may declare Your praise*" should be said before beginning the Shemoneh Esrei. One who has reached this high level of *kavanah* becomes completely passive, silent like a stone, unable to speak. G-d has to open his lips to enable him to utter

31 This is a higher level than the one described in Chapter 14. There he is still actively praying, whereas in the present chapter his self has been completely annihilated. *(Uvacharta Bachaim)*

the words of the *tefillah*.[32] In line with this the Gemara in *Berachos* 30b says: The pious men of old used to wait an hour before praying in order to concentrate their thoughts on their Father in Heaven.

32 The *Tur Orach Chaim* 98 says: Pious men would seclude themselves to concentrate on their *tefillah* to the point of *hispashtus hagashmius*, "divesting themselves of physicality" until they came close to the level of prophecy. The *Rambam* in *Hilchos Yesodei Hatorah* 7 says: When prophesying, the prophet's limbs tremble, he grows faint and loses control of his thoughts [he is free of any trace of physicality]. Therefore, if during prayer a person approaches this level, it is possible that he loses control of his limbs and is unable to speak, so that G-d has to open his lips. *(Uvacharta Bachaim)*

שער ג'

GATE THREE

HAMAKOM, G-D IS THE PLACE OF THE WORLD

The Mishnah in *Avos* 2:18 says: When you pray, do not make your prayer a set routine, but rather beg for compassion and favor before *HaMakom* (the Omnipresent; lit., "the Place"), blessed be He. In using the Divine Name of *HaMakom,* the Sages hinted at an important concept. Their profound intentions [in choosing the Name *HaMakom*] must be explained, and the verses that allude to this must be clarified.

The Mishnah in *Avos* 2:15 compares the words of the Sages to glowing coal. A glowing coal merely glimmers, but the more you stir it and fan it, the more its flame flares up, and the more you can enjoy its light and bask in its warmth — but only from a distance. You cannot touch it, and if you are not careful, you will get burned. The same applies to the words of the Sages. At first glance, they appear short and simple, but in reality they are "like a hammer that shatters a rock."[1] The deeper one delves into their words, examining and analyzing them, the more his eyes light up with the dazzling, blazing light [of the wisdom] that is evident in the profound concepts he discovers. As the Sages[2] said: Delve into [the Torah] and continue to delve into [the Torah], for it contains everything.

But one has to be very cautious [not to get too close to] their "glowing coal," that is to say, not to contemplate and reflect on things that we are not permitted to scrutinize too deeply. As the Mishnah[3] puts it: Warm yourself by the fire of the Sages.

1 Yirmiyah 23:29.
2 *Avos* 5:26.
3 Ibid. 2:15.

This means: Don't turn away completely from pondering the Rabbis' words, for then you will not benefit from their wisdom at all. On the other hand, don't get too close, so that you will not be burned. Stay at a safe distance, as the Mishnah continues: Beware of their glowing coal, lest you be burned.

The same holds true for the word *Makom*; everyone knows that its plain meaning is "place" or "space." When we reflect on it, we discover that [by choosing this appellation] the Sages hinted at an important idea. The reason for calling Hashem *HaMakom* is explained by the Rabbis[4] in connection with the verse, "*He [Yaakov] came* [bamakom] *to a familiar place*" (Bereishis 28:11): [The Gemara asks:] Why is the Holy One, blessed be He, given the byname of *Makom* (Place)? Because He is the *Makom* (Place) of the world, but the world is not His place.

Commenting on the verse, "*Behold, there is a place with Me*" (Shemos 33:21), the Midrash[5] says: [Hashem says:] The place [of the world] is dependent on Me, but I am not dependent on the place [of the world]. The simple meaning of this remark is that just as the place supports an object [standing on it], so is Hashem the Place that supports and sustains the worlds and all creations. If, G-d forbid, He would remove His attention from creation for an instant, all the worlds would cease to exist, as it says, "*You are keeping them all alive*" (Nechemiah 9:6).

This is the cornerstone of the Jewish faith, and for this reason, the Zohar describes G-d as "the Soul of all souls." Just as the soul animates and sustains the body [so Hashem animates and sustain the worlds]. [In the same vein,] the Gemara in

4 *Bereishis Rabbah* 68, *Tanchuma* to Shemos 33:21.

5 *Shemos Rabbah* 45; *Tanchuma, Parashas Ki Sisa.*

Sanhedrin 91b says: Can a piece of meat remain for even three days without salt and not become spoiled? It is Hashem who gives life [to the body] and to all the worlds.

Similarly, the Gemara in *Berachos* 10a draws a parallel between the existence of the universe through G-d's power and the existence of the body through the power of the soul, stating: Just as the Holy One, blessed be He, nourishes the whole world, so does the soul nourish the body. This is the simple meaning of the concept of Hashem being the "Place of the world."

Chapter 2 | פרק ב׳

THE WORLD ENDURES BY THE WILL OF HASHEM

On a deeper level, the description of Hashem as "the Place of the world" is based on a very profound concept. The fact that Hashem is called "the Place of the world" has nothing to do with a place supporting the object that rests on it. For in that case, the object has an independent existence; the place on which it stands merely prevents it from falling and breaking. The same goes for the body being kept alive by the soul. The body has an independent existence. It does not cease to exist when the soul departs.

By contrast, the continued existence of all the worlds depends completely on Hashem. If He would cease to will their continued existence, they would revert to absolute nothingness in an instant. That is why the Sages chose to call Hashem by the Name of *Makom*. Hashem in His wisdom chose to make the constant existence of His world dependent on His will. It is beyond human comprehension that all the worlds in reality are non-existent and merely an illusion, if not for the fact that, constantly, they are kept in existence by the will of Hashem.

Therefore, in an attempt to clarify this paradox, the Sages gave Hashem the byname *Makom*. [They meant to explain] that Hashem, in His wisdom, decides to keep the world in existence every single moment. This is something even the wisest man cannot grasp, for to the human mind it seems that the world continues to exist independent [of Hashem's will]. By calling G-d *Makom*, the Sages intimated that just as an object, even though it may exist independently, cannot exist without a place on which to stand, so, too, the tangible universe, which seems to exist independently, has a place on which it stands. Its place is Hashem. If not for His will to be the Place for the worlds, the universe most certainly would be non-existent . . .

Chapter 3 | פרק ג'

A WORD OF CAUTION

This idea is expressed in the verse, "*Do I not fill Heaven and earth?*" (Yirmiyah 23:24), and most explicitly in, "*Realize it today . . . Hashem is the Supreme Being in Heaven above and on the earth beneath — there is nothing else* (Devarim 4:39), and, *You are the ones who have been shown, so that you will know that Hashem is the Supreme Being, and there is none else beside Him*" (Devarim 4:35).

This means literally, that there is nothing in existence in all the worlds except Hashem's absolute Oneness . . .

We mentioned at the outset that the words of the Sages are compared to "glowing coal." One should take care not to ponder and reflect excessively on subjects that should not be studied in depth, for it may be harmful. The subject [of Kabbalah] is meant only for a wise man who is capable of understanding it and will be inspired by it to pray with a pure heart. But delving deeply [into Kabbalah] is fraught with danger, as *Sefer Yetzirah* cautions: If your heart runs forward, go back to your place.

I really should have restrained myself from discussing this topic altogether. The early authorities made it a point to conceal it, like the holy Rokeach who only spoke about Kabbalah in allusions and hidden references.

On reflection, I concluded that their approach was the appropriate course to follow for their generation. But at the present time, we have not had a leading authority for a long time, and everyone lets his thoughts wander in whatever directions he pleases. What is worse, some people think that it (Kabbalah) is for everyone, and there are fools who say that pure G-dliness can be found everywhere and in everything. All their thoughts are focused on studying mysticism; even young boys are behaving according to their own understanding.

How extremely careful one must be not to be swayed by such thoughts! One must guard himself against acting on the basis of [mystical] ideas, for this will do away with many fundamental principles of the Torah. One may easily become entangled in the snares of the *yetzer hara*. For example, it may convince him that it is permitted to meditate on the Torah in dirty alleyways, thinking that Hashem is present in all places. Yet our Sages spoke out emphatically against this, declaring that such a person does not have a share in the World to Come. The Gemara in *Berachos* 24b says that [a person who meditates on the Torah in dirty places] *"has denigrated Hashem's word"* (Bamidbar 15:32), and the verse ends, *"that person shall be utterly cut off [spiritually],"* which is interpreted to mean "being cut off both in this world and in the World to Come." There are many more errors that can result from following this way.

These are the considerations that led me to discuss this topic. I want to caution people to avoid the errors that may result from it, and I want them to understand clearly the things the Sages alluded to. *"For it is a time to act for Hashem"* (Tehillim 119:126).

Chapter 4 | פרק ד'

HASHEM FILLS AND SURROUNDS ALL WORLDS

[The beginning of this chapter has been omitted, as it deals with profound Kabbalistic concepts.]

It says in many places in the Zohar that "Hashem fills all worlds" and "surrounds all worlds." This means that from Hashem's perspective, He fills all worlds, and we, from our Torah-oriented vantage point, see Hashem as surrounding all worlds. The meaning of the concept of "Hashem filling all worlds" is concealed from us.

The truth is that from Hashem's perspective, even after creating the world, He fills all the worlds and all existence; literally, *"There is nothing else beside Him"* (Devarim 4:35). We express this thought before our Shacharis prayer: "It was You before the world was created; it is You since the world was created." This means that even after the worlds were created, Hashem is eternal and unchanging, unaffected by time or place. He is the same now as before Creation when all was filled by His Infinite Oneness, filling also the space where the worlds are now.

The Sages had this in mind when they compared the connection between Hashem and the worlds with the bond between the soul and the body, saying: Just as the pure soul resides within the body, so is the Holy One, blessed be He, pure in His world.[6] They meant to say: Although the soul pervades all parts of the human body, both the clean ones and the foul and unclean ones, the soul itself remains immaculately pure and holy. So, too, G-d, although He fills all worlds, even their clean and unclean places, His sanctity and Oneness are unaffected by them, as it says, *"For I Hashem have not changed"* (Malachi 3:6).

Chapter 5 | פרק ה'

HASHEM IS THE SOUL OF THE WORLD

Hashem, in His awesome power, withdrew into Himself, [making "room"] so to speak, for the worlds and creations to emerge into separate existence, in different places, some holy and pure, others impure and soiled. We, from the human point of view, perceive with our senses what appears to be the real world. The laws governing our conduct commanded by Hashem are based on this perception of ours, and with this perception, the Sages compared [Hashem's relationship with the world] to the relationship of the soul to the body. Indeed, the Zohar says: Hashem is the soul of the world. With his senses, man perceives only his body, whereas the soul, although it pervades the entire body, is invisible to the human eye, and is evident only to the intellect. Similarly, we perceive the physical world and its creatures with our senses, whereas Hashem, Who is present in all the limbs and organs

6 *Vayikra Rabbah*, 4.

of the body, and Who, like the soul, imparts life to them [is hidden from our eye].

All the Divine Names and Attributes mentioned in the Torah apply to Hashem only as we conceive of Him "from our perspective," as it were, from the human point of view, whereby the worlds are affirmed in their reality and separateness . . .

Not always is G-d described as One Who fills the entire world. The Midrash[7] says: When Hashem wills it, *"Do I not fill the Heaven and earth?"* (Yirmiyah 23:24), and if He so wishes, He [can confine Himself to the smallest of spaces, for it states that He] spoke to Moshe from between the two *Keruvim*. As R. Chanina says: Sometimes the entire world cannot contain His glory and Divinity, but other times, He can speak with a man from among the hairs of his head.

Chapter 6 | פרק ו'

DO NOT DELVE INTO HIDDEN THINGS

All the fundamentals of the Torah, all positive and negative mitzvos, are based on the concept that from our perspective [in the physical world], there definitely are different places. In places that are clean we are allowed, even obligated, to meditate on Torah themes, whereas in unclean places it is forbidden to think about Torah subjects. Indeed, all the Divine commandments regulating our conduct [are predicated on the human perspective of existence]. Without this human outlook, there is no reason at all for the Torah and the mitzvos. From Hashem's point of view, He fills all the worlds uniformly, without

7 *Bereishis Rabbah* 4.

any separation or differentiation. There is only complete Oneness, exactly as before creation. But we are unable, and even forbidden, to attempt to understand this awesome concept as to how Hashem's Presence fills all existence with undivided, absolute Oneness. As the Rokeach expresses it: "Do not delve into things that are beyond your comprehension." For it says in a *beraisa*: Restrain your mouth from talking about this. But if your heart runs, return to the place, for that is the reason it says, "*And the angels* (Chayos) *run and return*" (Yechezkel 1:14). This means: If you reflect on the essence of the Creator, wondering about His Omnipresence, prevent your mouth from talking and your mind from contemplating. Banish such thoughts from your mind. But if your heart runs after such thoughts, be quick to stop thinking about these things. Go back to praying to Hashem, and be in awe of Him. The greatest sages cannot understand these matters.

The heavenly legions of angels ask: "Where is the place of His glory?" They cannot grasp the concept of [Hashem being] "the Place of the world." The Gemara in *Chagigah* 13b says: Since [the angels] say, "Blessed is the glory of Hashem from His place" (Yechezkel 3:15), we can infer that no one knows His place. Moshe, eager to understand this concept, said, "*Please let me comprehend Your unique nature*" (Shemos 33:18). He desired to understand the place of Hashem's glory, but his request was not granted. Only Hashem Himself knows the essence of this hidden and unfathomable idea.

It says, "*The hidden things are for Hashem, our G-d*" (Devarim 29:28). We are permitted to reflect only on the things that were revealed and which we are able to grasp as seen from our vantage point where Hashem "surrounds all the worlds." [He transcends the world and is outside the world] because He confined His glory, [making "room"] for the physical world to come into existence with its forces and new creatures. Therefore, it is our duty to know and firmly etch in our consciousness the reality of Creation as it relates to the Halachah. This is the foundation of our faith and the basis of the Torah and all the mitzvos.

[The remaining chapters of Gate Three deal with Kabbalistic and mystical themes that do not lend themselves to translation.]

הקדמה
לשער ד׳

PROLOGUE TO GATE FOUR

Dear Reader,

I have guided you thus far on the path of truth, showing you the safe road for you to travel. This will help you to train yourself to reach ever higher spiritual levels. With pure intention and clear thinking, you will discover that the more you become used to all these virtuous qualities, the purer will be your intention in studying Torah, observing mitzvos, and your fear and love of Hashem.

THE BANE OF PRIDE

But you should be careful not to become conceited when you serve the Creator with pure intention. Instead of being proud of yourself, you should carefully analyze your motives, for it says, "*Every haughty heart is an abomination to Hashem*" (Mishlei 16:5). Even if you feel pride only in your heart without showing it to the world, it is still an abomination to G-d, for haughtiness is the root cause of all bad qualities. And so the Gemara in *Sotah* 4b, 5a says: A person who is haughty is considered as though he had erected a pagan altar. The *Shechinah* laments over every haughty person, saying, "I and he cannot live in the same world." The Sages[1] say that an arrogant person is considered as though he worships idols, denies the existence of G-d and commits adultery.

The Gemara in *Pesachim* 66b says: Whoever is conceited, if he is a wise sage, his wisdom will leave him. We learn this from Hillel. Surely, everyone knows of Hillel's extraordinary

1 *Sotah* 4b.

humility and meekness. Yet, when on one occasion he expressed some criticism that at first glance could be considered a sign of arrogance for a man of his self-effacing nature, he was punished immediately: When someone asked him a *halachah,* he had to admit that he had forgotten it. Just think, then, how much we have to scrutinize our thoughts constantly [for traces of arrogance].

Chapter 2 | פרק ב׳

DO NOT DISPARAGE YOUR FELLOW

It is possible for a devout man to be guilty of conceit, [for example,] if he looks down on someone who does not pray as ardently and sincerely as he does. Even more so, if he observes someone learning Torah, and, thinking that he is not learning *lishmah* (purely for the sake of Torah), sneers at him. In so doing, he commits a grave sin. For if one fulfills a mitzvah correctly, even without fervor and devotion, he is considered a servant of G-d and is beloved by Him.

You may not disdain a person who learns Torah *shelo lishmah* (not for its own sake), not even inwardly. On the contrary, you should show him respect, as it says, *"At [the Torah's] left are wealth and honor"* (Mishlei 3:16), which the Sages explain to refer to "those who study the Torah with their left hand" [i.e., not for its own sake]. The Zohar[2] says: Whoever exerts himself in Torah study will have life. Even one who does not study the Torah *lishmah* is rewarded in this world, and it will not be held against him in the World to Come.

2 *Parashas Vayeishev* 184b.

This tells us that even if someone did not learn Torah *lishmah,* but for some ulterior motive, he is rewarded, as long as he did not learn Torah in order to criticize it. About such a person the Sages say: "It would have been better had he not been born,"[3] and, "The Torah turns into poison for such a person."[4]

[One who learns Torah for an ulterior motive] is still rewarded by the Holy One, blessed be He, with wealth, honor and tranquility in this world. He will not be condemned in the World to Come for not learning *lishmah,* and all the more so if he learned Torah for no particular motive in mind he will not be denounced, for it would be reckoned as if had learnt it *lishmah.* So you see, learning Torah is very dear to G-d, more so than any other mitzvah.

TORAH STUDY EQUIVALENT TO ALL MITZVOS

The Gemara in *Arachin* 16b proves this: R. Yehudah the son of R. Shimon ben Pazzi asked R. Shimon ben Pazzi: What is preferable, reproof for the sake of Heaven or insincere humility [where a person alleges that he is not worthy to admonish, while in fact he does not want to arouse the other person's ire (*Rashi*)]? He answered: Wouldn't you agree that genuine humility is preferable [to reproof for its own sake], for the Master said: Humility is the greatest quality of all. Then, also insincere humility is better. For R. Yehudah said in the name of Rav: A person should always engage in the study of the Torah and observance of mitzvos, even not for their own sake, because by doing good for ulterior motives, he will eventually come to do good for its own sake. [Similarly, insincere

3 *Yerushalmi, Berachos* 1:2.
4 *Yerushalmi, Berachos* 88:2.

humility will eventually lead to genuine humility.]

The same is true for Torah study. You surely will agree that "Torah *lishmah*" is preferable to "mitzvah *lishmah*," for the Mishnah in *Pe'ah* 1 says: The study of Torah is equivalent to all the mitzvos. And similarly, the Gemara in *Sotah* 21a says that the merit and light of mitzvos protects one from punishment but does not save him from sinning, whereas the light of Torah — according to the conclusion of the Gemara — saves him also from sinning, at least while he is engaged in studying it [and according to one opinion even when he is not engaged in studying it]. Further, the Gemara in *Yerushalmi, Pe'ah* 1 says: All the mitzvos are not equal to even one word of the Torah. It follows that Torah study *shelo lishmah* is preferable to doing mitzvos for their own sake, the reason being that learning Torah *shelo lishmah* will eventually lead to learning *lishmah*.

Chapter 3 | פרק ג'

SHELO LISHMAH LEADS TO *LISHMAH*

When one begins to study Torah, it is almost impossible to learn on the level of *lishmah*. Just as one needs a ladder to climb to the upper floor, so, too, one begins by learning *shelo lishmah* so that eventually he reaches the level of *lishmah*. That is why one who learns *shelo lishmah* is also beloved by Hashem.

With that in mind, the Gemara in *Pesachim* 50b says: A person should always engage in Torah study and good deeds even if he does not do it for its own sake. The Sages pointedly say "always" to indicate learning "on a steady basis," meaning that at the outset, one is not required to learn day and night. And even if occasionally a selfish motive occurs to him, such as pride or honor and the like, that is no reason for him to abandon or cut back on his Torah study. On the contrary, he should redouble his efforts in the firm belief that through his learning *shelo lishmah* he will arrive at learning *lishmah*. The same is true for the performance of mitzvos.

Therefore, if one has the audacity to disparage and revile a person who learns Torah and performs mitzvos *shelo lishmah*, he will not go unpunished; he will have to answer for it in the hereafter. What's more, he is included among those who are denied a share in the World to Come,[5] namely, the heretics, denouncers and non-believers. They will forever burn in Gehinnom. The Gemara explains that "non-believers" include one who has contempt for a Torah scholar [even one who learns *shelo lishmah*]. Since he disgraces and disdains a person who learns Torah *shelo lishmah*, he discourages him from continuing to learn, thus preventing him from reaching the level of learning Torah *lishmah* and from becoming a full-fledged *talmid chacham* (Torah scholar).

There is no greater desecration of G-d and the Torah than this. He has lowered the prestige of the holy Torah and torn down the service of Hashem, for the entire service of Hashem is based on Torah scholars who are immersed in Torah learning day and night, providing guidance to the Jewish people. A man who brings about a decline in Torah scholarship destroys the Jewish faith; Klal Yisrael will be left without Torah and without teachers. Therefore, you should make an all-out effort to honor and elevate those who study the Torah as well as those who support Torah institutions, even if they do it *shelo lishmah*.

---

5 *Rosh Hashanah* 17a.

A REASSURING THOUGHT

Even if it is obvious that a Torah scholar was engaged in Torah study all his life *shelo lishmah* — for ulterior motives — you must treat him with respect, and certainly may not disparage him. Since he is learning Torah all the time, you may be sure that many times he does learn *lishmah*. As the Sages promised: "Through learning *shelo lishmah* one will eventually come to learning *lishmah*." This does not mean that eventually one will learn *lishmah* the rest of his life. What it means is that if one learns for several hours without interruption, even if he generally learns *shelo lishmah*, he cannot help but learn *lishmah* at least for a short while. As a result, all the *shelo lishmah* learning he did until now will be sanctified and purified through the short time that he studied *lishmah*.

Chapter 4 | פרק ד׳

THE *YETZER HARA*'S DECEPTION

We must be very careful about these things. The Gemara in *Sukkah* 52a points out: "The greater the man, the stronger is his *yetzer hara*." The greater a man's stature in Torah and service of Hashem, the more the *yetzer hara* (the evil impulse) tries to invade his mind. When a person is on such a high moral level that he would never stoop to commit a major or even a minor sin, the *yetzer hara* disguises himself as the *yetzer tov*. He blinds and poisons the pious man's mind, misleading him into thinking that the sin is really a mitzvah, showing him that it is a virtuous and kosher deed. Like a bird, the pious man is caught in the *yetzer hara*'s snare, oblivious of the mortal danger he is in.

So, be very cautious. Do not allow the *yetzer hara* to beguile you by telling you, "The main thing is to purify your thoughts properly, cleaving to G-d in your thoughts all the time. Don't let anything divert your thoughts from concentrating your thoughts on Heaven." It sounds like saintly advice. But the *yetzer hara* means to say is that Torah study and mitzvos are valid only if accompanied by deep devotion and true veneration, without which it is worthless. The *yetzer hara* will cite verses from the Torah, Mishnah, Gemara, Midrashim and the Zohar to support his argument. He will quote the Gemara in *Sanhedrin* 106a: "The Holy One, blessed be He, desires the heart" (*Sanhedrin* 106b), and many other proof texts like this. But if you examine his arguments with discernment, you will realize that the *yetzer hara* is showing you his kosher hooves, as it were, attesting to his purity and holiness, but in truth his feet are submerged in a swamp of death.

DOING MITZVOS AT THE PROPER TIME

Be alert to the *yetzer hara*'s maneuvers. Today he tells you: "Torah and mitzvos without devotion are worthless, so elevate your thoughts to Heaven. Before doing a mitzvah or praying, concentrate your thoughts on preparing for the mitzvah." But when you are finally ready, the time for the mitzvah or the *tefillah* has passed. The *yetzer hara* makes you believe that a mitzvah done with *kedushah* and pure intention — even after its set time has passed — is more precious to G-d than a mitzvah performed at the proper time but without deep *kavanah*. And with his smooth talk, he gets you accustomed to disregarding the time when a mitzvah or *tefillah* must be performed. You will end up thinking that it is permitted to do a mitzvah or *daven* after the prescribed time. Ultimately, you will be left having done the mitzvah neither at its set time nor with the proper *kavanah*.

Listening to the *yetzer hara*'s blandishments leads to the total ruination of the Torah. Imagine a Jew sitting at the *seder* on the first night of Pesach. If he would prepare for the mitzvah of eating a *kezayis* (the prescribed olive-measure) of matzah in holiness, purity and devotion, by the time he would be ready to eat the matzah, dawn will have broken! All his holy intentions are now unacceptable. But if one eats the *kezayis* of matzah at the prescribed time, even without the extraordinary holiness and purity, he will be blessed for fulfilling the mitzvah as prescribed in the Torah.

There are many other examples of what can happen if one does not do a mitzvah at the prescribed time. Certainly, our case is no different from the case of a man blowing the shofar with profound *kavanah* at the *seder* and eating a *kezayis* of matzah on Rosh Hashanah! He fasts on the day before Yom Kippur and shakes the *lulav* on Yom Kippur! Then, what has happened to the laws ordained by the Torah?

And if the *yetzer hara* fails to make you ignore the proper time for doing the mitzvos, he will make you spend all day on purification, to the point that you have no time left to make sure that you do the mitzvos correctly in all their details and not to transgress explicit laws of the Talmud and the Rabbis. And don't be misled by the *yetzer hara* assuring you that concentrating on purifying your thoughts ensures that you will not neglect any detail of the mitzvah. You should know that when you think that doing a mitzvah or learning Torah must be completely free of impure thoughts, you are being duped and led astray by the *yetzer hara*. He prevents you from meticulously observing the *halachos*, causing you to violate the mitzvos without you being aware of it.

Chapter 5 | פרק ה׳

PERFORMING THE MITZVAH IS WHAT COUNTS

To put it plain and simple: This misguided way of thinking is a blazing fire that obliterates many fundamental principles of the Torah. At the end of Gate One, we mentioned that the essential part of every mitzvah is the performance; purity of intention is of secondary concern. And so the Gemara in *Niddah* 23a says that a glutton who gorges himself on the *korban Pesach*, although he has not done the mitzvah in the preferred way, has indeed fulfilled the mitzvah. And a person who has the loftiest and purest *kavanos* about the *korban Pesach* but neglects to prepare it incurs *kareis*. The same applies to all mitzvos. [Performing the mitzvah is what counts.]

PRAYER MUST BE ENUNCIATED

Physically doing a mitzvah is crucial not only when it comes to "tangible mitzvos." It is essential also for the mitzvah of *tefillah*, prayer, which is called "service of the heart." One is required to clearly enunciate with his lips and tongue every word of *tefillah*, as the Gemara in *Berachos* 31a says: [When Channah prayed] "*Only her lips moved*" (I Shmuel 1:13) — from this we can learn that when you pray you should clearly enunciate the words." In the same vein, *Shocher Tov* says: You might think that you should pray by reflecting on the words. To teach you otherwise it says, "*Only her lips moved.*" Clearly, this means that if you did not enunciate the words, you have not fulfilled the mitzvah of *tefillah,* and you must repeat it.

[The rest of the chapter deals with Kabbalistic themes.]

Chapter 6 | פרק ו׳

KAVANAH IS NOT DECISIVE

It is quite true that our thoughts ascend to the highest spiritual worlds, and when one does a mitzvah with pure *kavanah,* his performance has a greater beneficial effect on these worlds. Nevertheless, the thought behind the mitzvah is not the decisive factor ....

A person who worships G-d, observes all the mitzvos of the Torah and the Rabbis, and believes in the first verse of the *Shema* in general terms, namely, that G-d is One, even though he does not understand the meaning of His Oneness and directs his *tefillah* to G-d without philosophic speculation — this person is considered an *oveid Hashem,* "one who worships G-d."

Thus, let us not dismiss any element of the performance of a mitzvah, not even a small detail ordained by the Rabbis, and all the more so may we not change the set time for the performance of a mitzvah. Whoever is conscientious about doing the mitzvos is praiseworthy.

Chapter 7 | פרק ז׳

OTHER DECEPTIONS OF THE *YETZER HARA*

There are other ruses your *yetzer hara* will use to trap you. It will tell you that the main thing is to do everything *l'sheim*

Shamayim, for the sake of Heaven, and even sinning is considered a mitzvah if done in order to set something right, and you do it *l'sheim Shamayim.* It will quote the Gemara, saying, "The Compassionate One desires the heart" (*Sanhedrin* 106b), and, "A transgression done for the sake of Heaven is better ..." (*Nazir* 23b), and many similar sayings. Then it will support its view saying: After all, you are commanded to follow in the footsteps of your saintly forefathers who lived before the Torah was given. They were totally immersed in worshipping G-d. All their thoughts, words and deeds in this world were done with ecstatic devotion and purity of thought, directed toward restoring and unifying the higher spiritual worlds. Their worship was not regulated by prescribed sacred procedures or set times. For example, the *maggid* told the *Beis Yosef*[6] that Chanoch (Bereishis 5:24) would sew shoes, and with each stitch, he would praise the Holy One, blessed be He.[7]

Although the Sages say, "The Patriarchs fulfilled the entire Torah," and "Noach studied the Torah," that does not mean that they were obligated to keep the Torah as a *halachic* requirement. They observed the Torah because they perceived with their superior intellect what specific mitzvah was needed for the restoration of the spiritual worlds [which had fallen as a result of Adam's transgression]. But they had permission to worship G-d by other means or to transgress a mitzvah when they understood that a certain action was needed for the restoration of the higher worlds.

An intelligent person will realize that the *yetzer hara*'s arguments are false; they do not hold water. The truth is, as we

---

6 Rabbi Yosef Karo, author of the *Shulchan Aruch.*

7 *Maggid Meisharim, Parashas Mikeitz.*

pointed out at the end of Chapter 1, this kind of Divine service applied only before the Giving of the Torah. But ever since Moshe brought the Torah down to earth, it is no longer in Heaven. We proved in connection with the dialogue that took place between King Chizkiyah and Yeshayah that we are forbidden to change even one mitzvah of the Torah, even for the sake of Heaven. And even should one foresee that his fulfillment of a certain mitzvah will bring destruction to the world [as Chizkiyah did when he foresaw that by marrying he would beget the evil Menasheh], we do not have the right to abstain from doing that mitzvah, as the reasons for the mitzvos were not revealed to us.

Chapter 8 | פרק ח'

ANOTHER FALSE LINE OF REASONING

There is one more specious proof the *yetzer hara* may bring in an attempt to lead you astray. He will tell you that the goal of serving G-d is to attain exalted fear of G-d, and this is what you should strive for. [The *yetzer hara* will say that serving G-d out of] fear of punishment and being embarrassed [in front of people] are deplorable reasons [for worshipping G-d] that you should banish from your mind. The *yetzer hara* will heighten your fear of G-d to the point that you are convinced that [serving G-d out of] fear of punishment and embarrassment is a sin. As a result, it may happen that at times, when you do not feel the exalted fear of G-d, you will not restrain yourself from doing forbidden things.

The outcome may be that if someone admonishes you, showing you that you are violating a certain law, you will not stop doing it while the critic is present, because that would show that you are in awe of man rather than of G-d. And the Gemara in *Berachos* 28b quotes Rabbi Yochanan's blessing to his students: "May it be G-d's will that your fear of G-d should be as great as your fear of mortals."

SUMMATION

I have shown you a few of the strategies of the *yetzer hara,* as the Gemara in *Kiddushin* 30b says: "The *yetzer hara* renews [his battle to incite man to sin] every day, for it says, "*His yetzer ... was evil every day*" (Bereishis 6:5). Not content with yesterday's ploys, the *yetzer hara* conjures up new tricks every day. He makes it appear as if he does not incite you to sin at all. Instead, he tells you that the Torah you learned and the mitzvos you performed are worthless and that you are a thoroughly evil person. As we read in *Sukkah* 52b: It says, "*The wicked [impulse] watches for the righteous and seeks to kill him*" (Tehillim 37:32).

Dear reader, do not think that I dreamed these things up. I have checked, examined and researched these matters. I have seen many people who, striving for closeness to G-d, stumbled with regard to these things as they themselves have told me. I have witnessed several people who had been accustomed to this practice for so long that they have almost forgotten that the Minchah prayer must be recited at a set time prescribed by the Rabbis. Instead, out of habit, they accepted as Halachah that the proper time for the Minchah prayer is mainly after the stars appear, and when a man says to his friend, "Come, let's *daven* Minchah," the other answers, "First let's make sure the stars have already appeared in the sky." May G-d forgive them and pardon the unwitting and the ignorant.

CONCLUSION

You should follow the guidelines of the Rabbis who taught us that the primary concern is doing the mitzvah at its set time with all its details and particulars. This is the definitive halachah, and purity of intent is a welcome addition to the mitzvah. [If you do that,] you will be rewarded both for performing the mitzvah and having the pure intentions.

The *Mishnah* in *Avos* 3:11 clearly expresses this thought: "Anyone whose good deeds exceed his wisdom, his wisdom will endure in holiness, purity and devotion." And let us not take lightly the words of the Sages: "Anyone whose good deeds exceed his wisdom, to what is he likened? To a tree whose branches are few but whose roots are numerous. Even if all the winds of the world were to come and blow against it, they could not budge it from its place." The wise will understand [what I mean by this].

שער ד׳

GATE FOUR

THE STUDY OF TORAH *LISHMAH* – FOR ITS OWN SAKE

STUDYING *MUSSAR* AT THE EXPENSE OF TORAH

At this point, I wish to speak about the overriding importance of Torah study. Regrettably, with the passage of time, the study of Torah has declined markedly, and in our generation, due to the pressures of earning a livelihood, it has reached a dangerous low.

There are many sincerely devout people who occupy themselves almost exclusively with the study of books on piety and religious devotion rather than making the study of Torah their main concern. They shy away from Torah and halachah texts, may G-d forgive them. They mean well, but this is not the way toward attaining the light of the Torah.[1]

Of course, books on piety and religious devotion have their place. [They came about] because, although the early generations, with burning love of G-d, spent their days delving into the Gemara, Rashi and *Tosafos*, and teaching these subjects to large numbers of dedicated students, over the course of time, evil trends made inroads in the yeshivos, and as a result, many students turned just to studying Talmud and nothing else. Yet the Mishnah says: Without the fear of G-d, there is no wisdom (*Avos* 3:17). So, in an effort to counteract this lack, a number of leading rabbis wrote books stressing the importance of piety and fear of G-d.

However, they did not mean for people to set aside Torah study and devote themselves totally to the study of such works.

1 Although they are not guilty of neglecting the Torah, they do not gain the light of the Torah, and attaining the light of the Torah is the closest one can come to G-d in this world.

On the contrary, they wanted the study of the Written and Oral Torah and halachah to be one's main concern, and the pursuit of piety and fear of G-d a virtuous adjunct.

AN INVERSION OF VALUES

Lamentably, in our generation the opposite is happening. Torah study, which should be the primary concern, has been downgraded. Many people occupy themselves exclusively with studying books on piety and ethics, which inspire one to become submissive, break one's evil impulse and refine one's character. But in so doing, they neglect the study of the Torah. I have noticed that this outlook has spread to the point that in the *batei midrash* (study halls) of a certain town, most of the *sefarim* are works on *mussar* (ethics and piety); they do not even have a complete set of *Shas* (Talmud). People don't understand that this goes against G-d's will. They don't realize that in the foreseeable future — G-d forbid — they will have no rabbi or teacher to guide them, and what will become of the Torah?

Therefore, I must speak out and point out to the faithful among Yisrael the right way to the light of the Torah. Woe is us when G-d reproves us for casting aside the Torah, when G-d zealously avenges the neglect of the Torah!

A MISCONCEPTION

Let me begin by speaking about *Torah lishmah,* "learning Torah for its own sake." What does this mean? There is a popular misconception that it means learning with constant deep religious devotion. Even worse, people think that learning Torah without religious devotion is worthless, G-d forbid. And so, feeling that they are not up to such nonstop devotion, they don't even begin to study.

In the coming chapters, I shall, with G-d's help, explain the virtue of the holy Torah and the person who studies it properly. For that purpose, I shall quote a number of sayings on the subject from the Gemara, the Midrashim and the Zohar. Although these are well-known, I collected them in order to inspire the reader with a love of Torah.

Chapter 2 | פרק ב׳

TORAH LISHMAH IS NOT FERVENT DEVOTION

At the outset, let me say clearly that *Torah lishmah* does not mean learning with religious devotion, as most people think nowadays. Evidence of this is found in the Midrash stating that David Hamelech prayed to Hashem that He should consider a person who recites Tehillim as worthy as if he were immersed in studying the tractates *Nega'im* and *Ohalos*.[2] This proves that G-d values the in-depth study of Gemara more than reciting Tehillim. Now, if you would say that *lishmah* means passionate devotion, and that learning Torah requires passionate devotion, then the highest form of devotion is reciting Tehillim all day! Besides, how do you even know that G-d agreed [to equate saying Tehillim with Torah study]? The Rabbis do not tell us the answer G-d gave to David. Moreover, if religious fervor is the criterion, it would be enough to take one tractate, one chapter, or one Mishnah and study it all day long with intense fervor. Our Sages say otherwise. They tell us[3] about Rabbi Yochanan ben Zakkai that he did not leave unstudied the

---

2 The two most difficult and complex tractates of the Talmud.

3 *Sukkah* 28a.

Tanach, Mishnah, Gemara, Halachah, Aggadah[4] ..., implying that he was obsessed with the thought that he had not fulfilled his obligation of learning *Torah lishmah* by what he had learned to that point. Thus, he pushed himself all his life to learn more and more, every day, every hour.

ANOTHER PROOF

In *Mishlei Rabbesa* 10 it states: Rabbi Yehudah says: Let me show you how harshly one is treated on Judgment Day. In time to come, the Holy One, blessed be He, will judge the entire world. If one has learned Tanach [Torah, Prophets and Writings] but does not know Mishnah, he is put on trial and is sent to Gehinnom. If one has learned two or three orders of the Mishnah, the Holy One, blessed be He, tells him: "Why didn't you learn the *halachos* of all the orders?" ... If one has learned all the Aggados, the Holy One, blessed be He, asks: "Why didn't you learn the entire Talmud?" If one has learned the entire Talmud, the Holy One, blessed be He, asks: "Did you study Kabbalah ...?"

It is easily understood [that Torah *lishmah* cannot possibly mean learning with ecstatic religious feeling], for there are a large number of *halachos* in the Talmud dealing with knotty mundane issues that require deep concentration, for example, the laws of bird offerings and the laws dealing with the beginning of menstrual periods, which are essential laws,[5] and the laws relating to commercial dealings and fraud. When probing such intricate laws, it is virtually impossible to feel ardent religious devotion.

4 The ethical and inspirational teachings of the Talmud.

5 *Avos* 4:23.

TORAH FOR TORAH'S SAKE

In the final analysis, the concept of *Torah lishmah* means "learning Torah for Torah's sake." This is in line with the saying of R. Elazar bar Tzadok: "Fulfill them [the Torah's commands] for the sake of their Maker, [i.e., because G-d commanded them,] and speak of them [i.e., study them] for their own sake" — to understand their meanings, rather than to gain honor and respect.[6] Notice that regarding mitzvos, R. Elazar says that they should be performed "for the sake of G-d Who commanded them," but when it comes to learning Torah, he changes the wording to "speak of them for their own sake."[7]

What R. Elazar means to say is this: When performing a mitzvah, one should have as pure an intention as he can muster in order to bring about a *tikkun* in the higher worlds for the sake of their Maker, as it says, *"Everything Hashem made, He made for His sake"* (Mishlei 16:4). The Sages expound: "For His praise." Of course, the important thing about a mitzvah is its performance. Nevertheless, a mitzvah done with pure and fervent intention achieves greater *tikkunim* in the higher worlds than a mitzvah done without holy thoughts. But when learning Torah and Halachah, he should "speak of them for their own sake," meaning: for the Torah's sake — to know,

6 *Nedarim* 62a.

7 Since the learning should be "for the Torah's sake" in order to understand and clarify the subject matter, engaging in avid religious devotion negates the intellectual effort of Talmudic research (*Uvacharta Bachaim*).

understand and develop new insights in Halachah.[8]

Chapter 4 | פרק ד'

YIRAS SHAMAYIM, FEAR OF G-D

However, this definitely does not imply that Torah study can be done without fear of Heaven, G-d forbid. The Mishnah explicitly says: "Without the fear of G-d, there is no wisdom." And, expounding the verse, "*What good is money in the hand of a fool, when he has no mind to purchase wisdom?*" (Mishlei 17:16), the Gemara in *Yoma* 72b comments: "Woe to the scholars who engage in Torah study but have no fear of Heaven!" Similarly, in *Shemos Rabbah* it says: "Whoever has knowledge but lacks fear of Heaven has nothing at all."

In the introduction to the Zohar, R. Shimon bar Yochai says: *Yiras Shamayim* (fear of G-d) is the portal to *emunah* (faith). It is the foundation on which the entire world rests the root of all the other mitzvos of the Torah. Whoever keeps the mitzvah of fearing G-d keeps everything. And whoever is not G-d-fearing does not observe any of the mitzvos of the Torah.

In the same vein, the Midrash on *Behar* says: "What does accepting 'the yoke of heavenly sovereignty' mean? Just as one places a yoke on the ox before he begins to plow, so one should first accept the yoke of Heaven before performing the service of G-d." Without the yoke of *yiras Shamayim*, one cannot serve

8 Knowing the superficial meaning of a *halachah* is not enough. One should do his best to understand the underlying principles of the law and perhaps discover novel ideas. (*Uvacharta Bachaim*)

G-d, as it says, "*Serve Hashem with fear* (Tehillim 2:11).[9] *Yirah* (fear) is the foundation of everything, because *yirah* is the gate that leads to *kedushah*. Without *yirah*, one cannot attain *kedushah*.

The Mishnah in *Avos* 3:11 says: "Anyone whose fear of sin takes priority over his wisdom, his wisdom will endure"—because the fear of G-d is what keeps the wisdom of the Torah intact. To prove the point the *Gemara* in *Shabbos* 31a quotes the verse, "*The faith of your times will be the strength of your salvations ... fear of Hashem—that is His storehouse*" (Yeshayah 33:3), and expounds: *Faith* refers to the order of *Zera'im* [the first order of the Mishnah, which deals with agricultural laws]. But although the six orders of the Mishnah encompass the essence of life, nevertheless, "*the fear of Hashem is His storehouse*." Thus, the verse compares the Torah to the harvest and the fear of G-d to the storehouse where the grain is stockpiled, for the fear of G-d is the storehouse where the Torah is preserved. If one has not prepared a "storehouse" of *yiras shamayim*, the harvest of Torah remains standing in the field to be trampled by animals; he will not retain the Torah he has learned.

Chapter 5 | פרק ה'

THE STOREHOUSE OF *YIRAH*

The larger the size of the storehouse of *yirah* one has prepared, the greater the harvest of Torah it will hold. A farmer who

9 The fear of G-d is like a yoke that compels a person to serve, making it impossible for him to stray (*Uvacharta Bachaim*).

distributes grain to his sons will give each son only as much as his storehouse will hold. Much as he wants to, he cannot give him more than the capacity of his storehouse. And if the son did not even have a small barn, the father will not give him anything.

The same is true with G-d. He is ready to bestow on each Jew an abundance of wisdom and clear understanding that should remain intact, so that upon arriving in the heavenly realm he will bring his learning with him.[10] It all depends on the storehouse of *yirah* he provided. If he prepared a large storehouse of *yirah*, G-d will give him as great a flow of wisdom as his storehouse will hold. If he did not even build a small shed of *yirah*, G-d will not grant him any wisdom at all, since it will not last.

This ties in with the verse, "*The beginning of wisdom is the fear of Hashem*" (Tehillim 111:10). The mitzvah of acquiring *yirah* is of paramount importance because it is essential to preserving and keeping the holy Torah. If a person lacks *yirah*, people look down on his Torah learning. Hence, *yiras Shamayim* must precede Torah study.

Chapter 6 | פרק ו'

CONNECTING WITH G-D

The right approach to Torah study is that before sitting down to learn, one should reflect for a moment on *yiras Hashem*. He should confess his sins from the depths of his heart so that his Torah study will be holy and pure, and have in mind that his learning will bring him closer to G-d. For the Zohar says that

10 *Pesachim* 50a.

G-d and His Will are One and the same, and every *halachah* is His Will. It is G-d's Will that something is kosher or non-kosher, pure or impure, permitted or prohibited, or a person is guilty or innocent.

And even when studying the Aggadic passages of the Gemara — teachings that have no bearing on any law — one connects with the word of G-d, for the entire Torah, down to its smallest detail, was given by G-d to Moshe on Sinai. For the Midrash says:[11] "When the Holy One, blessed be He, appeared on Sinai to give the Torah to Moshe, He related to Moshe Scripture, Mishnah, Halachah and Aggadah — even the questions a student asks his rebbi."[12]

But there is more. While engrossed in Torah study down on earth, every word he utters emanates at the same time from G-d's mouth, so to speak. This is evident from the Gemara in *Gittin* 6b where R. Aviyasar and R. Yonasan argue on the subject of "the concubine in Giv'ah." Soon afterwards, R. Aviyasar met Eliyahu and said to him: "What is the Holy One, blessed be He, doing?"

"He is discussing the question of the concubine in Giv'ah," replied Eliyahu.

"What does He say?" asked R. Aviyasar.

"He says: My son Aviyasar says such-and-such, and My son Yonasan says such-and-such." This was because at that very moment, R. Aviyasar and R. Yonasan were debating that issue.

---

11 *Shemos Rabbah* 43.

12 Rav Chaim Brisker asks: How is it possible to question the Torah? He answers: Since the questions are merely devices to bring out the true meaning of the text, the questions themselves become part of Torah. (*Uvacharta Bachaim*)

And when David said, "*The Torah of Your mouth is better for me than thousands in gold and silver*" (Tehillim 119:72), he meant to say: "I rejoice in my Torah study, realizing that it is the Torah 'of Your mouth,' that You are saying the words I am studying, together with me." Therefore, all parts of the Torah are equally holy, because every word of Torah literally emanated from G-d's mouth. And if a letter is missing in a Torah scroll, the scroll is invalid, whether a letter in the phrase "*aluf Timna* (the chief of Timna)," or in the Ten Commandments or in *Shema Yisrael.*

Chapter 7 | פרק ז׳

FEAR OF G-D IS A PRESERVATIVE

As was mentioned above, before sitting down to study Torah one should reflect on the importance of *yiras Shamayim* and repentance, so that through his learning he connects with the Creator. In addition, he should make up his mind to observe the Written and Oral Torah. And when exploring a halachic point, he should pray for guidance in arriving at the correct conclusion.

In the midst of studying Torah, one is permitted to pause briefly in order to "recharge" his *yiras Shamayim*. In this vein, the Gemara in *Shabbos* 31a offers the following analogy: "[Thinking devout thoughts] can be compared to a farmer who said to his worker, 'Carry up a *kor* of wheat to the loft,' and he went and did so.

"'Did you mix a *kav* of *chumtan* in the wheat?' the farmer asked him. [*Chumtan* is a sandy soil containing salty substances used for preservation of wheat.]

"'No,' he replied.

"'Then it would have been better that you had not carried it up,' the farmer retorted."

In a figurative sense, this applies to Torah study, for it is helpful to add a dose of *yiras Shamayim* to one's studies to preserve one's learning [just as *chumtan* preserves wheat].

The Gemara continues by stating a general rule: "A man may mix a *kav* of *chumtan* in a *kor* of grain and have no fear [of being dishonest when he sells the whole amount as grain, because that proportion is necessary for its preservation]." This ruling deals with an issue of fraud and misappropriation, and as such it should be placed in the Order of *Nezikin* (Damages). What is it doing here [in *Mo'ed*]? It teaches us that, although adding a *kav* of *chumtan* dust to the grain may look like shortchanging the buyer, however, since it acts as a preservative, it is not considered theft. By the same token, one is allowed to interrupt his learning to reflect briefly on *yiras Hashem*, and it is not considered neglecting his Torah study, because *yiras Hashem* preserves his knowledge of Torah.

Chapter 8 | פרק ח'

STOREHOUSE FOR TORAH

On the other extreme, there are many people who mistakenly devote all their time to studying books on *yirah*, piety and *mussar*. Their error may be explained with an analogy: Before bringing in the harvest, a farmer will build a storehouse to hold the crops. Would any farmer in his right mind spend all his time and energy building a large storehouse and then neglect harvesting the grain? Of course not. By the same token, how can anyone say that a Jew should devote all his time to building the storehouse of *yiras Hashem* only to leave it empty? Then all he gains is just one single mitzvah, namely the mitzvah of "*You will fear Hashem, your G-d*" (Devarim 6:2).

And when the Sages say: The Holy One, blessed be He, has nothing in His world except a storehouse of the fear of Heaven,[13] they had in mind a storehouse of *yirah* that is filled with a rich harvest of Torah, Mishnah, Halachah and other elements of Torah study. It is the *yirah* that preserves one's Torah learning, engraving it on one's heart and memory, ready for instant recall.

Chapter 9 | פרק ט'

THE TORAH BRINGS ON *YIRAH*

We mentioned above that one is permitted to interrupt his Torah study to reflect on *yirah*. We compared inserting *yirah* meditations into one's Torah studies to the permissible addition of a *kav* of *chumtan* to a *kor* of grain. The implication is that adding more than a *kav* of *chumtan* is considered theft, since it is more than is needed as preservative. The same is true regarding *yirah*. If one spends more time on *yirah* meditation than is needed to guard and preserve his Torah knowledge, he is stealing the time he could have devoted to Torah study.[14]

13 *Berachos* 33b

14 A *kav* is 1/180 of a *kor*. Thus, a kav of *yirah* is 1/180 of the time set aside for Torah study, which means that for 15 hours of Torah study, five minutes should be devoted to contemplating *yirah*. *(Uvacharta Bachaim)*

As a matter of fact, a person who learns Torah *lishmah* — for the sake of Torah — does not have to devote as much time to studying devotional books to acquire *yirah* as one who does not learn Torah *lishmah*. Torah study itself brings on *yirah*, as it says:[15] "Whoever engages in Torah study for its own sake ... the Torah clothes him in humility and the fear of G-d."

The prophet says, *"Along the stream will grow every species of food tree"* (Yechezkel 47:12). Commenting on this verse, *Tanna D'bei Eliyahu* says: "What kind of trees will grow alongside this stream? — The trees are the scholars who possess Torah, Mishnah, Halachah, Aggadah, good deeds and practical experience. Since they love the Torah, G-d has mercy on them, giving them wisdom, understanding, knowledge and insight to do good deeds and learn Torah, and everything is put in order for them."

Chapter 10 | פרק י'

BLUEPRINT OF THE WORLD

While learning Torah, one certainly does not need to strive for closer attachment to G-d, because by the very act of Torah study, he clings to His Will and His Word, for G-d and His will are One and the same.

This idea is expressed in a saying in [Midrash] *Shemos Rabbah*: "If a person buys an article, does he thereby acquire also the owner of the article? Of course not! But when the Holy One, blessed be He, gave the Torah to Yisrael, He told them:

15 *Avos* 6:1.

'You are acquiring Me together with the Torah.'"[16] Indeed, the Zohar on several occasions remarks that "the Holy One, blessed be He, and the Torah are One and the same."[17]

The Torah is G-d's word, and through the utterance of His mouth [in Bereishis] the myriad of higher worlds were created. As the Zohar[18] says: "When G-d wanted to create the world, He looked in the Torah and made the world." Thus, the Torah is the blueprint of the world. This is the underlying idea of the verse, *"I was then His nursemaid"* (Mishlei 8:30). The Torah cries out: When G-d created the world, *I was then His nursemaid* [i.e., I showed G-d how to do it].

The Torah existed before the world was created, and when G-d wanted to create the world, He looked into every word of the Torah and formed every detail of creation according to those words. Indeed, everything in existence in all the worlds can be found in the Torah. So, when G-d saw the words, *"In the beginning G-d created Heaven ...,"* He created Heaven. When He saw the words, *"Let there be light,"* He created light, and so on. That's why the Torah says, *"I was then His nursemaid."*

For this reason, the Torah, all the worlds and everything concerned with their existence and their contents are alluded

---

16 This does not mean that we acquire G-d Himself; that is unthinkable. It means that by perceiving His Will that is expressed in the Torah, we recognize His existence. Therefore, by giving the Torah to Yisrael, handing over to the Rabbis the power to decide the Halachah, which means determining the Will of G-d through their halachic rulings down on earth, G-d, in fact, made the Rabbis the masters of His Will. This is the meaning of "acquiring G-d along with the Torah." *(Uvacharta Bachaim)*

17 This does not refer to the Essence of G-d, which is completely beyond our comprehension. It means that through the Torah, we get a very clear understanding of His existence. In the Torah, we recognize G-d much more clearly than by contemplating G-d's works in nature. *(Uvacharta Bachaim)*

18 *Parashas Terumah* 161:1.

to in the ten utterances[19] of the story of Creation. Therefore, the Torah, whose hidden root is high above the World of Emanation, has been the soul, life and light of all the worlds ever since the world was created. Without the constant flow of light of the Torah, all the worlds would revert to absolute, primordial emptiness.

Chapter 11 | פרק י״א

G-D, THE TORAH AND YISRAEL ARE ONE

Therefore, all the worlds continue to exist and function properly only if we are engaged in studying the Torah, because the Holy One, blessed be He, the Torah and Yisrael are One. For the root of each Jew's soul is linked to a letter of the Torah. Thus, it says:[20] "[G-d's] thought of bringing Yisrael into being came before all else." This does not contradict the saying that the Torah preceded everything else, because the Torah and Yisrael stem from the same heavenly root.

In the same vein, the Sages comment on the word "*bereishis*":

"[G-d created the world] for the sake of the Torah, which is called *reishis*, as in the verse, "*The beginning* (reishis) *of His way*" (Mishlei 8:22), and for the sake of Yisrael, since they are called *reishis*, as in, "*the beginning* (reishis) *of his crops*" (Yirmiyah 2:3).

For this reason, the Gemara in *Mo'ed Katan* 25a says: "If one is present at the time a person's soul departs, he is required to

19 In the story of Creation it says ten times, "*G-d said.*"

20 *Bereishis Rabbah* 1.

tear his clothes. To what is this [the dying person] compared? To a Torah scroll that was burned in which case one [who witnessed it] is required to tear his clothes." For the holiness of every Jew's soul is identical with the holiness of a Torah scroll.

THE WORLD BEFORE THE GIVING OF THE TORAH

At Creation, the Torah was still hidden away, its light radiating on the higher worlds and keeping them in existence from a distance. It had not yet reached the lower world to allow those assembled there to engross themselves in it. As a result, the world was still precarious and unstable. As the Gemara in *Avodah Zarah* 9a puts it: During the first two thousand years, the world is to be devoid [of Torah]. The fate of the world was in the balance until the giving of the Torah, as it says:[21] "The Holy One, blessed be He, stipulated with the works of Creation and said to them: 'If Yisrael accepts the Torah, you will continue to exist; if not, I will turn you back to primordial emptiness and void.'"

Ever since the Torah was lowered to this world, when Moshe brought it down from Heaven, the continued existence of all the worlds is secured by our speaking and thinking Torah thoughts.

Unquestionably, therefore, if there would be one moment when not one person is engrossed in Torah study somewhere in the entire world, all the upper and lower worlds would instantly cease to exist, G-d forbid.

THE FRUITS OF TORAH STUDY

And so, in the *berachah* over the Torah, we say, "He implanted eternal life within us." We plant a tree so that it should bear

21 *Shabbos* 88a.

fruit for our benefit. So, too, if we take pains to learn Torah for its own sake, we shall inherit eternal life and bring an increase of holiness, blessing and spiritual light to all the higher worlds. We unite the higher and the lower worlds, as the Gemara in *Sanhedrin* 99b says: "Whoever engages in Torah study for its own sake promotes peace among the heavenly hosts above [i.e., the angels], and among the hosts below [i.e., men], as it says, '*Or let him take hold of My strength [the Torah] that he may make peace with Me*' (Yeshayah 27:5). Rav says: [When a person studies Torah for its own sake,] it is as if he built the heavenly and earthly palaces, for it says, '*For I have placed My words in your mouth ... to plant the heavens and lay the foundations of the earth*' (Yeshayah 51:16)."

UPHOLDING THE WORLD

The Midrash expounds on the verse, "*His loins are pillars of marble*" (Shir Hashirim 5:15), stating, "This refers to Torah scholars." Why are they compared to pillars? Because they are the pillars that hold up the world, as it says, "*If My covenant ... would not be, I had not set up the laws of Heaven and earth*" (Yirmiyah 33:25). Says the Holy One, blessed be He: "When someone learns Torah and wisdom, I consider it as if he had created the Heaven and established the entire world."

And the Zohar[22] says: "Whoever immerses himself in the Torah every day will have a share in the World to Come and will be considered as if he had built worlds, because the world is founded on the Torah. See, Hashem created the world with the breath of His mouth, and through the breath of those who learn Torah the world endures."

22 *Parashas Bereishis* 47:1.

The Zohar says further:[23] "When Hashem created the world, it was not meant to endure. Only when He resolved to create man who would learn Torah did He decide that the world should endure for man's sake. Thus, you might say that when one looks in the Torah and studies it, he keeps the world intact. To put it another way: G-d looked into the Torah and created the world; man looks into the Torah and upholds the world."

G-D'S FRIEND AND PARTNER

Expressing this idea, the Mishnah in *Avos* 6:1 says: "Whoever engages in Torah study for its own sake is called a 'comrade.'" By learning Torah he becomes the Creator's partner, so to speak. Through his learning, he keeps all the worlds intact; without his learning, the world would return to primordial void. As the Midrash says: "G-d says about the Jewish people, *'I have considered you My friend'* (Shir Hashirim 1:9) — You have become My friend because you accepted the Torah."

Chapter 12 | פרק י"ב

CREATING NEW TORAH INSIGHTS

When it comes to Torah study, by far the greatest benefit to the higher worlds is achieved by developing novel Torah insights. Every single word of a new insight is cherished dearly by G-d. He kisses it and builds a new world from it.[24] This is alluded to in the verse, *"Just as the new heavens and the new earth that I am making will endure"* (Yeshayah 66:22).

23 *Parashas Terumah* 161:1.

24 The Vilna Gaon in his sefer *Shenos Eliyahu* says that with every word of Torah one utters he performs a mitzvah.

In this vein, the Zohar in its introduction says: "A person should exert himself day and night learning Torah, for G-d listens to the voices of Torah students, and from each novel point a student develops, Hashem creates a heavenly firmament. This teaches us that when someone creates a new Torah insight, G-d takes that insight, kisses it, and crowns it with seventy crowns. Each new word flies aloft to 70,000 worlds ... and becomes a heavenly expanse ... G-d calls these insights 'the new heavens.' As it says, '*Just as the new heavens ... that I am making.*' It does not say, 'that I have made,' but 'that I am making continuously.'"

Chapter 13 | פרק י"ג

G-D'S JOY AND DELIGHT

Through the study of Torah, G-d's plan for Creation is brought to fruition, for He created the world solely in order that Klal Yisrael should learn Torah. As the Sages[25] put it: "The world was created for the sake of the Torah, for the sake of Yisrael, and for the sake of Moshe who was Hashem's mediator at the Receiving of the Torah." At that time, G-d was happy to have created the world, for now its purpose was fulfilled.

The Midrash[26] compares it to a king who had built a palace. Admiring the beautiful edifice, he exclaims, "Palace, O palace! May I always enjoy you as much as I delight in you today." So said G-d to His world [on the day of the giving of the Torah]: "My world, O My world! May you always please Me as much as you gladden Me today."

25 *Bereishis Rabbah.*

26 *Midrash Rabbah, Parashas Bereishis* 9.

Indeed, the Torah is characterized as *"a beloved doe, inspiring favor"* (Mishlei 5:19).[27]

Commenting on the verse, *"I have placed My words in your mouth ... to implant the heavens and make firm the earth"* (Yeshayah 51:16), the Zohar[28] says: "This teaches us that when a man learns Torah and his lips utter words of Torah ... he upholds the world. G-d is as happy with him as he was on the day He created Heaven and earth, as it says, '*to implant the heavens and make firm the earth.*'"

The Zohar[29] says further: "When people are learning Torah, G-d is happy with His world. What's more, G-d rallies all His angels and tells them: 'Look what a holy nation I have on earth, for they make a crown for the Torah.' When the angels see their Master's joy, they immediately proclaim, 'Who is like Your people Yisrael, a unique nation on earth!'"

The Zohar[30] continues: "Yisrael is happy, for G-d gave them the Torah, which is the source of His joy and delight, as it says, '*I will be then His delight every day*' (Mishlei 8:30)."

Chapter 14 | פרק י"ד

AS IF STANDING AT SINAI

[It is not only G-d who rejoices when people learn Torah *lishmah,*] all the higher worlds and the spiritual beings are also filled with joy when the radiance of the supernal light shines

27 Just as a doe remains beloved to her mate, the Torah is most beloved to those who study it (*Rashi*).

28 *Parashas Tzav* 35:1.

29 *Parashas Terumah* 155:2.

30 *Parashas Shemini.*

on them from the heavenly source of the Torah, as it says: "[Whoever engages in Torah study for its own sake] gladdens the Omnipresent and gladdens His creatures."[31]

The Zohar[32] says: "When a person immerses himself in Torah study *lishmah*, it is as if he were standing at Mount Sinai receiving the Torah, as it says, '*Today* [with the giving of all the commandments] *you have become a nation*' (Devarim 27:9)." The reason is this: Just as at the giving of the Torah, Yisrael attached themselves to G-d's word, so, too, at the present time, whenever a person reflects on Torah thoughts, he attaches himself to G-d's word, because he is learning the words G-d transmitted to Moshe. Therefore, even today when a person is learning Torah, each word he learns is a fiery utterance from the mouth of G-d, and he is considered as receiving it on Sinai.

BRINGING GOODNESS TO THE WORLD

Through a person's learning, an abundance of light and blessing flows to all the spiritual worlds, and the physical world, too, is illuminated and blessed with the glory of the Torah. As a result, his learning brings a profusion of goodness to the world.

It says in *Tanna D'bei Eliyahu:*[33] "A person who learns Torah brings goodness to the world. He can pray for Divine mercy; he can pierce the sky to bring rain upon the world." It says there also: "When Jews engage in Torah study and obey G-d's will, the Holy One, blessed be He, showers blessings on them, as

31 *Avos* 6:1.

32 *Parashas Acharei* 69a.

33 *Seder Eliyahu Rabbah*, ch. 18.

it says, *'Truth sprouts from earth, and righteousness looks down* [nishkaf] *from Heaven'* (Tehillim 85:12), and the word *nishkaf* (looks down) denotes blessing, as it says, *'Look down* [hashkifah] *from Your holy abode, and bless Your people Yisrael'* (Devarim 26:15)."

Chapter 15 | פרק ט"ו

THE POWER OF TORAH LEARNING

We have a rule: The one who blesses, receives blessing. Therefore, by bringing blessing on the higher worlds, the person who learns Torah *lishmah* is himself blessed, and the glory of G-d hovers over him all day. He attains a lofty soul in line with the level and the intensity of his learning. And so it says:[34] "If a person sanctifies himself a little, [Heaven] helps him to become very much sanctified. If he sanctifies himself below, he becomes sanctified above."

[The person who learns Torah *lishmah*] is master over everything; evil decrees have no power over him in this world. And so it says:[35] "R. Shimon ben Lakish said: If you study Torah, pain and suffering will depart from you." And it says:[36] "If someone's head hurts, let him engage in Torah study. If someone's throat is sore, let him study Torah ... If he feels pain all over his body, let him study Torah."

Similarly, in *Tanna D'bei Eliyahu* it says: "If a person committed many transgressions, and Heaven decreed that he should die for his sins, but he repents and studies Torah, Prophets and

34 *Yoma* 39a.
35 *Berachos* 5a.
36 *Eruvin* 54a.

Writings, and he also learns Mishnah, Midrash, Halachah and Aggadah, then even if a hundred decrees were passed against him, the Holy One, blessed be He, will revoke all of them."

Commenting on the verse, "*The King has brought me into His chambers*" (Shir Hashirim 1:4), *Tanna D'bei Eliyahu* says: "Just as the Holy One, blessed be He, has innermost chambers in His Torah, so, too, each Torah scholar has secluded chambers of profound Torah knowledge. And when you feel pain coming on, intensify your Torah studies, probe the inner chambers of Torah,[37] and your pain will disappear, as it says, '*Go, my people, enter your chambers and close your door behind you*' (Yeshayah 26:20)."

THE TORAH PROTECTS FROM HARM

The Zohar[38] says: "How beloved to G-d are the words of Torah, and how beloved to G-d are those who engage in Torah learning. Whoever engrosses himself in Torah study need not fear the destructive forces of the world. He is protected from harmful influences from above and from below. What's more, he can subdue the demons of the world, casting them down to the bottom of the vast depths."

The same idea is expressed in the Gemara in *Sotah* 21a [according to R. Yosef]: "The Torah you learn protects you [from punishment] and saves you [from the *yetzer hara*], whether you are engaged in studying or not, for "*She* [the Torah] *is good to him, never bad, all the days of her life*" (Shir Hashirim 31:12), meaning, even when one is not studying it, as long as one has in mind to resume one's studies."

---

37 Meaning, that he should delve deeper into the intricacies of the Torah (*Uvacharta Bachaim*).

38 *Parashas Vayechi* 242a.

RELIEF FROM ANXIETIES

[If someone learns Torah *lishmah*] all his worries and worldly concerns that interfere with his learning are removed, as it says:[39] "If someone accepts upon himself the yoke of Torah, the yoke of government and the yoke of worldly responsibilities are removed from him."

The Midrash[40] says: "It is for this reason that the Torah was given in the desert. Just as a desert is an area that is not plowed and where no crops grow, so, too, if someone accepts upon himself the yoke of Torah, his worries about earning a livelihood are taken away from him. And just as in a wilderness you do not have to pay taxes, so, too, a Torah scholar is exempt from paying taxes."

EXEMPT FROM PAYING TAXES

In fact, it is a halachic ruling that Torah scholars are exempt from paying taxes, as the Gemara in Nedarim 62b says: "Rava said, A Torah scholar is permitted to say, 'I will not pay the head tax [that was levied on the town since the town benefits from my Torah study],' as it says, '*[King Artaxerxes wrote to Ezra:] No one has the authority to impose upon them [the kohanim] any levy, tax or duty* (Ezra 7:24).'"

Likewise, it says in *Tanna D'bei Eliyahu, Eliyahu Rabbah*, Chapter 4: "A Torah scholar who studies full-time for the sake of Heaven does not need a sword, a spear or any protective

39 *Avos* 3:6.

40 *Tanchuma, Parashas Chukas.*

armor, because the Holy One, blessed be He, Himself guards him." And in Chapter 18 it says: "If a person conducts himself properly and knows only the Written Torah, he is given one angel to protect him. If he knows Tanach, he is given two angels to protect him, for it says, '*He will charge His angels for you*' (Tehillim 91:11). But if one knows Tanach, Mishnah, Midrash, Halachah and Aggadah, and has ministered to Torah scholars, the Holy One, blessed be He, Himself watches over him, for it says, '*G-d is your Guardian*' (Tehillim 121:5)."

The more dedicated one is to learning Torah *lishmah*, the more he will be granted relief from worldly worries, and a heavenly protective shield will hover over him. The Gemara in *Avodah Zarah* 17a says: "Whoever occupies himself with Torah study will have his wishes granted by the Holy One, blessed be He." And the Midrash[41] says: "Whoever occupies himself with Torah study will be successful in all his undertakings," and: "Whoever disseminates Torah to the public will earn his livelihood without strain and hard work. Hashem will provide his daily sustenance, as it says, '*She* [the Torah] *gives food for her household*' (Mishlei 31:15)."[42]

It says in *Tanna D'bei Eliyahu*: Torah scholars who learn Torah for the sake of Heaven, and at every possible opportunity, with *yirah* in their hearts, even if they were to ask for the whole world, G-d would give it to them instantly.

41 Tehillim 1:1.

42 The *Rambam* says in *Hilchos Shemittah* 13:13: Every person in the world whose spirit lifts him and whose wisdom guides him to keep away [from worldly pursuits] and devote himself to serving G-d and gaining knowledge of G-d ... casting off the yoke of mundane concerns, will be sanctified and will be holy of holies. G-d will be his portion and inheritance for all eternity ... All his needs are filled in this world. *(Uvacharta Bachaim)*

But there's more. We know that a Torah scholar who studies Torah *lishmah* shuns honor and greatness, as it says:[43] "Do not seek greatness for yourself, and do not crave honor." However, G-d will grant him joy and glory against his will, as it says, "*Only goodness and kindness shall pursue me all the days of my life*" (Tehillim 23:6), meaning: Although I run away from honor and greatness, the unwanted accolades pursue me against my will.

Chapter 17 | פרק י"ז

TORAH STUDY SAVES FROM GEHINNOM

The Gemara in *Chagigah* 27a says: "The fire of Gehinnom has no power over Torah scholars." And the Midrash[44] says: "The Holy One, blessed be He, said to Yisrael at Mount Sinai: If you accept the Torah and keep it, I will save you from three calamities: the war of Gog and Magog, the birthpangs of Mashiach, and the judgment of Gehinnom. And I will satiate you with the good that is set aside [for *tzaddikim*] in the hereafter, as it says, '*How abundant is Your goodness that You have stored away for those who fear You*' (Tehillim 31:20)." And the Midrash says further: "The only righteous act that saves man from Gehinnom is Torah study. Even if a person has committed a sin, the Torah he has studied can save him from harsh judgment."

And in Midrash Tehillim[45] it says: "In the time to come, Gehinnom will cease to exist. Instead, the sun will scorch the evildoers, as it says, '*For behold the day is coming,* [the sun will

43 *Avos* 6:5.
44 *Mishlei Rabbesa* 1.
45 Tehillim 19.

be] *burning like an oven, when all the wicked people and all the evildoers will be like straw, and the sun will burn them up'* (Malachi 3:19). Furthermore it says, *'There is no darkness and no shadow of death where evildoers can be hidden'* (Iyov 34:22). But who can hide [from the searing heat of the sun]? Those who occupy themselves with Torah study."

We can derive this with a *kal vachomer* (an *a fortiori* logical deduction) from Elisha-Acher.[46] For the Gemara in *Chagigah* 15b says: "When Acher [who rejected the Torah] died, they said in Heaven: 'We cannot sentence him to Gehinnom because he immersed himself in Torah study.'" [All the more would this be true of lesser evildoers.]

The Zohar[47] says: "Why was the Torah given amid fire and darkness?[48] To teach us that whoever studies Torah will be saved from the fire of Gehinnom and from the darkness that the nations of the world spread over Yisrael."

EVERLASTING LIFE

Raya Mehemna[49] says: "It is a mitzvah to learn Torah every day, for it discloses the mystery of the ways of Hashem. Whoever learns Torah gains merit in this world and the next. He is saved from all accusing angels, and the *Shechinah* rests on him."

Commenting on the verse, *"Unveil my eyes that I may perceive the wonders of Your Torah"* (Tehillim 119:18), *Raya Mehemna*[50] says: "How foolish are people who don't learn Torah,

---

46 Elisha ben Avuya, the mentor of Rabbi Meir, was a great Torah scholar. However, he renounced Judaism and became an apostate, after which he was referred to only as Acher, "the other one" (*Chagigah* 15a).

47 *Parashas Yisro* 83b.

48 See Devarim 4:11.

49 *Parashas Terumah* 134b.

50 *Parashas Chayei Sarah* 131b.

for the Torah means life, freedom and goodness in this world and the World to Come. Torah grants complete happiness in this world, a life of total freedom, without misery — freedom from oppression in this world and freedom in the World to Come — for whoever has learned Torah is free from Divine judgment in the hereafter."

The Zohar[51] says: "Anyone who makes an effort to learn Torah will have life in this world and the World to Come. Even if he did not study it *lishmah*, he is rewarded in this world and will not be judged in the World to Come. Proof of this is the verse, '*Length of days is at its right; at its left, wealth and honor*' (Mishlei 3:16). '*Length of days at its right*' means: everlasting life in the hereafter is given to one who learns Torah *lishmah*. '*At its left, wealth and honor*' means: he will be granted a rich reward and a life of tranquility in this world. What's more, when a person who learned Torah *lishmah* departs from this world, the Torah goes ahead of him, protecting him from accusing angels. When his body lies in the grave, the Torah watches over him, and when his soul ascends to its place in the hereafter, the Torah goes ahead of him, and many gates crumble before the Torah, until the soul reaches its destination. The Torah hovers over him until he awakens at the revival of the dead, and it defends him [before the heavenly tribunal]. And so it says, '*As you go forth, it will guide you; as you recline*' — in the grave —, '*it will guard you; and when you wake up, it will speak for you*' — it will defend you before the heavenly court" (Mishlei 6:22).

Further on this subject, the Midrash Tanchuma says in *Parashas Eikev* on the words, "inscribed (*charus*) on the tablets

---

51 *Parashas Vayeishev* 184b, 185a.

[of stone]": Do not read *charus* but *cherus*, "freedom," because a person is considered free from the grip of the angel of death if he studies Torah.

Chapter 18 | פרק י"ח

UNTOUCHED BY THE FORCES OF NATURE

A person who takes upon himself the yoke of learning Torah *lishmah*—for Torah's sake—lives under Hashem's special supervision. As such, worldly conditions do not affect him; he stands above the forces of nature and is immune to celestial influences. Being attached to the Torah and close to the Holy One, blessed be He, he is filled with the holiness of the Torah, which is infinitely higher than all the worlds. It is the source of life of all the worlds and all the forces of nature. Therefore, a person who occupies himself with studying the Torah infuses life into all the worlds and ranks higher than the worlds. So it is impossible for this person's destiny to be determined by the forces of nature.

This idea is expressed in the Gemara in *Pesachim* 50b: Rava contrasted two verses. It says, "*For Your kindness is great* until *the heavens*" (Tehillim 57:11); but another verse says, "*For your kindness is great* above *the heavens*" (108:5). How can this be explained? [Is Hashem's kindness until, or above, the heavens?] The Gemara answers: G-d's kindness reaches *above the heavens* for those who perform the mitzvos *lishmah* [i.e., they are beyond the laws of nature; meaning, miracles are performed for them]; it reaches only *until the heavens* for those who do the mitzvos *shelo lishmah* [i.e., they are governed by the laws of nature]." This concurs with the opinion of R. Yehudah who said:[52] "A man should always engage in Torah and mitzvos even *shelo lishmah,* for by doing them *shelo lishmah* he will come to engage in them *lishmah.*"

This means that a person who learns Torah *shelo lishmah,* although he has an ulterior motive, will eventually reach the level of learning *lishmah.* Nevertheless, at his present stage, he has not yet risen to the point where G-d would deal with him in a supernatural way.

This is expounded in *Raya Mehemna:*[53] "Before the Torah was given to Yisrael, the fate of humanity was determined by the position of the stars. After the Torah was given, the Jewish people were removed from the dictates of the planets and constellations. Therefore, if one learns Torah, he is set free from the predestined fate determined by the stars. Conversely, the destiny of one who neglects his Torah studies is unalterably decided by the position of the planets and the signs of the zodiac."

HE CONTROLS THE FORCES OF NATURE

Furthermore, the forces of nature do the bidding of one who learns Torah *lishmah* [i.e., he has the power to work miracles.] He can control the forces of nature, for they are in awe of him, as it says in *Avos* 6:1, "[The Torah] gives him kingship and dominion," for the Divine crown, the radiance of Torah, radiates from his head. The Zohar says: "'*I have placed My words in your mouth, and with the shade of My hand have I covered you*' (Yeshayah 51:16) — this teaches that whoever learns Torah, the Holy One, blessed be He, protects him, and the *Shechinah* spreads its wings over him."

52 *Pesachim* 50b.

53 *Parashas Pinchas* 216b.

In the same vein, the Zohar[54] says: "Look how powerful the Torah is, and how much higher it is above all else. Whoever learns Torah need not fear the higher and lower spiritual beings and need not be afraid of sickness and disease, because he holds on to the Tree of Life and eats its fruit all day. The Torah teaches man to walk in the path of truth."

And the Zohar[55] says: "Look how much G-d loves the Torah! Whoever learns Torah is beloved above and below. The Holy One, blessed be He, listens to his prayers and does not abandon him either in this world or the next." And the Zohar[56] says: "If a person does his best to serve his Master and study Torah, a multitude of angels come out to guard him, the *Shechinah* hovers over him and all angels proclaim before him: 'Honor to the image of the King! He is guarded in this world and the next. Fortunate is his lot!'"

Chapter 19 | פרק י״ט

THE TORAH COMPRISES THE NAMES OF G-D

G-d's name is associated with one who learns Torah, because the Torah is made up entirely of G-d's names, as it says in the Gemara in *Berachos* 21a: "Where do we find in the Torah that a *berachah* must be said prior to Torah study? For it says, '*When I proclaim the name of Hashem, praise G-d for His greatness*'

54 *Parashas Va'eschanan* 260a.
55 *Parashas Beshalach* 46a.
56 *Parashas Metzora* 52b.

(Devarim 32:3),[57] [meaning, when one learns Torah, which is made up of G-d's Names, he must recite a *berachah*, praising G-d's Name]."

The Sages taught also that when one learns Torah, the *Shechinah* hovers over him, for it says, "*Wherever I allow My name to be mentioned* [i.e., wherever a Torah scholar learns Torah, which is comprised of G-d's Name], *I will come to you and bless you*" (Shemos 20:21). Similarly, the Zohar[58] says: "Look how much G-d cherishes the Torah! Wherever someone is learning Torah, the Holy One, blessed be He, and all His hosts listen in, and G-d comes to dwell with him, as it says, '*Wherever I allow My name to be mentioned, I will come to you and bless you.*'"

The Zohar[59] also says: "Whoever observes the laws of the Torah and is occupied in studying it is considered as though he studied G-d's holy Name, because the entire Torah is one holy Divine Name that includes all Names. Therefore, [a scribe] who omits one letter in the Torah is reckoned as though he blemished the holy Name."

And the Zohar[60] further says: "Whoever forgets the Torah text and does not want to study it is considered as though he forgot the Holy One, blessed be He, because the Torah is made up entirely of G-d's Name. And whoever learns Torah is crowned with the crown of G-d's Name and will get to know

---

57 The *Ramban* in the introduction to his Torah commentary explains: We have a mystic tradition (Zohar, *Parashas Yisro* 87a) that the whole Torah is made up of Names of the Holy One, blessed is He, and that the letters of the words separate themselves into Divine Names when divided in a different way. For example: The verse *Bereishis bara Elokim* divides itself into the words: *berosh yisbarei Elokim* [or *Bara she'yisbarei*]. This principle applies likewise to the entire Torah.

58 *Parashas Bamidbar* 118a.

59 *Parashas Mishpatim* 124a.

60 *Parashas Vayikra* 13b.

the hidden ways and the deepest mysteries of the Torah."

G-D AND THE TORAH ARE ONE

For this reason, the Sages said that the Holy One, blessed be He, and the Torah are One, because He and His Name are One. And so it says in the Zohar:[61] "In reality, the entire Torah is one holy Name of G-d. Happy is one who acquires it, for he who learns Torah truly acquires G-d's holy Name. Rabbi Yose says: He actually acquires G-d Himself, for He and His Name are One."

In keeping with this, it says in *Tanna D'bei Eliyahu* 18: "Whoever quarrels with a Torah scholar is reckoned as though he quarrels with the Creator, for it says, '*Dasan and Aviram … who incited against Moshe and Aharon … when they contended against G-d*' (Bamidbar 26:9). Therefore, when a person comes in the name of G-d, everyone is in awe of him and trembles before him, as it says, '*All the nations of the world will realize that Hashem's Name is associated with You, and they will be in awe of You*' (Devarim 28:10)."

G-D LOVES TORAH SCHOLARS

The Zohar[62] says: "You can tell how much the Holy One, blessed be He, loves those who learn Torah, because even when the world is judged with strict Justice, and the destructive angel is permitted to wreak destruction, G-d warns him against harming Torah students. This is what G-d tells him [quoting Devarim 20:19], '*When you lay siege to a city*' — because of the many sins of its inhabitants, I should instruct you as to how to treat the

61 *Parashas Yisro* 90b.
62 *Parashas Balak* 202a.

members of My household. [The verse continues,] '*You must not destroy its trees*' — do not harm the Torah scholar in that city, for he is the tree of life that bears fruit. He advises the people and shows them the way; '*wielding an ax*' — do not swing the flaming sword against him. This is the order G-d gives the destructive angel regarding those who engage in Torah study."

Chapter 20 | פרק כ'

THE SECRETS OF THE TORAH ARE REVEALED TO HIM

A Torah scholar is the beloved son in the King's palace. Only he has permission to enter and probe the treasure house of the holy King. All heavenly gates swing open for him, as the Gemara in *Sotah* 49a says: "If a Torah scholar studies Torah in poverty, his prayers will be answered. R. Acha ben Chanina said, In addition, the partition [that separates mortal man from G-d] will not be closed to him, as it says, '*The teacher will no longer be hidden behind His garment*' (Yeshayah 30:19). He enters the gates of the holy Torah to perceive its inner light and penetrate its deep mysteries, as it says in *Avos* 6:1: 'The secrets of the Torah are revealed to him.'"

The Midrash[63] says: "[The Talmudic Sage] Shmuel said: 'I am as familiar with the pathways of Heaven as with the streets of Nahardea [his hometown].'" Obviously, Shmuel did not travel to outer space. But by exerting himself in his Torah studies, he derived from the Torah the wisdom and principles of astronomy.[64]

63 Tehillim 19.

64 The *Ramban* in the introduction to his commentary on the Torah explains at length that all the wisdom of Shlomo, whether mystical, worldly or scientific, is contained in the Torah.

And *Tanna D'bei Eliyahu*[65] says: "When the Torah scholars and their disciples are sitting and devoutly learning Torah *lishmah* in the synagogue, the *beis midrash* or any other available place, the Holy One, blessed be He, sits facing them and reveals to them the secrets of the Torah. *Ruach hakodesh,* Divine inspiration, rests on them, as the Zohar[66] says: 'A wise man is greater than a prophet. For a prophet receives *ruach hakodesh* only intermittently, whereas *ruach hakodesh* never leaves a wise man, even for a moment. Wise men know what transpires above and below, but they have no desire to reveal it.'"

And *Tanna D'bei Eliyahu*[67] further says: "When a person has learned *lishmah* the books of Torah, Prophets and Writings, and studied Midrash, Gemara, Halachah and Aggadah, *ruach hakodesh* comes to rest on him immediately, as it says, '*The spirit of Hashem spoke through me [King David]; His word is on my tongue*' (II Shmuel 23:2)."

And we read in *Avos* 6:1: "Whoever engages in Torah study, the Torah makes him great and exalts him above all things. In fact, a Torah scholar ranks higher than a prophet."[68]

---

65 *Eliyahu Rabbah* 27.

66 *Parashas Shemos* 6b.

67 Chapter 1.

68 *Bava Basra* 12a. The *Ramban* explains that since the destruction of the Beis Hamikdash, prophetic vision was taken away from prophets, but it was not taken away from Torah scholars. For Torah scholars arrive at prophetic insight through the wisdom of Torah and *ruach hakodesh.* *(Uvacharta Bachaim)*

TZADDIKIM ARE MORE POWERFUL AFTER DEATH

The stature of Torah scholars is certainly very high during their lifetime in this world of darkness, since with *ruach hakodesh* they perceive the Divine light. But after death, they are infinitely more powerful, as it says in *Chullin* 7b: "*Tzaddikim* are even greater in death than in life." When the *tzaddik*'s pure soul, saturated with Torah and mitzvos, returns to its source, all heavenly gates are opened for him; he splits the heavens, and is bound up in the bond of life with G-d."

Tanna D'bei Eliyahu[69] comments: "You might say that when Moshe died, he lost the radiance that crowned his face.[70] To teach you otherwise, it says, '*Never again has there arisen in Yisrael a prophet like Moshe, whom Hashem had known face to face*' (Devarim 343:10) — just as G-d's face endures forever, so did the luminescence of Moshe's face endure after his death. This applies not just to Moshe; rather, every Torah scholar who learned Torah all his life does not really die. He lives on for all eternity, as it says, '*May my lord's soul be bound up in the bond of life with Hashem your G-d*' (I Shmuel 25:29). The verse associates the righteous Torah scholar [David] with G-d. This tells us that just as G-d exists forever, so does a Torah scholar live on forever. And where does his soul reside? Beneath the Throne of Glory."

His soul is satiated with the glow of the heavenly light, as the Gemara in *Sotah* 49a says: "If a Torah scholar studies

69 *Eliyahu Rabbah* 4.

70 See Shemos 34:29.

Torah in poverty, his prayers will be answered. R. Abbahu said: He is rewarded in that he is satiated with the splendor of the *Shechinah*, for it says, '*Your eyes will behold your Teacher*' (Yeshayah 30:20)."

But the intensity of the heavenly light depends on the devotion with which the Torah scholar studied Torah. Now you might say: It makes no difference; the radiance of the scholar's face in the World to Come will be the same, regardless of whether he learned a great deal or only a little. Not so, for G-d shows no favoritism. Elsewhere it says, "*A righteous one has an advantage over his fellow*" (Mishlei 12:26). So, too, each person is rewarded according to the effort he puts into his Torah study.

THE ORIGINAL LIGHT OF CREATION

Herein lies the secret of the primordial light that came into being on the first day of Creation and that the Holy One, blessed be He, put away for the *tzaddikim*.[71] The Zohar expounds: "The Holy One, blessed be He, created man and arranged for him to be perfect in his service and rectify his ways properly so that he would merit the sublime light that Hashem set aside for the *tzaddikim*." And the Gemara in *Chagigah* 14a explains the verse, "*Those that pressed forward* (asher kumtu) *before their time*" (Iyov 22:16) as referring to Torah scholars who *mekamtin*, press sleep from their eyes in this world. The Holy One, blessed be He, reveals secrets to them in the World to Come, as the verse continues, "*Whose*

71 According to the Midrash, the original light was of an intense spiritual quality and G-d saw that the wicked were not worthy of benefiting from it. Therefore, He hid it and set it aside for the use of the righteous in the World to Come.

foundation was poured out like a stream" — this refers to the mystical meanings of the Torah, which are the sublime light of the first day of Creation that was hidden and stored away.

This is alluded to in *Avos* 6:1, "Whoever engages in Torah study *lishmah* merits many things." The Mishnah does not specify what the "many things" are. And you cannot say that the Mishnah means the things it goes on to enumerate ["he is called friend, beloved, he loves the Omnipresent ..."] because that list is introduced with the word, "and furthermore," implying that these things are merited *in addition* to the "many things." The truth is that "many things" allude to the delight of the radiance of the hidden light that is granted to the Torah scholar. Angels, holy *serafim* and prophets cannot grasp the essence of this light. Only Torah scholars perceive the hidden meanings of the Torah. That is what the Mishnah has in mind when it says "Whoever engages in Torah study *lishmah* merits many things."

Tanna D'bei Eliyahu[72] says: "Fortunate is the man who possesses words of Torah and who sits and learns Torah in a secluded place [so that people should not know that he is immersed in Torah study]. With whom does he reside? With the Holy One, blessed be He, as it says, '*Whoever sits in the shelter of the Most High, he shall dwell in the shadow of the Almighty*' (Tehillim 91:1).[73] Just as the Torah scholar secludes himself, living alone in this world, so will he be in the World to Come, dwelling alone in the company of the Holy One, blessed be He."

---

72 *Eliyahu Rabbah* 26.

73 Note that this verse is often interpreted differently by other commentators.

DECLINE IN TORAH STUDY LEADS TO DISASTER

If we learn with less vigor, G-d forbid, the flow of Divine light in all the worlds is diminished, and G-d sheds tears, so to speak. The Gemara in *Chagigah* 5b says: "Hashem weeps over three types [of people] every day, one of them being a man who has the opportunity to study Torah, but does not do so." The meaning of Hashem weeping is that the Attribute of [strict] Justice prevails as a result of the weakening of the Divine light — which is a manifestation of Hashem's great mercy in the hidden worlds.

A person who has never learned Torah is cast aside, G-d forbid, and handed over to the forces of evil, as the Gemara in *Berachos* 5a says: "Anyone who has the opportunity to engage in Torah study but does not do so, the Holy One, blessed be He, will bring upon him dreadful afflictions that make him repulsive (*ochrin*), as it says, '*I was dumb, silent; I kept quiet from the good thing, and my pain makes me repulsive* (ne'ecar)' (Tehillim 39:3)." He deprives himself and the entire world of much goodness, because he tipped the scale to the side of guilt for himself and the whole world. And so it says in *Bava Basra* 8a: "Misfortune comes to the world only because of the unlearned." If, G-d forbid, misfortune befalls an individual or a country even in the furthest corner of the world, it is the fault of the unlearned, may G-d spare us.

If one used to study Torah and then gave up his studies, he weakens the heavenly legions of angels and upsets the order of the higher worlds and the Divine chariot. He causes the destructive forces to gain the upper hand and undermines the power of the *Shechinah,* so to speak, for the *Shechinah* dwells among us through the study of Torah *lishmah.*

"A TIME TO ACT FOR G-D"

Commenting on the verse, *"For it is a time to act for Hashem; they have voided Your Torah"* (Tehillim 119:126), the Zohar[74] says: "When people are learning Torah, the Holy One, blessed be He, is happy with the worlds He created, and Heaven and earth are firmly established. But the moment the Jewish people stop learning, G-d's power wanes. When that happens, we have to act for G-d. The *tzaddikim* that are left in the world must gird their loins and intensify their own knowledge of the Torah to lend strength to the Holy One, blessed be he. Why? Because many have abandoned the Torah and do not study it as they should. On the other hand, when Klal Yisrael are learning Torah, the Jewish faith stands firm and is crowned with perfection." In short, the heavenly realm rises or falls, according to the way Klal Yisrael is studying Torah.

WHEN ONE BECOMES LAX IN TORAH LEARNING

When a person's Torah learning declines, G-d becomes distant from him, because He and the Torah are One. His Divine protection is removed, and he is handed over to the power of strict Justice, which he himself aroused, as the Gemara in Berachos 63a says: "Whoever weakens himself from words of Torah [by studying it without enthusiasm or diligence] will have no strength to stand in the time of distress, as it says, *"Your*

74 *Parashas Terumah* 155b.

strength will become limited" (Mishlei 24:10) [i.e., if you are slack in your learning, you will become too weak to help yourself.]" And the Midrash[75] says: "Hashem says to Klal Yisrael: If you keep the Torah, I will guard you, as it says, '*If you will observe* (shamor tishmerun) *all this Torah*' (Devarim 11:22)." The double expression thus means that if you keep (*shamor*) then you will be guarded (*tishmerun*).

And a well-known Midrash[76] says: "[Yitzchak said,] '*Hakol kol Yaakov, vehayadayim yedei Eisav,*'"[77] 'The voice is Yaakov's voice, but the hands are Eisav's hands' (Bereishis 27:22). [Why the repetitive *hakol kol?*] When the voice of Yaakov (i.e., the Torah, *kol* written with a *vav*) is heard in the synagogue and the study hall, the hands of Eisav are powerless, but when the voice of Yaakov is weak (*kol* written without the *vav*), the hands of Eisav dominate."

THE BOOK AND THE SWORD

In line with this it says:[78] "The book and the sword came down from Heaven tied together. Said the Holy One, blessed be He: If you will keep that which is written in the book, you will be saved from the sword. If you don't, the sword will obliterate you."

Similarly, *Tanna D'bei Eliyahu*[79] says: "We find that the Holy One, blessed be He, overlooked the sins of idol worship, sexual immorality and bloodshed, but not the sin of rejecting

75 *Tehillim* 57.

76 *Bereishis Rabbah* 65.

77 The first *kol* is written "weak" without a *vav* and can be read as *kal*, "light, weak"; the second *kol* is written full and strong, with a *vav*.

78 *Vayikra Rabbah* 35.

79 *Eliyahu Rabbah* 18.

the Torah, for it says, *'Why is the land in ruins, laid waste like a wilderness with none passing through?'* (Yirmiyah 9:11). It does not say that the calamity happened because of idol worship, sexual immorality or bloodshed. What then is the reason? G-d answers: Because they forsook the Torah I had set before them (9:12). *Tanna D'bei Eliyahu* expounds: "Look how grave is the sin of neglecting the Torah! Jerusalem and the Temple were destroyed for no other reason than the sin of the people spurning the Torah." For Klal Yisrael can survive only if they are engaged in Torah study. And since they turned away from learning Torah, the enemy came and ravaged the land and the Temple.

Chapter 23 | פרק כ"ג

AFTER DEATH

The Gemara in Bava Basra 79a says: "Anyone straying from the words of the Torah falls into Gehinnom. Rav Yehudah says: He is consumed by fire." And the Midrash[80] comments: "It says, *'One who abandons reproof goes astray* (mas'eh)' (Mishlei 10:17) — a Torah scholar who stops learning Torah is as if he mocked (*mesate'a*) the Creator. What's more, since he deserted Torah study in this world, G-d abandons him in the World to Come."

The Zohar[81] describes at great length the lofty stature enjoyed by Torah scholars in this world and the next: "Look at the person who did not learn Torah. He walks in darkness,

80 *Mishlei Rabbah* 10.
81 *Parashas Vayeishev* 185a.

and when he leaves this world, he is taken to the bottom rung of Gehinnom known as *'the pit of raging waters, the slimy mud'* (Tehillim 40:3), where those who did not learn Torah are judged and shown no mercy."

What's more, after a person's demise, the first question he is asked by the heavenly tribunal is whether or not he learned Torah, as it says, *"The rejection of water [i.e., the Torah] is the beginning of judgment"* (Mishlei 17:14).

THE FATE OF ONE WHO REFUSES TO LEARN TORAH

The Mishnah in Avos 6:2 says: "Every day a heavenly voice emanates from Mount Chorev, proclaiming: Whoever does not occupy himself with the Torah is called 'Banned.'"

He deserves to be branded "Banned," because he rejected life and true goodness for himself, for all of mankind and for all the worlds. By refusing to attach himself to G-d, he has diminished the flow of Divine light in all the worlds and disturbed and darkened the order of the heavenly realm. He has brought evil on himself, because he removed the holy garments and instead, put on soiled clothes that are formed from the lusts and pleasures of this world. In this sullied state, he surely is not admitted to heavenly places of holiness. All the angels that used to protect him shun him, because they cannot touch his soiled clothes. Aimlessly, he wanders about the world, crying out: "*Tamei! Tamei!* Unclean! Unclean!" For he associated with the demons of pollution that he himself conjured up.

The Zohar[82] spells it out: "Look how careful people should be about being in awe of the Holy One, blessed be He, not to veer from the right path or violate the laws of the Torah.

82 *Parashas Metzora* 52b.

Whoever makes no effort to study Torah is rebuked by G-d, the *Shechinah* does not rest on him and his guardian angels leave him. To make things worse, they call out in front of him: 'Stay away from So-and-so because he shows no regard for the honor of his Master!' Woe is him! He has no share in the path of everlasting life. But when he makes every effort to toil in Torah, countless guardian angels are ready to watch over him, the *Shechinah* rests on him and the angels proclaim before him: 'Give glory to the image of the King! Give glory to the prince!' He is then protected in this world and the next. How truly fortunate he is!"

ABANDONED THE TORAH

The Gemara in Chagigah 9a expounds the verse, "*A crooked thing cannot be made straight*" (Koheles 1:15): "R. Shimon bar Yochai says, 'One is not called crooked unless he was straight at first and then became crooked. Who is this? This is a Torah scholar who forsakes the Torah.' Woe to the people who see him and don't realize what an insult he is to the Torah!" One should keep this in mind and reflect on it at all times, so that one should not waste his life living in darkness. Driven by lust, he [the Torah scholar who gave up learning] lives as an outcast, spending the years G-d mercifully has allotted him removed from the Torah. It will cost him his soul — for when his life ends, and his body returns to dust, his spirit does not return to G-d to be bound up in the bond of higher life. His soul is given no rest, because he is censured on earth and in Heaven. Woe to the shame! May the Merciful G-d save us.

THE GRAVITY OF HIS PUNISHMENT

The Sages strongly condemn a person who had the opportunity to learn Torah and did not learn, or a person who has learned Torah but stopped learning. They deplore it so severely that with their *ruach hakodesh* they declare that this person is barred from the World to Come. And so the Gemara in Sanhedrin 99a says: "It says, '*Since he has shown contempt of Hashem's word and violated His commandment, that person shall be utterly cut off* (hikareis tikareis)' (Bamidbar 15:31). R. Nehorai says: This refers to anyone who has the opportunity to engage in Torah study but does not." The Sages explain the double expression "*hikareis tikareis,* that soul shall be utterly cut off," as implying that he shall be cut off both in this world and in the World to Come.

The *kareis* punishment of such a person is far graver than the *kareis* given for other sins. If one is condemned to *kareis* for any other sin, he has not lost his share in the World to Come. Only the small spark of the soul that committed the sin is cut off from its Divine root. But the present verse stresses emphatically "*hikareis tikareis,*" meaning that his entire soul has lost its share in the World to Come.

The *Rambam*[83] mentions this, and Rabbeinu Yonah[84] enumerates ten levels of sin. On the tenth level are sins for which the sinner is denied a share in the World to Come. Included in this group are "those who are able to study Torah but don't." The *Rambam* and the *Beis Yosef* both state that one who

83 *Hilchos Talmud Torah* 3:13.

84 *Sha'ar Hateshuvah* 3:153.

previously learned Torah but then took up worldly frivolities, abandoning his Torah studies, is judged as one who was able to study but didn't.

His punishment fits his misdeed. His deplorable deed keeps him away from goodness. He had the opportunity to study Torah but callously chose a bad deal for himself, for others and for all the [higher] worlds. He spurned the holy Torah, the light of all the worlds, the path to draw him close to the Holy One, blessed be He. He tried to tear down the King's palace and dimmed the abundant light that illuminates all the worlds and his soul. Why should he deserve everlasting life?[85] By not seeing the light of eternal life, he has cut himself off from Gan Eden. He refused to be bound up in the bond of life with G-d, going from bad to worse. Woe to the shame![86]

The Sages said that at the end of time, when the dead will awaken for everlasting life, he will not be resurrected. Commenting on the verse, "*May your dead come to life ... for Your dew is like the dew that revives vegetation, may You topple the wicked to the ground*" (Yeshayah 26:19), the Gemara in *Kesubos* 111b says: "A person who makes use of the light of the Torah will be revived by the light of Torah, but a person who does not make use of the light of the Torah will not be revived by the light

---

85 Interestingly, in all other cases where individuals are denied entrance to the World to Come, it is because they actively committed sins, whereas one who did not study Torah did not engage in a forbidden act. All he did was fail to observe a mitzvah. This is somewhat hard to understand. Rav Chaim therefore goes to great length to explain why one who had the opportunity to learn but didn't do so has no share in the World to Come. Rav Chaim clarifies the gravity of his wrongdoing. (*Uvacharta Bachaim*)

86 The *Chafetz Chaim* explains that although women do not engage in intensive Torah study, they merit everlasting life in the World to Come, because they have a share in the Torah their husbands and children are learning (*Uvacharta Bachaim*).

of Torah." And they found a remedy for the ignorant so that they, too, can be resurrected. Namely, if they support Torah scholars, letting them derive benefit from their resources, the Torah considers it as though they attached themselves to the *Shechinah*, and in that merit, *"You are all alive today"* (Devarim 5:4) — you will be revived for eternal life; not just the scholars, but anyone who assists Torah scholars or marries off his daughter to a Torah scholar will be resurrected.

Chapter 25 | פרק כ"ה

TORAH LEARNING PROTECTS THE WORLD FROM DESTRUCTION

The above applies as long as there are still Jews left in the world who cling to G-d and immerse themselves in intensive study of Torah *lishmah*. It is then that people who deliberately give up Torah study altogether will be cut off from eternal life. Although this world and the higher worlds have been diminished and have lost some of their holiness and spiritual light through the deplorable behavior of these people, the worlds continue to exist in the merit of the few remaining Torah scholars who learn day and night. [It is due to their Torah study] that the world is not destroyed and returned to the primeval emptiness and void.

Thus, *Tanna D'bei Eliyahu*[87] says: "'*For to Hashem are the pillars* (metzukei) *of the earth and upon them He established the world.*' (I Shmuel 2:8). The *metzukim* refer to the Torah scholars. When people stop learning Torah, the Holy One, blessed be He, seeks to destroy the world." Furthermore, it says there:

87 *Eliyahu Rabbah* 2.

"Every day, destructive angels go forth from before G-d to wipe out the entire world. If not for the synagogues and study halls where Torah scholars are sitting and learning, the destructive angels would instantly annihilate the entire world."

Indeed, the Gemara in *Sanhedrin* 99b says: "[The person who studies Torah *lishmah*] provides protection for the whole world." And the Mishnah in *Avos* 6:1 says: "The creation of the whole world is worthwhile for [the Torah scholar's] sake alone."

ONE MAN CAN SAVE THE WORLD

You cannot help but be overawed and filled with fear and terror if you realize that, G-d forbid, you may have slackened off somewhat on your Torah studies. You reflect that perhaps at this very moment no one in the entire world is learning Torah, and without your concentrating on Torah thoughts, the universe would turn to nothing this instant![88]

By studying Torah, one can sustain all the worlds and reap the immeasurable reward for keeping them intact. With that in mind, the Mishnah in *Sanhedrin* 37a says: "Every person is required to say, 'The world was created for my sake.'" Other sins have no negative effect on the multitude of higher worlds, but the sin of neglecting Torah learning surpasses all other sins, for it puts at risk the existence of all the worlds.

88 The *sefer Ruach Eliyahu*, p. 101, relates that for this reason, R. Chaim Volozhiner instituted that groups of students should take turns learning Torah around the clock, so that there should never be a moment without someone learning. On *motza'ei Yom Kippur*, when everyone left the Yeshivah to break the fast, he himself would sit and learn until midnight, for fear that there would not be anyone upholding the world by learning Torah. (*Uvacharta Bachaim*)

THE EXALTED ROOT OF THE TORAH

Why is this so? We explained earlier that the hidden root of the Torah is exalted above all worlds and situated in the mystical World of *Atzilus* (Emanation), as the holy Arizal[89] explains. From this loftiest of spiritual worlds, the Torah gradually descended to earth, which became illuminated with its splendor. [At the giving of the Torah,] G-d handed the Torah to us and planted it in our midst in order that we should grasp and uphold the Tree of Life [i.e., the Torah]. Ever since, the life and existence of all the higher worlds depends on the fervor with which we study and reflect on the Torah. If we study and support it properly, without laxness, we arouse its exalted source, the wellspring of holiness and blessing, causing it to shower an abundance of blessing and *kedushah* on all the worlds, each world according to the degree of *kedushah* it is able to absorb.

PRAYER DEPENDS ON TORAH STUDY

If, G-d forbid, we are careless about learning Torah, the exalted light of the Torah is gradually dimmed in all the higher worlds. And, G-d forbid, if all of us would cease learning Torah altogether, all the worlds would evaporate instantly. The abandonment of no other mitzvah would have such catastrophic consequences. Take even the mitzvah of prayer; if all Jews stopped

89 Rabbi Yitzchak Luria, the great Kabbalist, teaches in his *sefer Etz Chaim* that the totality of existence is composed of four worlds. In descending order they are: *Atzilus* (Emanation), *Beriah* (Creation), *Yetzirah* (Formation) and *Asiyah* (Action). In Kabbalistic literature, the four worlds are generally referred to by the acronym *Abiyah*.

praying to G-d, the worlds would not cease to exist. But Torah study touches the very life force of the upper worlds. That is why Jews are required to engage in Torah learning constantly to ensure the continued existence of all the worlds.

What's more, prayer itself depends completely on Torah learning. Without Torah study, prayer is not accepted, as it says, "*If one turns aside from hearing the Torah, his prayer, too, will be [considered] an abomination*" (Mishlei 28:9). And the Zohar interprets the verse: "*Desire fulfilled is a tree of life*" (Mishlei 13:12): "This teaches us that if you want the Holy One, blessed be He, to fulfill your prayer, you should study Torah, for it is the *tree of life*."

In light of that, the Gemara in *Megillah* 27a rules: "It is permissible to convert a synagogue into a *beis midrash* (study hall)," because a study hall is more sacred than a synagogue. Only a *beis midrash* has the power to draw down *kedushah* and spiritual light to all the worlds, for it ranks higher than all the worlds.[90]

Chapter 27 | פרק כ"ז

THE GRADUAL DESCENT OF *KEDUSHAH*

Indeed, the *kedushah* of the Torah is much greater than that of the higher worlds. Descending from the higher to the lower worlds, the radiance of the *kedushah* gradually decreases. G-d's radiance is most evident in the sublime World of *Atzilus* (Emanation), and it is almost completely obscured in our world, the World of

90 That's why the *Shulchan Aruch, Orach Chaim* 90:18, rules that it is preferable to *daven* in a *beis midrash* than in a *beis hakeneses* (synagogue) (*Uvacharta Bachaim*).

Asiyah (Action). As it says in the Zohar:[91] "The spiritual worlds, arranged one above the other, are all joined to each other. But each world has less *kedushah* and Divine light than the one above it, to the point that in our world, the World of *Asiyah*, the Divine light is totally obscured by mundane corporeality."

THE TORAH RETAINED ITS HEAVENLY *KEDUSHAH*

Although on its descent from its holy source above,[92] going from world to world, the Torah has passed through countless phases, its original *kedushah* has remained the same even in our material world, so that we are forbidden to treat it with disrespect. Therefore, we are forbidden to reflect on Torah thoughts in unclean places. Also, the Gemara in *Megillah* 32b says: "Anyone who grasps a Torah scroll with his bare hands[93] will be buried bare, without mitzvos." And moving a Torah scroll from one house to another is forbidden, even from one synagogue to another, because the Torah retained the original *kedushah* it had at its Divine source, without undergoing the slightest change.

This is the underlying idea of the saying in the Zohar: "The Holy One, blessed be He, and the Torah are One." The chain of worlds, where each world has less *kedushah* than the one above it, is true only as viewed from our human vantage point. From G-d's perspective, the concepts of "change" and "place" do not exist, as it says, *"For I, Hashem, have not changed"* (Malachi

---

91 *Parashas Yisro* 82b.

92 In each world, the Torah appeared in a form that was appropriate for it. For example, if it had been given to the world of the angels, it would not have had our wording with the prohibitions against stealing and bloodshed, which apply only to our physical world. (*Uvacharta Bachaim*)

93 Without placing a piece of material between it and his hands (*Rashi*).

3:6).[94] The same is true for the Torah. Although it came from the spiritual realm of Heaven down to the physical lower world, its *kedushah* and splendor are undiminished.

With that in mind, King David prayed, *"Unveil my eyes that I may perceive the wonders from Your Torah"* (Tehillim 119:18). In essence, the innermost mysteries of the Torah are obvious and can plainly be seen in the radiance of the exalted spiritual light. It is our eyes that cannot endure the immense *kedushah* and radiance of this light.[95]

Chapter 28 | פרק כ"ח

PROFOUND SECRETS HIDDEN IN THE TORAH TEXT

And so, on its journey from Heaven, passing from world to world, degree by degree, down to the physical world, the Torah confined itself, speaking in terms of the needs of each world, according to the degree of *kedushah* that world could accept. Arriving in our physical world, it adjusted itself to speaking in terms of the values and concerns of this world, relating to matters of this mundane world, so that the world can tolerate the *kedushah* of the Torah's light.

However, even while speaking about worldly matters, the Torah alludes to basic principles and the most profound mystical concepts. As the Zohar[96] says: "All the mystical secrets are locked in the Torah." This means that they are encased in the details of the myriad facets in which the Torah clothed

94 This metaphysical idea is beyond human comprehension (*Uvacharta Bachaim*).

95 Hence, we pray in *tefillas Shacharis,* "Enlighten our eyes in Your Torah."

96 *Parashas Toldos* 134b.

itself on its way down to this world.

For this reason, the Zohar repeatedly says that the entire Torah is "both hidden and revealed." Everyone understands that while the words of the verses express the plain meaning of the Torah, the individual words and letters of the Torah hint at the hidden and esoteric meaning of the Torah. As the Zohar[97] says: "How sweet is the Torah text, for hidden in every single word there are lofty secrets."

Everyone will understand the inner meaning of the Torah according to his intellect, perception, purity of intent and the time he devotes to Torah study. But remember, the true inner meanings of the Torah are concealed by G-d. No man can fathom them. Only the Father of us all, *Adam Harishon,* had the "soul of souls" and higher vision with which he could gaze into the soul of the holy Torah. The most lofty forms of wisdom were revealed to him. But after he transgressed, the spiritual splendor was taken from him, and the heavenly order [and the forces of good and evil] became mixed and intermingled. As a result, the paths of Torah wisdom he had been able to fathom with his "soul of souls" were closed to him.

The Gemara in *Shabbos* 146a says that when Klal Yisrael received the Torah, their lustfulness left them [and they became as pure as Adam was before he sinned]. Even so, they were able to grasp only the level of "soul of the Torah" but not the level of "soul of soul of the Torah" [the level of understanding reached by Adam before he sinned].

But when G-d will pour out His spirit on all mankind, the wondrous paths of higher wisdom, the "soul of soul of the

97 *Parashas Beha'alosecha* 149a.

Torah" will be revealed. As the Zohar[98] says: "The Torah has a garment, a body, and a soul. The fools of the world see only the garment; those with more understanding do not look at the garment, but see the body that is beneath the garment. The wise servants of the supreme King who stood at Sinai saw only the soul, which is the essence of the Torah. In time to come, they will perceive the 'soul of soul' of the Torah, as it says, '*Your Teacher will no longer be hidden behind His garment, and Your eyes will behold your Teacher*' (Yeshayah 30:20)." This is the underlying idea of "the light of the first day of Creation" that the Holy One, blessed be He, stored away for the *tzaddikim* in time to come.[99]

It says, "*Man does not know its worth*" (Iyov 28:13). The Midrash comments:[100] "The portions of the Torah were not given in their proper order. Had they been given in the proper order, anyone reading the Torah could [understand the profound mysteries of the Torah, which would have enabled him to] instantly create a world and revive the dead."

We will now explain that the *kedushah* of Torah study is greater than the *kedushah* of doing mitzvos.

Chapter 29 | פרק כ"ט

STUDY AND PRACTICE

The Gemara in *Sotah* 21a says: "It says, '*The mitzvah is a lamp, and the Torah is light*' (Mishlei 6:25). The verse compares the mitzvah to a lamp and the Torah to light to tell you that

98 *Parashas Beha'alosecha* 152a.
99 *Chagigah* 12a.
100 Tehillim 3.

just as a lamp burns only temporarily, so, too, the fulfillment of a mitzvah protects you only temporarily. The Torah is compared to light to tell you that just as light protects forever, so does the Torah protect forever." Rava challenged this, saying: "While you are occupied in learning Torah, it protects you [from punishment] and saves you [from sinning], but when you are not engaged in learning Torah, it protects you [from punishment] but does not save you [from sinning]. By contrast, a mitzvah, whether or not you are involved with it, protects you [from punishment], but it does not save you [from the sinning]." Furthermore, it says there: "A transgression cancels the merit of a mitzvah, but not the merit of Torah study."

HEALING FOR THE WHOLE BODY

In the same vein, the Zohar says that the 613 mitzvos correspond to the 613 limbs and connective tissues in the human body. And when one performs a mitzvah, the limb that correlates with that mitzvah is sanctified and vitalized. By the same token, if one has the opportunity to commit a sin and refrains from doing it, the limb with which he could have sinned is sanctified and vitalized, as it says, *"Keep My decrees and laws, since it is only by keeping them that a person can [truly] live"* (Vayikra 18:5), for then he is really alive.

However, when one learns Torah [not only is one limb vitalized, but his entire body is energized], as it says, *"For [the words of the Torah] are healing for his whole body"* (Mishlei 4:22). And so the Gemara in *Eruvin* 54a says: "If one's head aches, let him engage in Torah study ... if he feels pain all over his body, let him learn Torah, for it says, *'It is a healing for his whole body.'* Hence, the Gemara in *Shabbos* 127a says: "The study of Torah is equal to all [the mitzvos]."

Conversely, the sin of *bittul Torah* — the neglect of Torah study — is equivalent to all sins together. When one transgresses a mitzvah, only the corresponding limb is blemished, since the *kedushah* and the otherworldly light that hovers over every limb departs from the limb [that corresponds to the mitzvah that was violated]. Lacking that limb, the sinner becomes disabled. But *bittul Torah* afflicts all the limbs and blood vessels of the one who neglects Torah study, impairs his health and stamina, and causes the aura of *kedushah* to leave his body. He becomes like a lifeless creature, for it says, "*[The Torah] is your life and the length of your days*" (Devarim 30:20).

LIKE THE FISH OF THE SEA

This is in line with the Gemara in *Avodah Zarah* 3b: "What is the meaning of the verse, "*You have made man like the fish of the sea*" (Chavakuk 1:14)? Why is man compared to the fish of the sea? To tell you that just as the fish of the sea perish the moment they go on dry land, so, too, man perishes as soon as he ceases to study Torah." Similarly, *Raya Meheimna*[101] says: "Just as the fish of the sea live in water, so too, Torah scholars, being immersed in the Torah, will die the moment they are removed from their Torah study."

Likewise, the Gemara in *Berachos* 5a says: "If one feels afflictions coming on, he should examine his way of life. If he searched and found that he has done no wrong, he should attribute his suffering to *bittul Torah*, the neglect of Torah study." At first glance, this seems surprising. Since he is guilty of the grave offense of *bittul Torah* — how can he say that he found

101 End of *Parashas Shemini*.

nothing wrong! Rashi explains that he found no sin that warranted his pain. For G-d punishes measure for measure and afflicts the limb that committed the sinful act, so that one should understand for which failing he is being punished. He will then mend his ways and will be healed. Thus, the Gemara says: "If a person feels afflictions coming on, he should examine his way of life, and his pain will tell him which weakness he should correct. If he searched and found that he has done nothing wrong with the limb that hurts, he should attribute his pain to *bittul Torah*." For the sin of *bittul Torah* is so grave that it is not punished measure for measure, since *bittul Torah* affects the entire body, all limbs and all organs.

Chapter 30 | פרק ל׳

SUPERIORITY OF TORAH STUDY

Torah study outweighs all other mitzvos put together. This may be seen by the fact that even if a man observed all 613 mitzvos with true perfection and with the proper intention, the *kedushah* and supernal light inherent in the mitzvos that comes to rest on all his limbs and organs does not compare to the awesome *kedushah* and splendor of the holy Torah radiating on the person who immerses himself in learning Torah *lishmah*. Its source in *kedushah* is infinitely higher than the root of all the mitzvos combined. The Mishnah in *Avos* 6:1 expresses this thought: "[The study of Torah *lishmah*] makes him great and exalts above all things," meaning above all the other mitzvos combined. Similarly, the Sages say:[102] "All the other mitzvos

102 *Yerushalmi, Pei'ah* 1.

combined do not have the value of one word of the Torah."

Then consider this: The very *kedushah* and light of the mitzvos that rest on the object with which the mitzvah is performed lasts only for the duration of the mitzvah. As soon as the mitzvah is performed, the *kedushah* and the light depart without a trace. By contrast, any place where the Torah's light has shone remains sanctified forever, as the Gemara in *Megillah* 26b says: "Objects used for the performance of a mitzvah may be discarded [since no sanctity attaches to the object after its use]. But objects that are accessories to sacred items must be hidden away [and may not be put to any other use], such as a case for *tefillin* and *mezuzah*, because at one time they contained parchments on which Torah passages are written."

The verse, *"For a mitzvah is a lamp, and the Torah is light"* (Mishlei 6:23) — aside from the exposition given in the Gemara *Sotah* 21a — also alludes to the superiority of Torah study over the performance of mitzvos. In addition, the very *kedushah*, life and light of the mitzvos are derived from the *kedushah* and light of the Torah alone. A mitzvah itself has no life, *kedushah* or light at all except for the *kedushah* it receives from the letters in the Torah passage that describes that mitzvah. This idea is also alluded to in the verse, *"For a mitzvah is a lamp, and the Torah is light"* — a lamp itself does not give off any light; it only supports the flame.

TORAH STUDY WITHOUT DOING MITZVOS IS WORTHLESS

Of course, Torah study without the performance of mitzvos is worthless, as the Gemara in *Yevamos* 109b says: "Whoever says that he is interested only in the study of Torah [and not in the observance of the mitzvos] has no reward even for the study of Torah." And the Gemara in *Berachos* 17a says: "Rava was known to say the following: The goal of Torah wisdom is [that it should lead to] repentance and good deeds, so that a man should not study Torah and Mishnah [and become proud of his knowledge] and then despise his father, mother and his teacher, as it says, '*The beginning of wisdom is the fear of Hashem; all who do His commandments gain sound understanding*' (Tehillim 111:10). It doesn't say, 'all who *study* His commandments,' but 'all who *do* His commandments.'"

And the Midrash[103] says: "If one learns Torah but does not perform the mitzvos, it would be better had he not been born." And the Zohar[104] says: "Anyone who learns Torah in this world and does good deeds inherits a world of perfection. But he who learns Torah in this world and does not perform good deeds will inherit neither this world nor the World to Come." And the Gemara in *Avodah Zarah* 17b says: "Whoever engages only in Torah study [but neglects the mitzvos] is as though he has no G-d." If he does not fulfill the mitzvos, the light of the Torah has no way to attach itself to him and stay with him; it is like a flame without a wick.[105] However, as we mentioned above, the mitzvos themselves receive their light from the letters of the portion of the Torah that describes the mitzvah.

THE TORAH CONFERS EVERLASTING LIFE

The Mishnah in *Avos* 6:7 sums it up: "The Torah is great, for it confers life upon those who observe it." Now it does not say

103 *Shemos Rabbah* 40.

104 *Parashas Shemos* 5b.

105 The light of Torah can exist only through the fulfillment of the mitzvos. Therefore, the observance of mitzvos is the underpinning of the Torah. (*Uvacharta Bachaim*)

upon those who study it, or upon those who immerse themselves in it, but "upon those who observe it." This means that the Torah grants everlasting life and *kedushah* [to those who study it,] and to those who observe the mitzvos that are recorded in it. In light of this, the Midrash[106] says: "He may be a *tzaddik*, but if he does not study Torah, he has no reward even for his good deeds."

The reason for this is that, at their heavenly root, the mitzvos are linked to the exalted transcendental realm of the Torah. Since the Torah pervades the inner core of all the mitzvos, they receive their vitality and *kedushah* from the Torah. Thus, it is the Torah that infuses life, *kedushah* and light into the mitzvos.

Chapter 31 | פרק ל"א

TORAH STUDY IS LIKE OFFERING A SACRIFICE

[Because the Torah is rooted in the uppermost spiritual world,] the study of Torah *lishmah* has the potential to atone for all sins. And so the Gemara in *Menachos* 110a says: "What is implied by the verse, '*This is the Torah law of the burnt offering, the meal offering and the peace offering*' (Vayikra 7:37)? It teaches us that if a man is engaged in Torah study, it is as though he were offering a burnt offering, a meal offering, a sin offering and a guilt offering."

Likewise, the Midrash[107] says: "It says, '*Take words with you and return to Hashem*' (Hoshea 14:3). Yisrael says: We are poor, so we have no money to bring sacrifices. Replies G-d: All

106 *Tanchuma, Parashas Bechukosai.*

107 *Tanchuma, Parashas Tzav,* and *Midrash Rabbah* 38.

I want is words, and I will forgive you for all your sins. And surely 'words' implies 'words of Torah.'"

TORAH LEARNING BRINGS FORGIVENESS

In reference to the Holy Ark, the Midrash[108] says that the Ark grants forgiveness for the sins of Yisrael, because the Torah scroll that rests in it pardons Yisrael's sins.

In the same vein, *Tanna D'bei Eliyahu*[109] says: "A man committed numerous sins for which Heaven decreed death. If he repents and learns Torah, Prophets, Writings, Mishnah, Midrash, Halachah and Aggadah, and ministers to Torah scholars, then, even if a hundred decrees were pronounced against him, the Holy One, blessed be He, will revoke all of them."

And the Zohar[110] says: "Surely people should hold Torah study in high regard, for whoever learns Torah is considered as though he had offered to Hashem all the sacrifices in the world. What's more, the Holy One, blessed be He, forgives all his sins, and he is assured of a place in the World to Come."

Moreover, Torah study affords forgiveness even for those grave sins that cannot be atoned for by sacrifices, as the Gemara in *Rosh Hashanah* 18a says: "[Speaking about the sins of the sons of the prophet Eli, G-d says,] '*Therefore I have sworn concerning the house of Eli that the sin of the house of Eli will never be atoned for by sacrifice or meal offering*' (I Shmuel 3:14). [Commenting on this verse, Rabbah says:] With sacrifice and meal offering, the sin cannot be atoned for, but it can be atoned for through Torah study."

108 *Tanchuma, Parashas Vayakhel.*

109 *Eliyahu Rabbah* 5.

110 *Parashas Shelach* 159.

Likewise, the Gemara in *Megillah* 3b says: "Torah study is more important than offering the daily sacrifices." And the Zohar[111] says: "One who learns Torah needs no sacrifices and burnt offerings, for Torah study is better than everything. That's why it says, *'Its ways are ways of pleasantness'* (Mishlei 3:18)."

And the Midrash[112] says: "The sacrifices have ceased, but the Torah has not ceased. Therefore, since sacrifices can no longer be offered, one should devote himself to Torah study; it will be even more beneficial than sacrifices." Rabbi Kruspedai adds: "If one discusses the laws of the sacrifices in the *beis midrash*, he can be rest assured that the accusing angels who mention one's sins cannot do him any harm; they can only [point out his] good deeds."

TORAH LEARNING IS LIKE A *MIKVEH*

The Gemara in *Berachos* 16a says: "Why are tents mentioned in conjunction with streams in the verse, *'How good are your tents Yaakov ... They stretch out like streams'* (Bamidbar 24:5-6)? This comes to tell you that just as streams elevate a man from ritual impurity to ritual purity, so do the tents of Torah [i.e., halls of learning] elevate a man from the scale of guilt to the scale of merit."

Commenting on the verse, *"Pour out your heart like water in the presence of the Lord"* (Eichah 2:19), *Tanna D'bei Eliyahu* 18 says: "Just as water is a *mikveh* for the ritual purification of Yisrael and for all the creatures of the world, so are the words of Torah a *mikveh* that purifies Yisrael wherever they reside.

111 *Parashas Tzav* 35a.

112 *Midrash Hane'elam, Parashas Vayeira* 100a.

Look and see how powerful the Torah is, for it cleanses the transgressors in Yisrael even from as grave a sin as idol worship if they do *teshuvah*, for it says, '*Then I will sprinkle pure water on you, that you may become cleansed*' (Yechezkel 36:25)."

Perfect repentance is done out of love, and perfect *teshuvah* can be achieved only through learning Torah *lishmah*. As it says in *Avos* 6:1: "Whoever engages in Torah study *lishmah* ... shows that he loves the Omnipresent." And so we say in the Shemoneh Esrei: "Bring us back, our Father, to Your Torah ... and cause us to return in perfect *teshuvah* before You." And the Zohar[113] says: "When a man separates himself from the Torah, he becomes distant from the Holy One, blessed be He. But when he becomes close to the Torah, the Holy One, blessed be He, draws him near."

THE TORAH MAKES THE SINNER TURN BACK

It says, *Love covers up for all offenses* (Mishlei 10:12). *Tanna D'bei Eliyahu*[114] expounds: "Love of Torah covers up all offenses." And the Midrash[115] explains, "It is the light of the Torah that causes the sinner to mend his ways."

The Gemara in *Sukkah* 52b says: "If that contemptible scoundrel [the *yetzer hara*] comes up against you, drag him into the *beis midrash* [i.e., subdue him by learning Torah]. If he is made of stone, he will crumble."

And the Zohar[116] says: "If a man feels improper thoughts entering his mind, he should immerse himself in Torah study, and these thoughts will pass. R. Eliezer said: If the *yetzer hara*

113 *Parashas Vayikra* 21a.

114 *Eliyahu Rabbah* 3.

115 *Pesichta Eichah.*

116 *Parashas Vayeishev* 190a.

comes to seduce you, haul him into the *beis midrash,* and he will let go of you."

LIKE A FOUNTAIN

And this is how we can explain the maxim that "he [who has learnt Torah *lishmah*] is like a fountain that constantly gains strength."[117] For a surging fountain that became clogged with gravel and mud will continue to spout and gradually regain its strength. Eventually, it cascades again with full force as before. Similarly, a man may at first be soiled with sins and transgressions, and mired in a morass of evil. But once he engages in Torah study *lishmah,* his mind will be set straight because the light of Torah will surely transform him. The good in him will subdue his evil impulse to the point that the good impulse will take total command, completely cleansing him of his impurity. And so the Mishnah says: "[His Torah learning] makes him fit to be righteous and devout." The Hebrew word for "makes him fit" is *machsharto,* which literally means "makes him kosher." Torah learning "*kashers*" him as utensils acquired from non-Jews are "purged" by heating them in fire. And so it says, "*Look, My word is like fire*" (Yirmiyah 23:29).

Chapter 32 | פרק ל״ב

TORAH LEARNING BRINGS JOY TO ALL THE WORLDS

All this is as we said earlier that the Torah originates in the very highest spheres of the Divine realm. By learning Torah *lishmah,* one arouses the Torah's heavenly source, causing an

117 See *Avos* 6:1.

abundant flow of spiritual light and *kedushah* to descend on all the worlds. The Torah's fiery flame drives out and incinerates all the impurity and filth he injected into the higher worlds with his wrongful deeds, so that they radiate once again with celestial *kedushah* and are joined to one another. All defects are mended, all damages repaired and all ruins rebuilt, and joy, exultation and spiritual light abound in all the worlds.

We know that [a blemished soul can be rectified] only in its heavenly root. And the heavenly root of each Jew's soul is anchored in one of the letters of the Torah. Therefore, all flaws in the soul caused by sin can be restored through studying Torah *lishmah,* as it says, "*G-d's Torah is perfect, restoring the soul*" (Tehillim 19:8). Even if a man's soul has been cut off from its root and has sunk appallingly to the very depths of evil, the Torah he learns will raise it, free it from its shackles and restore its previous bond [with *kedushah*] with more Torah light than before. As the Gemara in *Taanis* 7a says: "R. Banaah used to say, Whoever studies Torah *lishmah,* his Torah study becomes an elixir of life for him, for it says, '*It is a tree of life for those who grasp it*' (Mishlei 3:18). And it also says, '*One who finds me [the Torah] finds life*' (Mishlei 8:35)."

And it says in *Mechilta*: "What is implied by the passage, '*I am Hashem who heals you*' (Shemos 15:26)? The Holy One, blessed be He, said to Moshe: Tell the Jewish people, 'The Torah I gave you means healing for you, it means life for you, as it says, "*For [the words of the Torah] are life to he who finds them, and healing for all his flesh*" (Mishlei 4:22).'"

With that in mind, the early authorities arranged the verses of the *viduy* prayer (confession of sins recited on Yom Kippur) according to the order of the twenty-two letters of the *alef-beis.* The heavenly root of the soul that is tied up with and dependent on the Torah will be aroused to cleanse and sanctify the soul of the one reciting the *viduy*.

IMMUNE TO THE BLANDISHMENTS OF THE *YETZER HARA*

When a man clings to the Torah and learns with ever-increasing fervor, the Torah in turn will light his way, protect him wherever he goes and help him in all his undertakings so that he will not fall into the trap of the *yetzer hara*, as the Midrash says:[118] "'*In my heart have I stored Your word, so that I would not sin against You*' (Tehillim 119:11) — the *yetzer hara* has no power over the Torah. If one has the Torah in his heart, the *yetzer hara* cannot touch him."

In *Avos D'Rabbi Nassan* it says: "R. Shimon bar Yochai says, If one takes to heart the words of the Torah, he will be spared ten great difficulties: [spared] from sinful thoughts, preoccupation about war, worry about oppression, frivolous thoughts, thoughts prompted by the *yetzer hara*, thoughts of adultery, distress because of a troublesome wife, thoughts of idolatry, concern about worldly responsibilities and idle thoughts.[119] [The Torah] will clothe him in humility, fear of G-d and virtuous qualities. He is not afraid of the *yetzer hara* tempting him with worldly pleasures and delights, for he is in firm control of his evil impulse. All his actions are guided by the light of the Torah, so that he uses worldly pleasures in moderation and only for proper ends."

118 *Midrash Tehillim* 119:11.

119 The *Rambam* in *Hilchos Ishus* 22:21 says: "Thoughts of forbidden relations gain a foothold in a mind empty of wisdom" (*Kiddushin* 30b).

A PERFECT REMEDY

In this vein, the Gemara in *Kiddushin* 30b says: "The word *v'samtem* [in the verse, '*Place these words of Mine [i.e., the Torah] on your heart and soul*'] (Devarim 11:18) may be read as *sam tam*, 'a perfect remedy.' The Torah is likened to a life-giving elixir. This may be compared to a man who struck his son a hard blow and then put a bandage on his wound, saying: "Son! As long as this bandage is on your wound, you can eat and drink anything you wish without fear. But if you remove it, your wound will break out into sores." Similarly, the Holy One, blessed be He, said to Yisrael: "My children! I created the *yetzer hara*, but I also created the Torah as its antidote. If you occupy yourselves with the Torah, you will not be delivered into the *yetzer hara*'s hand, for it says, '*If you do good* [i.e., engage in Torah study], *will you not be exalted* [*above the yetzer hara*]?' (Bereishis 4:7) But if you do not occupy yourselves with Torah study, you will be delivered into its hand, as that verse continues, '*sin is crouching at the door*.'"[120]

THE TORAH GUARDS THE TORAH SCHOLAR

The Midrash[121] says: "Fortunate is the man who acquired Torah learning. Why? Because it guards him from taking the wrong path, as it says, '*As you go forth, [the Torah] will guide you*' (Mishlei 6:22), for the Torah directs his heart to be faithful to Hashem, to serve Him with both his impulses [the *yetzer tov* and the *yetzer hara*]."

Further, the Gemara in *Chagigah* 3b says: "It states, '*The words of the wise [i.e., the Torah] are like goads*' (Koheles 12:11).

---

120 Meaning: When you give in to the *yetzer hara*, you become its slave.

121 *Mishlei Rabbah*.

Why are the words of the Torah compared to a goad? To teach you that just as a goad directs the cow [that pulls the plow] along its furrow in order to produce life-giving [grain] for the world, so do the words of the Torah direct their students away from the ways of death, toward the ways of life."

Furthermore, the Midrash[122] says that engaging in Torah study is the only method in the world to avoid the snare of the *yetzer hara,* which tries to destroy man to bring him to eternal death.[123] By engaging in Torah study, man becomes alive, for through Torah study he attaches himself to his share in the true eternal life, as it says, *"For [the Torah] is your life"* (Mishlei 4:13).

LIKE FISH IN WATER

The Gemara in *Avodah Zarah* 3b says: "What is the meaning of the verse, '*You have made man like the fish of the sea*' (Chavakuk 1:14)? Why is man compared to the fish of the sea? To tell you that just as the fish of the sea perish as soon as they are lifted onto dry land, so, too, man perishes as soon as they reject the Torah and the mitzvos."

In the same vein, the Gemara in *Berachos* 61b relates [a parable where the fish told the fox who wanted to entice them to come ashore]: "If in the environment that sustains our life [water] we are afraid, in the environment that will induce our death [i.e., on dry land] all the more so!"

122 *Bamidbar Rabbah* 14.

123 Women do not require the remedy of Torah study, since they do not have the same *yetzer hara* as men. The quality of *tz'nius* (modesty) is their shield against the *yetzer hara.* The Vilna Gaon in his letter published in "*Cheshbono shel Olam*" (B'nei B'rak, 1963) states explicitly: The remedy for men is Torah study; the remedy for women is modesty. (*Uvacharta Bachaim*)

And *Raya Mehemna*[124] says: "Just as the fish of the sea exist in water, so do Torah scholars thrive by learning Torah, for without Torah study they would perish instantly." Similarly, the Midrash[125] comments on the verse, *"For they are life to those who find them"* (Mishlei 4:22): "Whoever finds Torah teachings finds life."

THE TORAH IS YOUR LIFE

The Zohar[126] says: "The Jewish people are fortunate because the Torah teaches them the way of the Holy One, blessed be He. Fortunate is he who engages in Torah study constantly, for interrupting one's Torah study even for just a short while is like separating from eternal life, as it says, '*[The Torah] is your life*' (Mishlei 4:13) and '*[The Torah] adds to you length of days and years of life and peace*' (Mishlei 3:2)."

Furthermore, the Zohar says:[127] "How fortunate are the Jewish people, for Hashem favored them and gave them the Torah of truth, the tree of life. If a man grasps hold of it, he earns life in this world and in the hereafter. Those who exert themselves in Torah study are holding on to life. Those who forsake Torah learning forsake life, for the words of the Torah are life to those who find them."

124 End of *Parashas Shemini.*

125 *Tanchuma, Parashas Eikev.*

126 *Parashas Lech Lecha* 92a.

127 Beginning of *Parashas Beha'alosecha.*

STUDYING TORAH WITHOUT LETUP

Torah study is of such paramount importance that G-d commanded, *"Let not this Book of the Torah cease from your mouth; rather you should contemplate it day and night"* (Yehoshua 1:8). The introduction to the Zohar elaborates on this concept, saying: "Look how powerful and incomparably lofty is the Torah! That's why you should engage in Torah study day and night, without interruption. Rejecting Torah study is like turning your back on the tree of life."

Tanna D'bei Eliyahu[128] says: "[Although the supporters of Torah scholars have an equal share in the reward,] you should do your best to study Torah yourself, because Torah teachings are compared to bread and water to teach you that just as man cannot live without bread and water, so it is impossible for man to exist without Torah study, as it says, *'Let not this Book of the Torah cease from your mouth.'*"

GRASPING THE TREE OF LIFE

It says, *"[The Torah] is a tree of life to those who grasp her"* (Mishlei 3:18). Imagine that you were swept away in a raging river, and suddenly you see in front of you an overhanging tree. You would surely strain with all your might to grab hold of it, and not let go of it even for second, for releasing your grip means certain death! In the same way, the Torah is called the "tree of life." By holding on to it lovingly and learning it continually, you truly live a higher form of life. You are bound and tied, as it

128 *Eliyahu Zuta* 13.

were, to G-d, because G-d and the Torah are One.

If one eases up on his learning, giving up his regular study periods in favor of worldly delights and frivolities, he severs his connection with the spiritual life, becoming bogged down in the morass of evil.

The Zohar[129] says: "The Jewish people are fortunate in that G-d has given them the Torah in which to occupy themselves day and night. Whoever learns Torah achieves complete freedom — even freedom from death. [The angel of] death has no power over him, since by studying the Torah he holds on to the tree of life. But if he lets go of the tree of life, the tree of death seizes him."

WORDS OF ADMONITION

This awesome concept must be indelibly engraved on your mind. Remember that the totality of a man's life adds up to no more than the amount of time he devoted to the study of Torah. If he stops learning, being fascinated with the glitter of this world of darkness, he becomes a prisoner of his *yetzer hara*. If that happens, why should he go on living! He is mired in the swamp of perfidy. Although he is physically alive in this world, he is as good as dead. Stumbling downhill, he does not realize that his very soul is at risk.

The Torah herself warns, *"He who sins against me destroys his soul"* (Mishlei 8:36). And it says, *"However, take care and guard yourselves well, so that you do not forget the things that your eyes saw"* (Devarim 4:9). The Gemara in *Menachos* 99b says: "This can be compared to the case of a man who gave a swallow (type of bird) to his servant to safeguard, and said to him, 'Do you think that if you allow it to become lost, I will take from

129 *Parashas Vayetzei* 152a,

you only an *issar* [a coin]? I will in fact take your soul from you!' The Midrash[130] explains: "The Holy One, blessed be He, said to man: My lamp [the Torah] is in your hand, and your lamp [the soul] is in My hand. If you look after My lamp, I will guard your lamp. If you don't look after My lamp … I will take back your lamp."

Chapter 34 | פרק ל"ד

A SMALL-SCALE SANCTUARY

Ever since the destruction of the Beis Hamikdash, when the Jewish people were sent into exile, the *Shechinah* has had no tranquility. The only source of delight the *Shechinah* has left is the sound of Yisrael engrossed in studying Torah *lishmah*. By learning Torah, they turn [the *beis midrash*] into a miniature Sanctuary. The *Shechinah* dwells among them and spreads Her wings over them. In the process, the *Shechinah* enjoys a little cheer and serenity.

This idea is the subject of the Gemara in *Berachos* 8a: "Since the day the Beis Hamikdash was destroyed, the Holy One, blessed be He, has nothing in the world except the four cubits of halachah …" The Gemara asks: "From where do we know that even if only one person is learning Torah the *Shechinah* dwells with him? Because it says, '*Wherever I allow My name to be mentioned, I will come to you and bless you*' (Shemos 20:21)."

The Midrash[131] comments on the verse: "*For one who finds [the Torah] finds life*" (Mishlei 8:35): "The Holy One, blessed be

130 *Devarim Rabbah* 4.
131 *Mishlei* 8.

He, says: When I find you studying Torah, I will be found near you, wherever you may be."

TORAH STUDY IS SPIRITUAL FOOD

The Zohar[132] says: "*When you lay siege to a city ... you must not destroy its trees*" (Devarim 20:19) — this alludes to a Torah scholar, for he is the tree of life. The verse continues, "*for from it you will eat ...*" For the only desire that *ruach hakodesh* has in this world is the Torah that the Torah scholar learns. His learning is "food" for the *ruach hakodesh* in this world, so to speak, providing it with more "nourishment" than all the sacrifices in the world. Since the Beis Hamikdash was destroyed and the sacrifices have ceased, all G-d has left are the novel insights created by the Torah scholars.

That is the underlying meaning of the phrase, "*for from it you will eat.*" The only nourishment the *Shechinah* finds in this world is the learning of the Torah scholar and his colleagues.

This is also the deeper sense of the Gemara in *Taanis* 7a, which asks: What is meant by the verse, "*For a man is a tree in the field*" (Devarim 20:19)? The same verse says about trees, "*for from it you will eat, and you shall not cut it down.*" How does this apply to a human being? If you have a Torah scholar who is a worthy [i.e., G-d-fearing] person, learn [i.e., eat] from him and do not cut him down, but if he is not G-d-fearing, destroy him and cut him down.

By learning Torah, the scholar prepares a dwelling for G-d in the world below, so that His glory resides on earth. As the Midrash[133] puts it: Before the Torah was given to Yisrael,

132 *Parashas Balak* 202a.

133 *Shemos Rabbah* 33.

"Moshe ascended to G-d" (Shemos 19:3), but after the Torah was given, Hashem said, *"They shall make Me a sanctuary, and I shall dwell among them"* (Shemos 25:8).[134]

A CONCLUDING THOUGHT

A thoughtful person will understand from my words that he is to devote himself to Torah study every day of his life, and that he should despise evil and choose to do good, for himself, for all creations and for all the higher worlds, so that he will be a source of joy for his Creator.

May it be His will that He may open our heartt through His Torah, and imbue our heart with love and awe of Him. Thereby His intention of creating His world will come to fruition, to perfect the universe through the Almighty's sovereignty, and everything that has been created will know that You are its Maker, and all will accept upon themselves the yoke of Your kingship, according to Your exalted will, so that Hashem will be One and His name will be One. Amen, and may this be His will.

134 By engaging in the study of the Torah, a Jew turns himself into a sanctuary worthy of having the *Shechinah* dwell in it (*Uvacharta Bachaim*).

Index

A

Abandoning study, consequences of, 174, 178, 181–182
Acher and Gehinnom, 161
Acquiring G-d, 148, 167
Action, speech and thought. *See Ruach, nefesh and neshama*
Adam's spiritual level, 101
Adam's *teshuvah*, 67
Amram marrying his aunt, transgression, 69
Angels, destructive, 52, 167, 181
Angels and humankind, rank, 45–48

B

Banned, 177–178
Beis Hamikdash, destruction of, 34, 62*tn*
Beis midrash, conversion to a synagogue, 184
Beneficial speech, 52
Berachos, formulation of, 80–81
Berachos, meaning of, 78–80
Bereishis, 149
Bittul Torah, 190–191
Blessing. *See* Berachos.
B'nei Yisrael meriting sparks of *neshamah*, 59*n*
Book and the sword, 175–176

C

Cantillation marks correspondence, 99–100
Celestial influences, immunity, 162–165
Channah's plea, 93–94
Chanoch's spiritual level, 101
Cherubs. *See Keruvim*
Chizkiyah's refusal to marry, 70–71
Conceit, 119–121
Concubine in Giv'ah, 143
Creation, human partnership with, 87
Creation, ongoing and continual, 30–31
Creation and the Torah, 150, 153–154

D

Death and judgment, 177
Destiny, human influence on, 22, 31–33
Disparaging *shelo lishmah* learners, 123
Divine Light and *sefiros*, 37*n*

E

Eim Habanim, 58
Eliyahu's spiritual level, 101
Elokim term, choice of, 30
Enunciation of prayers, 127–128
Ethics and piety, study, 135–136, 145–146
Everlasting life, 161–162, 180–181, 193–194, 203
Evil speech, consequences of, 52–53

F

Faith and miracles, 43–45
Fate and punishment of the refuser, 177–181
Fate of humanity and the stars, 164
Fifty gates of understanding, 46*n*
Fish of the sea simile, 190, 202–203
Food, spiritual, 207–208
Forbearance, attribute of, 34
Forces of nature, control of and immunity from, 162–165
Forgiveness and Torah study, 195–196
Foundation Stone, 35*n*
Fountain cleansing simile, 198
Fraud and misappropriation, 144–145
Fruits of Torah study, 150–156

G

Garment simile, 188
Gates of understanding, fifty, 46*n*
G-d
  acquiring with the Torah, 148, 167
  connection to the Jewish people, 64–65
  connection with Torah study, 142–144
  existence, place of all the worlds, 109–116
  fills all the worlds, 112–113
  how we may speak of, 79–81
  image of, 22, 30
  Man's partnership with, 87–88
  names of, 80
  nourishing the mystical bond, 84–86
  prayers of the righteous, 88–89
  soul's reflection of, 82–84
  tefillah as nourishment, 87
  Torah and the names of, 165–167
  world, involvement in, 81–82
G-d is your shadow, 40
Gehinnom, 49–50, 160–161, 176–177
Glass blowing, three phases of, 57
Glowing coal, 107–108
Goad simile, 202
Good deeds' nourishment of the Higher Worlds, 84–85
Good intentions, 51*n*
Goodness, bringing into the world, 155–156
Great Deep, 52

H

HaMakom, 107–109
Hanged bodies, leaving, 83–84
Harmful influences, protection from, 157
Heavenly tribunal's judgment, 177
Hidden things, warning against, 111–112, 114–116
Higher Worlds, man's actions impact upon, 31–33, 39–40
  good deeds nourishing, 84–85
  human body, heavenly correspondence of, 35–39
  increasing blessing, 81–83
  pain and anguish, 92
  repercussions of, 48–56
Hikareis tikareis, 179
Human body, health, 189–191
Humility, 121–122

I

Ignorant, resurrection of, 181
Immoral thoughts of women, 66*n*
Improper thoughts, 55, 62
Impurity, spirit of, 50*n*
Indecent thoughts and sins, impact of, 35–36, 39
Influence, angel *vs.* humankind, 45–46
Intent and degree of punishment, 53–55

K

Kabbalah study, warning, 111–112
Kabbalistic concepts, 23
Kabbalist insight into *mitzvos*, 73
Kareis, 62–63, 179
Kavannah and prayer, 89–90
Kav of *yirah*, 146
Kayin marriage to his sister, transgression, 69
Kedushah, 39
  gradual descent of, 184–185
  of *mitzvos*, source, 191
  and *yiras Shamayim*, 141
Keruvim, position of, 40–41, 43, 44
King Chizkiyah
  and Yeshayah, 130
  refusal to marry, 70–71
Korbanos, 94, 96–97
Kosher offerings of Noach, 68

L

Lamp simile, 206
Law change and the prophets, 71
Laxness in study, consequences of, 174–175
Life everlasting, promise of, 161–162, 193–194
Light of Creation and *tzaddikim*, 171–172

M

Machsharto, 198
Maggidim, offer to the Vilna Gaon, 59*n*
Man as a speaking spirit, 36
Manna, miracle of, 43–44
Man's partnership with G-d, 87–88
Men of the Great Assembly, 30, 88, 90, 102

Metzukim, 181–182
Mikveh-like nature of Torah learning, 196–197
Miracles and faith, 43–45
Misappropriation and fraud, 144–145
Mitzvos
human body correspondence, 39, 189–191
Kabbalist's insight, 73
kavannah of, 128, 139–140
kedushah, source of, 191
at the proper time, 125–127
prophet's right to temporarily alter, 71
Rabbinic, 72
reward of, 49
Torah study's superiority to, 188–190, 191–203
understanding the deeper reasons for, 71
without Torah study, 191–192
Moshe
his *neshamah*, 57, 60*n*
his radiance, 170
Mother of Children *(Eim Habanim)*, 58
Mussar study *vs.* Torah study, 135–136, 145–146
Mystical bond with G-d, nourishing, 84–86

N

Names of G-d, 80, 165–167
Nature, ongoing creation and direction of, 30–31
Nature's forces, control of and immunity from, 162–165
Nefesh
action correspondence, 55–56
letters correspondence, 99–100
removing a stain from, 65–66
Nefesh, ruach and *neshamah*, 46, 48
Nefesh chayah, 97
Neshamah, 46, 48, 56–60
and brain correspondence, 56
immoral thoughts, damage of, 55, 62
removing a stain from, 66–67
root of, 101–102
thought correspondence, 56–58
understanding the root of, argument, 69
in Yaakov's dream, 63–64
Neshimah and the soul, 56–57
Netziv. See Berlin, R. Naftali Tzvi Yehudah, 21
Nevuchadnezar's success, 33–35
Noach's *teshuvah* of kosher offerings, 68
Nourishment, spiritual, 207–208

O

Olah offerings' intention, 90
Olam Haba, 49, 70, 123, 179–180
Oveid Hashem, 128

P

Patriarchs and the granting of the Torah, 68–69
Perek Shirah, recitation's significance, 47–48
Personal pleas and petitions, 90–93
Piety and ethics study, 135–136, 145–146
Place of the world, 107–116
Prayer
  clear enunciation of, 127–128
  dependent on Torah study, 183–184
  as G-d's food and nourishment, 84–85, 87
  how to pray, 94–98
  kavannah in, 86, 89–90
  personal pleas and petitions, 90–93
  of the righteous, 88–89
  suffering, relief of, 90–93
  in times of hardship, 94
Praying with your heart and soul, 77–78
Pride and conceit, 119–121
Prophets and law changes, 72
Punishment and fate of the refuser, 177–181
Punishment and intent, 53–55

R

Rachel's marriage to Yaakov, transgression, 68–69
Rank of angels and humankind, 45–46
Reed Sea, miraculous parting of, 45
Remedy, perfect, 201
Renewal, continual, 30–31
Resurrection, 180–181
Rokeach, 111
Root of the Torah, hidden, 183
Rosh Hashanah prayers theme, 90
Ruach
  see also Nefesh, ruach and *neshama*
  and heart correspondence, 56
  removing damage to, 66
  speech correspondence, 56
  vowel signs correspondence, 99–100
Ruach Hakodesh authorship of Shemoneh Esrei, 95
Ruach memallela, 97

S

Saintliness, 36*n*
Sanctuary creation, 206–208
Sefiros, 37*n*
Serving G-d with prayer, 77–78
Shameful deeds' damage to the Higher Worlds, 85
Shechinah, 91, 92, 178, 206
Shelo lishmah, 122–124, 164
Shemoneh Esrei, 88, 90
  kavannah verse, 102–103
  and personal pleas, 93–94
  praying, 95–98
  Ruach Hakodesh authorship, 95
Shlomo's wisdom, 65*n*
Shoresh haneshamah, 101–102
Sin
  Higher Worlds' pain, 92

indecent thoughts, impact of, 35–36, 39
intent and degree of punishment, 53–55
as its own punishment, 50–51
kareis punishment, 62–63, 179
punishment of, 86
ten levels of, 179–180
Torah neglect, 190–191
and *tumah*, 50*n*
Sinful deeds' damage to the Higher Worlds, 85
Soul, 113
formation of, 36–38
heavenly root of, 199–200
and *neshimah*, 56–57
as reflection of G-d, 82–84
three parts of, 46, 48, 99–100
women's immoral thoughts, 66*n*
Soul of the world, 113–114
Sparks of light of the *Neshamah*, 59–61
Speaking evil, gravity of, 52–53, 62
Speech, beneficial, 52
Speech and *ruach* correspondence, 56
Spiritual food, 207–208
Spiritual worlds linkage, 52
Stains, removal from *nefesh*, 66–67
Standing at Sinai, 154–155
Stars and fate of humanity, 164
Storehouse of *yirah*, 141–142, 145–146
Strict Justice, attribute of, 34
Suffering, prayers for the relief of, 90–93
Swallow simile, 205–206
Synagogue conversion from a *beis midrash*, 184

T

Tammasi, 91
Tanna D'bei Eliyahu, 147, 155
Tax paying exemption, 158–159
Tefillah. *See* Prayer.
Tefillah as Divine nourishment, 87
Ten great difficulties, 200
Teshuvah, 60–61, 66–67, 66, 67, 85, 197
Thought and *neshamah* correspondence, 56
Tikrei, reading instruction, 32*n*
Titus' success, 33–35
Torah
as a garment, 188
hidden root of, 183
kedushah of, 184–186
and the Patriarchs, 68–69
as the world's blueprint, 147–149
Torah *lishmah*. *See* Torah study
Torah scholar, resurrection of, 180–181
Torah scholars, G-d's love for, 167–171
Torah study, 22–23
anxiety and harm, protection from, 157–158
cleansing and healing nature of, 196–197, 199

decline and laxness, consequences of, 173–177
disparaging *shelo lishmah* learners, 123
equivalence to all *mitzvos,* 121–122
fate of the refuser, 177–178
fruits of, 150–156
heals the body, 189–190
and heavenly tribunal, 177
and the Higher Worlds, 67–68
for its own sake. *See* Torah *lishmah*
mitzvos, superiority to, 188–203
mussar study and, 135–136, 145–146
neshamah, removing a stain from, 66–67
new insights, 152–153
power and benefits from, 156–165
prayer acceptance, dependence on, 183–184
pride and conceit, avoiding, 119–121
protecting the world from destruction, 181–182
as a sacrificial act, 194–196
shelo lishmah, 122–124
superior to *mitzvos,* 188–203
upholds the world, 150, 151–152
without ceasing, 204
without *mitzvos,* 191–192
and women, 180*n*, 202*n*
and worldly pursuits, 41–44
and *yetzer hara,* deception of, 124–127
Torah text, secrets within, 186–188
Transgressions
canceling by study, 189
and degree of punishment, 53–55
intention for, 50*n*
Yaakov and Chizkiyah's, 68
Tree in the field simile, 207
Tree of Life, 22–23, 204–205
Tumah, 50*n*
Tzaddikim, 170–171
Tzelem Elokim, 22, 31
Tznius and *yetzer hara,* 202*n*

V

Viduy prayer, 199
Vilna Gaon's *maggidim* offer, 59*n*
Virtuous deeds, impact of, 38–39
Vowel signs correspondence, 99–100

W

Women and immoral thoughts, 66*n*
Women and Torah study, 180*n*, 202*n*
Women's *tznius* and *yetzer hara,* 202*n*
Words, impact of, 51–53
Worldly concerns, relief from, 158
World of Action, 48
World to Come, 49, 70, 123, 179–180

Y

Yaakov's transgression by marrying two sisters, 69
Yaakov's vision of the ladder, 46, 63–64
Yeshayah
  and King Chizkiyah's refusal to marry, 70–71
  dialogue with King Chizkiyah, 130
Yetzer hara, 200, 202
  deception of, 124–127
  ruses and deceptions, 128–131
  snares of, 111–112
  and women's *tznius*, 202*n*
Yiras Shamayim and Torah study, 140–142, 144–147
Yocheved's marriage to Amram, 69
Yoke of heavenly sovereignty, 140–141

Glossary

Adam Harishon — Adam, the first man
Aggadah, aggados — non-legal, homiletical sections of the Oral Torah
Alef-beis — the Hebrew alphabet
B'nei Yisrael — the Jewish people
Bamidbar — the Book of Numbers
Beis Hamikdash — the Holy Temple in Jerusalem
Berachah, berachos — blessing(s)
Beraisa (Aram.) — a Mishnaic text not codified in the main body of the Mishnah
Bereishis — the Book of Genesis
Chazzan — person leading the prayers
Devarim — the Book of Deuteronomy
Divrei Hayamim — the Book of Chronicles
Dovid Hamelech — King David
Eichah — the Book of Lamentations
Gan Eden — the Garden of Eden, Heaven
Gaon — genius
Gehinnom — the place where souls are cleansed of their sins after death
Gemara (Aram.) — the Talmud
Halachah, halachos — Jewish law(s)
Halachic — pertaining to Jewish law
Hashem — G-d
Hashem Yisbarach — G-d, may He be blessed
Haskamah — rabbinic approbation
Iyov — the Book of Job
Kabbalist — Torah scholar who is expert in mysticism
Kabbalistic — pertaining to Jewish mysticism
Kareis — spiritual excision
Kasher (Yidd.) — make kosher
Kavanah, kavanos — intention(s)
Kedushah — holiness
Keruv, keruvim — cherub(s) that were part of the cover of the Ark in the Holy Temple
Klal Yisrael — the Jewish people

Koheles — the Book of Ecclesiastes
Kohen Gadol — the High Priest
Kohen, kohanim — priest(s)
Korban, korbanos — offering(s)
Lishmah — for its own sake
L'sheim Shamayim — for the sake of Heaven
Lulav — palm branch taken as part of the Four Species, a mitzvah on the festival of Sukkos
Maggid, maggidim — heavenly messenger(s) who communicated with certain saintly individuals
Mashiach — the Messiah
Matzah — unleavened bread eaten on Passover
Megillah — the Book of Esther
Melachim — the Book of Kings
Midrash, midrashim — homiletical Torah work(s)
Mikveh — ritual bath
Minchah — afternoon prayers
Mishlei — the Book of Proverbs
Mitzvah, mitzvos — Torah commandment(s)
Motza'ei Yom Kippur — the night after Yom Kippur, the Day of Atonement
Mount Chorev — the mountain on which the Torah was given to the Jewish people
Mussar — ethical teachings
Nefesh — the animalistic element of the soul
Nefesh Hachaim — the soul of life
Neshamah — the most lofty component of the soul
Olah — offering in the Temple that was completely burnt on the Altar
Olam Haba — the World to Come, Heaven
Parashas — the weekly Torah portion of
Pesach — Passover
Pirkei Avos — Ethics of the Fathers
Rav — rabbi
Rebbi (Aram.) — Torah teacher
Rishonim — the leading Rabbis and halachic decisors who lived approximately during the 11th to 15th centuries
Rosh Hashanah — the Jewish New Year
Rosh yeshivah, rashei yeshivos — head(s) of Torah school(s)
Ruach — the intermediate level component of the soul
Ruach hakodesh — Divine inspiration
Seder — the festive meal on Passover, at which the miracles of the Exodus are recounted
Sefer, sefarim — Torah book(s)
Serafim — fiery angels
Shacharis — morning prayers

Shas — the Talmud
Shechinah — G-d's presence
Shelo lishmah — with ulterior motivest
Shema — the silent devotion, which is the central part of the daily prayers
Shemoneh Esrei — the silent devotion, which is the central part of the daily prayers
Shemos — the Book of Exodus
Shir Hashirim — the Book of Song of Songs
Shlit"a — acronym for "*sheyizkeh li'chayim tovim v'aruchim*," that he should merit a good, long life
Shmuel — the Book of Samuel
Sivan — the ninth month of the Jewish year
Tanach — the Five Books of Moses, the Prophets and the Holy Writings
Tefillah, tefillos — prayer(s)
Tehillim — the Book of Psalms
Teshuvah — repentance
Tikkun — rectification
Tishrei — the first month of the Jewish year
Tzaddik, tzaddikim — righteous one(s)
Tzedakah — charity
Tz'nius — modesty
Vav — the sixth letter of the Hebrew alphabet
Vayikra — the Book of Leviticus
Yamim tovim — festivals
Yechezkel — the Book of Ezekiel
Yehoshua — the Book of Joshua
Yerushalayim — Jerusalem
Yeshayah — the Book of Isaiah
Yeshivah, yeshivos — Torah school(s)
Yetzer hara — the evil inclination
Yirah — fear, awe
Yiras Shamayim — fear of Heaven
Yirmiyah — the Book of Jeremiah
Zohar — the primary work of Jewish mysticism

נפש החיים

שַׁעַר א'

פֶּרֶק א'

כְּתִיב (בראשית א, כז) "וַיִּבְרָא אֱלֹקִים אֶת הָאָדָם בְּצַלְמוֹ בְּצֶלֶם אֱלֹקִים בָּרָא אוֹתוֹ", וְכֵן כְּתִיב (שם ט, ו) "כִּי בְּצֶלֶם אֱלֹקִים עָשָׂה אֶת הָאָדָם".

הִנֵּה עֹמֶק פְּנִימִיּוּת עִנְיַן הַצֶּלֶם, הוּא מִדְּבָרִים הָעוֹמְדִים בְּרוּמוֹ שֶׁל עוֹלָם, וְהוּא כּוֹלֵל רוֹב סִתְרֵי פְּנִימִיּוּת הַזֹּהַר. אָמְנָם, כָּאן נְדַבֵּר בְּמִלַּת "צֶלֶם", בְּדֶרֶךְ הַפַּשְׁטָנִים הָרִאשׁוֹנִים ז"ל עַל פָּסוּק "נַעֲשֶׂה אָדָם בְּצַלְמֵנוּ כִּדְמוּתֵנוּ" (שם א, כו):

וְהוּא, כִּי מִלַּת "צֶלֶם" וּ"דְמוּת" כָּאן, אֵינוֹ כְּמַשְׁמָעוֹ, כִּי כָּתוּב מְפֹרָשׁ (ישעי' מ', יח) "וּמַה דְּמוּת תַּעַרְכוּ לוֹ", אֶלָּא פֵּרוּשׁוֹ, דִּמְיוֹן מַה בְּאֵיזֶה דָּבָר, כְּמוֹ "דָּמִיתִי לִקְאַת מִדְבָּר" (תהלים קב, ז), כִּי לֹא נַעֲשׂוּ לוֹ כְּנָפַיִם וְחַרְטוֹם, וְלֹא נִשְׁתַּנָּה צוּרָתוֹ לְצוּרַת הַקָּאַת, רַק שֶׁנִּדְמֶה אָז, בְּמִקְרֶה פְּעֻלּוֹתָיו שֶׁהָיָה נָע וָנָד, כְּמוֹ הַקָּאַת מִדְבָּר, שֶׁהוּא צִפּוֹר בּוֹדֵד וּמְעוֹפֵף מִמָּקוֹם לְמָקוֹם. כָּךְ הוּא לְפִי הַפַּשְׁטָנִים הָרִאשׁוֹנִים זִכְרוֹנָם לִבְרָכָה.

וְכֵן עַל דֶּרֶךְ זֶה הוּא עִנְיַן מִלַּת "צֶלֶם", כִּי הֵמָּה דּוֹמִים בְּמַשְׁמָעָם בְּצַד מַה:

פֶּרֶק ב'

אָמְנָם, לְהָבִין עִנְיַן אָמְרוֹ "בְּצֶלֶם אֱלֹקִים" דַּיְקָא, וְלֹא שֵׁם אַחֵר, כִּי שֵׁם "אֱלֹקִים" יָדוּעַ פֵּרוּשׁוֹ, שֶׁהוּא מוֹרֶה שֶׁהוּא יִתְבָּרַךְ שְׁמוֹ בַּעַל הַכֹּחוֹת כֻּלָּם, כְּמוֹ שֶׁמְּבֹאָר בְּטוּר אֹרַח חַיִּים סִימָן ה'.

וְעִנְיַן מַה שֶּׁהוּא יִתְבָּרַךְ נִקְרָא "בַּעַל הַכֹּחוֹת", כִּי לֹא כְּמִדַּת בָּשָׂר וָדָם – מִדַּת הַקָּדוֹשׁ בָּרוּךְ הוּא, כִּי הָאָדָם, כְּשֶׁבּוֹנֶה בִּנְיָן דֶּרֶךְ מָשָׁל מֵעֵץ, אֵין הַבּוֹנֶה בּוֹרֵא וּמַמְצִיא אָז מִכֹּחוֹ הָעֵץ, רַק שֶׁלּוֹקֵחַ עֵצִים שֶׁכְּבָר נִבְרְאוּ, וּמְסַדְּרָם בַּבִּנְיָן, וְאַחַר שֶׁכְּבָר סִדְּרָם לְפִי רְצוֹנוֹ, עִם שֶׁכֹּחוֹ הוּסַר וְנִסְתַּלֵּק מֵהֶם, עִם כָּל זֶה הַבִּנְיָן קַיָּם.

אֲבָל הוּא יִתְבָּרַךְ שְׁמוֹ, כְּמוֹ בְּעֵת בְּרִיאַת הָעוֹלָמוֹת כֻּלָּם, בְּרָאָם וְהִמְצִיאָם הוּא יִתְבָּרַךְ יֵשׁ מֵאַיִן, בְּכֹחוֹ הַבִּלְתִּי תַּכְלִית, כֵּן מֵאָז, כָּל יוֹם וְכָל רֶגַע מַמָּשׁ, כָּל כֹּחַ מְצִיאוּתָם וְסִדְרָם וְקִיּוּמָם, תָּלוּי רַק בְּמַה שֶׁהוּא יִתְבָּרַךְ שְׁמוֹ מַשְׁפִּיעַ בָּהֶם בִּרְצוֹנוֹ יִתְבָּרַךְ כָּל רֶגַע, כֹּחַ וְשִׁפְעַת אוֹר חָדָשׁ, וְאִלּוּ הָיָה הוּא יִתְבָּרַךְ מְסַלֵּק מֵהֶם כֹּחַ הַשְׁפָּעָתוֹ אַף רֶגַע אַחַת, כְּרֶגַע הָיוּ כֻּלָּם לְאֶפֶס וָתֹהוּ.

וּכְמוֹ שֶׁיָּסְדוּ אַנְשֵׁי כְּנֶסֶת הַגְּדוֹלָה (בְּבִרְכַּת יוֹצֵר אוֹר) "הַמְחַדֵּשׁ בְּטוּבוֹ בְּכָל יוֹם תָּמִיד מַעֲשֵׂה בְרֵאשִׁית", הַיְנוּ "תָּמִיד" מַמָּשׁ, כָּל עֵת וָרֶגַע, וּרְאָיָתָם מְפֹרֶשֶׁת כְּאָמוּר "לְעוֹשֵׂה אוֹרִים גְּדוֹלִים" (תהלים קלו, ז), שֶׁלֹּא אָמַר "עָשָׂה" אֶלָּא "עוֹשֶׂה":

וְזֶהוּ שֶׁנִּקְרָא הוּא יִתְבָּרַךְ שְׁמוֹ, "הָאֱלֹקִים", בַּעַל הַכֹּחוֹת כֻּלָּם. שֶׁכָּל כֹּחַ פְּרָטֵי הַנִּמְצָא בְּכָל הָעוֹלָמוֹת, הַכֹּל, הוּא יִתְבָּרַךְ שְׁמוֹ, הַבַּעַל כֹּחַ שֶׁלָּהֶם, שֶׁמַּשְׁפִּיעַ בָּהֶם הַכֹּחַ וּגְבוּרָה כָּל רֶגַע, וּתְלוּיִים בְּיָדוֹ תָּמִיד לְשַׁנּוֹתָם וּלְסַדְּרָם, כִּרְצוֹנוֹ יִתְבָּרַךְ:

פֶּרֶק ג'

כֵּן בְּדִמְיוֹן זֶה, כִּבְיָכוֹל, בָּרָא הוּא יִתְבָּרֵךְ אֶת הָאָדָם, וְהִשְׁלִיטוֹ עַל רִבֵּי רִבְבָן כֹּחוֹת וְעוֹלָמוֹת אֵין מִסְפָּר, וּמְסָרָם בְּיָדוֹ, שֶׁיְּהֵא הוּא הַמְּדַבֵּר וְהַמַּנְהִיג אוֹתָם, עַל פִּי כָּל פְּרָטֵי תְּנוּעוֹת מַעֲשָׂיו, וְדִבּוּרָיו, וּמַחְשְׁבוֹתָיו, וְכָל סִדְרֵי הַנְהָגוֹתָיו, הֵן לְטוֹב אוֹ לְהֶפֶךְ חַס וְשָׁלוֹם.

כִּי בְּמַעֲשָׂיו וְדִבּוּרָיו וּמַחְשְׁבוֹתָיו הַטּוֹבִים, הוּא מְקַיֵּם וְנוֹתֵן כֹּחַ בְּכַמָּה כֹּחוֹת וְעוֹלָמוֹת עֶלְיוֹנִים הַקְּדוֹשִׁים, וּמוֹסִיף בָּהֶם קְדֻשָּׁה וְאוֹר, כְּמוֹ שֶׁכָּתוּב (ישעי' נא, טז) "וָאָשִׂים דְּבָרַי בְּפִיךָ וגו' לִנְטֹעַ שָׁמַיִם וְלִיסֹד אָרֶץ", וּכְמַאֲמָרָם זִכְרוֹנָם לִבְרָכָה (ברכות סד.) אַל תִּקְרָא בָּנַיִךְ אֶלָּא בּוֹנָיִךְ, כִּי הֵמָּה הַמְסַדְּרִים עוֹלָמוֹת הָעֶלְיוֹנִים, כְּבוֹנֶה הַמְסַדֵּר בִּנְיָנוֹ, וְנוֹתְנִים בָּהֶם רֹב כֹּחַ.

וּבְהִפּוּךְ חַס וְשָׁלוֹם, עַל יְדֵי מַעֲשָׂיו אוֹ דִּבּוּרָיו וּמַחְשְׁבוֹתָיו אֲשֶׁר לֹא טוֹבִים, הוּא מְהָרֵס רָצָה לוֹמַר כַּמָּה כֹּחוֹת, וְעוֹלָמוֹת עֶלְיוֹנִים הַקְּדוֹשִׁים, לְאֵין עֵרֶךְ וְשִׁעוּר, כְּמוֹ שֶׁנֶּאֱמַר (שם מט, יז) "מְהָרְסַיִךְ וּמַחֲרִיבַיִךְ מִמֵּךְ יֵצֵאוּ", אוֹ מַחְשִׁיךְ, אוֹ מַקְטִין אוֹרָם וּקְדֻשָּׁתָם חַס וְשָׁלוֹם, וּמוֹסִיף כֹּחַ לְעֻמַּת זֶה, בִּמְדוֹרוֹת הַטֻּמְאָה ר"ל.

זֶהוּ "וַיִּבְרָא אֱלֹקִים אֶת הָאָדָם בְּצַלְמוֹ בְּצֶלֶם אֱלֹקִים וגו' (בראשית א, כז), כִּי בְּצֶלֶם אֱלֹקִים עָשָׂה" וגו' (שם ט, ו) שֶׁכְּמוֹ שֶׁהוּא יִתְבָּרַךְ שְׁמוֹ, הוּא הָאֱלֹקִים, בַּעַל הַכֹּחוֹת הַנִּמְצָאִים בְּכָל הָעוֹלָמוֹת כֻּלָּם, וּמְסַדְּרָם וּמַנְהִיגָם כָּל רֶגַע כִּרְצוֹנוֹ, כֵּן הִשְׁלִיט רְצוֹנוֹ יִתְבָּרַךְ אֶת הָאָדָם שֶׁיְּהֵא הוּא הַפּוֹתֵחַ וְהַסּוֹגֵר שֶׁל כַּמָּה אַלְפֵי רִבּוֹאוֹת כֹּחוֹת וְעוֹלָמוֹת, עַל פִּי כָּל פְּרָטֵי סִדְרֵי הַנְהָגוֹתָיו בְּכָל עִנְיָנָיו בְּכָל עֵת וְרֶגַע מַמָּשׁ, כְּפִי שָׁרְשׁוֹ הָעֶלְיוֹן שֶׁל מַעֲשָׂיו וְדִבּוּרָיו וּמַחְשְׁבוֹתָיו, כְּאִלּוּ הוּא גַּם כֵּן הַבַּעַל כֹּחַ שֶׁלָּהֶם כִּבְיָכוֹל.

וְאָמְרוּ זִכְרוֹנָם לִבְרָכָה בְּאֵיכָה רַבָּתִי (בַּפָּסוּק א, ו, וַיֵּלְכוּ בְלֹא כֹחַ גו') רַבִּי עֲזַרְיָה בְּשֵׁם רַבִּי יְהוּדָה בֶּן סִימוֹן אוֹמֵר, בִּזְמַן שֶׁיִּשְׂרָאֵל עוֹשִׂין רְצוֹנוֹ שֶׁל מָקוֹם, מוֹסִיפִין כֹּחַ בַּגְּבוּרָה שֶׁל מַעְלָה, כְּמָה דְּאַתְּ אָמַרְתְּ "בֵּאלֹקִים נַעֲשֶׂה חָיִל" (תהלים ס, יד), וּבִזְמַן שֶׁאֵין יִשְׂרָאֵל עוֹשִׂין רְצוֹנוֹ שֶׁל מָקוֹם, כִּבְיָכוֹל מַתִּישִׁין כֹּחַ גָּדוֹל שֶׁל מַעְלָה, דִּכְתִיב (דברים לב, יח) "צוּר יְלָדְךָ תֶּשִׁי" וגו'.

וּבְכַמָּה מְקוֹמוֹת בַּזֹּהַר הַקָּדוֹשׁ, דְּחוֹבֵי בַּר נָשׁ, עַבְדִין פְּגִימוּ לְעֵלָּא כו', [חֲטָאֵי בֶּן אָדָם עוֹשִׂים פְּגָם לְמַעְלָה] וְכֵן לְהֶפֶךְ כַּנַּ"ל. וְזֶהוּ שֶׁאָמַר הַכָּתוּב "תְּנוּ עֹז לֵאלֹקִים" (תהלים סח, לה). וּבַזֹּהַר רֵישׁ פָּרָשַׁת בֹּא, "וַיְהִי הַיּוֹם וַיָּבֹאוּ גו' לְהִתְיַצֵּב עַל ה'" (איוב א, ו), כַּד בָּעָאן לְקַיְּמָא עַל אִינוּן עוֹבָדִין דְּיִשְׂרָאֵל, עַל ה' וַדַּאי קַיָּמִין, דְּהָא כַּד יִשְׂרָאֵל עָבְדִין עוֹבְדִין דְּלָא כַּשְׁרָן, כִּבְיָכוֹל מַתִּישִׁין חֵילָא דְּקוּדְשָׁא בְּרִיךְ הוּא, וְכַד עָבְדִין עוֹבְדִין דְּכַשְׁרָן, יָהֲבִין תּוּקְפָּא וְחֵילָא לְקוּדְשָׁא בְּרִיךְ הוּא, וְעַל דָּא כְּתִיב "תְּנוּ עֹז לֵאלֹקִים", בְּמָה, בְּעוֹבְדִין דְּכַשְׁרָן, [כְּשֶׁרוֹצִים לַעֲמֹד (לְקַטְרֵג) עַל אוֹתָם מַעֲשִׂים שֶׁל יִשְׂרָאֵל, עַל ה' וַדַּאי עוֹמְדִים (לְקַטְרֵג), שֶׁכַּאֲשֶׁר יִשְׂרָאֵל עוֹשִׂים מַעֲשִׂים שֶׁלֹּא כְּשֵׁרִים, כִּבְיָכוֹל מַתִּישִׁים כֹּחוֹ שֶׁל הַקָּדוֹשׁ בָּרוּךְ הוּא, וְכַאֲשֶׁר עוֹשִׂים מַעֲשִׂים כְּשֵׁרִים, נוֹתְנִים תֹּקֶף וְכֹחַ לקב"ה, וְעַל זֶה כָּתוּב תְּנוּ עֹז לֵאלֹקִים — בַּמֶּה, בְּמַעֲשִׂים כְּשֵׁרִים.]

וְלָכֵן אָמַר "לֵאלֹקִים", וְכֵן "בֵּאלֹקִים נַעֲשֶׂה חָיִל" (תהלים ס, יד), שֶׁפֵּרוּשׁוֹ בַּעַל הַכֹּחוֹת כֻּלָּם וְכַנַּ"ל.

פֶּרֶק ד'

וְזֹאת תּוֹרַת הָאָדָם, כָּל אִישׁ יִשְׂרָאֵל, אַל יֹאמַר בְּלִבּוֹ חַס וְשָׁלוֹם, כִּי מָה אֲנִי וּמָה כֹּחִי לִפְעֹל בְּמַעֲשַׂי הַשְּׁפָלִים שׁוּם עִנְיָן בָּעוֹלָם.

אָמְנָם יָבִין וְיֵדַע וְיִקְבַּע בְּמַחְשְׁבוֹת לִבּוֹ, שֶׁכָּל פְּרָטֵי מַעֲשָׂיו וְדִבּוּרָיו וּמַחְשְׁבוֹתָיו כָּל עֵת וָרֶגַע, לָא אִתְאֲבִידוּ חַס וְשָׁלוֹם, וּמָה רַבּוּ מַעֲשָׂיו וּמְאֹד גָּדְלוּ וְרָמוּ, שֶׁכָּל אַחַת, עוֹלָה כְּפִי שָׁרְשָׁהּ, לִפְעֹל פְּעֻלָּתָהּ בְּגָבְהֵי מְרוֹמִים, בָּעוֹלָמוֹת וְצַחְצָחוֹת הָאוֹרוֹת הָעֶלְיוֹנִים.

וּבֶאֱמֶת, כִּי הָאִישׁ הֶחָכָם וְיָבֵן אֶת זֹאת לַאֲמִתּוֹ, לִבּוֹ יָחִיל בְּקִרְבּוֹ בְּחִיל וּרְעָדָה, בְּשׂוּמוֹ עַל לִבּוֹ עַל מַעֲשָׂיו אֲשֶׁר לֹא טוֹבִים חַס וְשָׁלוֹם, עַד הֵיכָן הֵמָּה מַגִּיעִים לְקַלְקֵל וְלַהֲרֹס בְּחֵטְא קַל חַס וְשָׁלוֹם, הַרְבֵּה יוֹתֵר מִמַּה שֶּׁהֶחֱרִיב נְבוּכַדְנֶצַּר וְטִיטוּס.

כִּי הֲלֹא נְבוּכַדְנֶצַּר וְטִיטוּס לֹא עָשׂוּ בְּמַעֲשֵׂיהֶם, שׁוּם פְּגַם וְקִלְקוּל כְּלָל לְמַעְלָה, כִּי לֹא לָהֶם חֵלֶק וְשֹׁרֶשׁ בָּעוֹלָמוֹת הָעֶלְיוֹנִים, שֶׁיִּהְיוּ יְכוֹלִים לִנְגֹּעַ שָׁם כְּלָל בְּמַעֲשֵׂיהֶם. רַק שֶׁבַּחֲטָאֵינוּ נִתְמַעֵט וְתָשׁ כִּבְיָכוֹל כֹּחַ גְּבוּרָה שֶׁל מַעְלָה, אֶת מִקְדַּשׁ ה' טִמְּאוּ כִּבְיָכוֹל הַמִּקְדָּשׁ הָעֶלְיוֹן, וְעַל יְדֵי כָּךְ הָיָה לָהֶם כֹּחַ לִנְבוּכַדְנֶצַּר וְטִיטוּס לְהַחֲרִיב הַמִּקְדָּשׁ שֶׁל מַטָּה, הַמְּכֻוָּן נֶגֶד הַמִּקְדָּשׁ שֶׁל מַעְלָה, כְּמוֹ שֶׁאָמְרוּ רַבּוֹתֵינוּ זִכְרוֹנָם לִבְרָכָה (איכה רבתי א, מג) קִמְחָא טְחִינָא טְחִינַת. הֲרֵי כִּי עֲוֹנוֹתֵינוּ הֶחֱרִיבוּ "נְוֵה מַעְלָה" — עוֹלָמוֹת עֶלְיוֹנִים הַקְּדוֹשִׁים, וְהֵמָּה הֶחֱרִיבוּ רַק "נְוֵה מַטָּה".

וְזֶהוּ שֶׁהִתְפַּלֵּל דָּוִד הַמֶּלֶךְ עָלָיו הַשָּׁלוֹם (תהלים עד, ה) "יִוָּדַע כְּמֵבִיא לְמָעְלָה בִּסְבָךְ עֵץ קַרְדֻּמּוֹת", בִּקֵּשׁ שֶׁיֵּחָשֵׁב לוֹ כְּאִלּוּ לְמַעְלָה בִּשְׁמֵי מְרוֹמִים הָרַס, אֲבָל בֶּאֱמֶת לֹא נָגְעוּ שָׁם מַעֲשָׂיו כְּלָל כנ"ל:

גַּם עַל זֹאת יֶחֱרַד לֵב הָאָדָם מֵעַם הַקֹּדֶשׁ, שֶׁהוּא כּוֹלֵל בְּתַבְנִיתוֹ כָּל הַכֹּחוֹת וְהָעוֹלָמוֹת כֻּלָּם, כְּמוֹ שֶׁיִּתְבָּאֵר אי"ה לְהַלָּן בְּפֶרֶק ו' וּבְשַׁעַר ב' פֶּרֶק ה', שֶׁהֵן הֵמָּה הַקֹּדֶשׁ וְהַמִּקְדָּשׁ הָעֶלְיוֹן, וְהַלֵּב שֶׁל הָאָדָם, אֶמְצָעִיתָא דְּגוּפָא, הוּא כְּלָלִיּוּת הַכֹּל, נֶגֶד הַבֵּית קָדְשֵׁי קָדָשִׁים, אֶמְצַע הַיִּשּׁוּב, אֶבֶן שְׁתִיָּה, כּוֹלֵל כָּל שָׁרְשֵׁי מְקוֹר הַקְּדֻשּׁוֹת כָּמוֹהוּ, וּרְמָזוּהוּ זִכְרוֹנָם לִבְרָכָה בַּמִּשְׁנָה פֶּרֶק תְּפִלַּת הַשַּׁחַר (ברכות כ, א) יְכַוֵּן אֶת לִבּוֹ כְּנֶגֶד בֵּית קָדְשֵׁי הַקֳּדָשִׁים.

וּבַזֹּהַר שְׁלַח (קס"א סוף ע"א) תָּא חֲזֵי, כַּד בְּרָא קוּדְשָׁא בְּרִיךְ הוּא בַּר נָשׁ בְּעָלְמָא, אַתְקִין לֵיהּ כְּגַוְנָא עִלָּאָה יַקִּירָא, וִיהַב לֵיהּ חֵילֵיהּ וְתוּקְפֵיהּ בְּאֶמְצָעִיתָא דְּגוּפָא דְּתַמָּן שַׁרְיָא לִבָּא כו', כְּגַוְנָא דָּא אַתְקִין קוּדְשָׁא בְּרִיךְ הוּא עָלְמָא, וְעָבִיד לֵיהּ חַד גּוּפָא, כו' וְלִבָּא שַׁרְיָא בְּאֶמְצָעוּתָא וכו' דְּהוּא תּוּקְפָּא דְּכֹלָּא, וְכֹלָּא בֵּיהּ תַּלְיָין כו', וְהַהֵיכָל לְבֵית קָדְשֵׁי הַקֳּדָשִׁים דְּתַמָּן שְׁכִינָה וְכַפֹּרֶת וּכְרוּבִים וְאָרוֹן, וְהָכָא הוּא לִבָּא דְּכָל אַרְעָא וְעָלְמָא, וּמֵהָכָא אִתְזָנוּ כו'. [בּוֹא וּרְאֵה, כַּאֲשֶׁר בָּרָא הַקָּדוֹשׁ בָּרוּךְ הוּא אָדָם בָּעוֹלָם, תִּקֵּן אוֹתוֹ כְּדוּגְמָה עֶלְיוֹנָה נִכְבָּדָה וְנָתַן לוֹ כֹּחוֹ וְתָקְפּוֹ בְּאֶמְצַע גּוּפוֹ שֶׁשָּׁם שׁוֹרֶה הַלֵּב,

וּבְאֹפֶן זֶה הִתְקִין הַקָּדוֹשׁ בָּרוּךְ הוּא אֶת הָעוֹלָם וַעֲשָׂהוּ גּוּף אֶחָד וכו' וְהַלֵּב שׁוֹרֶה בָּאֶמְצַע שֶׁהוּא תָּקְפּוֹ שֶׁל כֻּלָּם וְהַכֹּל תָּלוּי בּוֹ וכו', וְהַהֵיכָל [מַקִּיף] לְבֵית קֹדֶשׁ הַקֳּדָשִׁים שֶׁשָּׁם שְׁכִינָה וְכַפֹּרֶת וּכְרוּבִים וְאָרוֹן, וְכָאן הוּא הַלֵּב שֶׁל כָּל הָאָרֶץ וְהָעוֹלָם. וּמִכָּאן נִזּוֹנִים וכו'] עַיֵּן שָׁם בְּאֹרֶךְ.

אִם כֵּן, בְּעֵת אֲשֶׁר יָתוּר הָאָדָם לַחְשׁוֹב בִּלְבָבוֹ, מַחְשָׁבָה אֲשֶׁר לֹא טְהוֹרָה בְּנִאוּף ר"ל. הֲרֵי הוּא מַכְנִיס זוֹנָה, סֵמֶל הַקִּנְאָה, בְּבֵית קָדְשֵׁי הַקֳּדָשִׁים הָעֶלְיוֹן נוֹרָא בָּעוֹלָמוֹת הָעֶלְיוֹנִים הַקְּדוֹשִׁים חַס וְשָׁלוֹם, וּמַגְבִּיר רַחֲמָנָא לִצְלָן כֹּחוֹת הַטֻּמְאָה וְהַסִּטְרָא אַחֲרָא בְּבֵית קָדְשֵׁי הַקֳּדָשִׁים הָעֶלְיוֹן, הַרְבֵּה יוֹתֵר וְיוֹתֵר מִמַּה שֶּׁנִּגְרַם הִתְגַּבְּרוּת כֹּחַ הַטֻּמְאָה, עַל יְדֵי טִיטוּס בְּהַצִּיעוֹ זוֹנָה בְּבֵית קָדְשֵׁי הַקֳּדָשִׁים בְּמִקְדַּשׁ מַטָּה.

וְכֵן כָּל חֵטְא אֲשֶׁר כָּל אִישׁ יִשְׂרָאֵל מַכְנִיס בְּלִבּוֹ חַס וְשָׁלוֹם אֵשׁ זָרָה, בְּכַעַס אוֹ שְׁאָרֵי תַּאֲווֹת רָעוֹת ר"ל, הֲלֹא הוּא מַמָּשׁ כְּעִנְיַן הַכָּתוּב (ישעיה סד, י) "בֵּית קָדְשֵׁנוּ וְתִפְאַרְתֵּנוּ אֲשֶׁר וגו' הָיָה לִשְׂרֵפַת אֵשׁ", הָרַחֲמָן יִתְבָּרֵךְ שְׁמוֹ יַצִּילֵנוּ.

וְזֶה שֶׁאָמַר הַשֵּׁם לִיחֶזְקֵאל (מג ז) "אֶת מְקוֹם כִּסְאִי גו' אֲשֶׁר אֶשְׁכָּן שָׁם בְּתוֹךְ בְּנֵי יִשְׂרָאֵל לְעוֹלָם וְלֹא יְטַמְּאוּ עוֹד בֵּית יִשְׂרָאֵל שֵׁם קָדְשִׁי גו' בִּזְנוּתָם גו' עַתָּה יְרַחֲקוּ אֶת זְנוּתָם גו' וְשָׁכַנְתִּי בְתוֹכָם לְעוֹלָם":

וּבָזֶה יוּבַן הַכָּתוּב (בראשית ב, ז) "וַיִּיצֶר ה' אֱלֹקִים אֶת הָאָדָם עָפָר גו' וַיִּפַּח בְּאַפָּיו נִשְׁמַת חַיִּים, וַיְהִי הָאָדָם לְנֶפֶשׁ חַיָּה". וּפְשׁוּטוֹ שֶׁל מִקְרָא וַדַּאי הוּא כְּתַרְגּוּמוֹ — "וַהֲוַת בְּאָדָם לְרוּחַ מְמַלְּלָא", וְרָצָה לוֹמַר שֶׁכַּאֲשֶׁר הָיָה הַגּוּף לְבַדּוֹ, הָיָה עֲדַיִן עָפָר מַמָּשׁ בְּלֹא שׁוּם חִיּוּת וּתְנוּעָה, וְכַאֲשֶׁר נָפַח בּוֹ נִשְׁמַת חַיִּים, אָז נַעֲשָׂה אִישׁ חַי לְהִתְנוֹעֵעַ וּלְדַבֵּר. וְעַיֵּן רַמְבַּ"ן בְּפֵרוּשׁ הַתּוֹרָה.

אָמְנָם בַּקְּרָא "וַיְהִי בְּאָדָם" לֹא כְּתִיב, אֶלָּא "וַיְהִי הָאָדָם", לָזֹאת יֵשׁ מָקוֹם לְפָרְשׁוֹ עַל פִּי שֶׁנִּתְבָּאֵר, שֶׁהָאָדָם בְּנִשְׁמַת הַחַיִּים שֶׁבְּתוֹכוֹ, הוּא נַעֲשָׂה "נֶפֶשׁ חַיָּה" לְרִבּוּי עוֹלָמוֹת אֵין מִסְפָּר, שֶׁכְּמוֹ שֶׁכָּל פְּרָטֵי הַנְהָגוֹת הַגּוּף וּתְנוּעוֹתָיו, הוּא עַל יְדֵי כֹּחַ הַנֶּפֶשׁ שֶׁבְּקִרְבּוֹ, כֵּן הָאָדָם הוּא הַכֹּחַ וְנֶפֶשׁ הַחַיָּה שֶׁל עוֹלָמוֹת עֶלְיוֹנִים וְתַחְתּוֹנִים לְאֵין שִׁעוּר, שֶׁכֻּלָּם מִתְנַהֲגִים עַל יָדוֹ כַּנַּ"ל.

פֶּרֶק ה'

וּמַה שֶּׁעָלְתָה בִּרְצוֹנוֹ יִתְבָּרֵךְ שְׁמוֹ, לְהַרְכִּיב אֶת הָאָדָם הַתַּחְתּוֹן — לְרָאשֵׁי הָעוֹלָמוֹת עֶלְיוֹנִים, שֶׁיִּתְנַהֲגוּ עַל יָדוֹ:

כִּי יָדוּעַ בַּזֹּהַר וְכִתְבֵי הָאֲרִיזַ"ל בְּסֵדֶר הִשְׁתַּלְשְׁלוּת וְהִתְקַשְּׁרוּת הָעוֹלָמוֹת, שֶׁכָּל עוֹלָם הוּא מִתְנַהֵג, בְּסִדּוּר מַצָּבוֹ וְכָל פְּרָטֵי עִנְיָנָיו, כְּפִי נְטִיַּת כֹּחַ הָעוֹלָם שֶׁעָלָיו, שֶׁמַּנְהִיגוֹ כִּנְשָׁמָה אֶת הַגּוּף, וְכֵן הוֹלֵךְ עַל זֶה הַסֵּדֶר גָּבוֹהַּ מֵעַל גָּבוֹהַּ, עַד הוּא יִתְבָּרֵךְ שְׁמוֹ נִשְׁמַת כֻּלָּם.

עַיֵּן זֹהַר (בראשית כ' ע"א) וְכָל עָלְמָא כו' עֵילָּא וְתַתָּא מֵרֵישׁ רָזָא דִּנְקוּדָה עִלָּאָה עַד

סוֹפָא דְּכָל דַּרְגִּין, כֻּלָּא אִיהוּ, דָּא לְבוּשָׁא לְדָא וְדָא לְדָא כו' דָּא לְגוֹ מִן דָּא וְדָא לְגוֹ מִן דָּא כו', [וְכָל עוֹלָם וכו' עֶלְיוֹן וְתַחְתּוֹן, מֵרֵאשִׁית סוֹד נְקֻדָּה הָעֶלְיוֹנָה עַד סוֹף שֶׁל כָּל הַדְּרָגוֹת כֻּלָּם הֵם זֶה לְבוּשׁ לָזֶה וְזֶה לָזֶה וכו' זֶה בְּתוֹךְ זֶה וְזֶה בְּתוֹךְ זֶה.]

וּבְאִדְּרָא (זוּטָא רצ"א ב') וְכֻלְּהוּ נְהוֹרִין אֲחִידָן, נְהוֹרָא דָּא בִּנְהוֹרָא דָּא וּנְהוֹרָא דָּא בִּנְהוֹרָא דָּא, וְנַהֲרִין דָּא בְּדָא כו', נְהוֹרָא דְּאִתְגַּלְיָא אִקְרֵי לְבוּשָׁא דְּמַלְכָּא, נְהוֹרָא דִּלְגוֹ לְגוֹ כו', [וְכָל הָאוֹרוֹת אֲחוּזִים אוֹר זֶה בְּאוֹר זֶה וְאוֹר זֶה בְּאוֹר זֶה, וּמְאִירִים זֶה בָּזֶה וכו', הָאוֹר הַמִּתְגַּלֶּה נִקְרָא לְבוּשׁ הַמֶּלֶךְ, וְהָאוֹר הַפְּנִימִי שֶׁבִּפְנִים וכו'] עַיֵּן שָׁם.

וּפְרָטוּת הָעִנְיָן מְבֹאָר בְּעֵץ חַיִּים שַׁעַר פְּנִימִיּוּת וְחִיצוֹנִיּוּת דְּרוּשׁ ב', וּבִפְרִי עֵץ חַיִּים בְּהַקְדָּמַת שַׁעַר הַשַּׁבָּת פֶּרֶק ז' וּפֶרֶק ח', וּבְשַׁעַר הַשַּׁבָּת פֶּרֶק כ"ה, שֶׁחִיצוֹנִיּוּת שֶׁל כָּל פַּרְצוּף וְעוֹלָם, מִתְפַּשֵּׁט וּמִתְלַבֵּשׁ בְּהַפַּרְצוּף וְהָעוֹלָם שֶׁתַּחְתָּיו, וְנַעֲשָׂה לוֹ לִפְנִימִיּוּת וּנְשָׁמָה.

וְכָל הָעוֹלָמוֹת נִכְלָלִים וְנֶחְלָקִים לד' כַּיָּדוּעַ, שֶׁהֵן: הָאוֹפַנִּים, וְהַחַיּוֹת, וְכִסֵּא כְּבוֹדוֹ, וַאֲצִילוּת קָדְשׁוֹ יִתְבָּרַךְ.

וְנִשְׁמַת כָּל אֶחָד הוּא הָעוֹלָם שֶׁעָלָיו, כְּמוֹ שֶׁנֶּאֱמַר (יחזקאל א, יט) "וּבְהִנָּשֵׂא הַחַיּוֹת גו' יִנָּשְׂאוּ הָאוֹפַנִּים לְעֻמָּתָם כִּי רוּחַ הַחַיָּה בָּאוֹפַנִּים, בְּלֶכְתָּם יֵלֵכוּ וּבְעָמְדָם יַעֲמֹדוּ" וגו', וְהַחַיּוֹת גַּם כֵּן מִתְנַהֲגִים עַל יְדֵי עוֹלַם הַכִּסֵּא שֶׁעֲלֵיהֶם, כְּמוֹ שֶׁאָמְרוּ רַבּוֹתֵינוּ זִכְרוֹנָם לִבְרָכָה, שֶׁהַכִּסֵּא נוֹשֵׂא אֶת נוֹשְׂאָיו. וּבְזֹהַר חָדָשׁ יִתְרוֹ (בְּמַעֲשֵׂה מֶרְכָּבָה ל"ג א') דְּחַיוֹת נָטְלִין לְדִנָטְלִין לוֹן כו' כָּרְסַיָּא קַדִּישָׁא נָטִיל לְחַיוֹת. [הַחַיּוֹת נוֹשְׂאוֹת אֶת הַנּוֹשְׂאִין אוֹתָם וכו' הַכִּסֵּא הַקָּדוֹשׁ נוֹשֵׂא אֶת הַחַיּוֹת.]

וְנִשְׁמַת הַחַיִּים שֶׁל הַכִּסֵּא, הוּא סוֹד שֹׁרֶשׁ הָעֶלְיוֹן שֶׁל כְּלָלוּת נִשְׁמוֹת יִשְׂרָאֵל יַחַד, שֶׁהוּא יוֹתֵר גָּבוֹהַּ וּמְאֹד נַעֲלֶה גַּם מֵהַכִּסֵּא, שֶׁהוּא הָאָדָם שֶׁעַל הַכִּסֵּא, כְּמוֹ שֶׁנֶּאֱמַר שָׁם "וְעַל דְּמוּת הַכִּסֵּא" וגו'.

וְזֶהוּ שֶׁאָמְרוּ בַּזֹּהַר יִתְרוֹ ע' ע"ב בְּעִנְיַן הַפָּסוּק "אָחוֹר וָקֶדֶם צַרְתָּנִי" (תהלים קלט, ה), "אָחוֹר" – לְעוֹבְדָא דִבְרֵאשִׁית, "וְקֶדֶם" – לְעוֹבְדָא דְמֶרְכָּבָה. שֶׁמִּצַּד הַגּוּף – הוּא "אָחוֹר" לְמַעֲשֵׂי בְּרֵאשִׁית, וּמִצַּד שֹׁרֶשׁ הָעֶלְיוֹן שֶׁל הַנִּשְׁמַת חַיִּים שֶׁלּוֹ – הוּא "קֶדֶם" לְעוֹבְדָא דְמֶרְכָּבָה, גַּם מֵעוֹלַם הַכִּסֵּא. וְגַם כִּי הַנִּשְׁמַת חַיִּים הִיא סוֹד נְשִׁימַת פִּיו יִתְבָּרַךְ שְׁמוֹ כִּבְיָכוֹל, כְּמוֹ שֶׁיִּתְבָּאֵר אי"ה לְהַלָּן פֶּרֶק ט"ו עַיֵּן שָׁם.

לָכֵן הָעוֹלָמוֹת מִתְנַהֲגִים עַל יְדֵי מַעֲשֵׂי הָאָדָם, כִּי הֵמָּה כְּפִי נְטִיָּתָם מְעוֹרְרִים שֹׁרֶשׁ נִשְׁמָתוֹ הָעֶלְיוֹנָה שֶׁמֵּעֲלֵיהֶם, שֶׁהִיא הַ'נֶּפֶשׁ חַיָּה' שֶׁלָּהֶם, בְּהִתְנוֹעֲעוֹ יָנוּעוּ וּבְעָמְדוֹ תִּרְפֶּינָה.

זֶהוּ שֶׁאָמַר, כַּאֲשֶׁר נָפַח בְּאַפָּיו הַנִּשְׁמַת חַיִּים, שֶׁהִיא גָּבוֹהַּ מֵהָעוֹלָמוֹת וּפְנִימִיּוּתָם, אָז "וַיְהִי הָאָדָם לְנֶפֶשׁ חַיָּה" – לְהָעוֹלָמוֹת. וְכֵן כָּתַב רַבֵּנוּ חַיִּים וִיטַל זִכְרוֹנוֹ לִבְרָכָה בְּשַׁעַר הַקְּדֻשָּׁה חֵלֶק ג' שַׁעַר ב'. שֶׁנִּשְׁמַת הָאָדָם הִיא הַפְּנִימִי שֶׁבְּכֻלָּם:

פֶּרֶק ו'

אָמְנָם עֲדַיִן הָעִנְיָן צָרִיךְ בֵּאוּר, (כִּי הוּא זִכְרוֹנוֹ לִבְרָכָה דִּבֵּר בְּקָדְשׁוֹ דֶּרֶךְ קְצָרָה כְּדַרְכּוֹ בְּכָל כִּתְבֵי קָדְשׁוֹ בְּנִסְתָּרוֹת, כְּמוֹ שֶׁכָּתַב בְּעַצְמוֹ בְּהַקְדָּמָתוֹ שָׁם, שֶׁהוּא מְגַלֶּה טֶפַח וּמְכַסֶּה אַלְפַּיִם אַמָּה), שֶׁלֹּא כְּדַמַשְׁמַע לִכְאוֹרָה מִדְּבָרָיו זִכְרוֹנוֹ לִבְרָכָה שָׁם, שֶׁהָאָדָם אֶל הָעוֹלָמוֹת הוּא נֶפֶשׁ מַמָּשׁ, כְּמוֹ הַנֶּפֶשׁ הַנִּתָּן וְדָבוּק בְּתוֹךְ גּוּף הָאָדָם, אֲשֶׁר אֵיזֶה דָּבָר שֶׁהַנֶּפֶשׁ עוֹשָׂה, הוּא רַק עַל יְדֵי כְּלֵי הַגּוּף, שֶׁבְּבוֹאוֹ רֶגַע מַמָּשׁ גַּם הַגּוּף עוֹשֵׂהוּ, דְּזֶה וַדַּאי לֹא יִתָּכֵן:

אֲבָל עִקָּרוֹ שֶׁל דָּבָר, כִּי הוּא יִתְבָּרַךְ שְׁמוֹ, אַחַר שֶׁבָּרָא כָּל הָעוֹלָמוֹת, בָּרָא אֶת הָאָדָם אָחוֹר לְמַעֲשֵׂי בְּרֵאשִׁית, בְּרִיאָה נִפְלָאָה, כֹּחַ מְאַסֵּף לְכָל הַמַּחֲנוֹת, שֶׁכָּלַל בּוֹ כָּל צַחְצָחוֹת אוֹרוֹת הַנִּפְלָאוֹת וְהָעוֹלָמוֹת וְהֵיכָלִין הָעֶלְיוֹנִים שֶׁקָּדְמוּ לוֹ, וְכָל תַּבְנִית הַכָּבוֹד הָעֶלְיוֹן בְּסֵדֶר פִּרְקֵי הַמֶּרְכָּבָה, וְכָל הַכֹּחוֹת פְּרָטִים הַנִּמְצָאִים בְּכָל הָעוֹלָמוֹת עֶלְיוֹנִים וְתַחְתּוֹנִים, כֻּלָּם נָתְנוּ כֹּחַ וְחֵלֶק מֵעַצְמוּתָם בְּבִנְיָנוֹ, וְנִכְלְלוּ בּוֹ בְּמִסְפַּר פְּרָטֵי כֹּחוֹתָיו שֶׁבּוֹ.

כְּמוֹ שֶׁאָמְרוּ בְּזֹהַר יִתְרוֹ ע"ה ב': קוּדְשָׁא בְּרִיךְ הוּא כַּד בְּרָא לֵיהּ לְבַר נָשׁ סַדַּר בֵּיהּ כָּל דְּיוּקְנִין דְּרָזִין עִלָּאִין דְּעָלְמָא דִּלְעֵלָּא, וְכָל דְּיוּקְנִין דְּרָזִין תַּתָּאִין דְּעָלְמָא דִּלְתַתָּא, וְכֻלָּא מִתְחַקְקָא בְּבַר נָשׁ דְּאִיהוּ קָאִים בְּצֶלֶם אֱלֹקִים כו', דִּכְתִיב "וַיִּבְרָא אֱלֹהִים אֶת הָאָדָם בְּצַלְמוֹ", [הַקָּדוֹשׁ בָּרוּךְ הוּא כְּשֶׁבָּרָא אֶת הָאָדָם, סִדֵּר בּוֹ כָּל הַצּוּרוֹת שֶׁל סוֹדוֹת עֶלְיוֹנִים שֶׁל הָעוֹלָם הָעֶלְיוֹן וְכָל הַצּוּרוֹת שֶׁל הַסּוֹדוֹת הַתַּחְתּוֹנִים שֶׁל עוֹלָם הַתַּחְתּוֹן, וְכֻלָּם חֲקוּקִים בָּאָדָם שֶׁהוּא עוֹמֵד בְּצֶלֶם אֱלֹקִים וכו'] עַיֵּן שָׁם.

וּבְפָרָשַׁת תַּזְרִיעַ מ"ח א' תָּאנָא כֵּיוָן דְּנִבְרָא אָדָם כו', וּבְרֵישׁ פָּרָשַׁת בַּמִּדְבָּר רַבִּי אַבָּא פָּתַח וַיִּבְרָא אֱלֹקִים אֶת הָאָדָם בְּצַלְמוֹ" וגו' תָּא חֲזִי כו', וּבְאִדְּרָא רַבָּא קל"ה א' "כְּמַרְאֵה אָדָם" כו'. וְשָׁם בְּדַף קמ"א סוֹף ע"א דְּיוּקְנָא דְּכָלִיל כָּל דְּיוּקְנִין כו'. וּבְרַעְיָא מְהֵימְנָא פָּרָשַׁת פִּנְחָס רל"ח ב' "וַיֹּאמֶר אֱלֹקִים נַעֲשֶׂה אָדָם" כו' עַד וְהַיְנוּ "נַעֲשֶׂה אָדָם בְּצַלְמֵנוּ" כו'. וְכֵן אָמְרוּ זֶה הַלָּשׁוֹן יוֹתֵר בְּאֹרֶךְ בְּתִקּוּנֵי זֹהַר חָדָשׁ פ"ט ע"א עַיֵּן שָׁם, וּבְזֹהַר חָדָשׁ יִתְרוֹ בְּמַעֲשֵׂה מֶרְכָּבָה ל"ב ע"ג דְּיוּקְנָא דְּאָדָם דְּדָא אִיהוּ דְּיוּקְנָא דְּכָלִיל כָּל דְּיוּקְנִין כו', [דְּיוּקְנוֹ שֶׁל אָדָם זֶהוּ דְּיוּקָן שֶׁכּוֹלֵל כֹּל הַדְּיוּקָנִים] וְשָׁם דַּף ל"ג רֵישׁ ע"א, וְשָׁם בְּשִׁיר הַשִּׁירִים נ"ח ב' "וַיֹּאמֶר אֱלֹקִים נַעֲשֶׂה אָדָם בְּצַלְמֵנוּ" כו', עַיֵּן שָׁם הֵיטֵב בְּכָל הַמְּקוֹמוֹת הַנִּזְכָּרִים. וְעַיֵּן בְּעֵץ חַיִּים שַׁעַר הַצֶּלֶם פ"א, וּבְלִקּוּטֵי תּוֹרָה פָּרָשַׁת תִּשָּׂא וּפָרָשַׁת הַאֲזִינוּ.

וְזֶה כָּל הָאָדָם, שֶׁכָּל כֹּחַ פְּרָטִי שֶׁבּוֹ, מְסֻדָּר נֶגֶד עוֹלָם וְכֹחַ אֶחָד פְּרָטִי, מִסּוֹד הַ'שִּׁעוּר קוֹמָה' שֶׁל כְּלַל הַכֹּחוֹת וְהָעוֹלָמוֹת, שֶׁמְּסֻדָּרִים כִּבְיָכוֹל כְּתַבְנִית קוֹמַת אָדָם, כְּמוֹ שֶׁיִּתְבָּאֵר אי"ה בְּשַׁעַר ב' פֶּרֶק ה':

וְכֵן הַמִּצְוֹת, כֻּלָּן קְשׁוּרִין וּתְלוּיִין, בִּמְקוֹר שָׁרְשָׁן הָעֶלְיוֹן, בְּסִדְרֵי פִּרְקֵי הַמֶּרְכָּבָה וְשִׁעוּר קוֹמָה שֶׁל הָעוֹלָמוֹת כֻּלָּם, שֶׁכָּל מִצְוָה פְּרָטִית בְּשָׁרְשָׁהּ כּוֹלֶלֶת רִבֵּי רִבְבָן כֹּחוֹת וְאוֹרוֹת מִסִּדְרֵי הַשִּׁעוּר קוֹמָה.

כְּמוֹ שֶׁאָמַר בַּזֹּהַר יִתְרוֹ (פ"ה ב'): כָּל פִּקּוּדֵי אוֹרַיְתָא מִתְאַחֲדָן בְּמַלְכָּא קַדִּישָׁא עִלָּאָה,

מִנְּהוֹן בְּרֵישָׁא דְמַלְכָּא, וּמִנְּהוֹן בְּגוּפָא, וּמִנְּהוֹן בִּידֵי מַלְכָּא, וּמִנְּהוֹן בְּרַגְלוֹי כו', [כָּל מִצְוֹות הַתּוֹרָה מִתְאַחֲדִים בַּמֶּלֶךְ הַקָּדוֹשׁ הָעֶלְיוֹן, מֵהֶם בְּרֹאשׁ הַמֶּלֶךְ וּמֵהֶם בַּגּוּף וּמֵהֶם בִּידֵי הַמֶּלֶךְ, וּמֵהֶם בְּרַגְלָיו]. וְהָעִנְיָן יוֹתֵר מְבֹאָר בַּתִּקּוּנִים ת"ע קכ"ט ב' ק"ל א' עַיֵּן שָׁם.

וּבְזֹהַר תְּרוּמָה קס"ה ב' פִּקּוּדֵי אוֹרַיְתָא כֻּלְּהוּ שַׁיְפִין וְאֵבָרִין בְּרָזָא דִּלְעֵלָּא. וְכַד מִתְחַבְּרָן כֻּלְּהוּ כְּחַד, כְּדֵין כֻּלְּהוּ סַלְקִין לְרָזָא חַד. [מִצְווֹת הַתּוֹרָה כֻּלָּן אֵבָרִים בְּסוֹד הָעֶלְיוֹן, וְכַאֲשֶׁר מִתְחַבְּרִים כֻּלָּם כְּאֶחָד, אָז כֻּלָּם עוֹלִים לְסוֹד אֶחָד.]

וְשָׁם בְּדַף קס"ה ב' בְּהַאי שְׁמָא כְּלִילָן תַּרְיַ"ג פִּקּוּדֵי אוֹרַיְתָא, דְּאִנּוּן כְּלָלָא דְּכָל רָזִין עִלָּאִין וְתַתָּאִין כו', וְכֻלְּהוּ פִּקּוּדִין כֻּלְּהוּ שַׁיְפִין וְאֵבָרִין לְאִתְחֲזָאָה בְּהוּ רָזָא דִמְהֵימְנוּתָא, מָאן דְּלָא יַשְׁגַּח וְלָא אִסְתַּכַּל בְּרָזִין דְּפִקּוּדֵי אוֹרַיְתָא, לָא יָדַע וְלָא אִסְתַּכַּל הֵיךְ מִתְתַּקְּנָן שַׁיְפִין בְּרָזָא עִלָּאָה, שַׁיְפִין דְּגוּפָא כֻּלְּהוּ מִתְתַּקְּנָן עַל רָזָא דְּפִקּוּדֵי אוֹרַיְתָא, [בַּשֵּׁם הַזֶּה כְּלוּלִים תַּרְיַ"ג מִצְוֹות הַתּוֹרָה, שֶׁהֵם כְּלָלִים שֶׁל כָּל הַסּוֹדוֹת הָעֶלְיוֹנִים וְהַתַּחְתּוֹנִים, וְכֻלָּן חֲלָקִים וְאֵבָרִים לְהֵרָאוֹת בָּהֶם סוֹד הָאֱמוּנָה, מִי שֶׁלֹּא מַשְׁגִּיחַ וְלֹא מִסְתַּכֵּל בְּסוֹדוֹת שֶׁל מִצְווֹת הַתּוֹרָה, אֵינוֹ יוֹדֵעַ וְאֵינוֹ מִסְתַּכֵּל אֵיךְ מִתְתַּקְּנִים הָאֵבָרִים בְּסוֹד הָעֶלְיוֹן, אֵיבָרִים שֶׁל הַגּוּף כֻּלָּם מִתְתַּקְּנִים עַל סוֹד מִצְווֹת הַתּוֹרָה]. עַיֵּן שָׁם. וְכֵן כָּתַב הָאֲרִיזַ"ל בְּשַׁעַר הַיִּחוּדִים פֶּרֶק ב'.

וּבַעֲשׂוֹת הָאָדָם רְצוֹן קוֹנוֹ יִתְבָּרֵךְ שְׁמוֹ, וּמְקַיֵּם בְּאֵיזֶה אֵבֶר וְכֹחַ שֶׁבּוֹ, אַחַת מִמִּצְוֹת ה', הַתִּקּוּן נוֹגֵעַ לְאוֹתוֹ עוֹלָם וְכֹחַ הָעֶלְיוֹן הַמַּקְבִּילוֹ, לְתַקְּנוֹ, אוֹ לְהַעֲלוֹתוֹ, אוֹ לְהוֹסִיף אוֹר וּקְדֻשָּׁה עַל קְדֻשָּׁתוֹ, מֵחֵפֶץ וּרְצוֹן הָעֶלְיוֹן יִתְבָּרֵךְ שְׁמוֹ, כְּפִי עֵרֶךְ וְאֹפֶן עֲשִׂיָּתוֹ, וּלְפִי רֹב הַהִזְדַּכְּכוּת וְטָהֳרַת קְדֻשַּׁת מַחְשַׁבְתּוֹ בְּעֵת עֲשִׂיַּת הַמִּצְוָה, הַמִּצְטָרֶפֶת לְטוֹבָה לְמַעֲשֶׂה הָעִקָּרִית, וּכְפִי עֵרֶךְ מַדְרֵגַת אוֹתוֹ הָעוֹלָם וְהַכֹּחַ עֶלְיוֹן. וּמִשָּׁם נִמְשָׁךְ הַקְּדֻשָּׁה וְחִיּוּת גַּם עַל אוֹתוֹ הַכֹּחַ שֶׁל הָאָדָם שֶׁבּוֹ קִיֵּם מִצְוַת בּוֹרְאוֹ הַמְּכֻוֶּנֶת נֶגְדּוֹ.

וְכַאֲשֶׁר קִיֵּם כָּל הַמִּצְוֹת בִּשְׁלֵמוּת, בְּכָל פְּרָטֵיהֶם וְדִקְדּוּקֵיהֶם בְּעִקַּר הַמַּעֲשֶׂה, וְנוֹסָף עֲלֵיהֶם הִצְטָרֵף עֶצֶם טָהֳרַת וּקְדֻשַּׁת הַמַּחֲשָׁבָה, הֲרֵי תִּקֵּן כָּל הָעוֹלָמוֹת וְהַסְּדָרִים הָעֶלְיוֹנִים, וְנַעֲשָׂה כֻּלּוֹ בְּכֹל כֹּחוֹתָיו וְאֵבָרָיו מֶרְכָּבָה לָהֶם, וּמִתְקַדְּשִׁים מִקְּדֻשָּׁתָם הָעֶלְיוֹנָה, וּכְבוֹד ה' חוֹפֵף עָלָיו תָּמִיד.

וְעַיֵּן זֹהַר תְּרוּמָה קנ"ה א: "כֹּל הַנִּקְרָא בִשְׁמִי וְלִכְבוֹדִי בְּרָאתִיו" כו' (ישעיה מג, ז), וְלִכְבוֹדִי בְּרָאתִיו דַּיְקָא, וְרָזָא דָא כו' אוֹלִיפְנָא דְּהַאי כָּבוֹד כו', כְּלָא אִתְקַן לְעֵלָּא מִגּוֹ תִּקּוּנָא דִּבְנֵי עָלְמָא, כַּד אִנּוּן בְּנֵי נָשָׁא זַכָּאִין וַחֲסִידִין, וְיָדְעִין לְתַקְּנָא תִּקּוּנֵי [וְלִכְבוֹדִי בְּרָאתִיו הוּא בְּדַוְקָא, וְסוֹד זֶה וכו' לָמַדְנוּ כִּי זֶה הַכָּבוֹד וכו' כֻּלּוֹ נִתְקַן לְמַעְלָה מִתּוֹךְ הַתִּקּוּנִים שֶׁל בְּנֵי הָעוֹלָם, כַּאֲשֶׁר בְּנֵי הָאָדָם הֵם צַדִּיקִים וַחֲסִידִים, וְיוֹדְעִים לְתַקֵּן תִּקּוּנִים]. כו' עַיֵּן שָׁם בְּאֹרֶךְ. וְעַיֵּן הֵיטֵב בְּרַעְיָא מְהֵימְנָא פָּרָשַׁת פִּנְחָס רל"ט א'.

וְזֶהוּ שֶׁאָמְרוּ רַבּוֹתֵינוּ זִכְרוֹנָם לִבְרָכָה (ב"ר מ"ז), הָאָבוֹת הֵן הֵן הַמֶּרְכָּבָה. וְכֵן לְהֵפֶךְ חַס וְשָׁלוֹם, בִּפְגַם אֶחָד מִכֹּחוֹתָיו וְאֵבָרָיו, עַל יְדֵי חֶטְאתוֹ אֲשֶׁר חָטָא, גַּם כֵּן הַפְּגָם מַגִּיעַ לְפִי שָׁרְשׁוֹ, לְאוֹתוֹ הָעוֹלָם וְהַכֹּחַ הָעֶלְיוֹן הַמְּכֻוָּן נֶגְדּוֹ בְּסִדְרֵי הַשִּׁעוּר קוֹמָה כִּבְיָכוֹל, לְהָרְסוֹ

וּלְהַחֲרִיבוֹ חַס וְשָׁלוֹם, אוֹ לְהוֹרִידוֹ, אוֹ לְפָגְמוֹ, אוֹ לְהַחְשִׁיךְ וּלְהַקְטִין צַחְצוּחַ אוֹרוֹ, וּלְהַתִּישׁ וּלְהַחֲלִישׁ וּלְמַעֵט כֹּחַ טָהֳרַת קְדֻשָּׁתוֹ חַס וְשָׁלוֹם, הַכֹּל כְּפִי עֵרֶךְ הַחֵטְא וְאָפְנֵי עֲשִׂיָּתוֹ, וּכְפִי עֵרֶךְ וְעִנְיַן אוֹתוֹ הָעוֹלָם וְגֹבַהּ מַדְרֵגָתוֹ.

כִּי לֹא כָּל הָעוֹלָמוֹת שָׁוִו בְּשִׁעוּרָן בְּעִנְיַן הַפְּגָם וְהַקִּלְקוּל, שֶׁבְּתַחְתּוֹן — הוּא הֲרִיסָה וְחֻרְבָּן ר״ל, וּלְמַעְלָה — מְנִיעַת הָאוֹר, וּבָעֶלְיוֹן יוֹתֵר מִמֶּנּוּ — גּוֹרֵם רַק הִתְמַעֲטוּת שִׁפְעַת אוֹרוֹ אוֹ הַקְטָנָתוֹ, וּבְיוֹתֵר גָּבוֹהַּ וְנַעֲלֶה — גּוֹרֵם רַק הִתְמַעֲטוּת בְּגֹדֶל צַחְצוּחַ אוֹרוֹ וְטָהֳרַת קְדֻשָּׁתוֹ הַנִּפְלָאָה, וְכָהֵנָּה רַבּוֹת בְּחִינוֹת שׁוֹנוֹת:

וְזֶהוּ הָעִנְיָן שֶׁקָּרְאוּ רַבּוֹתֵינוּ זִכְרוֹנָם לִבְרָכָה בְּכַמָּה מְקוֹמוֹת לִפְגַם הֶעָוֹן פְּגַם אִיקוֹנִין שֶׁל מֶלֶךְ. וּבַזֹּהַר יִתְרוֹ פ״ה ב׳ וּבְגִין כָּךְ מַאן דְּפָשַׁע בְּפִקּוּדֵי אוֹרַיְתָא כְּמַאן דְּפָשַׁע בְּגוּפָא דְּמַלְכָּא, כְּמָה דִּכְתִּיב (ישעיה סו, כד) "וְיָצְאוּ וְרָאוּ בְּפִגְרֵי הָאֲנָשִׁים הַפּוֹשְׁעִים בִּי", בִּי מַמָּשׁ, וַי לְחַיָּבַיָּא דְּעָבְרִין עַל פִּתְגָּמֵי אוֹרַיְתָא וְלָא יָדְעִין מַאי קָא עָבְדִין. [וּמִשּׁוּם כָּךְ מִי שֶׁפּוֹשֵׁעַ בְּמִצְווֹת הַתּוֹרָה כְּמוֹ שֶׁפָּשַׁע בְּגוּף הַמֶּלֶךְ כמש״כ וְיָצְאוּ וְרָאוּ בְּפִגְרֵי הַפּוֹשְׁעִים בִּי, בִּי מַמָּשׁ. אוֹי לַחַיָּבִים הָעוֹבְרִים עַל דִּבְרֵי תּוֹרָה וְלֹא יוֹדְעִים מַה הֵם עוֹשִׂים] וּבַתִּקּוּנִים ת״ע קכ״ט ב׳ וְכָל מַאן דְּפָשַׁע בְּפִקּוּדָא כְּאִלּוּ פָּשַׁע בִּדְיוֹקְנָא דְּמַלְכָּא, [וְכָל מִי שֶׁפָּשַׁע בְּמִצְוֹת כְּאִלּוּ פָּשַׁע בְּדִיּוֹקַן הַמֶּלֶךְ] כנ״ל שֶׁהַפְּגָם נִמְשָׁךְ וְנוֹגֵעַ בְּפִרְקֵי וְסִדְרֵי הַכֹּחוֹת וְהָעוֹלָמוֹת הַשִּׁעוּר קוֹמָה, מִצַּד שֶׁכֻּלָּם נִכְלְלוּ בוֹ וְנָתְנוּ חֵלֶק מֵעַצְמוּתָם בְּבִנְיָנוֹ וּבְרִיאָתוֹ:

פֶּרֶק ז׳

וְעַתָּה מְבֹאָר הָעִנְיָן הנ״ל בְּפֶרֶק ה׳, שֶׁהָאָדָם נִקְרָא הַנֶּפֶשׁ וְנִשְׁמַת הַחַיִּים שֶׁל רִבֵּי רִבְבָן עוֹלָמוֹת. לֹא נֶפֶשׁ כְּנֶפֶשׁ הַנָּתוּן וְדָבוּק מַמָּשׁ בְּתוֹךְ גּוּף הָאָדָם, דְּזֶה לֹא יִתָּכֵן.

אָמְנָם הַיְינוּ שֶׁכְּמוֹ שֶׁכָּל פְּרָטֵי תְּנוּעוֹת וּנְטִיַּת אֶבְרֵי הַגּוּף, הֵם עַל יְדֵי הַנִּשְׁמַת חַיִּים שֶׁבּוֹ, כְּפִי תְּנוּעוֹת חִיּוּתוֹ וּנְטִיָּתוֹ, כֵּן הָעִנְיָן שֶׁכָּל נְטִיַּת הַכֹּחוֹת וְהָעוֹלָמוֹת וְסִדְרֵי הַמֶּרְכָּבָה, תִּקּוּנָם וּבִנְיָנָם וַהֲרִיסוּתָם חַס וְשָׁלוֹם, הוּא רַק כְּפִי עִנְיַן הַהִתְעוֹרְרוּת מִמַּעֲשֵׂי הָאָדָם לְמַטָּה, וּמִטַּעַם שֶׁהוּא כָּלוּל וּמְשֻׁכְלָל בְּמִסְפַּר פְּרָטֵי כֹּחוֹתָיו וְסִדְרֵיהֶם עַל פִּי סִדְרֵי הַשְׁתַּלְשְׁלוּת וְהִתְקַשְּׁרוּת הַכֹּחוֹת וְהָעוֹלָמוֹת עֶלְיוֹנִים וְתַחְתּוֹנִים כֻּלָּם, וְהוּא מִצַּד שֹׁרֶשׁ נִשְׁמָתוֹ הָעֶלְיוֹנָה, שֶׁהִיא הַגְּבוֹהָ וְהַפְּנִימִית מֵהָעוֹלָמוֹת הַנִּבְרָאִים כֻּלָּם, כַּנִּזְכָּר לְעֵיל בְּפֶרֶק ה׳, לָכֵן הוּא כּוֹלֵל אֶת כֻּלָּם.

וְהַטַּעַם שֶׁנִּתְבָּאֵר בְּפֶרֶק ה׳ — מֵחֲמַת שֹׁרֶשׁ נִשְׁמָתוֹ שֶׁהִיא גְּבוֹהָ וּפְנִימִית מֵהָעוֹלָמוֹת, וְהַטַּעַם שֶׁנִּתְבָּאֵר בְּפֶרֶק הֶעָבָר — מֵחֲמַת שֶׁהוּא כָּלוּל מִכָּל הָעוֹלָמוֹת, הַכֹּל אֶחָד כְּמוֹ שֶׁנִּתְבָּאֵר:

וְלָזֹאת, לוֹ לְבַדּוֹ נִתְּנָה מִשְׁפַּט הַבְּחִירָה, לְהַטּוֹת עַצְמוֹ וְאֶת הָעוֹלָמוֹת לְאֵיזֶה צַד אֲשֶׁר יַחְפֹּץ. אוֹ אַף אִם כְּבָר גָּרַם וְסִבֵּב חַס וְשָׁלוֹם בַּחֲטָאָיו הֲרִיסַת הָעוֹלָמוֹת וְסִדְרֵי הַמֶּרְכָּבָה, וְחֻרְבָּנָם וִירִידָתָם חַס וְשָׁלוֹם, יֵשׁ כֹּחַ וְסִפֵּק בְּיָדוֹ לְתַקֵּן אֶת אֲשֶׁר עִוֵּת וְלִבְנוֹת הַנֶּהֱרָסוֹת, מִצַּד שֶׁהוּא כָּלוּל וּמְשֻׁתָּף מִכֻּלָּם:

וְזֶה שֶׁאָמַר דָּוִד הַמֶּלֶךְ עָלָיו הַשָּׁלוֹם (תהלים קכא) "ה' צִלְּךָ עַל יַד יְמִינֶךָ". הַיְינוּ שֶׁכְּמוֹ שֶׁנְּטִיַּת הַצֵּל שֶׁל אֵיזֶה דָּבָר, הוּא מְכֻוָּן רַק כְּפִי תְּנוּעוֹת אוֹתוֹ הַדָּבָר לְאָן נוֹטֶה, כֵּן בְּדִמְיוֹן זֶה כִּבְיָכוֹל הוּא יִתְבָּרֵךְ שְׁמוֹ מִתְחַבֵּר לִנְטוֹת הָעוֹלָמוֹת כְּפִי תְּנוּעוֹת וּנְטִיַּת מַעֲשֵׂי הָאָדָם לְמַטָּה.

וְכֵן מְפֹרָשׁ בַּמִּדְרָשׁ, אָמַר לוֹ הַקָּדוֹשׁ בָּרוּךְ הוּא לְמֹשֶׁה לֵךְ אֱמוֹר לָהֶם לְיִשְׂרָאֵל כִּי שְׁמִי אקי"ק אֲשֶׁר אקי"ק. מַהוּ אקי"ק אֲשֶׁר אקי"ק, כְּשֵׁם שֶׁאַתָּה הֹוֶה עִמִּי, כָּךְ אֲנִי הֹוֶה עִמְּךָ. וְכֵן אָמַר דָּוִד (שם) "ה' צִלְּךָ עַל יַד יְמִינֶךָ". מַהוּ ה' צִלְּךָ, כְּצִלְּךָ, מַה צִלְּךָ אִם אַתָּה מְשַׂחֵק לוֹ הוּא מְשַׂחֵק לְךָ, וְאִם אַתָּה בּוֹכֶה הוּא בּוֹכֶה כְּנֶגְדְּךָ, וְאִם אַתָּה מַרְאֶה לוֹ פָּנִים זְעוּמוֹת אוֹ מְסֻבָּרוֹת אַף הוּא נוֹתֵן לְךָ כָּכָה, אַף הַקָּדוֹשׁ בָּרוּךְ הוּא "ה' צִלְּךָ", כְּשֵׁם שֶׁאַתָּה הֹוֶה עִמּוֹ הוּא הֹוֶה עִמְּךָ, עַד כָּאן.

וּבַזֹּהַר תְּצַוֶּה קפ"ד ב' תָּא חֲזֵי עָלְמָא תַּתָּאָה קַיְמָא לְקַבְּלָא תָּדִיר כו', וְעָלְמָא עִלָּאָה לָא יָהִיב לֵיהּ אֶלָּא כְּגַוְנָא דְּאִיהוּ קַיְמָא, אִי אִיהוּ קַיְמָא בִּנְהִירוּ דְּאַנְפִּין מִתַּתָּא, כְּדֵין הָכִי נַהֲרִין לֵיהּ מִלְּעֵלָּא, וְאִי אִיהוּ קַיְמָא בַּעֲצִיבוּ, יָהֲבִין לֵיהּ הַאי דִּינָא בְּקַבְלֵיהּ. כְּגַוְנָא דָּא "עִבְדוּ אֶת ד' בְּשִׂמְחָה" (תהלים כא), חֶדְוָה דְּבַר נָשׁ מָשִׁיךְ לְגַבֵּיהּ חֶדְוָה אָחֳרָא עִלָּאָה, הָכִי נָמֵי הַאי עָלְמָא תַּתָּאָה, כְּגַוְנָא דְּאִיהוּ אִתְּעַר הָכִי אַמְשִׁיךְ מִלְּעֵלָּא כו'. [בּוֹא וּרְאֵה עוֹלָם הַתַּחְתּוֹן עוֹמֵד לְקַבֵּל תָּמִיד וכו' וְלָעוֹלָם הָעֶלְיוֹן אֵינוֹ נוֹתֵן אֶלָּא כְּפִי שֶׁהוּא עוֹמֵד, אִם הוּא עוֹמֵד בְּהֶאָרַת פָּנִים מִלְּמַטָּה אָז כָּךְ מְאִירִים לוֹ מִלְמַעְלָה, וְאִם הוּא עוֹמֵד בְּעַצְבוּת נוֹתְנִים לוֹ דִּין זֶה כְּנֶגְדּוֹ, כְּעֵין זֶה עִבְדוּ אֶת ה' בְּשִׂמְחָה, כִּי שִׂמְחַת הָאָדָם מוֹשֶׁכֶת אֵלָיו שִׂמְחָה אַחֶרֶת עֶלְיוֹנָה, כָּךְ גַּם עוֹלָם הַתַּחְתּוֹן הַזֶּה כְּמוֹ שֶׁמִּתְעוֹרֵר כָּךְ הוּא מוֹשֵׁךְ מִלְמַעְלָה וכו'.]

וְהוּא עִנְיַן הַכְּרוּבִים שֶׁהָיוּ מְעוֹרִין כְּמַעַר אִישׁ וְלוֹיוֹת (מלכים א, ז, לו) "פְּנֵיהֶם אִישׁ אֶל אָחִיו" (שמות כה, כ). וּבִכְרוּבֵי שְׁלֹמֹה כְּתִיב (דה"י ב' ג, ו) "וּפְנֵיהֶם לַבָּיִת" כְּמוֹ שֶׁיִּתְבָּאֵר בְּעֶזְרַת ה'.

פֶּרֶק ח'

הִנֵּה רַבּוֹתֵינוּ זִכְרוֹנָם לִבְרָכָה אָמְרוּ בְּעִנְיַן הַכְּרוּבִים (בבא בתרא צ"ט א') כֵּיצַד הֵן עוֹמְדִין, ר' יוֹחָנָן ור' אֶלְעָזָר חַד אָמַר פְּנֵיהֶם אִישׁ אֶל אָחִיו, וְחַד אָמַר פְּנֵיהֶם לַבַּיִת. וּלְמַאן דְּאָמַר פְּנֵיהֶם אִישׁ אֶל אָחִיו הַכְּתִיב וּפְנֵיהֶם לַבַּיִת, לֹא קַשְׁיָא כָּאן בִּזְמַן שֶׁיִּשְׂרָאֵל עוֹשִׂין רְצוֹנוֹ שֶׁל מָקוֹם, כָּאן בִּזְמַן שֶׁאֵין יִשְׂרָאֵל עוֹשִׂין רְצוֹנוֹ שֶׁל מָקוֹם, וְעַיֵּן רַשְׁבַּ"ם: וּלְמַאן דְּאָמַר פְּנֵיהֶם לַבַּיִת, הַכְּתִיב וּפְנֵיהֶם אִישׁ אֶל אָחִיו, דִּמְצַדְּדֵי אִצְדּוּדֵי, רוֹצֶה לוֹמַר קְצָת לַבַּיִת וּקְצָת זֶה לָזֶה, וְעַיֵּן רַשְׁבַּ"ם ז"ל: וְהָא לֵיכָּא לְתָרוּצֵי כִּדְלְעֵיל, כָּאן בִּזְמַן שֶׁיִּשְׂרָאֵל עוֹשִׂין כו', דְּכֵיוָן דְּעִקַּר עֲשִׂיַּת כְּרוּבִים פְּנֵיהֶם לַבַּיִת, לֹא הָיָה לָהֶם לַעֲשׂוֹתוֹ לְסִימָן שֶׁאֵין יִשְׂרָאֵל עוֹשִׂין רְצוֹנוֹ שֶׁל מָקוֹם. וְכֵן כָּתְבוּ תּוֹסָפוֹת שָׁם (ד"ה דמצדדי) דְּמִסְתַּמָּא הֶעֱמִידוּם תְּחִלָּה לְפִי מַה שֶּׁהָיוּ עוֹשִׂין רְצוֹנוֹ שֶׁל מָקוֹם. וְלִכְאוֹרָה אַכַּתִּי תִּקְשֵׁי לָמָּה הֶעֱמִידוּם תְּחִלָּה כְּרוּבֵי שְׁלֹמֹה פְּנֵיהֶם מְצֻדָּדִין וְלֹא אִישׁ אֶל אָחִיו מַמָּשׁ.

וְהָעִנְיָן הוּא כְּמוֹ שֶׁאָמְרוּ פֶּרֶק כֵּיצַד מְבָרְכִין (ל"ה ב') תָּנוּ רַבָּנָן וְאָסַפְתָּ דְגָנֶךָ כו', לְפִי שֶׁנֶּאֱמַר (יהושע א) "לֹא יָמוּשׁ סֵפֶר הַתּוֹרָה הַזֶּה מִפִּיךָ" גו', יָכוֹל דְּבָרִים כִּכְתָבָן, תַּלְמוּד לוֹמַר (דברים יא) "וְאָסַפְתָּ דְגָנֶךָ" — הַנְהֵג בָּהֶן מִנְהַג דֶּרֶךְ אֶרֶץ, דִּבְרֵי רַבִּי יִשְׁמָעֵאל, רַשְׁבִּ"י אוֹמֵר אֶפְשָׁר אָדָם חוֹרֵשׁ בִּשְׁעַת חֲרִישָׁה כו' תּוֹרָה מַה תְּהֵא עָלֶיהָ, אֶלָּא בִּזְמַן שֶׁיִּשְׂרָאֵל עוֹשִׂין רְצוֹנוֹ שֶׁל מָקוֹם מְלַאכְתָּן נַעֲשֵׂית עַל יְדֵי אֲחֵרִים וכו' וּבִזְמַן שֶׁאֵין יִשְׂרָאֵל עוֹשִׂין רְצוֹנוֹ שֶׁל מָקוֹם מְלַאכְתָּן נַעֲשֵׂית עַל יְדֵי עַצְמָן, שֶׁנֶּאֱמַר "וְאָסַפְתָּ דְגָנֶךָ".

וְלִכְאוֹרָה תְּמוּהָ דְּמוֹקֵי לִקְרָא דְּוְאָסַפְתָּ דְגָנֶךָ, כְּשֶׁאֵין עוֹשִׂין רְצוֹנוֹ שֶׁל מָקוֹם, וְהָא לְעֵיל מִינֵּהּ כְּתִיב וְהָיָה אִם שָׁמוֹעַ תִּשְׁמְעוּ אֶל מִצְוֹתַי וגו' לְאַהֲבָה וגו' וּלְעָבְדוֹ בְּכָל לְבַבְכֶם וגו', וַעֲלָהּ קָאָמַר וְאָסַפְתָּ דְגָנֶךָ.

אֲבָל הָעִנְיָן, כִּי וַדַּאי שֶׁאֵין דַּעַת רַבִּי יִשְׁמָעֵאל שֶׁיְּהֵא הָרְשׁוּת נְתוּנָה לָאָדָם לִפְרֹשׁ חַס וְשָׁלוֹם אַף זְמַן מְעַט מֵעֵסֶק הַתּוֹרָה, וְלַעֲסֹק בְּפַרְנָסָה, וִיהְיֶה בָּטֵל אוֹתוֹ הָעֵת מֵעֵסֶק הַתּוֹרָה לְגַמְרֵי חַס וְשָׁלוֹם, אָמְנָם רָמַז רַבִּי יִשְׁמָעֵאל בִּלְשׁוֹנוֹ הַקָּדוֹשׁ, הַנְהֵג "בָּהֶן" מִנְהַג דֶּרֶךְ אֶרֶץ, רוֹצֶה לוֹמַר עִמָּהֶן עִם הַדִּבְרֵי תּוֹרָה, הַיְנוּ שֶׁגַּם בְּאוֹתוֹ הָעֵת וְשָׁעָה מְעֻטֶּת שֶׁאַתָּה עוֹסֵק בְּפַרְנָסָה כְּדֵי הַצֹּרֶךְ וְהַהֶכְרֵחַ לְחִיּוּת נֶפֶשׁ, עַל כָּל פָּנִים בְּרַעְיוֹנֵי מַחְשַׁבְתְּךָ תְּהֵא מְהַרְהֵר רַק בְּדִבְרֵי תּוֹרָה.

וְכֵן רָבָא אָמַר לְתַלְמִידָיו (ברכות לה:), בְּיוֹמֵי נִיסָן וְתִשְׁרֵי לָא תִּתְחֲזוּ קַמַּאי דַּיְקָא, שֶׁלֹּא לָבֹא לְבֵית מִדְרָשׁוֹ, אֲבָל וַדַּאי שֶׁתַּלְמִידֵי רָבָא לֹא הָיוּ בְּטֵלִים חַס וְשָׁלוֹם לְגַמְרֵי מֵעֵסֶק הַתּוֹרָה גַּם בְּבֵיתָם בְּאֵלּוּ הַיָּמִים.

וְאָמְרוּ שָׁם הַרְבֵּה עָשׂוּ כר' יִשְׁמָעֵאל וְעָלְתָה בְּיָדָם, וְהַרְבֵּה עָשׂוּ כְּרַשְׁבִּ"י וְלֹא עָלְתָה בְּיָדָם, הַיְנוּ רַבִּים דַּוְקָא, כִּי וַדַּאי שֶׁלִּכְלַל הֶהָמוֹן כִּמְעַט בִּלְתִּי אֶפְשָׁר שֶׁיַּתְמִידוּ כָּל יְמֵיהֶם רַק בְּעֵסֶק הַתּוֹרָה, שֶׁלֹּא לִפְנוֹת אַף שָׁעָה מְעֻטֶּת לָשׂוּם עֵסֶק פַּרְנָסַת מְזוֹנוֹת כְּלָל, וְעַל זֶה אָמְרוּ בְּאָבוֹת כָּל תּוֹרָה שֶׁאֵין עִמָּהּ מְלָאכָה וכו', אֲבָל יָחִיד לְעַצְמוֹ, שֶׁאֶפְשָׁר לוֹ לִהְיוֹת אַךְ עָסוּק כָּל יָמָיו בְּתוֹרָתוֹ וַעֲבוֹדָתוֹ יִתְבָּרַךְ שְׁמוֹ, וַדַּאי שֶׁחוֹבָה מֻטֶּלֶת עָלָיו שֶׁלֹּא לִפְרֹשׁ אַף זְמַן מְעַט מִתּוֹרָה וַעֲבוֹדָה לְעֵסֶק פַּרְנָסָה חַס וְשָׁלוֹם, וּכְדַעַת רַבִּי שִׁמְעוֹן בַּר יוֹחַאי:

וְהִנֵּה פָּסוּק "וְאָסַפְתָּ דְגָנֶךָ" וגו' הוּא מוּצָא מִכְּלַל פָּרָשַׁת "וְהָיָה" שֶׁכֻּלָּהּ נֶאֶמְרָה בִּלְשׁוֹן רַבִּים, וּפָסוּק "וְאָסַפְתָּ" נֶאֱמַר בִּלְשׁוֹן יָחִיד, לָכֵן קָרֵי לֵיהּ אֵין עוֹשֶׂה רְצוֹנוֹ שֶׁל מָקוֹם כְּשֶׁמְּפַנֶּה עַצְמוֹ אַף מְעַט לְעֵסֶק פַּרְנָסָה:

וְיָדוּעַ שֶׁהַכְּרוּבִים, הָאֶחָד — רֶמֶז עָלָיו יִתְבָּרַךְ שְׁמוֹ, וְהַשֵּׁנִי — עַל יִשְׂרָאֵל סְגֻלָּתוֹ. וּכְפִי שִׁעוּר הִתְקָרְבוּתָם וּדְבֵיקוּתָם שֶׁל יִשְׂרָאֵל אֵלָיו יִתְבָּרַךְ שְׁמוֹ, אוֹ לְהֶפֶךְ חַס וְשָׁלוֹם, הָיָה נִכָּר הַכֹּל בְּעִנְיַן עֲמִידַת הַכְּרוּבִים דֶּרֶךְ נֵס וָפֶלֶא. אִם פְּנֵיהֶם יָשָׁר יֶחֱזוּ אֵלָיו יִתְבָּרַךְ שְׁמוֹ, גַּם הַכְּרוּבִים עָמְדוּ אָז פְּנֵיהֶם אִישׁ אֶל אָחִיו, אוֹ אִם הָפְכוּ פְּנֵיהֶם מְעַט וּמִצַּדְּדֵי אִצְדוּדֵי, כֵּן הָיָה נִכָּר הָעִנְיָן תֵּכֶף בַּכְּרוּבִים, אוֹ אִם חַס וְשָׁלוֹם הִפְנוּ עֹרֶף, גַּם הַכְּרוּבִים כְּרֶגַע הִפְנוּ וְהָפְכוּ פְּנֵיהֶם אִישׁ מֵעַל אָחִיו לְגַמְרֵי חַס וְשָׁלוֹם.

וּכְעִנְיָן שֶׁאָמְרוּ זִכְרוֹנָם לִבְרָכָה בְּיוֹמָא (נ"ד א') שֶׁהָיוּ מְגַלְּלִין הַפָּרֹכֶת לְעוֹלֵי

רְגָלִים, וּמַרְאִין לָהֶם הַכְּרוּבִים שֶׁהָיוּ מְעוּרִין זֶה בָּזֶה, וְאוֹמְרִים לָהֶן: רְאוּ חִבַּתְכֶם לִפְנֵי הַמָּקוֹם כו'.

וּבַזֹּהַר תְּרוּמָה קנ"ב ב': אֵימָתַי אִיהִי בְּרַחֲמֵי, א"ל בְּשַׁעְתָּא דִּכְרוּבִים מְהַדְרָן כו', וּמִסְתַּכְּלָן אַנְפִּין בְּאַנְפִּין, כֵּיוָן דְּאִנּוּן כְּרוּבִים מִסְתַּכְּלָן אַנְפִּין בְּאַנְפִּין כְּדֵין כָּל גַּוְנִין מִתְתַּקְּנָן כו'. כְּמָה דְּמִסַּדְּרִין יִשְׂרָאֵל תִּקּוּנַיְהוּ לְגַבֵּי קוּדְשָׁא בְּרִיךְ הוּא, הָכִי קַיְמָא כֹּלָּא וְהָכִי אִתְסְדַר כו'. [מָתַי הִיא בְּרַחֲמִים א"ל בְּשָׁעָה שֶׁהַכְּרוּבִים מַחֲזִירִים וכו' וּמִסְתַּכְּלִים פָּנִים בְּפָנִים כֵּיוָן שֶׁהֵם הַכְּרוּבִים מִסְתַּכְּלִים פָּנִים בְּפָנִים אָז כָּל הַגְּוָנִים מִתְתַּקְּנִים וכו' כְּמוֹ שֶׁמְּסַדְּרִים יִשְׂרָאֵל תִּקּוּנֵיהֶם אֶל הַקָּדוֹשׁ בָּרוּךְ הוּא, כָּךְ עוֹמֵד הַכֹּל וְכָךְ מִסְתַּדֵּר וכו'.]

וּבְפָרָשַׁת אַחֲרֵי נ"ט רֵישׁ ע"ב: שֶׁבֶת אַחִים כו', בְּשַׁעְתָּא דַּהֲווּ חַד בְּחַד מַשְׁגִּיחִין אַנְפִּין בְּאַנְפִּין כְּתִיב: "מַה טּוֹב וּמַה נָּעִים" וגו', וְכַד מְהַדֵּר דְּכוּרָא אַנְפּוֹי מִן נוּקְבָא וַי לְעָלְמָא כו'. [שֶׁבֶת אַחִים וכו' כִּי בְּשָׁעָה שֶׁהָיוּ מִסְתַּכְּלִים זֶה בָּזֶה פָּנִים בְּפָנִים כָּתוּב מַה טּוֹב וּמַה נָּעִים וגו' וּכְשֶׁהַזָּכָר מַחֲזִיר פָּנָיו מִן הַנְּקֵבָה אוֹי לָעוֹלָם.]

וּבַזֹּהַר חָדָשׁ סוֹף פָּרָשַׁת תְּרוּמָה מ"ג א': בְּכָל זִמְנָא דְּיִשְׂרָאֵל הֲווּ זַכָּאִין, כְּרוּבִים הֲווּ דְּבִיקִין בִּדְבִיקוּ אַפִּין בְּאַפִּין. כֵּיוָן דַּהֲווּ סָרְחָן, הֲווּ מְהַדְּרִין אַפַּיְהוּ דָּא מִן דָּא כו', וְעַל דָּא כְּרוּבִים בְּהַהוּא זִמְנָא דַּהֲווּ יִשְׂרָאֵל זַכָּאִין, הֲווּ אַנְפִּין בְּאַנְפִּין כו'. וְעַל רָזִין אִלֵּין הֲווּ יָדְעֵי אִי יִשְׂרָאֵל זַכָּאִין אִי לָא כו'. כְּתִיב: "עִבְדוּ אֶת ה' בְּשִׂמְחָה", חֶדְוָתָא דִּתְרֵין כְּרוּבִין כו', כֵּיוָן דְּשָׁארֵי עֲלַיְהוּ, אִתְהַדַּר בְּחֶדְוָה כו', וְעָלְמָא אִתְהַדַּר בְּרַחֲמֵי כו'. [בְּכָל זְמַן שֶׁהָיוּ יִשְׂרָאֵל זַכָּאִים, הַכְּרוּבִים הָיוּ דְּבוּקִים בִּדְבֵקוּת פָּנִים בְּפָנִים, וְכֵיוָן שֶׁהָיוּ חוֹטְאִים הָיוּ מַחֲזִירִים פְּנֵיהֶם זֶה מִזֶּה וכו' וע"כ הַכְּרוּבִים בְּאוֹתוֹ זְמַן שֶׁהָיוּ יִשְׂרָאֵל זַכָּאִים הָיוּ פָּנִים בְּפָנִים וכו' וְעַל סוֹדוֹת אֵלּוּ הָיוּ יוֹדְעִים אִם יִשְׂרָאֵל הֵם זַכָּאִים אוֹ לֹא וכו' כָּתוּב עִבְדוּ אֶת ה' בְּשִׂמְחָה שִׂמְחָתָם שֶׁל שְׁנֵי הַכְּרוּבִים וכו' כֵּיוָן שֶׁשּׁוֹרָה עֲלֵיהֶם חוֹזֵר לִהְיוֹת בְּשִׂמְחָה וְהָעוֹלָם חוֹזֵר לִהְיוֹת בְּרַחֲמִים]. וְעַיֵּן שָׁם בָּאֹרֶךְ:

פֶּרֶק ט'

וְהִנֵּה דּוֹר הַמִּדְבָּר שֶׁזָּכוּ לִהְיוֹת מֵאוֹכְלֵי שֻׁלְחַן גָּבוֹהַּ, לֶחֶם מִן הַשָּׁמַיִם דְּבַר יוֹם בְּיוֹמוֹ, וְשִׂמְלָתָם לֹא בָלְתָה מֵעֲלֵיהֶם, וְלֹא הָיוּ צְרִיכִים לְשׁוּם עֵסֶק פַּרְנָסָה בָּעוֹלָם כְּלָל, לְדִבְרֵי הַכֹּל לֹא מִקְרוּ עוֹשִׂין רְצוֹנוֹ שֶׁל מָקוֹם אֶלָּא אִם כֵּן הָיוּ מִסְתַּכְּלִין כְּלַפֵּי מַעְלָה בְּיֹשֶׁר גָּמוּר, וּמְשַׁעְבְּדִין אֶת לִבָּם רַק לַתּוֹרָה וַעֲבוֹדָה, וְיִרְאָתוֹ יִתְבָּרַךְ שְׁמוֹ, יוֹמָם וָלַיְלָה לֹא יָמוּשׁ מִפִּיהֶם, דְּבָרִים כִּכְתָבָן מַמָּשׁ, בְּלִי נְטוֹת אֶל הַצַּד כְּלָל, אַף שָׁעָה קַלָּה לְעֵסֶק פַּרְנָסָה, וּכְמַאֲמָרָם זִכְרוֹנָם לִבְרָכָה (מכילתא בשלח י"ז) לֹא נִתְּנָה תּוֹרָה אֶלָּא לְאוֹכְלֵי מָן, לָכֵן הֶעֱמִידוּ אָז אֶת הַכְּרוּבִים לְפִי מַה שֶּׁהָיוּ עוֹשִׂין רְצוֹנוֹ שֶׁל מָקוֹם, פְּנֵיהֶם אִישׁ אֶל אָחִיו מַמָּשׁ, לְהַרְאוֹת כִּי יָשָׁר יֶחֱזוּ פָנֵימוֹ יִתְבָּרַךְ, פָּנִים בְּפָנִים עִם עַם קְדוֹשׁוֹ.

אָמְנָם בִּימֵי שְׁלֹמֹה, שֶׁהָיוּ כְּלַל הֲמוֹן יִשְׂרָאֵל צְרִיכִים וּמֻכְרָחִים לִנְטוֹת מְעַט אֶל הַצַּד לְעֵסֶק הַפַּרְנָסָה, עַל כָּל פָּנִים כְּדֵי חַיֵּי נֶפֶשׁ, שֶׁזֶּה עִקַּר אֲמִתַּת רְצוֹנוֹ יִתְבָּרַךְ לְדַעַת רַבִּי

יִשְׁמָעֵאל דְּסָבַר דִּלְרַבִּים טְפֵי אָרִיךְ לְמֶעֱבַד הָכִי, וּכְמוֹ שֶׁאָמְרוּ בְּאָבוֹת: "יָפֶה תַּלְמוּד תּוֹרָה עִם דֶּרֶךְ אֶרֶץ כוּ', וְכָל תּוֹרָה שֶׁאֵין עִמָּהּ מְלָאכָה" כוּ'. וְכָל מִלֵּי דְּאָבוֹת מִילֵּי דַּחֲסִידוּת נִינְהוּ, רַק שֶׁגַּם בְּעֵת עָסְקָם בְּפַרְנָסָה יְהֵא לִבָּם נוֹהֵג בְּחָכְמָה בְּהִרְהוּר דִּבְרֵי תּוֹרָה, לָכֵן הֶעֱמִידוּ אָז בַּתְּחִלָּה אֶת הַכְּרוּבִים, לְפִי מַה שֶּׁיִּהְיוּ עוֹשִׂין רְצוֹנוֹ שֶׁל מָקוֹם, פְּנֵיהֶם מְצֻדָּדִין מְעַט, וְעִם כָּל זֶה הָיוּ מְעוּרִים "כְּמַעַר אִישׁ וְלֹיוֹת" (מלכים א' ז, לו) בְּפָנִים שֶׁל חִבָּה, לְהַרְאוֹת חִבָּתוֹ יִתְבָּרַךְ אֶצְלֵנוּ, שֶׁזֶּה עִקַּר רְצוֹנוֹ יִתְבָּרַךְ כַּנַּ"ל. (וְסוֹבֵר כְּרַבִּי יִשְׁמָעֵאל. וּמַאן דְּאָמַר שֶׁגַּם בִּכְרוּבֵי שְׁלֹמֹה, הֶעֱמִידוּם תְּחִלָּה לְפִי מַה שֶּׁיִּהְיוּ עוֹשִׂין רְצוֹנוֹ שֶׁל מָקוֹם, פְּנֵיהֶם אִישׁ אֶל אָחִיו מַמָּשׁ, סוֹבֵר כְּרַשְׁבִּ"י).

וְלִכְאוֹרָה אַכַּתִּי לָמָּה הֻצְרְכוּ לְהַעֲמִיד ב' הַכְּרוּבִים מְצֻדָּדִין, הֲלֹא הַכְּרוּב הָאֶחָד שֶׁרָמַז עָלָיו יִתְבָּרַךְ שְׁמוֹ, הָיוּ צְרִיכִים לְהַעֲמִידוֹ יָשָׁר מַמָּשׁ.

אָמְנָם הָעִנְיָן כְּמוֹ שֶׁכָּתַבְנוּ, שֶׁהִתְחַבְּרוּתוֹ יִתְבָּרַךְ כִּבְיָכוֹל לְהָעוֹלָמוֹת וְהַכֹּחוֹת כֻּלָּם, וְכָל סִדְרֵיהֶם וְהִתְקַשְּׁרוּתָם, וְכֵן כָּל סִדְרֵי הַנְהָגָתוֹ יִתְבָּרַךְ אִתָּנוּ, הוּא כְּפִי שִׁעוּר הַתְּנוּעָה וְהַהִתְעוֹרְרוּת הַמַּגִּיעַ אֲלֵיהֶם מִמַּעֲשֵׂינוּ לְמַטָּה, וּכְפִי זֶה הַשִּׁעוּר מִשְׁתַּלְשֵׁל וְנִמְשָׁךְ גַּם אֵלֵינוּ לְמַטָּה פָּנִים שׂוֹחֲקוֹת וּמְסֻבָּרוֹת. לָכֵן, גַּם הַכְּרוּב שֶׁרָמַז עָלָיו יִתְבָּרַךְ שְׁמוֹ, הָיוּ גַּם כֵּן צְרִיכִים לְהַעֲמִידוֹ מְצֻדָּד מְעַט, כְּפִי שִׁעוּר הַצִּדּוּד שֶׁל הַכְּרוּב שֶׁרוֹמֵז עָלֵינוּ, מִזֶּה הַטַּעַם:

וְלָכֵן בְּעֵת קְרִיעַת יַם סוּף, אָמַר הוּא יִתְבָּרַךְ לְמֹשֶׁה: "מַה תִּצְעַק אֵלָי דַּבֵּר אֶל בְּנֵי יִשְׂרָאֵל וְיִסָּעוּ" (שמות יד, טו), רָצָה לוֹמַר דִּבְדִידְהוּ תַּלְיָא מִלְתָא, שֶׁאִם הֵמָּה יִהְיוּ בְּתֹקֶף הָאֱמוּנָה וְהַבִּטָּחוֹן, וְיִסְּעוּ הָלוֹךְ וְנָסוֹעַ אֶל הַיָּם, סָמוּךְ לִבָּם לֹא יִירָא, מֵעֹצֶם בִּטְחוֹנָם שֶׁוַּדַּאי יִקָּרַע לִפְנֵיהֶם, אָז יִגְרְמוּ עַל יְדֵי זֶה הִתְעוֹרְרוּת לְמַעְלָה, שֶׁיֵּעָשֶׂה לָהֶם הַנֵּס וְיִקָּרַע לִפְנֵיהֶם.

וְזֶהוּ "לְסֻסָתִי בְּרִכְבֵי פַרְעֹה דִּמִּיתִיךְ רַעְיָתִי" (שה"ש א, ט), רוֹצֶה לוֹמַר, כְּמוֹ בְּסוּסֵי פַרְעֹה שֶׁהָיָה הֵפֶךְ מִנְהָגוֹ שֶׁל עוֹלָם שֶׁהָרוֹכֵב מַנְהִיג לַסּוּס, וּבְפַרְעֹה וְחֵילוֹ — הַסּוּס הִנְהִיג אֶת רוֹכְבוֹ, כְּמוֹ שֶׁאָמְרוּ רַבּוֹתֵינוּ זִכְרוֹנָם לִבְרָכָה (שמו"ר כג ושהש"ר א, נ), כֵּן דִּמִּיתִיךְ וְהִמְשַׁלְתִּיךְ רַעְיָתִי עַל זֶה הָאֹפֶן מַמָּשׁ, שֶׁאַף שֶׁאֲנִי "רוֹכֵב עֲרָבוֹת", עִם כָּל זֶה כִּבְיָכוֹל אַתְּ מַנְהִיגָה אוֹתִי עַל יְדֵי מַעֲשַׂיִךְ, שֶׁעִנְיַן הִתְחַבְּרוּתִי כִּבְיָכוֹל לְהָעוֹלָמוֹת, הוּא רַק כְּפִי עִנְיַן הִתְעוֹרְרוּת מַעֲשַׂיִךְ לְאָן נוֹטִים, וְזֶהוּ שֶׁאָמַר הַכָּתוּב: (דברים לג, כו) "רוֹכֵב שָׁמַיִם בְּעֶזְרֶךָ", וְכֵן מַה שֶּׁאָמְרוּ רַבּוֹתֵינוּ זִכְרוֹנָם לִבְרָכָה (עי' שבת קטז: קלא:, יבמות ה: מנחות סד.) "הָעֲבוֹדָה צֹרֶךְ גָּבוֹהַּ":

פֶּרֶק י'

וְעַל פִּי זֶה יְבֹאַר פֵּשֶׁר דָּבָר, בְּעִנְיַן שִׁנּוּי דֵּעוֹת שֶׁבֵּין גְּדוֹלֵי הָרִאשׁוֹנִים ז"ל, אִם הָאָדָם מִיִּשְׂרָאֵל גָּדוֹל מֵהַמַּלְאָךְ, אוֹ מַלְאָךְ גָּדוֹל מִמֶּנּוּ, וְכָל אֶחָד מִשְּׁנֵי הַדֵּעוֹת מֵבִיא רְאָיוֹת מְפֹרָשׁוֹת מִמִּקְרָאוֹת מְפֹרָשִׁים. וְעַל פִּי דְּבָרֵינוּ הַנַּ"ל יִתְבָּאֵר אֲשֶׁר בֶּאֱמֶת אֵלּוּ וָאֵלּוּ דִּבְרֵי אֱלֹהִים חַיִּים, רַק בִּבְחִינוֹת חֲלוּקִים.

כִּי וַדַּאי מַלְאָךְ גָּדוֹל מֵהָאָדָם, הֵן בְּעֶצֶם מַהוּתוֹ, הֵן בְּגֹדֶל קְדֻשָּׁתוֹ וְנִפְלְאוֹת הַשָּׂגָתוֹ, אֵין עֵרֶךְ וְדִמְיוֹן בֵּינֵיהֶם כְּלָל.

וּכְמוֹ שֶׁכָּתוּב בְּזֹהַר חָדָשׁ בְּרֵאשִׁית בַּמִּדְרָשׁ הַנֶּעְלָם בְּפָרָשָׁה וַיִּקְרָא אֱלֹהִים לָאוֹר יוֹם: "הַשָּׂגַת הַמַּלְאָכִים הִיא הַשָּׂגָה גְּדוֹלָה, מַה שֶּׁאֵין כֵּן לְמַטָּה מֵהֶם, הַשָּׂגָה שְׁנִיָּה כו', הַשָּׂגָה שְׁלִישִׁית הִיא הַשָּׂגַת הַמַּדְרֵגָה הַתַּחְתּוֹנָה אֲשֶׁר בֶּעָפָר יְסוֹדָהּ, וְהִיא הַשָּׂגַת בְּנֵי אָדָם". וְשָׁם ט"ז ב': "הַמַּלְאָכִים הַקְּרוֹבִים מְקַבְּלִים כֹּחַ שֶׁפַע אַסְפַּקְלַרְיָא שֶׁל מַעְלָה תְּחִלָּה, וּמֵהֶם יוֹרֵד לַשָּׁמַיִם וְכָל צְבָאָם, וּמֵהֶם אֶל הָאָדָם", עַיֵּן שָׁם. וּבְזֹהַר תְּרוּמָה קכ"ט ב': "מַלְאֲכֵי עִלָּאֵי אִנּוּן קַדִּישִׁין יַתִּיר מִנָּן". [מַלְאָכִים עֶלְיוֹנִים, הֵם קְדוֹשִׁים יוֹתֵר מֵאִתָּנוּ.]

אָמְנָם בְּדָבָר אֶחָד, יִתְרוֹן גָּדוֹל לָאָדָם מֵהַמַּלְאָכִים, וְהוּא הַעֲלָאַת וְהִתְקַשְּׁרוּת הָעוֹלָמוֹת וְהַכֹּחוֹת וְהָאוֹרוֹת אֶחָד בַּחֲבֵרוֹ, אֲשֶׁר זֶה אֵין בְּכֹחַ כְּלָל לְשׁוּם מַלְאָךְ.

וְהוּא מִטַּעַם הַנַּ"ל, כִּי הַמַּלְאָךְ הוּא בְּעֶצֶם כֹּחַ אֶחָד פְּרָטִי לְבַד, שֶׁאֵין בּוֹ כְּלִילוּת כָּל הָעוֹלָמוֹת יַחַד. (וְכֵן כָּתוּב בְּעֵץ חַיִּים שַׁעַר פְּנִימִיּוּת וְחִיצוֹנִיּוּת רֵישׁ דְּרוּשׁ יו"ד, שֶׁהַמַּלְאָךְ אֵינוֹ רַק בְּחִינָה פְּרָטִית שֶׁל אוֹתוֹ הָעוֹלָם שֶׁעוֹמֵד בּוֹ, אֲבָל נִשְׁמַת הָאָדָם, בְּכָל ג' הַחֲלָקֵי נר"ן שֶׁלָּהּ, הִיא כְּלוּלָה מִכָּל הָעוֹלָמוֹת, עַיֵּן שָׁם) לָכֵן אֵין בְּכֹחַ וִיכֹלֶת הַמַּלְאָךְ כְּלָל לְהַעֲלוֹת וּלְקַשֵּׁר וּלְיַחֵד כֹּל עוֹלָם בְּהָעוֹלָם הַנָּטוּי עַל רָאשֵׁיהֶם, כֵּיוָן שֶׁאֵינוֹ כָּלוּל וּמְשֻׁתָּף מֵהֶם.

וְגַם עֲלִיַּת עַצְמוּתוֹ שֶׁל הַמַּלְאָךְ עַד מַדְרֵגָתוֹ, לְהִתְקַשֵּׁר בָּעוֹלָם שֶׁעָלָיו, אֵין תָּלוּי בּוֹ בְּעַצְמוֹ. לָכֵן נִקְרָאִים הַמַּלְאָכִים "עוֹמְדִים", כְּמוֹ שֶׁכָּתוּב (ישעיה ו'): "שְׂרָפִים עוֹמְדִים", "וְנָתַתִּי לְךָ מַהְלְכִים בֵּין הָעוֹמְדִים הָאֵלֶּה" (זכריה ג').

וְרַק הָאָדָם לְבַד הוּא הַמַּעֲלֶה וְהַמְקַשֵּׁר וּמְיַחֵד אֶת הָעוֹלָמוֹת וְהָאוֹרוֹת בְּכֹחַ מַעֲשָׂיו, מֵחֲמַת שֶׁהוּא כָּלוּל מִכֻּלָּם, וְאָז גַּם הַמַּלְאָךְ מַשִּׂיג עֲלִיָּה וְתוֹסֶפֶת קְדֻשָּׁה עַל קְדֻשָּׁתוֹ, אֲשֶׁר בָּא בְּכֹחַ מַעֲשֵׂה הָאָדָם, מִפְּנֵי שֶׁגַּם הוּא כָּלוּל בְּהָאָדָם. (וְעַיֵּן כְּעֵין זֶה בְּעֵץ חַיִּים שַׁעַר הָעִבּוּרִים רֵישׁ פֶּרֶק ד'):

וְגַם הַג' בְּחִינוֹת נר"ן שֶׁל הָאָדָם עַצְמוֹ, לֹא נִתַּן לָהֶם זֶה הַכֹּחַ הַהַעֲלָאָה וְהַהִתְקַשְּׁרוּת שֶׁל הָעוֹלָמוֹת וְשֶׁל עַצְמָם, עַד רִדְתָּם לְזֶה הָעוֹלָם הַמַּעֲשִׂי בְּגוּף הָאָדָם, וּכְמוֹ שֶׁכָּתוּב (בראשית ב. ז): "וַיִּפַּח בְּאַפָּיו נִשְׁמַת חַיִּים" בְּגוּף הָאָדָם, אָז "וַיְהִי הָאָדָם לְנֶפֶשׁ חַיָּה" שֶׁל כָּל הָעוֹלָמוֹת, כנ"ל בפ"ד:

וְהוּא גַּם כֵּן עִנְיַן מַרְאֵה הַסֻּלָּם שֶׁל יַעֲקֹב אָבִינוּ עָלָיו הַשָּׁלוֹם. עַיֵּן רַעְיָא מְהֵימְנָא נָשֹׂא קכ"ג ב' "וַיִּפַּח בְּאַפָּיו נִשְׁמַת חַיִּים כו', דְּאִתְּמַר בֵּיהּ (בראשית כח, ב): "וַיַּחֲלֹם וְהִנֵּה סֻלָּם", סֻלָּם וַדַּאי אִיהוּ נִשְׁמַת חַיִּים כו', עַיֵּן שָׁם, וּכְמוֹ שֶׁיִּתְבָּאֵר אי"ה לְהַלָּן בְּפֶרֶק י"ט, וְעַל יְדֵי זֶה "וְהִנֵּה מַלְאֲכֵי אֱלֹהִים עוֹלִים וְיוֹרְדִים בּוֹ", רוֹצֶה לוֹמַר, עַל יְדֵי הַנִּשְׁמַת חַיִּים שֶׁהוּא מֻצָּב אַרְצָה, מִתְלַבֶּשֶׁת קְצֵה הַתַּחְתּוֹן שֶׁלָּהּ בְּגוּף הָאָדָם:

פֶּרֶק י"א

וְזֶהוּ הַטַּעַם שֶׁהַמַּלְאָכִים הַמַּקְדִּישִׁים בִּשְׁמֵי מָרוֹם מַמְתִּינִים מִלְּשַׁלֵּשׁ קְדֻשָּׁתָם עַד אַחַר שֶׁאָנוּ מְשַׁלְּשִׁים קְדֻשָּׁה לְמַטָּה (כַּנַּ"ל פֶּרֶק ו' בְּהַגָּ"ה), אַף שֶׁקְּדֻשָּׁתָם לְמַעְלָה מִקְּדֻשָּׁתֵנוּ. לֹא שֶׁהֵם חוֹלְקִים כָּבוֹד לְיִשְׂרָאֵל, אֶלָּא שֶׁאֵין בְּכֹחָם וִיכָלְתָּם כְּלָל מִצַּד עַצְמָם לִפְתֹּחַ פִּיהֶם לְהַקְדִּישׁ לְיוֹצְרָם, עַד עֲלִיַּת קוֹל קְדֻשַּׁת יִשְׂרָאֵל אֲלֵיהֶם מִלְּמַטָּה.

כִּי עִנְיַן אֲמִירַת הַקְּדֻשָּׁה הוּא הַעֲלָאַת הָעוֹלָמוֹת וְהִתְקַשְּׁרוּתָם, כָּל עוֹלָם בָּעוֹלָם שֶׁמֵּעָלָיו, לְהוֹסִיף קְדֻשָּׁתָם וְצַחְצוּחַ אוֹרָם.

וְעַיֵּן בְּהֵיכָלוֹת דִּפְקוּדֵי בְּהֵיכְלָא תִּנְיָנָא רמ"ז סוֹף ע"ב בְּעִנְיַן קְדֻשַּׁת הַמַּלְאָכִים הַבָּא מִכֹּחַ אֲמִירַת קְדֻשָּׁתֵנוּ, ז"ל: "וְאִלֵּין דִּימִינָא אָמְרֵי שִׁירָתָא, וְסַלְקֵי רְעוּתָא לְעֵלָּא, וְאָמְרֵי קָדוֹשׁ, וְאִלֵּין דִּשְׂמָאלָא אָמְרֵי שִׁירָתָא, וְסַלְקֵי רְעוּתָא לְעֵלָּא, וְאָמְרֵי בָּרוּךְ כו', וּמִתְחַבְּרָאן בִּקְדוּשָׁה בְּכָל אִנּוּן דְּיָדְעֵי לְקַדְּשָׁא לְמָארֵיהוֹן בְּיִחוּדָא כו', וְכֻלְּהוּ כְּלִילָן אִלֵּין בְּאִלֵּין בְּיִחוּדָא חֲדָא, וּמִתְקַשְּׁרָאן דָּא בְּדָא, עַד דְּכֻלְּהוּ אִתְעֲבִידוּ קִשּׁוּרָא חֲדָא וְרוּחָא חַד, וּמִתְקַשְּׁרָן בְּאִנּוּן דִּלְעֵלָּא לְמֶהֱוֵי כֹּלָּא חַד, לְאִתְכַּלְלָא דָּא בְּדָא". [וְאֵלּוּ מִיָּמִין אוֹמְרִים שִׁירָה וּמַעֲלִים רָצוֹן לְמַעְלָה וְאוֹמְרִים קָדוֹשׁ, וְאֵלּוּ מִשְּׂמֹאל אוֹמְרִים שִׁירָה וּמַעֲלִים רָצוֹן לְמַעְלָה וְאוֹמְרִים בָּרוּךְ וכו' וּמִתְחַבְּרִים בִּקְדֻשָּׁה בְּכָל אֵלּוּ שֶׁיּוֹדְעִים לְקַדֵּשׁ לַאֲדוֹנָם בְּיִחוּדָא וכו' וְכֻלָּם כְּלוּלִים אֵלּוּ בְּאֵלּוּ בְּיִחוּד אֶחָד וּמִתְקַשְּׁרִים זֶה בָּזֶה עַד שֶׁכֻּלָּם עוֹשִׂים קֶשֶׁר אֶחָד וְרוּחַ אֶחָד וּמִתְקַשְּׁרִים בְּאֵלּוּ שֶׁלְּמַעְלָה לִהְיוֹת כֻּלָּם אֶחָד לְהִתְכַּלֵּל זֶה בָּזֶה.]

וְעַיֵּן בִּפְרִי עֵץ חַיִּים בְּכָל פֶּרֶק ג' מִשַּׁעַר חֲזָרַת הָעֲמִידָה, מְבֹאָר שָׁם כַּוָּנַת עִנְיַן אֲמִירַת הַקְּדֻשָּׁה, שֶׁהוּא הַעֲלָאַת וְהִתְקַשְּׁרוּת עוֹלָמוֹת עֶלְיוֹנִים, לְהוֹסִיף בָּהֶם עַל יְדֵי זֶה תּוֹסֶפֶת קְדוּשָׁה וְאוֹר עֶלְיוֹן. (וְאוּלַי מִזֶּה יָצָא מִנְהָגָן שֶׁל יִשְׂרָאֵל שֶׁנּוֹהֲגִים לְהַעֲלוֹת עַצְמָן בְּעֵת אֲמִירַת הַקְּדוּשָּׁה).

וְזֶה אֵין בְּכֹחַ שׁוּם מַלְאָךְ וְשָׂרָף לַעֲשׂוֹתוֹ בְּעַצְמוֹ תְּחִלָּה כנ"ל. לָזֹאת, לֹא יִפְתַּח פִּיו עַד עֲלִיַּת הֶבֶל פִּיהֶם שֶׁל קְדֻשַּׁת יִשְׂרָאֵל קְבוּצֵי מַטָּה.

וְאִלּוּ הָיוּ כָּל יִשְׂרָאֵל, מִסּוֹף הָעוֹלָם וְעַד סוֹפוֹ, שׁוֹתְקִים חַס וְשָׁלוֹם מִלּוֹמַר קְדֻשָּׁה, מִמֵּילָא בְּהֶכְרֵחַ הָיוּ גַּם הֵמָּה נִשְׁתָּקִים מִלְּהַקְדִּישׁ קְדֻשָּׁתָם. וְעַיֵּן בַּזֹּהַר בָּלָק ק"צ ע"ב. וְזֶהוּ שֶׁאָמַר הַנָּבִיא (יחזקאל א' כד כה): "בְּעָמְדָם תְּרַפֶּינָה כַנְפֵיהֶן", רָצָה לוֹמַר כְּשֶׁיִּשְׂרָאֵל לְמַטָּה עוֹמְדִים שׁוֹתְקִים, מִמֵּילָא תְּרַפֶּינָה כַּנְפֵיהֶם שֶׁל הֲמוֹנֵי מַעְלָה, כִּי עִנְיַן אֲמִירַת קְדֻשָּׁתָם הוּא גַּם בְּכַנְפֵיהֶם, וּכְמַאֲמָרָם זִכְרוֹנָם לִבְרָכָה (חגיגה י"ג ב'): כָּתוּב אֶחָד אוֹמֵר וכו', הֵי מִנַּיְהוּ אִמְעֲטוּ אָמַר רַבִּי חֲנַנְאֵל אָמַר רַב אוֹתָן שֶׁאוֹמְרוֹת בָּהֶן שִׁירָה כו'. וְעַיֵּן זֹהַר חָדָשׁ בְּרֵאשִׁית י"ג רֵישׁ ע"ב "קוֹל הֲמֻלָּה" כו' (יחזקאל שם), אֶלָּא שֶׁשָּׁם פֵּרֵשׁ כַּנְפֵיהֶם לְשׁוֹן כְּנוּפְיָא:

וְלָזֹאת, הֲמוֹן צִבְאוֹת מַעְלָה, כִּתּוֹת כִּתּוֹת יֵשׁ. אַחַת אוֹמֶרֶת "קָדוֹשׁ", וְהֵם הַשְּׂרָפִים, כמו"ש בְּהֵיכָלוֹת דִּבְרֵאשִׁית וּפְקוּדֵי בְּהֵיכְלָא תִּנְיָנָא שָׁם מ"ב א', וְשָׁם רמ"ז סוֹף ע"א) וכמו"ש (ישעי' ו'): "שְׂרָפִים עוֹמְדִים מִמַּעַל לוֹ" וגו', "וְקָרָא זֶה אֶל זֶה וְאָמַר קָדוֹשׁ" גו'.

וְהַשֵּׁנִית לְעֻמָּתָם מְשַׁבְּחִים וְאוֹמְרִים "בָּרוּךְ", וְהֵם הָאוֹפַנִּים וְחַיּוֹת, כְּמוֹ שֶׁאָמְרוּ רַבּוֹתֵינוּ זִכְרוֹנָם לִבְרָכָה (חולין צא.) רֵישׁ פֶּרֶק גִּיד הַנָּשֶׁה: "וְהָאִכָּא בָּרוּךְ, בָּרוּךְ, אוֹפַנִּים הוּא דְּאָמְרֵי לֵיהּ", וּכְמוֹ שֶׁסִּדְּרוּ אַנְשֵׁי כְּנֶסֶת הַגְּדוֹלָה בִּקְדֻשַּׁת יוֹצֵר, שֶׁכָּל כַּת מְקַדֶּשֶׁת כְּפִי מְקוֹרָהּ וְשָׁרְשָׁהּ בְּהָעוֹלָמוֹת.

אֲבָל יִשְׂרָאֵל קְבוּצֵי מַטָּה אוֹמְרִים שְׁנֵיהֶם "קָדוֹשׁ" וּ"בָרוּךְ", לִהְיוֹתָם כּוֹלְלִים כָּל הַמְּקוֹרוֹת וְהַשָּׁרָשִׁים יַחַד:

וְזֶהוּ גַּם כֵּן עִנְיַן אֲמִירַת פֶּרֶק שִׁירָה שֶׁאָמְרוּ ז"ל: "כָּל הָאוֹמֵר פֶּרֶק שִׁירָה בְּכָל יוֹם" כו', שֶׁעַל יְדֵי אֲמִירַת הָאָדָם אוֹתוֹ, שֶׁהוּא כּוֹלֵל כָּל הַכֹּחוֹת כֻּלָּם, הוּא נוֹתֵן כֹּחַ לְהַמַּלְאָכִים וְהַשָּׂרִים שֶׁל כָּל אֵלּוּ הַבְּרִיּוֹת שֶׁיֹּאמְרוּ אֵלּוּ הַשִּׁירוֹת, וְעַל יְדֵי זֶה הֵם מוֹשְׁכִים חִיּוּתָם וְשִׁפְעָם לְהַשְׁפִּיעַ בְּכָל הַתַּחְתּוֹנִים. וְעַיֵּן בָּזֶה בְּלִקּוּטֵי תּוֹרָה בְּטַעֲמֵי מִצְוֹת פָּרָשַׁת וָאֶתְחַנַּן:

פֶּרֶק י"ב

וּמַה שֶּׁהַנֶּפֶשׁ רוּחַ נְשָׁמָה שֶׁל הָאָדָם אֵין בִּיכָלְתָּם לְקַשֵּׁר הָעוֹלָמוֹת עַד רִדְתָּם לְמַטָּה בְּגוּף הָאָדָם כַּנַּ"ל (בפ"י), כִּי לְתַקֵּן "עוֹלַם הָעֲשִׂיָּה" הֻצְרְכוּ בְּהֶכְרֵחַ לְהִתְלַבֵּשׁ בַּגּוּף, בְּעוֹלַם הַמַּעֲשֶׂה. וְכֵן מָצִינוּ כַּמָּה מִקְרָאוֹת הַמְדַבְּרִים בְּאֵלּוּ הַג' בְּחִינוֹת הַנַּ"ל.

בְּעִנְיַן הַהִתְעוֹרְרוּת שֶׁלְּמַעְלָה עַל יְדֵי בְּחִינַת "הַמַּעֲשֶׂה" — אָמַר דָּוִד הַמֶּלֶךְ עָלָיו הַשָּׁלוֹם (תהלים לג, טו): "הַיֹּצֵר יַחַד לִבָּם הַמֵּבִין אֶל כָּל מַעֲשֵׂיהֶם", וּלְפִי פְּשׁוּטוֹ הָיָה רָאוּי לוֹמַר "הַמֵּבִין כָּל מַעֲשֵׂיהֶם", וְאָמַר "אֶל" כָּל מַעֲשֵׂיהֶם, רוֹצֶה לוֹמַר הַנּוֹגֵעַ לְמַעֲשֵׂיהֶם, וְהַיְנוּ, שֶׁהוּא הַיּוֹצְרָם יִתְבָּרַךְ שְׁמוֹ, הַיּוֹדֵעַ וּמֵבִין עַד הֵיכָן מַעֲשֵׂיהֶם מַגִּיעִים וְנוֹגְעִים בְּתִקּוּנֵי הָעוֹלָמוֹת, אוֹ לְהֶפֶךְ חַס וְשָׁלוֹם.

וְכֵן קֹהֶלֶת אָמַר (יב, יד) "כִּי אֶת כָּל מַעֲשֶׂה הָאֱלֹקִים יָבִיא בְמִשְׁפָּט עַל כָּל נֶעְלָם גו', וְלֹא אָמַר "כִּי הָאֱלֹקִים יָבִיא בְּמִשְׁפָּט אֶת כָּל מַעֲשֶׂה" וגו'. וְהַיְנוּ, כִּי "אֱלֹקִים" פֵּרוּשׁוֹ "בַּעַל הַכֹּחוֹת כֻּלָּם", וּבְעֵת עֲמֹד הָאָדָם לַמִּשְׁפָּט לְפָנָיו יִתְבָּרַךְ שְׁמוֹ, לֹא יְדוּנוּ אֶת הַמַּעֲשֶׂה לְבַדָּהּ כְּפִי שֶׁהִיא, אַךְ יַחְשְׁבוּ גַּם כָּל מַה שֶּׁגָּרַם וְסִבֵּב עַל יְדֵי מַעֲשָׂיו, אִם טוֹב וְאִם רַע, בְּכָל הַכֹּחוֹת וְהָעוֹלָמוֹת, זֶהוּ אָמְרוֹ "מַעֲשֶׂה הָאֱלֹקִים":

וְאָמַר "כִּי 'אֶת' כָּל מַעֲשֶׂה", וְלֹא "עַל" כָּל מַעֲשֶׂה, הָעִנְיָן כְּמוֹ שֶׁאָמַר (איוב לד, יא): "כִּי פֹעַל אָדָם יְשַׁלֶּם לוֹ". וְהוּא כְּמוֹ שֶׁנִּתְבָּאֵר לְמַעְלָה (בְּפֶרֶק ו' בהג"ה), שֶׁמִּיַּד שֶׁעוֹלֶה עַל טֹהַר מַחְשֶׁבֶת הָאָדָם לַעֲשׂוֹת מִצְוָה, תֵּכֶף נַעֲשֶׂה רְשׁוּמוֹ לְמַעְלָה, בְּשָׁרְשׁוֹ הָעֶלְיוֹן, לִבְנוֹת וְלִנְטֹעַ כַּמָּה עוֹלָמוֹת וְכֹחוֹת עֶלְיוֹנִים, כְּמוֹ שֶׁכָּתוּב (ישעי' נא, טז) "וָאָשִׂים דְּבָרַי בְּפִיךָ וגו' לִנְטֹעַ שָׁמַיִם" גו', וּכְמַאֲמָרָם זִכְרוֹנָם לִבְרָכָה (סוף ברכות סד, א) "אַל תִּקְרֵי בָּנַיִךְ אֶלָּא בּוֹנָיִךְ", כמש"ל (רפ"ג).

וּמִמֵּילָא מִתְעוֹרֵר וּמַמְשִׁיךְ גַּם עָלָיו "אוֹר מַקִּיף" מֵהַקְּדֻשָּׁה הָעֶלְיוֹנָה, וְהוּא הַמְסַיְּעוֹ לְגָמְרָהּ. וְאַחַר גָּמְרוֹ הַמִּצְוָה, הַקְּדֻשָּׁה וְהָאוֹר מִסְתַּלֵּק לְשָׁרְשׁוֹ.

וְזֶהוּ עִנְיַן שְׂכַר הָעוֹלָם הַבָּא, שֶׁהוּא מַעֲשֵׂי יְדֵי הָאָדָם עַצְמוֹ, שֶׁאַחַר פְּרִידַת נַפְשׁוֹ מֵהַגּוּף, הוּא הָעוֹלֶה לְהִתְעַדֵּן וּלְהַשְׂבִּיעַ נַפְשׁוֹ בְּצַחְצָחוּת הָאוֹרוֹת וְהַכֹּחוֹת וְהָעוֹלָמוֹת הַקְּדוֹשִׁים, שֶׁנִּתּוֹסְפוּ וְנִתְרַבּוּ מִמַּעֲשָׂיו הַטּוֹבִים.

וְזֶהוּ שֶׁאָמְרוּ רַבּוֹתֵינוּ זִכְרוֹנָם לִבְרָכָה (אבות): "כָּל יִשְׂרָאֵל יֵשׁ לָהֶם חֵלֶק לָעוֹלָם הַבָּא", וְלֹא אָמְרוּ "בָּעוֹלָם הַבָּא", שֶׁמַּשְׁמָעוּ הָיָה שֶׁהָעוֹלָם הַבָּא הוּא מוּכָן מֵעֵת הַבְּרִיאָה עִנְיָן וְדָבָר לְעַצְמוֹ, וְאִם יִצְדַּק הָאָדָם יִתְּנוּ לוֹ בִּשְׂכָרוֹ חֵלֶק מִמֶּנּוּ. אֲבָל הָאֱמֶת, שֶׁהָעוֹלָם הַבָּא הוּא הוּא מַעֲשֵׂה יְדֵי הָאָדָם עַצְמוֹ, שֶׁהִרְחִיב וְהוֹסִיף וְהִתְקִין חֵלֶק לְעַצְמוֹ בְּמַעֲשָׂיו. לְכָךְ אָמַר שֶׁכָּל יִשְׂרָאֵל יֵשׁ לָהֶם, לְכָל אֶחָד, חֵלֶק הַקְּדֻשָּׁה וְהָאוֹרוֹת וְהַצַּחְצָחוֹת, שֶׁהִתְקִין וְהוֹסִיף לָעוֹלָם הַבָּא מִמַּעֲשָׂיו הַטּוֹבִים.

וְכֵן עֹנֶשׁ הַגֵּיהִנֹּם, עִנְיָנוֹ גַּם כֵּן, שֶׁהַחֵטְא עַצְמוֹ הוּא עָנְשׁוֹ, כְּמוֹ שֶׁכָּתוּב (משלי ה׳ כב): "עֲוֹנוֹתָיו יִלְכְּדֻנוֹ אֶת הָרָשָׁע וּבְחַבְלֵי חַטָּאתוֹ יִתָּמֵךְ", "תְּיַסְּרֵךְ רָעָתֵךְ" גו׳ (ירמיה ב׳ יט), כְּמוֹ שֶׁנִּתְבָּאֵר, שֶׁכַּאֲשֶׁר הָאָדָם עוֹשֶׂה אַחַת מִמִּצְווֹת ה׳ אֲשֶׁר לֹא תֵעָשֶׂנָה, הַפְּגַם וְהַחֻרְבָּן נִרְשָׁם חַס וְשָׁלוֹם תֵּכֶף לְמַעְלָה בְּשָׁרְשׁוֹ. וּלְעֻמַּת זֶה "אִמָּלְאָה הָחֳרָבָה" (יחזקאל כו), הוּא מֵקִים וּמַגְבִּיר כֹּחוֹת וְחֵילֵי הַטֻּמְאָה וְהַקְּלִפּוֹת, הָרַחֲמָן יִתְבָּרֵךְ שְׁמוֹ יַצִּילֵנוּ.

וּמִשָּׁם מַמְשִׁיךְ גַּם עַל עַצְמוֹ "רוּחַ הַטֻּמְאָה", שֶׁמְּלַפַּפְתּוֹ בְּעֵת עֲשִׂיַּת הֶעָוֹן, וְאַחַר עֲשׂוֹתוֹ הָרוּחַ טֻמְאָה מִסְתַּלֵּק לִמְקוֹמוֹ, וְהוּא בְּחַיָּיו בְּגֵיהִנֹּם מַמָּשׁ, הַמַּקִּיפוֹ בְּעֵת עֲשִׂיַּת הַחֵטְא, רַק שֶׁאֵינוֹ מַרְגִּישׁ עֲדַיִן עַד אַחַר פְּטִירָתוֹ, שֶׁנִּלְכַּד אָז בְּרֶשֶׁת אֲשֶׁר הֵכִין, הֵן כֹּחוֹת הַטֻּמְאָה וְהַמַּזִּיקִין שֶׁנִּבְרְאוּ מִמַּעֲשָׂיו.

וְזֶהוּ שֶׁאָמְרוּ רַבּוֹתֵינוּ זִכְרוֹנָם לִבְרָכָה (עירובין יט.): "רְשָׁעִים מַעֲמִיקִין לָהֶם גֵּיהִנֹּם", רְצוֹנוֹ לוֹמַר שֶׁהֵן עַצְמָם הַמַּעֲמִיקִים לְעַצְמָם הַגֵּיהִנֹּם, וּמַרְחִיבִין אוֹתוֹ וּמַבְעִירִין אוֹתוֹ בְּחֶטְאֵיהֶם, וּכְמוֹ שֶׁכָּתוּב (ישעיה נ׳): "הֵן כֻּלְּכֶם קוֹדְחֵי אֵשׁ גו׳, לְכוּ בְּאוּר אֶשְׁכֶם וּבְזִקּוֹת בְּעַרְתֶּם מִיָּדִי הָיְתָה זֹּאת לָכֶם" וגו׳.

לָכֵן כְּשֶׁתָּפְסוּ אַנְשֵׁי כְּנֶסֶת הַגְּדוֹלָה לְהַיֵּצֶר הָרַע, נִכְבָּה אָז גַּם הַגֵּיהִנֹּם מֵעַצְמוֹ כְּמוֹ שֶׁכָּתוּב בַּזֹּהַר תְּרוּמָה ק"ט רֵישׁ ע"ב: "כְּגַוְנָא דְּחַיָּבַיָּא מִתְחַמְּמָן בְּנוּרָא דְּיֵצֶר הָרַע כו׳, בְּכָל חִמּוּמָא וְחִמּוּמָא כו׳, הָכִי אִתּוֹקַד נוּרָא דְּגֵיהִנֹּם. זִמְנָא חֲדָא לָא אִשְׁתְּכַח יֵצֶר הָרַע בְּעָלְמָא כו׳, וְכָל הַהוּא זִמְנָא כָּבָה נוּרָא דְּגֵיהִנָּם וְלָא אִתּוֹקַד כְּלָל. אַהֲדַר יֵצֶר הָרַע לְאַתְרֵיהּ, שָׁארוּ חַיָּבֵי עָלְמָא לְאִתְחַמְּמָא בֵּיהּ, שָׁארֵי נוּרָא דְּגֵיהִנֹּם לְאִתּוֹקְדָא, דְּהָא גֵיהִנֹּם לָא אִתּוֹקַד אֶלָּא בַּחֲמִימוּ דְּתוּקְפָּא דְּיֵצֶר הָרַע דְּחַיָּבַיָּא. [בְּאֹפֶן שֶׁהָרְשָׁעִים מְחַמְּמִים עַצְמָם בְּאֵשׁ הַיֵּצֶר הָרַע וכו׳ בְּכָל חִמּוּם וְחִמּוּם וכו׳ כָּךְ בּוֹעֵר אֵשׁ הַגֵּיהִנֹּם, פַּעַם אַחַת לֹא נִמְצָא יֵצֶר הָרַע בָּעוֹלָם וכו׳ וְכָל אוֹתוֹ זְמַן כָּבָה אֵשׁ הַגֵּיהִנֹּם וְלֹא בָּעַר כְּלָל, חָזַר הַיֵּצֶר הָרַע לִמְקוֹמוֹ וְרִשְׁעֵי עוֹלָם הִתְחִילוּ לְהִתְחַמֵּם בּוֹ הִתְחִיל אֵשׁ הַגֵּיהִנֹּם לִבְעֹר כִּי הַגֵּיהִנֹּם לֹא בּוֹעֵר אֶלָּא בְּכֹחַ הַחֹם שֶׁל יֵצֶר הָרַע שֶׁל הָרְשָׁעִים.]

זֶהוּ שֶׁאָמַר הַכָּתוּב (איוב לד, יא): "כִּי פֹעַל אָדָם יְשַׁלֶּם לוֹ", שֶׁהַפְּעֻלָּה עַצְמָהּ, הַטּוֹבָה הִיא אִם רָעָה חַס וְשָׁלוֹם, הִיא הִיא עַצְמָהּ הַתַּשְׁלוּמִין שֶׁלּוֹ כַּנַּ"ל, וְעַיֵּן זֹהַר קֹרַח קע"ז א׳.

וְזֶהוּ שֶׁאָמְרוּ בְּאָבוֹת (פ"ד, מ"ב) "שֶׁשְּׂכַר מִצְוָה מִצְוָה וּשְׂכַר עֲבֵרָה עֲבֵרָה", וְזֶהוּ שֶׁכָּתוּב (קהלת יב, יד): "כִּי אֶת כָּל מַעֲשֶׂה וגו' [יָבִיא בְמִשְׁפָּט"], רָצָה לוֹמַר הַמַּעֲשֶׂה עַצְמָהּ, הָעוֹמֶדֶת וְנִרְשֶׁמֶת כְּמוֹת שֶׁהִיא, כְּמוֹ שֶׁנִּתְבָּאֵר לְעֵיל:

וְלָכֵן אָמְרוּ רַבּוֹתֵינוּ זִכְרוֹנָם לִבְרָכָה (בבא קמא נ' ע"א) "כָּל הָאוֹמֵר הַקָּדוֹשׁ בָּרוּךְ הוּא וַתְּרָן הוּא, יְוַתְּרוּ חַיָּיו" כו'. וְכֵן הוּא בִּירוּשַׁלְמִי פֶּרֶק חֲמִישִׁי דִּשְׁקָלִים, וּבִבְרֵאשִׁית רַבָּה פָּרָשָׁה ס"ז, וּבְתַנְחוּמָא פָּרָשַׁת תִּשָּׂא, וּבְשׁוֹחֵר טוֹב תְּהִלִּים. וְלִכְאוֹרָה יִפָּלֵא, הֲלֹא אֲפִלּוּ אָדָם אִישׁ חֶסֶד מִתְנַהֵג בְּמִדַּת וַתְּרָנוּת.

אָמְנָם הוּא כְּמוֹ שֶׁכָּתַבְנוּ לְעֵיל, שֶׁאֵינוּ עַל דֶּרֶךְ הָעֹנֶשׁ וּנְקִימָה חַס וְשָׁלוֹם, רַק "חַטָּאִים תְּרַדֵּף רָעָה" (משלי יג כא), שֶׁהַחֵטְא עַצְמוֹ הוּא עָנְשׁוֹ. כִּי מֵעֵת הַבְּרִיאָה קָבַע הוּא יִתְבָּרַךְ שְׁמוֹ כָּל סִדְרֵי הַנְהָגַת הָעוֹלָמוֹת, שֶׁיִּהְיוּ תְּלוּיִים כְּפִי הִתְעוֹרְרוּת מַעֲשֵׂה הָאָדָם, הַטּוֹבִים וְאִם רָעִים חַס וְשָׁלוֹם, שֶׁכָּל מַעֲשָׂיו וְעִנְיָנָיו נִרְשָׁמִים מֵאֲלֵיהֶם, כָּל אֶחָד בִּמְקוֹרוֹ וְשָׁרְשׁוֹ.

וְהוּא מֻכְרָח לְקַבֵּל דִּינוֹ עַל יְדֵי אוֹתָן כֹּחוֹת הַטֻּמְאָה שֶׁהִגְבִּיר בְּמַעֲשָׂיו, כְּפִי עֵרֶךְ וְעִנְיַן הַפְּגָם. וּבָזֶה מְמֵילָא יְתֻקַּן הַפְּגָם שֶׁל הָעוֹלָמוֹת וְשֶׁל נַפְשׁוֹ.

אוֹ עַל יְדֵי כֹּחַ הַתְּשׁוּבָה, שֶׁמַּגַּעַת עַד שָׁרְשָׁהּ הָעֶלְיוֹן, עוֹלַם הַתְּשׁוּבָה, עָלְמָא דְּחֵירוּ וּנְהִירוּ דְּכֹלָּא, וּמִשָּׁם מִתְאַצֵּל וְנִשְׁפָּע תּוֹסֶפֶת קְדֻשָּׁה עֶלְיוֹנָה וְאוֹר מַבְהִיק, לְהָתֵם וּלְכַלּוֹת כָּל טֻמְאָה וּלְתַקֵּן הָעוֹלָמוֹת כְּמִקֹּדֶם, וּבְיִתְרוֹן אוֹר חָדָשׁ מֵעוֹלַם הַתְּשׁוּבָה הַמּוֹפִיעַ עֲלֵיהֶם.

לָזֹאת, אֵין שַׁיָּךְ וַתְּרָנוּת בָּזֶה. וְזֶהוּ שֶׁאָמְרוּ בְּאָבוֹת (פ"ב, מ"א) "וְכָל מַעֲשֶׂיךָ בַּסֵּפֶר נִכְתָּבִים", הַיְנוּ שֶׁמֵּעַצְמָן נִכְתָּבִים וְנִרְשָׁמִים לְמַעְלָה:

פֶּרֶק יג

וְכֵן בְּעִנְיַן הַהִתְעוֹרְרוּת שֶׁלְּמַעְלָה עַל יְדֵי בְּחִינַת "הַדִּבּוּר", אָמַר עָמוֹס הַנָּבִיא עָלָיו הַשָּׁלוֹם (ד, יג): "כִּי הִנֵּה יוֹצֵר הָרִים וּבֹרֵא רוּחַ וּמַגִּיד לְאָדָם מַה שֵּׂחוֹ". כִּי אָמְרוּ בַּזֹּהַר (לֶךְ לְךָ פ"ו ב', וַיְחִי רל"ד ב' ורמ"ט א', יִתְרוֹ פ' ע"א, תַּזְרִיעַ נ' ע"ב, שְׁלַח קס"א א', ובא"ז רֵישׁ דַּף רצ"ג, וּבְזֹהַר חָדָשׁ שִׁיר הַשִּׁירִים נ"ה ע"ד), שֶׁלְּשׁוֹן "הַגָּדָה" שַׁיָּךְ עַל רָזָא דְּמִלְּתָא.

הִזְהִיר כָּאן אֶת הָאָדָם, מֵחֲמַת הֱיוֹתוֹ עַתָּה בָּזֶה הָעוֹלָם הַשָּׁפָל, שֶׁאֵינוֹ רוֹאֶה וּמַשִּׂיג הַבִּנְיָן אוֹ הַהֲרִיסָה, חַס וְשָׁלוֹם, הַנַּעֲשֶׂה לְמַעְלָה בְּהָעוֹלָמוֹת מִכָּל דִּבּוּר וְדִבּוּר שֶׁלּוֹ, וְיָכוֹל לְהַעֲלוֹת עַל דַּעְתּוֹ חַס וְשָׁלוֹם לוֹמַר, בַּמֶּה נֶחְשָׁב דִּבּוּר וְשִׂיחָה קַלָּה, שֶׁתִּפְעַל שׁוּם פְּעֻלָּה וְעִנְיָן בָּעוֹלָם, אֲבָל יֵדַע נֶאֱמָנָה שֶׁכָּל דִּבּוּר וְשִׂיחָה קַלָּה שֶׁלּוֹ, לְכָל אֲשֶׁר יְבַטֵּא בִשְׂפָתָיו, לֹא אִתְאֲבִיד וְאֵינוֹ הוֹלֵךְ לְבַטָּלָה חַס וְשָׁלוֹם.

וּכְמוֹ שֶׁכָּתוּב בסבא ק' ע"ב: "אֲפִלּוּ הֶבֶל דְּפוּמָא אֲתַר וְדוּכְתָּא אִית לֵיהּ, וְקוּדְשָׁא בְּרִיךְ הוּא עָבִיד מִינֵּיהּ מַה דְּעָבִיד, וַאֲפִלּוּ מִלָּה דְּבַר נָשׁ, וַאֲפִלּוּ קָלָא, לָא הֲוֵי בְּרֵיקַנְיָא, וַאֲתַר וְדוּכְתָּא אִית לְהוּ לְכֹלָּא". [אֲפִילוּ הֶבֶל פֶּה, מָקוֹם וּמַעֲמָד יֵשׁ לוֹ, וְהַקָּדוֹשׁ בָּרוּךְ הוּא עוֹשֶׂה מִמֶּנּוּ מַה שֶּׁעוֹשֶׂה, וַאֲפִילוּ מִלָּה שֶׁל אָדָם, וַאֲפִילוּ קוֹל אֵינָם לָרִיק וּמָקוֹם וּמַעֲמָד

לָהֶם לְכֻלָּם] וּבְפָרָשַׁת מְצֹרָע נ"ה א': "כָּל מִלָּה וּמִלָּה דְּאַפִּיק בַּר נָשׁ מִפּוּמֵיהּ, סַלְקָא לְעֵלָּא וּבָקְעָא רְקִיעִין וְעָאלַת לַאֲתַר דְּעָאלַת". [כָּל מִלָּה וּמִלָּה שֶׁהָאָדָם מוֹצִיא מִפִּיו עוֹלָה לְמַעְלָה וּבוֹקַעַת רְקִיעִים וְנִכְנֶסֶת לְמָקוֹם שֶׁנִּכְנֶסֶת וכו']. וּבְרֵישׁ פָּרָשַׁת נָשֹׂא: "דְּהַהוּא מִלָּה דְּאַפִּיק בַּר נַשׁ מִפּוּמֵיהּ, סַלְקָא וּבָקַע רְקִיעִין וְקַיְמָא בַּאֲתַר דְּקַיְמָא". [הַמִּלָּה הַהִיא שֶׁהָאָדָם הוֹצִיא מִפִּיו עוֹלָה וּבוֹקַעַת רְקִיעִים וְעוֹמֶדֶת בְּמָקוֹם שֶׁעוֹמֶדֶת וכו'.]

שֶׁכְּכָל הַיּוֹצֵא מִפִּיו יֵעָשֶׂה לְמַעְלָה, וּמְעוֹרֵר כֹּחַ עֶלְיוֹן, הֵן בְּדִבּוּר טוֹב מוֹסִיף כֹּחַ בַּכֹּחוֹת הַקְּדוֹשִׁים כְּמוֹ שֶׁכָּתוּב (ישעיה נ"א טז): "וָאָשִׂים דְּבָרַי בְּפִיךָ" וגו' "לִנְטֹעַ שָׁמַיִם" גו'.

וּבַזֹּהַר אֱמֹר ק"ה א': "דְּלֵית לָךְ מִלָּה וּמִלָּה כו', וּמַאן דְּאַפִּיק מִלָּה קַדִּישָׁא מִפּוּמֵיהּ, מִלָּה דְּאוֹרַיְתָא, אִתְעֲבִיד מִנֵּיהּ קָלָא וְסַלִּיק לְעֵלָּא, וְאִתְּעָרוּ קַדִּישֵׁי מַלְכָּא עִלָּאָה וּמִתְעַטְּרָן בְּרֵישֵׁיהּ, וּכְדֵין אִשְׁתְּכַח חֶדְוָתָא לְעֵלָּא וְתַתָּא". [כִּי אֵין לְךָ מִלָּה וּמִלָּה וכו' וּמִי שֶׁמּוֹצִיא דִּבּוּר קָדוֹשׁ מִפִּיו, דִּבּוּר שֶׁל תּוֹרָה, נַעֲשֶׂה מִמֶּנּוּ קוֹל וְעוֹלֶה לְמַעְלָה וּמִתְעוֹרְרִים קְדוֹשֵׁי מֶלֶךְ הָעֶלְיוֹן, וּמִתְעַטְּרִים בְּרֹאשׁוֹ וְאָז נִמְצָא שִׂמְחָה לְמַעְלָה וּלְמַטָּה] וְעַיֵּן בְּאֹרֶךְ בְּפָרָשַׁת וַיַּקְהֵל רי"ז א' נוֹרָאוֹת נִפְלָאוֹת עִנְיַן הַדִּבּוּר שֶׁל מִלִּין קַדִּישִׁין דְּאוֹרַיְתָא, שֶׁכָּל עָלְמִין נְהִירִין מֵחֶדְוָתָא, וְשִׂמְחוֹת וְגִיל תְּבוּאָנָה בְּהֵיכְלִין קַדִּישִׁין עִלָּאִין, וּמְעַטְּרָן לְהוּ בְּעִטְרִין קַדִּישִׁין. וְעַיֵּן בְּפָרָשַׁת קְדוֹשִׁים פ"ה סוֹף ע"א.

וְכֵן מְבֹאָר בִּמְקוֹמוֹת רַבּוֹת בַּתִּקּוּנִים, שֶׁמִּכָּל דִּבּוּר וְקוֹל וְהֶבֶל דְּאוֹרַיְתָא אוֹ דִּצְלוֹתָא נִבְרָאִים כַּמָּה מַלְאָכִים קְדוֹשִׁים.

וּבְהֵפֶךְ, בְּדִבּוּר אֲשֶׁר לֹא טוֹב חַס וְשָׁלוֹם, הוּא בּוֹנֶה רְקִיעִים וְעוֹלָמוֹת שֶׁל שָׁוְא לס"מ ר"ל, וְגוֹרֵם חַס וְשָׁלוֹם הֲרִיסַת וְחֻרְבַּן הָעוֹלָמוֹת סִדְרֵי הַמֶּרְכָּבָה הַקְּדוֹשָׁה הַנּוֹגְעִים לְשֹׁרֶשׁ הַדִּבּוּר.

וְעַיֵּן זֹהַר צַו ל"א ב': "דְּהָא לֵית לָךְ טַב וּבִישׁ כו', וְאוֹי לָהֶם לַבְּרִיּוֹת שֶׁרוֹאוֹת וְאֵינָן יוֹדְעוֹת מַה הֵם רוֹאוֹת, כִּי אֵין לְךָ דִּבּוּר שֶׁאֵין לוֹ מָקוֹם, "כִּי עוֹף הַשָּׁמַיִם יוֹלִיךְ אֶת הַקּוֹל" (קהלת י, כ), וְכַמָּה אַלְפֵי מָארֵי דְּגַדְפֵי דְּאַחֲדִין לָהּ, וְסַלְקִין לָהּ לְמָארֵי דמדין, וְדַיְנִין לָהּ", [וְכַמָּה אֲלָפִים בַּעֲלֵי כְּנָפַיִם שֶׁאוֹחֲזִים בָּהּ וּמַעֲלִים אוֹתָהּ לְבַעֲלֵי הַדִּין וְדָנִין אוֹתָהּ] הֵן לְטוֹב אוֹ לְהֵפֶךְ חַס וְשָׁלוֹם, כְּמוֹ שֶׁכָּתוּב בַּזֹּהַר לֶךְ לְךָ צ"ב א'. וּבְפָרָשַׁת קְדוֹשִׁים הַנַּ"ל: "וְלֵית לָךְ מִלָּה וּמִלָּה וכו' וְכַמָּה קַסְטוֹרִין מִתְחַבְּרִין עִמֵּיהּ דְּהַהוּא קָלָא, עַד דְּסַלְקָא וְאִתְּעַר אֲתַר דִּתְהוֹם רַבָּה כו', וְכַמָּה מִתְעָרִין עָלֵיהּ דְּהַהוּא בַּר נַשׁ, וַי לְמָאן דְּאַפִּיק מִלָּה בִּישָׁא מִפּוּמֵיהּ". [וְכַמָּה מַלְאֲכֵי חַבָּלָה מִתְחַבְּרִין עִם אוֹתוֹ הַקּוֹל עַד שֶׁעוֹלֶה וְנִתְעוֹרֵר הַמָּקוֹם שֶׁל תְּהוֹם הַגָּדוֹל וכו' וְכַמָּה מִתְעוֹרְרִים עַל הָאָדָם הַהוּא, אוֹי לְמִי שֶׁמּוֹצִיא דִּבּוּר רַע מִפִּיו ע"ש] עַיֵּן שָׁם.

וּכְתִיב (קהלת ה' ה): "לָמָּה יִקְצֹף הָאֱלֹהִים עַל קוֹלֶךָ וְחִבֵּל אֶת מַעֲשֵׂה יָדֶיךָ". וְאָמְרוּ (ערכין טו.): "גָּדוֹל הָאוֹמֵר בְּפִיו מִן הָעוֹשֶׂה מַעֲשֶׂה" כו', וְאָמְרוּ זִכְרוֹנָם לִבְרָכָה (סנהדרין צ"ב א'): "כָּל הַמַּחֲלִיף בְּדִבּוּרוֹ כְּאִלּוּ עוֹבֵד עֲבוֹדַת כּוֹכָבִים":

זֶהוּ שֶׁכָּתוּב (עמוס ד, יג): "וּמַגִּיד לְאָדָם מַה שֵּׂחוֹ", רָצָה לוֹמַר שֶׁבְּעֵת עֲמֹד הָאָדָם

לָתֵת דִּין וְחֶשְׁבּוֹן לְפָנָיו יִתְבָּרַךְ, אָז הוּא יִתְבָּרַךְ מַגִּיד לוֹ הַסּוֹד, רָזָא דְּמִלְּתָא, מַה שֶּׁגָּרַם שִׂחוֹ לְמַעְלָה בָּעוֹלָמוֹת הָעֶלְיוֹנִים, כְּמוֹ שֶׁנִּתְבָּאֵר לְעֵיל שֶׁלְּשׁוֹן "הַגָּדָה" פֵּרוּשׁוֹ רָזָא דְּמִלְּתָא:

פֶּרֶק י"ד

וְכֵן עַל הַהִתְעוֹרְרוּת שֶׁלְּמַעְלָה עַל יְדֵי בְּחִינַת "הַמַּחֲשָׁבָה". אָמַר דָּוִד הַמֶּלֶךְ עָלָיו הַשָּׁלוֹם (תהלים לג): "הַיּוֹצֵר יַחַד לִבָּם הַמֵּבִין אֶל כָּל מַעֲשֵׂיהֶם", וְהָיָה צָרִיךְ לוֹמַר "הַמֵּבִין כָּל מַעֲשֵׂיהֶם", וּלְמַעְלָה בְּפֶרֶק י"ב פֵּרַשְׁנוּ עַל בְּחִינַת "הַמַּעֲשֶׂה". וְיֵשׁ לְפָרְשׁוֹ גַּם כֵּן עַל בְּחִינַת "הַמַּחֲשָׁבָה".

וְהוּא, כִּי יִתָּכֵן שֶׁשְּׁנֵי אֲנָשִׁים עוֹשִׂין עֲבֵרָה אַחַת, וְעִם כָּל זֶה אֵין עָנְשָׁן שָׁוֶה, אוֹ מִפְּנֵי שֶׁהָאֶחָד שִׂכְלוֹ וְהַשָּׂגָתוֹ יוֹתֵר גְּדוֹלָה מֵחֲבֵרוֹ, מִצַּד שֶׁשֹּׁרֶשׁ נִשְׁמָתוֹ מִמָּקוֹם גָּבוֹהַּ וְעֶלְיוֹן מִשֶּׁל חֲבֵרוֹ, וְהָעֹנֶשׁ הוּא כְּפִי עִנְיַן הַפְּגָם שֶׁגָּרַם לְמַעְלָה, וְהַפְּגָם שֶׁל כָּל אֶחָד מַגִּיעַ עַד שֹׁרֶשׁ נִשְׁמָתוֹ.

כְּמוֹ שֶׁכָּתוּב בַּתִּקּוּנִים סוֹף תמ"ג: "מַאן דְּפָגֵם לְתַתָּא, פָּגִים לְעֵלָּא, לַאֲתַר דְּאִתְגְּזַר נִשְׁמָתֵיהּ". [מִי שֶׁפּוֹגֵם לְמַטָּה פּוֹגֵם לְמַעְלָה, לַמָּקוֹם שֶׁמִּשָּׁם נֶחְצְבָה נִשְׁמָתוֹ] וְשָׁם בת"ע קכ"ג א': "וְכַד בַּר נַשׁ עָבִיד חוֹבִין, כְּפוּם הַהוּא בַּר נַשׁ הָכִי סָלִיק חוֹבֵיהּ לַאֲתַר דְּאִתְגְּזַר נִשְׁמָתֵיהּ כו', וְעוֹנְשֵׁיהּ אִיהוּ סַגֵּי כְּפוּם דַּרְגֵיהּ" [וּכְשֶׁהָאָדָם עוֹשֶׂה חֲטָאִים, כְּפִי אוֹתוֹ הָאָדָם כָּךְ עוֹלֶה חֶטְאוֹ לַמָּקוֹם שֶׁנֶּחְצְבָה נִשְׁמָתוֹ וכו', וְעָנְשׁוֹ גָּדוֹל כְּפִי דַּרְגָּתוֹ] וְכֵן כָּתַב הָאֲרִיזַ"ל בְּשַׁעַר הַיִּחוּדִים רֵישׁ תִּקּוּן עֲוֹנוֹת, וּבִפְרִי עֵץ חַיִּים בְּהַקְדָּמַת שַׁעַר הַשַּׁבָּת פֶּרֶק א' וּבְגִלְגּוּלִים. וְאֵינוֹ דּוֹמֶה הַמְּטַנֵּף חֲצַר הַמֶּלֶךְ לִמְטַנֵּף פַּלְטִין שֶׁל מֶלֶךְ, וְכָל שֶׁכֵּן הַכִּסֵּא אוֹ בִּגְדֵי תִפְאַרְתּוֹ, וְכָל שֶׁכֵּן הַכֶּתֶר.

וְאַף שֶׁבְּכָל עוֹלָם שֶׁהוּא יוֹתֵר גָּבוֹהַּ וְנַעֲלֶה, אֵין בְּכֹחַ הֶעָוֹן לִפְעֹל בּוֹ פְּגָם וְרֹשֶׁם גָּדוֹל כָּל כָּךְ, עִם כָּל זֶה עָנְשׁוֹ גָּדוֹל יוֹתֵר. כִּי מִי שֶׁהוּא מְמֻנֶּה לְטַהֵר וּלְצַחְצֵחַ כִּתְרוֹ שֶׁל מֶלֶךְ, אִם הִשְׁאִיר עָלָיו אֲפִלּוּ אָבָק מְעַט לְבַד, אֵין עֵרֶךְ וְדִמְיוֹן לְעָנְשׁוֹ, לְעֹנֶשׁ הַמְּמֻנֶּה לְנַקּוֹת חֲצַר הַמֶּלֶךְ אַף אִם הִשְׁאִיר אוֹ הִנִּיחַ בְּתוֹכוֹ הַרְבֵּה רֶפֶשׁ וָטִיט. וְלָכֵן רַבּוּ מִשְׁפְּטֵי ה' אֱמֶת, בְּשִׁנּוּי חִלּוּקֵי הָעֳנָשִׁים לְאֵין קֵץ, לְכָל אֶחָד כְּפִי מַדְרֵגַת הַפְּגָם בְּשֹׁרֶשׁ נִשְׁמָתוֹ, מֵאֵיזֶה עוֹלָם חֻצְּבָה.

גַּם לֹא יִהְיֶה שָׁוֶה עֹנֶשׁ שְׁנֵי הָאֲנָשִׁים, מִטַּעַם שֶׁלֹּא הָיְתָה מַחֲשֶׁבֶת שְׁנֵיהֶם שָׁוָה בְּעֵת עֲשִׂיַּת הֶעָוֹן, וְהַפְּגָם נִמְשָׁךְ בְּהָעוֹלָמוֹת גַּם לְפִי עִנְיַן הַמַּחֲשָׁבָה בִּשְׁעַת הָעֲשִׂיָּה, וְאִם הָאֶחָד הִדְבִּיק יוֹתֵר מַחֲשַׁבְתּוֹ לְהָעֲבֵירָה, וַדַּאי שֶׁהוּא רָאוּי לְעֹנֶשׁ יוֹתֵר גָּדוֹל, כִּי אָז הַפְּגָם מַגִּיעַ חַס וְשָׁלוֹם לְעוֹלָמוֹת יוֹתֵר עֶלְיוֹנִים. וּמִטַּעַם זֶה הַשּׁוֹגֵג עָנְשׁוֹ יוֹתֵר קַל מֵהַמֵּזִיד. וְלָכֵן אָמְרוּ (יומא כ"ט) שֶׁהִרְהוּרֵי עֲבֵרָה קָשִׁין מֵעֲבֵרָה:

זֶהוּ שֶׁכָּתוּב (תהלים שם): "הַיּוֹצֵר יַחַד לִבָּם" (הַיְנוּ שֶׁרוֹאֶה יַחַד מַחְשְׁבוֹת לִבָּם כְּמוֹ שֶׁפֵּרְשׁוּ רַבּוֹתֵינוּ זִכְרוֹנָם לִבְרָכָה בְּמַסֶּכֶת רֹאשׁ הַשָּׁנָה י"ח א') "הַמֵּבִין אֶל כָּל מַעֲשֵׂיהֶם",

רָצָה לוֹמַר שֶׁהַיּוֹצֵר עֶלְיוֹן יִתְבָּרַךְ שְׁמוֹ רוֹאֶה וּמֵבִין מַחְשְׁבוֹת לִבָּם הַמִּצְטָרֵף אֶל מַעֲשֵׂיהֶם, וְדָן אֶת כָּל אֶחָד כְּפִי עִנְיַן מַחְשֶׁבֶת לִבּוֹ שֶׁהָיָה בְּעֵת עֲשִׂיַּת הֶעָוֹן:

וְכֵן אָמַר שְׁלֹמֹה הַמֶּלֶךְ עָלָיו הַשָּׁלוֹם (קהלת יב, יד): "כִּי אֶת כָּל מַעֲשֶׂה הָאֱלֹהִים יָבִא בְמִשְׁפָּט עַל כָּל נֶעְלָם" גו'. רָצָה לוֹמַר שֶׁמִּלְּבַד הָעֹנֶשׁ עַל מַעֲשֵׂה הֶעָוֹן בְּפֹעַל, עוֹד יָבִיא הָאֱלֹהִים יִתְבָּרַךְ שְׁמוֹ בְּמִשְׁפָּט אֶת "כָּל מַעֲשֶׂה", לְגַלְגֵּל עָלֶיהָ לְדוּנָהּ גַּם עַל הַמַּחְשָׁבָה הַנֶּעְלָמָה, אֵיךְ וּבְאֵיזֶה אֹפֶן הָיְתָה בְּעֵת הָעֲשִׂיָּה.

וְכֵן אָמַר (משלי ג' יט): "ה' בְּחָכְמָה יָסַד אָרֶץ כּוֹנֵן שָׁמַיִם בִּתְבוּנָה בְּדַעְתּוֹ תְּהוֹמוֹת נִבְקָעוּ". כָּלַל כָּאן דֶּרֶךְ כְּלָל אֶת כָּל הָעוֹלָמוֹת: "אֶרֶץ" — הוּא עוֹלָם הָאֶמְצָעִי, "שָׁמַיִם" — הֵם כְּלַל הָעוֹלָמוֹת הָעֶלְיוֹנִים, "וּתְהוֹמוֹת" — הֵם כְּלַל הַתַּחְתּוֹנִים.

וְאָמַר אַחַר זֶה: "בְּנִי אַל יָלֻזוּ מֵעֵינֶיךָ", וּלְשׁוֹן "עַיִן" מָצִינוּ כַּמָּה פְּעָמִים בַּמִּקְרָא נֶאֱמַר עַל עִנְיַן הַמַּחְשָׁבָה, כְּמוֹ שֶׁכָּתוּב (קהלת א, טז): "וְלִבִּי רָאָה" גו'. "הֶחָכָם עֵינָיו בְּרֹאשׁוֹ" (שם ב, יד), "וְיָלִיזוּ" — מָצִינוּ בַּמִּשְׁנָה שֶׁהוּא לְשׁוֹן עַקְמוּמִית, כְּמוֹ "נָלוֹז הוּא וּמֵלִיז אֶת אָבִיו שֶׁבַּשָּׁמַיִם עָלָיו" (סוֹף כִּלְאַיִם). זֶהוּ שֶׁכָּתוּב, בְּנִי חוּס נָא וַחֲמֹל עַל עוֹלָמוֹת הַיְקָרִים, שֶׁנִּבְרְאוּ בְּחָכְמָה וּבִתְבוּנָה וּבְדַעַת, וְהִזָּהֵר שֶׁלֹּא תִּגְרֹם חַס וְשָׁלוֹם עִקּוּם וְקִלְקוּל לְכֻלָּם בְּמַחְשָׁבָה אַחַת אֲשֶׁר לֹא טוֹבָה חַס וְשָׁלוֹם:

וְאֵלּוּ הַשְּׁלשָׁה בְּחִינוֹת מַעֲשֶׂה דִּבּוּר מַחְשָׁבָה, הֵן כְּלַל הַבְּחִינוֹת פְּנִימִיּוֹת שֶׁל הָאָדָם, שֶׁהֵם הַשְּׁלשָׁה בְּחִינוֹת נֶפֶשׁ רוּחַ נְשָׁמָה.

כִּי הַמַּעֲשֶׂה — הוּא מִבְּחִינַת הַנֶּפֶשׁ, כְּמוֹ שֶׁכָּתוּב (במדבר טו, ל): "וְהַנֶּפֶשׁ אֲשֶׁר תַּעֲשֶׂה" "הַנְּפָשׁוֹת הָעוֹשׂוֹת" (ויקרא יח, כט), וְהַרְבֵּה כַּיּוֹצֵא. "כִּי הַדָּם הוּא הַנָּפֶשׁ" (דברים יב, כג), שֶׁהַנֶּפֶשׁ שׁוֹרֶה וּמִתְלַבֵּשׁ בְּדַם הָאָדָם, וְלָכֵן עִקַּר מִשְׁכָּנָהּ בַּכָּבֵד, שֶׁהוּא כֻּלּוֹ דָּם, וּמְרוּצַת הַדָּם בְּכָל פְּרָטֵי חֶלְקֵי הָאֵבָרִים, כְּלֵי הַמַּעֲשֶׂה, הוּא הַנּוֹתֵן לָהֶם חִיּוּת הַתְּנוּעָה וְהַהִתְעוֹרְרוּת, שֶׁיּוּכְלוּ לִפְעֹל וְלַעֲשׂוֹת אֶת אֲשֶׁר בְּכֹחָם. וְאִם יִמָּנַע מְרוּצַת הַדָּם מֵאֵבֶר אֶחָד, אוֹתוֹ הָאֵבֶר מִתְיַבֵּשׁ וְאֵין בּוֹ שׁוּם תְּנוּעָה לַעֲשׂוֹת שׁוּם דָּבָר, וְהוּא אֵבֶר מֵת.

וְהַדִּבּוּר — הוּא מִבְּחִינַת הָרוּחַ, כְּמוֹ שֶׁכָּתוּב (ש"ב כ"ג ב): "רוּחַ ה' דִּבֶּר בִּי", "וּבְרוּחַ שְׂפָתָיו" (ישעיה י"א ד), וּכְמוֹ שֶׁתִּרְגֵּם אוּנְקְלוֹס עַל פָּסוּק (בראשית ב' ז): "וַיְהִי הָאָדָם לְנֶפֶשׁ חַיָּה", — לְרוּחַ מְמַלְּלָא. וְכֵן נִרְאֶה לָעַיִן, שֶׁבְּכָל דִּבּוּר שֶׁהָאָדָם מוֹצִיא מִפִּיו, יוֹצֵא רוּחַ וְהֶבֶל מֵהַפֶּה, וּמִשְׁכַּן הָרוּחַ עִקָּרוֹ הוּא בַּלֵּב, כִּי רוּחַ וְהֶבֶל הַדִּבּוּר, עִקָּרוֹ וְרֵאשִׁיתוֹ הוּא עוֹלֶה מֵהַלֵּב.

וּמַחְשָׁבָה — הִיא בְּחִינַת הַנְּשָׁמָה, שֶׁהִיא הַמְלַמֶּדֶת לָאָדָם דֵּעָה וּבִינָה בַּתּוֹרָה הַקְּדוֹשָׁה, לָכֵן עִקַּר מִשְׁכָּנָהּ הוּא בַּמֹּחַ, כְּלִי הַמַּחְשָׁבָה, וְהִיא הַבְּחִינָה הָעֶלְיוֹנָה שֶׁבָּהֶם. וְכֵן אָמְרוּ בִּבְרֵאשִׁית רַבָּה פָּרָשָׁה י"ד: "חֲמִשָּׁה שֵׁמוֹת נִקְרְאוּ לָהּ כו', נֶפֶשׁ — זֶה הַדָּם כו', רוּחַ כו', נְשָׁמָה — זוֹ הָאוֹפְיָה דִּבְרִיָּתָא", רָצָה לוֹמַר דַּעְתּוֹ וּמַחְשַׁבְתּוֹ, כְּמוֹ שֶׁפֵּרְשׁוּ הֶעָרוּךְ וְרַשִׁ"י זִכְרוֹנָם לִבְרָכָה:

פֶּרֶק ט"ו

וְכִי יִפָּלֵא, הֲלֹא "נְשָׁמָה" פֵּרוּשׁוֹ הוּא נְשִׁימָה, וַהֲרֵי נִרְאֶה לָעַיִן שֶׁנְּשִׁימַת הָאָדָם הוּא הַהֶבֶל הָעוֹלֶה מֵהַלֵּב מִמַּטָּה לְמַעְלָה. וְגַם כִּי הֲרֵי הוּא בְּחִינַת אוֹר חוֹזֵר, וְאֵינוֹ בְּחִינָה עֶלְיוֹנָה.

אָמְנָם הָעִנְיָן שֶׁנִּקְרֵאת בִּלְשׁוֹן "נְשִׁימָה", אֵין הַכַּוָּנָה בְּחִינַת נְשִׁימַת הָאָדָם, אֶלָּא כִּבְיָכוֹל נְשִׁימַת פִּיו יִתְבָּרַךְ שְׁמוֹ, כְּמוֹ שֶׁכָּתוּב (בראשית ב, ז): "וַיִּפַּח בְּאַפָּיו נִשְׁמַת חַיִּים".

וּכְבָר הִמְשִׁילוּ רַבּוֹתֵינוּ זִכְרוֹנָם לִבְרָכָה (סנהדרין צא. ריש פֶּרֶק חלק) עִנְיַן הִשְׁתַּלְשְׁלוּת הָרוּחַ חַיִּים בָּאָדָם – לַעֲשִׂיַּת כְּלֵי זְכוּכִית, לְעִנְיַן תְּחִיַּת הַמֵּתִים, וְאָמְרוּ: "קַל וָחֹמֶר מִכְּלֵי זְכוּכִית שֶׁעֲמָלָן בְּרוּחַ בָּשָׂר וָדָם כו', בָּשָׂר וָדָם שֶׁבְּרוּחוֹ שֶׁל הַקָּדוֹשׁ בָּרוּךְ הוּא עַל אַחַת כַּמָּה וְכַמָּה". וְכֵן הוּא בְּשׁוֹחֵר טוֹב תְּהִלִּים מִזְמוֹר ב', עַיֵּן שָׁם.

כִּי הַנִּדּוֹן דּוֹמֶה לָרְאָיָה, שֶׁכְּשֶׁנַּבְחִין בִּנְשִׁימַת פִּי הָאוּמָן בִּכְלִי הַזְּכוּכִית בְּעֵת עֲשִׂיָּתוֹ, נִמְצָא בּוֹ שְׁלֹשָׁה בְּחִינוֹת. בְּחִינָה הָרִאשׁוֹנָה הוּא כְּשֶׁנְּשִׁימַת הַהֶבֶל הוּא עֲדַיִן תּוֹךְ פִּיו, קֹדֶם בֹּאוֹ לְתוֹךְ חֲלַל הַשְּׁפוֹפֶרֶת הַחֲלוּלָה, אֵין לִקְרוֹתָהּ אָז אֶלָּא בְּשֵׁם "נְשִׁימָה". וְהַבְּחִינָה הַשֵּׁנִית – כְּשֶׁנִּכְנָס הַהֶבֶל וּבָא לְתוֹךְ הַשְּׁפוֹפֶרֶת וְנִמְשֶׁכֶת כְּמוֹ קַו, אָז נִקְרָא "רוּחַ". וְהַבְּחִינָה הַשְּׁלִישִׁית הַתַּחְתּוֹנָה – הוּא כְּשֶׁיּוֹצֵא הָרוּחַ מֵהַשְּׁפוֹפֶרֶת לְתוֹךְ הַזְּכוּכִית, וּמִתְפַּשֶּׁטֶת בְּתוֹכָהּ, עַד שֶׁנַּעֲשֵׂית כְּלִי כְּפִי רְצוֹן הַמְּזַגֵּג, אָז מַכְלִיא רוּחוֹ, וְנִקְרָא אָז "נֶפֶשׁ", לְשׁוֹן שְׁבִיתָה וּמְנוּחָה:

כֵּן בְּדִמְיוֹן זֶה, הוּא עִנְיַן הַשְּׁלֹשָׁה בְּחִינוֹת נר"ן, שֶׁמֻּשְׁפָּעִים כִּבְיָכוֹל מִנְּשִׁימַת פִּיו יִתְבָּרַךְ שְׁמוֹ, שֶׁבְּחִינַת הַנֶּפֶשׁ – הִיא הַבְּחִינָה הַתַּחְתּוֹנָה, שֶׁהִיא כֻּלָּהּ בְּתוֹךְ גּוּף הָאָדָם.

וּבְחִינַת הָרוּחַ – הוּא בָּא דֶּרֶךְ עֵרוּי מִלְמַעְלָה, שֶׁחֵלֶק וְקָצֶה הָעֶלְיוֹן שֶׁלּוֹ קָשׁוּר וְנֶאֱחָז לְמַעְלָה בַּבְּחִינָה הַתַּחְתּוֹנָה שֶׁל הַנְּשָׁמָה, וּמִשְׁתַּלְשֶׁלֶת וְנִכְנֶסֶת גַּם בְּתוֹךְ גּוּף הָאָדָם, וּמִתְקַשֶּׁרֶת שָׁם בַּבְּחִינָה הָעֶלְיוֹנָה שֶׁל הַנֶּפֶשׁ, כְּמוֹ שֶׁכָּתוּב (ישעיה לב, טו): "עַד יֵעָרֶה עָלֵינוּ רוּחַ מִמָּרוֹם", "אֶשְׁפּוֹךְ אֶת רוּחִי" וגו' (יואל ג, א), שֶׁהוּא מֻשְׁפָּע בָּאָדָם דֶּרֶךְ שְׁפִיכָה וְעֵרוּי כַּנַּ"ל, וּכְמוֹ שֶׁיִּתְבָּאֵר עוֹד לְהַלָּן אי"ה [פי"ז] עִנְיַן הִתְקַשְּׁרוּתָם בְּאֹרֶךְ:

אָמְנָם בְּחִינַת הַנְּשָׁמָה – הִיא הַנְּשִׁימָה עַצְמָהּ שֶׁפְּנִימִיּוּת עַצְמוּתָהּ מִסְתַּתֶּרֶת בְּהֶעְלֵם, וּמְקוֹרָהּ בָּרוּךְ כִּבְיָכוֹל בְּתוֹךְ נְשִׁימַת פִּיו יִתְבָּרַךְ שְׁמוֹ, שֶׁאֵין עַצְמוּת מַהוּתָהּ נִכְנֶסֶת כְּלָל בְּתוֹךְ גּוּף הָאָדָם. וְאָדָם הָרִאשׁוֹן – קֹדֶם הַחֵטְא – זָכָה לְעַצְמוּתָהּ, וּבְסִבַּת הַחֵטְא נִסְתַּלְּקָה מִתּוֹכוֹ, וְנִשְׁאֲרָה רַק חוֹפֶפֶת עָלָיו.

לְבַד מֹשֶׁה רַבֵּנוּ עָלָיו הַשָּׁלוֹם, שֶׁזָּכָה לְעַצְמוּתָהּ תּוֹךְ גּוּפוֹ, וְלָכֵן נִקְרָא "אִישׁ הָאֱלֹקִים" (דברים לג, א), כַּיָּדוּעַ שֶׁבְּכָל שְׁלֹשָׁה עוֹלָמוֹת, בְּרִיאָה יְצִירָה עֲשִׂיָּה, מִבְּחִינַת הַנְּשָׁמָה דִּלְהוֹן וּלְמַעְלָה, הוּא אֱלֹקוּת גָּמוּר, כְּמוֹ שֶׁכָּתוּב בְּעֵץ חַיִּים שַׁעַר הַצֶּלֶם פֶּרֶק א', וּבְרֵישׁ שַׁעַר צִיּוּר עוֹלָמוֹת אֲצִילוּת בְּרִיאָה יְצִירָה עֲשִׂיָּה, בְּהַקְדָּמַת הר"ח ויטל זִכְרוֹנוֹ לִבְרָכָה, וּבְשַׁעַר הַשֵּׁמוֹת פֶּרֶק א'.

וְזוּלָתוֹ לֹא זָכָה אֵלֶיהָ שׁוּם אָדָם, רַק בְּהִירוּת נִצוֹצֵי אוֹר מִתְנוֹצְצִים מִמֶּנָּה, עַל רֹאשׁ הָאָדָם הַזּוֹכֶה אֵלֶיהָ, כָּל אֶחָד לְפִי מַדְרֵגָתוֹ וּלְפוּם שִׁעוּרָא דִּילֵיהּ.

וְעַיֵּן רַעְיָא מְהֵימְנָא נָשֹׂא קכ"ג ב': "וַיִּפַּח בְּאַפָּיו נִשְׁמַת חַיִּים, דָּא אִיהִי דְּיוֹקְנָא דְּעַל בַּר נַשׁ" כו', וּבְזֹהַר חָדָשׁ רוּת ס"ד ע"ג: "וְאִי זָכֵי כו', כְּדֵין נָחֲתָא עֲלֵיהּ רְבוּ יַתִּיר מִלְעֵלָּא כו', אִתְעַר עֲלֵיהּ מִלְעֵלָּא אִתְעָרוּ קַדִּישָׁא, וְשַׁרְיָא עֲלֵיהּ דְּבַר נַשׁ, וְסַחֲרָא לֵיהּ מִכָּל סִטְרִין. וְהַהוּא אִתְעָרוּ דְּשַׁרְיָא עֲלֵיהּ, מֵאֲתַר עִלָּאָה הוּא, וּמַאי שְׁמֵיהּ, נְשָׁמָה שְׁמֵיהּ". [וְאִם זוֹכֶה וכו' אָז יוֹרֶדֶת עָלָיו גַּדְלוּת יְתֵרָה מִלְּמַעְלָה וכו' מִתְעוֹרֶרֶת עָלָיו מִלְּמַעְלָה הִתְעוֹרְרוּת קְדֻשָּׁה וְשׁוֹרָה עַל הָאָדָם וּמְסַבַּבְתּוֹ מִכָּל הַצְּדָדִים, וְאוֹתָהּ הִתְעוֹרְרוּת הַשּׁוֹרָה עָלָיו, מִמָּקוֹם עֶלְיוֹן הִיא. וּמַה שְּׁמָהּ, נְשָׁמָה שְׁמָהּ] עַיֵּן שָׁם.

וְהִיא הַנּוֹתֶנֶת לְהָאָדָם בִּינָה יְתֵרָה, לְהַשְׂכִּיל הַשִּׂכְלִיּוֹת הַפְּנִימִיִּים הַגְּנוּזִים בְּתוֹרָה הַקְּדוֹשָׁה. וּכְמוֹ שֶׁכָּתוּב בס"ת לֶךְ לְךָ ע"ט ב': "נְשָׁמָה אִתְעָרַת לְאֵינַשׁ בְּבִינָה". וּבְזֹהַר חָדָשׁ רוּת ס"ד א': "וְאִתְעַר בֵּיהּ בְּחָכְמְתָא עִלָּאָה" כו'.

וְעַיֵּן בְּעֵץ חַיִּים (שַׁעַר מוֹחִין דְּקַטְנוּת פֶּרֶק ג') ז"ל: "אָמְנָם לֹא כָּל אָדָם זוֹכֶה לָזֶה. וְדַע כִּי מִי שֶׁיֵּשׁ בְּיָדוֹ כֹּחַ בְּמַעֲשָׂיו כו' אָז יִהְיֶה לוֹ זְכִירָה נִפְלָאָה בַּתּוֹרָה, וְיָבִין כָּל רָזֵי הַתּוֹרָה כו' וְיִתְגַּלּוּ לוֹ רָזֵי הַתּוֹרָה כְּתִקּוּנָן", עַד כָּאן. וְעַיֵּן לְהַלָּן [פֶּרֶק ט"ז] הָעִנְיָן בְּשָׁרְשׁוֹ הָעֶלְיוֹן, וְתָבִין.

וְזֶהוּ שֶׁאָמַר הַכָּתוּב (אִיּוֹב ל"ב ח): "אָכֵן רוּחַ הִיא בֶאֱנוֹשׁ וְנִשְׁמַת שַׁדַּי תְּבִינֵם", רָצָה לוֹמַר, שֶׁבְּחִינַת הָרוּחַ הוּא מִשְׁתַּלְשֵׁל וּמֻשְׁפָּע וְנִכְנָס בְּתוֹךְ הָאָדָם, אֲבָל הַנְּשָׁמָה שֶׁהִיא "נִשְׁמַת שַׁדַּי", רָצָה לוֹמַר, נְשִׁימַת פִּיו יִתְבָּרַךְ, אֵין עַצְמוּתָהּ מֻשְׁפָּע וּמִתְגַּלָּה בְּתוֹךְ הָאָדָם, כִּי הִיא מְרוֹמִים תִּשְׁכֹּן, בְּתוֹךְ פִּיו יִתְבָּרַךְ כִּבְיָכוֹל, רַק שֶׁהִיא הַנּוֹתֶנֶת לוֹ בִּינָה בְּנִצוֹצֵי אוֹרָהּ עָלָיו, לְהַשְׂכִּילוֹ בְּעִמְקֵי מַצְפּוּנֵי הַתּוֹרָה הַקְּדוֹשָׁה.

וּמַה שֶּׁכָּתוּב בַּזֹּהַר וְהַמְקֻבָּלִים זִכְרוֹנָם לִבְרָכָה, שֶׁבְּחִינַת הַנְּשָׁמָה מִשְׁכָּנָהּ בְּמֹחַ הָאָדָם, כַּוָּנָתָם זִכְרוֹנָם לִבְרָכָה עַל הַנִּצוֹצֵי זִיו אוֹרָהּ הַמַּשְׂכֶּלֶת מֹחוֹ וְשִׂכְלוֹ, לֹא עַצְמוּתָהּ מַמָּשׁ.

וְעִקַּר כַּוָּנָתָם זִכְרוֹנָם לִבְרָכָה, עַל בְּחִינַת שְׁלֹשָׁה רֵישִׁין שֶׁל הָרוּחַ סוֹד הַמֹּחִין, שֶׁהֵן פְּעָמִים מִתְנוֹצְצִים פְּעָמִים מִסְתַּלְּקִין, וּבָאִים בְּסוֹד תּוֹסֶפֶת לְמִי שֶׁזּוֹכֶה לָזֶה, כַּיָּדוּעַ, לֹא עַל בְּחִינַת הַנְּשָׁמָה הָעִקָּרִית. וְכֵן כָּתַב רַבֵּנוּ הַגָּדוֹל הַגָּאוֹן הֶחָסִיד מוהר"א זִכְרוֹנוֹ לִבְרָכָה בְּבֵאוּרוֹ עַל הַהֵיכָלוֹת בְּהֵיכָלָא תִּנְיָנָא.

וְהַכֹּל אֶחָד, שֶׁבְּחִינָה הַתַּחְתּוֹנָה שֶׁל הַנְּשָׁמָה הַמִּתְנוֹצֶצֶת בְּדַעוֹ וְשִׂכְלוֹ לְהַשְׂכִּילוֹ, הִיא הִיא הַשְּׁלֹשָׁה רֵישִׁין שֶׁל הָרוּחַ בְּמוֹחִין שֶׁלּוֹ, כְּמוֹ שֶׁיִּתְבָּאֵר לְפָנֵינוּ אי"ה:

פֶּרֶק ט"ז

וְהַמַּשְׂכִּילִים יָבִינוּ, שֶׁכֵּן הוּא הָעִנְיָן גַּם בְּשָׁרְשׁוֹ הָעֶלְיוֹן. שֶׁרַק בְּחִינָה הַתַּחְתּוֹנָה שֶׁל אֵם הַבָּנִים, סוֹד נִשְׁמַת חַיִּים עִלָּאָה, הִיא נִכְנֶסֶת וּמִתְפַּשֶּׁטֶת בִּפְנִימִיּוּת הָאָדָם הָעֶלְיוֹן בְּסוֹד תּוֹסֶפֶת, אַחַר הַתִּקּוּן, עַל יְדֵי מַעֲשֵׂי הַתַּחְתּוֹנִים הָרְצוּיִים.

וְהוּא סוֹד הַמּוֹחִין קַדִּישִׁין, ג' רֵישִׁין דִּילֵיהּ, שֶׁעִקָּרוֹ הוּא ו"ק כַּיָּדוּעַ, כַּמְבֹאָר לַמֵּבִין בְּעֵץ חַיִּים שַׁעַר או"א פֶּרֶק ח', וּבְשַׁעַר פִּרְטֵי עי"מ, וּבְשַׁעַר הַזִּוּוּגִים רֵישׁ פֶּרֶק ד', וּבְסוֹף שַׁעַר מוֹחִין דְּצֶלֶם, וּבְשַׁעַר דְּרוּשֵׁי הַצֶּלֶם דְּרוּשׁ ב', עַיֵּן שָׁם הֵיטֵב בְּכָל הַדְּרוּשׁ, וּבִדְרוּשׁ ח' שָׁם, וּבִפְרִי עֵץ חַיִּים פֶּרֶק ג' מִשַּׁעַר הַתְּפִלִּין, וּבְשַׁעַר הַיִּחוּדִים פֶּרֶק ה' מִתִּקּוּן עֲוֹנוֹת.

וְהוּא שֶׁאָמְרוּ שֶׁהַנְּשָׁמָה שׁוֹרָה בַּמֹּחַ, כְּמוֹ שֶׁכָּתַב שָׁם בְּשַׁעַר אנ"ך פֶּרֶק ו', וּבְשַׁעַר הַמֹּחִין בְּכָל פֶּרֶק ז', וּבְפֶרֶק ח', וּבְפֶרֶק י"ב, וּבְשַׁעַר דְּרוּשֵׁי הַצֶּלֶם רֵישׁ דְּרוּשׁ ב'. וְיוֹתֵר מְבֹאָר הָעִנְיָן שָׁם בְּהַגָּהַת הרח"ו ז"ל, וּבְשַׁעַר הַפַּרְצוּפִים רֵישׁ פֶּרֶק א'. וּבְשַׁעַר פְּנִימִיּוּת וְחִיצוֹנִיּוּת דְּרוּשׁ ד' וּדְרוּשׁ ט', וּבְשַׁעַר קְלִפַּת נֹגַהּ רֵישׁ פֶּרֶק א'. וְהוּא מְבֹאָר לַמְּדַקְדֵּק הֵיטֵב בְּכָל דְּרוּשֵׁי הַצֶּלֶם.

וּקְצָתָהּ חוֹפֵף וּמַקִּיף וּמֵאִיר עַל רֹאשׁוֹ בְּקֵרוּב מָקוֹם, סוֹד "בָּעֲטָרָה שֶׁעִטְּרָה לוֹ אִמּוֹ" (שה"ש ג, יא), בְּסוֹד הַנְּשִׁימָה וְהַהֶבֶל הַיּוֹצֵא "מִפֶּה" אִמָּא, לְאוֹר מַקִּיף אֵלָיו. כְּמוֹ שֶׁכָּתוּב בְּעֵץ חַיִּים שַׁעַר הַכְּלָלִים סוֹף פֶּרֶק י"א, וּבְלִקּוּטֵי תַּנַ"ךְ בִּתְהִלִּים (נג, ד) בְּפָסוּק כֻּלּוֹ סָג כו', כְּמוֹ שֶׁנִּתְבָּאֵר לְעֵיל, שֶׁבְּחִינַת הַנְּשָׁמָה הִיא נְשִׁימַת "הַפֶּה הָעֶלְיוֹן", אֲבָל עִקָּרָהּ הִיא כֻּלָּהּ לְמַעְלָה, גְּנוּזָה וְנֶעֱלָמָה בִּמְקוֹרָהּ הָעֶלְיוֹן בְּתוֹךְ הַפֶּה, וּמֵאִיר בְּרִחוּק מָקוֹם:

וּבָזֶה יוּבַן כַּוָּנָתָם זִכְרוֹנָם לִבְרָכָה בִּשְׁמוֹת רַבָּה פָּרָשָׁה מ"א, עַל פָּסוּק "כִּי ה' יִתֵּן חָכְמָה מִפִּיו דַּעַת וּתְבוּנָה" (משלי ב, ו), שֶׁאָמְרוּ: "לְמָה הַדָּבָר דּוֹמֶה, לְמֶלֶךְ שֶׁהָיָה לוֹ בֵּן, בָּא בְּנוֹ מִבֵּית הַסֵּפֶר מָצָא תַּמְחוּי לִפְנֵי אָבִיו, נָטַל אָבִיו חֲתִיכָה אַחַת וּנְתָנָהּ לוֹ כו', אָמַר לוֹ אֵינִי מְבַקֵּשׁ אֶלָּא מִמַּה שֶּׁבְּתוֹךְ פִּיךָ, מֶה עָשָׂה, נְתָנוֹ לוֹ" כו'. הַיְנוּ, שֶׁבַּקָּשַׁת הַבֵּן יַקִּיר לְהַשִּׂיג, שֶׁיֻּשְׁפַּע בּוֹ מִנִּצוֹצֵי אוֹר בְּחִינַת הַנְּשָׁמָה, אֲשֶׁר מְקוֹרָהּ נֶעֱלָמָה בִּנְשִׁימַת "פִּיו" יִתְבָּרַךְ שְׁמוֹ.

וְרָמְזוּ עוֹד בִּלְשׁוֹנָם הַקָּדוֹשׁ, שֶׁהִמְשִׁילוּ לְתִינוֹק הַבָּא מִ'בֵּית הַסֵּפֶר' דַּוְקָא, הוֹדִיעוּ נֶאֱמָנָה, שֶׁאֵין מָבוֹא בָּעוֹלָם לְהַשִּׂיג בְּחִינַת נִצוֹצֵי אוֹר הַנְּשָׁמָה, אִם לֹא עַל יְדֵי הָעֵסֶק וְהָעִיּוּן וְהִתְבּוֹנְנוּת בַּתּוֹרָה הַקְּדוֹשָׁה בִּקְדֻשָּׁה, כִּי שְׁנֵיהֶם מִמָּקוֹר אֶחָד בָּאִים, כַּיָּדוּעַ לַמֵּבִין:

וְזֶהוּ שֶׁאָמְרוּ שָׁם (בשמו"ר), בְּשָׁעָה שֶׁעָמְדוּ יִשְׂרָאֵל עַל הַר סִינַי לְקַבֵּל אֶת הַתּוֹרָה, הָיוּ מְבַקְּשִׁים לִשְׁמֹעַ הַדִּבְּרוֹת "מִפִּי" הַקָּדוֹשׁ בָּרוּךְ הוּא, וּכְמוֹ שֶׁכָּתוּב (שה"ש א, ב): "יִשָּׁקֵנִי מִנְּשִׁיקוֹת פִּיהוּ".

שֶׁבְּעֵת הַמַּעֲמָד הַמְקֻדָּשׁ, זָכוּ כֻּלָּם, שֶׁהָיָה חוֹפֵף וּמֵאִיר עֲלֵיהֶם, זִיו נִצוֹצֵי זֹהַר בְּחִינַת הַנְּשָׁמָה, מִנִּשְׁמַת פִּיו יִתְבָּרַךְ כִּבְיָכוֹל. וְהוּא סוֹד הַכְּתָרִים שֶׁזָּכוּ בְּסִינַי (שבת פח, א), "וְשִׂמְחַת עוֹלָם עַל רֹאשָׁם", (ישעיה לה, י. נא, יא).

וְעַל יְדֵי כָךְ, זָכוּ לְהַשִּׂיג סִתְרֵי פְּנִימִיּוּת נִשְׁמַת הַתּוֹרָה הַקְּדוֹשָׁה, כְּמוֹ שֶׁכָּתוּב בַּזֹּהַר בְּהַעֲלוֹתְךָ קנ"ב א': "אוֹרַיְתָא אִית לָהּ גּוּפָא כו', חַכִּימִין עַבְדֵי דְּמַלְכָּא עִלָּאָה, אִנּוּן דְּקָיְמוּ בְּטוּרָא דְּסִינַי, לָא מִסְתַּכְּלֵי אֶלָּא בְּנִשְׁמָתָא, דְּאִיהוּ עִקָּרָא דְּכֹלָּא אוֹרַיְתָא מַמָּשׁ". [הַתּוֹרָה יֵשׁ לָהּ גּוּף וכו', הַחֲכָמִים עַבְדֵי הַמֶּלֶךְ הָעֶלְיוֹן – אוֹתָם שֶׁעָמְדוּ בְּהַר סִינַי – אֵינָם מִסְתַּכְּלִים אֶלָּא בַּנְּשָׁמָה (שֶׁבַּתּוֹרָה), שֶׁהוּא עִקַּר כָּל הַתּוֹרָה מַמָּשׁ.]

וְהוּא שֶׁאָמְרוּ בְּכַמָּה מְקוֹמוֹת בְּמִדְרַשׁ רַבָּה: "זַיִן הָיָה לָהֶם בְּסִינַי וְשֵׁם הַמְּפֹרָשׁ חָקוּק עָלָיו", שֶׁהוּא הַהַשָּׂגָה עֶלְיוֹנָה בְּנִשְׁמְתָא וְסִתְרִין דְּאוֹרַיְתָא, שְׁמָא מְפֹרָשׁ:

כִּי כֵן הָיָה הָעִנְיָן אָז לְמַעְלָה בְּשָׁרְשׁוֹ הָעֶלְיוֹן, כַּנַּ"ל בְּפֶרֶק הָעֲבָר, סוֹד "בָּעֲטָרָה שֶׁעִטְּרָה לוֹ אִמּוֹ" (שה"ש ג, יא), וְדָרְשׁוּ עַל זֶה בְּחָזִית (שהש"ר): "בְּיוֹם חֲתֻנָּתוֹ" — זֶה סִינַי, "וּבְיוֹם שִׂמְחַת לִבּוֹ" — אֵלּוּ דִּבְרֵי תוֹרָה. וְזֶהוּ "בָּעֲטָרָה" כו', הֵם הַכְּתָרִים הַנַּ"ל שֶׁהָיוּ בְּסִינַי, חַיֵּי הַמֶּלֶךְ. וְעַיֵּן בְּעֵץ חַיִּים שַׁעַר הַכְּלָלִים סוֹף פֶּרֶק ה':

פֶּרֶק י"ז

וּנְבָאֵר עִנְיַן הִתְקַשְּׁרוּת הַשְּׁלֹשָׁה בְּחִינוֹת נר"ן אֶחָד בַּחֲבֵרוֹ. וְהוּא יְסוֹד וְעִקַּר עִנְיַן הַתְּשׁוּבָה. וְזֶה כָּל פְּרִי הָסֵר הַחַטָּאוֹת מִנֶּפֶשׁ הַחוֹטֵאת, וּלְטַהֲרָהּ מֵחֶלְאַת טֻמְאָתָהּ.

וְיִתְבּוֹנֵן הָאָדָם כַּמָּה הוּא צָרִיךְ לְהַשְׁגִּיחַ וּלְהִתְבּוֹנֵן עַל כָּל פְּרָטֵי עִנְיְנֵי עֲבוֹדָתוֹ לְבוֹרְאוֹ יִתְבָּרַךְ שְׁמוֹ, שֶׁתְּהֵא עֲבוֹדָתוֹ תַּמָּה וּשְׁלֵמָה, קְדוֹשָׁה וּטְהוֹרָה. וְיִרְאֶה לְפַשְׁפֵּשׁ וּלְמַשְׁמֵשׁ תָּמִיד בְּכָל מַעֲשָׂיו וְדִבּוּרָיו וּמַחְשְׁבוֹתָיו, שֶׁהֵם הַשְּׁלֹשָׁה בְּחִינוֹת הַנַּ"ל, אוּלַי לֹא הִשְׁלִים עֲדַיִן חֶפְצוֹ וּרְצוֹנוֹ יִתְבָּרַךְ, לְפִי שֹׁרֶשׁ נִשְׁמָתוֹ, בְּהַשָּׂגָה, וְכָל יָמָיו יוֹסִיף אֹמֶץ בְּתוֹרָה וּמִצְוֹת, לְהַשְׁלִים נַפְשׁוֹ וְרוּחוֹ וְנִשְׁמָתוֹ מְטֹהָרִים כַּאֲשֶׁר נְתָנָם, אַחַר שֶׁיִּרְאֶה בְּעֵין שִׂכְלוֹ אֵיךְ שֶׁחָפֵץ הוּא יִתְבָּרַךְ בְּחַסְדּוֹ הַגָּדוֹל לְהֵטִיב אַחֲרִיתוֹ, וְשׁוֹקֵד עַל תַּקָּנַת הַנֶּפֶשׁ הַחוֹטֵאת, שֶׁגַּם אִם כְּבָר נִטְבְּעָה בְּעֹמֶק מְצוּלוֹת הָרַע, עִם כָּל זֶה תַּחֲזֹר כָּל דָּבָר לִמְקוֹמוֹ וּמְקוֹרוֹ, בִּלְתִּי יִדַּח מִמֶּנּוּ נִדָּח:

וְהָעִנְיָן, כִּי יָדוּעַ בְּסֵדֶר הִשְׁתַּלְשְׁלוּת הָעוֹלָמוֹת, שֶׁהַבְּחִינָה הָעֶלְיוֹנָה שֶׁבְּכָל עוֹלָם, מִתְקַשֵּׁר עִם הַבְּחִינָה הַתַּחְתּוֹנָה שֶׁל הָעוֹלָם שֶׁעָלָיו. וְעַיֵּן זֹהַר וַיִּקְרָא י' ע"ב: "דְּכֻלְּהוּ עָלְמִין מִתְקַשְּׁרָן דָּא בְּדָא וְדָא בְּדָא, כְּהַאי שַׁלְשֶׁלֶת דְּאִתְקַשַּׁר דָּא בְּדָא". וְכַיָּדוּעַ בְּכִתְבֵי הָאֲרִיזַ"ל שֶׁחִיצוֹנִיּוּת מַלְכוּת שֶׁל כָּל עוֹלָם וּפַרְצוּף, נַעֲשֶׂה פְּנִימִיּוּת כֶּתֶר לְהָעוֹלָם אוֹ הַפַּרְצוּף שֶׁתַּחְתָּיו, (הַיְנוּ שֶׁבְּקַבָּלַת הָאָדָם עַל מַלְכוּתוֹ יִתְבָּרַךְ, לְהַעֲלוֹת כָּל מַעֲשָׂיו וְדִבּוּרָיו וּמַחְשְׁבוֹתָיו בַּתּוֹרָה וּמִצְוֹת לְמַדְרֵגָה יוֹתֵר גְּבוֹהָה, מִזֶּה נַעֲשֶׂה לוֹ רָצוֹן פְּנִימִי, לְשַׁעְבֵּד מֹחוֹ וְדִבּוּרוֹ וּמַעֲשָׂיו בַּתּוֹרָה וּמִצְווֹת), בְּסוֹד כֶּתֶר מַלְכוּת.

וְכֵן הוּא הָעִנְיָן הַשְּׁלֹשָׁה הַבְּחִינוֹת נר"ן שֶׁל הָאָדָם. כִּי כָּל בְּחִינָה מִדָּבָר שֶׁבִּקְדֻשָּׁה, כָּלוּל מֵעֶשֶׂר בְּחִינוֹת פְּרָטִיִּים, שֶׁהֵם הָעֶשֶׂר סְפִירוֹת שֶׁלּוֹ. וְהַבְּחִינָה הָעֶלְיוֹנָה שֶׁל הַנֶּפֶשׁ, נֶאֱחֶזֶת וּמִתְקַשֶּׁרֶת עִם הַבְּחִינָה הַתַּחְתּוֹנָה הָעֲשִׂירִית שֶׁל בְּחִינַת הָרוּחַ, וְהַבְּחִינָה הָעֶלְיוֹנָה שֶׁל הָרוּחַ מִתְקַשֶּׁרֶת עִם בְּחִינָה הַתַּחְתּוֹנָה שֶׁל הַנְּשָׁמָה, וְהַנְּשָׁמָה גַּם כֵּן מִתְקַשֶּׁרֶת וּמִתְדַּבֶּקֶת בִּבְחִינַת שֹׁרֶשׁ הַנְּשָׁמָה, סוֹד כְּנֶסֶת יִשְׂרָאֵל, שֶׁהִיא שֹׁרֶשׁ הַכְּנֵסִיָּה שֶׁל כָּל נִשְׁמוֹת כְּלַל יִשְׂרָאֵל יַחַד. וְכֵן עַל זֶה הַדֶּרֶךְ גַּם בְּחִינַת שֹׁרֶשׁ הַנְּשָׁמָה גַּם כֵּן מִתְקַשֶּׁרֶת לְמַעְלָה מַעְלָה, מִמַּדְרֵגָה לְמַדְרֵגָה, עַד עַצְמוּת אֵין סוֹף בָּרוּךְ הוּא.

וְזֶהוּ שֶׁאָמְרָה אֲבִיגַיִל לְדָוִד (שמו"א כה, כט) "וְהָיְתָה נֶפֶשׁ אֲדֹנִי צְרוּרָה בִּצְרוֹר הַחַיִּים אֵת ה' אֱלֹקֶיךָ", רָצָה לוֹמַר, שֶׁגַּם בְּחִינַת "נַפְשׁוֹ" תִּתְדַּבֵּק כִּבְיָכוֹל בּוֹ יִתְבָּרַךְ שְׁמוֹ.

וּכְמוֹ שֶׁכָּתוּב בַּזֹּהַר תְּרוּמָה קמ"ב ב': "כַּד הַהִיא רוּחַ סָלְקָא וְאִתְעַטְּרָא כו', הַהִיא נֶפֶשׁ מִתְקַשְּׁרָא בְּהַהִיא רוּחַ, וְאִתְנְהִירַת מִנֵּיהּ כו', וְרוּחַ מִתְקַשְּׁרָא גּוֹ הַהִיא נִשְׁמָתָא, וְהַהִיא נִשְׁמָתָא מִתְקַשְּׁרָא גּוֹ סוֹף מַחֲשָׁבָה דְּאִיהִי רָזָא, וְהַהִיא נֶפֶשׁ אִתְקַשְּׁרַת גּוֹ הַהוּא רוּחַ עִלָּאָה, וְהַהוּא רוּחַ אִתְקַשַּׁר גּוֹ הַהִיא נְשָׁמָה עִלָּאָה, וְהַהוּא נְשָׁמָה אִתְקַשְּׁרַת בְּאֵין סוֹף, וּכְדֵין אִיהוּ נַיְחָא דְּכֹלָּא וְקִשּׁוּרָא דְּכֹלָּא, עֵלָּא וְתַתָּא כֻּלָּא בְּרָזָא חֲדָא כו', וּכְדֵין אִיהוּ נַיְחָא דְּנֶפֶשׁ דִּלְתַתָּא, וְעַל דָּא כְּתִיב: "וְהָיְתָה נֶפֶשׁ אֲדוֹנִי צְרוּרָה בִּצְרוֹר הַחַיִּים אֵת ה' אֱלֹהֶיךָ". [כְּשֶׁהָרוּחַ הַהִיא עוֹלָה וּמִתְעַטֶּרֶת וכו' נֶפֶשׁ הַהִיא מִתְקַשֶּׁרֶת בָּרוּחַ הַהִיא וְנַעֲשֵׂת מוּאֶרֶת מִמֶּנּוּ וכו' וְהָרוּחַ מִתְקַשֵּׁר בַּנְּשָׁמָה הַהִיא, וּנְשָׁמָה הַהִיא מִתְקַשֶּׁרֶת תּוֹךְ סוֹף הַמַּחְשָׁבָה שֶׁהִיא סוֹד, וְנֶפֶשׁ הַהִיא מִתְקַשֶּׁרֶת בָּרוּחַ הַהוּא הָעֶלְיוֹן, וְרוּחַ הַהוּא מִתְקַשֵּׁר בַּנְּשָׁמָה הַהִיא הָעֶלְיוֹנָה, וּנְשָׁמָה הַהִיא מִתְקַשֶּׁרֶת בְּאֵין סוֹף, וְאָז הִיא מְנוּחָה לַכֹּל וְקֶשֶׁר הַכֹּל לְמַעְלָה וּלְמַטָּה הַכֹּל בְּסוֹד אֶחָד וכו' וְאָז הִיא מְנוּחַת הַנֶּפֶשׁ לְמַטָּה.]

וּבְפָרָשַׁת אַחֲרֵי ע"א ב': תָּאנָא כְּתִיב: "וְהָיְתָה נֶפֶשׁ אֲדוֹנִי צְרוּרָה" גו', "נִשְׁמַת" אֲדוֹנִי מִבָּעֵי לֵיהּ, אֶלָּא כְּמָה דְּאָמְרָן דְּזַכָּאָה חוּלָקֵיהוֹן דְּצַדִּיקַיָּא, דְּכֹלָּא אִתְקַשַּׁר דָּא בְּדָא, נֶפֶשׁ בְּרוּחַ, וְרוּחַ בִּנְשָׁמָה, וּנְשָׁמָה בְּקוּדְשָׁא בְּרִיךְ הוּא, אִשְׁתַּכַּח דְּנֶפֶשׁ צְרוּרָה בִּצְרוֹר הַחַיִּים" כו'. [לָמַדְנוּ כָּתוּב וְהָיְתָה "נֶפֶשׁ" אֲדוֹנִי צְרוּרָה וגו', "נִשְׁמַת" אֲדוֹנִי הָיָה צָרִיךְ לוֹמַר, אֶלָּא כְּמוֹ שֶׁאָמַרְנוּ שֶׁאַשְׁרֵי חֶלְקָם שֶׁל הַצַּדִּיקִים שֶׁהַכֹּל נִקְשָׁר זֶה בָּזֶה, הַנֶּפֶשׁ בָּרוּחַ, וְרוּחַ בַּנְּשָׁמָה, וְהַנְּשָׁמָה בְּקוּדְשָׁא בְּרִיךְ הוּא, נִמְצָא שֶׁהַנֶּפֶשׁ צְרוּרָה בִּצְרוֹר הַחַיִּים]. וְעַיֵּן עוֹד בְּפָרָשַׁת וַיִּקְרָא רֵישׁ דַּף כ"ה.

וְזֶהוּ עִנְיַן "כִּי חֵלֶק ה' עַמּוֹ יַעֲקֹב חֶבֶל נַחֲלָתוֹ", כִּי הֵם כְּחֵלֶק ה', מְדֻבָּקִים כִּבְיָכוֹל בּוֹ יִתְבָּרַךְ שְׁמוֹ, עַל יְדֵי הִתְקַשְּׁרוּת הג' בְּחִינוֹת הַנַּ"ל, כְּחֶבֶל הַקָּשׁוּר לְמַעְלָה, וּמִשְׁתַּלְשֵׁל וְיוֹרֵד עַד לְמַטָּה:

פֶּרֶק י"ח

וְכָל זֶה מֵרֹב טוּבוֹ וְחַסְדּוֹ הַגָּדוֹל יִתְבָּרַךְ שְׁמוֹ, אֲשֶׁר חָפֵץ לְהַצְדִּיקֵנוּ לְהֵטִיב אַחֲרִיתֵנוּ, לָזֹאת הִפְלִיא עֵצָה, וּקְבָעָם בְּעִנְיָן זֶה, שֶׁכָּל בְּחִינָה מֵהַשְּׁלֹשָׁה אֵלּוּ, תִּתְקַשֵּׁר בְּהַבְּחִינָה שֶׁעָלֶיהָ, כְּדֵי שֶׁעַל יְדֵי זֶה יוּכַל הָאָדָם לַעֲלוֹת וּלְהִתְקַשֵּׁר מִמַּטָּה לְמַעְלָה, מְעַט מְעַט, לְפִי רֹב עִסְקוֹ בְּתוֹרָתוֹ וַעֲבוֹדָתוֹ יִתְבָּרַךְ שְׁמוֹ, וְטָהֳרַת לִבּוֹ וְאַהֲבָתוֹ וְיִרְאָתוֹ, עַד שֶׁיַּעֲלֶה וְיִתְדַּבֵּק בִּצְרוֹר הַחַיִּים כִּבְיָכוֹל אֶת ה' אֱלֹקָיו יִתְבָּרַךְ שְׁמוֹ, לְפִי שָׁרְשׁוֹ וּמַדְרֵגָתוֹ.

זֹאת וְעוֹד אַחֶרֶת, כִּי יֵשׁ כַּמָּה עֲוֹנוֹת שֶׁהַנֶּפֶשׁ הַחוֹטֵאת בְּאַחַת מֵהֵנָּה, נִתְחַיְּבָה כָּרֵת אוֹ אֲבַדּוֹן חַס וְשָׁלוֹם. וְעִנְיַן הַכָּרֵת הוּא, שֶׁבְּחִינַת הַנֶּפֶשׁ נִפְסָק וְנִכְרַת מִשָּׁרְשׁוֹ הָעֶלְיוֹן, וְיִנָּתֵק הַחֶבֶל שֶׁהָיָה קָשׁוּר וּמְדֻבָּק בּוֹ עַד הֵנָּה עַל יְדֵי הִתְקַשְּׁרוּת הַנַּ"ל.

וּכְמוֹ שֶׁכָּתוּב בַּזֹּהַר תְּרוּמָה הַנַּ"ל: "וְאִית נַפְשָׁא כו', דִּכְתִיב בָּהּ (ויקרא כב, ג): "וְנִכְרְתָה הַנֶּפֶשׁ הַהִיא מִלְּפָנַי אֲנִי ה'". מַאי מִלְּפָנַי, דְּלָא שַׁרְיָא עֲלָהּ רוּחָא. וְכַד רוּחָא לָא שַׁרְיָא עֲלָהּ, לֵית לָהּ שׁוּתָּפוּ כְּלָל בְּמַה דִּלְעֵלָּא" כו' [וְיֵשׁ נֶפֶשׁ וכו' שֶׁכָּתוּב בָּהּ וְנִכְרְתָה הַנֶּפֶשׁ

הַהִיא מִלְּפָנַי אֲנִי ה'. מַהוּ מִלְּפָנַי, שֶׁלֹּא שׁוֹרֶה עָלָיו הָרוּחַ, וּכְשֶׁהָרוּחַ אֵינָהּ שׁוֹרָה עָלֶיהָ אֵין לָהּ חִבּוּר כְּלָל בְּמַה שֶּׁלְּמַעְלָה וכו']. וְעַיֵּן שָׁם. וְעַיֵּן בְּלִקּוּטֵי תּוֹרָה פָּרָשָׁה בֹּא, וּבִמְכִילְתָּא פָּרָשַׁת בֹּא, וּבְסוֹף פָּרָשַׁת תִּשָּׂא, וּבְסִפְרֵי פָּרָשַׁת בְּהַעֲלוֹתְךָ וּפָרָשַׁת שְׁלַח, "וְנִכְרְתָה" אֵין הַכְּרָתָה אֶלָּא הַפְסָקָה.

וְזֶה שֶׁכָּתוּב (ישעיה נ"ט ב): "כִּי אִם עֲוֹנוֹתֵיכֶם הָיוּ מַבְדִּילִים בֵּינֵיכֶם לְבֵין אֱלֹקֵיכֶם", הַיְנוּ לְבֵין אֱלֹקֵיכֶם מַמָּשׁ כַּנַּ"ל, וְאָז נִטְבַּעַת בְּעִמְקֵי הַטֻּמְאָה וְהַקְּלִפּוֹת רַחֲמָנָא לִיצְלַן.

עַיֵּן בְּעֵץ חַיִּים שַׁעַר כְּלָלוּת אבי"ע רֵישׁ פֶּרֶק א', וּבְשַׁעַר הַיִּחוּדִים סוֹף פֶּרֶק ד', וְשָׁם פֶּרֶק א' מִתִּקּוּנֵי עֲוֹנוֹת, וּבְלִקּוּטֵי תַּנַּ"ךְ בִּישַׁעְיָה בְּפָסוּק "כִּי רוּחַ מִלְּפָנַי יַעֲטֹף" (נז, טז), וּבַגִּלְגּוּלִים סוֹף פֶּרֶק ל"ה. וְכֵן כָּתוּב בְּכִתְבֵי קָדְשׁוֹ שֶׁל רַבֵּינוּ הַגָּדוֹל מוהר"א ז"ל, בְּפֵרוּשׁ עַל הַהֵיכָלוֹת בְּהֵיכְלָא תִּנְיָנָא.

וּלְבַל יִדַּח מִמֶּנּוּ נִדָּח, גָּזְרָה רְצוֹנוֹ יִתְבָּרַךְ, שֶׁלֹּא יִכָּרְתוּ חַס וְשָׁלוֹם לְגַמְרֵי כָּל הָעֲשָׂרָה חֶלְקֵי בְּחִינַת הַנֶּפֶשׁ, רַק הַתִּשְׁעָה בְּחִינוֹת הַתַּחְתּוֹנִים, מֵחָכְמָה דִּילָהּ וּלְמַטָּה הֵם הַנִּכְרָתִים, אֲבָל בְּחִינָה הָעֶלְיוֹנָה סוֹד הַכֶּתֶר דִּילָהּ (א) אֵינָהּ נִכְרֶתֶת, שֶׁמִּצַּד דְּבֵקוּתָהּ וְהִתְקַשְּׁרוּתָהּ עִם בְּחִינַת הָרוּחַ כַּנַּ"ל, (ב) נִדּוֹנֵית כִּבְחִינַת הָרוּחַ שֶׁאֵין בּוֹ כָּרֵת, כְּמוֹ שֶׁכָּתַבְנוּ לְהַלָּן. וְהוּא מֵחֶסֶד הָעֶלְיוֹן בָּרוּךְ הוּא, שֶׁעַל יְדֵי בְּחִינַת הָרוּחַ הַיְנוּ עַל יְדֵי וִדּוּי דְּבָרִים מִלֵּב שֶׁהוּא בְּחִינַת רוּחַ כַּנַּ"ל, יִתְעַלּוּ גַּם הַתִּשְׁעָה בְּחִינוֹת הַנֶּפֶשׁ לְהִתְקַשֵּׁר כֻּלָּם בִּבְחִינַת הָרוּחַ כְּמִקֹּדֶם:

וְכֵן אִם פָּגַם וְקִלְקֵל חַס וְשָׁלוֹם בְּחִינַת הַדִּבּוּר שֶׁלּוֹ עַל יְדֵי עֲוֹנוֹת הַתְּלוּיִם בְּדִבּוּר, בְּלָשׁוֹן הָרַע וְכַיּוֹצֵא, אוֹ שְׁאָרֵי עֲוֹנוֹת הַתְּלוּיִים בְּשָׁרְשָׁם בִּבְחִינַת הָרוּחַ, וְנִתְקַלְקֵל בָּזֶה בְּחִינַת הָרוּחַ, (וְהַגַּם שֶׁאֵין בְּחִינַת הָרוּחַ נִכְרַת כְּלָל, כִּי לֹא מָצִינוּ בַּתּוֹרָה עִנְיַן הַכָּרֵת רַק אֵצֶל בְּחִינַת הַנֶּפֶשׁ לְבַד, "וְנִכְרְתָה הַנֶּפֶשׁ הַהִיא" (ויקרא כב, ג), "וְנִכְרְתוּ הַנְּפָשׁוֹת הָעֹשֹׂת" (שם יח, יט) וְכַיּוֹצֵא הַרְבֵּה, וְכֵן כָּתַב בְּלִקּוּטֵי תּוֹרָה פָּרָשַׁת בֹּא שָׁם, וּבְפֶרֶק ו' מֵהַגִּלְגּוּלִים וּבְסוֹפוֹ שָׁם, עִם כָּל זֶה עַל יְדֵי הָעֲוֹנוֹת הַתְּלוּיִים בְּשָׁרְשָׁם בִּבְחִינַת "הָרוּחַ", הוּא מְקַלְקְלוֹ וּפוֹגְמוֹ, וּמַגְבִּיר לְעֻמַּת זֶה כֹּחַ "רוּחַ" הַטֻּמְאָה רַחֲמָנָא לִיצְלַן). מִצַּד שֶׁהַבְּחִינָה הָעֶלְיוֹנָה, סוֹד כֶּתֶר שֶׁלּוֹ, קָשׁוּר וְדָבוּק לְעוֹלָם בַּבְּחִינָה הַתַּחְתּוֹנָה שֶׁל הַנְּשָׁמָה כַּנַּ"ל, יוּכַל הוּא לְהִתָּקֵן עַל יְדֵי בְּחִינַת הַנְּשָׁמָה, בְּהִרְהוּרֵי תְּשׁוּבָה בְּמַחְשֶׁבֶת הַלֵּב, שֶׁהוּא בְּחִינַת הַנְּשָׁמָה:

אֲבָל בְּחִינַת הַנְּשָׁמָה אֵינָהּ נִפְגֶּמֶת כְּלָל לְעוֹלָם, כִּי מְקוֹר שָׁרְשָׁהּ הוּא מֵעוֹלָם הַמְּשֻׁמָּר מִמַּגַּע זָרִים, וּדְבוּקָה לְעוֹלָם בְּשֹׁרֶשׁ הַנְּשָׁמָה כַּיָּדוּעַ, שֶׁהֵם רְעִין דְּלָא מִתְפָּרְשִׁין לְעָלְמִין, וְאֵין מַעֲשֵׂי הָאָדָם מַגִּיעִים עָדֶיהָ כְּלָל לְקַלְקֵל חַס וְשָׁלוֹם. וְאִם הָאָדָם חוֹטֵא בְּמַחֲשָׁבָה אֲשֶׁר לֹא טוֹבָה חַס וְשָׁלוֹם, הוּא גּוֹרֵם רָעָה לְעַצְמוֹ לְבַד, שֶׁיִּסְתַּלֵּק וְיִתְעַלֵּם מִמֶּנּוּ נִצּוֹצֵי אוֹר הַנְּשָׁמָה, אֲבָל לֹא שֶׁהִיא נִפְגֶּמֶת חַס וְשָׁלוֹם:

פֶּרֶק י"ט

וְזֶהוּ עִנְיַן הַכָּתוּב (משלי יח, יד) "רוּחַ אִישׁ יְכַלְכֵּל מַחֲלֵהוּ וְרוּחַ נְכֵאָה מִי יִשָּׂאֶנָּה", רָצָה לוֹמַר הַמַּחֲלָה וְחֶלְאַת הֶעָוֹן שֶׁל בְּחִינַת הַנֶּפֶשׁ (שֶׁסְּתָם רֹב הָעֲוֹנוֹת מְצוּיוֹת בִּבְחִינַת

הַנֶּפֶשׁ, שֶׁהִיא הַתַּחְתּוֹנָה הַקְּרוֹבָה אֶל הַסִּטְרָא אַחֲרָא, "רַגְלֶיהָ יוֹרְדוֹת מָוֶת" (משלי ה, ה), וּכְמוֹ שֶׁכָּתוּב (ויקרא ה, א) "וְנֶפֶשׁ כִּי תֶחֱטָא". "הַחַטָּאִים הָאֵלֶּה בְּנַפְשׁוֹתָם" (במדבר יז, ג) וְהַרְבֵּה כַּיּוֹצֵא. וְעַיֵּן עֵץ חַיִּים שַׁעַר הָעֲקוּדִים סוֹף פֶּרֶק ה', וּפְרִי עֵץ חַיִּים שַׁעַר קְרִיאַת שְׁמַע שֶׁעַל הַמִּטָּה פֶּרֶק ח'), יְכוֹלָה הִיא לְהִתָּקֵן, וְגַם לַעֲלוֹת, עַל יְדֵי בְּחִינַת הָרוּחַ כַּנַּ"ל. וְאִם הָ'רוּחַ נְכֵאָה' – שֶׁפָּגַם וְקִלְקֵל בְּחִינַת רוּחוֹ עַל יְדֵי עֲוֹנוֹת הַתְּלוּיִים בִּבְחִינַת הָרוּחַ, אָז "מִי יִשָּׂאֶנָּה", תִּקּוּנוֹ הוּא עַל יְדֵי בְּחִינַת הַנְּשָׁמָה שֶׁנִּקְרֵאת "מִ"י", כַּיָּדוּעַ בַּזֹּהַר:

וְאִישׁ תְּבוּנוֹת יָבִין, שֶׁכְּלַל הַדְּבָרִים הַנַּ"ל בְּעִנְיַן הַשְּׁלֹשָׁה בְּחִינוֹת נר"ן שֶׁל הָאָדָם, הֵם גַּם כֵּן עַל זֶה הַדֶּרֶךְ, גַּם בְּשָׁרְשָׁם הָעֶלְיוֹן שֶׁל אֵלּוּ הַשְּׁלֹשָׁה בְּחִינוֹת, שֶׁהֵם קוּדְשָׁא בְּרִיךְ הוּא וּשְׁכִינְתֵּיהּ וְאֵם הַבָּנִים. שֶׁעֲוֹנוֹת הַתַּחְתּוֹנִים גּוֹרְמִים לִשְׁכִינַת עֻזֵּנוּ, רָזָא דְ'נֶפֶשׁ' דִּלְעֵלָּא, שֶׁנּוֹדֶדֶת מֵהִתְקַשְּׁרוּתָהּ הָעֶלְיוֹן, בְּסוֹד גָּלוּת (הַיְנוּ כְּשֶׁנַּפְשׁוֹת יִשְׂרָאֵל מִשְׁקָעִים בְּתַאֲוֹת רָעוֹת חַס וְשָׁלוֹם).

וְעַיֵּן עֵץ חַיִּים שַׁעַר מִעוּט הַיָּרֵחַ פֶּרֶק ב, וּבְשַׁעַר סֵדֶר אבי"ע פֶּרֶק ב', וּבְשַׁעַר הַקְּלִפּוֹת כָּל פֶּרֶק ג', וּבְהַקְדָּמַת פְּרִי עֵץ חַיִּים בִּכְלָלֵי ז"א ונוק', וּבְשַׁעַר הַיִּחוּדִים פֶּרֶק א' מִתִּקּוּנֵי עֲוֹנוֹת.

אָמְנָם לֹא כָּל עֶשֶׂר בְּחִינוֹתֶיהָ, רַק הַתֵּשַׁע בְּחִינוֹתֶיהָ מֵחָכְמָה וּלְמַטָּה, כַּנַּ"ל בְּעִנְיַן הָאָדָם, אֲבָל בְּחִינָה הָעֶלְיוֹנָה, סוֹד כִּתְרָהּ, שֶׁהִיא נְקֻדָּה הַשָּׁרְשִׁית דִּילָהּ, הִיא קְשׁוּרָה וּדְבוּקָה לְעוֹלָם בַּעֲטֶרֶת יְסוֹד בְּחִינַת הָרוּחַ, וְאֵינָהּ נִפְרֶדֶת מִשָּׁם לְעוֹלָם (וְלָכֵן נִקְרֵאת "עֲטָרָה" שֶׁהוּא כִּתְרָהּ).

וְעַיֵּן בְּהַקְדָּמַת פְּרִי עֵץ חַיִּים הַנַּ"ל, וּבְשַׁעַר הָעֲמִידָה שָׁם בְּעִנְיַן בִּרְכַּת הַמִּינִים, וְכֵן כָּתַב רַבֵּינוּ הַגָּדוֹל זִכְרוֹנָם לִבְרָכָה בְּפֵרוּשׁ עַל הַהֵיכָלוֹת בְּהֵיכְלָא תִּנְיָנָא שָׁם. (וְעַיֵּן בְּעֵץ חַיִּים שַׁעַר הַמְּלָכִים פֶּרֶק ז', וּבְשַׁעַר מִעוּט הַיָּרֵחַ, וּבְשַׁעַר הַקְּלִפּוֹת, וְתָבִין בְּמ"ש בִּפְרִי עֵץ חַיִּים בְּאֵלּוּ ב' הַמְּקוֹמוֹת הַנַּ"ל, וְעַיֵּן עוֹד בִּפְרִי עֵץ חַיִּים שַׁעַר ר"ה פֶּרֶק ב' וְתָבִין כָּל הַנַּ"ל).

אֲבָל בְּחִינַת הָ'רוּחַ' עִלָּאָה, אֵינוֹ נִפְרָד חַס וְשָׁלוֹם מִמְּקוֹמוֹ עַל יְדֵי עֲוֹנוֹת הַתַּחְתּוֹנִים אֶלָּא שֶׁגּוֹרְמִים בּוֹ פְּגַם וְקִלְקוּל חַס וְשָׁלוֹם בו"ק שֶׁלּוֹ, כַּיָּדוּעַ.

אָמְנָם בִּבְחִינַת הַ'נְּשָׁמָה', שֶׁהוּא סוֹד הַמּוֹחִין, ג' רִאשׁוֹנוֹת דִּילֵיהּ, כַּנַּ"ל בְּפֶרֶק ט"ו, שָׁם אֵין מַעֲשֵׂה הַתַּחְתּוֹנִים מַגִּיעִים כְּלָל, לְקַלְקְלָם אוֹ לְפָגְמָם חַס וְשָׁלוֹם, אֶלָּא שֶׁיְּכוֹלִים לִגְרֹם בְּמַעֲשֵׂיהֶם הִסְתַּלְּקוּתָם הֵימֶנּוּ חַס וְשָׁלוֹם, כַּיָּדוּעַ בְּעֵץ חַיִּים, שֶׁהֵם בָּאִים בְּסוֹד תּוֹסֶפֶת לְבַד, וּתְלוּיִים בְּמַעֲשֵׂי הַתַּחְתּוֹנִים, כִּי הֵם בָּאִים מֵהִתְפַּשְּׁטוּת בְּחִינָה הַתַּחְתּוֹנָה שֶׁל אֵם הַבָּנִים בּוֹ כַּיָּדוּעַ, וכמש"ה (משלי ג, יט) "כּוֹנֵן שָׁמַיִם בִּתְבוּנָה", וְהוּא עוֹלָם הַמְּשֻׁמָּר מִמַּגַּע זָרִים, כַּיָּדוּעַ:

וְהוּא עִנְיַן מַרְאֵה הַסֻּלָּם מֻצָּב אַרְצָה גו' (בראשית כח, יב), וְלֹא אָמַר מֻצָּב "בָּאָרֶץ", אֶלָּא "אַרְצָה", שֶׁפֵּרוּשׁוֹ לָאָרֶץ, וּמַשְׁמָעוֹ שֶׁרֹאשׁ עִקַּר שָׁרְשׁוֹ – בַּשָּׁמַיִם מִמַּעַל, וּמִשָּׁם הוּא מִשְׁתַּלְשֵׁל וְיוֹרֵד, עַד לָאָרֶץ יַגִּיעַ. וְהוּא הַנִּשְׁמַת חַיִּים שֶׁל הָאָדָם, שֶׁמִּתְאַצֶּלֶת כִּבְיָכוֹל

מִנִּשְׁמַת פִּיו יִתְבָּרַךְ שְׁמוֹ, וּמִשָּׁם מִשְׁתַּלְשֶׁלֶת כְּסֻלָּם וְשַׁלְשֶׁלֶת, וּמִתְקַשֶּׁרֶת עִם הָרוּחַ, וְהָרוּחַ בַּנֶּפֶשׁ, עַד רִדְתָּהּ לְזֶה הָעוֹלָם בְּגוּף הָאָדָם.

וְכֵן מְפֹרָשׁ בְּרַעְיָא מְהֵימְנָא נָשֹׂא קכ"ג ב': "וַיִּפַּח בְּאַפָּיו נִשְׁמַת חַיִּים" גו' (בראשית ב, ז) דְּאִתְמַר בֵּיהּ (שם כח, יב): "וַיַּחֲלֹם וְהִנֵּה סֻלָּם", סֻלָּם וַדַּאי אִיהִי נִשְׁמַת חַיִּים כו', עַיֵּן שָׁם. "וְהִנֵּה מַלְאֲכֵי אֱלֹקִים עוֹלִים וְיוֹרְדִים בּוֹ", כְּמוֹ שֶׁכָּתַבְתִּי לְעֵיל בְּאֹרֶךְ, שֶׁהִיא הַנֶּפֶשׁ חַיָּה שֶׁל הָעוֹלָמוֹת וְהַכֹּחוֹת וּמַלְאֲכֵי עֶלְיוֹן, שֶׁכָּל עֲלִיָּתָם וִירִידָתָם וְכָל סִדְרֵי הַנְהָגָתָם כָּל רֶגַע, תָּלוּי רַק כְּפִי נְטִיַּת מַעֲשֶׂיהָ דִּבּוּרָהּ וּמַחְשַׁבְתָּהּ בְּגוּף הָאָדָם כָּל רֶגַע. (וּמ"ש "עוֹלִים" תְּחִלָּה, וְאַחַר כָּךְ "יוֹרְדִים", כִּי כָּל עִקַּר תּוֹרַת הָאָדָם – לְהַעֲלוֹת תְּחִלָּה כָּל עוֹלָם מִמַּטָּה לְמַעְלָה, וְאַחַר כַּךְ נִמְשָׁכִים אוֹרוֹת מִלְמַעְלָה לְמַטָּה) עַד שֶׁאַחַר כָּךְ וְהִנֵּה הֲוָיָ"ה בָּרוּךְ הוּא נִצָּב עָלָיו כַּנַּ"ל:

וּמַה נָּעֲמוּ אִמְרֵי רַבּוֹתֵינוּ זִכְרוֹנָם לִבְרָכָה בִּירוּשַׁלְמִי תַּעֲנִית פֶּרֶק ב': רֵישׁ לָקִישׁ בְּשֵׁם רַבִּי יוֹחָנָן אָמַר, שִׁתֵּף הַקָּדוֹשׁ בָּרוּךְ הוּא שְׁמוֹ בְּיִשְׂרָאֵל. מָשָׁל לְמֶלֶךְ שֶׁהָיָה לוֹ מַפְתֵּחַ שֶׁל פַּלְטֵרִין קְטַנָּה, אָמַר אִם אֲנִי מַנִּיחָהּ כְּמוֹת שֶׁהִיא הֲרֵי הִיא אֲבוּדָה, אֶלָּא הֲרֵינִי קוֹבֵעַ בָּהּ שַׁלְשֶׁלֶת, שֶׁאִם אָבְדָה, תְּהֵא שַׁלְשֶׁלֶת מֻנַּחַת עָלֶיהָ. כָּךְ אָמַר הַקָּדוֹשׁ בָּרוּךְ הוּא, אִם אֲנִי מַנִּיחַ אֶת יִשְׂרָאֵל כְּמוֹ שֶׁהֵן, הֵן נִבְלָעִין בְּאֻמּוֹת הָעוֹלָם, אֶלָּא הֲרֵינִי מְשַׁתֵּף אֶת שְׁמִי הַגָּדוֹל בָּהֶם". וְהֵם זִכְרוֹנָם לִבְרָכָה דִּבְּרוּ לְעִנְיַן כְּלַל הָאֻמָּה יְחִידָה.

אָמְנָם עֵינֵיהֶם זִכְרוֹנָם לִבְרָכָה מְטִיפָן כְּדַרְכָּם בַּקֹּדֶשׁ, וְרָמְזוּ גַּם עַל הָאָדָם יְחִידִי. וְשִׂיחָתָם זִכְרוֹנָם לִבְרָכָה צְרִיכָה תַּלְמוּד, שֶׁהִמְשִׁילוּ הָעִנְיָן לְמַפְתֵּחַ וְשַׁלְשֶׁלֶת, כְּמוֹ שֶׁכָּתַבְתִּי לְעֵיל, שֶׁהָאָדָם הוּא הַפּוֹתֵחַ וְהַסּוֹגֵר שֶׁל הַכֹּחוֹת וְהָעוֹלָמוֹת, פַּלְטֵרִין שֶׁל מַעְלָה וּפַלְטֵרִין שֶׁל מַטָּה, שֶׁכֻּלָּם מִתְנַהֲגִים עַל יְדֵי כֹּחַ מַעֲשָׂיו בִּבְחִינַת נֶפֶשׁ, שֶׁהוּא עִקָּרָא וְשָׁרְשָׁא דִּבְחִינַת נֶפֶשׁ כָּל עָלְמִין.

וַאֲדוֹן כֹּל בָּרוּךְ הוּא, בְּטוּבוֹ הַגָּדוֹל לְהֵטִיב לִבְרוּאָיו, שָׁקַד עַל תַּקָּנָתֵינוּ וְאָמַר, אִם אֲנִי מַנִּיחָהּ כְּמוֹת שֶׁהִיא, שֶׁלֹּא יִהְיֶה הִתְקַשְּׁרוּת בֵּין הַג' בְּחִינוֹת נר"ן, "אִלּוּ הָאֶחָד שֶׁיִּפֹּל" בְּחִינַת נֶפֶשׁ הַתַּחְתּוֹנָה לְעִמְקֵי מְצוּלוֹת הָרַע חַס וְשָׁלוֹם, אֵין שֵׁנִי לַהֲקִימוֹ, וַהֲרֵי הִיא אֲבוּדָה שָׁם לְעוֹלָם חַס וְשָׁלוֹם, כְּעִנְיַן הַכָּתוּב "וְהַאֲבַדְתִּי אֶת הַנֶּפֶשׁ הַהִיא" (ויקרא כג, ל), וְנֶפֶשׁ הַחוֹטֵאת בַּמֶּה תִּתְכַּפֵּר.

לָזֹאת, הִפְלִיא עֵצָה יִתְבָּרַךְ שְׁמוֹ, וְקָבַע הַשְּׁלֹשָׁה מַדְרֵגוֹת נר"ן, שֶׁכָּל אַחַת מֵהֶם תִּתְקַשֵּׁר בְּחִינָה הָרִאשׁוֹנָה שֶׁלָּהּ הָעֶלְיוֹנָה בִּבְחִינָה הַתַּחְתּוֹנָה שֶׁל הַמַּדְרֵגָה שֶׁעָלֶיהָ, כְּעִנְיַן הַשַּׁלְשֶׁלֶת, שֶׁכָּל טַבַּעַת מִמֶּנָּה, קָצֶה הָעֶלְיוֹן שֶׁלָּהּ נֶאֱחֶזֶת וְנִכְנֶסֶת תּוֹךְ קָצֶה הַתַּחְתּוֹן שֶׁל הַטַּבַּעַת שֶׁעָלֶיהָ, וְעַל יְדֵי כֵן גַּם אִם יִכָּרֵת הַנֶּפֶשׁ וְתִפֹּל לְעִמְקֵי כֹּחוֹת הַטֻּמְאָה חַס וְשָׁלוֹם, יְכוֹלָה הִיא לְהִתָּקֵן וְלַעֲלוֹת עַל יְדֵי הִתְקַשְּׁרוּת בְּחִינוֹת עֶלְיוֹנוֹת שֶׁלָּהּ בִּבְחִינַת הָרוּחַ, וְכֵן עַל דֶּרֶךְ זֶה בְּקִלְקוּל וּפְגַם הָרוּחַ כַּנַּ"ל.

וְזֶהוּ שֶׁאָמַר שָׁם, אֶלָּא הֲרֵינִי מְשַׁתֵּף אֶת שְׁמִי הַגָּדוֹל בָּהֶם, שֶׁהַשְּׁלֹשָׁה דְּרָגִין נר"ן וְשֹׁרֶשׁ הַנְּשָׁמָה, מְקוֹר שָׁרְשָׁם הוּא מֵהָאַרְבַּע אוֹתִיּוֹת הַשֵּׁם הַגָּדוֹל יִתְבָּרַךְ שְׁמוֹ:

פֶּרֶק כ׳

וּבֵאוּר פְּרָטוּת סֵדֶר תִּקּוּנָם וְהִתְקַשְּׁרוּתָם עַל יְדֵי הַתְּשׁוּבָה, שֶׁכַּאֲשֶׁר פָּגַם הָאָדָם בְּחִינַת "נַפְשׁוֹ", אוֹ אַף אִם גָּרַם חַס וְשָׁלוֹם שֶׁנִּפְסְקוּ וְנִכְרְתוּ כָּל הַתֵּשַׁע סְפִירוֹתֶיהָ — מֵחָכְמָה וּלְמַטָּה — מֵהִתְקַשְּׁרוּתָהּ הַנַּ"ל, וַתֵּרֶד פְּלָאִים לְעִמְקֵי מְצוּלוֹת הַקְּלִפּוֹת חַס וְשָׁלוֹם. אָז עַל יְדֵי וִדּוּי דְּבָרִים בֶּאֱמֶת מֵעֻמְקָא דְּלִבָּא, בַּעֲקִימַת שְׂפָתָיו, בְּחִינַת נֶפֶשׁ דְּרוּחַ, מְעוֹרֵר בְּקוֹל דְּבָרִים שֶׁלּוֹ עַד לְעֵלָּא וּלְעֵלָּא, וְגוֹרֵם שֶׁיִּתְאַצֵּל תּוֹסֶפֶת קְדֻשָּׁה מִמֶּנּוּ יִתְבָּרַךְ שְׁמוֹ עַד "שֹׁרֶשׁ הַנְּשָׁמָה" תְּחִלָּה, וּמִשָּׁם לְ"נִשְׁמָתוֹ וְרוּחוֹ", וְהָרוּחַ מַבְהִיק אוֹרוֹ הַגָּדוֹל הַנִּשְׁפָּע עָלָיו גַּם עַל בְּחִינַת הַ"נֶּפֶשׁ", מִצַּד הַהִתְקַשְּׁרוּת שֶׁנִּשְׁאַר עֲדַיִן בֵּינֵיהֶם כַּנַּ"ל, לְכַלּוֹת וּלְהָתֵם הַכֹּחוֹת הָרַע וּמַדְרֵגוֹת הַטֻּמְאָה, וּלְהוֹצִיא מִמַּסְגֵּר אָסִיר כָּל בְּחִינוֹתֶיהָ, וְלַחֲזֹר וּלְקַשְּׁרָם כְּבָרִאשׁוֹנָה עִם בְּחִינַת הָרוּחַ:

וְכֵן אִם פָּגַם וְקִלְקֵל בְּחִינַת רוּחוֹ חַס וְשָׁלוֹם, בְּדִבּוּרִים אֲשֶׁר לֹא טוֹבִים, אוֹ בִּשְׁאָר עֲוֹנוֹת הַתְּלוּיִים בִּבְחִינַת הָרוּחַ, וּבִטּוּל תּוֹרָה כְּנֶגֶד כֻּלָּם, וְהִגְבִּיר לְעֻמַּת זֶה כֹּחַ רוּחַ הַטֻּמְאָה רַחֲמָנָא לִיצְלַן, וְאָז גַּם נַפְשׁוֹ אֵינָהּ שְׁלֵמָה כְּמִקֹּדֶם, כִּי הִיא מְקַבֶּלֶת שֶׁפַע חִיּוּתָהּ וְאוֹרָהּ עַל יְדֵי הָרוּחַ כַּיָּדוּעַ, הִנֵּה עַל יְדֵי הַחֲרָטָה אֲמִתִּית בַּלֵּב, וּמִתְמַרְמֵר עַל גֹּדֶל חֶטְאוֹ, כְּעִנְיַן "צָעַק לִבָּם אֶל ה'" (איכה ב, יח), וּמְהַרְהֵר הִרְהוּרֵי תְּשׁוּבָה בְּמַחֲשָׁבָה, שֶׁהִיא מִשְׁכַּן נִצּוֹצֵי אוֹר הַנְּשָׁמָה, (וְהוּא מַלְכוּת דִּתְבוּנָה), מְעוֹרֵר גַּם כֵּן עַד לְעֵלָּא, לְהַשְׁפִּיעַ תְּחִלָּה תּוֹסֶפֶת קְדֻשָּׁה וְאוֹר עַל "שֹׁרֶשׁ הַנְּשָׁמָה", וּמִשָּׁם לְ"נִשְׁמָתוֹ", וְהִיא מַבְהֶקֶת זִיו אוֹרָהּ שֶׁנִּשְׁפָּע עָלֶיהָ גַּם עַל בְּחִינַת "הָרוּחַ", וְזִבְחֵי אֱלֹקִים רוּחַ נִשְׁבָּרָה (תהלים נא, יט), וְשׁוֹבֵר כֹּחַ רוּחַ הַטֻּמְאָה שֶׁהִגְבִּיר בַּעֲוֹנוֹ, וּמְטַהֵר בְּחִינַת רוּחוֹ הַקָּדוֹשׁ לְהִתְקַשֵּׁר בִּבְחִינַת הַנְּשָׁמָה כְּבַתְּחִלָּה, וּמִשָּׁם מִמֵּילָא יֻשְׁפַּע גַּם עַל "נַפְשׁוֹ" לְהַשְׁלִימָהּ בִּשְׁלֵמוּתָהּ הָרִאשׁוֹן:

וְכֵן אִם חָטָא חַס וְשָׁלוֹם בְּמַחֲשָׁבָה אֲשֶׁר לֹא טְהוֹרָה, וְגָרַם בָּזֶה שֶׁיִּסְתַּלְּקוּ מֵעָלָיו נִצּוֹצֵי זֹהַר נִשְׁמָתוֹ, שֶׁהָיְתָה עַד הֵנָּה בְּהִלָּהּ נֵרָהּ עֲלֵי רֹאשׁוֹ, אָז עַל יְדֵי עֵסֶק הַתּוֹרָה בְּבִינָה יְתֵרָה בְּעֹמֶק תְּבוּנָתוֹ, מְעוֹרֵר שֶׁיִּתְאַצֵּל תּוֹסֶפֶת קְדֻשָּׁה עַל "שֹׁרֶשׁ נִשְׁמָתוֹ", וּמִשָּׁם לְ"נִשְׁמָתוֹ", לְהַחֲזִירָהּ שֶׁתָּאִיר עָלָיו אוֹרָהּ, לְהַשְׂכִּילוֹ בַּתּוֹרָה הַקְּדוֹשָׁה בְּבִינָה יְתֵרָה בְּסִתְרֵי טְהוֹרֶיהָ, וּמֵאוֹתוֹ הַקְּדֻשָּׁה וְהָאוֹר מִשְׁתַּלְשֵׁל וְנִשְׁפָּע גַּם עַל "רוּחוֹ וְנַפְשׁוֹ" לְהַשְׁלִימָם בִּשְׁלֵמוּתָם:

וְלָכֵן אָמְרוּ זִכְרוֹנָם לִבְרָכָה (שבת קיט, ב): "כָּל הָעוֹנֶה 'אָמֵן יְהֵא שְׁמֵיהּ רַבָּא מְבָרַךְ' בְּכָל כֹּחוֹ, קוֹרְעִים לוֹ גְּזַר דִּינוֹ, וַאֲפִלּוּ יֵשׁ בּוֹ שֶׁמֶץ שֶׁל עֲבוֹדָה זָרָה מוֹחֲלִים לוֹ".

כִּי עִקַּר כַּוָּנַת זֶה הַשֶּׁבַח, הוּא שֶׁיִּתְאַצֵּל וְיֻשְׁפַּע תּוֹסֶפֶת בְּרָכָה וְשִׁפְעַת אוֹר עֶלְיוֹן לְכָל הָאַרְבַּע עוֹלָמוֹת אבי"ע . וְזֶהוּ יְהֵא שְׁמֵיהּ רַבָּא מְבָרַךְ, הַיְנוּ, שֶׁיִּתְאַצֵּל בְּרָכָה וְתוֹסֶפֶת קְדֻשָּׁה מִמֶּנּוּ יִתְבָּרַךְ שְׁמוֹ, עַד "לְעָלַם" — הוּא עוֹלַם הָאֲצִילוּת, וּמִשָּׁם גַּם "לְעָלְמֵי" — הֵם ב' עוֹלָמוֹת בְּרִיאָה יְצִירָה, "עָלְמַיָּא" — הוּא עוֹלַם הָעֲשִׂיָּה, וְהֵם שֹׁרֶשׁ הַד' דַּרְגִּין שֶׁל הָאָדָם, שֹׁרֶשׁ הַנְּשָׁמָה, ונר"ן.

וּכְשֶׁמְּכַוֵּן הָאָדָם בִּקְדֻשַּׁת מַחֲשַׁבְתּוֹ בַּאֲמִירַת זֶה הַשֶּׁבַח, לְעוֹרֵר וּלְהַשְׁפִּיעַ עַל יָדוֹ תּוֹסֶפֶת קְדֻשָּׁה וּבְרָכָה עַל שֹׁרֶשׁ נִשְׁמָתוֹ, וּמִשָּׁם עַל נִשְׁמָתוֹ וְרוּחוֹ וְנַפְשׁוֹ, גּוֹרֵם בָּזֶה לְהָתֵם

וּלְכַלֵּה כָּל עָוֹן וְחֵטְא אֲשֶׁר חָטָא בְּאֵיזֶה בְּחִינָה מֵאֵלּוּ הַשְּׁלֹשָׁה, וְהָיוּ כְּלֹא הָיוּ, וְזֶה כָּל עִקַּר הַתְּשׁוּבָה הָאֲמִתִּית כַּנַּ"ל, לָכֵן מוֹחֲלִין לוֹ עַל כָּל עֲוֹנוֹתָיו:

וְזֶה גַּם כֵּן עִנְיַן מַאֲמָרָם זִכְרוֹנָם לִבְרָכָה (ע"ז ח' א'): "שׁוֹר שֶׁהִקְרִיב אָדָם הָרִאשׁוֹן, קַרְנוֹתָיו קוֹדְמוֹת לְפַרְסוֹתָיו הָיוּ", שֶׁכֵּוֵן בְּהַקְרָבָתוֹ לְתַקֵּן אֲשֶׁר עִוֵּת, לִבְנוֹת הַנֶּהֱרָסוֹת, לְקָרֵב אֲשֶׁר הִרְחִיק וּלְיַחֵד אֲשֶׁר הִפְרִיד, וְהֶעֱלָה טֹהַר קְדֻשַּׁת מַחְשַׁבְתּוֹ וְכַוָּנָתוֹ, לְהַאֲצִיל תְּחִלָּה שִׁפְעַת אוֹר וּקְדֻשָּׁה עַל הַבְּחִינוֹת וּמַדְרֵגוֹת הָעֶלְיוֹנוֹת שֶׁבּוֹ, דִּמְיוֹן הַקְּרָנַיִם, הֵם שֹׁרֶשׁ נִשְׁמָתוֹ וְנִשְׁמָתוֹ, וּמִשָּׁם הִמְשִׁיךְ אַחַר זֶה עַל רוּחוֹ וְנַפְשׁוֹ, לְטַהֵר כָּל אֵבָרָיו מֵרֹאשׁוֹ וְעַד רַגְלָיו, עַל דֶּרֶךְ "וְהָיָה עֵקֶב תִּשְׁמְעוּן" וגו', מִצְוֹת שֶׁאָדָם דָּשׁ בַּעֲקֵבָיו, וְהוּא הַפַּרְסוֹת שֶׁל נֶפֶשׁ הַבְּהֵמִית. וְזֶהוּ שֶׁאָמַר (בְּוַיִּקְרָא רַבָּה פָּרָשָׁה ב' וְקֹהֶלֶת ז') שֶׁתַּפּוּחַ עֲקֵבוֹ הָיָה מַכְהֶה גַּלְגַּל חַמָּה וכו':

פֶּרֶק כ"א

וְזֹאת תּוֹרַת הָאָדָם, שֶׁבְּעֵת עָסְקוֹ בַּתּוֹרָה לִשְׁמָהּ, לִשְׁמֹר וּלְקַיֵּם כְּכָל הַכָּתוּב בָּהּ, מְטַהֵר אֶת גּוּפוֹ מֵרֹאשׁוֹ וְעַד רַגְלָיו. כְּמִדְרָשָׁם זִכְרוֹנָם לִבְרָכָה (ברכות טז, א) "לָמָּה נִסְמְכוּ אֹהָלִים לִנְחָלִים כו', מַה נְּחָלִים מַעֲלִין אֶת הָאָדָם מִטֻּמְאָה לְטָהֳרָה, אַף אֹהָלִים מַעֲלִין אֶת הָאָדָם מִכַּף חוֹבָה לְכַף זְכוּת". וּכְעִנְיַן שֶׁדָּרְשׁוּ זִכְרוֹנָם לִבְרָכָה (עירובין ד:) גַּבֵּי טָהֳרַת הַטְּמֵאִים בְּמִקְוֶה, "כָּל בְּשָׂרוֹ בַּמַּיִם", מַיִם שֶׁכָּל גּוּפוֹ עוֹלֶה בָּהֶם, כָּךְ בְּדִבְרֵי תּוֹרָה כָּל גּוּפוֹ שֶׁל אָדָם עוֹלֶה בָּהֶם. (וְשִׁעֲרוּ חֲכָמִים אַמָּה עַל אַמָּה בְּרוּם שָׁלֹשׁ אַמּוֹת (עיין פסחים קז ועוד), הֵן הַשְּׁלֹשָׁה עוֹלָמוֹת, ונר"ן, מַעֲשֶׂה דִּבּוּר מַחֲשָׁבָה בַּתּוֹרָה).

וּכְשֵׁם שֶׁכָּל גּוּפוֹ שֶׁל אָדָם עוֹלֶה וּמִזְדַּכֵּךְ עַל יְדֵי עֵסֶק הַתּוֹרָה וְהַמִּצְוֹת, כָּךְ הָעוֹלָמוֹת כֻּלָּם, אֲשֶׁר הֵן הֵמָּה שִׁעוּר קוֹמַת אָדָם, כְּמוֹ שֶׁכָּתַבְתִּי לְעֵיל פֶּרֶק ו', הֵם מִזְדַּכְּכִים וּמִתְטַהֲרִים וּמִתְעַלִּים.

וְהָאָדָם הַיָּשָׁר הָעוֹבֵד אֲמִתִּי, לֹא יִפְנֶה דַּעְתּוֹ וּמַחְשַׁבְתּוֹ בְּעֵת עֲבוֹדָתוֹ לוֹ יִתְבָּרַךְ שְׁמוֹ, אֲפִלּוּ כְּדֵי לַעֲלוֹת וּלְטַהֵר גּוּפוֹ וְנַפְשׁוֹ, אֶלָּא שֶׁיַּעֲלֶה טֹהַר מַחְשַׁבְתּוֹ וְכַוָּנָתוֹ וּפָנָה לְמַעְלָה – לְתִקּוּן וְטָהֳרַת הָעוֹלָמוֹת הַקְּדוֹשִׁים.

וְזוֹ הָיְתָה גַּם כָּל עִנְיַן עֲבוֹדָתָם שֶׁל הָאָבוֹת, וְכָל הַצַּדִּיקִים הָרִאשׁוֹנִים, שֶׁקִּיְּמוּ אֶת הַתּוֹרָה קֹדֶם נְתִינָתָהּ. כְּמוֹ שֶׁדָּרְשׁוּ רַבּוֹתֵינוּ זִכְרוֹנָם לִבְרָכָה עַל פָּסוּק "מִן הַבְּהֵמָה הַטְּהוֹרָה" גו' (בראשית ז, ח), וְאָמְרוּ: "מִכָּאן שֶׁלָּמַד נֹחַ תּוֹרָה", וְאָמְרוּ (יומא כ"ח ב'): "קִיֵּם אַבְרָהָם אָבִינוּ אֶת כָּל הַתּוֹרָה" (וְכֵן אִיתָא בִּבְרֵאשִׁית רַבָּה פָּרָשָׁה צ"ב, וּבְבַמִּדְבָּר רַבָּה פָּרָשָׁה י"ה, וּבְתַנְחוּמָא בְּהַ"ה, וּבְמִדְרַשׁ תְּהִלִּים מִזְמוֹר א').

לֹא שֶׁהָיוּ מְצֻוִּים וְעוֹשִׂים כָּךְ מִצַּד הַדִּין, דְּאִם כֵּן לֹא הָיוּ מַעֲמִידִים חַס וְשָׁלוֹם עַל דַּעְתָּם וְהַשָּׂגָתָם, אַף שֶׁהִשִּׂיגוּ שֶׁלְּפִי עִנְיַן שֹׁרֶשׁ נִשְׁמָתָם הֶהְכְרֵחַ לָהֶם לַעֲבֹר וּלְשַׁנּוֹת אַף מִקְצָת מֵאַחַת מִכָּל מִצְוֹת ה', וְלֹא הָיָה יַעֲקֹב אָבִינוּ עָלָיו הַשָּׁלוֹם נוֹשֵׂא שְׁתֵּי אֲחָיוֹת, וְלֹא הָיָה עַמְרָם נוֹשֵׂא דּוֹדָתוֹ חַס וְשָׁלוֹם.

רַק מִצַּד הַשָּׂגָתָם בְּטֹהַר שִׂכְלָם הַתִּקּוּנִים הַנּוֹרָאִים הַנַּעֲשִׂים בְּכָל מִצְוָה בְּהָעוֹלָמוֹת וְכֹחוֹת הָעֶלְיוֹנִים וְתַחְתּוֹנִים, וְהַפְּגָמִים הַגְּדוֹלִים וְהַחֻרְבָּן וַהֲרִיסָה חַס וְשָׁלוֹם שֶׁיִּגָּרְמוּ בָּהֶם אִם לֹא יְקַיְּמוּם.

וְכֵן נֹחַ הִקְרִיב דַּוְקָא מִן הַבְּהֵמָה הַטְּהוֹרָה, כִּי רָאָה וְהִשִּׂיג הַכֹּחַ וְהַשֹּׁרֶשׁ הָעֶלְיוֹן שֶׁל כָּל בְּהֵמָה וְחַיָּה, אֵיזֶה מֵהֶם כֹּחַ שָׁרְשׁוֹ מִצַּד הַקְּדֻשָּׁה, וְהִקְרִיבָהּ, וְאֵיזֶה מֵהֶם כֹּחַ נַפְשָׁהּ מִצַּד הַטֻּמְאָה וְהַסִּטְרָא אַחֲרָא, וְלֹא בָּחַר בָּהּ לְהַקְרִיבָהּ לְפָנָיו יִתְבָּרַךְ, כִּי לֹא יֵרָצֶה.

וְזֶהוּ "וַיִּתְהַלֵּךְ חֲנוֹךְ אֶת הָאֱלֹקִים" (בראשית ה, כד), "אֶת הָאֱלֹקִים הִתְהַלֶּךְ נֹחַ" (שם ו, ט), "הָאֱלֹקִים אֲשֶׁר הִתְהַלְּכוּ אֲבוֹתַי לְפָנָיו" (שם מח, טו), שֶׁפֵּרוּשׁ "אֱלֹקִים" — בַּעַל הַכֹּחוֹת כֻּלָּם, הַיְנוּ, שֶׁהִשִּׂיגוּ עִנְיְנֵי הַכֹּחוֹת הָעֶלְיוֹנִים וְתַחְתּוֹנִים, וְחֻקּוֹת שָׁמַיִם וָאָרֶץ וּמִשְׁטָרָם, וְסִדְרֵי הַנְהָגָתָם וְהִתְקַשְּׁרוּתָם וְהַרְכָּבָתָם עַל יְדֵי כָּל עִנְיְנֵי מַעֲשֵׂי הָאָדָם, וְעַל פִּי סֵדֶר וְעִנְיָן זֶה הָיָה כָּל אֶחָד מֵהֶם מִתְהַלֵּךְ וּמִתְנַהֵג בְּכָל עִנְיָנָיו, כְּפִי שֶׁרָאָה וְהִשִּׂיג הַתִּקּוּנִים הָעֶלְיוֹנִים לְפִי שֹׁרֶשׁ נִשְׁמָתוֹ:

לָכֵן כְּשֶׁהִשִּׂיג יַעֲקֹב אָבִינוּ עָלָיו הַשָּׁלוֹם, שֶׁלְּפִי שֹׁרֶשׁ נִשְׁמָתוֹ יִגְרֹם תִּקּוּנִים גְּדוֹלִים בְּכֹחוֹת וְעוֹלָמוֹת הָעֶלְיוֹנִים אִם יִשָּׂא הַשְּׁתֵּי אֲחָיוֹת אֵלּוּ רָחֵל וְלֵאָה, וְהֵמָּה יִבְנוּ שְׁתֵּיהֶן אֶת בֵּית יִשְׂרָאֵל, יָגַע כַּמָּה יְגִיעוֹת וַעֲבוֹדוֹת לְהַשִּׂיגָם שֶׁיִּנָּשְׂאוּ לוֹ. וְכֵן הָעִנְיָן בְּעַמְרָם, שֶׁנָּשָׂא יוֹכֶבֶד דּוֹדָתוֹ שֶׁיָּצְאוּ מִמֶּנָּה מֹשֶׁה, אַהֲרֹן וּמִרְיָם:

וְזֶה גַּם כֵּן אֶחָד מֵהַטְּעָמִים שֶׁלֹּא נִתְּנָה הַתּוֹרָה לְנֹחַ וְהָאָבוֹת הַקְּדוֹשִׁים, שֶׁאִם הָיְתָה נִתֶּנֶת לָהֶם, לֹא הָיָה יַעֲקֹב רַשַּׁאי לִישָּׂא שְׁתֵּי אֲחָיוֹת, וְלֹא עַמְרָם דּוֹדָתוֹ, אַף אִם הָיוּ מַשִּׂיגִים שֶׁכֵּן רָאוּי לָהֶם לְפִי שֹׁרֶשׁ נִשְׁמָתָם, וּבֶאֱמֶת זֶה הָיָה כָּל בְּנִיַּת בֵּית יִשְׂרָאֵל עַם סְגֻלָּה וְתִקּוּן כָּל הָעוֹלָמוֹת עֶלְיוֹנִים וְתַחְתּוֹנִים. כְּעִנְיַן מַאֲמָרָם זִכְרוֹנָם לִבְרָכָה (סנהדרין נח, ב) וְאִם תֹּאמַר קַיִן נָשָׂא אֲחוֹתוֹ, "עוֹלָם חֶסֶד יִבָּנֶה" (תהלים פט, ג):

פֶּרֶק כ"ב

וּמִשֶּׁבָּא מֹשֶׁה וְהוֹרִידָהּ לָאָרֶץ, לֹא בַּשָּׁמַיִם הִיא. וּלְבַל יִתְחַכֵּם הָאָדָם הַגָּדוֹל שֶׁהַשָּׂגָתוֹ מְרֻבָּה, לוֹמַר, אָנֹכִי הָרוֹאֶה סוֹד וְטַעֲמֵי הַמִּצְוֹת בְּכֹחוֹת וְעוֹלָמוֹת הָעֶלְיוֹנִים שֶׁרָאוּי לִי לְפִי שֹׁרֶשׁ נִשְׁמָתִי, אוֹ לְמִי וָמִי לְפִי שָׁרְשׁוֹ, לַעֲבֹר חַס וְשָׁלוֹם עַל אֵיזֶה מִצְוָה, אוֹ לִדְחוֹת שׁוּם פְּרָט מִפְּרָטֵי הַמַּעֲשֶׂה, לַעֲשׂוֹתָהּ בְּמִגְרַעַת אַף דִּקְדּוּק אֶחָד מִדִּבְרֵי סוֹפְרִים, אוֹ לְשַׁנּוֹת זְמַנָּהּ חַס וְשָׁלוֹם.

וְלָזֶה סִיְּמָה הַתּוֹרָה (דברים לד, י) "וְלֹא קָם נָבִיא כְּמֹשֶׁה", וּכְמוֹ שֶׁלָּמְדוּ זִכְרוֹנָם לִבְרָכָה "אֵלֶּה הַמִּצְוֹת" (ויקרא כז, לד), שֶׁאֵין נָבִיא רַשַּׁאי לְחַדֵּשׁ דָּבָר מֵעַתָּה (שבת קד, א), וּכְמוֹ שֶׁסָּמְכָה הַתּוֹרָה (דברים יג) "אֵת כָּל הַדָּבָר אֲשֶׁר אָנֹכִי מְצַוֶּה גו' לֹא תוֹסֵף עָלָיו וְלֹא תִגְרַע מִמֶּנּוּ" וגו', שֶׁגַּם "כִּי יָקוּם בְּקִרְבְּךָ נָבִיא" וגו' רָצָה לוֹמַר לְהוֹסִיף אוֹ לִגְרֹעַ חַס וְשָׁלוֹם "לֹא תִשְׁמַע אֶל דִּבְרֵי הַנָּבִיא הַהוּא. אַחֲרֵי ה' אֱלֹקֵיכֶם תֵּלֵכוּ" וגו'.

וַהֲרֵי חִזְקִיָּהוּ הַמֶּלֶךְ שֶׁרָאָה בְּרוּחַ הַקֹּדֶשׁ דִּנְפְקִין מִנֵּיהּ בְּנִין דְּלָא מַעֲלֵי, וְלָכֵן לָא נְסִיב

אִתְּתָא (ברכות י, א), וְכַוָּנָתוֹ לְשֵׁם שָׁמַיִם שֶׁלֹּא לְהַרְבּוֹת רִשְׁעֵי עוֹלָם, עִם כָּל זֶה בָּא אֵלָיו יְשַׁעְיָה בִּדְבַר ה' וְאָמַר לוֹ (מלכים ב' כ, א): "כִּי מֵת אַתָּה" וגו', "וְלֹא תִחְיֶה" — לָעוֹלָם הַבָּא, מִשּׁוּם דְּלָא עָסַקְתְּ בִּפְרִיָּה וּרְבִיָּה, וְלֹא הוֹעִיל לוֹ כָּל עֹצֶם צִדְקוֹתָיו הַנּוֹרָאִים לַהֲבִיאוֹ לְחַיֵּי עוֹלָם הַבָּא, בִּשְׁבִיל שֶׁסָּבַר לְהִפָּטֵר מִמִּצְוָה אַחַת מִתּוֹרַת מֹשֶׁה, אַף שֶׁכֵּן רָאָה בְּהַשָּׂגַת רוּחַ קָדְשׁוֹ דְּיִפְקוּן מִנֵּיהּ בְּנִין דְּלָא מַעֲלֵי, וְגַם שֶׁהָיָה בְּשֵׁב וְאַל תַּעֲשֶׂה.

כִּי טַעֲמֵי מִצְוֹת עַד תַּכְלִיתָם, לֹא נִתְגַּלּוּ עֲדַיִן לְשׁוּם אָדָם בָּעוֹלָם, אַף לְמֹשֶׁה רַבֵּנוּ עָלָיו הַשָּׁלוֹם, רַק לְאָדָם הָרִאשׁוֹן קֹדֶם הַחֵטְא, וְהוּא הַיַּיִן הַמְּשֻׁמָּר בַּעֲנָבָיו מִשֵּׁשֶׁת יְמֵי בְּרֵאשִׁית (ברכות ל"ד ע"ב), וְהָאוֹר שֶׁשִּׁמֵּשׁ בְּיוֹם רִאשׁוֹן שֶׁהָיָה אָדָם הָרִאשׁוֹן צוֹפֶה וּמַבִּיט בּוֹ מִסּוֹף הָעוֹלָם (חגיגה יב, א) וכו'.

כִּי הַתּוֹרָה הַקְּדוֹשָׁה אֲצוּלָה מִלְּמַעְלָה רֹאשׁ, מֵעַל כָּל הַהַשָּׂגוֹת, וְאֵיךְ אֶפְשָׁר שֶׁיְּהֵא הַדָּבָר מָסוּר לְהַשָּׂגַת הָאָדָם, לְשַׁנּוֹת מֵהִלְכָתָם וְסֵדֶר זְמַנָּם עַל פִּי רֹחַב דַּעְתּוֹ וְהַשָּׂגָתוֹ, וּכְמוֹ שֶׁהֵשִׁיבוֹ יְשַׁעְיָה לְחִזְקִיָּה: "בַּהֲדֵי כַּבְשֵׁי דְּרַחֲמָנָא לָמָּה לָךְ, מַאי דְּמִפַּקְדַתְּ אִבָּעֵי לָךְ לְמֶעֱבַד, וּמַאי דְּנִיחָא קַמֵּי קוּדְשָׁא בְּרִיךְ הוּא לֶעֱבִיד":

וַעֲדַיִן כְּשֶׁהָיְתָה נְבוּאָה בְּיִשְׂרָאֵל, הָיָה נָבִיא רַשַּׁאי לְחַדֵּשׁ דָּבָר לְהוֹרָאַת שָׁעָה לְבַד, וְאַף גַּם לַעֲבֹר עַל אַחַת מִמִּצְוֹת ה', כְּגוֹן אֵלִיָּהוּ בְּהַר הַכַּרְמֶל וְכַיּוֹצֵא.

אָמְנָם זֶה עַצְמוֹ הוּא מֵאֲשֶׁר נִצְטַוִּינוּ בְּתוֹרַת מֹשֶׁה "אֵלָיו תִּשְׁמָעוּן" (דברים י"ח), שֶׁהוּא צִוּוּי וְאַזְהָרָה לִשְׁמֹעַ אֶל דִּבְרֵי הַנָּבִיא, גַּם כְּשֶׁיִּתְנַבֵּא בִּשְׁמוֹ יִתְבָּרַךְ לַעֲבֹר עַל אֵיזֶה מִצְוָה, בְּשָׁעָה הַצְּרִיכָה לְכָךְ, כְּמוֹ שֶׁדָּרְשׁוּ רַבּוֹתֵינוּ זִכְרוֹנָם לִבְרָכָה (יבמות צ:) לְבַד מֵעֲבוֹדָה זָרָה.

אֲבָל לֹא חָלִילָה לְחַדֵּשׁ דָּבָר לְקָבְעוֹ לְדוֹרוֹת. שֶׁהֲרֵי אֶסְתֵּר שֶׁהָיְתָה אַחַת מִשֶּׁבַע נְבִיאוֹת (מגילה י"ד א'), עִם כָּל זֶה כְּשֶׁשָּׁלְחָה לַחֲכָמִים כִּתְבוּנִי "לְדוֹרוֹת", הֵשִׁיבוּהָ: "הֲלֹא כָתַבְתִּי לְךָ שָׁלִשִׁים", (משלי כב, כ), עַד שֶׁמָּצְאוּ לָהּ אַחַר כָּךְ סָמַךְ מִן הַמִּקְרָא (שם ז' א'). וְכֵן נֵרוֹת חֲנֻכָּה, וַדַּאי שֶׁמָּצְאוּ לָהֶם גַּם כֵּן סָמַךְ מֵהַמִּקְרָא, וְעַיֵּן בַּמִּדְרָשׁ שֶׁהֵבִיא הָרַמְבַּ"ן זִכְרוֹנוֹ לִבְרָכָה בְּפָרָשָׁה בְּהַעֲלֹתְךָ מִשֵּׁם רַבֵּנוּ נִסִּים גָּאוֹן ז"ל:

וּמֵעֵת שֶׁבַּעֲוֹנֵינוּ פָּסְקָה נְבוּאָה מִיִּשְׂרָאֵל, אַף אִם יִתְאַסְּפוּ כָּל חַכְמֵי יִשְׂרָאֵל, אֲשֶׁר נִמְסַר לָהֶם מַעֲשֵׂה בְרֵאשִׁית וּמַעֲשֵׂה מֶרְכָּבָה, וְיַעֲמִיקוּ הַשָּׂגָתָם וְטֹהַר שִׂכְלָם לְשַׁנּוֹת אַף אֵיזֶה פְּרָט מֵאֵיזֶה מִצְוָה, אוֹ לְהַקְדִּים וּלְאַחֵר זְמַנָּהּ חַס וְשָׁלוֹם, לֹא נֹאבֶה וְלֹא נִשְׁמַע אֲלֵיהֶם. וְאַף בְּבַת קוֹל אָמְרוּ (בבא מציעא נ"ט ב'): "לֹא בַשָּׁמַיִם הִיא".

וַעֲדַיִן בִּימֵי חַכְמֵי הַתַּלְמוּד הָיוּ רַשָּׁאִים לְחַדֵּשׁ מִצְוֹת דְּרַבָּנָן כְּשֶׁמָּצְאוּ סָמַךְ מֵהַתּוֹרָה, כְּגוֹן נֵרוֹת חֲנֻכָּה וְכַיּוֹצֵא, כַּנַּ"ל, וְכֵן לִגְזֹר גְּזֵרוֹת, כְּמוֹ י"ח דָּבָר (שבת יג:) וְכַיּוֹצֵא.

וְכַאֲשֶׁר נֶחְתַּם הַתַּלְמוּד הַקָּדוֹשׁ, אָנוּ אֵין לָנוּ אֶלָּא לִשְׁמֹר וְלַעֲשׂוֹת כְּכָל הַכָּתוּב בַּתּוֹרָה הַקְּדוֹשָׁה שֶׁבִּכְתָב וּבְעַל פֶּה, כְּכָל מִשְׁפָּטָם וְחֻקָּתָם וּבִזְמַנָּם וּפְרָטֵיהֶם וְדִקְדּוּקֵיהֶם, בְּלִי נְטוֹת מֵהֶם נְטִיָּה כָּל דְּהוּ.

וּכְשֶׁיְּקַיְּמֵם אִישׁ יִשְׂרָאֵל כָּרָאוּי, אַף אִם לֹא יְכַוֵּן, וְגַם לֹא יֵדַע כְּלָל טַעֲמֵי הַמִּצְוֹת

וְסוֹדוֹת כַּוָּנָתָם, עִם כָּל זֶה נִתְקַיְּמוּ הַמִּצְוֹת, וִיתֻקְּנוּ עַל יְדֵיהֶם הָעוֹלָמוֹת, וְיִתְרַבֶּה בָּהֶם קְדֻשָּׁה וְאוֹר, בְּכָל מִצְוָה לְפִי שָׁעְתָהּ וּמְקוֹרָהּ וְעִנְיָנָהּ, וְיִתֵּן עֹז לֵאלֹקִים יִתְבָּרַךְ שְׁמוֹ. שֶׁכֵּן קָבַע הַבּוֹרֵא יִתְבָּרַךְ שְׁמוֹ טִבְעָם שֶׁל הָעוֹלָמוֹת, שֶׁיִּתְנַהֲגוּ עַל יְדֵי מַעֲשֵׂי הָאָדָם, וְכָל מִצְוָה, הִיא הָעוֹלָה מֵעַצְמָהּ לִפְעֹל פְּעֻלָּתָהּ הַמְּיֻחָד לָהּ:

וּמִי שֶׁזִּכָּהוּ יִתְבָּרַךְ שְׁמוֹ לְהַשִּׂיג נִסְתָּרוֹת תּוֹרָתֵנוּ הַקְּדוֹשָׁה, אֲשֶׁר הִשְׁאִירוּ לָנוּ בְּרָכָה קַדִּישֵׁי עֶלְיוֹנִין חַכְמֵי הַתַּלְמוּד, כְּגוֹן רַבִּי שִׁמְעוֹן בֶּן יוֹחַאי וַחֲבֵרָיו וְתַלְמִידָיו, וְשֶׁשּׁוֹתִין מֵימָיו בַּדּוֹרוֹת הָאַחֲרוֹנִים כְּמוֹ הָרַב הַקָּדוֹשׁ אִישׁ אֱלֹקִים נוֹרָא הָאֲרִיזַ"ל, אֲשֶׁר הֵאִירוּ עֵינֵינוּ בִּקְצָת טַעֲמֵי וְכַוָּנוֹת הַמִּצְוֹת, הוּא רַק כְּדֵי שֶׁיִּתְבּוֹנֵן כָּל אֶחָד לְפִי שִׂכְלוֹ וְהַשָּׂגָתוֹ, עַד הֵיכָן מַגִּיעִים כָּל פְּרָטֵי מַעֲשָׂיו וְדִבּוּרָיו וּמַחְשְׁבוֹתָיו וְכָל עִנְיָנָיו בְּהָעוֹלָמוֹת וְהַכֹּחוֹת עֶלְיוֹנִים וְתַחְתּוֹנִים, וְיִתְפַּעֵל וְיִתְעוֹרֵר מִזֶּה לַעֲשׂוֹת וּלְקַיֵּם כָּל מִצְוָה, וְכָל עִנְיְנֵי עֲבוֹדָתוֹ לְבוֹרְאוֹ יִתְבָּרַךְ שְׁמוֹ, בְּתַכְלִית הַדִּקְדּוּק וּבְאֵימָה וְיִרְאָה וְאַהֲבָה עֲצוּמָה וּבִקְדֻשָּׁה וְטָהֳרַת הַלֵּב, וְעַל יְדֵי זֶה יִגְרֹם תִּקּוּנִים יוֹתֵר גְּדוֹלִים בְּהָעוֹלָמוֹת, מֵאִם הָיָה מְקַיֵּם הַמִּצְוָה בְּלֹא קְדֻשַּׁת וְטָהֳרַת הַכַּוָּנָה. אָמְנָם הָעִקָּר בְּכָל הַמִּצְוֹת לְעִכּוּבָא, הוּא פְּרָטֵי הַמַּעֲשֶׂה שֶׁבָּהֶם:

שַׁעַר ב'

פֶּרֶק א'

כְּתִיב (דברים יא, יג): "לְאַהֲבָה אֶת ה' אֱלֹקֵיכֶם וּלְעָבְדוֹ בְּכָל לְבַבְכֶם וּבְכָל נַפְשְׁכֶם", וְאָמְרוּ רַבּוֹתֵינוּ זִכְרוֹנָם לִבְרָכָה בְּפֶרֶק קַמָּא דְּתַעֲנִית (ב.) וּבְסִפְרִי: "אֵיזוֹהִי עֲבוֹדָה שֶׁבַּלֵּב, הֱוֵי אוֹמֵר זוֹ תְּפִלָּה".

הִנֵּה הָאַהֲבָה שֶׁאָמַר שֶׁצְּרִיכָה לִהְיוֹת "בְּכָל לֵב", הוּא פָּשׁוּט, כִּי הִיא מִמִּצְוֹת הַתְּלוּיוֹת בַּלֵּב. וְכֵן עִנְיַן הָאַהֲבָה "בְּכָל נֶפֶשׁ" שֶׁאָמַר, הַיְנוּ אַף גַּם לִמְסֹר נַפְשׁוֹ עָלָיו יִתְבָּרַךְ שְׁמוֹ, מֵעֹצֶם נִפְלְאַת הָאַהֲבָה לוֹ יִתְבָּרַךְ. וּכְמוֹ שֶׁכָּתוּב בְּפָרָשָׁה רִאשׁוֹנָה: "וְאָהַבְתָּ אֵת ה' אֱלֹקֶיךָ בְּכָל לְבָבְךָ וּבְכָל נַפְשְׁךָ" (שם) גו'.

אָמְנָם בְּפָרָשָׁה זוֹ חִדּוּשׁ הוּא שֶׁחִדְּשָׁה, שֶׁגַּם הָעֲבוֹדָה, הִיא הַתְּפִלָּה, צְרִיכָה לִהְיוֹת "בְּכָל לֵב וּבְכָל נֶפֶשׁ". (וּלְהָכִי נַמִּי לֹא כְּתִיב "וּבְכָל מְאֹדְכֶם" בְּפָרָשָׁה זוֹ, כְּמוֹ בְּפָרָשָׁה רִאשׁוֹנָה דִּכְתִיב בָּהּ נַמִּי "וּבְכָל מְאֹדֶךָ", כִּי פָּרָשָׁה רִאשׁוֹנָה מַיְירֵי מֵעִנְיַן מִצְוַת הָאַהֲבָה לְחוּד, שַׁיָּךְ לוֹמַר שֶׁתִּהְיֶה הָאַהֲבָה גַּם "בְּכָל מְאֹד", זֶה הַמָּמוֹן, כְּמוֹ שֶׁאָמְרוּ רַבּוֹתֵינוּ זִכְרוֹנָם לִבְרָכָה (ברכות סא, ב): "אִם יֵשׁ לְךָ אָדָם שֶׁמָּמוֹנוֹ חָבִיב עָלָיו מִגּוּפוֹ, לְכָךְ נֶאֱמַר "וּבְכָל מְאֹדֶךָ". אֲבָל בְּפָרָשָׁה זוֹ דִּכְתִיב בָּהּ נַמִּי עֲבוֹדָה הִיא תְּפִלָּה, לֹא שַׁיָּךְ עָלֶיהָ כָּל כָּךְ "וּבְכָל מְאֹד"):

וְהִנֵּה מַה שֶּׁנֶּאֱמַר "בְּכָל לְבַבְכֶם" עַל עִנְיַן הַתְּפִלָּה, הוּא פָּשׁוּט וּמְבֹאָר כַּוָּנַת הַכָּתוּב לִשְׁנֵי עִנְיָנִים, הא' הַיְנוּ לְפַנּוֹת לִבּוֹ מִטִּרְדַּת הַמַּחְשָׁבוֹת, וּלְהַטּוֹתָהּ אֶל הַכַּוָּנָה הַשְּׁלֵמָה

לְתֵבוֹת הַתְּפִלָּה, בְּלֵבָב שָׁלֵם וּמֵעֻמְקָא דְּלִבָּא, כְּמַאֲמָרָם זִכְרוֹנָם לִבְרָכָה בִּבְרַיְתָא רֵישׁ פֶּרֶק אֵין עוֹמְדִין (ברכות לא, א): "הַמִּתְפַּלֵּל צָרִיךְ שֶׁיְּכַוֵּן אֶת לִבּוֹ לַשָּׁמַיִם, שֶׁנֶּאֱמַר (תהלים י) "תָּכִין לִבָּם" גו', וְכִדְמַשְׁמַע לְהוּ נַמִּי הָתָם מִקְרָאֵי דְּחַנָּה "וְחַנָּה הִיא מְדַבֶּרֶת עַל לִבָּהּ" (שמו"א א. יג): מִכָּאן לַמִּתְפַּלֵּל צָרִיךְ שֶׁיְּכַוֵּן לִבּוֹ. וּכְמוֹ שֶׁאָמַר דָּוִד הַמֶּלֶךְ עָלָיו הַשָּׁלוֹם (תהלים קיט י) "בְּכָל לִבִּי דְרַשְׁתִּיךָ".

וּבַזֹּהַר בְּשַׁלַּח ס"ג ב': "כָּל מַאן דִּמְצַלֵּי צְלוֹתָא קָמֵי מַלְכָּא קַדִּישָׁא, בָּעֵי לְמִבְעֵי בְּעוּתֵיהּ וּלְצַלָּאָה מֵעוּמְקָא דְּלִבָּא, בְּגִין דְּיִשְׁתְּכַּח לִבֵּיהּ שְׁלִים בְּקוּדְשָׁא בְּרִיךְ הוּא, וִיכַוֵּין לִבָּא וּרְעוּתָא" [כָּל מִי שֶׁמִּתְפַּלֵּל תְּפִלָּה לִפְנֵי הַמֶּלֶךְ הַקָּדוֹשׁ, צָרִיךְ לְבַקֵּשׁ בַּקָּשׁוֹתָיו וּלְהִתְפַּלֵּל מֵעֹמֶק הַלֵּב כְּדֵי שֶׁיִּמָּצֵא לִבּוֹ שָׁלֵם בְּהַקָּדוֹשׁ בָּרוּךְ הוּא, וִיכַוֵּן לִבּוֹ וּרְצוֹנוֹ.]

וְלָכֵן אָמְרוּ זִכְרוֹנָם לִבְרָכָה שָׁם סוֹף פֶּרֶק תְּפִלַּת הַשַּׁחַר (ברכות ל, ב) שֶׁהַמִּתְפַּלֵּל צָרִיךְ לִשְׁהוֹת וכו', כְּדֵי שֶׁתִּתְחוֹנֵן דַּעְתּוֹ עָלָיו. וְהַיְנוּ "בְּכָל לְבַבְכֶם", שֶׁתִּתְמַלֵּא כָּל הַלֵּב רַק בְּכַוָּנַת תֵּבוֹת הַתְּפִלָּה. שֶׁאִם יַעֲלֶה בְּלִבּוֹ אֵיזֶה מַחֲשָׁבָה אַחֶרֶת, הֲרֵי הַלֵּב חֲלוּקָה בִּשְׁנֵי מַחֲשָׁבוֹת:

והב' הַיְנוּ גַּם לְשָׁרֵשׁ מִלִּבּוֹ בַּעֲבוֹדַת הַתְּפִלָּה תַּעֲנוּגֵי הָעוֹלָם וַהֲנָאוֹתָיו מִכֹּל וָכֹל, וְאַךְ לְהִסְתַּכֵּל כְּלַפֵּי מַעְלָה בְּרוֹמְמוּת הַבּוֹרֵא יִתְבָּרַךְ. כְּמוֹ שֶׁאָמְרוּ (יבמות ק"ה ב'): "הַמִּתְפַּלֵּל צָרִיךְ שֶׁיִּתֵּן לִבּוֹ לְמַעְלָה", עַד שֶׁיְּהֵא כָּל כֹּחַ לִבּוֹ מְשׁוּכָה רַק לְמַעְלָה, לְהִתְעַנֵּג עַל ה' לְבַד בְּתֵבוֹת הַתְּפִלָּה. וּכְעִנְיַן הַחֲסִידִים הָרִאשׁוֹנִים, שֶׁהָיוּ שׁוֹהִים שָׁעָה אַחַת, כְּדֵי שֶׁיְּכַוְּנוּ אֶת לִבָּם לַמָּקוֹם, (ברכות ל, ב) וּכְעִנְיַן שֶׁפֵּרֵשׁ רַבֵּנוּ יוֹנָה זִכְרוֹנָם לִבְרָכָה שָׁם עִנְיָנָהּ, עַיֵּן שָׁם וְלִבְּךָ תָּשִׁית, וּכְמוֹ שֶׁאָמְרוּ בִּשְׁמוֹת רַבָּה פָּרָשָׁה כ"ב: "אָדָם צָרִיךְ שֶׁיְּטַהֵר לִבּוֹ קֹדֶם שֶׁיִּתְפַּלֵּל".

(אָמְנָם כָּל עִקַּר עִנְיַן טָהֳרַת הַלֵּב, הִיא רַק לְמִצְוָה וְלֹא לְעִכּוּבָא, גַּם לְעִנְיַן הַתְּפִלָּה, אַף שֶׁנִּקְרֵאת "עֲבוֹדָה שֶׁבַּלֵּב", כְּמוֹ שֶׁנִּתְבָּאֵר קְצָת לְעֵיל סוֹף שַׁעַר א', שֶׁהָעִקָּר בְּכָל הַמִּצְוֹת הִיא הַמַּעֲשֶׂה. עַיֵּן שָׁם):

וּלְהָבִין עִנְיַן מַה שֶּׁאָמַר הַכָּתוּב "וּבְכָל נַפְשְׁכֶם" עַל עֲבוֹדַת הַתְּפִלָּה, צָרִיךְ לְבָאֵר תְּחִלָּה פֵּרוּשׁ וְעִנְיַן הַ"בְּרָכָה" כִּבְיָכוֹל לוֹ יִתְבָּרַךְ שְׁמוֹ. שֶׁמָּצִינוּ כַּמָּה פְּעָמִים בַּמִּקְרָא (דברים ח, י) "וּבֵרַכְתָּ אֶת ה' אֱלֹקֶיךָ", "בָּרוּךְ ה' לְעוֹלָם" (תהלים פט, ו) גו', "בָּרְכִי נַפְשִׁי אֶת ה'" (שם קג, א), וְהַרְבֵּה כַּיּוֹצֵא. וְכֵן בְּדִבְרֵי רַבּוֹתֵינוּ זִכְרוֹנָם לִבְרָכָה מָצִינוּ (ברכות ז, א) שֶׁאָמַר כִּבְיָכוֹל לְרַבִּי יִשְׁמָעֵאל, יִשְׁמָעֵאל בְּנִי בָּרְכֵנִי. וְכֵן כָּל נוּסַח מַטְבֵּעַ תְּפִלּוֹת וְהַבְּרָכוֹת כֻּלָּם, שֶׁיְּסָדוּ אַנְשֵׁי כְּנֶסֶת הַגְּדוֹלָה, הֵם פּוֹתְחִים וּמְסַיְּמִים בְּ"בָרוּךְ":

פֶּרֶק ב'

וְהָעִנְיָן כִּי מִלַּת "בָּרוּךְ", אֵינוֹ לְשׁוֹן תְּהִלָּה וְשֶׁבַח, כְּמוֹ שֶׁשּׁוּמָה בְּפִי הֶהָמוֹן, שֶׁהֲרֵי (ברכות ז, א) כְּשֶׁאָמַר לְרַבִּי יִשְׁמָעֵאל, "יִשְׁמָעֵאל בְּנִי בָּרְכֵנִי", לֹא אָמַר שָׁם שׁוּם שֶׁבַח בְּבִרְכָתוֹ, אֶלָּא תְּפִלָּה וּבַקָּשַׁת רַחֲמִים (ברכות ז, א). וְכֵן בְּבָבָא מְצִיעָא (קיח, א) אַמְרִינַן:

"וּבֵרַכְךָ" (דברים כד) יָצָא הֶקְדֵּשׁ שֶׁאֵין צָרִיךְ בְּרָכָה. וּפָרִיךְ הַשַּׁ"ס – וְלֹא, וְהָא כְּתִיב "וְאָכַלְתָּ וְשָׂבָעְתָּ וּבֵרַכְתָּ אֶת ה'" (דברים ח, י) כו'.

אֲבָל הָאֱמֶת, כִּי "בָּרוּךְ" פֵּרוּשׁוֹ לְשׁוֹן תּוֹסֶפֶת וְרִבּוּי, וּכְעִנְיַן "קַח נָא אֶת בִּרְכָתִי" (בראשית לג, יא) גו', "וּבֵרַךְ אֶת לַחְמְךָ" (שמות כג, כה) "וּבֵרַךְ פְּרִי בִטְנְךָ" (דברים ז, יג) וגו', וְהַרְבֵּה כַּיּוֹצֵא בַּמִּקְרָא, שֶׁאִי אֶפְשָׁר לְפָרְשָׁם לְשׁוֹן תְּהִלָּה וְשֶׁבַח, אֶלָּא לְשׁוֹן תּוֹסֶפֶת וְרִבּוּי.

וּבַזֹּהַר אָמַר בְּכַמָּה מְקוֹמוֹת לְאַמְשָׁכָא בִּרְכָאן כו'. לְאַרְקָא בִּרְכָאן, לְאוֹסוּפֵי בִּרְכָאן, תּוֹסֶפֶת רִבּוּיָא דְּבִרְכָאן כו'. וְעַיֵּן בְּרַעְיָא מְהֵימְנָא (רֵישׁ פָּרָשַׁת עֵקֶב ע"א וע"ב) שֶׁ"בָּרוּךְ אַתָּה הֲוָיָ"ה" פֵּרוּשׁוֹ כְּמַשְׁמָעוֹ, לְאַמְשָׁכָא וּלְאַרְקָא חַיִּין מִמְּקוֹרָא דְּחַיֵּי, לִשְׁמֵיהּ דְּקוּדְשָׁא בְּרִיךְ הוּא קַדִּישָׁא כו', וּכְתִיב (שם): "וְאָכַלְתָּ וְשָׂבָעְתָּ וּבֵרַכְתָּ אֶת ה' אֱלֹהֶיךָ", וְאִנּוּן בִּרְכָאן אָרִיק בַּר נָשׁ בְּאִנּוּן מִלִּין כו', [לְהַמְשִׁיךְ וּלְהָרִיק חַיִּים מִמְּקוֹר הַחַיִּים לִשְׁמוֹ שֶׁל הַקָּדוֹשׁ בָּרוּךְ הוּא וגו', וְאֵלּוּ הַבְּרָכוֹת מֵרִיק אָדָם בְּמִלִּים אֵלּוּ וכו'], עַיֵּן שָׁם בְּאֹרֶךְ.

וְכֵן כָּתוּב בִּפְרִי עֵץ חַיִּים שַׁעַר הַקַּדִּישִׁים פֶּרֶק א', זֶה לְשׁוֹנוֹ: "סוֹד בָּרוּךְ בְּכָל מִינֵי רִבּוּיִין", וְכֵן הוּא שָׁם סוֹף שַׁעַר הַבְּרִיאָה, וְסוֹף פֶּרֶק ב' מִשַּׁעַר הָעֲמִידָה, וּבְרֵישׁ פֶּרֶק שְׁלִישִׁי שָׁם, וּבְשַׁעַר הַשַּׁבָּת רֵישׁ פי"ב, וּבְשַׁעַר תְּפִלַּת ר"ה פ"ג, ע"ש. וְכֵן כָּתַב הָרַשְׁבָּ"א זִכְרוֹנוֹ לִבְרָכָה בְּעִנְיַן יִשְׁמָעֵאל בְּנִי בָּרְכֵנִי, עַיֵּן שָׁם:

אָמְנָם, עִנְיַן הַבְּרָכָה לוֹ יִתְבָּרַךְ שְׁמוֹ, אֵין הַכַּוָּנָה לְעַצְמוּת אָדוֹן יָחִיד בָּרוּךְ הוּא כִּבְיָכוֹל, חָלִילָה וְחָלִילָה, כִּי הוּא מְרוֹמָם מֵעַל כָּל בְּרָכָה.

אֲבָל הָעִנְיָן, כְּמוֹ שֶׁאָמְרוּ בַּזֹּהַר (אמור צח: ועוד בכ"מ), דְּקוּדְשָׁא בְּרִיךְ הוּא סָתִים וְגַלְיָא, כִּי עַצְמוּת "אֵין סוֹף" בָּרוּךְ הוּא – סָתִים מִכָּל סְתִימִין, וְאֵין לְכַנּוֹתוֹ חַס וְשָׁלוֹם בְּשׁוּם שֵׁם כְּלָל, אֲפִלּוּ בְּשֵׁם "הֲוָיָ"ה" בָּרוּךְ הוּא, וַאֲפִלּוּ בְּקוֹצוֹ שֶׁל יוּ"ד דְּבֵיהּ.

(וְאַף גַּם מַה שֶּׁבַּזֹּהַר הַקָּדוֹשׁ מְכַנֵּהוּ יִתְבָּרַךְ בְּשֵׁם "אֵין סוֹף", אֵינֶנּוּ כִּנּוּי עָלָיו יִתְבָּרַךְ שְׁמוֹ, אֶלָּא הַכַּוָּנָה עַל הַשָּׂגָתֵנוּ אוֹתוֹ מִצַּד כֹּחוֹת הַנִּשְׁפָּעִים מֵאִתּוֹ בְּהִתְחַבְּרוּתוֹ בִּרְצוֹנוֹ לְהָעוֹלָמוֹת. וְלָזֹאת כִּנּוּהוּ "אֵין סוֹף", וְלֹא "אֵין רֵאשִׁית", כִּי בֶּאֱמֶת מִצַּד עַצְמוּתוֹ יִתְבָּרַךְ שְׁמוֹ, אֵין לוֹ לֹא סוֹף וְלֹא רֵאשִׁית, רַק מִצַּד הַשָּׂגָתֵנוּ כֹּחוֹתָיו יִתְבָּרַךְ, הֲלֹא כָּל הַשָּׂגָתֵנוּ הוּא רַק "רֵאשִׁית", אֲבָל "אֵין סוֹף" לְהַגִּיעַ בְּהַשָּׂגָה לְהַשִּׂיג אֶת כֹּחוֹתָיו יִתְבָּרַךְ שְׁמוֹ הַנִּשְׁפָּעִים).

וּמַה שֶּׁמֻּשָּׂג אֶצְלֵנוּ קְצָת, וְאָנוּ מְכַנִּים וּמְתָאֲרִים כַּמָּה תְּאָרִים וְשֵׁמוֹת וְכִנּוּיִים וּמִדּוֹת, כְּמוֹ שֶׁמְּצִיאוּם בַּתּוֹרָה וּבְכָל מַטְבֵּעַ הַתְּפִלָּה, כֻּלָּם הֵם רַק מִצַּד הִתְחַבְּרוּתוֹ יִתְבָּרַךְ אֶל הָעוֹלָמוֹת וְהַכֹּחוֹת מֵעֵת הַבְּרִיאָה, לְהַעֲמִידָם וּלְהַחֲיוֹתָם וּלְהַנְהִיגָם כִּרְצוֹנוֹ יִתְבָּרַךְ שְׁמוֹ, (וְהֵם אֲשֶׁר קְרָאוּם בְּשֵׁם "הִשְׁתַּלְשְׁלוּת הַסְּפִירוֹת").

וּלְפִי כָּל שִׁנּוּיֵי פְּרָטֵי סִדְרֵי הַהַנְהָגָה, שֶׁמִּשְׁתַּלְשֵׁל וְנִמְשָׁךְ לָזֶה הָעוֹלָם, אִם לְדִין, אִם לְחֶסֶד, אִם לְרַחֲמִים, עַל יְדֵי כֹּחוֹת הָעֶלְיוֹנִים וְהִתְמַזְּגוּתָם, מִשְׁתַּנִּים הַשֵּׁמוֹת וְהַכִּנּוּיִים וְהַתְּאָרִים. שֶׁלְּכָל עִנְיַן פְּרָטִי מִסִּדְרֵי הַהַנְהָגָה – מְיֻחָד לוֹ כִּנּוּי וְשֵׁם פְּרָטִי, שֶׁכֵּן מוֹרִים

פֵּרוּשָׁם שֶׁל כָּל הַתְּאָרִים שֶׁהֵם מִצַּד הַכֹּחוֹת הַבְּרוּאִים, כְּמוֹ "רַחוּם" וְ"חַנּוּן", פֵּרוּשָׁם, רַחְמָנוּת וַחֲנִינָה עַל הַבְּרוּאִים.

וַאֲפִלּוּ הַשֵּׁם הָעֶצֶם הַמְּיֻחָד הֲוָיָ"ה בָּרוּךְ הוּא, לֹא עַל עַצְמוּתוֹ יִתְבָּרַךְ לְבַד אָנוּ מְיַחֲדִים לוֹ, אֶלָּא מִצַּד הִתְחַבְּרוּתוֹ יִתְבָּרַךְ עִם הָעוֹלָמוֹת, כְּפֵרוּשׁוֹ הָיָה וְהֹוֶה וְיִהְיֶה וּמְהַוֶּה הַכֹּל, רָצָה לוֹמַר, הוּא יִתְבָּרַךְ מִתְחַבֵּר בִּרְצוֹנוֹ לְהָעוֹלָמוֹת לְהַוָּם וּלְקַיְּמָם כָּל רֶגַע . וְזֶה שֶׁאָמַר הָאֲרִיזַ"ל בִּלְשׁוֹנוֹ הַקָּדוֹשׁ, הוּבָא בְּהַקְדָּמַת פְּרִי עֵץ חַיִּים (בסוף הקדמה שניה), שֶׁכָּל הַכִּנּוּיִים וְהַשֵּׁמוֹת, הֵם שְׁמוֹת הָעַצְמוּת הַמִּתְפַּשְּׁטִים בַּסְּפִירוֹת, וְעַיֵּן שָׁם:

פֶּרֶק ג'

וְהוּא מַאֲמָרָם זִכְרוֹנָם לִבְרָכָה בִּשְׁמוֹת רַבָּה פָּרָשָׁה ג': "אֱלֹקֵי אֲבוֹתֵיכֶם שְׁלָחַנִי אֲלֵיכֶם" (שם ג, יג), אוֹתָהּ שָׁעָה נִתְבָּרֵר מֹשֶׁה עַל עֲסָקָיו כוּ', בְּאוֹתָהּ שָׁעָה הָיָה מְבַקֵּשׁ מֹשֶׁה שֶׁיּוֹדִיעֵנוּ הַקָּדוֹשׁ בָּרוּךְ הוּא אֶת הַשֵּׁם הַגָּדוֹל כוּ', אָמַר לוֹ הַקָּדוֹשׁ בָּרוּךְ הוּא לְמֹשֶׁה, שְׁמִי אַתָּה מְבַקֵּשׁ לֵידַע, לְפִי מַעֲשַׂי אֲנִי נִקְרָא, פְּעָמִים אֲנִי נִקְרָא בְּ'אֵל שַׁדַּי', בִּ'צְבָאוֹת' אוֹ בֶּ'אֱלֹהִים', בַּ'הֲוָיָה'. כְּשֶׁאֲנִי דָּן אֶת הַבְּרִיּוֹת – אֲנִי נִקְרָא "אֱלֹקִים", וּכְשֶׁאֲנִי עוֹשֶׂה מִלְחָמָה בָּרְשָׁעִים – אֲנִי נִקְרָא "צְבָאוֹת", וּכְשֶׁאֲנִי תּוֹלֶה חֲטָאָיו שֶׁל אָדָם – אֲנִי נִקְרָא "אֵ–ל שַׁדַּי", וּכְשֶׁאֲנִי מְרַחֵם עַל עוֹלָמִי – אֲנִי נִקְרָא "הֲוָיָה" כוּ', הֱוֵי "אֶהְיֶ"ה אֲשֶׁר אֶהְיֶ"ה" (שמות ג, יד), אֲנִי נִקְרָא לְפִי מַעֲשַׂי".

וּבְרַעְיָא מְהֵימְנָא פָּרָשַׁת בֹּא דַּף מ"ב ב': "כִּי לֹא רְאִיתֶם כָּל תְּמוּנָה" (דברים ד, טו) וגו', דְּהָא כְּתִיב (במדבר יב, ח) "וּתְמוּנַת ה' יַבִּיט" וגו', דַּאֲפִלּוּ הַאי תְּמוּנָה לֵית לֵיהּ בְּאַתְרֵיהּ, אֶלָּא כַּד נָחִית לְאַמְלָכָא עֲלַיְהוּ, וְיִתְפַּשֵּׁט עַל בְּרִיָּן [יִתְחַזֵי לוֹן לְכָל חַד כְּפוּם מַרְאֶה וְחֶזְיוֹן וְדִמְיוֹן דִּלְהוֹן] כוּ', דְּהָא קֹדֶם דְּבָרָא דְּיוֹקְנָא בְּעָלְמָא וְצִיֵּר צוּרָה, הֲוָה הוּא יְחִידָאִי בְּלָא צוּרָה וְדִמְיוֹן, וּמַאן דְּאִשְׁתְּמוֹדַע לֵיהּ קֹדֶם "בְּרִיאָה", דְּאִיהוּ לְבַר מִדְּיוֹקְנָא, אָסוּר לְמֶעְבַּד לֵיהּ צוּרָה וּדְיוֹקְנָא בְּעָלְמָא וכו', וַאֲפִלּוּ בִּשְׁמָא קַדִּישָׁא וְלָא בְּשׁוּם אוֹת וּנְקֻדָּה בְּעָלְמָא, וְהַאי אִיהוּ "כִּי לֹא רְאִיתֶם כָּל תְּמוּנָה" גו', אֲבָל בָּתַר דַּעֲבִיד הָא דְּיוֹקְנָא דְּמֶרְכָּבָה דְּאָדָם עִלָּאָה, נָחִית תַּמָּן וְאִתְקְרֵי בְּהַהוּא דְּיוֹקְנָא "הֲוָיָ"ה", בְּגִין דְּאִשְׁתְּמוֹדְעוּן לֵיהּ בִּדְמוּת דִּילֵיהּ כוּ', אֵל, אֱלֹהִים, שַׁדַּי, צְבָאוֹת, אֶהְיֶ"ה, בְּגִין דְּיִשְׁתְּמוֹדְעוּן לֵיהּ בְּכָל מִדָּה וּמִדָּה, אֵיךְ יִתְנַהֵג עָלְמָא בְּחֶסֶד וּבְדִינָא כוּ'. וַי לֵיהּ לְמַאן דְּיַשְׁוֵי לֵיהּ בְּשׁוּם מִדָּה כוּ', אֶלָּא דִּמְיוֹנָא דִּילֵיהּ כְּפוּם שָׁלְטָנוּתֵיהּ עַל הַהוּא מִדָּה, וַאֲפִלּוּ עַל כָּל בִּרְיָן כוּ', כַּד אִסְתַּלִּיק מִנָּהּ, לֵית לֵיהּ מִדָּה וְלָא דִּמְיוֹן", [כִּי לֹא רְאִיתֶם כָּל תְּמוּנָה וגו', הֲרֵי כָּתוּב "וּתְמוּנַת ה' יַבִּיט" וגו', שֶׁאֲפִילוּ תְּמוּנָה זוֹ אֵין לוֹ בִּמְקוֹמוֹ, אֶלָּא כְּשֶׁיּוֹרֵד לִמְלֹךְ עֲלֵיהֶם וּמִתְפַּשֵּׁט עַל הַבְּרִיּוֹת וכו', שֶׁהֲרֵי קֹדֶם שֶׁבָּרָא תְּמוּנָה בָּעוֹלָם וְצִיֵּר צוּרָה – הָיָה הוּא יָחִיד בְּלֹא צוּרָה וְדִמְיוֹן, וּמִי שֶׁמַּשִּׂיגוֹ קֹדֶם הַ"בְּרִיאָה", שֶׁהוּא עוֹד מִחוּץ לְכָל צוּרָה, אָסוּר לוֹ לַעֲשׂוֹת צוּרָה וּדְמוּת בָּעוֹלָם וכו', וַאֲפִילוּ בַּשֵּׁם הַקָּדוֹשׁ וְלֹא בְּשׁוּם אוֹת וּנְקֻדָּה בָּעוֹלָם, וְזֶה שֶׁאוֹמֵר הַכָּתוּב "כִּי לֹא רְאִיתֶם" וגו'. אֲבָל אַחַר שֶׁעָשָׂה אוֹתָהּ הַצּוּרָה שֶׁל הַמֶּרְכָּבָה שֶׁל אָדָם הָעֶלְיוֹן, יָרַד שָׁם וְהוּא נִקְרָא

בַּצּוּרָה הַהִיא הֲוָיָ"ה, כְּדֵי שֶׁיַּשִּׂיגוּ אוֹתוֹ בִּדְמוּת שֶׁלּוֹ וכו', אֵל, אֱלוֹקִים, שַׁדַּי, צְבָאוֹת, אֶהְיֶה, כְּדֵי שֶׁיַּכִּירוּ אוֹתוֹ בְּכָל מִדָּה וּמִדָּה אֵיךְ מַנְהִיג הָעוֹלָם בְּחֶסֶד וּבְדִין וכו', אוֹי לְמִי שֶׁיְּדַמֶּה אוֹתוֹ לְאֵיזֶה מִדָּה וכו', אֶלָּא הַדִּמְיוֹן שֶׁלּוֹ הוּא כְּפִי הַשְּׁלִיטָה שֶׁלּוֹ עַל אוֹתוֹ הַמִּדָּה, וַאֲפִילוּ עַל כָּל הַבְּרִיּוֹת וכו'. וּכְשֶׁהוּא מִסְתַּלֵּק מִמֶּנָּה אֵין לוֹ מִדָּה וְלֹא דִּמְיוֹן] עַיֵּן שָׁם.

וּבְפָרָשַׁת פִּנְחָס רכ"ה א': "וְאִיהוּ לָא אִתְקְרֵי הֲוָיָ"ה וּבְכָל שְׁמָהָן אֶלָּא בְּאִתְפַּשְּׁטוּת נְהוֹרֵיהּ עֲלַיְהוּ, וְכַד אִסְתַּלֵּק מִנַּיְהוּ, לֵית לֵיהּ מִגַּרְמֵיהּ שֵׁם כְּלָל" כו' [וְהוּא אֵינוֹ נִקְרָא "הֲוָיָ"ה" וּבְכָל הַשֵּׁמוֹת, אֶלָּא בְּהִתְפַּשְּׁטוּת אוֹרוֹ עֲלֵיהֶם. וּכְשֶׁמִּסְתַּלֵּק מֵהֶם אֵין לוֹ מֵעַצְמוּתוֹ שׁוּם שֵׁם כְּלָל וכו'.] עַיֵּן שָׁם.

וּבְתִקּוּנִים ת"ע קכ"א ב', הֶאֱרִיךְ בְּעִנְיַן פִּרְקֵי אֵבְרֵי הַשִּׁעוּר קוֹמָה כִּבְיָכוֹל, אָמַר אַחַר זֶה, שֶׁכָּל הָעִנְיָן הוּא לְאַחְזָאָה בְּכָל אֵבֶר וְאֵבֶר דְּגוּפֵיהּ – שׁוּלְטָנוּתֵיהּ, לְאִשְׁתְּמוֹדְעָא לְבַר נַשׁ אֵיךְ אִתְנְהִיג עָלְמָא, וְיִנְדַּע לְמִקְרֵי לֵיהּ בְּכָל אֵבֶר כִּדְקָא יָאוּת, וְאֵיךְ אִשְׁתַּנֵּי שְׁמֵיהּ לְפוּם הַהוּא אֵבֶר, וְאִית אֵבֶר דְּאִתְקְרֵי בֵּיהּ "הֲוָיָ"ה" – רַחֲמֵי, וְאִית אֵבֶר דְּאִתְקְרֵי בֵּיהּ "אֱלֹקִים", וְאִית אֵבֶר דְּאִתְקְרֵי בֵּי' כו', "אקי"ק" אַחְזֵי עַל עִלַּת הָעִלּוֹת כו', דְּעִלַּת עַל כָּל הָעִלּוֹת אִיהוּ חַד בְּכָל שְׁמָהָן, וְלָא אִשְׁתַּנֵּי בְּכֻלְּהוּ, דְּשִׁנּוּיִין בִּשְׁמָהָן אִנּוּן, וְלָאו בֵּיהּ כו', [לְהַרְאוֹת בְּכָל אֵבֶר וְאֵבֶר שֶׁבְּגוּפוֹ (אֶת) שִׁלְטוֹנוֹ, לְהוֹדִיעַ לָאָדָם אֵיךְ מִתְנַהֵג הָעוֹלָם, וְיֵדַע לִקְרֹא לוֹ בְּכָל אֵבֶר כָּרָאוּי, וְאֵיךְ מִשְׁתַּנֶּה שְׁמוֹ לְפִי הָאֵבֶר הַהוּא, וְיֵשׁ אֵבֶר שֶׁנִּקְרָא בּוֹ "הֲוָיָ"ה" רַחֲמִים, וְיֵשׁ אֵבֶר שֶׁנִּקְרָא בּוֹ "אֱלֹקִים", וְיֵשׁ אֵבֶר שֶׁנִּקְרָא בּוֹ וכו'. "אֶהְיֶה" מַרְאֶה וּמְלַמֵּד עַל מַהוּת עִלַּת הָעִלּוֹת וכו', שֶׁעִלַּת עַל כָּל הָעִלּוֹת הוּא אֶחָד בְּכָל הַשֵּׁמוֹת וְלֹא יִשְׁתַּנֶּה בְּכֻלָּם. שֶׁהַשִּׁנּוּיִים בַּשֵּׁמוֹת הֵם, וְלֹא בּוֹ]. עַיֵּן שָׁם. וְעַיֵּן עוֹד בְּרַעְיָא מְהֵימְנָא פִּנְחָס רנ"ז ב' ורנ"ח א', וְעַיֵּן בְּעֵץ חַיִּים רֵישׁ שַׁעַר עִגּוּלִים וְיֹשֶׁר, וְשָׁם בְּסוֹף זֶה הַשַּׁעַר רֵישׁ הַמַּהֲדוּרָא תִּנְיָנָא, וְתָבִין שָׁם עַל פִּי דְּבָרֵינוּ.

וְזֶה כָּל הַשָּׂגָתֵנוּ כִּבְיָכוֹל אוֹתוֹ יִתְבָּרֵךְ, הַכֹּל מִצַּד עִנְיַן הִתְחַבְּרוּתוֹ אֶל הָעוֹלָמוֹת וְהִתְפַּשְּׁטוּתוֹ יִתְבָּרֵךְ בְּתוֹכָם. כְּמוֹ שֶׁכָּתוּב בְּרַעְיָא מְהֵימְנָא פ' בֹּא הַנִּזְכָּר לְעֵיל, דַּאֲפִילוּ הַאי תְּמוּנָה לֵית לֵיהּ בְּאַתְרֵיהּ, אֶלָּא כַּד נָחִית לְאַמְלָכָא עֲלַיְהוּ, וְיִתְפַּשֵּׁט עַל בִּרְיָן, יִתְחֲזֵי לְכָל חַד כְּפוּם מַרְאֶה וְחֶזְוָן וְדִמְיוֹן דִּלְהוֹן, וְהַאי אִיהוּ "וּבְיַד הַנְּבִיאִים אֲדַמֶּה" (הושע יב, יא):

וְלָכֵן קָבְעוּ אַנְשֵׁי כְּנֶסֶת הַגְּדוֹלָה, הַנּוּסָח שֶׁל כָּל בִּרְכוֹת הַמִּצְוֹת בִּלְשׁוֹן נוֹכֵחַ וְנִסְתָּר. תְּחִלָּתָם "בָּרוּךְ אַתָּה" – הוּא לְשׁוֹן נוֹכֵחַ, וּמְסַיְּמִים "אֲשֶׁר קִדְּשָׁנוּ כו' וְצִוָּנוּ" – לְשׁוֹן נִסְתָּר.

שֶׁמִּצַּד הִתְחַבְּרוּתוֹ יִתְבָּרֵךְ בִּרְצוֹנוֹ אֶל הָעוֹלָמוֹת, שֶׁעַל יְדֵי זֶה יֵשׁ לָנוּ קְצָת הַשָּׂגָה כָּל דְּהוּ, אָנוּ מְדַבְּרִים לְנוֹכֵחַ – "בָּרוּךְ אַתָּה ה'" כו', כִּי הָעוֹלָמוֹת הֵם הַצְּרִיכִים לְעִנְיַן הַתּוֹסֶפֶת וְרִבּוּי בְּרָכָה מֵעַצְמוּתוֹ יִתְבָּרֵךְ הַמִּתְחַבֵּר אֲלֵיהֶם, וְזֶהוּ "מֶלֶךְ הָעוֹלָם", כְּמוֹ שֶׁאָמְרוּ בְּרַעְיָא מְהֵימְנָא הַנִּזְכָּר לְעֵיל "כַּד נָחִית לְאַמְלָכָא עֲלַיְהוּ וְיִתְפַּשֵּׁט עַל בִּרְיָן" כו'.

וְהַמְצַוֶּה אוֹתָנוּ וּמְקַדְּשֵׁנוּ, הוּא עַצְמוּתוֹ יִתְבָּרֵךְ אֵין סוֹף בָּרוּךְ הוּא לְבַדּוֹ, הַסָּתוּם מִכָּל סְתִימִין, לָכֵן תִּקְּנוּ בִּלְשׁוֹן נִסְתָּר "אֲשֶׁר קִדְּשָׁנוּ וְצִוָּנוּ":

פֶּרֶק ד'

וְטַעְמוֹ שֶׁל דָּבָר, שֶׁנִּכְלָל בְּכָל בְּרָכָה שְׁנֵי הַבְּחִינוֹת הַנַּ"ל, כִּי יְסוֹד פִּנַּת אֱמוּנָתֵנוּ הַקְּדוֹשָׁה, שֶׁכָּל מְגַמַּת כַּוָּנַת לִבֵּנוּ בְּכָל הַבְּרָכוֹת וְהַתְּפִלּוֹת וּבַקָּשׁוֹת — אַךְ רַק לִיחִידוֹ שֶׁל עוֹלָם, אָדוֹן יָחִיד אֵין סוֹף בָּרוּךְ הוּא.

אָמְנָם לֹא שֶׁאָנוּ מְדַבְּרִים אֵלָיו כִּבְיָכוֹל עַל עַצְמוּתוֹ יִתְבָּרַךְ לְבַד, בִּבְחִינַת הֱיוֹתוֹ מֻפְשָׁט וּמֻפְרָשׁ כִּבְיָכוֹל לְגַמְרֵי מֵהָעוֹלָמוֹת, כְּעִנְיָן שֶׁהָיָה קֹדֶם הַבְּרִיאָה, דְּאִם כֵּן אֵיךְ נִתְאַרֵהוּ חַס וְשָׁלוֹם בְּכָל בִּרְכוֹתֵינוּ וּתְפִלָּתֵנוּ בְּשׁוּם שֵׁם וְכִנּוּי בָּעוֹלָם כְּלָל.

וְגַם, דְּאִם לֹא מִצַּד שֶׁהֶרְאָנוּ יִתְבָּרַךְ שֶׁרְצוֹנוֹ לְהִתְחַבֵּר לְהָעוֹלָמוֹת, וּלְאַמְלָכָא עַל בְּרָיָן כְּפוּם עוֹבָדֵיהוֹן, לֹא הָיִינוּ רַשָּׁאִים כְּלָל לְהִתְפַּלֵּל לְעַצְמוּתוֹ יִתְבָּרַךְ שֶׁיִּתְחַבֵּר לְהָעוֹלָמוֹת וּלְאַשְׁגָּחָא עַל בְּרָיָן.

וְלָכֵן מַקְדִּימִין אֲנַחְנוּ לוֹמַר "אַתָּה ה' מֶלֶךְ הָעוֹלָם", פֵּרוּשׁ, אַחַר שֶׁרְצוֹנְךָ הָיָה לְהַוּוֹת הָעוֹלָמוֹת וּלְהִתְחַבֵּר אֲלֵיהֶם לְאַמְלָכָא עֲלֵיהוֹן, לָזֹאת, בַּקָּשָׁתֵנוּ שֶׁיִּתְבָּרַךְ מְקוֹר הָרָצוֹן לְאַמְלָכָא כֵּן לְעָלְמִין.

וְגַם שֶׁלְּפִי בְּחִינַת עַצְמוּתוֹ יִתְבָּרַךְ, בִּלְתִּי הִתְחַבְּרוּתוֹ אֶל הָעוֹלָמוֹת, אֵין מָקוֹם לְתוֹרָה וּמִצְוֹת כְּלָל. וְעַל זֶה נֶאֱמַר (איוב לה): "אִם חָטָאתָ מַה תִּפְעָל בּוֹ וגו', אִם צָדַקְתָּ מַה תִּתֶּן לוֹ אוֹ מַה מִיָּדְךָ יִקָּח", וְכֵן כְּתִיב (משלי ט, יב): "אִם חָכַמְתָּ חָכַמְתָּ לָּךְ", כִּי לְעַצְמוּת אֲדוֹן כֹּל בָּרוּךְ הוּא, כֹּל מַעֲשֵׂה הָאָדָם, הֲטוֹבָה הִיא אִם רָעָה, אֵינֶנָּה נוֹגַעַת לוֹ בְּעֶצֶם כְּלָל חַס וְשָׁלוֹם.

וְהוּא מַאֲמָרָם זִכְרוֹנָם לִבְרָכָה בִּבְרֵאשִׁית רַבָּה רֵישׁ פָּרָשָׁה מ"ד: (תהלים יח, לא) "אִמְרַת ה' צְרוּפָה" גו', אָמַר רַב, לֹא נִתְּנוּ הַמִּצְוֹת אֶלָּא לְצָרֵף כו', וְכִי מָה אִכְפַּת לֵיהּ לְהַקָּדוֹשׁ בָּרוּךְ הוּא לְמִי שֶׁשּׁוֹחֵט מִן הַצַּוָּאר אוֹ מִי שֶׁשּׁוֹחֵט מִן הָעֹרֶף" כו', וְכֵן הוּא בְּתַנְחוּמָא פָּרָשַׁת שְׁמִינִי (סימן ז וסימן ח) בְּפָסוּק זֹאת הַחַיָּה כו', וּבְמִדְרַשׁ תְּהִלִּים מִזְמוֹר י"ח, עַיֵּן שָׁם.

וּבַתִּקּוּנִים תִּקּוּן ע' ק"ל סוֹף ע"א: "עִלַּת הָעִלּוֹת מִתְעַלָּה עַל כֹּלָּא, אִיהוּ בָּרִיךְ לְכֹלָּא, וְלָא צָרִיךְ אִיהוּ בִּרְכָאָן מֵאָחֳרָא, דְּלֵית עָלֵיהּ מָאן דְּאַשְׁפַּע לֵיהּ, הֲדָא הוּא דִכְתִיב (נחמיה ט, ה): "וּמְרוֹמַם עַל כָּל בְּרָכָה וּתְהִלָּה": [עִלַּת הָעִלּוֹת מִתְעַלָּה עַל הַכֹּל הוּא מְבָרֵךְ לְכֻלָּם וְאֵין הוּא צָרִיךְ בְּרָכוֹת מֵאֲחֵרִים, שֶׁאֵין מִישֶׁהוּ שֶׁיַּשְׁפִּיעַ לוֹ זֶהוּ שֶׁכָּתוּב "וּמְרוֹמַם עַל כָּל בְּרָכָה וּתְהִלָּה"].

אֶלָּא שֶׁכָּל כַּוָּנַת לִבֵּנוּ — בְּכָל הַבְּרָכוֹת וְהַתְּפִלּוֹת — צָרִיךְ שֶׁתִּהְיֶה לְעַצְמוּת אֵין סוֹף בָּרוּךְ הוּא, מִצַּד הִתְחַבְּרוֹ כִּרְצוֹנוֹ יִתְבָּרַךְ אֶל הָעוֹלָמוֹת, שֶׁמִּצִּדָּם הֵם כָּל הַתְּאָרִים וְהַשֵּׁמוֹת מִתְחַלְּפִים, לִפְעֹל וּלְהַמְשִׁיךְ בָּהֶם אוֹר וְשִׁפְעַת קְדֻשָּׁה מֵעַצְמוּתוֹ יִתְבָּרַךְ, כְּפִי הִתְעוֹרְרוּת הַמַּגִּיעַ אֲלֵיהֶם מִמַּעֲשֵׂי הָאָדָם שֶׁל כָּל אִישׁ מֵעַם סְגֻלָּה, אִם בְּחֶסֶד, אִם בְּמִשְׁפָּט, אִם בִּצְדָקָה, אִם בְּרַחֲמִים, הַמְעַט וְאִם רַב, כָּכָה הוּא עַל זֶה הָאֹפֶן וְהַשִּׁעוּר בְּדִקְדּוּק עָצוּם בְּמִדָּה וּבְמִשְׁקָל, עִנְיַן הִתְחַבְּרוּתוֹ יִתְבָּרַךְ אֶל הַכֹּחוֹת וְהָעוֹלָמוֹת, לְשַׁנּוֹת

סֵדֶר הִתְקַשְּׁרוּתָם לְהַמְשָׁכַת שִׁפְעַת אוֹרָם, וְכָל פְּרָטֵי הַנְהָגָתָם, אִם לְדִין וְרֹגֶז, אִם לְחֶסֶד וְרַחֲמִים, וְגַם שִׁעוּר הַדִּין וְהַחֶסֶד הַמְעַט וְאִם רַב:

זֶהוּ שֶׁאָמְרוּ בְּהַמַּאֲמָרִים הַנַּ"ל, "שֶׁלֹּא נִתְּנוּ הַמִּצְוֹת אֶלָּא לְצָרֵף בָּהֶן אֶת הַבְּרִיּוֹת", הַיְנוּ שֶׁצֹּרֶךְ גָּדוֹל הֵמָּה לְצָרֵף וּלְזַקֵּק, לְהַפְרִיד הַסִּיגִים מִכָּל הַכֹּחוֹת וְהָעוֹלָמוֹת הַבְּרוּאִים יִתְצָרֵף וְיִתְלַבֵּן. וְגַם כֵּן בְּמַשְׁמָע. "לְצָרֵף" — הַיְנוּ לְחַבֵּר וּלְקַשֵּׁר כָּל הַכֹּחוֹת וְהָעוֹלָמוֹת הַבְּרוּאִים מְתֻקָּנִים וּמְסֻדָּרִים כְּפִי הַכַּוָּנָה וְהָרָצוֹן הָעֶלְיוֹן בָּרוּךְ הוּא, וּמִמֵּילָא גַּם בֵּית יִשְׂרָאֵל עַם סְגֻלָּה יִתְאַחֲדוּ בַּשֵּׁם הַמְיֻחָד יִתְבָּרֵךְ לְחֶלְקוֹ וְנַחֲלָתוֹ, שֶׁרַק עַל זֶה הַתַּכְלִית בָּאוּ כָּל הַמִּצְוֹת וְהָעֲבוֹדָה הַקְּדוֹשָׁה כֻּלָּהּ בִּכְלָלָהּ:

זֶהוּ עִנְיַן הַבְּרָכָה לוֹ יִתְבָּרֵךְ בְּכָל הַבְּרָכוֹת וְהַתְּפִלּוֹת, שֶׁפֵּרוּשׁוֹ הוּא, תּוֹסֶפֶת וְרִבּוּי מַמָּשׁ כְּמַשְׁמָעוֹ כַּנַּ"ל (פֶּרֶק ב), שֶׁזֶּהוּ רְצוֹנוֹ יִתְבָּרֵךְ מִטַּעַם כָּמוּס אִתּוֹ יִתְבָּרֵךְ, שֶׁנִּתְקַן וּנְיַחֵד עַל יְדֵי הַבְּרָכוֹת וְהַתְּפִלּוֹת הַכֹּחוֹת וְהָעוֹלָמוֹת הָעֶלְיוֹנִים, שֶׁיִּהְיוּ מוּכָנִים וּרְאוּיִם לְקַבֵּל שִׁפְעַת קְדֻשַּׁת אוֹר עֶלְיוֹן, וּלְהַמְשִׁיךְ וּלְהוֹסִיף בָּהֶם קְדֻשַּׁת הָאוֹר וְרֹב בְּרָכוֹת, מֵעַצְמוּתוֹ יִתְבָּרַךְ הַמִּתְחַבֵּר אֲלֵיהֶם וּמִתְפַּשֵּׁט בְּתוֹכָם, וּמִמֵּילָא יֻשְׁפַּע זֶה הַתּוֹסֶפֶת בְּרָכָה וְהַקְּדֻשָּׁה גַּם עַל עַם סְגֻלָּה שֶׁגָּרְמוּ וְסִבְּבוּ לְכָל הַכָּבוֹד הַזֶּה.

וְזֶה שֶׁאָמַר רַבִּי יִשְׁמָעֵאל, כְּשֶׁבִּקֵּשׁ הוּא יִתְבָּרֵךְ מֵאִתּוֹ, "יִשְׁמָעֵאל בְּנִי בָּרְכֵנִי", "יְהִי רָצוֹן שֶׁיִּכְבְּשׁוּ רַחֲמֶיךָ אֶת כַּעַסְךָ, וְיִגֹּלּוּ רַחֲמֶיךָ כו', וְתִתְנַהֵג עִם בָּנֶיךָ בְּמִדַּת הָרַחֲמִים, וְתִכָּנֵס לָהֶם לִפְנִים מִשּׁוּרַת הַדִּין" (ברכות ז, א).

וְעַיֵּן זֹהַר חָדָשׁ רוּת ס"ז ב', "רַבִּי נְחֶמְיָה פָּתַח, "וְאָכַלְתָּ גו' וּבֵרַכְתָּ אֶת ה' אֱלֹהֶיךָ" גו' (דברים ח, ו), וְאָמַר רַבִּי יוּדָא "גָּדוֹל כֹּחַ בִּרְכַּת הַמָּזוֹן שֶׁמּוֹסִיף כֹּחַ בְּרָכָה בְּפָמַלְיָא שֶׁל מַעְלָה". וְלָכֵן אָמְרוּ רַבּוֹתֵינוּ זִכְרוֹנָם לִבְרָכָה (ברכות לה: ר"פ כֵּיצַד מְבָרְכִין) וּבְזֹהַר חָדָשׁ שָׁם: "כָּל הָאוֹכֵל וְאֵינוֹ מְבָרֵךְ נִקְרָא גַּזְלָן, שֶׁנֶּאֱמַר "גּוֹזֵל אָבִיו וְאִמּוֹ" גו', וְאֵין אָבִיו אֶלָּא הַקָּדוֹשׁ בָּרוּךְ הוּא כו', כִּי הוּא גּוֹזֵל וּמוֹנֵעַ מֵהָעוֹלָמוֹת — שִׁפְעַת הַבְּרָכָה וְהַקְּדֻשָּׁה, שֶׁהָיָה צָרִיךְ לְהַשְׁפִּיעַ בָּהֶם עַל יְדֵי בִּרְכָתוֹ.

וְכֵן כָּל הַמִּקְרָאוֹת "בָּרְכִי נַפְשִׁי אֶת ה'" (תהלים קג), "בָּרוּךְ אַתָּה ה' אֱלֹהֵי יִשְׂרָאֵל" גו' (דה"י א' כט, יא), וְכָל כַּיּוֹצֵא בּוֹ, הַכֹּל הוּא עַל זֶה הָעִנְיָן. וּמִצַּד רְצוֹנוֹ יִתְבָּרֵךְ לְהִתְחַבֵּר אֶל הַבְּרִיאָה, עַל זֶה נֶאֱמַר (עי' מנחות סד. שבת קטז:) "הָעֲבוֹדָה צֹרֶךְ גָּבוֹהַּ":

פֶּרֶק ה'

אָמְנָם, לְהָבִין עִקָּרוֹ שֶׁל עִנְיַן הַתּוֹסֶפֶת וְרִבּוּי בְּרָכָה בְּהָעוֹלָמוֹת — עַל יְדֵי מַעֲשֵׂי הָאָדָם, וּמַהוּת הָעִנְיָן צֹרֶךְ הָעוֹלָמוֹת לָזֶה.

הִנֵּה רַבּוֹתֵינוּ זִכְרוֹנָם לִבְרָכָה אָמְרוּ (ברכות י, א): "הַנֵּי חֲמִשָּׁה "בָּרְכִי נַפְשִׁי", כְּנֶגֶד מִי אֲמָרָן דָּוִד, לֹא אֲמָרָן אֶלָּא כְּנֶגֶד הַקָּדוֹשׁ בָּרוּךְ הוּא וּכְנֶגֶד הַנְּשָׁמָה, מַה הַקָּדוֹשׁ בָּרוּךְ הוּא מָלֵא כָּל הָעוֹלָם — אַף הַנְּשָׁמָה מְלֵאָה כָּל הַגּוּף" כו'. וְכֵן אָמְרוּ בְּוַיִּקְרָא רַבָּה פָּרָשָׁה ד', וּדְבָרִים רַבָּה סוֹף פָּרָשָׁה ב', וּבְמִדְרַשׁ תְּהִלִּים מִזְמוֹר ק"ג, וּבַתִּקּוּנִים רֵישׁ תִּקּוּן י"ג, וּכְמוֹ

שֶׁבֵּאֵר בְּרַעְיָא מְהֵימְנָא פָּרָשַׁת פִּנְחָס רנ"ז ב' ורנ"ח א'. וְעַיֵּן בְּעֵץ חַיִּים שַׁעַר פְּנִימִיּוּת וְחִיצוֹנִיּוּת סוֹף דְּרוּשׁ י"א.

וְזֶה שֶׁאָמְרוּ רַבּוֹתֵינוּ זִכְרוֹנָם לִבְרָכָה בְּמַסֶּכֶת רֹאשׁ הַשָּׁנָה (כה, ב) וּבַעֲבוֹדָה זָרָה (מג, ב) בַּבְּרַיְתָא, כָּל הַפַּרְצוּפוֹת מֻתָּרִים חוּץ מִפַּרְצוּף אָדָם, וּמְפָרֵשׁ טַעְמָא דִּכְתִיב (שמות כ, כ): "לֹא תַעֲשׂוּן אִתִּי" – לֹא תַעֲשׂוּן אוֹתִי. וְכֵן מָצִינוּ בַּזֹּהַר יִתְרוֹ פ"ו סוֹף ע"א, עַיֵּן שָׁם.

וּבִבְרֵאשִׁית רַבָּה רֵישׁ פָּרָשָׁה כ"ז אָמְרוּ: כְּתִיב (קהלת ב, כא) "כִּי יֵשׁ אָדָם שֶׁעֲמָלוֹ בְּחָכְמָה" גו', אָמַר רַבִּי יוּדָן גָּדוֹל כֹּחָן שֶׁל נְבִיאִים שֶׁמְּדַמִּין צוּרָה לְיוֹצְרָהּ, שֶׁנֶּאֱמַר (דניאל ח, טז): "וָאֶשְׁמַע קוֹל אָדָם בֵּין אוּלָי", אָמַר רַבִּי יְהוּדָה בַּ"ר סִימוֹן אִית לָן קְרָיָא אוֹחֲרָן דִּמְחַוַּר יָתִיר מִן דֵּין, [יֵשׁ לָנוּ מִקְרָא אַחֵר מְפֹרָשׁ יוֹתֵר מִזֶּה], שֶׁנֶּאֱמַר (יחזקאל ו, כא): "וְעַל דְּמוּת הַכִּסֵּא דְּמוּת כְּמַרְאֵה אָדָם" גו'. וּבְבַמִּדְבַּר רַבָּה פָּרָשָׁה י"ט "חָכְמַת אָדָם תָּאִיר פָּנָיו" (קהלת ח, א), אָמַר רַבִּי יוּדָן גָּדוֹל כֹּחָן שֶׁל נְבִיאִים שֶׁמְּדַמִּין דְּמוּת גְּבוּרָה שֶׁל מַעְלָה לְצוּרַת אָדָם כו', עַיֵּן שָׁם. וְכֵן הוּא בְּקֹהֶלֶת רַבָּה סִימָן ח' פָּסוּק א', וּבְתַנְחוּמָא פָּרָשַׁת חֻקַּת.

וְלִכְאוֹרָה יִפָּלֵא, כִּי "אֶל מִי תְּדַמְּיוּן" (ישעיה מ, יח) וגו'. אָמְנָם הָעִנְיָן כְּמוֹ שֶׁכָּתַבְתִּי לְעֵיל (סוֹף"ג), שֶׁכָּל הַשָּׂגָתֵנוּ כִּבְיָכוֹל אוֹתוֹ יִתְבָּרַךְ שְׁמוֹ, הוּא רַק מִצַּד הִתְחַבְּרוּתוֹ יִתְבָּרַךְ לְהָעוֹלָמוֹת. וְסֵדֶר מַצַּב הָעוֹלָמוֹת וְהַכֹּחוֹת כֻּלָּם, הָעֶלְיוֹנִים וְתַחְתּוֹנִים יַחַד בִּכְלָל, מְסֻדָּרִים כִּבְיָכוֹל בְּכָל פְּרָטֵיהֶם כְּתַבְנִית קוֹמַת אָדָם, בְּסִדּוּר כָּל פִּרְקֵי אֵבָרָיו וְגִידָיו וְכָל פְּרָטֵי הָעִנְיָנִים שֶׁבּוֹ וְהִתְאַחֲדוּתָם אֶחָד בַּחֲבֵרוֹ, שֶׁהוּא כּוֹלְלָם יַחַד בְּתוֹכוֹ כָּל הַכֹּחוֹת וְהָעוֹלָמוֹת, כְּמוֹ שֶׁנִּתְבָּאֵר לְעֵיל בְּשַׁעַר א'.

וְהוּא עִנְיַן "הַשִּׁעוּר קוֹמָה" – הַנִּזְכָּר בְּדִבְרֵיהֶם זִכְרוֹנָם לִבְרָכָה בַּמִּדְרָשִׁים. וְעַיֵּן בְּעֵץ חַיִּים שַׁעַר עִגּוּלִים וְיֹשֶׁר עָנָף ב' וג' וד' שָׁם, וְשָׁם בְּסוֹף הַשַּׁעַר בְּרֵישׁ מַהֲדוּרָא תִּנְיָנָא. וְכָתַב שָׁם שֶׁזֶּה רֶמֶז הַכָּתוּב (בראשית א, כז) "וַיִּבְרָא אֱלֹקִים אֶת הָאָדָם בְּצַלְמוֹ בְּצֶלֶם אֱלֹקִים". וְעַיֵּן עוֹד בְּרֵישׁ שַׁעַר הַצֶּלֶם, וּבְשַׁעַר צִיּוּר עוֹלָמוֹת אבי"ע שָׁם.

וְעַצְמוּתוֹ יִתְבָּרַךְ מִתְפַּשֵּׁט וּמִסְתַּתֵּר בְּתוֹךְ כֻּלָּם, וּמְמַלְּאָם, וְהוּא נִשְׁמְתָא דִּלְהוֹן, כִּבְיָכוֹל כְּעִנְיַן הַנְּשָׁמָה הַמִּתְפַּשֶּׁטֶת וּמִסְתַּתֶּרֶת בְּגוּף הָאָדָם, לָכֵן הִרְשִׁינוּ לְתָאֲרוֹ יִתְבָּרַךְ עַל זֶה הָאֹפֶן.

וְגַם הָרַמְבַּ"ם זִכְרוֹנוֹ לִבְרָכָה כָּתַב בַּמּוֹרֶה בְּפֶרֶק ע"ב מֵחֵלֶק הא', שֶׁכָּל זֶה הָעוֹלָם בִּכְלָלוֹ נִקְרָא "שִׁעוּר קוֹמָה", וְהֶאֱרִיךְ לְהַמְשִׁיל כְּלַל חֶלְקֵי הָעוֹלָם לְחֶלְקֵי אֵבְרֵי הָאָדָם וְכָל עִנְיָנָיו שֶׁבּוֹ, וְשֶׁהוּא יִתְבָּרַךְ הוּא נִשְׁמַת הָעוֹלָם כְּעִנְיַן הַנְּשָׁמָה לְגוּף הָאָדָם עַיֵּן שָׁם, וּדְבָרָיו זִכְרוֹנוֹ לִבְרָכָה רְאוּיִים לְמִי שֶׁאֲמָרָם, שֶׁכֵּן מְבֹאָר בַּזֹּהַר (תולדות קל"ד ע"ג) עַיֵּן שָׁם. וּמִדְּבָרָיו זִכְרוֹנוֹ לִבְרָכָה נִשְׁמַע לְדִידָן, לְעִנְיַן סֵדֶר כְּלַל הָעוֹלָמוֹת כֻּלָּם יַחַד.

וּשְׁגוּרָה בְּפִי רַבּוֹתֵינוּ זִכְרוֹנָם לִבְרָכָה שֶׁהָאָדָם הוּא אִיקוֹנִין וּדְיוֹקָן מַלְכּוֹ שֶׁל עוֹלָם יִתְבָּרַךְ שְׁמוֹ, כְּמוֹ שֶׁאָמְרוּ בְּסַנְהֶדְרִין (מו, א' וב'): "לֹא תָלִין נִבְלָתוֹ גו' כִּי קִלְלַת אֱלֹהִים תָּלוּי" (דברים כא, כג) תַּנְיָא אָמַר רַבִּי מֵאִיר, מָשְׁלוּ מָשָׁל לְמָה הַדָּבָר דּוֹמֶה, לִשְׁנֵי אַחִים

תְּאוֹמִים כו', אֶחָד מִנּוּהוּ מֶלֶךְ וְאֶחָד יָצָא לְלִסְטִיּוּת, צִוָּה הַמֶּלֶךְ וּתְלָאוּהוּ, כָּל הָרוֹאֶה אוֹתוֹ אוֹמֵר, הַמֶּלֶךְ תָּלוּי כו', וּפֵרֵשׁ רַשִׁ"י, אַף אָדָם עָשׂוּי בִּדְיוֹקְנוֹ שֶׁל מָקוֹם. וּבִשְׁמוֹת רַבָּה פָּרָשָׁה ל' (טז), "מַכֵּה אִישׁ וָמֵת" (שמות כא. יב) וגו', מָשָׁל לְאָדָם שֶׁקִּפֵּחַ אִיקוֹנִין שֶׁל מֶלֶךְ כו', אָמַר הַמֶּלֶךְ לֹא קְרָאתָ כו', שֶׁכָּל מִי שֶׁהוּא נוֹגֵעַ בְּאִיקוֹנִין שֶׁלִּי הוּא אָבֵד [מִיִּשְׂרָאֵל], כָּךְ אִם הָרַג אָדָם נֶפֶשׁ כו' כְּאִלּוּ הוּא מַעֲבִיר אִיקוֹנִין שֶׁל מֶלֶךְ, רוֹצֶה לוֹמַר, זֶה שֶׁסִּיֵּם בְּסֵיפֵיהּ דִּקְרָא הַטַּעַם עַל זֶה "כִּי בְּצֶלֶם אֱלֹקִים עָשָׂה אֶת הָאָדָם":

פֶּרֶק ו'

וּכְמוֹ שֶׁעִנְיַן חִבּוּר וְקִיּוּם נִשְׁמַת הָאָדָם בְּגוּפוֹ, הוּא עַל יְדֵי אֲכִילָה וּשְׁתִיָּה, וּבִלְתָּם תִּפָּרֵד וְתִסְתַּלֵּק מֵהַגּוּף, כֵּן חִבּוּר עַצְמוּתוֹ יִתְבָּרֵךְ אֶל הָעוֹלָמוֹת, שֶׁהֵן סוֹד "הָאָדָם הַגָּדוֹל", כְּדֵי לְהַעֲמִידָם וּלְקַיְּמָם, וְלֹא תִּגְעַל נַפְשׁוֹ אוֹתָם, גָּזְרָה רְצוֹנוֹ יִתְבָּרֵךְ שֶׁיְּהֵא תָּלוּי בְּעֵסֶק הַתּוֹרָה וּמַעֲשֵׂי הַמִּצְוֹת וַעֲבוֹדַת הַתְּפִלָּה שֶׁל עַם סְגֻלָּה, וּבִלְתָּם הָיָה הוּא יִתְבָּרֵךְ מְסַלֵּק עַצְמוּתוֹ יִתְבָּרֵךְ מֵהֶם, וּכְרֶגַע הָיוּ חוֹזְרִים כֻּלָּם לְאֶפֶס וָאַיִן.

וְלָכֵן אָמְרוּ רַבּוֹתֵינוּ זִכְרוֹנָם לִבְרָכָה (תענית ג' ע"ב): "מַאי דִּכְתִיב (זכריה ב, י) "כִּי כְּאַרְבַּע רוּחוֹת הַשָּׁמַיִם פֵּרַשְׂתִּי אֶתְכֶם" כו', כְּשֵׁם שֶׁאִי אֶפְשָׁר לָעוֹלָם בְּלֹא רוּחוֹת, כָּךְ אִי אֶפְשָׁר לָעוֹלָם בְּלֹא יִשְׂרָאֵל".

וְהוּא שֶׁאָמְרוּ בְּוַיִּקְרָא רַבָּה סוֹף פָּרָשָׁה ד': "בָּרְכִי נַפְשִׁי אֶת ה'" (תהלים קד) גו', וְכִי מָה רָאָה דָּוִד לִהְיוֹת מְקַלֵּס "בְּנַפְשׁוֹ" לְהַקָּדוֹשׁ בָּרוּךְ הוּא, אֶלָּא אָמַר, הַנֶּפֶשׁ הַזּוֹ כו', הַנֶּפֶשׁ הַזֹּאת אֵינָהּ אוֹכֶלֶת בַּגּוּף, וְהַקָּדוֹשׁ בָּרוּךְ הוּא אֵין לְפָנָיו אֲכִילָה" כו', וְכֵן אָמְרוּ בְּסִגְנוֹן זֶה בְּמִדְרַשׁ תְּהִלִּים מִזְמוֹר ק"ג, "וּמַה הַנֶּפֶשׁ אֵינָהּ אוֹכֶלֶת וְאֵינָהּ שׁוֹתָה, כָּךְ הַקָּדוֹשׁ בָּרוּךְ הוּא אֵינוֹ אוֹכֵל וְאֵינוֹ שׁוֹתֶה".

בְּהַזְכִּירָם "אֲכִילָה וּשְׁתִיָּה" יוֹתֵר מִשְּׁאָר הַהֲנָאוֹת, הִשְׁמִיעוּנוּ זֶה הָעִנְיָן הַנַּ"ל. וְהוּא, שֶׁהֲגַם שֶׁהַנֶּפֶשׁ עַצְמָהּ לֹא אוֹכֶלֶת וְלֹא שׁוֹתָה, עִם כָּל זֶה, הֲרֵי כָּל עִקַּר חִבּוּר הַנֶּפֶשׁ עִם הַגּוּף כְּאֶחָד, וְקִיּוּמוֹ מִסְפַּר יָמָיו הַקְּצוּבִים, הוּא תָּלוּי עַל יְדֵי הַמַּאֲכָל וּשְׁתִיַּת הַגּוּף. כֵּן הָעִנְיָן, עִם כִּי וַדַּאי שֶׁלְּעַצְמוּת אָדוֹן יָחִיד אֵין סוֹף בָּרוּךְ הוּא, אֵינֶנּוּ נוֹגֵעַ חַס וְשָׁלוֹם שׁוּם מַעֲשֵׂה הַמִּצְוֹת, וְתוֹרָה וַעֲבוֹדָה כְּלָל, וְלֹא אִכְפַּת לֵיהּ כְּלָל, כְּמוֹ שֶׁכָּתוּב "כָּךְ הַקָּדוֹשׁ בָּרוּךְ הוּא אֵינוֹ אוֹכֵל וְאֵינוֹ שׁוֹתֶה", וּכְמוֹ שֶׁכָּתַבְתִּי לְעֵיל בְּהַמַּאֲמָרִים הַנִּזְכָּרִים בְּפֶרֶק ד'.

אָמְנָם כָּל עִקַּר עִנְיַן הִתְחַבְּרוּתוֹ יִתְבָּרֵךְ אֶל הָעוֹלָמוֹת, שֶׁמְּסֻדָּרִים כְּאֶחָד כְּתַבְנִית אָדָם בְּכָל הַפְּרָטִים וְאֵבְרֵי הָאֲכִילָה כֻּלָּם, גָּזְרָה רְצוֹנוֹ יִתְבָּרֵךְ שֶׁיְּהֵא תָּלוּי בְּמַעֲשֵׂיהֶם הַטּוֹבִים שֶׁל עַם קְדוֹשׁוֹ, שֶׁהֵן הֵמָּה עִנְיַן אֲכִילָה וּשְׁתִיָּה אֶל הָעוֹלָמוֹת, (*א) (*ב) לְהַעֲמִידָם וּלְקַיְּמָם וּלְהוֹסִיף כֹּחַ קְדֻשָּׁתָם וְאוֹרָם עַל יְדֵי הִתְחַבְּרוּתוֹ יִתְבָּרֵךְ אֲלֵיהֶם כָּרָאוּי, כְּפִי הָרָצוֹן הָעֶלְיוֹן יִתְבָּרֵךְ שְׁמוֹ, הַכֹּל לְפִי רֹב הַמַּעֲשֶׂה שֶׁל עַם סְגֻלָּה, שֶׁהֵמָּה הַמְּתַקְּנִים וּמְאַחֲדִים הָעוֹלָמוֹת, שֶׁיִּהְיוּ רְאוּיִים לְקַבֵּל שִׁפְעַת הָאוֹר וְתוֹסֶפֶת קְדֻשָּׁתוֹ יִתְבָּרֵךְ, (*ג) כְּעִנְיַן הַמָּזוֹן שֶׁהוּא מוֹסִיף כֹּחַ בַּגּוּף וּמְעַדֵּן אוֹתוֹ.

וְזֶהוּ עִנְיַן הַכָּתוּב (משלי ט, ה) "לְכוּ לַחֲמוּ בְלַחְמִי", שֶׁפֵּרְשׁוּהוּ רַבּוֹתֵינוּ זִכְרוֹנָם לִבְרָכָה (חגיגה יד, א) וּבְרַעְיָא מְהֵימְנָא צַו ל"ג ב', וּבְפָרָשַׁת עֵקֶב רע"א ב' עַל הַתּוֹרָה, עַיֵּן שָׁם, הַיְנוּ "בְלַחְמִי" מַמָּשׁ, כִּבְיָכוֹל לַחֲמוּ יִתְבָּרֵךְ. וּכְמוֹ שֶׁאָמְרוּ בְּפָרָשַׁת עֵקֶב שָׁם, תַּקִּין פָּתוֹרָא לְמָארָךְ [הָכֵן שֻׁלְחָן לַאֲדוֹנְךָ] כו', עַיֵּן שָׁם.

וּבְפָרָשַׁת בָּלָק ר"ב סוֹף ע"א "כִּי מִמֶּנּוּ תֹאכֵל" (דברים כ, יט) הַהוּא טַנָּרָא תַּקִּיפָא כו', דְּהַהוּא זַכָּאָה כִּבְיָכוֹל, אִיהוּ מְפַרְנֵס לָהּ וְיָהִיב לָהּ מְזוֹנָא כו', בְּגִין כָּךְ "כִּי מִמֶּנּוּ תֹאכֵל", וְלֵית מְזוֹנָא בְּהַאי עָלְמָא אֶלָּא מִמֶּנּוּ, [כִּי מִמֶּנּוּ תֹאכַל, אוֹתוֹ הַסֶּלַע הַקָּשֶׁה וכו' שֶׁאוֹתוֹ הַזַּכַּאי כִּבְיָכוֹל, הוּא מְפַרְנֵס אוֹתָהּ וְנוֹתֵן לָהּ מְזוֹנוֹת וכו' מִשּׁוּם זֶה "כִּי מִמֶּנּוּ תֹאכֵל" וְאֵין מָזוֹן בָּעוֹלָם הַזֶּה אֶלָּא מִמֶּנּוּ (מֵהַתַּלְמִיד חָכָם)] עַיֵּן שָׁם. וְעַיֵּן עוֹד בְּרַעְיָא מְהֵימְנָא בְּהַר ק"י ע"א, וּבְפָרָשַׁת פִּנְחָס שָׁם רכ"ד רֵישׁ ע"ב, וּבַזֹּהַר שָׁם רכ"ה רֵישׁ ע"ב בָּזֶה.

וְכֵן אָמַר הַמַּגִּיד לְהַבֵּית יוֹסֵף (בְּפָרָשַׁת בְּשַׁלַּח) בְּעִנְיַן הַמָּן, דְּכָל הַנִּבְרָאִים צְרִיכִים מָזוֹן כו'. וַאֲפִלּוּ סְפִירוֹת דְּאִינוּן נֶאֱצָלִים צְרִיכֵי כִּבְיָכוֹל מְזוֹנָא כו', וְהָא מְזוֹנָא דִּסְפִירָן אִיהִי תּוֹרָה וּמַעֲשִׂים טוֹבִים דְּעָבְדִין לְתַתָּא. [וְהַמָּזוֹן שֶׁל הַסְּפִירוֹת הוּא הַתּוֹרָה וּמַעֲשִׂים טוֹבִים שֶׁעוֹשִׂים לְמַטָּה] עַיֵּן שָׁם בְּאֹרֶךְ.

וּבְרַעְיָא מְהֵימְנָא מִשְׁפָּטִים קכ"א א': "קֹדֶשׁ יִשְׂרָאֵל לַה' רֵאשִׁית תְּבוּאָתֹה" (ירמיה ב, ג) כו', וְיִשְׂרָאֵל אִתְקְרִיאוּ אִילָנָא רַבָּה וְתַקִּיף, וּמָזוֹן לְכֹלָּא בֵּיהּ, בֵּיהּ אוֹרַיְתָא דְּאִיהוּ מְזוֹנָא לְעֵלָּא, בֵּיהּ צְלוֹתָא דְּאִיהוּ מְזוֹנָא כו'. וַאֲפִלּוּ מַלְאָכִים לֵית לוֹן מְזוֹנָא אֶלָּא בְּיִשְׂרָאֵל, דְּאִי לָאו דְּיִשְׂרָאֵל יִתְעַסְקוּן בְּאוֹרַיְתָא, לָא הֲוָה נָחִית לוֹן מְזוֹנָא מִסִּטְרָא דְּאוֹרַיְתָא דְּאִמְתִּילָא לְעֵץ, הֲדָא הוּא דִכְתִיב: "עֵץ חַיִּים הִיא" וגו' וּלְאִבָּא דְּאִיהִי מִצְוָה". ['קֹדֶשׁ יִשְׂרָאֵל לַה'" וגו', וְיִשְׂרָאֵל נִקְרְאוּ אִילָן גָּדוֹל וְחָזָק, וּמָזוֹן לַכֹּל (צוֹמֵחַ) בּוֹ. בּוֹ הַתּוֹרָה שֶׁהִיא מָזוֹן לְמַעְלָה, בּוֹ הַתְּפִלָּה שֶׁהִיא מָזוֹן וכו', וַאֲפִילוּ הַמַּלְאָכִים אֵין לָהֶם מָזוֹן אֶלָּא עַל יְדֵי יִשְׂרָאֵל. שֶׁאִם לֹא הָיוּ יִשְׂרָאֵל עוֹסְקִים בַּתּוֹרָה לֹא הָיָה יוֹרֵד לָהֶם מָזוֹן מִצַּד הַתּוֹרָה שֶׁנִּמְשְׁלָה לְ'עֵץ', הֲדָא הוּא דִכְתִיב "עֵץ חַיִּים הִיא" וגו', וְלַ'פְּרִי' שֶׁהוּא מִצְוָה.]

והרמ"ק זִכְרוֹנוֹ לִבְרָכָה רָמַז הָעִנְיָן בְּסֵפֶר אֵלִימָה, הוּבְאוּ דְּבָרָיו בְּזֶה בְּסֵפֶר שׁוֹמֵר אֱמוּנִים, עַיֵּן שָׁם, וּבְתוֹלַעַת יַעֲקֹב, וּבְרֵישׁ סֵפֶר דֶּרֶךְ אֱמוּנָה שֶׁלּוֹ. וְזֶהוּ עִנְיַן מַאֲמָרָם ז"ל (זוהר ויקרא ז ריש ע"ב): "יִשְׂרָאֵל מְפַרְנְסִין לַאֲבִיהֶם שֶׁבַּשָּׁמַיִם":

פֶּרֶק ז'

וְכֵן בְּהֵפֶךְ, הַמַּעֲשִׂים אֲשֶׁר לֹא טוֹבִים חַס וְשָׁלוֹם, הֵם אֶל הָעוֹלָמוֹת כְּעִנְיַן הַמַּאֲכָלִים רָעִים, אֲשֶׁר יִתְבָּאֵר עִנְיָנוֹ בְּעֶזְרַת ה'.

וּכְמוֹ שֶׁאָמְרוּ בְּרַעְיָא מְהֵימְנָא פָּרָשַׁת אֱמוֹר דַּף צ"ט ב' וְדַף ק' ע"א, ז"ל: "בְּיוֹמָא דְּרֹאשׁ הַשָּׁנָה נָפִיק יִצְחָק בִּלְחוֹדוֹי, וְקָרֵי לְעֵשָׂו לְאַטְעָמָא לֵיהּ תַּבְשִׁילִין דְּכָל עָלְמָא, כָּל חַד כְּפוּם אָרְחוֹי כו', וְשָׁכִיב עַל עַרְסֵיהּ דְּדִינָא, וְקָרֵי לְעֵשָׂו וְאָמַר (בראשית כז, ג): "וְצוּדָה לִּי צָיִד, וַעֲשֵׂה לִי מַטְעַמִּים" כו', וַיְהִי אַךְ יָצֹא כו' וְעֵשָׂו אָחִיו בָּא מִצֵּידוֹ" טָעִין טְעוּנֵי

מֵעוֹבָדֵי דְעָלְמָא, "וַיַּעַשׂ גַּם הוּא מַטְעַמִּים" – חָדִיד לְשׁוֹנֵיהּ לְמִטְעַן טְעָנוֹת כו', "וַיֹּאמֶר יָקֻם אָבִי" – יִתְעַר בְּדִינוֹי "וְיֹאכַל", כַּמָּה עוֹבָדִין בִּישִׁין דְּכָל עָלְמָא" כו' [בְּיוֹם רֹאשׁ הַשָּׁנָה יוֹצֵא יִצְחָק בִּלְבַדּוֹ, וְהוּא קוֹרֵא לְעֵשָׂו לְהַטְעִים לוֹ תַּבְשִׁילִים שֶׁל כָּל הָעוֹלָם, כָּל אֶחָד לְפִי דַּרְכּוֹ. וְשׁוֹכֵב עַל מִטַּת הַדִּין וְקוֹרֵא לְעֵשָׂו וְאָמַר "וְצוּדָה לִי צָיִד וַעֲשֵׂה לִי מַטְעַמִּים וכו' וַיְהִי אַךְ יָצֹא וכו' וְעֵשָׂו אָחִיו בָּא מִצֵּידוֹ" – טָעוּן מַשָּׂאוֹת מִמַּעֲשֵׂי הָעוֹלָם, "וַיַּעַשׂ גַּם הוּא מַטְעַמִּים" – חִדֵּד לְשׁוֹנוֹ לִטְעֹן טְעָנוֹת וכו', "וַיֹּאמֶר יָקוּם אָבִי" – שֶׁיִּתְעוֹרֵר בְּדִינָיו "וְיֹאכַל" – כַּמָּה מַעֲשִׂים רָעִים שֶׁמִּכָּל הָעוֹלָם.]

וּבַתִּקּוּנִים תִּקּוּן כ' מ"ז ב': "וַעֲשֵׂה לִי מַטְעַמִּים כַּאֲשֶׁר אָהַבְתִּי" מִפִּקּוּדִין דַּעֲשֵׂה כו', וּפִקּוּדִין דְּלֹא תַעֲשֶׂה – פַּרְנָסָה לס"מ לְמַאן דַּעֲבַר עֲלַיְהוּ, וְאִלֵּין הֲוָה קָרִיב עֵשָׂו לְיִצְחָק וְאָמַר לֵיהּ: "יָקֻם אָבִי וְיֹאכַל מִצֵּיד בְּנוֹ", וס"מ בְּגִינַיְהוּ הֲוָה קָרִיב לִשְׂמָאלָא, לְאַטְעָמָא לְקוּדְשָׁא בְּרִיךְ הוּא מֵחוֹבִין דִּבְנֵיהּ, דְּאִנּוּן מַאֲכְלִין מְרִירָן כו'. ["וַעֲשֵׂה לִי מַטְעַמִּים כַּאֲשֶׁר אָהַבְתִּי", מִמִּצְוֹת עֲשֵׂה וכו', וּמִמִּצְוֹת לֹא תַעֲשֶׂה פַּרְנָסָה לס"מ לְמִי שֶׁעוֹבֵר עֲלֵיהֶם. וְאֵלֶּה הָיָה מְקָרֵב עֵשָׂו לְיִצְחָק וְאָמַר לוֹ "יָקוּם אָבִי וְיֹאכַל מִצֵּיד בְּנוֹ". וס"מ בִּגְלָלָם הָיָה מְקָרֵב אֶל שְׂמֹאל, לְהַטְעִים לְהַקָּדוֹשׁ בָּרוּךְ הוּא מֵחֶטְאֵי בָנָיו, שֶׁהֵם מַאֲכָלִים מָרִים וכו'.]

וּבְרַעְיָא מְהֵימְנָא פָּרָשַׁת פִּנְחָס רל"ב סוֹף ע"א: "וְהַהוּא לֵב לָאו אָרְחוֹי כו', בַּעֲכִירוּ דְּעוֹבָדִין דְּעַמֵּיהּ, אֶלָּא נָקִיט כָּל בְּרִירוּ כו', וְכָל זַכְוָן וְכָל עוֹבָדִין טָבִין. וְכָל הַהוּא עֲכִירוּ וְטִנּוּפִין וְלִכְלוּכָא, דְּאִנּוּן עוֹבָדִין בִּישִׁין, אֲנַח לְכָבֵד דְּאִתְּמַר בֵּיהּ (בראשית כז, יא) "עֵשָׂו אִישׁ שָׂעִיר" כו', "וְנָשָׂא הַשָּׂעִיר עָלָיו אֶת כָּל עֲוֹנֹתָם" (ויקרא טז, כ). [וְלֵב הַהוּא אֵין דַּרְכּוֹ וכו' בַּעֲכִירוּת הַמַּעֲשִׂים שֶׁל עַמּוֹ, אֶלָּא לוֹקֵחַ כָּל הַמְבוֹרָרִים וכו', וְכָל הַזְּכֻיּוֹת וְכָל הַמַּעֲשִׂים טוֹבִים. וְכָל אוֹתָהּ הָעֲכִירוּת וְהַטִּנּוּף וְהַלִּכְלוּךְ, שֶׁהֵם הַמַּעֲשִׂים רָעִים, מַנִּיחַ בִּשְׁבִיל הַכָּבֵד שֶׁנֶּאֱמַר בּוֹ "עֵשָׂו אִישׁ שָׂעִיר" וכו', זֶה שֶׁכָּתוּב "וְנָשָׂא הַשָּׂעִיר עָלָיו אֶת כָּל עֲוֹנֹתָם"] וְכֵן אִיתָא עוֹד שָׁם כְּעִנְיָן זֶה בְּסוֹף הָעַמּוּד, עַיֵּן שָׁם:

וּכְשֵׁם שֶׁמַּאֲכַל הַגּוּף, כַּאֲשֶׁר אֵינֶנּוּ טוֹב, וְאֵינוֹ מִתְקַבֵּל אֶל הַגּוּף, אֵינוֹ זָן וְסוֹעֵד אֶת הַגּוּף, אֶלָּא נֶהְפָּךְ בְּתוֹכוֹ לְפֶסֹלֶת וְזֻהֲמָא וְצוֹאָה, וְגַם הוּא מַתִּישׁ וּמַחֲלִישׁ אֶת כָּל הַגּוּף, כִּי עַל יְדֵי זֶה אֵין הַנֶּפֶשׁ מִתְפַּשֵּׁט בְּתוֹכוֹ כָּרָאוּי, וְלִפְעָמִים יֶחֱלֶה מִזֶּה. כֵּן הָעִנְיָן, שֶׁהַמַּעֲשִׂים אֲשֶׁר לֹא טוֹבִים וּרְצוּיִים, חַס וְשָׁלוֹם, הֵמָּה נֶהְפָּכִים בְּתוֹךְ הָעוֹלָמוֹת לְפֶסֹלֶת וְלִכְלוּךְ כִּבְיָכוֹל, וְהוּא הִתְגַּבְּרוּת כֹּחוֹת הַטֻּמְאָה וְהַקְּלִיפּוֹת, הָרַחֲמָן יַצִּילֵנוּ, שֶׁנִּקְרָאִים "קִיא צוֹאָה" (עיין זוהר א' קצ: וח"ב קנ: קנג: רנב. רסה:) כְּמַאֲמָרָם זִכְרוֹנָם לִבְרָכָה בַּפָּסוּק "צֵא תֹּאמַר לוֹ" (ישעיה ל, כב).

וְכֵן אָמַר בְּרַעְיָא מְהֵימְנָא פִּנְחָס בְּדַף ל"ב הַנַּ"ל, וְעַיֵּן שָׁם, וְשָׁם בְּפָרָשַׁת תֵּצֵא רפ"ב א', שֶׁנִּקְרֵאת אִשָּׁה מְטֻנֶּפֶת וְצוֹאָה. וְכֵן אִיתָא בַּתִּקּוּנִים תִּקּוּן ע' קכ"ט א'. וּבְזֹהַר חָדָשׁ בס"א פָּרָשַׁת בְּרֵאשִׁית ו' ע"ג בַּפָּסוּק "אֵיכָכָה אֲטַנְּפֵם" (שה"ש ה, ג) שֶׁהוּא הס"א מְסָאֲבָא, וְשָׁם בְּפָרָשַׁת בְּהַר ל"ט ע"ה, וְאֵין צוֹאָה אֶלָּא יֵצֶר הָרָע כו'. וְעַיֵּן בְּטַעֲמֵי מִצְוֹת

לְהָאֲרִיזַ"ל פָּרָשַׁת יִתְרוֹ בָּזֶה, וְכֵן הוּא מְקוֹם יְנִיקָתָם בַּשֹּׁרֶשׁ הָעֶלְיוֹן, עַיֵּן בְּעֵץ חַיִּים שַׁעַר הָאָרַת הַמּוֹחִין פֶּרֶק ה'.

וְזֶה הָיָה גַּם כֵּן עִנְיַן עֲבוֹדַת פְּעוֹר, וּכְמוֹ שֶׁכָּתוּב בְּמַאֲמַר הַתִּקּוּנִים הַנַּ"ל, וּפִקּוּדִין דְּלָא תַעֲשֶׂה פַּרְנָסָה לס"מ, לְמַאן דְּעָבַר עֲלַיְהוּ כו'. [וּמִצְווֹת לֹא תַעֲשֶׂה פַּרְנָסָה לס"מ לְמִי שֶׁעוֹבֵר עֲלֵיהֶם]. וְזֶהוּ עִנְיַן הַכָּתוּב (ישעיה ד, ד): "אִם רָחַץ ה' אֵת צֹאַת בְּנוֹת צִיּוֹן".

וְזֶה שֶׁאָמְרוּ בְּזֹהַר חָדָשׁ פָּרָשַׁת אַחֲרֵי ס"ט א', בְּעִנְיַן יָרָבְעָם, כַּד עָבַד תְּרֵי עֶגְלֵי, שֶׁאָמַר הַקָּדוֹשׁ בָּרוּךְ הוּא לְהַמַּלְאָכִים, הֲרֵי כָּל שֶׁפַע דַּהֲוָה יָהִיב לְכוֹן אִתְהַפֵּךְ לְכוֹן בְּזוּהֲמָא, [כָּל שֶׁפַע שֶׁהָיָה נוֹתֵן לָכֶם הִתְהַפֵּךְ לָכֶם בְּזֻהֲמָה.]

וְגוֹרֵם בָּזֶה פְּגַם וְחִלּוּי וְקִלְקוּל גָּדוֹל וּתְשׁוּשׁוּת כֹּחַ חַס וְשָׁלוֹם בְּהָעוֹלָמוֹת, לְפִי עִנְיַן וְאֹפֶן הַמַּעֲשֶׂה, וּלְפִי מַדְרֵגָתוֹ בְּשָׁרְשׁוֹ בְּהָעוֹלָמוֹת. כִּי אָז בְּאוֹתָן הָעוֹלָמוֹת שֶׁאוֹתָן הַמַּעֲשִׂים מַגִּיעִים עֲדֵיהֶם, אֵין הַהִתְפַּשְּׁטוּת וְהִתְחַבְּרוּת עַצְמוּתוֹ יִתְבָּרַךְ בָּהֶם עַל הַשְּׁלֵמוּת הָאֲמִתִּי כָּרָאוּי, כְּפִי כַּוָּנַת רְצוֹנוֹ יִתְבָּרַךְ, דְּלָא שָׁרֵי בַּאֲתַר פְּגִים כָּל עוֹד אֲשֶׁר עֲדַיִן חֶלְאָתָהּ בְּתוֹכָהּ וּמִצּוֹאָתָהּ לֹא רֻחָץ. וּמֵאַחַר שֶׁכָּל הָעוֹלָמוֹת בִּכְלָל, הֵם מְקֻשָּׁרִים וּמְיֻחָדִים כְּאֶחָד, מִמֵּילָא גַּם כָּל הָעוֹלָמוֹת מַרְגִּישִׁים מְעַט בְּמִקְצָת מִזֶּה הַפְּגָם.

וְאֵינָם חוֹזְרִים לְאֵיתָן בְּרִיאוּתָם וְתִקּוּנָם הָאֲמִתִּי כְּמִקֹּדֶם, עַד אֲשֶׁר יִתְרוֹקְנוּ אֵלּוּ כֹּחוֹת הַטֻּמְאָה, עַל יְדֵי קִבּוּל הָאָדָם עָנְשׁוֹ הָרָאוּי לוֹ. וּכְמוֹ שֶׁכָּתוּב בְּרַעְיָא מְהֵימְנָא פִּנְחָס רל"ד סוֹף ע"א, וְרֵישׁ ע"ב שָׁם, עַיֵּן שָׁם, שֶׁעַל יְדֵי זֶה מִמֵּלָא מִגּוֹ יִגְרְשׁוּ, וּכְרֶגַע סָפוּ תַּמּוּ. וְעַיֵּן לְעֵיל בְּשַׁעַר א' (פֶּרֶק י"ב). וְאָז מִמֵּילָא מִתְרַפֵּא הַפְּגָם וְהַקִּלְקוּל שֶׁל הָעוֹלָמוֹת, וְנִטְהָרִים מֵחֶלְאַת זֻהֲמָתָם וְחוֹזְרִים לְתִקּוּנָם הָרִאשׁוֹן.

אוֹ עַל יְדֵי הַתְּשׁוּבָה שְׁלֵמָה אֲמִתִּית, שֶׁמַּגַּעַת עַד שָׁרְשָׁהּ הָעֶלְיוֹן, הַנִּקְרָא "עוֹלַם הַתְּשׁוּבָה", עָלְמָא דְּחִירוּ וּנְהִירוּ עִלָּאָה דְּכֹלָּא, וּמִשָּׁם מִתְעוֹרֵר וְנִמְשָׁךְ אוֹר עֶלְיוֹן קָדוֹשׁ, אֲשֶׁר הוּא מֵי מִקְוֶה טָהֳרָה, לִרְחֹץ וּלְטַהֵר כָּל לִכְלוּךְ פְּסֹלֶת כֹּחוֹת הַטֻּמְאָה, וְהֵם בְּטֵלִים וְכָלִים. וְהוּא עִנְיַן הַכָּתוּב (שם) "אִם רָחַץ אֲדֹנָי אֶת צֹאַת בְּנוֹת צִיּוֹן", וְכֵן (יחזקאל לו, כה) "וְזָרַקְתִּי עֲלֵיכֶם מַיִם טְהוֹרִים" וגו':

פֶּרֶק ח'

וְזֶהוּ מַאֲמָרָם זִכְרוֹנָם לִבְרָכָה (בבא קמא נ, א): "כָּל הָאוֹמֵר הַקָּדוֹשׁ בָּרוּךְ הוּא וַתְּרָן הוּא יְוַתְּרוּן חַיּוֹהִי", אֲשֶׁר לִכְאוֹרָה נִפְלָאת, וּכְבָר נִתְבָּאֵר קְצָת לְמַעְלָה בְּשַׁעַר א' פֶּרֶק י"ב.

וּלְדְבָרֵינוּ כָּאן, הָעִנְיָן יוֹתֵר מְבֹאָר בְּטוּב טַעַם, שֶׁאֵינוֹ עַל דֶּרֶךְ הַנְּקִימָה חַס וְשָׁלוֹם, אֶלָּא שֶׁכְּמוֹ שֶׁמִּטֶּבַע הָאָדָם, שֶׁאִם יֹאכַל מַאֲכָל שֶׁבְּטִבְעוֹ הוּא מְקַלְקֵל וּמַזִּיק לְגוּפוֹ, יַזִּיק לוֹ אוֹתוֹ הַמַּאֲכָל אוֹ גַּם יֶחֱלֶה מִמֶּנּוּ, וְאִם סַם הַמָּוֶת הוּא, יָמוּת מִמֶּנּוּ, וּבְעַצְמוֹ נִתְחַיֵּב בְּנַפְשׁוֹ. כֵּן הוּא בְּעִנְיַן הָעֲוֹנוֹת שֶׁל הַנֶּפֶשׁ הַחוֹטֵאת חַס וְשָׁלוֹם, כֵּיוָן שֶׁכֵּן קָבַע הוּא יִתְבָּרַךְ בִּרְצוֹנוֹ, טֶבַע סִדּוּר מַצָּבָם וְעִנְיְנֵיהֶם שֶׁל הָעוֹלָמוֹת, שֶׁמַּעֲשֵׂי הָאָדָם הַטּוֹבִים אוֹ רָעִים חַס וְשָׁלוֹם הֵם כְּעִנְיַן מַאֲכָל וּמָזוֹן לָהֶם, אֵין שַׁיָּךְ וַתְּרָנוּת בָּזֶה,

וְהוּא מֻכְרָח לְהָרִיק לִכְלוּךְ הַטֻּמְאָה שֶׁהִגְבִּיר בַּעֲוֹנוֹ בְּהָעוֹלָמוֹת, עַל יְדֵי אֶחָד מִשְּׁנֵי הַתִּקּוּנִים הנ״ל:

וְעַתָּה תֶּחֱזֶה וּבִין תָּבִין עִנְיַן הַתּוֹסֶפֶת וְרִבּוּי בְּרָכָה, וּמַה רַב עֹצֶם צֹרֶךְ עֲבוֹדָתֵנוּ הַקְּדוֹשָׁה בִּכְלָלָהּ אֶל עַצְמוּת קִיּוּם הַעֲמָדַת הָעוֹלָמוֹת, וּלְהַמְשִׁיךְ וּלְהַשְׁפִּיעַ בְּתוֹכָם רֹב בְּרָכוֹת וְתוֹסֶפֶת קְדֻשָּׁה, מִצַּד הִתְחַבְּרוּת עַצְמוּתוֹ יִתְבָּרֵךְ אֲלֵיהֶם כְּפִי הָרָצוֹן הָעֶלְיוֹן יִתְבָּרֵךְ שְׁמוֹ, כְּעִנְיַן הָאֲכִילָה וְהַמָּזוֹן כַּנַּ״ל, וְזֶהוּ רְצוֹנוֹ וּכְבוֹדוֹ יִתְבָּרֵךְ מִטַּעַם כָּמוּס אִתּוֹ יִתְבָּרֵךְ שְׁמוֹ אֲשֶׁר אֵין בִּיכָלְתֵּנוּ לְהַשִּׂיג:

וְרָאוּי לְכָל אִישׁ מֵעַם הַקֹּדֶשׁ, אֲשֶׁר לִבּוֹ חָרֵד שֶׁיִּהְיוּ מַעֲשָׂיו רְצוּיִים לְפָנָיו יִתְבָּרֵךְ, לְצָרֵף זֹאת הַמַּחֲשָׁבָה וְטֹהַר הַכַּוָּנָה הָרְצוּיָה, בְּעֵסֶק הַתּוֹרָה וּמַעֲשֵׂי הַמִּצְוֹת כֻּלָּם, לְהַמְשִׁיךְ וּלְהוֹסִיף, עַל יְדֵי אוֹתוֹ הַמָּזוֹן, קְדֻשָּׁה וְאוֹר חָדָשׁ בְּהָעוֹלָמוֹת:

פֶּרֶק ט׳

וּבִפְרָט בְּעֵת עָמְדוֹ לְהִתְפַּלֵּל לְפָנָיו יִתְבָּרֵךְ, אֲשֶׁר בְּשַׁעְתָּהּ הַמְיֻחֶדֶת לָהּ הִיא עִקַּר הַמָּזוֹן לְהָעוֹלָמוֹת וּלְנֶפֶשׁ הָאָדָם עַצְמוֹ. וּכְמוֹ שֶׁכָּתוּב בַּזֹּהַר בְּרֵאשִׁית כ״ד א׳, מְזוֹנָא דִּילֵיהּ צְלוֹתָא, דַּחֲשִׁיבָא לְקָרְבְּנָא. [מָזוֹן שֶׁלּוֹ תְּפִלָּה, הַנֶּחְשֶׁבֶת לְקָרְבָּן.]

וּבְרַעְיָא מְהֵימְנָא פָּרָשַׁת אֱמוֹר (הַנַּ״ל בְּפֶרֶק ז׳), "וְרִבְקָה אָמְרָה אֶל יַעֲקֹב" (בראשית כז, ו) כו׳, לְאִתְעֲרָא אִיהוּ בְּאִנּוּן מַטְעַמִּים דִּילֵיהּ. וְיַעֲקֹב אִתְּעַר מִתַּתָּא מִתְלַבֵּשׁ בִּצְלוֹתִין וּבָעוּתִין כו׳. "וַיֹּאמֶר מִי אֵיפֹה הַצָּד צַיִד" (שם) בְּכַמָּה צְלוֹתִין וּבָעוּתִין "וָאוֹכַל מִכֹּל" וכו׳. [וְרִבְקָה אָמְרָה לְיַעֲקֹב" וכו׳ שֶׁיִּתְעוֹרֵר הוּא בְּאֵלּוּ מַטְעַמִּים שֶׁלּוֹ, וְיַעֲקֹב נִתְעוֹרֵר מִלְּמַטָּה מִתְלַבֵּשׁ בִּתְפִלּוֹת וּבַקָּשׁוֹת וכו׳ "וַיֹּאמֶר מִי אֵיפֹה הַצָּד צַיִד" בְּכַמָּה תְּפִלּוֹת וּבַקָּשׁוֹת וָאֹכַל מִכֹּל וכו׳] וּבְפָרָשַׁת פִּנְחָס רל״ה א׳ "וַיֹּאכַל מִצֵּיד בְּנוֹ" אִלֵּין אִנּוּן צְלוֹתִין דְּאָזְלִין וּמִתְתָּרְכִין כו׳. ["וַיֹּאכַל מִצֵּיד בְּנוֹ" אֵלּוּ הֵם הַתְּפִלּוֹת הַהוֹלְכוֹת וּמִתְגָּרְשׁוֹת.]

וּבַזֹּהַר שָׁם רכ״ו א׳ וב׳ בֵּאֵר כָּל סֵדֶר הַכָּתוּב "אָכַלְתִּי יַעְרִי" (שה״ש ה, א) וגו׳ גַּם עַל סֵדֶר מַטְבֵּעַ הַתְּפִלָּה כֻּלָּהּ מֵרֵאשִׁיתָהּ עַד סוֹפָהּ, עַיֵּן שָׁם. וְכֵן בְּרַעְיָא מְהֵימְנָא שָׁם רמ״ד א׳, פֵּרְשׁוּ גַּם כֵּן עַל סֵדֶר הַתְּפִלָּה בְּאֹפֶן אַחֵר קְצָת, עַיֵּן שָׁם.

וְשָׁם רמ״א ב׳, אָמַר רַבִּי שִׁמְעוֹן, עַל רָזָא דָּא אָסִיר לְבַר נַשׁ לְטְעוֹם כְּלוּם עַד דְּיֵיכוּל מַלְכָּא עִלָּאָה, וּמַה אִיהוּ, צְלוֹתָא כו׳. עַד דְּמַלְכָּא עִלָּאָה אָכִיל, וְהַיְנוּ שָׁלֹשׁ רִאשׁוֹנוֹת וְשָׁלֹשׁ אַחֲרוֹנוֹת, כֵּיוָן דְּאִיהוּ אָכִיל כו׳, [אָמַר רַבִּי שִׁמְעוֹן עַל סוֹד זֶה אָסוּר לָאָדָם לִטְעֹם כְּלוּם עַד שֶׁיֹּאכַל מֶלֶךְ הָעֶלְיוֹן, וּמַה הִיא, תְּפִלָּה וכו׳. עַד שֶׁמֶּלֶךְ הָעֶלְיוֹן אוֹכֵל וְהַיְינוּ שָׁלֹשׁ רִאשׁוֹנוֹת וְשָׁלֹשׁ אַחֲרוֹנוֹת, כֵּיוָן שֶׁהוּא אָכַל וכו׳] עַיֵּן שָׁם בְּאֹרֶךְ. וְהַכֹּל עַל הַכַּוָּנָה הַנַּ״ל, שֶׁהוּא הַמְשָׁכַת תּוֹסֶפֶת קְדֻשָּׁה וּבְרָכָה וּנְהִירוּ לְכָל עָלְמִין, וְכַמְפֹרָשׁ בַּזֹּהַר וַיְחִי הַנַּ״ל, עַיֵּן שָׁם הֵיטֵב. וְצָרִיךְ הָעוֹבֵד הָאֲמִתִּי לְכַוֵּן לָזֶה:

פֶּרֶק י׳

וְלֹא זוֹ בִּלְבַד בְּתֵיבַת "בָּרוּךְ אַתָּה", שֶׁפֵּרוּשׁוֹ הוּא תּוֹסֶפֶת רִבּוּי בְּרָכָה וְשֶׁפַע, שַׁיָּךְ זֹאת הַכַּוָּנָה, אֶלָּא שֶׁגַּם בְּכָל תֵּבָה וְתֵבָה מִכָּל נֹסַח הַתְּפִלָּה, שַׁיָּךְ גַּם כֵּן זֹאת הַכַּוָּנָה הַקְּדוֹשָׁה. כִּי כָּל תֵּבָה מֵהַתְּפִלָּה, אוֹ שֶׁל אֵיזֶה בְּרָכָה, הִיא הָעוֹלָה לְמַעְלָה מַעְלָה, עַל יְדֵי מָארֵי קָלִין וְגַדְפִין דְּנָטְלִין לָהּ, לִפְעֹל פְּעֻלָּתָהּ בְּשָׁרְשָׁהּ הָעֶלְיוֹן הַמְיֻחָד לָהּ, וְהוּא נַעֲשָׂה בָּזֶה כִּבְיָכוֹל שֻׁתָּפוֹ שֶׁל יוֹצֵר בְּרֵאשִׁית, לִבְנוֹת וְלִנְטֹעַ כַּמָּה וְכַמָּה עוֹלָמוֹת.

כְּמוֹ שֶׁכָּתוּב בַּתִּקּוּנִים תִּקּוּן י"ח ל"ה ב׳: "וְכַד בַּר נַשׁ אַפִּיק הֲבָלִים וְדִבּוּרִים בִּצְלוֹתֵיהּ, כַּמָּה עוֹפִין פַּתְחִין גַּדְפַיְהוּ וּפוּמַיְהוּ לְקַבְּלָא לוֹן. הֲדָא הוּא דִכְתִיב (קהלת י, כ) "כִּי עוֹף הַשָּׁמַיִם יוֹלִיךְ אֶת הַקּוֹל וּבַעַל כְּנָפַיִם" גו׳, וְנָטִיל קוּדְשָׁא בְּרִיךְ הוּא אִנּוּן מִלִּין וּבָנֵי בְּהוֹן עָלְמִין, דְּאִתְּמַר בְּהוֹן (ישעיה סו, כב) "כִּי כַאֲשֶׁר הַשָּׁמַיִם הַחֲדָשִׁים וְהָאָרֶץ הַחֲדָשָׁה" גו׳, וְרָזָא דְמִלָּה "וָאָשִׂים דְּבָרַי בְּפִיךָ וגו׳ לִנְטֹעַ שָׁמַיִם" (שם נא, טז) וגו׳ [וּכְשֶׁהָאָדָם מוֹצִיא הֲבָלִים וְדִבּוּרִים בִּתְפִלָּתוֹ, כַּמָּה עוֹפוֹת פּוֹתְחִים כַּנְפֵיהֶם וּפִיהֶם לְקַבְּלָם. זֶה שֶׁכָּתוּב "כִּי עוֹף הַשָּׁמַיִם יוֹלִיךְ אֶת הַקּוֹל וּבַעַל כְּנָפַיִם" וגו׳, וְלוֹקֵחַ הַקָּדוֹשׁ בָּרוּךְ הוּא אוֹתָם מִלִּים וּבוֹנֶה בָּהֶם עוֹלָמוֹת, שֶׁכָּתוּב בָּהֶם "כִּי כַאֲשֶׁר הַשָּׁמַיִם הַחֲדָשִׁים וְהָאָרֶץ הַחֲדָשָׁה" וגו׳, וְסוֹד הַדָּבָר "וָאָשִׂים דְּבָרַי בְּפִיךָ וגו׳ לִנְטֹעַ שָׁמַיִם" וגו׳] "וְלֵאמֹר לְצִיּוֹן עַמִּי אָתָּה", אַל תִּקְרֵי "עַמִּי" אֶלָּא "עִמִּי", בְּשֻׁתָּפִי". וְכֵן הוּא שָׁם בְּתִקּוּן ס"ט ק"ו ב׳.

וְהַמַּשְׂכִּיל יָבִין מִדַּעְתּוֹ, שֶׁלֹּא לְחִנָּם הֻצְרְכוּ לְתִקּוּן תְּחִנָּה קְטַנָּה וּתְפִלָּה קְצָרָה כָּזוֹ, מֵאָה וְעֶשְׂרִים זְקֵנִים וּמֵהֶם כַּמָּה נְבִיאִים. אֶלָּא שֶׁהֵמָּה הִשִּׂיגוּ בְּרוּחַ קָדְשָׁם וְהַשָּׂגַת נְבוּאָתָם הָעֶלְיוֹנָה, וְנַהִירָא לְהוּ שְׁבִילִין דְּכָל סִדְרֵי בְּרֵאשִׁית וּפִרְקֵי הַמֶּרְכָּבָה, לָזֹאת יָסְדוּ וְתִקְּנוּ מַטְבֵּעַ בְּרָכוֹת וְהַתְּפִלּוֹת בְּאֵלּוּ הַתֵּבוֹת דַּוְקָא, מֵאֲשֶׁר רָאוּ וְהִשִּׂיגוּ אֵיזֶה דֶּרֶךְ יִשְׁכֹּן אוֹרָהּ שֶׁל כָּל תֵּבָה פְּרָטִית מֵהֶם, אֲשֶׁר הִיא נִצְרֶכֶת מְאֹד לְתִקּוּן רִבּוּי עוֹלָמוֹת וְכֹחוֹת עֶלְיוֹנִים וְסִדּוּר הַמֶּרְכָּבָה. וּכְמַאֲמָרָם זִכְרוֹנָם לִבְרָכָה (עי׳ שבת קטז: מנחות סה.) "הָעֲבוֹדָה צֹרֶךְ גָּבוֹהַּ".

וְזֶהוּ עִנְיַן מַאֲמָרָם זִכְרוֹנָם לִבְרָכָה (יבמות סד): "שֶׁהַקָּדוֹשׁ בָּרוּךְ הוּא מִתְאַוֶּה לִתְפִלָּתָן שֶׁל צַדִּיקִים". וּבְתַנְחוּמָא פָּרָשַׁת תּוֹלְדוֹת אָמְרוּ: "וְלָמָּה נִתְעַקְּרוּ הָאִמָּהוֹת, אָמַר רַבִּי לֵוִי שֶׁהָיָה הַקָּדוֹשׁ בָּרוּךְ הוּא מִתְאַוֶּה לִתְפִלָּתָם". וּבַזֹּהַר תּוֹלְדוֹת קל"ז א׳: "תָּא חֲזֵי עֶשְׂרִין שְׁנִין אִשְׁתַּהֵי יִצְחָק עִם אִתְּתֵיהּ וְלָא אוֹלִידַת, עַד דְּצַלֵּי צְלוֹתֵיהּ, בְּגִין דְּקוּדְשָׁא בְּרִיךְ הוּא אִתְרְעֵי בִּצְלוֹתְהוֹן דְּצַדִּיקַיָּא כו׳, מַאי טַעֲמָא, בְּגִין דְּיִתְרַבֵּי וְיִתּוֹסַף רְבוּת קוּדְשָׁא, לְכָל מָאן דְּאִצְטְרִיךְ, בִּצְלוֹתְהוֹן דְּצַדִּיקַיָּא". [בּוֹא וּרְאֵה עֶשְׂרִים שָׁנָה נִשְׁתַּהָה יִצְחָק עִם אִשְׁתּוֹ וְלֹא יָלְדָה עַד שֶׁהִתְפַּלֵּל תְּפִלָּתוֹ. וְהוּא מִשּׁוּם שֶׁהַקָּדוֹשׁ בָּרוּךְ הוּא חָפֵץ בִּתְפִלָּתָם שֶׁל צַדִּיקִים וכו׳ מַהוּ הַטַּעַם כְּדֵי שֶׁיִּתְרַבֶּה וְיִתּוֹסֵף תּוֹסֶפֶת קְדֻשָּׁה לְכָל מִי שֶׁצָּרִיךְ, עַל יְדֵי תְּפִלָּתָם שֶׁל הַצַּדִּיקִים]. וְכָתוּב מְפֹרָשׁ (משלי טו, ח): "וּתְפִלַּת יְשָׁרִים רְצוֹנוֹ":

וְלָכֵן קָרְאוּ רַבּוֹתֵינוּ זִכְרוֹנָם לִבְרָכָה אֶת עִנְיַן הַתְּפִלָּה, "דְּבָרִים הָעוֹמְדִים בְּרוּמוֹ שֶׁל עוֹלָם" (ברכות ו, ב). הַיְנוּ, שֶׁהַדְּבָרִים עַצְמָם, הֵם תֵּבוֹת הַתְּפִלָּה, עוֹמְדִים בְּרוּם הָעוֹלָמוֹת.

וּבַזֹּהַר וַיַּקְהֵל ר"א א׳: "צְלוֹתָא דְּבַר נַשׁ אִיהוּ פּוּלְחָנָא דְּרוּחָא, אִיהִי קַיְמָא בְּרָזִין

עִלָּאִין, וּבְנֵי נָשָׁא לָא יַדְעִין דְּהָא צְלוֹתָא דְּבַר נַשׁ בַּקְעַת אֲוִירִין, בַּקְעַת רְקִיעִין, פַּתְחַת פִּתְחִין וְסַלְקָא לְעֵלָּא". [תְּפִלָּתוֹ שֶׁל אָדָם הִיא עֲבוֹדַת הָרוּחַ, הִיא עוֹמֶדֶת בְּסוֹדוֹת עֶלְיוֹנִים, וּבְנֵי אָדָם אֵינָם יוֹדְעִים שֶׁתְּפִלָּתוֹ שֶׁל אָדָם בּוֹקַעַת אֲוִירִים וּבוֹקַעַת רְקִיעִים פּוֹתַחַת פְּתָחִים וְעוֹלָה לְמַעְלָה] וְעַיֵּן בע"ב שָׁם, וּבְדַף ר"ב ע"א וְרֵישׁ ע"ב, נוֹרָאוֹת נִפְלָאוֹת עִנְיַן עֲלִיַּת כָּל מִלָּה וּמִלָּה דִּצְלוֹתָא. וּבְרֵישׁ פָּרָשַׁת וָאֶתְחַנַּן ר"ס רֵישׁ ע"ב: "וּבְשַׁעֲתָא דִּצְלוֹתָא קַיְמָא, כָּל אִנּוּן מִלִּין דְּאַפִּיק בַּר נַשׁ מִפּוּמֵיהּ בְּהַהִיא צְלוֹתָא, כֻּלְּהוּ סַלְּקָן לְעֵלָּא, וּבַקְעִין רְקִיעִין, עַד דְּמָטוּ כו׳, וּמִתְעַטְּרֵי" כו׳: [וּבִשְׁעַת הַתְּפִלָּה כָּל אֵלּוּ הַמִּלִּים שֶׁהָאָדָם מוֹצִיא מִפִּיו בַּתְּפִלָּה הַהִיא, כֻּלָּם עוֹלִים לְמַעְלָה וּבוֹקְעִים רְקִיעִים עַד שֶׁמַּגִּיעִים וכו׳ וּמִתְעַטְּרִים.]

וְהוּא מְעוֹרֵר בְּקוֹלוֹ דִּלְתַתָּא אֶת הַקּוֹל הָעֶלְיוֹן, "קוֹל גָּדוֹל" הַיָּדוּעַ בַּזֹּהַר (יתרו פא: ועי׳ ואתחנן רפא). (וּכְמוֹ שֶׁכָּתוּב בְּכַמָּה מְקוֹמוֹת בַּזֹּהַר (ויחי רכט:, ואתחנן רסה:, בשלח סג:), דִּצְלוֹתָא סַלְקָא לְאַמְשָׁכָא בִּרְכָאָן מֵעוּמְקָא דְּכֹלָּא, וְהוּא "הַקּוֹל גָּדוֹל"). וְזֶה שֶׁכָּתוּב "הַקֹּל קוֹל יַעֲקֹב". (בראשית כז, כב), שֶׁלְּקוֹל תְּפִלַּת הָאָדָם – מִתְעוֹרֵר לְעֻמָּתוֹ הַקּוֹל הָעֶלְיוֹן.

וְלָכֵן דָּרְשׁוּ רַבּוֹתֵינוּ זִכְרוֹנָם לִבְרָכָה (תענית טז, ב): עַל פָּסוּק "נָתְנָה עָלַי בְּקוֹלָהּ עַל כֵּן שְׂנֵאתִיהָ" (ירמיה יב, ח) וְאָמְרוּ זֶה שְׁלִיחַ צִבּוּר שֶׁאֵינוֹ הָגוּן, רָצָה לוֹמַר, שֶׁאֵין נִמְצָא רַק "קוֹלוֹ" לְבַד, וְלֹא גָּרַם קוֹלוֹ לְעוֹרֵר גַּם הַ'קּוֹל הָעֶלְיוֹן' עִמּוֹ, זֶה שֶׁכָּתוּב "נָתְנָה עָלַי בְּקוֹלָהּ" לְבַד "עַל כֵּן כו׳" וְזֶה שֶׁאָמַר הַכָּתוּב (יואל ב, יא): "וה׳ נָתַן קוֹלוֹ לִפְנֵי חֵילוֹ".

וְלָזֹאת, אַף שֶׁקָּרְאוּ רַבּוֹתֵינוּ זִכְרוֹנָם לִבְרָכָה (ברכות לא, ב) אֶת עִנְיַן הַתְּפִלָּה "עֲבוֹדָה שֶׁבַּלֵּב", עִם כָּל זֶה, אַגְמְרוּ מִקְּרָאֵי דְּחַנָּה, שֶׁצָּרִיךְ שֶׁיַּחְתֹּךְ בִּשְׂפָתָיו:

פֶּרֶק י"א

וּמַה שֶּׁכָּתוּב "לִפְנֵי חֵילוֹ" (יואל שם) רָמַז זֶה הָעִקָּר הַגָּדוֹל שֶׁל עִנְיַן הַתְּפִלָּה, שֶׁכְּלַל כַּוָּנָתָהּ הוּא, לְכַוֵּן רַק לְהוֹסִיף כֹּחַ בִּקְדֻשָּׁה. שֶׁכְּמוֹ שֶׁהָאִישׁ מֵאַנְשֵׁי הַחַיִל מַשְׁלִיךְ כָּל עִנְיָנָיו וְצָרְכֵי עַצְמוֹ מִנֶּגֶד, וּמוֹסֵר נַפְשׁוֹ בִּרְצוֹנוֹ רַק עַל כְּבוֹד הַמֶּלֶךְ, שֶׁיַּשִּׂיג הַכֶּתֶר מְלוּכָה שֶׁל אוֹתָהּ הַמְּדִינָה וְתִנָּשֵׂא מַלְכוּתוֹ. כֵּן רָאוּי מְאֹד לְהָאָדָם הַיָּשָׁר, לָשׂוּם כָּל כַּוָּנָתוֹ וְטֹהַר מַחְשַׁבְתּוֹ בִּתְפִלָּתוֹ רַק לְהוֹסִיף תֵּת כֹּחַ בְּהָעוֹלָמוֹת הַקְּדוֹשִׁים, וּלְעוֹרֵר בְּקוֹלוֹ – הַקּוֹל הָעֶלְיוֹן, לְאַמְשָׁכָא מִנֵּיהּ בִּרְכָאָן וּנְהִירוּ לְכֹלָּא, [לְהַמְשִׁיךְ מִמֶּנּוּ בְּרָכוֹת וְאוֹר לַכֹּל] לְהַעֲבִיר רוּחַ הַטֻּמְאָה מִן הָעוֹלָם, וִיתֻקַּן עוֹלָם בְּמַלְכוּתוֹ יִתְבָּרַךְ שְׁמוֹ, וְלֹא עַל עִנְיָנָיו וְצָרְכֵי עַצְמוֹ כְּלָל.

וְעֵינֵינוּ הָרוֹאוֹת בְּנֹסַח תְּפִלַּת רֹאשׁ הַשָּׁנָה, שֶׁהוּא מְסֻדָּר מֵרֹאשׁוֹ עַד סוֹפוֹ רַק עַל כְּבוֹד מַלְכוּתוֹ יִתְבָּרַךְ שְׁמוֹ, שֶׁתִּתְעַלֶּה כְּבַתְּחִלָּה קֹדֶם חֵטְא אָדָם הָרִאשׁוֹן. וְגַם נֹסַח תְּפִלַּת כָּל הַשָּׁנָה, אַף שֶׁלְּפִי פְּשׁוּטוֹ הַנִּרְאֶה רֻבּוֹ כְּכֻלּוֹ מְסֻדָּר עַל עִנְיְנֵי צָרְכֵי עַצְמֵנוּ, וַדַּאי בָּרוּר לְכָל מֵבִין, וּמִמְּקוֹמוֹ הוּא מֻכְרָע, שֶׁלֹּא כִּוְּנוּ אַנְשֵׁי הַכְּנֶסֶת הַגְּדוֹלָה עַל הַנִּרְאֶה מִפְּשׁוּטֵי פֵּרוּשׁ הַמִּלּוֹת לְבַד, וּכְמוֹ שֶׁכָּתַבְתִּי לְעֵיל פֶּרֶק י׳.

וּתְפִלּוֹת נֶגֶד תְּמִידִין תִּקְּנוּם (ברכות כו, ב), שֶׁהָיוּ עוֹלוֹת כָּלִיל לָאִשִּׁים, כֻּלָּהּ לְגָבוֹהַּ סָלְקָא, וְלֹא הָיָה בָּהֶם חֵלֶק הֶדְיוֹט כְּלָל:

וְאַף דְּהִלְכְתָא גְּמִירָא לָהּ בַּשַּׁ"ס (עבודה זרה ח, א) שֶׁהַיָּחִיד רַשַּׁאי לְחַדֵּשׁ דָּבָר בִּתְפִלָּתוֹ עַל צָרְכֵי עַצְמוֹ וְצַעֲרוֹ, בְּכָל בְּרָכָה לְפִי עִנְיָנָהּ, גַּם בָּזֶה צָרִיךְ שֶׁלֹּא תְּהֵא תַּכְלִית כַּוָּנָתוֹ עַל צַעֲרוֹ, וְלֹא זוֹ הַדֶּרֶךְ הַנְּכוֹנָה לַיְשָׁרִים בְּלִבּוֹתָם.

כִּי בֶּאֱמֶת יִפָּלֵא, אֵיךְ שַׁיָּךְ לְבַקֵּשׁ לְהִתְחַנֵּן כְּלָל לְפָנָיו יִתְבָּרַךְ שְׁמוֹ, לְהָסִיר מֵעָלָיו צַעֲרוֹ וְיִסּוּרָיו. כְּמוֹ בְּעִנְיַן רְפוּאַת הַגּוּף, הָרוֹפֵא מַשְׁקֵהוּ סַמָּנִים חֲרִיפִים, אוֹ אִם הָרוֹפֵא מֻכְרָח אַף גַּם לַחְתֹּךְ אֵבֶר אֶחָד לְגַמְרֵי, שֶׁלֹּא יִתְפַּשֵּׁט אֶרֶס הַחֹלִי יוֹתֵר, הַאִם יִתְחַנֵּן אֵלָיו הַחוֹלֶה שֶׁלֹּא יַשְׁקֵהוּ הַסַּמָּנִים אוֹ שֶׁלֹּא יַחְתֹּךְ הָאֵבֶר, הֲלֹא הַחוֹלֶה עַצְמוֹ שׂוֹכְרוֹ לְכָךְ, כֵּן אֵיךְ יִשְׁפֹּךְ שִׂיחַ לְפָנָיו יִתְבָּרַךְ שְׁמוֹ לְהָסִיר מֵעָלָיו הַיִּסּוּרִים, הֲלֹא הֵמָּה רְטִיָּה וְסַמָּא דְּחַיֵּי לְכַפֵּר עֲוֹנוֹתָיו, כְּמַאֲמָרָם זִכְרוֹנָם לִבְרָכָה (שבת נה, א): "אֵין יִסּוּרִין בְּלֹא עָוֹן", וְאִם לֹא, אֵפוֹא, נֶפֶשׁ הַחוֹטֵאת בַּמֶּה תִּתְכַּפֵּר:

אָמְנָם תַּכְלִית הַכַּוָּנָה, צְרִיכָה שֶׁתִּהְיֶה רַק צֹרֶךְ גָּבוֹהַּ, כִּי בְּמָקוֹם שֶׁיֵּשׁ חִלּוּל שְׁמוֹ יִתְבָּרַךְ, כְּגוֹן צָרַת כְּלַל יִשְׂרָאֵל, "בֶּאֱמוֹר עַם ה' אֵלֶּה" – וְהֵמָּה מֻכִּים וּמְעֻנִּים, מְחֻיָּבִים לְבַקֵּשׁ וְלִשְׁפֹּךְ שִׂיחַ לְפָנָיו יִתְבָּרַךְ שְׁמוֹ עַל חִלּוּל שְׁמוֹ יִתְבָּרַךְ, וְאַךְ לְמַעַן שְׁמוֹ יַעֲשֶׂה.

וְגַם הַיָּחִיד עַל צַעֲרוֹ, אַף אִם אֵין חִלּוּל הַשֵּׁם בַּדָּבָר, יֵשׁ מָקוֹם גַּם כֵּן, (א) לְבַקֵּשׁ לְפָנָיו יִתְבָּרַךְ עַל גֹּדֶל הַצַּעַר שֶׁל מַעְלָה בִּזְמַן שֶׁהָאָדָם שָׁרוּי בְּצַעַר לְמַטָּה. כְּמַאֲמָרָם זִכְרוֹנָם לִבְרָכָה בַּמִּשְׁנָה פֶּרֶק ו' דְּסַנְהֶדְרִין (מו.): "אָמַר רַבִּי מֵאִיר, בִּזְמַן שֶׁהָאָדָם מִצְטַעֵר שְׁכִינָה מַה לָּשׁוֹן אוֹמֶרֶת, קַלַּנִי מֵרֹאשִׁי קַלַּנִי מִזְּרוֹעִי".

וְאָמְרוּ בִּשְׁמוֹת רַבָּה פָּרָשָׁה ב', וּבְחָזִית בְּפָסוּק אֲנִי יְשֵׁנָה: "תַּמָּתִי" (שה"ש ה, ב) גו' מַה הַתְּאוֹמִים הַלָּלוּ, אִם חָשַׁשׁ אֶחָד בְּרֹאשׁוֹ חֲבֵרוֹ מַרְגִּישׁ, כֵּן אָמַר הַקָּדוֹשׁ בָּרוּךְ הוּא (תהלים צא, טו) "עִמּוֹ אָנֹכִי בְצָרָה". וּבְתַנְחוּמָא סוֹף פָּרָשַׁת אַחֲרֵי: "כָּל יְשׁוּעָה שֶׁבָּאָה לְיִשְׂרָאֵל, הִיא שֶׁל הַקָּדוֹשׁ בָּרוּךְ הוּא, שֶׁנֶּאֱמַר: "עִמּוֹ אָנֹכִי בְצָרָה" גו' (רוֹצֶה לוֹמַר וּמְסַיֵּם "וְאַרְאֵהוּ בִּישׁוּעָתִי"). הַיְשׁוּעָה שֶׁלְּךָ הִיא שֶׁנֶּאֱמַר (שם פ, ג) "וּלְכָה לִישֻׁעָתָה לָּנוּ", וּבְשׁוֹחֵר טוֹב תְּהִלִּים מִזְמוֹר י"ג: "יָגֵל לִבִּי בִּישׁוּעָתֶךָ" אָמַר רַב אַבָּהוּ זֶה אֶחָד מִן הַמִּקְרָאוֹת הַקָּשִׁים, שֶׁיְשׁוּעָתוֹ שֶׁל הַקָּדוֹשׁ בָּרוּךְ הוּא הִיא יְשׁוּעָתָן שֶׁל יִשְׂרָאֵל, "בִּישׁוּעָתֵנוּ" אֵין כְּתִיב אֶלָּא "בִּישׁוּעָתְךָ" כו', יְשׁוּעָתְךָ הִיא יְשׁוּעָתֵנוּ". וְעַיֵּן זֹהַר אֱמוֹר צ' רֵישׁ ע"ב, בְּעִנְיַן הַכָּתוּב "לַה' הַיְשׁוּעָה".

וְזֶהוּ "עִמּוֹ אָנֹכִי בְצָרָה" (שם צא, טו), הַיְנוּ, שֶׁמִּן הַמֵּצַר מְשַׁתֵּף אוֹתוֹ יִתְבָּרַךְ שְׁמוֹ, אָז "אֲחַלְּצֵהוּ" וכו'. וּכְשֶׁהָאָדָם אֵין מַרְגִּישׁ צַעֲרוֹ מִיִּסּוּרָיו, מִגֹּדֶל מְרִירוּתוֹ מִצַּעֲרוֹ כִּבְיָכוֹל, הַמְּרוֹרוֹת הַלָּלוּ הֵן הֵן עֶצֶם מֵרוּק פְּשָׁעָיו, וּמִתְכַּפֵּר בָּזֶה עַד שֶׁיִּסּוּרֵי עַצְמוֹ בְּדֵלִין הֵימֶנּוּ (וְהֵן הֵן הַגְּבוּרוֹת קְדוֹשׁוֹת, כְּדַרְכּוֹ יִתְבָּרַךְ שְׁמוֹ לְהַמְתִּיק מַר בְּמַר, וְהוּא תִּקּוּן הַמִּדּוֹת בְּשָׁרְשָׁן):

פֶּרֶק י"ב

וְלָכֵן אָמְרוּ רַבּוֹתֵינוּ זִכְרוֹנָם לִבְרָכָה (ברכות סג, א): "כָּל הַמְשַׁתֵּף שֵׁם שָׁמַיִם בְּצַעֲרוֹ כּוֹפְלִין לוֹ פַּרְנָסָתוֹ". וְהָעִנְיָן, כִּי מִלְּבַד זֶה הַצַּעַר שֶׁנַּעֲשָׂה לְמַעְלָה כְּשֶׁמְּקַבֵּל עָנְשׁוֹ בְּיִסּוּרִים רַחֲמָנָא לִיצְלַן, אֵין עֵרֶךְ וְדִמְיוֹן כְּלָל זֶה הַצַּעַר שֶׁל מַעְלָה נֶגֶד עֹצֶם הַצַּעַר שֶׁגָּרַם לְמַעְלָה בְּעֵת עֲשׂוֹתוֹ הֶעָוֹן רַחֲמָנָא לִיצְלַן.

כְּעִנְיַן הַבֵּן יַקִּיר שֶׁנִּתְפַּתָּה בְּיֵינוֹ וְנָפַל לָאָרֶץ וְנִשְׁבַּר מַפְרַקְתּוֹ וְגוּפוֹ וְהוּא מְסֻכָּן. וְהוּא עַצְמוֹ אֵינוֹ מַרְגִּישׁ אָז כְּלָל סַכָּנַת נַפְשׁוֹ, כְּמוֹ שֶׁכָּתוּב (משלי כג, לה) "הִכּוּנִי בַל חָלִיתִי הֲלָמוּנִי בַּל יָדָעְתִּי". אָמְנָם, אָבִיו לִבּוֹ מִתְמַרְמֵר מְאֹד עַל זֶה, וְכַאֲשֶׁר הָרוֹפְאִים קָשְׁרוּ הַשְּׁבָרִים וְהִנִּיחוּ רְטִיָּה וְתַחְבֹּשֶׁת מְסַמָּנִים חֲרִיפִים, וְהַבֵּן מַר צוֹרֵחַ עַל הַכְּאֵב שֶׁלּוֹ מֵהַסַּמָּנִים הַחֲרִיפִים הָאוֹכְלִים בְּשָׂרוֹ, וְעִם כִּי אָבִיו מִצְטַעֵר לְצַעֲקָתוֹ וְרִבּוּת אַנְחוֹתָיו עַתָּה, אֵין עֵרֶךְ כְּלָל הַצַּעַר שֶׁל עַתָּה נֶגֶד הַצַּעַר וְהַיָּגוֹן הָרִאשׁוֹן שֶׁהָיָה לְאָבִיו בְּעֵת שֶׁנָּפַל וְשִׁבֵּר עַצְמוֹתָיו אֲשֶׁר כִּמְעַט נִתְיָאֵשׁ מֵחַיָּיו אָז.

כֵּן מַמָּשׁ, עַל זֶה הָאֹפֶן, הוּא עִנְיַן הֶעָוֹן רַחֲמָנָא לִיצְלַן. שֶׁבְּעֵת שֶׁהָאָדָם עוֹשֵׂהוּ, הוּא גּוֹרֵם לְמַעְלָה צַעַר גָּדוֹל וְעָצוּם לְאֵין עֵרֶךְ, וְהָאָדָם עַצְמוֹ אֵינוֹ מַרְגִּישׁ אָז בָּזֶה כְּלָל, וְלֹא יָדַע כִּי בְנַפְשׁוֹ הוּא, כִּי הוּא נֶחְשָׁב אָז כְּמֵת חַס וְשָׁלוֹם, כְּמַאֲמָרָם זִכְרוֹנָם לִבְרָכָה (בְּרֵישׁ פֶּרֶק מִי שֶׁמֵּתוֹ ברכות יח, ב) "רְשָׁעִים בְּחַיֵּיהֶם קְרוּיִים מֵתִים". וְיֵשׁ עֲוֹנוֹת שֶׁעַל יְדֵיהֶם נַפְשׁוֹ נִכְרֶתֶת חַס וְשָׁלוֹם לְגַמְרֵי מֵהִתְקַשְּׁרוּת חֶבֶל הַקֹּדֶשׁ, אֲבָל הוּא יִתְבָּרַךְ שְׁמוֹ, אָב הָרַחֲמָן, כִּבְיָכוֹל בְּצָרָתוֹ לוֹ צָעַר, וּמֵרֹב רַחֲמָיו וַחֲסָדָיו יִתְבָּרַךְ שְׁמוֹ, שׁוֹלֵחַ לוֹ יִסּוּרִין אֲשֶׁר הֵמָּה רְטִיָּה וְתַחְבֹּשֶׁת לְמָרֵק עֲוֹנוֹ, וְאָז הָאָדָם מַרְגִּישׁ כְּאֵב יִסּוּרָיו וּמִצְטַעֵר, וּבָזֶה מִתְעוֹרֵר גַּם כֵּן צַעַר לְמַעְלָה כַּנַּ"ל. אָמְנָם אֵין עֵרֶךְ כְּלָל זֶה הַצַּעַר נֶגֶד הַצַּעַר שֶׁגָּרַם לְמַעְלָה בְּעֵת עֲשׂוֹתוֹ הֶעָוֹן חַס וְשָׁלוֹם.

וְלָכֵן כְּשֶׁכָּל תַּכְלִית תְּפִלַּת הָאָדָם לְפָנָיו יִתְבָּרַךְ שְׁמוֹ לְהָסִיר מֵעָלָיו צַעֲרוֹ, הוּא רַק עַל הַצַּעַר שֶׁל מַעְלָה הַמִּשְׁתַּתֵּף עִמּוֹ בְּצַעֲרוֹ, וְשָׁב וּמִתְחָרֵט בֶּאֱמֶת עַל עֲוֹנוֹ שֶׁגָּרַם עַל יָדוֹ הַצַּעַר שֶׁל מַעְלָה, אָז הַיִּסּוּרִין מִסְתַּלְּקִין מֵעָלָיו. וְלֹא עוֹד אֶלָּא שֶׁמּוֹדְדִין לוֹ כְּמִדָּתוֹ וְ"כוֹפְלִין" לוֹ פַּרְנָסָתוֹ, נֶגֶד הַשְּׁנֵי מִינֵי צַעַר שֶׁגָּרַם לְמַעְלָה, וְעַתָּה מִתְחָרֵט עַל שְׁנֵיהֶם, זְדוֹנוֹת מִתְהַפְּכִין לוֹ לִזְכֻיּוֹת:

וְהוּא שֶׁדָּרְשׁוּ רַבּוֹתֵינוּ זִכְרוֹנָם לִבְרָכָה בְּחַנָּה (ברכות לא, ב) "וְהִיא מָרַת נָפֶשׁ וַתִּתְפַּלֵּל עַל ה'" (שמו"א א, י), שֶׁהֵטִיחָה דְּבָרִים כְּלַפֵּי מַעְלָה. רוֹצֶה לוֹמַר, הֲגַם שֶׁהִיא עַצְמָהּ הָיְתָה מָרַת נֶפֶשׁ, עִם כָּל זֶה, הִשְׁלִיכָה צַעֲרָהּ מִנֶּגֶד, וְלֹא אִכְפַּת לָהּ לְהִתְפַּלֵּל עַל זֶה כְּלָל, אֶלָּא שֶׁהֵטִיחָה דִּבְרֵי תְּפִלָּתָהּ לְפָנָיו יִתְבָּרַךְ שְׁמוֹ עַל הַצַּעַר שֶׁל מַעְלָה, הַנַּעֲשָׂה מֵחֲמַת שֶׁהִיא שְׁרוּיָה עַתָּה בְּצַעַר.

וְלָכֵן אָמְרוּ שָׁם (ברכות לב, א) שֶׁגַּם מֹשֶׁה הֵטִיחַ דְּבָרִים כְּלַפֵּי מַעְלָה כו', אַל תִּקְרֵי (במדבר יא, ב) "אֶל ה'" אֶלָּא "עַל ה'". וּלְפִי פְּשׁוּטוֹ, מִי הִכְרִיחָם לְרַבּוֹתֵינוּ זִכְרוֹנָם לִבְרָכָה לִדְרֹשׁ אַל תִּקְרֵי, וְלוֹמַר שֶׁהֵטִיחַ דְּבָרִים כְּלַפֵּי מַעְלָה. אָמְנָם לְמַעְלְיוּתָא הוּא דְּדָרְשׁוּ הָכִי, וּכְמוֹ שֶׁבֵּאַרְנוּ.

(וְאֶת פְּנֵי מֵבִין לְהָבִין, עַל דֶּרֶךְ זֶה, מַה שֶּׁאָמְרוּ שָׁם עוֹד, שֶׁגַּם אֵלִיָּהוּ הֵטִיחַ דְּבָרִים כְּלַפֵּי מַעְלָה, שֶׁנֶּאֱמַר "וְאַתָּה הֲסִבֹּתָ אֶת לִבָּם אֲחֹרַנִּית" (מלכים א' יח). וְהוּא כְּעִנְיַן "צוּר לְבָבִי" (תהלים עג, כו) וגו'. וְעַיֵּן זֹהַר תְּרוּמָה קכ"ח רֵישׁ ע"ב, וּכְמוֹ שֶׁכָּתוּב (ישעיה נ, א) "וּבְפִשְׁעֵיכֶם שֻׁלְּחָה אִמְּכֶם", "הֵשִׁיב אָחוֹר יְמִינוֹ" (איכה ב, ג) זֶהוּ "וְאַתָּה הֲסִבֹּתָ אֶת לִבָּם אֲחוֹרַנִּית", וְכֵן מְפֹרָשׁ בִּפְרִי עֵץ חַיִּים שַׁעַר הק"ש פֶּרֶק ח', עַיֵּן שָׁם):

וְאִם בְּעִנְיַן תְּפִלַּת הַיָּחִיד עַל צַעֲרוֹ, צָרִיךְ שֶׁתְּהֵא כַּוָּנָתוֹ רַק צֹרֶךְ גָּבוֹהַּ לְבַד, כָּל שֶׁכֵּן בְּמַטְבֵּעַ בִּרְכוֹת הַתְּפִלָּה הַקְּבוּעָה וּסְדוּרָה מֵאַנְשֵׁי הַכְּנֶסֶת הַקְּדוֹשִׁים, וַדַּאי רָאוּי שֶׁלֹּא לְכַוֵּן בָּהֶם כְּלָל צֹרֶךְ עַצְמוֹ הַנִּרְאֶה מִפְּשׁוּטָם, אֶלָּא צֹרֶךְ גָּבוֹהַּ לְבַד, לְהַמְשִׁיךְ תּוֹסֶפֶת רִבּוּי בְּרָכָה וּקְדֻשָּׁה לְהָעוֹלָמוֹת, מִצַּד הִתְחַבְּרוּתוֹ יִתְבָּרֵךְ שְׁמוֹ אֲלֵיהֶם, כְּמוֹ שֶׁנִּתְבָּאֵר לְעֵיל בָּאֹרֶךְ:

וְאַף שֶׁגַּם רַבּוֹתֵינוּ זִכְרוֹנָם לִבְרָכָה אָמְרוּ (ערובין סה, א): "יָכֹלְנִי לִפְטֹר כָּל הָעוֹלָם מִדִּין תְּפִלָּה שֶׁנֶּאֱמַר (ישעי' נא, כא) "שְׁכֻרַת וְלֹא מִיָּיִן", וּמַה נֹּאמַר עַתָּה בַּדּוֹרוֹת הַלָּלוּ, אֲשֶׁר כָּל אִישׁ הוּא כְּשׁוֹכֵב בְּרֹאשׁ חִבֵּל וּבְלֵב יַמִּים (מלה"כ משלי כג, לד), כָּל הַיָּמִים מֵעֹל יְגִיעַת הַפַּרְנָסוֹת, וְלָזֹאת, אֵין אִישׁ שָׂם עַל לֵב לְפַנּוֹת לִבּוֹ וּמַחֲשַׁבְתּוֹ, מִבִּלְבּוּלֵי טְרָדוֹתָיו הָעֲצוּמִים בְּהַבְלֵי זֶה הָעוֹלָם הַשָּׁפָל, לְהָכִין עַצְמוֹ לִקְרַאת אֱלֹקָיו יִתְבָּרֵךְ שְׁמוֹ.

עִם כָּל זֶה וַדַּאי שֶׁכָּל אֶחָד לְפִי שִׂכְלוֹ וְהַשָּׂגָתוֹ, מְחֻיָּב לָשִׁית עֵצוֹת בְּנַפְשׁוֹ וּלְבַקֵּשׁ תַּחְבּוּלוֹת מִלְחֶמֶת מִצְוָה, לְהִמָּלֵט מִבִּלְבּוּל הַמַּחְשָׁבוֹת אֲשֶׁר לֹא טְהוֹרִים, שֶׁתִּתְחוֹנֵן דַּעְתּוֹ עָלָיו לַעֲבוֹדַת הַתְּפִלָּה כָּרָאוּי, כִּי עֲבוֹדַת הַתְּפִלָּה הִיא לָנוּ עַתָּה בִּמְקוֹם עֲבוֹדַת הַקָּרְבָּן, שֶׁהָיָה תָּלוּי כֻּלּוֹ בְּמַחֲשַׁבְתּוֹ שֶׁל הַכֹּהֵן, שֶׁבְּמַחֲשַׁבְתּוֹ הָיָה יָכוֹל לְפַגְּלוֹ, וְעַל יְדֵי קְדֻשַּׁת מַחֲשַׁבְתּוֹ הָיָה הַקָּרְבָּן מִתְעַלֶּה לְרֵיחַ נִיחוֹחַ לְפָנָיו, יִתְבָּרֵךְ שְׁמוֹ.

פֶּרֶק י"ג

וְהָעֵצָה הַיְּעוּצָה עַל זֶה, הוּא כְּמוֹ שֶׁאָמַר הַמַּגִּיד לְהַבֵּית יוֹסֵף בְּאַזְהָרָה הַשֵּׁנִית שֶׁבְּרֵישׁ הַסֵּפֶר מַגִּיד מֵישָׁרִים, זֶה לְשׁוֹנוֹ: "לִיזָּהֵר מִלַּחֲשֹׁב בִּשְׁעַת תְּפִלָּה בְּשׁוּם מַחֲשָׁבָה, אֲפִלּוּ שֶׁל תּוֹרָה וּמִצְוֹת, כִּי אִם בְּתֵבוֹת הַתְּפִלָּה עַצְמָם".

דַּק בִּדְבָרָיו, שֶׁלֹּא אָמַר לְכַוֵּן בְּ'כַוָּנַת' הַתֵּבוֹת, כִּי בֶּאֱמֶת בְּעֹמֶק פְּנִימִיּוּת כַּוָּנַת הַתְּפִלָּה, אֵין אִתָּנוּ יוֹדֵעַ עַד מָה, כִּי גַּם מַה שֶּׁנִּתְגַּלָּה לָנוּ קְצָת כַּוָּנוֹת הַתְּפִלָּה מֵרַבּוֹתֵינוּ הָרִאשׁוֹנִים זִכְרוֹנָם לִבְרָכָה קַדִּישֵׁי עֶלְיוֹנִין, וְעַד אַחֲרוֹן הָרַב הַקָּדוֹשׁ אִישׁ אֱלֹקִים נוֹרָא הָאֲרִיזַ"ל, אֲשֶׁר הִפְלִיא הִגְדִּיל לַעֲשׂוֹת כַּוָּנוֹת נִפְלָאִים, אֵינָם בְּעֵרֶךְ אַף כְּטִפָּה מִן הַיָּם כְּלָל נֶגֶד פְּנִימִיּוּת עֹמֶק כַּוָּנַת אַנְשֵׁי כְּנֶסֶת הַגְּדוֹלָה מְתַקְּנֵי הַתְּפִלָּה, שֶׁהָיוּ מֵאָה וְעֶשְׂרִים זְקֵנִים וּמֵהֶם כַּמָּה נְבִיאִים.

וְכָל מֵבִין יָבִין, דְּלָא אִיתֵי אֱנָשׁ עַל יַבֶּשְׁתָּא שֶׁיּוּכַל לְתַקֵּן תִּקּוּן נִפְלָא וְנוֹרָא כָּזֶה, לִכְלֹל וְלִגְנֹז בְּמַטְבֵּעַ תְּפִלָּה קְבוּעָה וּסְדוּרָה בְּנוּסַח אֶחָד, הַתִּקּוּנִים שֶׁל כָּל הָעוֹלָמוֹת, עֶלְיוֹנִים וְתַחְתּוֹנִים, וְסִדְרֵי פִּרְקֵי הַמֶּרְכָּבָה. וְשֶׁבְּכָל פַּעַם שֶׁמִּתְפַּלְּלִין, יִגְרֹם תִּקּוּנִים חֲדָשִׁים בְּסִדּוּר הָעוֹלָמוֹת וְהַכֹּחוֹת, וְהַמְשָׁכַת מוֹחִין חֲדָשִׁים אֲחֵרִים, שֶׁמֵּעֵת שֶׁתִּקְּנוּהָ עַד בִּיאַת הַגּוֹאֵל בִּמְהֵרָה בְיָמֵינוּ, לֹא הָיָה וְלֹא יִהְיֶה שׁוּם תְּפִלָּה בִּפְרָטוּת דּוֹמָה לַחֲבֶרְתָּהּ שֶׁקָּדַם

לָהּ וְאַחֲרֶיהָ כְּלָל. דִּלְבוּשִׁין דִּלְבִישׁ בְּצַפְרָא לָא לָבִישׁ בְּרַמְשָׁא וּדְלָבִישׁ בְּרַמְשָׁא כו׳ כְּמוֹ שֶׁכָּתוּב בַּתִּקּוּנִים תִּקּוּן כ״ב [שֶׁלְּבוּשִׁים שֶׁלּוֹבֵשׁ בַּבֹּקֶר אֵינוֹ לוֹבֵשׁ בָּעֶרֶב, וְשֶׁלּוֹבֵשׁ בָּעֶרֶב וכו׳]. וְכֵן כָּל יוֹם לַחֲבֵרוֹ שֶׁלְּפָנָיו וְאַחֲרָיו. וְלָכֵן אָמְרוּ רַבּוֹתֵינוּ זִכְרוֹנָם לִבְרָכָה (חגיגה ט, ב וּבְרַבָּה בְּמִדְבַּר פָּרָשָׁה ט׳): ״מְעֻוָּת לֹא יוּכַל לִתְקֹן (קהלת א, טו) זֶה שֶׁבִּטֵּל קְרִיאַת שְׁמַע כו׳ אוֹ תְּפִלָּה״ כו׳. וּכְמוֹ שֶׁכָּתוּב בְּאֹרֶךְ בִּפְרִי עֵץ חַיִּים פֶּרֶק ז׳ מִשַּׁעַר הַתְּפִלָּה, עַיֵּן שָׁם.

וְהוּא בִּלְתִּי אֶפְשָׁר אִם לֹא עַל יְדֵי הַנְּבוּאָה הָעֶלְיוֹנָה, וְרוּחַ קָדְשׁוֹ יִתְבָּרַךְ, אֲשֶׁר הוֹפִיעַ עֲלֵיהֶם הוֹפָעָה עֲצוּמָה, בְּעֵת תִּקּוּן נוּסַח מַטְבֵּעַ הַתְּפִלָּה וְהַבְּרָכוֹת, שָׂם הוּא יִתְבָּרַךְ שְׁמוֹ בְּפִיהֶם אֵלּוּ הַתֵּבוֹת סְפוּרוֹת, וּגְנוּזוֹת בְּתוֹכָם כָּל הַתִּקּוּנִים. לָזֹאת, מִי הוּא אֲשֶׁר עָמַד בְּסוֹד ה׳, עַל עֹמֶק כַּוָּנָתוֹ יִתְבָּרַךְ שְׁמוֹ, אֵיזֶה דֶּרֶךְ יִשְׁכֹּן אוֹרָהּ שֶׁל כָּל תֵּבָה פְּרָטִית מֵהֶם:

אֶלָּא הָעִקָּר בַּעֲבוֹדַת הַתְּפִלָּה, שֶׁבְּעֵת שֶׁהָאָדָם מוֹצִיא מִפִּיו כָּל תֵּבָה מֵהַתְּפִלָּה, יְצַיֵּר לוֹ אָז בְּמַחְשַׁבְתּוֹ אוֹתָהּ הַתֵּבָה בְּאוֹתִיּוֹתֶיהָ כְּצוּרָתָהּ , וּלְכַוֵּן לְהוֹסִיף עַל יָדָהּ כֹּחַ הַקְּדֻשָּׁה, שֶׁיַּעֲשֶׂה פְּרִי לְמַעְלָה לְהַרְבּוֹת קְדֻשָּׁתָם וְאוֹרָם, כְּמוֹ שֶׁכָּתַבְתִּי לְעֵיל בְּפֶרֶק י׳, שֶׁלָּכֵן נִקְרֵאת הַתְּפִלָּה ״דְּבָרִים הָעוֹמְדִים בְּרוּמוֹ שֶׁל עוֹלָם״ (ברכות ו:), שֶׁכָּל תֵּבָה בְּצוּרָתָהּ מַמָּשׁ, הִיא הָעוֹלָה לְמַעְלָה מַעְלָה, כָּל אַחַת לִמְקוֹרָהּ וְשָׁרְשָׁהּ, לִפְעֹל פְּעֻלּוֹת וְתִקּוּנִים נִפְלָאִים.

וְהִיא סְגֻלָּה נִפְלָאָה, בָּדוּק וּמְנֻסֶּה, לַמַּרְגִּילִים עַצְמָם בָּזֶה, לְבַטֵּל וּלְהָסִיר מֵעָלָיו בָּזֶה כָּל מַחְשְׁבוֹת הַהֲבָלִים הַטּוֹרְדוֹת, וּמְנִיעוֹת טָהֳרַת הַמַּחְשָׁבָה וְהַכַּוָּנָה, וְכָל אֲשֶׁר יוֹסִיף הֶרְגֵּלוֹ בָּזֶה יִתְוַסֵּף לוֹ טָהֳרָה בְּמַחְשַׁבְתּוֹ בִּתְפִלָּה, וְהִיא כַּוָּנָה פַּשְׁטִית:

פֶּרֶק י״ד

אָמְנָם בֵּאוּר הַכָּתוּב הַנַּ״ל בִּתְחִלַּת דְּבָרֵינוּ (פֶּרֶק א) ״וּלְעָבְדוֹ כו׳ וּבְכָל נַפְשְׁכֶם״, שֶׁעֲבוֹדַת הַתְּפִלָּה הַשְּׁלֵמָה צְרִיכָה שֶׁתִּהְיֶה עִם הַנֶּפֶשׁ, הוּא עִנְיָן גָּדוֹל לַיּוֹדְעִים וּמְבִינִים קְצָת. וְכַאֲשֶׁר יַתְמִיד הָאָדָם תְּפִלָּתוֹ בְּזֹאת הַמַּדְרֵגָה, שֶׁיִּתְבָּאֵר אי״ה, יִתְוַסֵּף לוֹ טָהֳרָה עַל טָהֳרָתוֹ.

כִּי מָצִינוּ בְּכַמָּה מְקוֹמוֹת בַּמִּקְרָא וּבְדִבְרֵי רַבּוֹתֵינוּ זִכְרוֹנָם לִבְרָכָה, שֶׁהַתְּפִלָּה נִקְרָאָה בְּשֵׁם ״נֶפֶשׁ״, כִּי כַּמָּה הִלְכְתָא גַּבְרְוָתֵי בְּעִקְּרֵי הַתְּפִלָּה אִכָּא לְמִשְׁמַע מִקְּרָאֵי דְּחַנָּה, וּכְתִיב בָּהּ (שמו״א, א, טו): ״וָאֶשְׁפֹּךְ אֶת נַפְשִׁי לִפְנֵי ה׳״, וּכְתִיב (תהלים קג, א) ״בָּרְכִי נַפְשִׁי אֶת ה׳״, ״הַלְלִי נַפְשִׁי אֶת ה׳״ (שם קמו, א). וְרַבּוֹתֵינוּ זִכְרוֹנָם לִבְרָכָה בְּפֶרֶק קַמָּא דִּבְרָכוֹת (ה, ב) אָמְרוּ: ״שְׁנַיִם שֶׁנִּכְנְסוּ לְהִתְפַּלֵּל, וְקָדַם אֶחָד מֵהֶם לְהִתְפַּלֵּל, וְלֹא הִמְתִּין אֶת חֲבֵרוֹ וְיָצָא, טוֹרְפִין לוֹ תְּפִלָּתוֹ בְּפָנָיו, שֶׁנֶּאֱמַר (איוב יח, ד) ״טֹרֵף נַפְשׁוֹ בְּאַפּוֹ״ וגו׳, פֵּרֵשׁ רַשִׁ״י: לְךָ אוֹמֵר, אֲשֶׁר גָּרַמְתָּ לְךָ לִטְרֹף אֶת נַפְשְׁךָ בְּפָנֶיךָ, וּמַה הִיא הַנֶּפֶשׁ, זוֹ תְּפִלָּה, כְּמוֹ שֶׁנֶּאֱמַר ״וָאֶשְׁפֹּךְ אֶת נַפְשִׁי״ (שמואל א׳ א, טו) כו׳.

וְהָעִנְיָן, שֶׁעֲבוֹדַת הַתְּפִלָּה הִיא בִּמְקוֹם עֲבוֹדַת הַקָּרְבָּן. וּכְמוֹ שֶׁעִנְיַן הַקָּרְבָּן הָיָה,

לְהַעֲלוֹת "נֶפֶשׁ" הַבְּהֵמָה לְמַעְלָה, וְלָכֵן עִקַּר הַכַּפָּרָה הָיָה תָּלוּי בִּזְרִיקַת הַדָּם הוּא הַ'נֶּפֶשׁ', וְכֵן הַקְטָרַת הָאֵמוּרִים עִקָּרָם הָיָה לְכַוָּנַת הַעֲלָאַת הַ'נֶּפֶשׁ', כֵּן עִקַּר עִנְיַן הַתְּפִלָּה הוּא, לְהַעֲלוֹת וְלִמְסֹר וּלְדַבֵּק "נַפְשׁוֹ" לְמַעְלָה. כִּי כֹּחַ הַדִּבּוּר שֶׁל הָאָדָם נִקְרָא "נֶפֶשׁ", כְּמוֹ שֶׁכָּתוּב (בראשית ב, ז): "וַיְהִי הָאָדָם לְנֶפֶשׁ חַיָּה", וְתִרְגֵּם אוּנְקְלוּס, לְרוּחַ מְמַלְּלָא. וְכֵן נִרְאֶה לָעַיִן, שֶׁבְּכָל דִּבּוּר שֶׁהָאָדָם מוֹצִיא מִפִּיו, יוֹצֵא מִפִּיו רוּחַ וְהֶבֶל הַלֵּב. וְהַדִּבּוּר הוּא עִקַּר נֶפֶשׁ הָאָדָם, שֶׁזֶּה יִתְרוֹן הָאָדָם מִן הַבְּהֵמָה, אִם כֵּן, כָּל תֵּבָה הַיּוֹצֵאת מִפִּי הָאָדָם הִיא כֹּחַ וְחֵלֶק מִנַּפְשׁוֹ:

לָזֹאת, בְּעֵת עָמְדוֹ לְהִתְפַּלֵּל לִפְנֵי קוֹנוֹ יִתְבָּרֵךְ שְׁמוֹ, יַפְשִׁיט גּוּפוֹ מֵעַל נַפְשׁוֹ , הַיְנוּ, שֶׁיָּסִיר כָּל רַעְיוֹנֵי הַהֲבָלִים הַבָּאִים מִכֹּחוֹת הַ'גּוּף', שֶׁנֶּחְקְקוּ וְנִתְדַּבְּקוּ בְּ'נַפְשׁוֹ', שֶׁלֹּא תִּהְיֶה עֲבוֹדַת תְּפִלָּתוֹ רַק בְּהַ'נֶּפֶשׁ' וּרְעוּתָא עִלָּאָה דִּילֵיהּ.

וְהוּא, שֶׁקֹּדֶם עָמְדוֹ בִּתְפִלָּה, צָרִיךְ לְבַטֵּל וּלְהָסִיר מֵעָלָיו בְּמַחְשַׁבְתּוֹ כָּל תַּעֲנוּגֵי הַגּוּף וְהַנְאוֹתָיו וְכָל עִנְיָנָיו, עַד שֶׁיִּקְבַּע בְּמַחְשַׁבְתּוֹ לִמְאֹס הַגּוּף, כְּאִלּוּ אֵינוֹ בַּעַל גּוּף כְּלָל, וְרַק נַפְשׁוֹ לְבַדָּהּ הִיא הַמְדַבֶּרֶת תְּפִלָּתָהּ.

וּבְדַבְּרוֹ כָּל תֵּבָה, שֶׁהִיא כֹּחַ וְחֵלֶק מִנַּפְשׁוֹ, יַדְבִּיק בָּהּ רְעוּתֵיהּ מְאֹד, לִיתֵּן וְלִשְׁפֹּךְ בָּהּ נַפְשׁוֹ מַמָּשׁ לְגַמְרֵי, וּלְהַדְבִּיקָהּ בְּשֹׁרֶשׁ הָעֶלְיוֹן שֶׁל תֵּבוֹת הַתְּפִלָּה הָעוֹמְדִים בְּרוּמוֹ שֶׁל עוֹלָם, וּכְמוֹ שֶׁכָּתוּב בַּזֹּהַר וַיַּקְהֵל הַנִּזְכָּר בַּהַגָּה"ה — וּבְעוֹד דְּפוּמֵיהּ וְשִׂפְוָתֵיהּ מְרַחֲשָׁן, לִבֵּיהּ יְכַוֵּין רְעוּתֵיהּ יִסְתַּלֵּק לְעֵלָּא לְעֵלָּא, לְיַחֲדָא כֹּלָּא בְּרָזָא דְרָזִין דְּתַמָּן תְּקִיעוּ דְּכָל רְעוּתִין וּמַחְשְׁבִתִּין בְּרָזָא דְקַיְמָא בְּאֵין סוֹף, [וּבְעוֹד שֶׁפִּיו וּשְׂפָתָיו נָעוֹת יְכַוֵּן לִבּוֹ, וּרְצוֹנוֹ יַעֲלֶה לְמַעְלָה לְמַעְלָה, לְיַחֵד הַכֹּל בְּסוֹד הַסּוֹדוֹת שֶׁשָּׁמָּה נִתְקָעִים כָּל הָרְצוֹנוֹת וְהַמַּחְשָׁבוֹת בְּסוֹד אֵין סוֹף.]

וְאָז יֵחָשֵׁב כְּאִלּוּ הוּא מְסֻלָּק מִזֶּה הָעוֹלָם, וְהוּא מִ"בְּנֵי עֲלִיָּה" לְמַעְלָה, עַד שֶׁגַּם אַחַר הַתְּפִלָּה יִקְשֶׁה לוֹ מְאֹד לְהַפְנוֹת מַחְשַׁבְתּוֹ לְעִנְיְנֵי זֶה הָעוֹלָם. וִיהֵא בְּעֵינָיו כְּאִלּוּ נוֹפֵל וּמְטַפֵּס וְיוֹרֵד מֵאִגְרָא רָמָא לְבֵירָא עֲמִיקְתָּא. וּכְעִנְיַן (ברכות לב, ב) חֲסִידִים הָרִאשׁוֹנִים שֶׁהָיוּ שׁוֹהִים שָׁעָה אַחַת גַּם אַחַר הַתְּפִלָּה. וְהוּא שֶׁכָּתַב גַּם כֵּן הָאֲרִ"י זִכְרוֹנוֹ לִבְרָכָה הַטַּעַם עַל זֶה, כְּדֵי לְהַשְׁהוֹת עוֹד הַמּוֹחִין וכו', וְהוּא עִנְיַן מַאֲמָרָם זִכְרוֹנָם לִבְרָכָה (יבמות קה, ב) הַמִּתְפַּלֵּל צָרִיךְ שֶׁיִּתֵּן לִבּוֹ לְמַעְלָה.

וְכָל כַּךְ תִּרְבֶּה וְתִתְלַהֵט אַהֲבָתוֹ יִתְבָּרֵךְ בְּכֹחַ נַפְשׁוֹ, עַד שֶׁיְּהֵא חוֹשֵׁק וּמִתְאַוֶּה בֶּאֱמֶת, שֶׁבְּדַבְּרוֹ עַתָּה אוֹתוֹ הַדִּבּוּר הַקָּדוֹשׁ שֶׁל אֵיזֶה תֵּבָה מִנֹּסַח הַתְּפִלָּה, תְּהֵא נַפְשׁוֹ יוֹצֵאת מֵהַגּוּף לְגַמְרֵי, וְתִתְעַלֶּה לְהִתְדַּבֵּק כִּבְיָכוֹל בּוֹ יִתְבָּרֵךְ שְׁמוֹ.

זֶה שֶׁכָּתוּב כָּאן "וּלְעָבְדוֹ כוּ', וּבְכָל נַפְשְׁכֶם", וְכֵן מַה שֶּׁאָמְרָה חַנָּה "וָאֶשְׁפֹּךְ אֶת נַפְשִׁי לִפְנֵי ה'", וְהוּא מְבֹאָר. וְכֵן יֵשׁ לְפָרֵשׁ מַאֲמָרָם זִכְרוֹנָם לִבְרָכָה (תענית ח' ע"א): "אֵין תְּפִלָּתוֹ שֶׁל אָדָם נִשְׁמַעַת אֶלָּא אִם כֵּן מֵשִׂים נַפְשׁוֹ בְּכַפּוֹ", הַיְנוּ, לְהַעֲלוֹת וּלְדַבֵּק בִּתְפִלָּתוֹ אֶת נַפְשׁוֹ לְמַעְלָה, וְ"כַפּוֹ" פֵּרוּשׁ "שָׁרְשׁוֹ", מִלְּשׁוֹן "וְכִפָּתוֹ לֹא רַעֲנָנָה" (איוב טו, לב):

פֶּרֶק ט"ו

וּמַה שֶּׁנֶּאֱמַר "וּבְכָל נַפְשְׁכֶם", יָדוּעַ פְּלוּגְתַּת רַבּוֹתֵינוּ זִכְרוֹנָם לִבְרָכָה בְּכַמָּה דּוּכְתֵּי בַּשַּׁ"ס (סנהדרין עח, א) לְחַד מַאן דְּאָמַר תֵּבַת "כֹּל" פֵּרוּשׁוֹ כֻּלּוֹ, וּלְחַד מַאן דְּאָמַר פֵּרוּשׁוֹ מִקְצָת וְכָל שֶׁהוּא. וְכֵן הוּא הָעִנְיָן כָּאן שְׁנֵיהֶם אֱמֶת.

כִּי כַּמָּה בְּחִינוֹת וּמַדְרֵגוֹת יֵשׁ בָּזֶה, כָּל אָדָם לְפִי כֹּחַ טָהֳרַת לִבּוֹ וּמַחְשַׁבְתּוֹ, שֶׁהָאָדָם שֶׁכֹּחוֹ יָפֶה בְּטָהֳרַת הַמַּחְשָׁבָה וְהַכַּוָּנָה, יוּכַל לְדַבֵּק אֶת "כָּל נַפְשׁוֹ", מִגֹּדֶל הָאַהֲבָה וְהַתְּשׁוּקָה לוֹ יִתְבָּרַךְ שְׁמוֹ. וְכָל אֶחָד לְפִי כֹּחוֹ, וְגַם לְפִי עִנְיַן הֲכָנַת טָהֳרַת לִבּוֹ אָז, כִּי גַּם לֹא כָּל הָעִתִּים שָׁווֹת בָּאָדָם בְּטָהֳרַת הַמַּחְשָׁבָה, רַק זֹאת רָאוּי וְנָכוֹן, שֶׁעַל כָּל פָּנִים יִרְאֶה שֶׁתְּהֵא כַּוָּנָתוֹ רְצוּיָה, לְדַבֵּק לוֹ יִתְבָּרַךְ בְּאַהֲבָתוֹ וְטָהֳרַת לִבּוֹ "מִקְצָת נַפְשׁוֹ" בְּכָל תֵּבָה. לָכֵן אָמַר הַכָּתוּב "וּבְכָל נַפְשְׁכֶם", דְּלֶהֱוֵי מַשְׁתַּמַּע לִתְרֵי אַפֵּי כַּנַּ"ל, כָּל אֶחָד לְפִי כֹּחוֹ וּמַדְרֵגָתוֹ וַהֲכָנָתוֹ.

וְעִקַּר הַהֲכָנָה לָזֶה הוּא לְפִי הַנְהָגָתוֹ כָּל הַיּוֹם וְהַלַּיְלָה בְּתַלְמוּד תּוֹרָה וּמִצְוֹת.

וּמַדְרֵגַת חַנָּה הָיְתָה, שֶׁשָּׁפְכָה בִּתְפִלָּתָהּ לְפָנָיו יִתְבָּרַךְ שְׁמוֹ "כָּל נַפְשָׁהּ", לָכֵן אָמְרָה "וָאֶשְׁפֹּךְ אֶת נַפְשִׁי" כו', וּ"שְׁפִיכָה" פֵּרוּשׁוֹ לְגַמְרֵי, כַּיָּדוּעַ בַּשַּׁ"ס. (וְהַיְנוּ שֶׁלֹּא נִשְׁאַר לָהּ שׁוּם רָצוֹן לְעִנְיְנֵי עוֹלָם הַזֶּה, כִּי "נֶפֶשׁ" פֵּרוּשׁוֹ "רָצוֹן", כְּמוֹ שֶׁכָּתוּב (שמואל א' כ) "מַה תֹּאמַר נַפְשְׁךָ וְאֶעֱשֶׂה לָךְ", וְ'רָצוֹן הַכְּלָלִי' קָשׁוּר בִּ'כְלַל הַנֶּפֶשׁ'):

וְהִנֵּה, כָּל הַנַּ"ל בְּעִנְיַן הַתְּפִלָּה, שֶׁעִקָּרָהּ שְׁפִיכַת הַנֶּפֶשׁ לְדָבְקָה לוֹ יִתְבָּרַךְ בְּכָל תֵּבָה, הַיְנוּ, שְׁפִיכַת "כְּלַל" הַנֶּפֶשׁ לוֹ יִתְבָּרַךְ, בְּלֹא כַּוָּנָה וְהַבְחָנָה בִּבְחִינַת "הַפְּרָטִים" הַכְּלוּלִים בַּנֶּפֶשׁ.

אָמְנָם יֵשׁ מַדְרֵגָה יוֹתֵר גָּבוֹהַּ בָּזֶה, וְהוּא לְכַוֵּן בִּבְחִינַת הַפְּרָטִים הַכְּלוּלִים בַּנֶּפֶשׁ. אֶלָּא שֶׁצָּרִיךְ חִנּוּךְ לְהַרְגִּיל עַצְמוֹ מִמַּדְרֵגָה לְמַדְרֵגָה. שֶׁאַחַר שֶׁכְּבָר הֻרְגַּל בִּתְפִלָּתוֹ אֵיזֶה זְמַן בְּעִנְיַן שְׁפִיכַת וְהִתְדַּבְּקוּת כְּלַל הַנֶּפֶשׁ, אַחַר זֶה יַעְתִּיק עַצְמוֹ לְכַוֵּן בִּבְחִינַת הַפְּרָטִים שֶׁנַּפְשׁוֹ כְּלוּלָה מֵהֶם:

פֶּרֶק ט"ז

כִּי יָדוּעַ שֶׁנֶּפֶשׁ הָאָדָם בִּכְלָלָהּ, הִיא כְּלוּלָה מִשְּׁלֹשָׁה בְּחִינוֹת פְּרָטִים, וְהֵם נר"ן, שֶׁהֵם עַצְמָם הַשְּׁלֹשָׁה בְּחִינוֹת: מַעֲשֶׂה, דִּבּוּר וּמַחְשָׁבָה, שֶׁזֶּה כָּל הָאָדָם.

וְגַם בְּכָל תֵּבָה יֵשׁ שָׁלֹשׁ בְּחִינוֹת, מַעֲשֶׂה, דִּבּוּר, מַחְשָׁבָה, — נר"ן, וְהֵם "אוֹתִיּוֹת" וּ"נְקֻדּוֹת" וּ"טְעָמִים" שֶׁבָּהּ, כְּמוֹ שֶׁכָּתוּב בְּהַקְדָּמַת הַתִּקּוּנִים ז' ע"ב: "טַעֲמֵי אִנּוּן 'נִשְׁמָתִין', וְנִקּוּדִין — 'רוּחִין', וְאַתְוָון — 'נַפְשִׁין'". וְכֵן אִיתָא שָׁם בְּרֵישׁ תִּיקּוּן ס"ז, עַיֵּן שָׁם.

הָאוֹתִיּוֹת — הֵם בְּחִינַת "מַעֲשֶׂה", כִּי מְצִיאוּת אוֹתִיּוֹת גְּרֵידָא, בְּלֹא נְקֻדּוֹת, אִי אֶפְשָׁר שֶׁיִּהְיוּ אֶלָּא בִּבְחִינַת מַעֲשֶׂה, הַיְנוּ מַעֲשֵׂה הַכְּתִיבָה כְּמוֹ שֶׁהֵם כְּתוּבִים בְּסֵפֶר תּוֹרָה בְּלֹא נְקֻדּוֹת, כִּי בְּדִבּוּר אִי אֶפְשָׁר לְהוֹצִיאָם מֵהַפֶּה אִם לֹא עַל יְדֵי צֵרוּף הַנְּקֻדּוֹת אֲלֵיהֶם. לָכֵן הָאוֹתִיּוֹת לְבַד, בְּלֹא נְקֻדּוֹת נִקְרָאִים בְּחִינַת "נֶפֶשׁ", (הַיְנוּ עִם הַתָּגִים כְּמוֹ שֶׁכָּתוּב בהג"ה), שֶׁהוּא בְּחִינַת "מַעֲשֶׂה" כַּיָּדוּעַ.

וְהַנְּקֻדּוֹת — הֵם בְּחִינַת "רוּחַ" שֶׁלָּהֶם כַּנַּ"ל, שֶׁהַנְּקֻדּוֹת בָּאִים עִם הָאוֹתִיּוֹת עַל יְדֵי

הַדִּבּוּר שֶׁל הָאָדָם שֶׁהוּא בְּחִינַת "רוּחַ", וּכְמוֹ שֶׁעִקַּר חִיּוּת הָאָדָם – עַל יְדֵי בְּחִינַת הָרוּחַ שֶׁבּוֹ, שֶׁבְּצֵאת מִמֶּנּוּ הָרוּחַ הוּא מֵת, אַף שֶׁחֵלֶק מִנַּפְשׁוֹ נִשְׁאָר בּוֹ עֲדַיִן כַּיָּדוּעַ, כֵּן עִקַּר חִיּוּת תְּנוּעוֹת הָאוֹתִיּוֹת – הֵם הַנְּקֻדּוֹת, שֶׁבִּלְתָּם אִי אֶפְשָׁר לְהוֹצִיא הָאוֹתִיּוֹת מֵהַפֶּה, וּכְמוֹ שֶׁכָּתוּב בְּכַמָּה מְקוֹמוֹת בַּתִּקּוּנִים "וְהַמַּשְׂכִּילִים" – אִלֵּין נְקוּדֵי, "יַזְהִירוּ" – דְּנַהֲרִין בְּאַתְוָן. ["וְהַמַּשְׂכִּילִים" הֵם נְקֻדּוֹת, "יַזְהִירוּ" שֶׁזּוֹהֲרִים בָּאוֹתִיּוֹת.]

וְהַטְּעָמִים שֶׁל הַתֵּבוֹת – הֵם בְּחִינַת הַמַּחֲשָׁבָה וְכַוָּנַת הַלֵּב, שֶׁהוּא בְּחִינַת "הַנְּשָׁמָה" כַּיָּדוּעַ, כִּי הֵם תְּנוּעוֹת וְהַנְהָגַת הַנְּקֻדּוֹת וְהָאוֹתִיּוֹת, וּנְטִיָּתָם לְאֵיזֶה צַד שֶׁהוּא, דָּבָר הַתָּלוּי בַּמַּחֲשָׁבָה, בַּשֵּׂכֶל.

וּבְזֹהַר חָדָשׁ שִׁיר הַשִּׁירִים נ"ז ע"ה, "תּוֹרֵי זָהָב" (שיר השירים א, א) אִינוּן תְּנוּעֵי דְּטַעֲמֵי כו', בְּגִין דְּאִנּוּן אַתְיָן מֵרֵישָׁא דְּמַלְכָּא, לְמֵיהַב דַּעְתָּא וְסָכְלְתָנוּ לְאַתְוָן כֻּלְּהוּ. ["תּוֹרֵי זָהָב" הֵם תְּנוּעוֹת הַטְּעָמִים וכו' מִשּׁוּם שֶׁהֵם בָּאִים מֵרֹאשׁ הַמֶּלֶךְ לָתֵת דַּעַת וּתְבוּנָה לְאוֹתִיּוֹת כֻּלָּן] וְעַיֵּן שָׁם עוֹד בְּעִנְיַן הַשְּׁלֹשָׁה בְּחִינוֹת: ט' נ' א' בְּאֹרֶךְ.

וְשָׁם דַּף נ"ח ע"ג, תְּנוּעָה דְּטַעֲמֵי, דְּאִנּוּן תִּקּוּנָא וּשְׁלִימוּ בְּדַעְתָּא וְסוּכְלְתָנוּ, לְמִנְדַּע יְדִיעָה כו', כֻּלְּהוּ מַטְלָנֵיהוֹן בְּחָכְמְתָא וּבְסָכְלְתָנוּ כו', תְּנוּעֵי דְּאִיהוּ שְׁלִימוּ דְּכֹלָּא, אָן אִנּוּן בְּבַר נַשׁ, אֶלָּא רָזָא דָּא כו' לְגוֹ סוּכְלְתָנוּ וּמַדַּע כו' הֵן בִּזְקִיפוּ, הֵן לְמֵיזַל כו' כֹּלָּא אִיהוּ מִנְדַּע וְסָכְלְתָנוּ כו', [תְּנוּעוֹת הַטְּעָמִין, שֶׁהֵם תִּקּוּן וּשְׁלֵימוּת בְּדַעַת וּתְבוּנָה, לָדַעַת יְדִיעָה וכו', כָּל מַסְעֵיהֶם הֵם בְּחָכְמָה וּבִתְבוּנָה וכו'. הַתְּנוּעוֹת שֶׁהֵן שְׁלֵמוּת הַכֹּל, אֵיפֹה הֵם בָּאָדָם, אֶלָּא סוֹד זֶה וכו', מִבִּפְנִים הוּא תְּבוּנָה וָדַעַת וכו', הֵן בַּעֲמִידָה, הֵן לָלֶכֶת וכו', הַכֹּל הוּא דַּעַת וּתְבוּנָה וכו']. עַיֵּן שָׁם.

וְלָכֵן נִקְרָאִים "טְעָמִים", כְּמוֹ שֶׁהַטַּעַם וְהַפֵּרוּשׁ שֶׁל כָּל עִנְיָן, הוּא הַשֵּׂכֶל הַנִּסְתָּר שֶׁבָּעִנְיָן, שֶׁמִּתּוֹכוֹ יוּכַל הָאָדָם לַהֲבִינוֹ בְּמַחֲשַׁבְתּוֹ.

וּבְתִקּוּן י"ח ל"ה ב', וְאַתְוָן אִנּוּן לְגַבֵּי נְקוּדִין כְּגוּפָא לְגַבֵּי רוּחָא כו'. וּמָאנָא דִּנְקוּדִין אִיהוּ נֶפֶשׁ, נִשְׁמְתָא אִיהִי כֶּתֶר עַל כֻּלְּהוּ, וּמִנָּהּ כִּתְרִין דְּאִנּוּן טַעֲמֵי תְּנוּעָה דִּנְקוּדִין וְאַתְוָן, וְאִיהִי תַּלְיָא בְּמַחֲשַׁבְתָּא, וּנְקוּדִין תַּלְיָן בַּאֲמִירָה, וְאַתְוָן בַּעֲשִׂיָּה. [וְאוֹתִיּוֹת לְגַבֵּי נְקֻדּוֹת הֵם כְּגוּף לְגַבֵּי רוּחַ וכו', וּכְלִי שֶׁל הַנְּקֻדּוֹת הוּא נֶפֶשׁ. נְשָׁמָה הִיא כֶּתֶר עַל כֻּלָּם, וּמִמֶּנָּה כְּתָרִים, שֶׁהֵם טַעֲמֵי הַתְּנוּעָה שֶׁל הַנְּקֻדּוֹת וְהָאוֹתִיּוֹת. וְהִיא תְּלוּיָה בְּמַחֲשָׁבָה, וּנְקֻדּוֹת תְּלוּיוֹת בַּאֲמִירָה, וְאוֹתִיּוֹת בַּעֲשִׂיָּה.]

וְלָכֵן הָעוֹבֵד הָאֲמִתִּי בְּכַוָּנָה רְצוּיָה, יְכַוֵּן לִשְׁפֹּךְ וּלְדַבֵּק יַחַד בִּתְפִלָּתוֹ כָּל הַשְּׁלֹשָׁה בְּחִינוֹת נֶפֶשׁ רוּחַ נְשָׁמָה, אֲשֶׁר נַפְשׁוֹ כְּלוּלָה בָּהֶם. שֶׁבְּעֵת שֶׁמּוֹצִיא מִפִּיו כָּל תֵּבָה מֵהַתְּפִלָּה, שֶׁיֵּשׁ בָּהּ כָּל הַשְּׁלֹשָׁה בְּחִינוֹת נר"ן בְּאוֹתִיּוֹתֶיהָ וּנְקֻדּוֹתֶיהָ וְטַעֲמֶיהָ, יִתְעַצֵּם בְּטֹהַר לִבּוֹ, בְּעֹצֶם הַתְּשׁוּקָה, לְקַשֵּׁר וּלְדַבֵּק עַל יָדָהּ מִמַּטָּה לְמַעְלָה בְּסֵדֶר הַמַּדְרֵגוֹת: נַפְשׁוֹ בְּרוּחוֹ וְרוּחוֹ בְּנִשְׁמָתוֹ, וְיִתְעַלּוּ כֻּלָּם לְשֹׁרֶשׁ אוֹתָהּ הַתֵּבָה בָּעוֹלָמוֹת הָעֶלְיוֹנִים.

וְזֶהוּ הָעִנְיָן שֶׁאָמְרוּ בְּתִקּוּנֵי זֹהַר חָדָשׁ ע"ו רֵישׁ ע"א: "וְהַמַּשְׂכִּילִים" כו', אִנּוּן דְּאִית בְּהוֹן שֵׂכֶל לְאִשְׁתְּמוֹדַע בִּצְלוֹתָא, אֵיךְ סַלְקָא כו', בְּאַתְוָן וּנְקוּדֵי וְטַעֲמֵי" כו', ["וְהַמַּשְׂכִּילִים"

אֵלֶּה שֶׁיֵּשׁ בָּהֶם שֵׂכֶל לָדַעַת בִּתְפִלָּה אֵיךְ עוֹלֶה וכו׳ בְּאוֹתִיּוֹת וּנְקֻדּוֹת וּטְעָמִים] עַיֵּן שָׁם. וְשָׁם בְּדַף ע״ח רֵישׁ ע״ג: "וַאֲשֶׁר כֹּחַ בָּהֶם לַעֲמֹד בְּהֵיכַל הַמֶּלֶךְ" (דניאל א, ד) בַּעֲמִידָה דִּצְלוֹתָא כו׳, כְּלִילָא מִכָּלָּא טַעֲמֵי וּנְקוּדֵי וְאַתְוָן: ["וַאֲשֶׁר כֹּחַ בָּהֶם לַעֲמֹד בְּהֵיכַל הַמֶּלֶךְ" בַּעֲמִידָה שֶׁל תְּפִלָּה וכו׳ כְּלוּלָה מֵהַכֹּל טְעָמִים וּנְקֻדּוֹת וְאוֹתִיּוֹת.]

פֶּרֶק י״ז

אָמְנָם עוֹד יֵשׁ לֶאֱלוֹהַּ מִלִּין, לִפְנֵי הָעוֹבֵד אֱלֹהִים בִּקְדֻשָּׁה, בִּבְחִינָה יוֹתֵר פְּרָטִית, וְהוּא בִּבְחִינַת "שֹׁרֶשׁ הַנְּשָׁמָה", הִיא "נִשְׁמְתָא לְנִשְׁמְתָא", הַנִּזְכָּר בַּזֹּהַר, וְנִקְרֵאת "חַיָּה".

וְאָדָם הָרִאשׁוֹן הִשִּׂיגָהּ, וְלִבְחִינַת "הַיְחִידָה" הַנִּכְלֶלֶת בָּהּ, סוֹד עוֹלָם אָדָם קַדְמָאָה, וְכַמְבֹאָר לַמֵּבִין בְּעֵץ חַיִּים סוֹף שַׁעַר הַמּוֹחִין, שֶׁאָדָם הָרִאשׁוֹן זָכָה לִבְחִינַת "חַיָּה" "יְחִידָה" הָאֲמִתִּיִּים בִּמְקוֹמָם הָעִקָּרִי. וְעַיֵּן רֵישׁ גִּלְגּוּלִים וּבְפֶרֶק י״ז שָׁם.

וְזֶהוּ עִקַּר כַּוָּנָתָם זִכְרוֹנָם לִבְרָכָה (עי׳ ב״ר ז, ה; ח, א) שֶׁדָּרְשׁוּ בַּפָּסוּק "תּוֹצֵא הָאָרֶץ נֶפֶשׁ חַיָּה" (בראשית א, כד) אֲפִלּוּ נַפְשׁוֹ שֶׁל אָדָם הָרִאשׁוֹן, אֲפִלּוּ נַפְשׁוֹ שֶׁל מָשִׁיחַ. כִּי זֹאת הַבְּחִינָה הִיא סוֹד כְּנֶסֶת יִשְׂרָאֵל, אֶרֶץ הַחַיִּים הָעֶלְיוֹנָה, (הַיְנוּ שֹׁרֶשׁ יְסוֹד הֶעָפָר מהד׳ יְסוֹדִין, שָׁרְשִׁין קַדְמָאִין, אַבְהָן דְּכֻלְּהוּ עָלְמִין, הַנִּזְכָּר בַּזֹּהַר וָאֵרָא כ״ג ע״ב, ע״שׁ.

וְעַיֵּן זֹהַר שְׁמוֹת י״ב א׳, וּבְפָרָשַׁת שְׁלַח קע״ד ב׳, רָזָא דִּכְתִיב "תּוֹצֵא הָאָרֶץ נֶפֶשׁ חַיָּה" וכו׳, וּבְפָרָשַׁת שְׁמִינִי ל״ט ב׳ "וְאֵת כָּל נֶפֶשׁ הַחַיָּה" כו׳. וְעַיֵּן סוֹף פָּרָשַׁת וָאֶתְחַנַּן בְּמַתְנִיתִין. וְעַיֵּן רַמְבַּ״ן זִכְרוֹנוֹ לִבְרָכָה בַּפָּסוּק "נַעֲשֶׂה אָדָם" (בראשית א, כו), כִּי רוּחַ ה׳ דִּבֵּר בּוֹ.

וְלָכֵן הָיָה אָדָם הָרִאשׁוֹן מוּכָן לִחְיוֹת לְעוֹלָם, כִּי הִיא "הַחָכְמָה תְּחַיֶּה בְעָלֶיהָ" (קהלת ז, יב), וְלָכֵן נִקְרֵאת "חַיָּה", וְזֶהוּ "תּוֹצֵא הָאָרֶץ נֶפֶשׁ חַיָּה". וּבְחֶטְאוֹ נִסְתַּלְּקָה הֵימֶנּוּ. וְעַיֵּן מַה שֶּׁכָּתַב הָאֲרִ״י זִכְרוֹנוֹ לִבְרָכָה בְּפֶרֶק ט״ו, וּבְרֵישׁ פֶּרֶק כ״א, וּבְפֶרֶק ל״ה מֵהַגִּלְגּוּלִים. וּמֵאָז לֹא זָכָה אֵלֶיהָ שׁוּם אָדָם בְּעוֹדוֹ בְּזֶה הָעוֹלָם. וַחֲנוֹךְ כְּשֶׁהִגִּיעַ לְזֹאת הַמַּדְרֵגָה, וְיָרַשׁ מַעֲלָתוֹ שֶׁל אָדָם הָרִאשׁוֹן, כְּמוֹ שֶׁכָּתוּב בְּזֹהַר חָדָשׁ תְּרוּמָה ל״ה ע״ג, וְשָׁם בְּשִׁיר הַשִּׁירִים נ״ד ע״ד עַיֵּן שָׁם וּבְרַעְיָא מְהֵימְנָא קְדוֹשִׁים פ״ג, וּבְמַתְנִיתִין סוֹף פָּרָשַׁת וָאֶתְחַנַּן, כְּמוֹ שֶׁפֵּרְשָׁם הָאֲרִיזַ״ל בְּפָרָשַׁת בְּרֵאשִׁית בִּדְרוּשׁ אָדָם הָרִאשׁוֹן, וּבְגִלְגּוּלִים פֶּרֶק י״ח עַיֵּן שָׁם, וּכְמוֹ שֶׁכָּתוּב שָׁם פֶּרֶק ל״ה, לָא הֲוָה יָכִיל עָלְמָא לְמִסְבְּלֵיהּ, וְהֻכְרַח לְהִסְתַּלֵּק מִזֶּה הָעוֹלָם. וְכֵן אֵלִיָּהוּ, נִסְתַּלֵּק מִזֶּה הָעוֹלָם כְּשֶׁהִשִּׂיג קְצָת מֵאוֹתָהּ הַזִּיהֲרָא עִלָּאָה, כְּמוֹ שֶׁכָּתוּב בְּפֶרֶק י״ט מֵהַגִּלְגּוּלִים, וּכְמוֹ שֶׁכָּתוּב בַּזֹּהַר וַיִּגַּשׁ ר״ט רֵישׁ ע״ב: "אֲמַר לֵיהּ קוּדְשָׁא בְּרִיךְ הוּא כו׳, וְעָלְמָא לָא יָכִיל לְמִסְבְּלָךְ עִם בְּנֵי נָשָׁא". [אָמַר לוֹ הַקָּדוֹשׁ בָּרוּךְ הוּא וכו׳ וְהָעוֹלָם אֵינוֹ יָכוֹל לִסְבֹּלְךָ שֶׁתִּמָּצֵא עִם בְּנֵי אָדָם] וַאֲנַחְנוּ מְקַוִּים לְהַשִּׂיגָהּ אַחַר הַתְּחִיָּה אי״ה, שֶׁיֵּעָרֶה עָלֵינוּ "רוּחַ" מִמָּרוֹם (מלה״כ ישעי׳ לב, טו):

וְהוּא בְּחִינַת שֹׁרֶשׁ הַמַּחְשָׁבָה שֶׁל אָדָם, כִּי בְּחִינַת "הַמַּחְשָׁבָה" הוּא — כְּשֶׁמְּדַבֵּק מַחֲשַׁבְתּוֹ לַחְשֹׁב אֵיזֶה עִנְיָן פְּרָטִי, וְהוּא בְּחִינַת "נְשָׁמָה", כְּמוֹ שֶׁכָּתוּב "וְנִשְׁמַת שַׁדַּי

תְּבִינֵם" (איוב לב, ח), וְאָז הַמַּחְשָׁבָה מֻשֶּׂגֶת עכ"פ לְהָאָדָם עַצְמוֹ הַמְּחַשֵּׁב. אֲבָל "שֹׁרֶשׁ" מְקוֹר מוֹצָא כְּלָלִיּוּת כֹּחַ הַמַּחְשָׁבָה – הוּא טָמִיר וְנֶעְלָם לְגַמְרֵי, שֶׁאֵינוֹ מֻשָּׂג גַּם לְהָאָדָם עַצְמוֹ מֵאַיִן תִּמָּצֵא, וְהוּא בְּחִינַת "שֹׁרֶשׁ נִשְׁמָתוֹ".

וְזֹאת הַבְּחִינָה הַנֶּעְלָמָה, הִיא בְּחִינַת צֵרוּפֵי הָאוֹתִיּוֹת שֶׁל הַתֵּבָה, שֶׁהוּא שֹׁרֶשׁ נִשְׁמַת הָאוֹתִיּוֹת, וְכֹחַ רוּחָנִיּוּתֵיהֶם בְּשָׁרְשָׁם הָעֶלְיוֹן.

וַאֲמִתַּת מַהוּת סִדְרֵי צֵרוּפָם בְּשָׁרְשָׁם הָעֶלְיוֹן, אֵינוֹ מֻשָּׂג לָנוּ עַתָּה, אַחַר שֶׁאֵין אֲנַחְנוּ מַשִּׂיגִים עַתָּה בְּחִינַת שֹׁרֶשׁ הַנְּשָׁמָה. וְאַחַר הַתְּחִיָּה נִתְבּוֹנֵן בִּינָה בְּסוֹד סִדְרֵי צֵרוּפֵי הָאוֹתִיּוֹת בְּשֹׁרֶשׁ קְדֻשָּׁתָם. וְהוּא שֶׁאָמְרוּ בַּזֹּהַר בְּהַעֲלוֹתְךָ קנ"ב א': "אוֹרַיְתָא כו' וּלְעָלְמָא דְּאָתֵי זְמִינִין לְאִסְתַּכָּלָא בְּנִשְׁמְתָא לְנִשְׁמְתָא דְּאוֹרַיְתָא": [תּוֹרָה וכו' וְלֶעָתִיד לָבוֹא מְזֻמָּנִים לְהִסְתַּכֵּל בִּנְשָׁמָה שֶׁל נְשָׁמָה שֶׁבַּתּוֹרָה.]

וְהוּא בְּחִינַת שֹׁרֶשׁ נִשְׁמוֹת כְּלַל יִשְׂרָאֵל יַחַד, מַלְכוּת דַּאֲצִילוּת, לְזֹאת נִקְרֵאת "כְּנֶסֶת יִשְׂרָאֵל":

פֶּרֶק י"ח

וְהִנֵּה אַחַר שֶׁכְּבָר הֻרְגַּל וּסְדוּרָה לוֹ תְּפִלָּתוֹ, בְּהִתְקַשְּׁרוּת הַשְּׁלֹשָׁה בְּחִינוֹת נר"ן שֶׁבִּכְלָלוּת נַפְשׁוֹ, עַל יְדֵי הָאוֹתִיּוֹת וּנְקֻדּוֹת וּטְעָמִים שֶׁבְּכָל תֵּבָה, כְּמוֹ שֶׁנִּתְבָּאֵר לְעֵיל פֶּרֶק ט"ז, יִתְעַצֵּם בְּטֹהַר מַחְשַׁבְתּוֹ וְכַוָּנָתוֹ, לְדַבֵּק אַחַר זֶה כָּל הַשְּׁלֹשָׁה בְּחִינוֹת נר"ן, בִּבְחִינַת "נִשְׁמְתָא לְנִשְׁמְתָא" הַנַּ"ל, שֶׁהוּא "שֹׁרֶשׁ נִשְׁמָתוֹ" , עַל יְדֵי צֵרוּפֵי הָאוֹתִיּוֹת שֶׁל הַתֵּבָה בְּשֹׁרֶשׁ קְדֻשָּׁתָם הָעֶלְיוֹן.

וּכְשֶׁיִּתְדַּבֵּק בְּזֹאת הַמַּדְרֵגָה, אָז יוּכַל לְהֵחָשֵׁב כְּאִלּוּ אֵינוֹ בָּעוֹלָם כְּלָל, וּמִמֵּילָא יִתְבַּטֵּל בְּעֵינָיו מִכֹּל וָכֹל. כִּי בְּחִינָה זֹאת הִיא נַעֲלָה מִמַּדְרֵגַת הָאָדָם עַתָּה, כְּמוֹ שֶׁכָּתַבְתִּי לְעֵיל, וְיִכְלֹל עַצְמוֹ בְּשֹׁרֶשׁ נִשְׁמָתוֹ בִּכְלַל שֹׁרֶשׁ הָעֶלְיוֹן שֶׁל כְּלַל נִשְׁמוֹת יִשְׂרָאֵל יַחַד:

לָכֵן קָבְעוּ אַנְשֵׁי כְּנֶסֶת הַגְּדוֹלָה, לוֹמַר קֹדֶם הַתְחָלַת תְּפִלַּת הָעֲמִידָה, הַפָּסוּק "אֲדֹנָי שְׂפָתַי תִּפְתָּח", כִּי מִי שֶׁזּוֹכֶה לְמַדְרֵגָה זוֹ בְּעֵת הַתְּפִלָּה, הֲרֵי מֵהִתְקַשְּׁרוּת הַמַּחְשָׁבָה זוֹ יוּכַל לִהְיוֹת גּוּפוֹ כְּאֶבֶן דּוֹמֵם, וּכְאִלֵּם לֹא יִפְתַּח פִּיו, רַק שֶׁהוּא יִתְבָּרַךְ יִפְתַּח שְׂפָתָיו לְדַבֵּר לְפָנָיו תֵּבוֹת הַתְּפִלָּה.

וְלָכֵן אָמַר שֵׁם "א–ד–נ–י" דַּוְקָא, שֶׁהוּא סוֹד "כְּנֶסֶת יִשְׂרָאֵל" הַנַּ"ל. וְעַיֵּן בִּפְרִי עֵץ חַיִּים סוֹף שַׁעַר הַבְּרִיאָה, בְּעִנְיַן זֶה הַפָּסוּק קֹדֶם הַתְּפִלָּה, שֶׁאָמְרוּ רַבּוֹתֵינוּ זִכְרוֹנָם לִבְרָכָה (ברכות ד, ב) עָלָיו שֶׁהוּא כִּתְפִלָּה אֲרִיכְתָּא. וְזֶהוּ שֶׁאָמְרוּ רַבּוֹתֵינוּ זִכְרוֹנָם לִבְרָכָה (יבמות קה, ב): "הַמִּתְפַּלֵּל צָרִיךְ שֶׁיִּתֵּן לִבּוֹ לְמַעְלָה", וּכְעֵין שֶׁפֵּרֵשׁ רַבֵּנוּ יוֹנָה זִכְרוֹנוֹ לִבְרָכָה שָׁם. וְכֵן חֲסִידִים הָרִאשׁוֹנִים שֶׁהָיוּ שׁוֹהִים שָׁעָה אַחַת וכו', כְּדֵי שֶׁיְּכַוְּנוּ אֶת לִבָּם לַמָּקוֹם (ברכות ל, ב), וְהוּא מְבֹאָר:

שַׁעַר ג'

פֶּרֶק א'

וּמַה שֶּׁאָמְרוּ כָּאן (ברכות ל:) "לַמָּקוֹם". וְכֵן בְּאָבוֹת (ב, יג) אָמְרוּ: "וּכְשֶׁאַתָּה מִתְפַּלֵּל אַל תַּעַשׂ תְּפִלָּתְךָ קֶבַע, אֶלָּא רַחֲמִים וְתַחֲנוּנִים לִפְנֵי הַמָּקוֹם בָּרוּךְ הוּא". רָמְזוּ זִכְרוֹנָם לִבְרָכָה בְּתֵיבַת "מָקוֹם" לְעִנְיָן גָּדוֹל. וְהָעִנְיָן צָרִיךְ בֵּאוּר, לְהָבִין עֹמֶק כַּוָּנָתָם זִכְרוֹנָם לִבְרָכָה בָּזֶה, וּלְמִסְפַּר קְרָאֵי הָרוֹמְזִים עַל זֶה:

וּכְבָר אָמְרוּ זִכְרוֹנָם לִבְרָכָה בְּאָבוֹת (ב, טו), שֶׁ"כָּל דִּבְרֵיהֶם כְּגַחֲלֵי אֵשׁ", שֶׁכְּמוֹ הַגַּחֶלֶת, שֶׁאַף שֶׁלֹּא נִרְאָה בָּהּ רַק "נִצּוֹץ" אֵשׁ, אִם תָּשִׂים כֹּחֲךָ בָּהּ לְהָפְכָהּ וּלְנָפְחָהּ, כָּל שֶׁתְּנַפְּחָהּ יוֹתֵר, תִּתְלַהֵב וְתִתְפַּשֵּׁט בָּהּ הַנִּצּוֹץ, עַד שֶׁתֵּעָשֶׂה כֻּלָּהּ לוֹחֶשֶׁת, וְתוּכַל לֵיהָנוֹת מִמֶּנָּה לְהִשְׁתַּמֵּשׁ לְאוֹרָהּ וּלְהִתְחַמֵּם נֶגְדָּהּ, אֲבָל רַק נֶגְדָּהּ, וְלֹא לַאֲחֹזָה, שֶׁכֵּיוָן שֶׁנַּעֲשֵׂית לוֹחֶשֶׁת צָרִיךְ זְהִירוּת שֶׁלֹּא תִּכָּוֶה בָּהּ.

כֵּן בְּדִמְיוֹן זֶה נִמְשְׁלוּ כָּל דִּבְרֵי חֲכָמִים, שֶׁאַף שֶׁנִּרְאִים דְּבָרִים קְצָרִים וּפְשׁוּטִים, אֲבָל הֵם כְּפַטִּישׁ יְפוֹצְצוּ, שֶׁכָּל שֶׁהָאָדָם מְהַפֵּךְ וּמְסַלְסֵל וּמְדַקְדֵּק בָּהֶם, יָאוֹרוּ עֵינָיו מִשַּׁלְהֶבֶת אוֹרָם הַגָּדוֹל, שֶׁיִּמְצָא בְּתוֹכָם עִנְיָנִים עֲמֻקִּים, כְּאָמְרָם זִכְרוֹנָם לִבְרָכָה (אבות ה, כח): "הֲפֹךְ בָּהּ וכו' דְּכֹלָּא בָהּ".

אֲבָל צָרִיךְ לְהִזָּהֵר מְאֹד בְּגַחַלְתָּן, שֶׁלֹּא לִיכָּנֵס לְהִתְבּוֹנֵן וְלַחְקֹר בִּדְבָרִים שֶׁאֵין הָרְשׁוּת נְתוּנָה לְהִתְבּוֹנֵן בָּהֶם יוֹתֵר מִדַּי, כְּאָמְרָם שָׁם "וֶהֱוֵי מִתְחַמֵּם כְּנֶגֶד אוּרָן שֶׁל חֲכָמִים", הַיְנוּ, שֶׁלֹּא לְהִתְרַחֵק מִלְּהִתְבּוֹנֵן כְּלָל בְּדִבְרֵיהֶם, כִּי לֹא יֵהָנֶה מֵאוֹרָם כְּלָל, וְגַם לֹא יִתְקָרֵב יוֹתֵר מִדַּי, שֶׁלֹּא יִכָּוֶה כַּנַּ"ל, רַק מְנֻגָּד, כְּמוֹ שֶׁסִּיֵּם אַחַר זֶה "וֶהֱוֵי זָהִיר בְּגַחַלְתָּן" וכו':

וְהִנֵּה כָּאן בְּתֵבַת "מָקוֹם" גַּם כֵּן, הֲגַם שֶׁפְּשׁוּטוֹ מוּבָן, אֲבָל כְּשֶׁנְּדַקְדֵּק בּוֹ נִמְצָא שֶׁכָּלְלוּ וְרָמְזוּ בָּזֶה עוֹד עִנְיָן גָּדוֹל.

כִּי עִנְיַן מַה שֶּׁהוּא יִתְבָּרַךְ נִקְרָא "מָקוֹם". פֵּרְשׁוּהוּ זִכְרוֹנָם לִבְרָכָה בִּבְרֵאשִׁית רַבָּה (פס"ח) עַל פָּסוּק "וַיִּפְגַּע בַּמָּקוֹם" (בראשית כח, יא): "רַב הוּנָא בְּשֵׁם רַב אַמִּי אָמַר, מִפְּנֵי מַה מְכַנִּין שְׁמוֹ שֶׁל הַקָּדוֹשׁ בָּרוּךְ הוּא וְקוֹרְאִין אוֹתוֹ "מָקוֹם", שֶׁהוּא מְקוֹמוֹ שֶׁל עוֹלָם וְאֵין עוֹלָמוֹ מְקוֹמוֹ". וּבִשְׁמוֹת רַבָּה סוֹף פָּרָשָׁה מ"ה, וּבְתַנְחוּמָא פָּרָשַׁת תִּשָּׂא "וַיֹּאמֶר ה' הִנֵּה מָקוֹם אִתִּי" (שמות לג, כא) אָמַר רַבִּי יוֹסֵי ב"ר חֲנִינָא וכו', אַתְרִי טְפֵלָה לִי וְאֵין אֲנִי טָפֵל לְאַתְרִי. וְכֵן אִיתָא בְּשׁוֹחֵר טוֹב תְּהִלִּים מִזְמוֹר צ'.

וּלְפִי פְּשׁוּטוֹ רָצָה לוֹמַר, כְּמוֹ שֶׁהַמָּקוֹם, הוּא סוֹבֵל וּמַחֲזִיק אֵיזֶה דָּבָר וְחֵפֶץ הַמֻּנָּח עָלָיו, כֵּן בְּדִמְיוֹן זֶה הַבּוֹרֵא אֲדוֹן כֹּל יִתְבָּרַךְ שְׁמוֹ, הוּא הַמָּקוֹם הָאֲמִתִּי, הַסּוֹבֵל וּמְקַיֵּם הָעוֹלָמוֹת וְהַבְּרִיּוֹת כֻּלָּם, שֶׁאִם חַס וְשָׁלוֹם יְסַלֵּק כֹּחוֹ מֵהֶם אַף רֶגַע אַחַת, אֶפֶס מְקוֹם קִיּוּם וְחִיּוּת כָּל הָעוֹלָמוֹת, וּכְמוֹ שֶׁכָּתוּב (נחמיה ט, ו) "וְאַתָּה מְחַיֶּה אֶת כֻּלָּם".

וְהוּא פִּנַּת יְסוֹד אֱמוּנַת יִשְׂרָאֵל, כְּמוֹ שֶׁכָּתַב הָרַמְבַּ"ם זִכְרוֹנוֹ לִבְרָכָה בְּרֵישׁ סִפְרוֹ.

וְלָכֵן קוֹרֵא בַּזֹּהַר לַאֲדוֹן כֹּל יִתְבָּרַךְ שְׁמוֹ — "נִשְׁמְתָא דְּכָל נִשְׁמָתִין", כְּמוֹ שֶׁהַנְּשָׁמָה

מְחַיָּה וּמְקַיֶּמֶת הַגּוּף, וכמ"ש (סנהדרין צ"א:) וְכִי אֶפְשָׁר לַחֲתִיכַת בָּשָׂר ג' יָמִים וכו', כֵּן הוּא יִתְבָּרַךְ שְׁמוֹ הוּא לְבַדּוֹ חֵי הָעוֹלָמִים כֻּלָּם, וְכַיָּדוּעַ בִּמְקוֹמוֹת רַבּוֹת בַּתִּקּוּנִים וְרַעְיָא מְהֵימְנָא. וְעַיֵּן בְּרֵישׁ הַקְדָּמָה שְׁנִיָּה שֶׁל הַתִּקּוּנִים, בְּמַאֲמַר פָּתַח אֵלִיָּהוּ וכו'.

וְכֵן רַבּוֹתֵינוּ זִכְרוֹנָם לִבְרָכָה דִּמּוּ קִיּוּם כָּל הָעוֹלָם עַל יְדֵי כֹּחוֹ יִתְבָּרַךְ, לְקִיּוּם הַגּוּף עַל יְדֵי כֹּחוֹת הַנְּשָׁמָה, אָמְרוּ (ברכות י.): "מַה הַנְּשָׁמָה מְלֵאָה וְזָנָה אֶת כָּל הַגּוּף, אַף הַקָּדוֹשׁ בָּרוּךְ הוּא מָלֵא וְזָן" כו'. זֶהוּ פַּשְׁטוּת עִנְיַן שֶׁהוּא יִתְבָּרַךְ נִקְרָא "מְקוֹמוֹ שֶׁל עוֹלָם":

פֶּרֶק ב'

אָמְנָם פְּנִימִיּוּת עִנְיַן "מְקוֹמוֹ שֶׁל עוֹלָם", הוּא עִנְיָן גָּדוֹל מְאֹד. כִּי מַה שֶּׁכִּנּוּהוּ יִתְבָּרַךְ שְׁמוֹ "מְקוֹמוֹ שֶׁל עוֹלָם", אֵין עֶרֶךְ כְּלָל לְעִנְיַן מָקוֹם הַנּוֹשֵׂא כָּל חֵפֶץ הָעוֹמֵד עָלָיו, שֶׁעַצְמוּת הִתְהַוּוּת וְקִיּוּם הַכְּלִי יֵשׁ לָהּ מְצִיאוּת בִּפְנֵי עַצְמָהּ, וְהַמָּקוֹם רַק מַצֶּלֶת אוֹתָהּ שֶׁלֹּא תִּפֹּל וְתִשָּׁבֵר. וְכֵן עִנְיַן חִיּוּת וְקִיּוּם הַגּוּף עַל יְדֵי הַנְּשָׁמָה, הַגּוּף יֵשׁ לוֹ מְצִיאוּת בִּפְנֵי עַצְמוֹ, וְאֵינוֹ מִתְבַּטֵּל מִמְּצִיאוּתוֹ גַּם בְּצֵאת הַנְּשָׁמָה מִמֶּנּוּ.

אֲבָל הָעוֹלָמוֹת כֻּלָּם, כָּל עִקַּר הִתְהַוּוּת מְצִיאוּתָם כָּל רֶגַע, הוּא רַק מֵאִתּוֹ יִתְבָּרַךְ שְׁמוֹ, וְאִלּוּ הָיָה מְסַלֵּק רְצוֹנוֹ יִתְבָּרַךְ מִלְּהַוּוֹת אוֹתָם כָּל רֶגַע, הָיוּ לְאַיִן וָאֶפֶס מַמָּשׁ.

וְרַק מֵחֲמַת שֶׁאֵין בְּכֹחַ שׁוּם נִבְרָא, אַף עֶלְיוֹן שֶׁבָּעֶלְיוֹנִים, לְהַשִּׂיג מַהוּת הָעִנְיָן, אֵיךְ כָּל הָעוֹלָמוֹת וְכָל צְבָאָם הֵמָּה בְּעֶצֶם אַיִן, וְרַק כָּל רֶגַע הֵמָּה מִתְהַוִּים לִמְצִיאוּת מִמֶּנּוּ יִתְבָּרַךְ. לָזֹאת בָּחֲרוּ לְהַמְשִׁילֵהוּ יִתְבָּרַךְ, וּלְהַסְבִּיר לְאֹזֶן שׁוֹמַעַת בְּקֶרֶב חֲכָמִים, בְּתֵבַת "מָקוֹם".

שֶׁאַף שֶׁכָּךְ גָּזְרָה חָכְמָתוֹ יִתְבָּרַךְ, לִיתֵּן מְצִיאוּת לְעוֹלָמוֹ, בְּאֹפֶן שֶׁיִּלְאֶה כָּל שֵׂכֶל לְהַשִּׂיג אֵיךְ הוּא הַמְשָׁכַת הִתְהַוּוּתָם מִמֶּנּוּ יִתְבָּרַךְ שְׁמוֹ כָּל רֶגַע, וְיוּכַל לְהִדַּמּוֹת בְּעֵינֵי בָּשָׂר שֶׁהָעוֹלָם הוּא מְצִיאוּת וְקִיּוּם בִּפְנֵי עַצְמוֹ חַס וְשָׁלוֹם.

הֵאִירוּ חז"ל עֵינֵי הַשֵּׂכֶל, בְּהַמְשִׁילָם לְעִנְיַן "מָקוֹם", שֶׁכְּמוֹ שֶׁהַכְּלִי הָעוֹמֶדֶת עַל אֵיזֶה מָקוֹם, הֲגַם שֶׁהַכְּלִי הֲרֵי יֵשׁ לָהּ בֶּאֱמֶת מְצִיאוּת בִּפְנֵי עַצְמָהּ, עִם כָּל זֶה אִם לֹא הָיָה לְהַכְּלִי מָקוֹם שֶׁתַּעֲמֹד עָלָיו, הָיְתָה כְּלֹא הָיָה, כֵּן אַף שֶׁהָעוֹלָם כֻּלּוֹ מֻרְגָּשׁ וְנִדְמֶה כִּמְצִיאוּת בִּפְנֵי עַצְמוֹ, הוּא יִתְבָּרַךְ שְׁמוֹ הוּא מְקוֹמוֹ, שֶׁאִלְמָלֵא הָיָה מָקוֹם בִּרְצוֹנוֹ לְהִתְהַוּוּת הָעוֹלָמוֹת, עַל אַחַת כַּמָּה וְכַמָּה שֶׁהָיוּ כֻּלָּם כְּלֹא הָיוּ.

וז"ש בְּסֵפֶר יְצִירָה (פֶּרֶק א' מִשְׁנָה ח'): עֶשֶׂר סְפִירוֹת בְּלִימָה, בְּלֹם פִּיךָ מִלְּדַבֵּר וְלִבְּךָ מִלְּהַרְהֵר, וְאִם רָץ לִבְּךָ שׁוּב לַמָּקוֹם, שֶׁלְּכָךְ נֶאֱמַר "רָצוֹא וָשׁוֹב" (יחזקאל א, יד).

אָמַר לַ"מָּקוֹם" דַּיְקָא, הַיְנוּ, שֶׁאִם יָרוּץ מַחְשֶׁבֶת לֵב הָאָדָם לְהַשִּׂיג הַמּוּשְׂכָּל אֵיךְ נִמְשַׁךְ הִתְהַוּוּתָם כָּל רֶגַע מִמֶּנּוּ ית"ש, "שׁוּב לַמָּקוֹם" לְהַשִּׂיג עֶרֶךְ הַמֻּשְׂכָּל מִדִּמְיוֹן הַמֻּרְגָּשׁ בִּבְחִינַת מָקוֹם, כַּנַּ"ל. וְעַיֵּן פֵּרוּשׁ רַמְבַּ"ן זִכְרוֹנוֹ לִבְרָכָה עַל מִשְׁנָה זוֹ:

וְעַל זוֹ הַכַּוָּנָה דָּרְכוּ רַבּוֹתֵינוּ זִכְרוֹנָם לִבְרָכָה הַקְּדוֹשִׁים, לְהַמְשִׁיל מְשָׁלִים בְּעִנְיַן הִתְחַבְּרוּתוֹ יִתְבָּרַךְ לְהָעוֹלָמוֹת, אַף שֶׁאֵין עֶרֶךְ וְדִמְיוֹן כְּלָל בֵּין הַמָּשָׁל וְהַנִּמְשָׁל רַק בְּאֵיזֶה דָּבָר פְּרָטִי. וְאַף גַּם זֹאת רַק בְּדִמְיוֹן מַה.

וּכְמוֹ שֶׁכָּתוּב בְּרַעְיָא מְהֵימְנָא פָּרָשַׁת פִּנְחָס רנ"ז ב' ורנ"ח א': "וְאִית לְמִנְדַּע כו', כְּגַוְנָא דָּא בָּרָא נִשְׁמְתָא כו', וּמָה רִבּוֹן עָלְמִין לֵית לֵיהּ שֵׁם יְדִיעַ וְלָא אֲתַר יְדִיעַ, אֶלָּא בְּכָל סְטַר שָׁלְטָנוּתֵיהּ, אוּף הָכִי לֵית לָהּ לְנִשְׁמְתָא כו', אֶלָּא בְּכָל סְטַר שׁוּלְטָנוּתָא, לֵית אֵבֶר פָּנוּי מִנַּהּ כו', בְּכָל אִנּוּן שְׁמָהָן וְכִנּוּיִן אִתְקְרֵי עַל שֵׁם כָּל עָלְמִין כו', לְאִתְחֲזָאָה שׁוּלְטָנוּתֵיהּ עֲלַיְהוּ, אוּף הָכִי נִשְׁמְתָא עַל שׁוּלְטָנוּתָא דְּכָל אֵבָרִים דְּגוּפָא אַמְתִיל לָהּ לְגַבֵּיהּ, לָאו דְּאִדַּמְיָא לֵיהּ אִיהִי בְּעַצְמָהּ, דְּהוּא בָּרָא לָהּ וכו', וְעוֹד כו'. וּבְגִין דָּא אִיהִי אִדַּמְיָא לְגַבֵּיהּ בְּשׁוּלְטָנוּתָא דִּילָהּ עַל כָּל אֵבְרֵי גוּפָא, אֲבָל לָא בְּמִלָּה אָחֳרָא". [וְיֵשׁ לָדַעַת וכו', כְּעֵין זֶה בָּרָא נְשָׁמָה וכו', וּמָה רִבּוֹן הָעוֹלָמִים אֵין לוֹ שֵׁם יָדוּעַ, וְלֹא מָקוֹם יָדוּעַ אֶלָּא מֶמְשַׁלְתּוֹ בְּכָל צַד, אַף כָּךְ אֵין לַנְּשָׁמָה וכו', אֶלָּא מֶמְשַׁלְתָּהּ הִיא בְּכָל צַד, וְאֵין אֵבֶר פָּנוּי מִמֶּנָּה וכו'. בְּכָל אֵלּוּ הַשֵּׁמוֹת וְכִנּוּיִים נִקְרָא עַל שֵׁם כָּל הָעוֹלָמוֹת וכו', לְהַרְאוֹת שֶׁמֶּמְשַׁלְתּוֹ עֲלֵיהֶם, אַף הַנְּשָׁמָה בַּעֲבוּר מֶמְשַׁלְתָּהּ עַל כָּל אֶבְרֵי הַגּוּף הִמְשִׁילָהּ אֵלָיו, אֲבָל לֹא שֶׁהַנְּשָׁמָה דּוֹמָה לוֹ בְּעַצְמוּתָהּ שֶׁהֲרֵי הוּא בָּרָא אוֹתָהּ וכו', וְעוֹד וכו'. וּמִשּׁוּם זֶה הַנְּשָׁמָה דּוֹמָה לוֹ בְּמֶמְשַׁלְתָּהּ עַל כָּל אֶבְרֵי הַגּוּף, אֲבָל לֹא בְּדָבָר אַחֵר] וְעַיֵּן שָׁם בְּאֹרֶךְ.

וְכֵן כָּל הַדְּבָרִים שֶׁמָּנוּ חֲזַ"ל שָׁם בְּעִנְיַן הִתְדַּמּוּתוֹ יִתְבָּרַךְ לְהַנְּשָׁמָה בַּגּוּף, הַכֹּל הוּא רַק עַל עִנְיַן הִתְפַּשְּׁטוּתוֹ יִתְבָּרַךְ שְׁמוֹ בְּהָעוֹלָמוֹת וּמְמַלְּאָם וּשְׁלִיטָתוֹ עֲלֵיהֶם כַּנַּ"ל, שֶׁרַק בְּדָבָר זֶה לְבַד מִתְדַּמִּין בְּעִנְיָנָם.

וְכֵן רָמְזוּ בַּתִּקּוּנִים סוֹף תל"ח, אָמְרוּ: "דְּאִשְׁתְּמַע קָלֵיהּ וְדִבּוּרֵיהּ מִן כָּרְסְיָא, וּמַלְאֲכַיָּא וּשְׁמַיָּא וְאַרְעָא דְּיִשְׁתְּמוֹדְעוּן לֵיהּ בְּכֹלָּא, עֵלָּא וְתַתָּא, כְּנִשְׁמְתָא דְּשָׁלְטָנוּתָהּ בְּכָל גּוּפָא, אֲפִילוּ בְּאֵבֶר זְעִירָא, וְלֵית אֵבֶר פָּנוּי מִנַּהּ". [שֶׁיִּשָּׁמַע קוֹלוֹ וְדִבּוּרוֹ מִן הַכִּסֵּא וּמַלְאָכִים וְשָׁמַיִם וָאָרֶץ שֶׁיִּוָּדַע לָהֶם בַּכֹּל, מַעְלָה וּמַטָּה כַּנְּשָׁמָה הַשּׁוֹלֶטֶת בְּכָל הַגּוּף אֲפִלּוּ בְּאֵבֶר קָטָן וְאֵין אֵבֶר פָּנוּי מִמֶּנָּה.]

דַּיֵּק בְּאָמְרוֹ "כְּנִשְׁמְתָא דְּשָׁלְטָנוּתָהּ" וכו', וּמִמֵּילָא נִשְׁמַע שֶׁגַּם בְּזֶה הָעִנְיָן עַצְמוֹ שֶׁדִּמּוּהוּ ז"ל, לֹא הִשְׁווּ בָּהּ לְגַמְרֵי, כִּי אַף שֶׁאָמְרוּ "מָה הַנְּשָׁמָה מְלֵאָה אֶת כָּל הַגּוּף אַף הַקָּדוֹשׁ בָּרוּךְ הוּא מָלֵא אֶת כָּל הָעוֹלָם", וְכֵן מ"ש בְּמַאֲמַר הַתִּקּוּנִים הַנַּ"ל כְּנִשְׁמְתָא כו' וְלֵית אֵבֶר מִנַּהּ, וְשָׁם בַּתִּקּוּן ע' בְּכָל אֵבֶר אִיהוּ הֲוָיָ"ה וכו', לֵית אֲתַר פָּנוּי מִנֵּיהּ, כְּנִשְׁמְתָא דְּאִשְׁתַּכְחַת בְּכָל אֵבֶר וְאֵבֶר דְּגוּפָא, [בְּכָל אֵבֶר הוּא הֲוָיָ"ה וכו', אֵין מָקוֹם פָּנוּי מִמֶּנּוּ, כַּנְּשָׁמָה שֶׁנִּמְצֵאת בְּכָל אֵבֶר וְאֵבֶר שֶׁבַּגּוּף.]

אֵין עִנְיַן מִלּוּי הַקָּדוֹשׁ בָּרוּךְ הוּא אֶת הָעוֹלָם כְּעִנְיַן מִלּוּי הַנְּשָׁמָה אֶת הַגּוּף, שֶׁעִם כָּל זֶה, גַּם הַגּוּף יֶשְׁנוֹ לְעַצְמוֹ חוּצָץ בִּפְנֶיהָ, רַק שֶׁמִּתְפַּשֶּׁטֶת בִּפְנִימִיּוּת כָּל פְּרָטֵי חֲלָקָיו וּמְקַיְּמוֹ, שֶׁהֲרֵי גַּם בְּצֵאת הַנְּשָׁמָה מֵהַגּוּף — אֵין הַגּוּף מִתְבַּטֵּל עַל יְדֵי זֶה מִמְּצִיאוּת.

אֲבָל אֲדוֹן כֹּל יִתְבָּרַךְ שְׁמוֹ, הוּא מָלֵא אֶת כָּל הָעוֹלָמוֹת וְהַנִּבְרָאִים, וְאֵינָם חוֹצְצִים חָלִילָה נֶגְדּוֹ יִתְבָּרַךְ כְּלָל בֶּאֱמֶת, וְאֵין עוֹד מִלְּבַדּוֹ יִתְבָּרַךְ מַמָּשׁ שׁוּם דָּבָר כְּלָל בְּכָל הָעוֹלָמוֹת, מֵהָעֶלְיוֹן שֶׁבָּעֶלְיוֹנִים עַד הַתְּהוֹם הַתַּחְתּוֹן שֶׁבִּתְהוֹמוֹת הָאָרֶץ, עַד שֶׁתּוּכַל לוֹמַר שֶׁאֵין כָּאן שׁוּם נִבְרָא וְעוֹלָם כְּלָל, רַק הַכֹּל מָלֵא עַצְמוּת אַחְדּוּתוֹ הַפָּשׁוּט יִתְבָּרַךְ שְׁמוֹ.

וְעַיֵּן רוֹקֵחַ בְּסוֹף שֹׁרֶשׁ קְדֻשַּׁת הַיִּחוּד ז"ל: "הַבּוֹרֵא אֵינוֹ צָרִיךְ לְמָקוֹם וּמָכוֹן, כִּי הָיָה קֹדֶם כָּל הֱיוֹת, וְאֵין קִירוֹת וְהַקּוֹרוֹת חוֹצְצִין לְפָנָיו, כִּי לֹא הָיָה בּוֹרֵא דָּבָר שֶׁהוּא מַזִּיק כְּנֶגְדּוֹ".

פֶּרֶק ג'

וְהוּא עִנְיַן הַכָּתוּב (ירמיה כ"ג כ"ד) "הֲלֹא אֶת הַשָּׁמַיִם וְאֶת הָאָרֶץ אֲנִי מָלֵא". וְיוֹתֵר מְפֹרָשׁ בְּמִשְׁנֵה תוֹרָה "וְיָדַעְתָּ הַיּוֹם וגו', כִּי ה' הוּא הָאֱלֹהִים בַּשָּׁמַיִם מִמַּעַל וְעַל הָאָרֶץ מִתָּחַת אֵין עוֹד" (דברים ד, לט) וְכֵן "אַתָּה הָרְאֵתָ לָדַעַת כִּי ה' הוּא הָאֱלֹהִים אֵין עוֹד מִלְּבַדּוֹ" (שם ד, לה) וְהוּא מַמָּשׁ כְּמַשְׁמָעוֹ, שֶׁאֵין עוֹד מִלְּבַדּוֹ יִתְבָּרַךְ כְּלָל, בְּשׁוּם בְּחִינָה וּנְקֻדָּה פְּרָטִית שֶׁבְּכָל הָעוֹלָמוֹת, עֶלְיוֹנִים וְתַחְתּוֹנִים וְהַבְּרִיּוֹת כֻּלָּם, רַק עַצְמוּת אַחְדוּתוֹ הַפָּשׁוּט יִתְבָּרַךְ שְׁמוֹ לְבַד.

וְהוּא פְּנִימִיּוּת אָמְרָם זִכְרוֹנָם לִבְרָכָה בִּדְבָרִים רַבָּה (פ"ב י"ט): דָּבָר אַחֵר "כִּי ה' הוּא הָאֱלֹהִים" וגו', יִתְרוֹ נָתַן מַמָּשׁ וכו', רָחָב וכו', מֹשֶׁה שָׂמָהוּ אַף בַּחֲלָלוֹ שֶׁל עוֹלָם, שֶׁנֶּאֱמַר (שם) "כִּי ה' כו' בַּשָּׁמַיִם מִמַּעַל וְעַל הָאָרֶץ מִתַּחַת אֵין עוֹד", מַהוּ "אֵין עוֹד", אֲפִלּוּ בַּחֲלָלוֹ שֶׁל עוֹלָם:

וְזֶה גַּם כֵּן בִּכְלַל מַאֲמָרָם ז"ל שֶׁהוּא יִתְבָּרַךְ מְקוֹמוֹ שֶׁל עוֹלָם וְאֵין הָעוֹלָם מְקוֹמוֹ, הַיְנוּ, שֶׁאַף כָּל הַמְּקוֹמוֹת שֶׁמֻּרְגָּשִׁים לַחוּשׁ בִּמְצִיאוּת, אֵין הַמְּקוֹמוֹת עַצְמִיִּים, אֶלָּא הוּא יִתְבָּרַךְ שְׁמוֹ, הוּא הַמָּקוֹם שֶׁל כָּל הַמְּקוֹמוֹת, שֶׁמִּצִּדּוֹ יִתְבָּרַךְ נֶחְשָׁבִים כֻּלָּם כְּאִלּוּ אֵינָם בִּמְצִיאוּת כְּלָל, גַּם עַתָּה כְּקֹדֶם הַבְּרִיאָה:

אָמְנָם כְּבָר הִקְדַּמְנוּ בִּתְחִלַּת דְּבָרֵינוּ, שֶׁהִמְשִׁילוּ דִּבְרֵיהֶם זִכְרוֹנָם לִבְרָכָה כְּ"גַחֲלֵי אֵשׁ", שֶׁיְּהֵא זָהִיר מְאֹד בְּגַחַלְתָּן שֶׁלֹּא לִיכָּנֵס לְהִתְבּוֹנֵן וְלַחְקֹר יוֹתֵר מִדַּי, בִּדְבָרִים שֶׁאֵין הָרְשׁוּת נְתוּנָה לְהִתְבּוֹנֵן הַרְבֵּה, וְיִכָּוֶה חַס וְשָׁלוֹם.

וְכֵן הוּא זֶה הָעִנְיָן הַנּוֹרָא. אֵין הַדָּבָר אָמוּר, אֶלָּא לְחָכָם וּמֵבִין מִדַּעְתּוֹ פְּנִימִיּוּת הָעִנְיָן בְּשִׁעוּרָא דְּלִבָּא לְבַד בְּרָצוֹא וָשׁוֹב, לְהַלְהִיב בָּזֶה טֹהַר לִבּוֹ לַעֲבוֹדַת הַתְּפִלָּה, אֲבָל רֹב הַהִתְבּוֹנְנוּת בָּזֶה הוּא סַכָּנָה עֲצוּמָה, וְעַל זֶה נֶאֱמַר בְּסֵפֶר יְצִירָה: "וְאִם רָץ לִבְּךָ, שׁוּב לַמָּקוֹם". כְּמוֹ שֶׁכָּתַבְתִּי לְעֵיל פֶּרֶק ב', וּכְמוֹ שֶׁאֶכְתֹּב אי"ה לְהַלָּן פֶּרֶק ו'.

וּבֶאֱמֶת הָיִיתִי מוֹנֵעַ עַצְמִי מִלְּדַבֵּר בְּעִנְיָן זֶה כְּלָל, כִּי הָרִאשׁוֹנִים זִכְרוֹנָם לִבְרָכָה הִסְתִּירוּ הָעִנְיָן מְאֹד, כְּמוֹ שֶׁתִּרְאֶה דִּבְרֵי קָדוֹשׁ ה' הָרוֹקֵחַ ז"ל, הוּבָא לְעֵיל (סוֹף"ב), שֶׁלֹּא דִּבֵּר בָּזֶה רַק בְּרֶמֶז, כִּי נֶאֱמְנָה אֶת אֵל רוּחַם וְכִסּוּ דָּבָר.

אֲבָל שַׁבְתִּי וְרָאִיתִי, שֶׁכָּךְ הָיָה יָפֶה לָהֶם לְפִי דּוֹרוֹתֵיהֶם. אֲבָל עַתָּה, הֵן יָמִים רַבִּים לְלֹא מוֹרֶה, וְכָל דֶּרֶךְ אִישׁ יָשָׁר בְּעֵינָיו לַהֲלֹךְ אַחֲרֵי נְטִיַּת שִׂכְלוֹ, וְכָל יֵצֶר מַחְשְׁבוֹת לֵב הָאָדָם מָלֵא רַק לָעוּף בְּמַחְשַׁבְתּוֹ אֶל כָּל אֲשֶׁר יִטֶּנּוּ שִׂכְלוֹ.

וְהָעוֹלָה עַל כֻּלָּם, שֶׁזֶּה תּוֹרַת כָּל הָאָדָם, וְנַעֲשָׂה מָשָׁל גַּם בְּפִי כְּסִילִים, לֵאמֹר, הֲלֹא בְּכָל מָקוֹם וְכָל דָּבָר הוּא אֱלֹקוּת גָּמוּר, וְעֵינָם וְלִבָּם כָּל הַיָּמִים לְהַעֲמִיק וּלְעַיֵּן

בָּזֶה, עַד שֶׁגַּם נְעָרִים מְנֹעָרִים מִמְּשְׁכָא לְהוּ לְבַיְהוּ לִקְבֹּעַ כָּל מַעֲשֵׂיהֶם וְהַנְהָגָתָם בָּזֶה לְפִי שִׂכְלָם זֶה.

וְכַמָּה זְהִירוּת יְתֵרָה, צָרִיךְ הָאָדָם לְהִזָּהֵר בָּזֶה, וְלִשְׁמֹר אֶת נַפְשׁוֹ מְאֹד בְּמִשְׁמֶרֶת לְמִשְׁמֶרֶת. שֶׁאִם חַס וְשָׁלוֹם יִקָּחֶנּוּ לִבֵּנוּ לִקְבֹּעַ לָנוּ מַחְשָׁבָה זוֹ, לְהַתִּיר לְעַצְמֵנוּ לְהִתְנַהֵג גַּם בְּמַעֲשֶׂה לְפִי הַמַּחְשָׁבָה זוֹ, הֲלֹא יוּכַל לְהִוָּלֵד מִזֶּה חַס וְשָׁלוֹם הֲרִיסַת כַּמָּה יְסוֹדוֹת הַתּוֹרָה הַקְּדוֹשָׁה ר״ל.

וּבְנָקֵל יוּכַל לְהִלָּכֵד חַס וְשָׁלוֹם בְּרֶשֶׁת הַיֵּצֶר, שֶׁיַּרְאֶה לוֹ הֶתֵּרָא עַל פִּי מַחְשָׁבָה זוֹ דֶּרֶךְ מָשָׁל – לְהַרְהֵר בְּדִבְרֵי תוֹרָה בִּשְׁאָט נֶפֶשׁ אַף בִּמְקוֹמוֹת הַמְּטֻנָּפִים, אַחַר שֶׁיִּקְבַּע אֶצְלוֹ תְּחִלָּה שֶׁהַכֹּל אֱלֹקוּת גָּמוּר. ורז״ל הִפְלִיגוּ בָּזֶה מְאֹד, וּכְרָתוּהוּ בְּרוּחַ קָדְשָׁם מֵהְיוֹת לוֹ חֵלֶק לָעוֹלָם הַבָּא, רַחֲמָנָא לִיצְלָן, כְּמוֹ שֶׁכָּתוּב (ברכות כ״ד ב׳) שֶׁבִּכְלַל "כִּי דְּבַר ה׳ בָּזָה" (דברים טו, לא) הוּא גַּם הַמְהַרְהֵר דִּבְרֵי תוֹרָה בַּמְּבוֹאוֹת הַמְּטֻנָּפִים, וּמִמֵּילָא נִשְׁמַע סֵיפֵיהּ דְּהַאי קְרָא "הִכָּרֵת תִּכָּרֵת" וכו׳, וּפֵירְשׁוּהוּ ז״ל בְּפֶרֶק חֵלֶק (צ׳ ע״ב) "הִכָּרֵת" – בָּעוֹלָם הַזֶּה, "תִּכָּרֵת" – לָעוֹלָם הַבָּא. וְעוֹד כַּמָּה טָעֻיּוֹת שֶׁיּוּכַל לָצֵאת חַס וְשָׁלוֹם, אִם הָיָה נִקְבַּע הַהַנְהָגָה בְּמַעֲשֶׂה עַל פִּי זֶה הַדֶּרֶךְ.

וְזֶה שֶׁהֱבִיאַנִי לְהִכָּנֵס לְדַבֵּר בְּזֶה הָעִנְיָן, וּלְהַזְהִיר וּלְהַרְחִיק מִטָּעוּת שֶׁיּוּכַל לְהִוָּלֵד מִזֶּה חַס וְשָׁלוֹם, וּלְהָבִין עַל בּוּרְיוֹ כָּל מַה שֶּׁרָמְזוּ לָנוּ רַבּוֹתֵינוּ זִכְרוֹנָם לִבְרָכָה בָּזֶה, וְהִנָּם כְּכָל דַּרְכֵי ה׳ הַיְשָׁרִים, וְעֵת לַעֲשׂוֹת:

פֶּרֶק ד׳

וּלְהָשֵׁב הַדָּבָר עַל מְכוֹנוֹ, נְבָאֵר מַאֲמַר קַדִּישִׁין רז״ל, שֶׁמְּבֹאָר בְּעֵץ חַיִּים, לָקוּחַ מֵהַתִּקּוּנִים בְּכַמָּה מְקוֹמוֹת, שֶׁהוּא יִתְבָּרַךְ שְׁמוֹ מְמַלֵּא כָּל עָלְמִין בְּהַשְׁוָאָה גְּמוּרָה.

וַהֲרֵי מָצִינוּ שֶׁגַּם בָּעוֹלָמוֹת הָעֶלְיוֹנִים, כָּל עוֹלָם חָלוּק וּמְשֻׁנֶּה מֵחֲבֵרוֹ בִּבְחִינוֹת שׁוֹנִים, בְּעִנְיַן הִתְחַבְּרוּתוֹ יִתְבָּרַךְ אֲלֵיהֶם, וכמ״ש בְּהַקְדָּמַת הַתִּקּוּנִים (דף ג׳ ע״ב) דְּעֶשֶׂר סְפִירוֹת דַּאֲצִילוּת מַלְכָּא בְּהוֹן, אִיהוּ וְגַרְמֵיהּ חַד בְּהוֹן, אִינוּן וְחַיֵּיהוֹן חַד בְּהוֹן, מַה דְּלָאו הָכִי בְּעֶשֶׂר סְפִירוֹת דִּבְרִיאָה, דְּלָאו אִנּוּן וְאִיהוּ חַד וכו׳. [שֶׁעֶשֶׂר סְפִירוֹת שֶׁאֲצִילוּת הַמֶּלֶךְ בָּהֶם, הוּא וְעַצְמוֹ אֶחָד בָּהֶם, הֵם וְחַיֵּיהֶם אֶחָד בָּהֶם, מַה שֶּׁאֵין כֵּן בְּעֶשֶׂר סְפִירוֹת שֶׁל בְּרִיאָה שֶׁאֵין הֵם וְהוּא אֶחָד.]

וְעַיֵּן בְּעֵץ חַיִּים שַׁעַר הִשְׁתַּלְשְׁלוּת הָעֲשָׂרָה סְפִירוֹת בְּרֵישׁ סֵדֶר הָאֲצִילוּת בִּקְצוּר, כָּתַב שֶׁ"אֵין סוֹף" בָּרוּךְ הוּא, בִּבְחִינַת הִתְלַבְּשׁוּתוֹ וְהִתְפַּשְּׁטוּתוֹ בְּכָל הָעוֹלָמוֹת, אֵינוֹ נוֹגֵעַ וְדָבֵק, זוּלָתִי בְּעוֹלַם אֲצִילוּת לְבַד, וְלֹא בִּבְרִיאָה יְצִירָה עֲשִׂיָּה, וְלָכֵן מִשָּׁם וּלְמַטָּה יִשְׁתַּנֶּה מַהוּתָם.

וְשָׁם בְּשַׁעַר דְּרוּשֵׁי אבי״ע פֶּרֶק ז׳, בְּפֵרוּשׁ מַאֲמַר הַתִּקּוּנִים הַנַּ״ל, כָּתַב, שֶׁהָאֲצִילוּת כֻּלּוֹ, גַּם בְּחִינַת הַכֵּלִים נִקְרָא אֱלָהוּת גָּמוּר, מַה שֶּׁאֵין כֵּן בבי״ע, עַיֵּן שָׁם.

וְכֵן מְבֹאָר שָׁם הַחִלּוּק הָעַצְמִי שֶׁבֵּין הָאֲצִילוּת לג׳ עוֹלָמוֹת בי״ע בְּעִנְיַן הָאֱלָהוּת, עַיֵּן שָׁם בְּרֵישׁ שַׁעַר צִיּוּר עוֹלָמוֹת אבי״ע, בְּהַקְדָּמַת הרח״ו, וּבְשַׁעַר הִשְׁתַּלְשְׁלוּת הי׳ סְפִירוֹת

פֶּרֶק ג׳, וְשַׁעַר הַצֶּלֶם פֶּרֶק א׳, וְשַׁעַר הַשֵּׁמוֹת פֶּרֶק א׳, וְשַׁעַר סֵדֶר אבי״ע פֶּרֶק ב׳ וְרֵישׁ פֶּרֶק ג׳, וְכַיּוֹצֵא כַּמָּה חִלּוּקֵי בְּחִינוֹת וְעִנְיָנִים שׁוֹנִים בֵּין הָעוֹלָמוֹת, פְּרָטֵי פְּרָטִים, הַמְּבֹאָר בְּכָל הַזֹּהַר וְדִבְרֵי הָאֲרִיזַ״ל.

וְעַיֵּן הֵיטֵב בְּסוֹף סֵפֶר אַרְבַּע מֵאוֹת שֶׁקֶל כֶּסֶף, בְּעִנְיַן יְדִיעָתוֹ יִתְבָּרַךְ שְׁמוֹ מִקֹּדֶם בְּמַעֲשֵׂי הָאָדָם, שֶׁחִלֵּק הָאֲרִיזַ״ל בָּזֶה בֵּין הָעוֹלָמוֹת.

וְיָתֵר עַל כֵּן, שֶׁמָּצִינוּ כַּמָּה מִקְרָאוֹת, כְּמוֹ ״אֵל עֶלְיוֹן״ (בראשית יד, יט) ״יוֹשֵׁב בַּשָּׁמַיִם״ (תהלים ב, ד), אֲשֶׁר אִלְמָלֵא מִקְרָא כָּתוּב אִי אֶפְשָׁר לְאָמְרָם. וְכֵן מָנוּ רַבּוֹתֵינוּ זִכְרוֹנָם לִבְרָכָה (כלים א, ו) ״עֶשֶׂר קְדֻשּׁוֹת״, ו״ג׳ מַחֲנוֹת״ מְקֻדָּשׁוֹת זוֹ לְמַעְלָה מִזּוֹ. אֲבָל אֲמִתַּת הָעִנְיָן הַט אָזְנְךָ, וְלִבְּךָ תָּשִׁית, וְתֵלֵךְ לָבֶטַח:

כִּי מְבֹאָר בְּכַמָּה מְקוֹמוֹת בַּזֹּהַר, שֶׁאָדוֹן יָחִיד אֵין סוֹף בָּרוּךְ הוּא, מְמַלֵּא כָּל עָלְמִין וְסוֹבֵב כָּל עָלְמִין, וְהַיְנוּ, שֶׁ״מִּצִּדּוֹ יִתְבָּרַךְ״ נִקְרָא בִּבְחִינַת ״מְמַלֵּא כָּל עָלְמִין״, וּ״מִצִּדֵּנוּ״ כְּפִי אֲשֶׁר נִצְטַוֵּינוּ בַּתּוֹרָה הַקְּדוֹשָׁה בְּעִנְיַן הַנְהָגוֹתֵינוּ בַּתּוֹרָה וּמִצְוֹת, וּכְפִי הַשָּׂגָתֵנוּ בְּחוּשׁ, נִקְרָא יִתְבָּרַךְ שְׁמוֹ בִּבְחִינַת ״סוֹבֵב כָּל עָלְמִין״, שֶׁבְּחִינַת ״מְמַלֵּא כָּל עָלְמִין״ הוּא כְּבוֹד אֱלֹהִים הַסְתֵּר דָּבָר מִצִּדֵּנוּ.

וְהָעִנְיָן כִּי וַדַּאי הָאֱמֶת, שֶׁמִּצִּדּוֹ יִתְבָּרַךְ, גַּם עַתָּה אַחַר שֶׁבָּרָא וְחִדֵּשׁ הָעוֹלָמוֹת בִּרְצוֹנוֹ, הוּא מְמַלֵּא כָּל הָעוֹלָמוֹת וְהַמְּקוֹמוֹת וְהַבְּרִיּוֹת כֻּלָּם בְּשִׁוּוּי גָּמוּר וְאַחְדוּת פָּשׁוּט, ״וְאֵין עוֹד מִלְּבַדּוֹ״ כְּמַשְׁמָעוֹ מַמָּשׁ, וּכְמוֹ שֶׁכָּתַבְתִּי לְעֵיל מִמִּקְרָאוֹת מְפֹרָשִׁים וּבְשֵׁם הָרוֹקֵחַ ז״ל.

וּכְמוֹ שֶׁתִּקְּנוּ לָנוּ קַדְמוֹנֵינוּ זִכְרוֹנָם לִבְרָכָה לוֹמַר קֹדֶם הַתְּפִלָּה ״אַתָּה הוּא עַד שֶׁלֹּא נִבְרָא הָעוֹלָם אַתָּה הוּא מִשֶּׁנִּבְרָא הָעוֹלָם״, רוֹצֶה לוֹמַר, אַף שֶׁכְּבָר נִבְרְאוּ הָעוֹלָמוֹת בִּרְצוֹנוֹ הַפָּשׁוּט יִתְבָּרַךְ, עִם כָּל זֶה אֵין שׁוּם שִׁנּוּי וְהִתְחַדְּשׁוּת חַס וְשָׁלוֹם, וְלֹא שׁוּם חֲצִיצָה מֵחֲמָתָם בְּעַצְמוּת אַחְדּוּתוֹ הַפָּשׁוּט, וְהוּא הוּא גַּם עַתָּה כְּקֹדֶם הַבְּרִיאָה, שֶׁהָיָה הַכֹּל מָלֵא עַצְמוּת אֵין סוֹף בָּרוּךְ הוּא, גַּם בְּמָקוֹם שֶׁעוֹמְדִים הָעוֹלָמוֹת עַתָּה.

וְלִבְּךָ תָּשִׁית לְדִבְרֵי קָדוֹשׁ ה׳ רַבֵּנוּ שְׁמוּאֵל, אָבִיו שֶׁל הַקָּדוֹשׁ רַבִּי יְהוּדָה חָסִיד, בְּשִׁיר הַיִּחוּד שֶׁחִבֵּר, בְּיִחוּד יוֹם ב׳ ״אֵין קָצֶה כו׳ וְאֵין תָּוֶךְ מַבְדִּיל בֵּינוֹתֶיךָ״ כו׳, עַיֵּן שָׁם, וּבְיִחוּד יוֹם ג׳ ״סוֹבֵב אֶת הַכֹּל וּמָלֵא אֶת כֹּל, וּבִהְיוֹת הַכֹּל אַתָּה בַּכֹּל״ כו׳, עַיֵּן שָׁם עוֹד בָּזֶה:

וְזֶה שֶׁאָמְרוּ רַבּוֹתֵינוּ זִכְרוֹנָם לִבְרָכָה בְּהַדְּבָרִים שֶׁדִּמּוּ הִתְחַבְּרוּתוֹ יִתְבָּרַךְ לְהָעוֹלָמוֹת, לְהִתְחַבְּרוּת הַנְּשָׁמָה לְהַגּוּף, ״מַה הַנֶּפֶשׁ טְהוֹרָה בַּגּוּף אַף הַקָּדוֹשׁ בָּרוּךְ הוּא טָהוֹר בְּעוֹלָמוֹ״ (וַיִּקְרָא רַבָּה סוֹף פָּרָשָׁה ד׳), רוֹצֶה לוֹמַר, כְּעִנְיַן הַנְּשָׁמָה, אַף שֶׁמִּתְפַּשֶּׁטֶת בְּכָל פְּרָטֵי אֵבְרֵי הָאָדָם, הַנְּקִיִּים וְגַם הַמְּלֵאִים לִכְלוּךְ טִנֹּפֶת וְזֻהֲמָא, וְעִם כָּל זֶה אֵינָם חוֹצְצִים כְּלָל לְעִנְיַן טָהֳרָתָהּ, וּבִקְדֻשָּׁתָהּ וְטָהֳרָתָהּ עוֹמֶדֶת.

כֵּן הָעִנְיָן, אִם שֶׁהוּא יִתְבָּרַךְ מְמַלֵּא אֶת כֹּל, וְכָל הַמְּקוֹמוֹת, מְקוֹמוֹת הַטְּהוֹרִים וְהַמְקֻדָּשִׁים וַאֲשֶׁר אֵינָם טְהוֹרִים, אַף עַל פִּי כֵן אֵינָם חוֹצְצִים כְּלָל, וְלֹא גוֹרְמִים שׁוּם שִׁנּוּי חָלִילָה לִקְדֻשַּׁת טָהֳרַת עַצְמוּתוֹ וְאַחְדּוּתוֹ הַפָּשׁוּט יִתְבָּרַךְ. וז״ש (מלאכי ג, ו) ״אֲנִי ה׳ לֹא שָׁנִיתִי״.

וכמ"ש בְּתִקּוּנֵי זֹהַר חָדָשׁ דַּף פ"ח סוֹף ע"ד: "וְכָל יִשְׂרָאֵל דְּקַבִּילוּ מִנֵּיהּ אוֹרַיְתָא, אִנּוּן עָבְדִין לֵיהּ אֶחָד בָּהּ, וּבְכָל אָתְוָן וּשְׁמָהָן קַדִּישִׁין דִּילֵיהּ, וּבְכָל מַשִׁרְיָן עִלָּאִין וְתַתָּאִין דְּאִתְבְּרִיאוּ בְהוּ, וּבְכָל בִּרְיָן עִלָּאִין וְתַתָּאִין. וּלְעֵלָּא מִכֻּלְּהוּ אֶחָד, וּלְתַתָּא מִכֻּלְּהוּ, וּמִלְּגָאו דְּכֻלְּהוּ, וּמִלְּבַר דְּכֻלְּהוּ, אִיהוּ אֶחָד כו', הָכִי אִיהוּ מִלְּגָאו דְּכָל עָלְמִין, כְּמוֹ מִלְּבַר דְּכָל עָלְמִין, לָא אִשְׁתַּנֵּי כו': [וְכָל יִשְׂרָאֵל שֶׁקִּבְּלוּ הֵימֶנּוּ הַתּוֹרָה, הֵם עוֹשִׂים אוֹתוֹ אֶחָד בָּהּ, וּבְכָל אוֹתִיּוֹת וּשְׁמוֹת הַקֹּדֶשׁ שֶׁלּוֹ, וּבְכָל מַחֲנוֹת הָעֶלְיוֹנִים וְתַחְתּוֹנִים שֶׁנִּבְרְאוּ בָּהֶם, וּבְכָל בְּרִיּוֹת עֶלְיוֹנִים וְתַחְתּוֹנִים וּלְמַעְלָה מִכֻּלָּם "אֶחָד", וּלְמַטָּה מִכֻּלָּם, וּבְתוֹךְ כֻּלָּם, וּמִבַּחוּץ לְכֻלָּם, הוּא "אֶחָד" וכו', כָּךְ הוּא מִבִּפְנִים לְכָל הָעוֹלָמוֹת כְּמוֹ מִבַּחוּץ לְכָל הָעוֹלָמוֹת לֹא נִשְׁתַּנָּה.]

פֶּרֶק ה'

אֲבָל עִם כָּל זֶה, הֵן הֵן גְּבוּרוֹתָיו וְנוֹרְאוֹתָיו יִתְבָּרַךְ שְׁמוֹ, שֶׁאַף עַל פִּי כֵן צִמְצֵם כִּבְיָכוֹל כְּבוֹדוֹ יִתְבָּרַךְ, שֶׁיּוּכַל לְהִמָּצֵא עִנְיַן מְצִיאוּת עוֹלָמוֹת וְכֹחוֹת וּבְרִיּוֹת נִבְרָאִים וּמְחֻדָּשִׁים, בִּבְחִינוֹת שׁוֹנִים וְעִנְיָנִים מְחֻלָּקִים, וְחִלּוּקֵי מְקוֹמוֹת שׁוֹנִים, מְקוֹמוֹת קְדוֹשִׁים וּטְהוֹרִים, וּלְהֵפֶךְ טְמֵאִים וּמְטֻנָּפִים.

וְהוּא הַבְּחִינָה אֲשֶׁר "מִצִּדֵּנוּ", הַיְנוּ, שֶׁהַשָּׂגָתֵנוּ אֵינָהּ מַשֶּׂגֶת בְּחוּשׁ רַק עִנְיַן מְצִיאוּתָם כְּמוֹ שֶׁהֵם נִרְאִים, שֶׁעַל פִּי זֹאת הַבְּחִינָה נִבְנוּ כָּל סִדְרֵי חִיּוּב הַנְהָגָתֵנוּ, שֶׁנִּצְטַוֵּינוּ מִפִּיו יִתְבָּרַךְ, חֹק וְלֹא יַעֲבֹר.

וּמִצַּד זֹאת הַבְּחִינָה, הוּא שֶׁדִּמּוּהוּ רַבּוֹתֵינוּ זִכְרוֹנָם לִבְרָכָה כִּבְיָכוֹל כְּעִנְיַן הַנְּשָׁמָה אֶל הַגּוּף, וכמ"ש בַּזֹּהַר שֶׁהוּא יִתְבָּרַךְ הוּא "נִשְׁמָתָא דְּכָל עָלְמִין", שֶׁכְּמוֹ שֶׁבָּאָדָם לֹא נִרְאֶה בְּחוּשׁ רַק הַגּוּף, וְהַנְּשָׁמָה אַף שֶׁהִיא מְלֵאָה אֶת כָּל הַגּוּף הִיא בִּבְחִינַת הֶסְתֵּר לְעֵינֵי בָּשָׂר, וְנִגְלֵית לְעֵינֵי שֵׂכֶל, כֵּן כְּפִי הַשָּׂגָתֵנוּ הַנִּגְלֵית, נִרְאֶה מְצִיאוּת הָעוֹלָמוֹת וְהַבְּרִיּוֹת כֻּלָּם, וְשֶׁהוּא יִתְבָּרַךְ שְׁמוֹ מִתְפַּשֵּׁט וּמִסְתַּתֵּר כִּבְיָכוֹל בִּפְנִימִיּוּת כֻּלָּם לְהַחֲיוֹתָם וּלְקַיְּמָם, כְּעִנְיַן הַנְּשָׁמָה שֶׁמִּתְפַּשֶּׁטֶת וּמִסְתַּתֶּרֶת בִּפְנִימִיּוּת כָּל פְּרָטֵי חֶלְקֵי אֵבְרֵי הַגּוּף, לְהַחֲיוֹתוֹ.

וְכָל הַשֵּׁמוֹת וְהַכִּנּוּיִים וְהַתְּאָרִים וְהַמִּדּוֹת עָלָיו יִתְבָּרַךְ שֶׁמָּצִינוּ בַּתּוֹרָה הַקְּדוֹשָׁה, כֻּלָּם מְדֻבָּרִים מִצַּד זֹאת הַבְּחִינָה — כְּפִי שֶׁהוּא "מִצִּדֵּנוּ", וְסִדְרֵי חִיּוּב הַנְהָגוֹתֵינוּ, שֶׁהוּא מִצַּד הִתְחַבְּרוּתוֹ יִתְבָּרַךְ אֶל הָעוֹלָמוֹת, שֶׁמִּצִּדָּם וְעַל יְדֵיהֶם נִמְשָׁךְ כָּל הַשִּׁנּוּיִים שֶׁל פְּרָטֵי סִדְרֵי הַהַנְהָגָה כֻּלָּם, כְּמוֹ שֶׁנִּתְבָּאֵר לְעֵיל בְּשַׁעַר ב' (פֶּרֶק ב'):

וְזֶה שֶׁכָּתוּב בְּהַקְדָּמַת הַתִּקּוּנִים הַנַּ"ל דְּעֶשֶׂר סְפִירוֹת דַּאֲצִילוּת מַלְכָּא בְּהוֹן, אִיהוּ וְגַרְמֵיהּ חַד בְּהוֹן, אִנּוּן וְחַיֵּיהוֹן חַד בְּהוֹן, מַה דְּלָאו הָכִי בְּעֶשֶׂר סְפִירוֹת דִּבְרִיאָה, דְּלָאו אִנּוּן וְאִיהוּ חַד, לָאו אִנּוּן וְגַרְמֵיהוֹן חַד. וְעִלַּת עַל כֹּולָּא הוּא נָחִית בְּעֶשֶׂר סְפִירָן דַּאֲצִילוּת, וְנָהִיר בְּעֶשֶׂר סְפִירוֹת דִּבְרִיאָה, וּבְעֶשֶׂר כִּתּוֹת דְּמַלְאֲכַיָּא, וּבְעֶשֶׂר גַּלְגַּלֵּי דִּרְקִיעָא. וְלָא אִשְׁתַּנֵּי בְּכָל אֲתַר, [עֶשֶׂר סְפִירוֹת שֶׁאֲצִילוּת מֶלֶךְ בָּהֶם, הוּא וְעַצְמוֹ אֶחָד בָּהֶם, הֵם וְחַיֵּיהֶם אֶחָד בָּהֶם, מַה שֶּׁאֵין כֵּן בְּעֶשֶׂר סְפִירוֹת שֶׁל בְּרִיאָה שֶׁאֵין הֵם וְהוּא אֶחָד אֵין הֵם וְעַצְמוּתָם אֶחָד. וְעֶלְיוֹן עַל כֻּלָּם הוּא יוֹרֵד בְּעֶשֶׂר סְפִירוֹת שֶׁל אֲצִילוּת וּמֵאִיר בְּעֶשֶׂר סְפִירוֹת שֶׁל

בְּרִיאָה וּבְעֶשֶׂר כִּתּוֹת שֶׁל מַלְאָכִים וּבַעֲשָׂרָה גַּלְגַּלִּים שֶׁל הָרָקִיעַ וְלֹא מִשְׁתַּנֶּה בְּשׁוּם מָקוֹם] רָמַז לב׳ הַבְּחִינוֹת הַנַּ״ל, כַּמְבֹאָר.

וּבִבְרֵאשִׁית רַבָּה פָּרָשָׁה ד׳ אָמְרוּ: ״כְּשֶׁהוּא רוֹצֶה ״הֲלֹא אֶת הַשָּׁמַיִם וְאֶת הָאָרֶץ אֲנִי מָלֵא״ (ירמיה כג, כד). וּכְשֶׁהוּא רוֹצֶה, הָיָה מְדַבֵּר עִם מֹשֶׁה מִבֵּין שְׁנֵי בַּדֵּי הָאָרוֹן. אָמַר רַבִּי חֲנִינָא בַּר אִיסִי, פְּעָמִים שֶׁאֵין הָעוֹלָם וּמְלֹאוֹ מַחֲזִיקִים כְּבוֹד אֱלֹהוּתוֹ, פְּעָמִים שֶׁהוּא מְדַבֵּר עִם הָאָדָם מִבֵּין שַׂעֲרוֹת רֹאשׁוֹ״ כו׳. וְכֵן הוּא בִּשְׁמוֹת רַבָּה פָּרָשָׁה ג׳, רָמְזוּ גַּם כֵּן לְאֵלּוּ ב׳ הַבְּחִינוֹת, כַּמְבֹאָר לַמֵּבִין:

וְלָכֵן נִקְרָא הוּא יִתְבָּרַךְ בְּכָל דִּבְרֵי רַבּוֹתֵינוּ זִכְרוֹנָם לִבְרָכָה בְּשֵׁם ״הַקָּדוֹשׁ בָּרוּךְ הוּא״. כִּי כָּלְלוּ בְּזֶה הַשֵּׁם הַנִּכְבָּד, אֵלּוּ הב׳ בְּחִינוֹת יַחַד. כִּי ״קָדוֹשׁ״ פֵּרוּשׁוֹ מֻבְדָּל וְנַעֲלֶה, וְהוּא כְּפִי אֲשֶׁר מִצִּדּוֹ יִתְבָּרַךְ, שֶׁהוּא בֶּאֱמֶת מֻפְרָשׁ וּמֻבְדָּל וּמְאֹד נַעֲלֶה מִכָּל עִנְיְנֵי הַחִלּוּקִים וְשִׁנּוּיִים חָלִילָה, רַק הַכֹּל מָלֵא אַחְדּוּת גָּמוּר לְבַד בְּהַשְׁוָאָה גְּמוּרָה, וּמְרוֹמָם מֵעַל כָּל בְּרָכָה וּתְהִלָּה, וְאֵינֶנּוּ צָרִיךְ לְהִתְבָּרֵךְ חַס וְשָׁלוֹם. וְעַיֵּן תִּקּוּנִים תִּקּוּן ע׳ ק״ל סוֹף עַמּוּד א׳, וְגַם לֹא שַׁיָּךְ כְּלָל לְפִי זֹאת הַבְּחִינָה שׁוּם עִנְיַן תּוֹסֶפֶת וְרִבּוּי בְּרָכָה, כֵּיוָן שֶׁהַכֹּל אַחְדּוּת פָּשׁוּט לְבַד כְּקֹדֶם הַבְּרִיאָה, וּכְמוֹ שֶׁכָּתוּב (ישעיה מ׳ כה) ״וְאֶל מִי תְדַמְּיוּנִי וְאֶשְׁוֶה יֹאמַר קָדוֹשׁ״, שֶׁזֶּה הַכָּתוּב נֶאֱמַר עַל עַצְמוּת אַחְדּוּתוֹ יִתְבָּרַךְ, כַּיָּדוּעַ בְּרַעְיָא מְהֵימְנָא וְתִקּוּנִים.

וּמִצַּד בְּחִינַת הַשָּׂגָתֵנוּ מְצִיאוּת הַכֹּחוֹת וְהָעוֹלָמוֹת, הוּא נִקְרָא ״בָּרוּךְ״ כִּבְיָכוֹל, מִצַּד הִתְחַבְּרוּתוֹ יִתְבָּרַךְ אֲלֵיהֶם, כִּי הֵם הַצְּרִיכִים לְעִנְיַן הַתּוֹסֶפֶת, וְרִבּוּי בְּרָכָה וְשֶׁפַע, עַל יְדֵי מַעֲשֵׂי הָאָדָם הָרְצוּיִים, כְּמוֹ שֶׁכָּתַבְתִּי לְעֵיל בְּשַׁעַר ב׳.

וְזֶהוּ ״הַקָּדוֹשׁ בָּרוּךְ הוּא״, רוֹצֶה לוֹמַר שֶׁהוּא מִצִּדּוֹ יִתְבָּרַךְ ״קָדוֹשׁ״, וְהוּא הוּא עַצְמוֹ נִקְרָא ״בָּרוּךְ״ כִּבְיָכוֹל מִצִּדֵּנוּ, וְהַכֹּל אֶחָד.

וְעַל זֹאת הַבְּחִינָה שֶׁמִּצִּדֵּנוּ, הוּא שֶׁנֶּאֶמְרוּ הַמִּקְרָאוֹת, ״אֵל עֶלְיוֹן״, ״יוֹשֵׁב בַּשָּׁמַיִם״, וְהַרְבֵּה כַּיּוֹצֵא:

פֶּרֶק ו׳

וְהִנֵּה כָּל יְסוֹדֵי תּוֹרָה הַקְּדוֹשָׁה, בְּכָל הָאַזְהָרוֹת וְהַמִּצְוֹת כֻּלָּם, עֲשֵׂה וְלֹא תַעֲשֶׂה, כֻּלָּם הוֹלְכִים עַל פִּי זֹאת הַבְּחִינָה – שֶׁמִּצַּד הַשָּׂגָתֵנוּ, שֶׁוַּדַּאי יֵשׁ חִלּוּק וְשִׁנּוּי מְקוֹמוֹת, שֶׁבַּמְּקוֹמוֹת הַטְּהוֹרִים מֻתָּרִים וְגַם חַיָּבִים אֲנַחְנוּ לְדַבֵּר אוֹ לְהַרְהֵר דִּבְרֵי תוֹרָה, וּבַמְּקוֹמוֹת הַמְטֻנָּפִים נֶאֱסַרְנוּ בָּהֶם אַף הַהִרְהוּר דִּבְרֵי תוֹרָה.

וְכֵן כָּל עִנְיְנֵי וְסִדְרֵי חִיּוּב הַנְהָגוֹתֵינוּ שֶׁנִּצְטַוִּינוּ מִפִּיו בַּתּוֹרָה הַקְּדוֹשָׁה, וּבִלְתִּי זֹאת הַבְּחִינָה שֶׁמִּצִּדֵּינוּ, אֵין מָקוֹם לַתּוֹרָה וּמִצְוֹת כְּלָל.

וְאַף שֶׁבֶּאֱמֶת שֶׁמִּצִּדּוֹ יִתְבָּרַךְ הַמַּשִּׂיג עַצְמוּתוֹ, הוּא מָלֵא אֶת כֹּל בְּהַשְׁוָאָה גְּמוּרָה, בְּלֹא שׁוּם חֲצִיצָה, וְלֹא שׁוּם חִלּוּק וְשִׁנּוּי מְקוֹמוֹת כְּלָל, רַק הַכֹּל אַחְדּוּת פָּשׁוּט כְּקֹדֶם הַבְּרִיאָה מַמָּשׁ. אֲבָל אֵין אֲנַחְנוּ יְכוֹלִים, וְגַם לֹא הֻרְשֵׁינוּ, לִיכָּנֵס כְּלָל לְהִתְבּוֹנֵן בִּינָה בְּזֶה

הָעִנְיָן הַנּוֹרָא, לֵידַע וּלְהַשִּׂיג אֵיךְ אָדוֹן יָחִיד בָּרוּךְ הוּא מָלֵא אֶת כֹּל, וְכָל הַמְּקוֹמוֹת, בְּאַחְדּוּת פָּשׁוּט וְשִׁוּוּי גָּמוּר חָלִילָה וְחָלִילָה.

וּכְמוֹ שֶׁכָּתַב הָרוֹקֵחַ זִכְרוֹנוֹ לִבְרָכָה בְּשֹׁרֶשׁ קְדֻשַּׁת הַיִּחוּד זֶה לְשׁוֹנוֹ הַקָּ׳: "בַּמֻּפְלָא מִמְּךָ אַל תַּחְקֹר" כו׳, זֶה שֶׁכָּתוּב בְּרֵישׁ בְּרַיְתָא דְּסֵפֶר יְצִירָה, "הָשֵׁב הַיּוֹצֵר עַל מְכוֹנוֹ הוּא הַיּוֹצֵר כֹּל" כו׳. וּבִבְרַיְתָא אַחֶרֶת, "וְאִם רָץ לִבְּךָ, שׁוּב לַמָּקוֹם, שֶׁלְּכָךְ נֶאֱמַר (יחזקאל א, יד) "וְהַחַיּוֹת רָצוֹא וָשׁוֹב". פֵּרוּשׁ, כְּשֶׁתַּחְשֹׁב בְּלִבְּךָ עַל בּוֹרֵא עוֹלָם מַה הוּא וְאֵיךְ חֲנָיָתוֹ בְּכָל מָקוֹם וּמַעֲשָׂיו, "בְּלֹם פִּיךָ מִלְּדַבֵּר, וְלִבְּךָ מִלְּהַרְהֵר", – הָסֵר הַמַּחְשָׁבָה מִלִּבְּךָ, "וְאִם רָץ לִבְּךָ" – לְמַחְשָׁבָה זֹאת, חוּשָׁה וּמַהֵר וְאַל תְּהַרְהֵר, וְשׁוּב לְיִחוּד מְקוֹמוֹ שֶׁל עוֹלָם לַעֲבוֹדָתוֹ וּלְיִרְאָתוֹ וכו׳. וְעַל דָּבָר זֶה נִכְרַת בְּרִית, שֶׁלֹּא לַחְשֹׁב בֶּאֱלָקוּתוֹ, שֶׁאֵין כָּל הַחֲכָמִים יְכוֹלִין לֵידַע". עַד כָּאן לְשׁוֹנוֹ, וְעַיֵּן שָׁם בְּאֹרֶךְ.

וְכָל צִבְאוֹת הֲמוֹנֵי מַעְלָה שׁוֹאֲלִין אַיֵּה מְקוֹם כְּבוֹדוֹ, שֶׁאֵין יְכוֹלִין לְהַשִּׂיג מַהוּת עִנְיַן בְּחִינַת "מְקוֹמוֹ שֶׁל עוֹלָם" הַנַּ"ל. וְהוּא מַאֲמָרָם זִכְרוֹנָם לִבְרָכָה חֲגִיגָה בְּפֶרֶק אֵין דּוֹרְשִׁין (י"ג ב׳): "דְּמִדְּאָמְרֵי "בָּרוּךְ כְּבוֹד ה׳ מִמְּקוֹמוֹ" (יחזקאל ג, יב) מִכְּלָל דִּמְקוֹמוֹ לֵיכָּא דְּיָדַע לֵיהּ". וּמֹשֶׁה רַבֵּנוּ בִּקֵּשׁ בַּקָּשָׁה נַפְשׁוֹ לְהַשִּׂיג הָעִנְיָן בְּאָמְרוֹ (שמות לג יח) "הַרְאֵנִי נָא אֶת כְּבוֹדֶךָ", הַיְנוּ בְּחִינַת מְקוֹם כְּבוֹדוֹ הַנַּ"ל, וְלֹא נִתַּן לוֹ.

וְרַק הוּא לְבַדּוֹ יִתְבָּרַךְ הַמַּשִּׂיג עַצְמוּתוֹ, הוּא הַיּוֹדֵעַ עַצְמוּת מַהוּת זֶה הָעִנְיָן הַמֻּפְלָא וּמְכֻסֶּה, "וְהַנִּסְתָּרוֹת לַה׳ אֱלֹהֵינוּ" (דברים כט, כח) וַאֲנַחְנוּ אֵין רְשׁוּת לְהִתְבּוֹנֵן אֶלָּא בְּמַה שֶּׁהֻרְשֵׁינוּ "וְהַנִּגְלֹת לָנוּ" – לְהַשָּׂגָתֵנוּ, וְהוּא בְּהַבְּחִינָה שֶׁ"מִּצִּדֵּנוּ", שֶׁנִּקְרָא הוּא יִתְבָּרַךְ שְׁמוֹ בִּבְחִינַת "סוֹבֵב כָּל עָלְמִין". מֵחֲמַת שֶׁעִם כָּל זֶה, צִמְצֵם בִּרְצוֹנוֹ הַפָּשׁוּט כְּבוֹדוֹ יִתְבָּרַךְ, שֶׁיִּתְרָאֶה לְעֵין הַהַשָּׂגָה מְצִיאוּת עוֹלָמוֹת וְכֹחוֹת וּבְרִיּוֹת נִבְרָאִים מְחֻדָּשִׁים.

וְלָזֹאת, חַיָּבִים אֲנַחְנוּ לֵידַע וְלִקְבֹּעַ בְּלִבֵּנוּ אֱמוּנַת אֹמֶן בְּלִי תְּמוּט: שֶׁמִּצִּדֵּנוּ וַדַּאי שֶׁיֵּשׁ חִלּוּק מְקוֹמוֹת וְעִנְיָנִים שׁוֹנִים לְעִנְיַן דִּינָא וְהִלְכְתָא רַבָּתֵי, כְּמוֹ שֶׁכָּתַבְתִּי לְעֵיל, כִּי הִיא פִּנַּת יְסוֹד הָאֱמוּנָה וְעִקַּר שֹׁרֶשׁ הַתּוֹרָה וְהַמִּצְוֹת כֻּלָּם.

וְהוּא גַּם כֵּן אֶחָד מֵהַטְּעָמִים, שֶׁאַחַר יִחוּד פָּסוּק רִאשׁוֹן דִּקְרִיאַת שְׁמַע, אוֹמְרִים "בָּרוּךְ שֵׁם כְּבוֹד מַלְכוּתוֹ לְעוֹלָם וָעֶד". וְהוּא כְּמוֹ שֶׁנִּתְבָּאֵר לְהַלָּן בְּפֶרֶק י"א, שֶׁעִנְיַן יִחוּד פָּסוּק רִאשׁוֹן בְּתֵבַת "אֶחָד", הַיְנוּ, לְכַוֵּן שֶׁאָדוֹן יָחִיד בָּרוּךְ הוּא, הוּא אֶחָד בְּכָל הָעוֹלָמוֹת וְהַבְּרִיּוֹת כֻּלָּם, אַחְדּוּת פָּשׁוּט כְּמַשְׁמָעוֹ, וְכֻלָּם נֶחְשָׁבִים לְאַיִן, וְאֵין עוֹד מִלְּבַדּוֹ יִתְבָּרַךְ לְגַמְרֵי. וְשֶׁלֹּא נָבֹא לְהִתְבּוֹנֵן חָלִילָה עַל מַהוּת הָעִנְיָן אֵיךְ וּמָה, לָזֹאת אֲנַחְנוּ אוֹמְרִים אַחַר זֶה "בָּרוּךְ שֵׁם כְּבוֹד מַלְכוּתוֹ לְעוֹלָם וָעֶד", שֶׁיִּתְבָּאֵר שָׁם שֶׁהַכַּוָּנָה הוּא עַל הַבְּחִינָה שֶׁמִּצַּד הַשָּׂגָתֵנוּ, שֶׁמִּתְרָאֶה מְצִיאוּת עוֹלָמוֹת וּבְרִיּוֹת מְחֻדָּשִׁים בִּרְצוֹנוֹ יִתְבָּרַךְ הַצְּרִיכִים לְהִתְבָּרֵךְ מֵאִתּוֹ, וְהוּא הַמּוֹלֵךְ עֲלֵיהֶם, זֶהוּ "בָּרוּךְ שֵׁם כְּבוֹד מַלְכוּתוֹ" וכו׳. (וְזֶהוּ הָעִנְיָן שֶׁפָּסוּק רִאשׁוֹן נִקְרָא בַּזֹּהַר "יִחוּדָא עִלָּאָה", וּפָסוּק "בָּרוּךְ שֵׁם כְּבוֹד מַלְכוּתוֹ לְעוֹלָם וָעֶד" נִקְרָא "יִחוּדָא תַּתָּאָה", וְהוּא מְבֹאָר):

פֶּרֶק ז'

וְאֵלּוּ הב' בְּחִינוֹת הַנַּ"ל: שֶׁמִּצִּדּוֹ יִתְבָּרֵךְ וּמִצִּדֵּנוּ, הֵן הֵן עַצְמָן עִנְיַן הַצִּמְצוּם וְהַקַּו הַנִּזְכָּר בְּדִבְרֵי הָאֲרִיזַ"ל. וַאֲשֶׁר מְבֹאָר שָׁם שֶׁמִּצַּד הַ"צִּמְצוּם" לֹא יִצְדַּק בּוֹ שׁוּם שִׁנּוּי וְחִלּוּק מָקוֹם, מַעְלָה וּמַטָּה פָּנִים וְאָחוֹר, רַק הַשְׁוָאָה גְּמוּרָה אֲמִתִּית, וְכָל עִנְיְנֵי הַשִּׁנּוּיִים וְחִלּוּק הַמְּקוֹמוֹת וְכָל הַשֵּׁמוֹת וְכִנּוּיִים, כֻּלָּם נֶאֱמָרִים רַק מִצַּד בְּחִינַת הַ"קַּו". וְעַיֵּן בְּרֵישׁ סֵפֶר אוֹצְרוֹת חַיִּים.

וּמוּדַעַת שֶׁכָּל דִּבְרֵי הָאֲרִיזַ"ל בְּנִסְתָּרוֹת מָשָׁל הֵם, וּפְנִימִיּוּת עִנְיַן הַצִּמְצוּם וְהַקַּו, הַכַּוָּנָה עַל אֵלּוּ הַשְּׁנֵי בְּחִינוֹת הַנַּ"ל, שֶׁהֵן בְּעֶצֶם בְּחִינָה אַחַת וְעִנְיָן אֶחָד לְגַמְרֵי.

כִּי בֵּאוּר מִלַּת "צִמְצוּם" כָּאן, אֵינוֹ לְשׁוֹן סִלּוּק וְהֶעְתֵּק מִמָּקוֹם לְמָקוֹם, לְהִתְכַּנֵּס וּלְהִתְחַבֵּר עַצְמוֹ אֶל עַצְמוֹ כִּבְיָכוֹל, לְהַמְצִיא מָקוֹם פָּנוּי חַס וְשָׁלוֹם, אֶלָּא כְּעִנְיַן שֶׁאָמְרוּ בִּבְרֵאשִׁית רַבָּה סוֹף פָּרָשָׁה מ"ה, וְצִמְצְמָה פָּנֶיהָ וְלֹא רָאֲתָה הַמֶּלֶךְ. וּבְאֵיכָה רַבָּתִי בְּרֵישׁ א"ב דְּאֲנִי הַגֶּבֶר, הָלְכָה וְצִמְצְמָה פָּנֶיהָ אַחַר הָעַמּוּד, שֶׁפֵּרוּשׁוֹ שָׁם, לְשׁוֹן הֶסְתֵּר וְכִסּוּי (עַיֵּן בְּעָרוּךְ עֵרֶךְ צמצם). כֵּן כָּאן מִלַּת "צִמְצוּם" הַיְנוּ הֶסְתֵּר וְכִסּוּי.

וְהַכַּוָּנָה, שֶׁאַחְדּוּתוֹ יִתְבָּרֵךְ שְׁמוֹ, בִּבְחִינַת עַצְמוּתוֹ הַמְּמַלֵּא כָּל עָלְמִין בְּהַשְׁוָאָה גְּמוּרָה, מְכַנִּים אֲנַחְנוּ בְּשֵׁם "צִמְצוּם", מֵחֲמַת שֶׁאַחְדּוּתוֹ יִתְבָּרֵךְ הַמְּמַלֵּא כָּל עָלְמִין הוּא מְצֻמְצָם וּמֻסְתָּר מֵהַשָּׂגָתֵנוּ, וּכְעִנְיַן "אָכֵן אַתָּה אֵל מִסְתַּתֵּר" (ישעיה מ"ה, ט"ו).

וְהַשָּׂגָתֵנוּ מַה שֶּׁאֲנַחְנוּ מַשִּׂיגִים מְצִיאוּת הִשְׁתַּלְשְׁלוּת עוֹלָמוֹת זֶה לְמַעְלָה מִזֶּה בִּבְחִינוֹת שׁוֹנִים, מְכַנִּים אֲנַחְנוּ בְּשֵׁם "קַו", שֶׁהוּא כְּעֵין קַו הַמִּשְׁתַּלְשֵׁל.

וְזֶה שֶׁכָּתַב הָאֲרִיזַ"ל, שֶׁמִּצַּד "הַצִּמְצוּם", הַיְנוּ, מִצַּד עַצְמוּת אַחְדּוּתוֹ יִתְבָּרֵךְ שֶׁבְּהָעוֹלָמוֹת הַמָּלֵא אֶת כֹּל, אֲשֶׁר אַף שֶׁמֵּאִתָּנוּ הוּא מְצֻמְצָם וּמֻסְתָּר, אֲבָל בִּבְחִינַת עַצְמוּתוֹ לֹא יִצְדַּק עִנְיַן מַעְלָה וּמַטָּה, רַק מִצַּד "הַקַּו", הַיְנוּ, מִצַּד הַשָּׂגָתֵנוּ, שֶׁאֲנַחְנוּ מִצִּדֵּנוּ מַשִּׂיגִים סֵדֶר הָעוֹלָמוֹת דֶּרֶךְ הִשְׁתַּלְשְׁלוּת כְּעֵין קַו, יִצְדַּק מִצִּדֵּנוּ מַעְלָה וּמַטָּה.

(וְאַף גַּם זֹאת, שֶׁמִּצַּד הַ"צִּמְצוּם", הַיְנוּ, אַף שֶׁהוּא יִתְבָּרֵךְ שְׁמוֹ צִמְצֵם וְהִסְתִּיר מֵהַשָּׂגָתֵנוּ אוֹר עַצְמוּת אַחְדּוּתוֹ הַמְּמַלֵּא כֹּל, עִם כָּל זֶה, לֹא יִצְדַּק בּוֹ מַעְלָה וּמַטָּה אַף מִצַּד הַשָּׂגָתֵנוּ, אִם הָיִינוּ מַשִּׂיגִים הֶסְתֵּר שָׁוֶה בְּהַשְׁוָאָה גְּמוּרָה בְּכָל הַמְּקוֹמוֹת, כְּעִנְיַן עִגּוּל הַמַּקִּיף שֶׁלֹּא יִצְדַּק בּוֹ עִנְיַן מַעְלָה וּמַטָּה וְחִלּוּק מָקוֹם.

אַךְ מִצַּד הַ"קַּו", הַיְנוּ, שֶׁמֵּאַחַר שֶׁגָּזְרָה רְצוֹנוֹ יִתְבָּרֵךְ, שֶׁגַּם אַחַר הַצִּמְצוּם וְהַהֶסְתֵּר, אֵין הַהֶסְתֵּר שָׁוֶה לְהַשָּׂגָתֵנוּ בְּכָל הַמְּקוֹמוֹת בְּשָׁוֶה, וַאֲנַחְנוּ מַשִּׂיגִים הַשָּׂגוֹת שׁוֹנִים בְּחִלּוּק בְּחִינוֹת פְּרָטִיִּים, דֶּרֶךְ הִשְׁתַּלְשְׁלוּת כְּעֵין קַו אוֹר, הַמֵּאִיר הַשָּׂגָתֵנוּ לְהַשִּׂיג הִתְגַּלּוּת אוֹרוֹ יִתְבָּרֵךְ בְּעוֹלָמוֹת וְכֹחוֹת חֲלוּקִים, שֶׁכָּל עוֹלָם וְכֹחַ הַיּוֹתֵר עֶלְיוֹן, הַהִתְגַּלּוּת אוֹר הָאֱלֹקִי בּוֹ יוֹתֵר.

וְגַם הַשָּׂגָתֵנוּ הִתְגַּלּוּת אוֹרוֹ יִתְבָּרֵךְ בְּזֶה הָעוֹלָם, הוּא גַּם כֵּן בִּבְחִינוֹת וּמַדְרֵגוֹת שׁוֹנִים בִּמְקוֹמוֹת חֲלוּקִים, כְּמוֹ שֶׁמָּנוּ רַבּוֹתֵינוּ זִכְרוֹנָם לִבְרָכָה (כלים א, ו) "עֶשֶׂר קְדֻשּׁוֹת" וְ"שָׁלֹשׁ מַחֲנוֹת מְקֻדָּשׁוֹת", זוֹ לְמַעְלָה מִזּוֹ בְּעֵרֶךְ קְדֻשָּׁתָם, אָז מִצַּד קַו אוֹר הַשָּׂגָתֵנוּ הִתְגַּלּוּת אוֹרוֹ

יִתְבָּרַךְ, הוּא שֶׁיִּצְדַּק בּוֹ מַעְלָה וּמַטָּה, וְכָל חִלּוּקֵי הַמְּקוֹמוֹת וְהַבְּחִינוֹת שׁוֹנִים וּפְרָטֵיהֶם, הַמְבֹאָרִים בְּדִבְרֵי הָאֲרִיזַ"ל.

וְכֵן עִנְיַן הַמִּקְרָאוֹת "אֵל עֶלְיוֹן" (בראשית יד, יט) וֶ"אֱלֹהֵינוּ בַּשָּׁמַיִם" (תהלים קלו, ג) "יוֹשֵׁב בַּשָּׁמַיִם" (תהלים ב. ד) וְהַרְבֵּה כַּיּוֹצֵא, שֶׁמִּצַּד הַשָּׂגָתֵנוּ יִצְדַּק לוֹמַר שֶׁבְּמָקוֹם זֶה נִכָּר יוֹתֵר גַּם אֶצְלֵנוּ הִתְגַּלּוּת אוֹר אֱלָקוּתוֹ יִתְבָּרַךְ שְׁמוֹ, מִבְּמָקוֹם אַחֵר שֶׁהִתְגַּלּוּת אוֹרוֹ יִתְבָּרַךְ הוּא בִּבְחִינַת הֶסְתֵּר מֵהַשָּׂגָתֵנוּ, וּכְעִנְיַן שֶׁאָמַר יַעֲקֹב אָבִינוּ עָלָיו הַשָּׁלוֹם בְּעָמְדוֹ עַל מְקוֹם הַמִּקְדָּשׁ, כְּמוֹ שֶׁקִּבְּלוּ רַבּוֹתֵינוּ זִכְרוֹנָם לִבְרָכָה, "אֵין זֶה כִּי אִם בֵּית אֱלֹהִים" (בראשית כח. יז) רוֹצֶה לוֹמַר שֶׁבְּזֶה הַמָּקוֹם מֻשָּׂג, גַּם לְהַשָּׂגַת הָאָדָם, שֶׁאֵין בּוֹ רַק הִתְגַּלּוּת אוֹר אֱלָקוּתוֹ יִתְבָּרַךְ לְבַד):

וְזֶהוּ עִנְיַן הֶ"חָלָל וּמָקוֹם פָּנוּי" שֶׁהִזְכִּיר ז"ל, וְשֶׁכְּלַל עִנְיַן הַצִּמְצוּם הָיָה לְהִתְגַּלּוּת הַכֵּלִים. הַיְנוּ, שֶׁגָּזְרָה רְצוֹנוֹ, מִטַּעַם הַכָּמוּס אִתּוֹ יִתְבָּרַךְ, לְהַסְתִּיר אוֹר אַחְדּוּת עַצְמוּתוֹ יִתְבָּרַךְ בְּזֶה הַמָּקוֹם, שִׁעוּר עֲמִידַת הָעוֹלָמוֹת וְהַבְּרִיּוֹת כֻּלָּם, הֶסְתֵּר עָצוּם, לְהַמְצִיא עַל יְדֵי זֶה עִנְיָן נִפְלָא כָּזֶה, שֶׁיִּתְרָאֶה וְיֻשַּׂג מְצִיאוּת עוֹלָמוֹת וְכֹחוֹת אֵין מִסְפָּר דֶּרֶךְ הַדְרָגָה וְהִשְׁתַּלְשְׁלוּת, וּלְהָאִיר בָּהֶם הִתְגַּלּוּת אוֹרוֹ יִתְבָּרַךְ אוֹר דַּק, בְּשִׁעוּר וְדִקְדּוּק עָצוּם וְדֶרֶךְ מְסַכִּים אֵין קֵץ, וְעַד שֶׁיּוּכְלוּ לְהִמָּצֵא דֶּרֶךְ הִשְׁתַּלְשְׁלוּת וּמְסַכִּים עֲצוּמִים גַּם מְקוֹמוֹת אֲשֶׁר אֵינָם טְהוֹרִים, וְכֹחוֹת הַטֻּמְאָה וְהָרַע וְהַקְּלִפּוֹת, בְּשֵׁפֶל הַמַּדְרֵגוֹת הַתַּחְתּוֹנִים, וְנִרְאֶה וּמִתְדַּמֶּה כְּאִלּוּ חַס וְשָׁלוֹם הוּא חָלָל פָּנוּי מֵאוֹר אַחְדּוּת עַצְמוּתוֹ יִתְבָּרַךְ שְׁמוֹ, וְאֵין אֲנַחְנוּ מַשִּׂיגִים רַק רְשִׁימָה דַּקָּה מֻעֶטֶת וְאוֹר מְעַט כְּעֵין קַו דֶּרֶךְ מָשָׁל, עַד שֶׁבְּהַגִּיעוֹ דֶּרֶךְ סֵדֶר הַהַדְרָגוֹת וְהַמְּסַכִים הָרַבִּים אֶל הַכֹּחוֹת תַּחְתּוֹנֵי הַתַּחְתּוֹנִים כֹּחוֹת הַטֻּמְאָה וְהָרַע, אֵין הִתְגַּלּוּת אוֹרוֹ יִתְבָּרַךְ נִכָּר כְּלָל לְהַשָּׂגָתֵנוּ, וְזֶה שֶׁאָמְרוּ שָׁם: שֶׁהַקַּו הָאוֹר לֹא הִגִּיעַ עַד קָצֶה הַתַּחְתּוֹן וְלֹא נִדְבַּק בְּתַחְתִּיתוֹ, וְעַל יְדֵי זֶה יִמָּצֵא בְּחִינוֹת מַעְלָה וָמַטָּה כו' עַיֵּן שָׁם, וְהוּא מְבֹאָר לַמֵּבִין.

וְהַצִּמְצוּם וְהַקַּו הַכֹּל אֶחָד וְעִנְיָן אֶחָד, וְרָצָה לוֹמַר, עִם כִּי וַדַּאי שֶׁגַּם בִּמְקוֹם כָּל הָעוֹלָמוֹת וְהַבְּרוּאִים, הַכֹּל מָלֵא גַּם עַתָּה רַק עַצְמוּתוֹ יִתְבָּרַךְ שְׁמוֹ לְבַד, כְּקֹדֶם הַבְּרִיאָה, אָמְנָם הוּא בִּבְחִינַת צִמְצוּם, הַיְנוּ בִּבְחִינַת הֶסְתֵּר לְבַד, מֻפְלָא וּמְכֻסֶּה מֵהַשָּׂגָתֵנוּ, כְּדֵי שֶׁעַל יְדֵי זֶה הַצִּמְצוּם וְהַהֶסְתֵּר תְּהֵא כָּל הַשָּׂגָתֵנוּ אֶת הָעוֹלָמוֹת דֶּרֶךְ הִשְׁתַּלְשְׁלוּת, וְהַמְשָׁכַת הִתְגַּלּוּת אוֹרוֹ יִתְבָּרַךְ בָּהֶם בְּסֵדֶר הַהַדְרָגָה לְבַד כְּעֵין קַו דֶּרֶךְ מָשָׁל, כַּנַּ"ל.

וְזֶהוּ שֶׁאָמַר שָׁם בְּשַׁעַר עִגּוּלִים וְיֹשֶׁר עָנָף ב', "שֶׁהַקַּו חוּט הָאוֹר לֹא נִמְשַׁךְ וְנִתְפַּשֵּׁט תֵּכֶף עַד לְמַטָּה, אֶלָּא לְאַט לְאַט", רוֹצֶה לוֹמַר דֶּרֶךְ הַדְרָגוֹת רַבּוֹת מְאֹד, בְּשִׁעוּר מְדֻקְדָּק, כְּפִי הַצֹּרֶךְ לְהַשָּׂגָתֵנוּ עִנְיַן הָעוֹלָמוֹת וְסֵדֶר הַדְרָגָתָם. וְהַמֵּבִין יָבִין עַל פִּי זֶה מִדַּעְתּוֹ כָּל שֹׁרֶשׁ הָעִנְיָן הַמְבֹאָר שָׁם, כִּי אִי אֶפְשָׁר לְפָרֵט וּלְהַסְבִּיר הֵיטֵב כָּל דְּבָרָיו ז"ל שָׁם:

פֶּרֶק ח'

וְלָכֵן נֶאֱסַר הַחֲקִירָה וְהַהִתְבּוֹנְנוּת בְּמַהוּת עִנְיַן הַצִּמְצוּם, כְּמוֹ שֶׁכָּתַב הָאֲרִיזַ"ל, כְּמוֹ שֶׁכָּתַבְתִּי לְעֵיל, שֶׁלֹּא הֻרְשֵׁנוּ לְהִתְבּוֹנֵן כְּלָל, לֵידַע וּלְהַשִּׂיג מַהוּת "עִנְיַן מְקוֹמוֹ שֶׁל עוֹלָם",

אֵיךְ שֶׁהַכֹּל מָלֵא רַק אַחְדּוּתוֹ הַפָּשׁוּט יִתְבָּרַךְ, וְאֵין עוֹד מִלְּבַדּוֹ כְּלָל לְגַמְרֵי מִצִּדּוֹ יִתְבָּרַךְ. וְהָאֱמֶת שֶׁהוּא בִּכְלָל שְׁאֵלַת וַחֲקִירַת "מַה לְּפָנִים", שֶׁלִּמְּדוּהוּ זִכְרוֹנָם לִבְרָכָה (חגיגה ר"פ אֵין דּוֹרְשִׁין) מִכָּתוּב מְפֹרָשׁ (דברים ד, לב) "כִּי שְׁאַל נָא לְיָמִים רִאשֹׁנִים [אֲשֶׁר הָיוּ לְפָנֶיךָ] לְמִן הַיּוֹם אֲשֶׁר בָּרָא אֱלֹהִים אָדָם [עַל הָאָרֶץ וּלְמִקְצֵה הַשָּׁמַיִם וְעַד קְצֵה הַשָּׁמָיִם"], (וְאִי אַתָּה שׁוֹאֵל וכו').

וְהָאֲרִיזַ"ל אֲשֶׁר הִרְשָׁה וְהִפְלִיא לְגַלּוֹת סוֹדוֹת עֲמֻקִּים וְרָמִים, כְּבָר פֵּרֵשׁ הוּא זִכְרוֹנוֹ לִבְרָכָה, שֶׁפְּנִימִיּוּת כַּוָּנַת הַכָּתוּב "לְמִן הַיּוֹם אֲשֶׁר בָּרָא אֱלֹהִים אָדָם" וכו', הוּא עַל עוֹלַם אָדָם קַדְמָאָה.

וְגַם בְּעִנְיַן אָדָם קַדְמָאָה כָּתַב, שֶׁאֵין אֲנַחְנוּ רַשָּׁאִין לְדַבֵּר וְלַחְקֹר בְּעִנְיַן עַצְמוּת פְּנִימִיּוּתוֹ, רַק בָּאוֹרוֹת הַיּוֹצְאִים מִמֶּנּוּ לְבַד, וְגַם זֹאת רַק מֵאוֹרוֹת דס"ג שֶׁבּוֹ וְאֵילָךְ, וְלֹא בְּאוֹרוֹת ע"ב שֶׁבּוֹ, כָּל שֶׁכֵּן שֶׁלֹּא הִרְשָׁנוּ לְהִתְבּוֹנֵן חָלִילָה בְּמַהוּת עִנְיַן הַצִּמְצוּם, כְּפִי אֲשֶׁר הוּא מִצִּדּוֹ יִתְבָּרַךְ.

וְרַק בְּעִנְיַן הַקַּו, הַיְנוּ בְּהִשְׁתַּלְשְׁלוּת הָעוֹלָמוֹת שֶׁכְּפִי הַשָּׂגָתֵנוּ, בָּזֶה הוּא שֶׁהֶעֱמִיק הִרְחִיב הַדִּבּוּר, אֲבָל בְּעִנְיַן הַצִּמְצוּם, דִּבֵּר בּוֹ בְּרָצוֹא וָשׁוֹב, וְלֹא דִּבֵּר בְּ'מַהוּת' עִנְיָנוֹ בִּפְרָטוּת. וְעַיֵּן בְּרֵישׁ סֵפֶר אוֹצְרוֹת חַיִּים דַּף ב' רֵישׁ ע"ג. וְלֹא גִּלָּהוּ, רַק "מְצִיאוּתוֹ" דֶּרֶךְ כְּלָל לְבַד, לְחָכָם וּמֵבִין מִדַּעְתּוֹ.

מִטַּעַם שֶׁוַּדַּאי רָאוּי לְהָאָדָם הַיָּשָׁר חֲכַם לֵבָב, הַקָּבוּעַ כָּל הַיָּמִים בְּתַלְמוּד תּוֹרָה וּמִצְוֹת, אֲשֶׁר נֶאֶמְנָה אֶת אֵל רוּחוֹ, לֵידַע מְצִיאוּת זֶה הָעִנְיָן הַנּוֹרָא דֶּרֶךְ כְּלָל, שֶׁאָדוֹן יָחִיד יִתְבָּרַךְ שְׁמוֹ מָלֵא אֶת כֹּל וְאֵין עוֹד מִלְּבַדּוֹ יִתְבָּרַךְ, לְהַלְהִיב מִזֶּה טֹהַר קֹדֶשׁ מַחְשַׁבְתּוֹ לַעֲבוֹדַת הַתְּפִלָּה, לְכַוֵּן לִבּוֹ בְּאֵימָה וְיִרְאָה וְרֶתֶת לַמָּקוֹם, הוּא מְקוֹמוֹ שֶׁל עוֹלָם, ("וּמְקוֹמוֹ שֶׁל עוֹלָם" הוּא הוּא כַּוָּנַת עִנְיַן הַצִּמְצוּם, וְהוּא מְבֹאָר כַּנַּ"ל), כְּמַאֲמָרָם זִכְרוֹנָם לִבְרָכָה (ברכות ל ע"ב) שֶׁהַמִּתְפַּלֵּל צָרִיךְ שֶׁיְּכַוֵּן לִבּוֹ לַמָּקוֹם. וְכֵן אָמְרוּ (אבות ב, יג) וּכְשֶׁאַתָּה מִתְפַּלֵּל אַל תַּעַשׂ וכו', אֶלָּא רַחֲמִים וְתַחֲנוּנִים לִפְנֵי הַמָּקוֹם ב"ה. וּכְעִנְיַן שֶׁאָמַר רַבִּי אֱלִיעֶזֶר לְתַלְמִידָיו (ברכות כ"ח ע"ב) דְּעוּ לִפְנֵי מִי אַתֶּם מִתְפַּלְּלִים.

וְכֵן בְּיִחוּד פָּסוּק רִאשׁוֹן דִּקְרִיעַת שְׁמַע בְּתֵיבַת "אֶחָד", רָאוּי לְהָעוֹבֵד אֲמִתִּי לְכַוֵּן בִּקְדֻשַּׁת מַחְשַׁבְתּוֹ, שֶׁהוּא יִתְבָּרַךְ שְׁמוֹ מִצִּדּוֹ, הוּא "אֶחָד" כְּמַשְׁמָעוֹ, גַּם בְּכָל הַבְּרוּאִים כֻּלָּם, אַחְדּוּת פָּשׁוּט לְבַד כְּקֹדֶם הַבְּרִיאָה, וּכְמוֹ שֶׁיִּתְבָּאֵר אי"ה לְהַלָּן.

גַּם לִהְיוֹת יָרֵא וְחָרֵד מִזֶּה מִלַּעֲבֹר חַס וְשָׁלוֹם עַל אַחַת מִמִּצְוֹתָיו יִתְבָּרַךְ, כִּי מְלֹא כָל הָאָרֶץ כְּבוֹדוֹ, כְּמוֹ שֶׁאָמַר הַכָּתוּב (ירמיה כג, כד): "אִם יִסָּתֵר אִישׁ בַּמִּסְתָּרִים וַאֲנִי לֹא אֶרְאֶנּוּ כו', הֲלוֹא אֶת הַשָּׁמַיִם וְאֶת הָאָרֶץ אֲנִי מָלֵא", וּכְעֵין שֶׁאָמַר דָּוִד הַמֶּלֶךְ עָלָיו הַשָּׁלוֹם (תהלים טז, ח): "שִׁוִּיתִי ה' לְנֶגְדִּי תָמִיד".

וְהוּא עִנְיַן "חִלּוּל ה'" הַנֶּאֱמַר בְּכָל מָקוֹם. כְּעֵין שֶׁפֵּרֵשׁ בַּזֹּהַר פָּסוּק "מְחַלְלֶיהָ" וכו' שֶׁהוּא לְשׁוֹן חָלָל וּפְנִיַּת מָקוֹם, כֵּן הָעִנְיָן כָּאן, שֶׁמַּרְאֶה חַס וְשָׁלוֹם כְּאִלּוּ הַמָּקוֹם שֶׁעוֹמֵד בּוֹ הוּא חָלוּל, פָּנוּי מִמֶּנּוּ יִת', וְאֵינוֹ חוֹשֵׁשׁ מִלַּעֲבֹר עַל מִצְוֹתָיו יִתְבָּרַךְ. וּכְעֵין

זֶה מַאֲמָרָם זִכְרוֹנָם לִבְרָכָה (ספ"ק דְּקִדּוּשִׁין לא, ע"א) "כָּל הָעוֹבֵר עֲבֵרָה בַּסֵּתֶר כְּאִלּוּ דּוֹחֵק רַגְלֵי הַשְּׁכִינָה".

(וּבָזֶה יִתְיַשֵּׁב מַאי דְּקַשְׁיָא טוּבָא וּבְעֵינֵי כָּל חֲכַם לֵב יִפָּלֵא, מֵאַיִן הִתִּיר הָאֲרִיזַ"ל לְעַצְמוֹ לְדַבֵּר וּלְהַזְכִּיר כְּלַל עִנְיַן הַצִּמְצוּם, כֵּיוָן שֶׁהַהִתְבּוֹנְנוּת בּוֹ אֲסוּרָה. וּלְפִי מַה שֶּׁבֵּאַרְנוּ עִנְיַן הַצִּמְצוּם, בֶּאֱמֶת הָעִנְיָן נוֹהֵג בְּכָל מָקוֹם וּזְמַן, גַּם בְּזֶה הָעוֹלָם, לַשְּׂרִידִים אֲשֶׁר ה' קוֹרֵא, לֵידַע מְצִיאוּת זֶה הָעִנְיָן הַנּוֹרָא מִטְּעָמִים הַנַּ"ל. וְכֵן בְּרַעְיָא מְהֵימְנָא וְתִקּוּנִים, וּקְדוֹשׁ ה' רַבֵּנוּ שְׁמוּאֵל בַּעַל שִׁיר הַיִּחוּד הַנַּ"ל, וְהָרוֹקֵחַ זִכְרוֹנוֹ לִבְרָכָה, שֶׁהִזְכִּירוּ הָעִנְיָן בְּרֶמֶז לַמֵּבִין, הַכֹּל מֵאֵלּוּ הַטְּעָמִים הַנִּזְכָּרִים, וְכַמְבֹאָר לַמֵּבִין בָּרוֹקֵחַ שָׁם בְּשֹׁרֶשׁ קְדֻשַּׁת הַיִּחוּד, ע"ש).

אָמְנָם הִזָּהֵר מְאֹד בְּנַפְשְׁךָ, זְכֹר וְאַל תִּשְׁכַּח אֲשֶׁר נִתְבָּאֵר לְמַעְלָה, שֶׁאֵין הַדָּבָר אָמוּר אֶלָּא לָדַעַת הָעִנְיָן יְדִיעַת הַלֵּב דֶּרֶךְ כְּלָל בְּשִׁעוּרָא דְּלִבָּא לְבַד, אֲבָל לֹא לַחֲקֹר וּלְהִתְבּוֹנֵן חַס וְשָׁלוֹם בְּמַהוּת הָעִנְיָן. וְגַם לְהִזָּהֵר מְאֹד, שֶׁלֹּא יְהֵא מִמְּשָׁכָא לָבֹא לִקְבֹּעַ כָּל סֵדֶר הַהַנְהָגָה בְּמַעֲשֶׂה עַל פִּי זֶה הָעִנְיָן הַנּוֹרָא, כִּי בְּקַל יוּכַל לְהִוָּלֵד מִזֶּה לְהִתְנַהֵג בְּכַמָּה דְּבָרִים גַּם נֶגֶד חֻקֵּי וִיסוֹדֵי תּוֹרָתֵנוּ הַקְּדוֹשָׁה, וְלֹא יַעֲבֹר כְּתִיב. וּכְמוֹ שֶׁאָמַר הַכָּתוּב (דברים ד, לט) "וְיָדַעְתָּ הַיּוֹם וַהֲשֵׁבֹתָ אֶל לְבָבֶךָ כִּי ה' כו', בַּשָּׁמַיִם מִמַּעַל וכו', אֵין עוֹד", "אֶל לְבָבֶךָ" דַּוְקָא, הַיְנוּ, רַק בְּאוּבַנְתָּא דְּלִבָּא וְשִׁעוּרָא דְּלִבָּא לְבַד, וּכְעִנְיָן שֶׁאָמְרוּ בִּתְפִלָּה "יְכַוֵּן 'לִבּוֹ' לַמָּקוֹם":

פֶּרֶק ט'

וּמַה שֶּׁכָּתוּב (דברים ד, לט) "וְיָדַעְתָּ הַיּוֹם וכו', כִּי ה' הוּא הָאֱלֹקִים", הַהֶבְדֵּל שֶׁבֵּין אֵלּוּ שְׁנֵי הַשֵּׁמוֹת הוּא, שֶׁשֵּׁם "אֱלֹקִים" נֶאֱמַר גַּם עַל אֵיזֶה כֹּחַ פְּרָטִי הַנִּמְשָׁךְ מִמֶּנּוּ יִתְבָּרַךְ, וְשֵׁם "הֲוָיָ"ה" נֶאֱמַר עַל מְקוֹר הַכֹּחוֹת כֻּלָּם, שֶׁנִּמְשָׁכִים מִמֶּנּוּ יִתְבָּרַךְ שְׁמוֹ.

וּכְמוֹ שֶׁאָמְרוּ זִכְרוֹנָם לִבְרָכָה בִּבְרֵאשִׁית רַבָּה (יג, ג), שֶׁהִזְכִּיר אַחַר גְּמַר כָּל מַעֲשֵׂי בְּרֵאשִׁית "שֵׁם מָלֵא (הַיְנוּ הֲוָיָ"ה אֱלֹקִים), עַל עוֹלָם מָלֵא". שֶׁשֵּׁם הֲוָיָ"ה בָּרוּךְ הוּא, הוּא מְקוֹרָא דְּכֹלָּא בֵּיהּ, וּבְעֵת הַבְּרִיאָה נִמְשַׁךְ בְּכָל מַאֲמָר, כֹּחַ אוֹ כֹּחוֹת פְּרָטִיִּים מִמְּקוֹרָא דְּכֹלָּא, לְהִתְהַוּוֹת וּלְהִבָּרְאוֹת אוֹתוֹ הַדָּבָר וְקִיּוּמוֹ, לָזֹאת לֹא נִזְכַּר בְּכָל מַעֲשֵׂי בְּרֵאשִׁית רַק שֵׁם "אֱלֹקִים" לְבַד, וְאַחַר שֶׁנִּגְמְרוּ הַמְשָׁכַת כָּל הַכֹּחוֹת, כְּפִי שֶׁגָּזְרָה רְצוֹנוֹ יִתְבָּרַךְ לְצֹרֶךְ הָעוֹלָם, אָז נֶאֱמַר (בראשית ב, ד) "בְּיוֹם עֲשׂוֹת הֲוָיָ"ה אֱלֹקִים", שֵׁם מָלֵא.

וְזֶהוּ "וְיָדַעְתָּ הַיּוֹם וַהֲשֵׁבֹתָ אֶל לְבָבֶךָ כִּי ה' הוּא הָאֱלֹקִים" (דברים שם) וכו'. הַיְנוּ, שֶׁלֹּא לְכַוֵּן לְהִשְׁתַּעְבֵּד וּלְהִתְדַּבֵּק בְּשׁוּם עֲבוֹדָה, לְאֵיזֶה כֹּחַ אוֹ כֹּחוֹת פְּרָטִיִּים אֲשֶׁר בַּשָּׁמַיִם מִמַּעַל וַאֲשֶׁר בָּאָרֶץ מִתָּחַת, רַק לְכַוֵּן הַכֹּל לְשֵׁם הָעֶצֶם הַמְיֻחָד הֲוָיָ"ה יִתְבָּרַךְ שְׁמוֹ, מְקוֹרָא וּכְלָלָא שֶׁל כְּלַל הַכֹּחוֹת כֻּלָּם שֶׁנִּמְשְׁכוּ מִמֶּנּוּ.

וְזוֹ הָיְתָה כָּל עִנְיַן הָעֲבוֹדָה זָרָה שֶׁל דּוֹרוֹת הָרִאשׁוֹנִים מִימֵי דּוֹר אֱנוֹשׁ, שֶׁאָז הִתְחִילוּ בָּעוֹלָם עִנְיַן הָעֲבוֹדָה זָרָה, כְּמוֹ שֶׁכָּתוּב (בראשית ד, כו) "אָז הוּחַל לִקְרֹא בְּשֵׁם ה'", שֶׁהָיוּ עוֹבְדִים לְכֹחוֹת הַכּוֹכָבִים וְהַמַּזָּלוֹת, כָּל אֶחָד לְכוֹכָב וּמַזָּל מְיֻחָד שֶׁבֵּרֵר לְעַצְמוֹ.

לֹא שֶׁחָשַׁב כָּל אֶחָד שֶׁאוֹתוֹ הַכּוֹכָב הוּא אֱלוֹהַּ שֶׁבָּרָא אֶת כֹּל, שֶׁהֲרֵי מֵעוֹלָם הָיָה שׁוּמָה בְּפִיהֶם שֶׁל הָאוּמּוֹת לִקְרוֹתוֹ יִתְבָּרַךְ שְׁמוֹ "אֱלָהּ דֶּאֱלָהִין" (דניאל ב, מז), כְּמוֹ שֶׁאָמְרוּ רַבּוֹתֵינוּ זִכְרוֹנָם לִבְרָכָה (מנחות קי ע"א). וְכֵן אָמַר מַלְאָכִי הַנָּבִיא בְּתוֹכַחְתּוֹ לְיִשְׂרָאֵל (א, יא): "כִּי מִמִּזְרַח שֶׁמֶשׁ וְעַד מְבוֹאוֹ גָּדוֹל שְׁמִי בַּגּוֹיִם כו', כִּי גָדוֹל שְׁמִי בַּגּוֹיִם אָמַר ה' צְבָאוֹת".

אֶלָּא שֶׁתְּחִלַּת טָעוּת דּוֹר אֱנוֹשׁ הָיָה, שֶׁחָשְׁבוּ בְּשִׁבּוּשׁ דַּעְתָּם כִּי רָם ה' וְעַל הַשָּׁמַיִם כְּבוֹדוֹ, וְאֵין כְּבוֹדוֹ לְהַשְׁגִּיחַ עַל בְּרוּאֵי זֶה הָעוֹלָם הַשָּׁפֵל, וְלָכֵן חָשְׁבוּ שֶׁהֵסִיר הוּא יִתְבָּרַךְ הַשְׁגָּחָתוֹ מֵהֶם, וּמְסָרָם לְכֹחוֹת הַגַּלְגַּלִּים וְהַמַּזָּלוֹת שֶׁהֵמָּה יַנְהִיגוּ זֶה הָעוֹלָם כִּרְצוֹנָם, וְהָיָה נֶחְשָׁב אֶצְלָם חוּלִין וְאִסּוּר גָּמוּר וְחֻצְפָּה גְּדוֹלָה נֶגְדּוֹ יִתְבָּרַךְ, לְהִתְפַּלֵּל לִשְׁמוֹ הַנִּכְבָּד וְהַנּוֹרָא, לְבַקֵּשׁ מֵאִתּוֹ צָרְכֵיהֶם הַשְּׁפֵלִים, לָזֹאת הִשְׁתַּעְבְּדוּ עַצְמָם, וְכִוְּנוּ כָּל עִנְיְנֵי עֲבוֹדָתָם וּבַקָּשָׁתָם לְכֹחוֹת הַכּוֹכָבִים וְהַמַּזָּלוֹת. (וְאֹפֶן עֲשִׂיָּתָם הָעֲבוֹדָה זָרָה, וְזִבּוּחָם וְקִטּוּרָם אֵלֶיהָ, עַיֵּן בְּתִקּוּן ס"ו).

וְהָיוּ יוֹדְעִים גַּם כֵּן, לְהַשְׁבִּיעַ הַמַּלְאָכִים הַמְמֻנִּים עַל הַמַּזָּלוֹת, לָדַעַת טוֹב וָרָע, וְשֶׁיַּשְׁפִּיעוּ לָהֶם עַל יְדֵי זֶה טוֹבוֹת וַהֲנָאוֹת עוֹלָם הַזֶּה, מִכֹּחָם שֶׁנִּתְמַנּוּ עָלָיו מֵאֲדוֹן כֹּל יִתְבָּרַךְ שְׁמוֹ. וּמְעַטִּים יְחִידֵי סְגֻלָּה הָיוּ, שֶׁהִכִּירוּ וְיָדְעוּ בֶּאֱמֶת, שֶׁאַף שֶׁהוּא יִתְבָּרַךְ שְׁמוֹ "מַגְבִּיהִי לָשָׁבֶת", עִם כָּל זֶה הוּא "מַשְׁפִּילִי לִרְאוֹת בַּשָּׁמַיִם וּבָאָרֶץ" (תהלים קיג, ו).

וּמֵהֶם שֶׁהָיוּ עוֹבְדִים לְחַיּוֹת וְעוֹפוֹת, כְּמוֹ שֶׁכָּתוּב (מְלָכִים ב' יז, ל), גַּם כֵּן כַּוָּנָתָם הָיָה לְהִתְדַּבֵּק עַצְמָם עַל יְדֵי זֶה לְהַכֹּחַ וְהַמַּזָּל הָעֶלְיוֹן שֶׁל אוֹתָהּ הַבְּרִיָּה, שֶׁיַּשְׁפִּיעַ עֲלֵיהֶם מִכֹּחוֹ וּמֶמְשַׁלְתּוֹ שֶׁנִּתְמַנָּה עָלָיו מֵהַבּוֹרֵא יִתְבָּרַךְ. וְזֶה שֶׁאָמְרוּ הַנָּשִׁים הָאֲרוּרוֹת לְיִרְמְיָהוּ: "וּמִן אָז חָדַלְנוּ לְקַטֵּר לִמְלֶכֶת הַשָּׁמַיִם וְהַסֵּךְ לָהּ נְסָכִים חָסַרְנוּ כֹל" כו' (ירמיה מד, יח).

וּמֵהֶם שֶׁהָיוּ מִשְׁתַּעְבְּדִים וּמְזַבְּחִים וּמְקַטְּרִים לְאֵיזֶה אָדָם שֶׁרָאוּ שֶׁכֹּחַ מֶמְשֶׁלֶת מַזָּלוֹ גָּדוֹל מְאֹד, בְּחָשְׁבָם שֶׁעַל יְדֵי הִשְׁתַּעְבְּדָם וַעֲבוֹדָתָם אֵלָיו יַעֲלֶה מַזָּלָם עִם מַזָּלוֹ.

וּמֵהֶם, אַף שֶׁלֹּא הָיְתָה כַּוָּנַת עֲבוֹדָתָם לְהַשְׁפָּעַת הֲנָאוֹת עוֹלָם הַזֶּה, אֲבָל כַּוָּנָתָם הָיְתָה לְהַשִּׂיג עַל יְדֵי זֶה אֵיזֶה הַשָּׂגוֹת שִׂכְלִיִּים שֶׁחָמְדוּ לָהֶם, כְּמוֹ חָכְמַת הַקְּסָמִים, וְכַיּוֹצֵא אֵיזֶה הַשָּׂגוֹת.

וּמֵהֶם שֶׁהִתְדַּבְּקוּ לַעֲבוֹדַת אֵיזֶה אֲנָשִׁים, כְּדֵי לְהַמְשִׁיךְ הַשְׁפָּעַת אֱמוּנַת אָמוֹן וְעִנְיְנֵי עֲתִידוֹת. וְזֶהוּ הַכֹּל עֲבוֹדָה זָרָה גְּמוּרָה, וּבִכְלָל "לֹא יִהְיֶה לְךָ אֱלֹהִים אֲחֵרִים" (שמות כ, ג), כְּמוֹ שֶׁכָּתַב הַכֹּל הָרַמְבַּ"ן זִכְרוֹנוֹ לִבְרָכָה בְּפֵרוּשׁוֹ עַל הַתּוֹרָה שָׁם. וְעַיֵּן לִיקּוּטֵי תּוֹרָה סוֹף פָּרָשַׁת נֹחַ בְּעִנְיַן דּוֹר הַהַפְלָגָה.

וַאֲפִלּוּ לְהִשְׁתַּעְבֵּד וּלְהִתְדַּבֵּק בְּאֵיזֶה עֲבוֹדָה, לִבְחִינַת רוּחַ הַקֹּדֶשׁ שֶׁבְּאֵיזֶה אָדָם נָבִיא וּבַעַל רוּחַ הַקֹּדֶשׁ, גַּם זֶה נִקְרָא עֲבוֹדָה זָרָה מַמָּשׁ.

כְּמוֹ שֶׁמָּצִינוּ בִּנְבוּכַדְנֶצַּר שֶׁהִשְׁתַּחֲוָה לְדָנִיֵּאל, גַּם כֵּן לֹא בַּעֲבוּר שֶׁהֶחֱזִיקוֹ לֶאֱלוֹהַּ בּוֹרֵא כֹּל, אֶלָּא שֶׁכִּוֵּן בְּהִשְׁתַּחֲוָיָתוֹ לְהִשְׁתַּעְבֵּד וּלְהִתְדַּבֵּק לְרוּחַ הַקֹּדֶשׁ שֶׁבּוֹ, כְּמוֹ שֶׁכָּתוּב (דניאל

ב, מו): "בֵּאדַיִן מַלְכָּא נְבוּכַדְנֶצַּר נְפַל עַל אַנְפּוֹהִי וּלְדָנִיֵּאל סְגִד וּמִנְחָה וְנִיחֹחִין וכו', מִן קְשֹׁט דִּי אֱלָהֲכוֹן הוּא אֱלָהּ אֱלָהִין כו', וְגָלֵה רָזִין, דִּי יְכֵלְתָּ לְמִגְלֵא רָזָא דְנָה". וְשָׁם (ה, ה) "וְעַד אָחֳרֵין עַל קֳדָמַי דָּנִיֵּאל כו', וְדִי רוּחַ אֱלָהִין קַדִּישִׁין בֵּהּ" וכו' [אָז נָפַל הַמֶּלֶךְ נְבוּכַדְנֶצַּר עַל אַפָּיו וְהִשְׁתַּחֲוָה לְדָנִיֵּאל וּמִנְחָה וּקְטֹרֶת (אָמַר לְנַסֵּךְ לוֹ, עָנָה הַמֶּלֶךְ לְדָנִיֵּאל וְאָמַר) הָאֱמֶת הִיא שֶׁאֱלֹקֵיכֶם הוּא אֱלוֹקֵי הָאֱלוֹהִים (וַאֲדוֹן מְלָכִים) וּמְגַלֶּה סוֹדוֹת, כִּי הִנֵּה יָכֹלְתָּ לְגַלּוֹת סוֹד זֶה. וְשָׁם (ה, ה) עַד אֲשֶׁר אַחֲרוֹן בָּא לְפָנַי דָּנִיֵּאל וגו' וַאֲשֶׁר רוּחַ אֱלֹקִים קְדוֹשִׁים בּוֹ]. וְרַבּוֹתֵינוּ זִכְרוֹנָם לִבְרָכָה אָמְרוּ (סנהדרין צ"ג) הַטַּעַם שֶׁלֹּא הָיָה דָּנִיֵּאל בְּעֵת צִוּוּי הַהִשְׁתַּחֲוָיָה לַצֶּלֶם, שֶׁאָמַר דָּנִיֵּאל, אֵיזִיל מֵהָכָא, דְּלָא לְקַיֵּם "בִּי פְּסִילֵי אֱלָהֵיהֶם תִּשְׂרְפוּן", וּנְבוּכַדְנֶצַּר אָמַר גַּם כֵּן, יֵזִיל דָּנִיֵּאל מֵהָכָא דְּלָא לֵימְרוּ קַלְיֵהּ לֶאֱלָהֵיהּ בְּנוּרָא. וְעַיֵּן זֹהַר חָדָשׁ רוּת ס' ע"ב. וּבִבְרֵאשִׁית רַבָּה פָּרָשָׁה צ"ו, וּבְתַנְחוּמָא רֵישׁ פָּרָשַׁת וַיְחִי. וְכֵן אַתָּה מוֹצֵא בְּדָנִיֵּאל (שם) וכו', מַה כְּתִיב "בֵּאדַיִן מַלְכָּא נְבוּכַדְנֶצַּר וכו', וּמִנְחָה וְנִיחֹחִין אֲמַר לְנַסָּכָא לֵהּ", אֲבָל דָּנִיֵּאל לֹא קִבֵּל, לָמָּה, שֶׁכְּשֵׁם שֶׁנִּפְרָעִין מֵעוֹבְדֵי עֲבוֹדָה זָרָה כָּךְ נִפְרָעִין מֵהָעֲבוֹדָה זָרָה עַצְמָהּ.

וְכֵן אָמְרוּ שָׁם זֶה הַטַּעַם, גַּם עַל יַעֲקֹב אָבִינוּ עָלָיו הַשָּׁלוֹם, שֶׁלֹּא רָצָה לִיקָּבֵר בְּמִצְרַיִם, הֲרֵי שֶׁקָּרְאוּ זִכְרוֹנָם לִבְרָכָה עִנְיָן זֶה "עֲבוֹדָה זָרָה", אַף שֶׁהַכַּוָּנָה הָיְתָה לְרוּחַ אֱלָהִין קַדִּישִׁין דְּבֵיהּ.

וְיֵשׁ לְפָרֵשׁ עַל פִּי זֶה הַכָּתוּב (שמות כ, ג) "לֹא יִהְיֶה לְךָ אֱלֹהִים אֲחֵרִים עַל פָּנָי", רָצָה לוֹמַר שֶׁלֹּא לְכַוֵּן חַס וְשָׁלוֹם בְּשׁוּם דָּבָר לְאֵיזֶה בְּחִינָה וְכֹחַ פְּרָטִי, אֲפִילוּ אִם יִהְיֶה אוֹתוֹ הַכֹּחַ בְּחִינַת "פָּנָי", הַיְנוּ, אֲפִלּוּ לִפְרָט רוּחַ הַקֹּדֶשׁ שֶׁבְּאֵיזֶה אָדָם, אוֹ פְּרָט בְּחִינַת הַקְּדֻשָּׁה שֶׁבְּאֵיזֶה כֹּחַ עֶלְיוֹן שֶׁבָּעֶלְיוֹנִים, וּכְעִנְיַן מַאֲמָרָם זִכְרוֹנָם לִבְרָכָה (ר"ה כד, ב) עַל "לֹא תַעֲשׂוּן אִתִּי" (שמות כ, כג) אֲפִלּוּ דְּמוּת שַׁמָּשַׁי הַמְשַׁמְּשִׁין לְפָנַי בַּמָּרוֹם, כְּגוֹן אוֹפַנִּים וּשְׂרָפִים וְחַיּוֹת הַקֹּדֶשׁ.

וְעִם כִּי עִקַּר אַזְהָרַת הַכָּתוּב עַל כָּל הָעֲבוֹדָה זָרָה הַנַּ"ל, הַיְנוּ בְּאַרְבַּע עֲבוֹדוֹת דַּוְקָא, אָמְנָם עַתָּה שֶׁעֲבוֹדַת הַתְּפִלָּה בְּהִשְׁתַּעְבְּדוּת כַּוָּנַת הַלֵּב הוּא בִּמְקוֹם עֲבוֹדַת הַקָּרְבָּן, וַדַּאי גַּם עַל זֶה שַׁיָּךְ הָאַזְהָרָה.

וְזֶהוּ שֶׁאָמַר הַכָּתוּב (שמות כב, יט) "זוֹבֵחַ לָאֱלֹהִים יָחֳרָם בִּלְתִּי לַה' לְבַדּוֹ", הַיְנוּ שֶׁלֹּא לְכַוֵּן חַס וְשָׁלוֹם בְּשׁוּם עֲבוֹדָה וְעִנְיָן לְאֵיזֶה כֹּחַ פְּרָטִי מִכֹּחוֹת שֶׁקָּבַע הַבּוֹרֵא יִתְבָּרֵךְ (כִּי שֵׁם אֱלֹקִים מְשֻׁתָּף לְכָל בַּעַל כֹּחַ פְּרָטִי שֶׁיִּהְיֶה כַּיָּדוּעַ, וּכְמוֹ שֶׁנִּתְבָּאֵר לְעֵיל), רַק לְכַוֵּן לְשֵׁם הָעֶצֶם הַמְיֻחָד לוֹ יִתְבָּרֵךְ לְבַד, שֶׁפֵּרוּשׁוֹ מְהַוֶּה הַכֹּל, הַיְנוּ כְּלָלָא וּמְקוֹרָא דְּכָל הַכֹּחוֹת כֻּלָּם כַּנַּ"ל, (וְזֶהוּ "שְׁמַע יִשְׂרָאֵל ה' אֱלֹקֵינוּ ה' אֶחָד", רָצָה לוֹמַר שֶׁכָּל הַכֹּחוֹת פְּרָטִיִּים שֶׁנִּמְשָׁכִים מֵהֲוָיָ"ה בָּרוּךְ הוּא, הֵמָּה מְאֻחָדִים וְנִקְבָּצִים בְּכֹחוֹ יִתְבָּרֵךְ שְׁמוֹ, כְּלַל מְקוֹר אַחְדוּתוֹ), וְהוּא מִצַּד הִתְחַבְּרוּתוֹ יִתְבָּרֵךְ עִם הָעוֹלָמוֹת.

וְלָזֹאת, בְּכָל מָקוֹם שֶׁצִּוְּתָה הַתּוֹרָה עַל עִנְיַן הַקָּרְבָּנוֹת, בֵּאֲרָה בְּפֵירוּשׁ לְ"הֲוָיָ"ה" דַּוְקָא, וּכְאָמְרָם זִכְרוֹנָם לִבְרָכָה (מנחות קי.) "בֹּא וּרְאֵה מַה כְּתִיב בְּפָרָשַׁת קָרְבָּנוֹת, שֶׁלֹּא נֶאֱמַר

בָּהֶם לֹא "אֵל" וְלֹא "אֱלֹהִים" אֶלָּא לה', שֶׁלֹּא לִתֵּן פִּתְחוֹן פֶּה לְבַעַל הַדִּין לַחֲלֹק". וְעַיֵּן זֹהַר חָדָשׁ בְּרֵאשִׁית ו' ע"ד, וז' ע"א וע"ב), הָעִנְיָן יוֹתֵר מְבֹאָר.

פֶּרֶק י'

וּלְפִי דַּרְכֵּנוּ בְּעִנְיַן הַשֵּׁנִי בְּחִינוֹת הַנַּ"ל: שֶׁמִּצִּדּוֹ יִתְבָּרֵךְ, וּמִצִּדֵּנוּ. שֶׁנִּתְבָּאֵה, יְבֹאַר עוֹד הֶפְרֵשׁ וְחִלּוּק שֶׁבֵּין הַשְּׁנֵי שֵׁמוֹת הֲוָיָ"ה וֶאֱלֹקִים.

כִּי שֵׁם "אֱלֹקִים" פֵּרוּשׁוֹ, בַּעַל הַכֹּחוֹת כֻּלָּם, וּקְצָת בֵּאוּר עִנְיָנוֹ עַיֵּן בְּרֵישׁ שַׁעַר א', וּבְיוֹתֵר בֵּאוּר עִנְיַן "בַּעַל הַכֹּחוֹת", כִּי כָּל כֹּחַ, מֵהַתַּחְתּוֹן שֶׁבַּתַּחְתּוֹנִים עַד הָעֶלְיוֹן שֶׁבָּעֶלְיוֹנִים, הַמְשָׁכַת קִיּוּמוֹ וְחִיּוּתוֹ הוּא עַל יְדֵי הַכֹּחַ שֶׁלְּמַעְלָה הֵימֶנּוּ, שֶׁהוּא נִשְׁמָתוֹ, הַמִּתְפַּשֵּׁט בִּפְנִימִיּוּתוֹ. וְכַיָּדוּעַ בְּדִבְרֵי הָאֲרִיזַ"ל, שֶׁהָאוֹר וּפְנִימִיּוּת נִשְׁמַת כָּל כֹּחַ וְעוֹלָם, הוּא עַצְמוֹ הַחִיצוֹנִיּוּת שֶׁל הַכֹּחַ וְהָעוֹלָם שֶׁעָלָיו, וְכֵן הוֹלֵךְ עַל זֶה הַסֵּדֶר גָּבוֹהַּ מֵעַל גָּבוֹהַּ, בֵּין בִּכְלָלוּת הַכֹּחוֹת.

כִּי כְּלָלֵי כָּל הַבְּרוּאִים וְכֹחוֹת הַתַּחְתּוֹנִים, הֵם מֵהִתְמַזְּגוּת הָאַרְבַּע יְסוֹדוֹת, וְשֹׁרֶשׁ הָאַרְבַּע יְסוֹדוֹת הֵם מֵהָאַרְבָּעָה מַלְאָכִים הַנִּקְרָאִים אַרְבַּע מַחֲנוֹת שְׁכִינָה שֶׁסִּימָנָם א'ו'ר'ג'ס'מ' ן'. וְהָאַרְבָּעָה מַלְאָכִים אֵלּוּ שָׁרְשָׁם מֵאַרְבַּע חַיּוֹת הַמֶּרְכָּבָה, שֶׁהֵם כְּלָלֵי כָּל שָׁרְשֵׁי נַפְשׁוֹת כָּל הַבְּרוּאִים הַתַּחְתּוֹנִים. שֶׁכָּל הָאַלְפֵי רִבּוּיֵי מִינֵי הַחַיּוֹת, שֹׁרֶשׁ נַפְשׁוֹתָם מִשְׁתַּלְשֵׁל מִן פְּנֵי "אַרְיֵה" שֶׁבַּמֶּרְכָּבָה, וְנַפְשׁוֹת כָּל מִינֵי הַבְּהֵמוֹת מִשְׁתַּלְשְׁלִים מִפְּנֵי "שׁוֹר", וְשֶׁל כָּל מִינֵי הָעוֹפוֹת מִפְּנֵי "נֶשֶׁר", וּכְמוֹ שֶׁכָּתוּב בַּזֹּהַר פִּנְחָס ר"מ ע"ב: רָזָא דְקָרְבְּנִין כו', פְּנֵי שׁוֹר אִתְפַּשַּׁט לִבְעִירֵי רוּחָא מִנֵּי' וכו', [סוֹד הַקָּרְבָּנוֹת וכו' פְּנֵי שׁוֹר, מִתְפַּשֵּׁט רוּחַ לַבְּהֵמוֹת מִמֶּנּוּ] ע"ש.

וְלָכֵן בְּכָל אֶחָד מוֹלֵךְ עֲלֵיהֶם אוֹתוֹ הַמִּין שֶׁצּוּרָתוֹ וּשְׁמוֹ הוּא כְּצוּרַת וְשֵׁם הַפָּנִים שֶׁבַּמֶּרְכָּבָה, כְּמוֹ שֶׁאָמְרוּ זִכְרוֹנָם לִבְרָכָה (חגיגה י"ג ב'), וּבִשְׁמוֹת רַבָּה (פכ"ג): אַרְיֵה מֶלֶךְ בַּחַיּוֹת, וכו'. וְנֶפֶשׁ הָאָדָם הוּא מִ"פְּנֵי אָדָם", לָכֵן הָאָדָם מִתְגָּאֶה עַל כֻּלָּם, כִּי כֵן עִקָּרָם וּכְלָלָם שֶׁל כָּל הָאַרְבַּע פְּנֵי הַמֶּרְכָּבָה הוּא פְּנֵי אָדָם, כְּמוֹ שֶׁכָּתוּב (יחזקאל א, ה) "וּמִתּוֹכָהּ דְּמוּת אַרְבַּע חַיּוֹת וְזֶה מַרְאֵיהֶן דְּמוּת אָדָם לָהֵנָּה". וְעַיֵּן בָּזֶה בַּזֹּהַר יִתְרוֹ פ' ע"ב, אָדָם כָּלִיל כּוּלְּהוּ וכו'.

וּבְפָרָשַׁת תַּזְרִיעַ מ"ח סוֹף ע"א כְּתִיב "וּדְמוּת פְּנֵיהֶם" וכו', וּבְפָרָשַׁת בַּמִּדְבָּר קי"ח ב' "וּדְמוּת פְּנֵיהֶם" וכו', וְעַיֵּן זֹהַר חָדָשׁ יִתְרוֹ בְּמַעֲשֵׂה מֶרְכָּבָה ל"ב ע"ג ול"ג רֵישׁ ע"א, (וְשֹׁרֶשׁ שָׁרְשׁוֹ שֶׁל הָאָדָם הוּא מֵאָדָם שֶׁעַל הַכִּסֵּא כַּנַּ"ל בְּשַׁעַר א' פ"ו), וְשָׁרְשָׁם וְחִיּוּתָם שֶׁל הָאַרְבַּע חַיּוֹת הוּא מֵהָעוֹלָם שֶׁעֲלֵיהֶם, וְכֵן עַד לְעֵלָּא וּלְעֵלָּא.

וְעַיֵּן זֹהַר יִתְרוֹ פ"ב ב', תָּאנָא בְּרָזָא עִלָּאָה, אַרְבַּע חֵיוָן אִית דְּאִינְהוּ לְגוֹ וכו', וְאִנּוּן קַדְמָאֵי עַתִּיקִין דְּעַתִּיקָא קַדִּישָׁא כו', תָּאנָא כְּגַוְנָא דִּלְעֵלָּא אִית לְתַתָּא מִנַּיְהוּ, וְכֵן בְּכֻלְּהוּ עָלְמִין כֻּלְּהוּ אֲחִידָן דָּא בְּדָא וְדָא בְּדָא. [לָמַדְנוּ בְּסוֹד הָעֶלְיוֹן אַרְבַּע חַיּוֹת יֵשׁ שֶׁהֵם לְפָנִים וכו' וְהֵן הָרִאשׁוֹנוֹת עַתִּיקִין מֵעַתִּיקָא קַדִּישָׁא וכו'. לָמַדְנוּ כְּעֵין שֶׁיֵּשׁ לְמַעְלָה כֵּן יֵשׁ לְמַטָּה

מֵהֶן, וְכֵן בְּכָל הָעוֹלָמוֹת כֻּלָּם אֲחוּזִים זֶה בָּזֶה וְזֶה בָּזֶה] וּבְרַעְיָא מְהֵימְנָא, וְאִית חֵיוָן דְּסַחֲרָן לְכוּרְסְיָא דִּבְרִיאָה כו', וְאִית חֵיוָן דִּיצִירָה כו', וְאִית אַרְבַּע חֵיוָן דְּאַרְבַּע יְסוֹדוֹת וכו'. [יֵשׁ חַיּוֹת הַסּוֹבְבוֹת לְכִסֵּא שֶׁל עוֹלַם הַבְּרִיאָה וכו', וְיֵשׁ חַיּוֹת וכו'] וְעַיֵּן עֵץ חַיִּים שַׁעַר קִצּוּר אבי"ע ספ"ח, וְשָׁם בְּסוֹף הַשַּׁעַר בְּעִנְיַן כֹּחוֹת נֶפֶשׁ הָאָדָם ע"ש.

וְשֹׁרֶשׁ כָּל הַשָּׁרָשִׁים דִּלְהוֹן הוּא מֵאַרְבַּע אוֹתִיּוֹת שֵׁם הֲוָיָ"ה בָּרוּךְ הוּא, וְהֵן הַשָּׁרָשִׁין קַדְמָאִין, רָזָא דִּמְהֵימְנוּתָא, אַבָהָן דְּכֻלְּהוּ עָלְמִין הַנִּזְכָּר בַּזֹּהַר וָאֵרָא כ"ג סוֹף ע"ב.

וְכֵן פְּרָטֵי הַכֹּחוֹת וְהַמִּינִים כֻּלָּם: לְכָל אֶחָד יֵשׁ שֹׁרֶשׁ, וְשֹׁרֶשׁ לְשֹׁרֶשׁ לְמַעְלָה מַעְלָה. כְּמַאֲמָרָם ז"ל (בראשית רבה פ"י): "אֵין לְךָ כָּל עֵשֶׂב וָעֵשֶׂב שֶׁאֵין לוֹ מַזָּל בָּרָקִיעַ שֶׁמַּכֶּה אוֹתוֹ וְאוֹמֵר לוֹ גְּדַל" שֶׁנֶּאֱמַר (איוב לח לג) "הֲיָדַעְתָּ חֻקּוֹת שָׁמָיִם", וכו'. וְעַיֵּן זֹהַר תְּרוּמָה קנ"א ב', וּבְפָרָשַׁת קְדוֹשִׁים פ"ו א', הָעִנְיָן בְּאֹרֶךְ קְצָת.

כִּי אוֹתוֹ הַכּוֹכָב וְהַמַּזָּל הוּא פְּנִימִיּוּת נַפְשׁוֹ וְחִיּוּתוֹ וְשָׁרְשׁוֹ שֶׁל אוֹתוֹ הַצֶּמַח, שֶׁמִּמֶּנּוּ מְקַבֵּל כֹּחַ הַצְּמִיחָה שֶׁהִיא נַפְשׁוֹ, כַּיָּדוּעַ. וְשֹׁרֶשׁ וְנֶפֶשׁ אוֹתוֹ הַכּוֹכָב וְהַמַּזָּל הוּא הַמַּלְאָךְ הַמְּמֻנֶּה עָלָיו, שֶׁמִּמֶּנּוּ מְקַבֵּל הַכּוֹכָב כֹּחַ הַצְּמִיחָה לְהַצְמִיחַ וּלְגַדֵּל אוֹתוֹ הַצֶּמַח, כְּמוֹ שֶׁכָּתוּב בַּזֹּהַר תְּרוּמָה הַנַּ"ל, וְעַל הַהוּא כּוֹכְבָא מְמַנָּא חַד וכו'. וְשֹׁרֶשׁ וְנֶפֶשׁ הַמַּלְאָךְ הוּא מֵהַכֹּחַ וְהָעוֹלָם שֶׁעָלָיו.

וְלָכֵן מַשְׁבִּיעִין אֶת הַמַּלְאָכִים בְּשֵׁמוֹת, כִּי אוֹתוֹ הַשֵּׁם הוּא נַפְשׁוֹ וְחִיּוּתוֹ וּנְהוֹרָא דִּילֵיהּ שֶׁל אוֹתוֹ הַמַּלְאָךְ בְּהָעוֹלָם וְהַכֹּחַ שֶׁעָלָיו שֶׁמֵּאִירוֹ וּמְקַיְּמוֹ.

וְעַיֵּן זֹהַר בָּלָק ר"ח א', כָּל אִלֵּין מַלְאָכִין קַדִּישִׁין דִּלְעֵלָּא, לָא קַיְמִין וְלָא יָכְלִין לְמֵיקַם, בַּר בִּנְהוֹרָא עִלָּאָה, דְּנָהַר לוֹן וְקַיֵּם לוֹן. וְאִי פָּסַק מִנַּיְהוּ נְהוֹרָא דִּלְעֵלָּא, לָא יָכְלִין לְמֵיקַם. [כָּל אֵלּוּ מַלְאָכִים קְדוֹשִׁים שֶׁלְּמַעְלָה, אֵינָם עוֹמְדִים וְאֵינָם יְכוֹלִים לַעֲמֹד רַק בָּאוֹר הָעֶלְיוֹן הַמֵּאִיר לָהֶם וּמְקַיֵּם אוֹתָם. וְאִם נִפְסַק מֵהֶם אוֹר שֶׁלְּמַעְלָה אֵינָם יְכוֹלִים לַעֲמֹד] וְעַיֵּן עֵץ חַיִּים שַׁעַר צִיּוּר עוֹלָמוֹת אבי"ע, בְּהַקְדָּמַת הרח"ו, וְשָׁם סוֹף פֶּרֶק א', וּבְשַׁעַר הַשֵּׁמוֹת פֶּרֶק ז', שֶׁהַמַּלְאָכִים הֵם בְּחִינַת "כֵּלִים", וְהַשֵּׁמוֹת הֵם "הָעַצְמוּת" שֶׁלָּהֶם וּפְנִימִיּוּת נִשְׁמָתָם, וְלָכֵן הוּא פּוֹעֵל בּוֹ וּמַנְהִיגוֹ לְכָל אֲשֶׁר יַטֵּהוּ, כִּנְשָׁמָה שֶׁמַּנְהֶגֶת הַגּוּף, וְכֵן עַל זֶה הַדֶּרֶךְ עַד לְעֵלָּא לְעֵלָּא:

וְכֵן בְּעִנְיַן הַנְּשָׁמוֹת שֶׁבְּכָל עוֹלָם, כָּל נְשָׁמָה שָׁרְשָׁהּ וּמְקוֹר חִיּוּתָהּ הוּא מִבְּחִינַת הַנְּשָׁמָה שֶׁל הָעוֹלָם שֶׁעָלֶיהָ, שֶׁהִיא נַעֲשֵׂית וְנִקְרֵאת אֶצְלָהּ "נְשָׁמָה לִנְשָׁמָה", וְכֵן כֻּלָּם:

וְהוּא יִתְבָּרַךְ שְׁמוֹ, הוּא הָאֱלֹקִים – "בַּעַל הַכֹּחוֹת כֻּלָּם" – שֶׁהוּא נִשְׁמַת וְחִיּוּת וְשֹׁרֶשׁ הַשָּׁרָשִׁים שֶׁל הַכֹּחוֹת כֻּלָּם, כְּמוֹ שֶׁכָּתוּב (נחמיה ט, ו) "וְאַתָּה מְחַיֶּה אֶת כֻּלָּם", כָּל רֶגַע מַמָּשׁ, וְלָכֵן נִקְרָא הוּא יִתְבָּרַךְ, נִשְׁמְתָא דְּכָל נִשְׁמָתִין, וְעִקָּרָא וְשָׁרְשָׁא דְּכָל עָלְמִין:

פֶּרֶק י"א

וְהָעִנְיָן כַּיָּדוּעַ בַּזֹּהַר, שֶׁהוּא יִתְבָּרַךְ וְדִבּוּרוֹ חַד, וְכָל דִּבּוּר וּמַאֲמָר שֶׁל הַקָּדוֹשׁ בָּרוּךְ הוּא בְּמַעֲשֵׂה בְרֵאשִׁית, שֶׁאָמַר וַיְהִי, הוּא הַנֶּפֶשׁ וְחִיּוּת אוֹתוֹ הַדָּבָר שֶׁנִּבְרָא בּוֹ, וְכָל

רִבֵּי רִבְבוֹת הַמִּינִים שֶׁבּוֹ, עִם הַמַּזָּלוֹת הַמְּמֻנִּים עֲלֵיהֶם, וְהַמַּלְאָכִים הַמְּמֻנִּים עַל אוֹתָם הַמַּזָּלוֹת, וְשָׁרְשָׁם וְשֹׁרֶשׁ שָׁרְשָׁם לְמַעְלָה מַעְלָה שֶׁבִּכְלַל עוֹלָם. וּמֵאָז וָהָלְאָה, עוֹד כָּל יְמֵי עוֹלָם, דְּבָרוֹ יִתְבָּרַךְ נִצָּב בָּהֶם לְהַאִירָם וּלְקַיְּמָם כָּל רֶגַע, בְּכָל פְּרָטֵי עִנְיְנֵיהֶם וְשִׁנּוּיֵיהֶם וְסִדּוּר מַצָּבָם.

לָכֵן בְּכָל הָעֶשֶׂר מַאֲמָרוֹת לֹא נִזְכַּר רַק שֵׁם "אֱלֹקִים", שֶׁאוֹתוֹ הַמַּאֲמָר הוּא בַּעַל הַכֹּחוֹת שֶׁל אוֹתוֹ הַדָּבָר, וְכָל הַמִּינִים שֶׁבּוֹ שֶׁנִּבְרְאוּ בּוֹ, שֶׁהוּא נַפְשָׁם הַמִּתְפַּשֵּׁט בִּפְנִימִיּוּת כָּל פְּרָטֵי חֲלָקֵיהֶם. רַק שֶׁעַתָּה טַח עֵינֵינוּ מֵרְאוֹת בְּעֵינֵי הַבָּשָׂר — אֵיךְ וּבְאֵיזֶה אֹפֶן דִּבּוּרוֹ יִתְבָּרַךְ מִתְפַּשֵּׁט בָּהֶם.

וּלְעָתִיד לָבֹא כְּתִיב (ישעיה מ, ה): "וְרָאוּ כָל 'בָּשָׂר' יַחְדָּו כִּי פִּי הֲוָיָ"ה דִּבֵּר", הַיְנוּ שֶׁיִּזְדַּכֵּךְ הַשָּׂגָתֵנוּ עַד שֶׁנִּזְכֶּה לְהַשִּׂיג וְלִרְאוֹת גַּם — בְּעֵין הַ"בָּשָׂר" — עִנְיַן הִתְפַּשְּׁטוּת דִּבּוּרוֹ יִתְבָּרַךְ בְּכָל דָּבָר בָּעוֹלָם, כְּמוֹ שֶׁכְּבָר הָיְתָה הַהַשָּׂגָה מֵעֵין זֶה בְּעֵת מַתַּן תּוֹרָה דִּכְתִיב (שמות כ, יח): "וְכָל הָעָם רוֹאִים אֶת הַקּוֹלוֹת". וְהוּא גַּם כֵּן בִּכְלַל מַאֲמָרָם זִכְרוֹנָם לִבְרָכָה סוֹף פֶּרֶק אֵלּוּ עוֹבְרִין (פסחים), לֹא כְּהָעוֹלָם הַזֶּה הָעוֹלָם הַבָּא, הָעוֹלָם הַזֶּה נִכְתָּב בְּי"ה וְנִקְרָא בְּא'ד'נ'י', אֲבָל הָעוֹלָם הַבָּא נִכְתָּב בְּי"ה וְנִקְרָא בְּי"ה, וְהָבֵן.

וְהוּא עִנְיַן הַכָּתוּב (ישעיה ל, כ): "וְלֹא יִכָּנֵף עוֹד מוֹרֶיךָ וְהָיוּ עֵינֶיךָ רוֹאוֹת אֶת מוֹרֶיךָ". וְעַיֵּן זֹהַר חָדָשׁ יִתְרוֹ ל"ד סוֹף ע"א, כְּנָפַיִם כִּסּוּיִין לְאִתְכַּסָּאָה שְׁמָהָן וכו', עַיֵּן שָׁם הֵיטֵב כָּל הָעִנְיָן:

וְלָכֵן פָּתַח יִתְבָּרַךְ שְׁמוֹ רֵאשִׁית עֲשֶׂרֶת הַדְּבָרִים "אָנֹכִי הֲוָיָ"ה אֱלֹהֶיךָ", כִּי זֶה כָּל עִקַּר יְסוֹד הָאֱמוּנָה, שֶׁצָּרִיךְ כָּל אִישׁ יִשְׂרָאֵל לִקְבֹּעַ בְּלִבּוֹ, שֶׁרַק הוּא יִתְבָּרַךְ שְׁמוֹ הוּא הַבַּעַל כֹּחַ הָאֲמִתִּי, וְנִשְׁמַת וְחִיּוּת וְשֹׁרֶשׁ הָעִקָּר שֶׁלּוֹ, וְשֶׁל כָּל הַבְּרוּאִים וְהַכֹּחוֹת וְהָעוֹלָמוֹת כֻּלָּם: זֶהוּ עִנְיַן וּפֵרוּשׁ שֶׁל שֵׁם "אֱלֹקִים" — בַּעַל הַכֹּחוֹת כֻּלָּם.

אֲבָל עִם כָּל זֶה, לְפִי פֵּרוּשׁוֹ וְעִנְיָנוֹ שֶׁל זֶה הַשֵּׁם, מַשְׁמַע, שֶׁיֵּשׁ בִּמְצִיאוּת גָּמוּר גַּם עוֹלָמוֹת וְכֹחוֹת מְחֻדָּשִׁים מֵרְצוֹנוֹ הַפָּשׁוּט יִתְבָּרַךְ, שֶׁצִּמְצֵם כְּבוֹדוֹ וְהִנִּיחַ מָקוֹם כִּבְיָכוֹל לִמְצִיאוּת כֹּחוֹת וְעוֹלָמוֹת, אֶלָּא שֶׁהוּא יִתְבָּרַךְ, הוּא נִשְׁמָתָם וּמְקוֹר שֹׁרֶשׁ כֹּחַ חִיּוּתָם שֶׁמְּקַבְּלִים מֵאִתּוֹ יִתְבָּרַךְ, שֶׁמִּתְפַּשֵּׁט וּמִסְתַּתֵּר בְּתוֹכָם כִּבְיָכוֹל.

כְּעִנְיַן הִתְפַּשְּׁטוּת הַנְּשָׁמָה בְּגוּף הָאָדָם, שֶׁאַף שֶׁהִיא מִתְפַּשֶּׁטֶת בְּכָל חֵלֶק וּנְקֻדָּה פְּרָטִית שֶׁבּוֹ, עִם כָּל זֶה לֹא נוּכַל לוֹמַר שֶׁהַגּוּף מִתְבַּטֵּל נֶגְדָּהּ כְּאִלּוּ אֵינוֹ בִּמְצִיאוּת כְּלָל. וְכֵן בְּכָל כֹּחַ וְעוֹלָם עֶלְיוֹן, שֶׁמִּתְפַּשֵּׁט בְּכָל עַצְמוּת הַכֹּחַ וְהָעוֹלָם שֶׁתַּחְתָּיו, עִם כָּל זֶה, גַּם הַכֹּחַ וְהָעוֹלָם הַתַּחְתּוֹן יֶשְׁנוֹ בִּמְצִיאוּת. וְהוּא כְּפִי אֲשֶׁר מִצִּדֵּנוּ בְּעִנְיַן הַשָּׂגָתֵנוּ כְּמוֹ שֶׁנִּתְבָּאֵר לְמַעְלָה.

אֲבָל שֵׁם הָעֶצֶם "הֲוָיָ"ה" בָּרוּךְ הוּא מוֹרֶה עַל הַבְּחִינָה וְהָעִנְיָן כְּפִי אֲשֶׁר הוּא מִצִּדּוֹ יִתְבָּרַךְ, שֶׁנִּתְבָּאֵר לְמַעְלָה (וְאַף שֶׁגַּם שֵׁם "הֲוָיָ"ה" בָּרוּךְ הוּא — נִקְרָא גַּם כֵּן מִצַּד הִתְחַבְּרוּתוֹ יִתְבָּרַךְ בִּרְצוֹנוֹ לְהָעוֹלָמוֹת, כִּי עַצְמוּת אָדוֹן יָחִיד אֵין סוֹף בָּרוּךְ הוּא, בִּבְחִינַת הֱיוֹתוֹ מֻפְשָׁט מֵהָעוֹלָמוֹת, לֹא אִתְרְמִיז בְּשׁוּם שֵׁם כְּלָל, אַף עַל פִּי כֵן, הָעוֹלָמוֹת הֵמָּה

בְּטֵלִים וּמְבֻטָּלִים בִּמְצִיאוּת נֶגְדּוֹ יִתְבָּרֵךְ מִצַּד זֶה הַשֵּׁם הַנִּכְבָּד וְהוּא מֵעֵין הַבְּחִינָה כְּפִי אֲשֶׁר מִצִּדּוֹ יִתְבָּרֵךְ) וְלָכֵן נִקְרָא שֵׁם הָעֶצֶם "שֵׁם הַמְיֻחָד" בָּרוּךְ הוּא.

וְזֶהוּ שֶׁאָמַר הַכָּתוּב (דברים ד, לט) "כִּי הֲוָיָ"ה הוּא הָאֱלֹקִים" כו', רָצָה לוֹמַר, עִם כִּי מִצַּד הַשְׁגָּחָתֵנוּ הוּא נִקְרָא בְּשֵׁם "אֱלֹקִים", וּמִצִּדּוֹ יִתְבָּרֵךְ נִקְרָא בִּבְחִינַת שֵׁם "הֲוָיָ"ה" בָּרוּךְ הוּא, בֶּאֱמֶת הַכֹּל אֶחָד "וַהֲוָיָ"ה הוּא הָאֱלֹקִים" כו', כְּמוֹ שֶׁנִּתְבָּאֵר לְעֵיל פֶּרֶק ז' עִנְיַן הַצִּמְצוּם וְהַקַּו דִּכֹלָּא חַדָא.

וְזֶהוּ גַּם כֵּן בִּכְלַל עִנְיַן יִחוּד פָּסוּק רִאשׁוֹן דִּקְרִיאַת שְׁמַע "ה' אֱלֹקֵינוּ ה' אֶחָד", רָצָה לוֹמַר, לְכַוֵּן שֶׁהוּא יִתְבָּרֵךְ הוּא אֱלֹקֵינוּ בַּעַל הַכֹּחוֹת, וּמְקוֹר שֹׁרֶשׁ נִשְׁמָתֵנוּ וְחִיּוּתֵנוּ, וְשֶׁל כָּל הַבְּרוּאִים וְהָעוֹלָמוֹת. וְאַף שֶׁבָּרָא וְהִמְצִיא מְצִיאוּת כֹּחוֹת וְעוֹלָמוֹת וּבְרִיּוֹת, עִם כָּל זֶה הוּא בִּבְחִינַת הֲוָיָ"ה וְאֶחָד מִצִּדּוֹ יִתְבָּרֵךְ, שֶׁאֵין הַבְּרוּאִים כֻּלָּם חוֹצְצִים חַס וְשָׁלוֹם כְּלָל נֶגֶד אַחְדּוּתוֹ הַפָּשׁוּט יִתְבָּרֵךְ הַמְמַלֵּא כֹּל, וְנִקְרָא גַּם עַתָּה הֲוָיָ"ה וְאֶחָד:

פֶּרֶק י"ב

וְזֶהוּ הָעִנְיָן שֶׁדָּרְשׁוּ זִכְרוֹנָם לִבְרָכָה (חולין ז, ב) עַל פָּסוּק "כִּי ה' הוּא הָאֱלֹקִים אֵין עוֹד מִלְבַדּוֹ" (דברים ד, לט), אָמַר רַבִּי חֲנִינָא, אֲפִלּוּ כְּשָׁפִים.

כִּי כָּל עִנְיְנֵי פְּעֻלּוֹת הַכְּשָׁפִים, נִמְשָׁךְ מֵהַכֹּחוֹת הַטֻּמְאָה שֶׁל הַמֶּרְכָּבָה טְמֵאָה, וְהוּא עִנְיַן חָכְמַת הַכִּשּׁוּף שֶׁהָיוּ הַסַּנְהֶדְרִין צְרִיכִין לֵידַע, הַיְנוּ, חָכְמַת שְׁמוֹת הַטֻּמְאָה, וִידִיעַת עִנְיְנֵי כֹּחוֹת הַמֶּרְכָּבָה טְמֵאָה בִּשְׁמוֹתֵיהֶם, שֶׁעַל יָדָם יִפְעֲלוּ בַּעֲלֵי הַכִּשּׁוּפִים פְּעֻלּוֹת וְעִנְיָנִים מְשֻׁנִּים, כְּשֶׁמַּשְׁבִּיעִין כֹּחוֹת הַטֻּמְאָה בִּבְחִינַת הַטּוֹב שֶׁבּוֹ, שֶׁיַּשְׁפִּיעַ בְּתוֹכוֹ חִיּוּת לַעֲשׂוֹת נִפְלָאוֹת, הֵפֶךְ סֵדֶר כֹּחוֹת הַטְּבָעִים וְהַמַּזָּלוֹת. וְעַיֵּן עֵץ חַיִּים שַׁעַר קְלִפַּת נֹגַהּ רֵישׁ פֶּרֶק ד'.

מֵחֲמַת שֶׁכֵּן קָבַע הַבּוֹרֵא, אֲדוֹן כֹּל יִתְבָּרֵךְ, עִנְיְנֵי כֹּחוֹתֵיהֶם לְמַעְלָה מִכֹּחוֹת הַטְּבָעִים הַנִּמְשָׁכִים מֵהַכּוֹכָבִים וְהַמַּזָּלוֹת, שֶׁעַל יְדֵי זֶה יְהֵא בְּכֹחָם לַעֲשׂוֹת פְּעֻלּוֹת, גַּם הִפּוּךְ טִבְעֵי כֹּחוֹת הַכּוֹכָבִים וּמַזָּלוֹת שֶׁהִקְבִּיעַ בָּהֶם בְּעֵת הַבְּרִיאָה. כַּיָּדוּעַ שֶׁכָּל כֹּחַ וְעוֹלָם, קָבַע בּוֹ הַבּוֹרֵא יִתְבָּרֵךְ כֹּחַ וִיכֹלֶת, לְהַנְהִיג וּלְהַטּוֹת אֶת הַכֹּחַ וְהָעוֹלָם שֶׁתַּחְתָּיו, לְכָל אֲשֶׁר יִהְיֶה שָׁמָּה הָרוּחַ וכו'.

וּמַה שֶּׁאָמְרוּ שָׁם "שֶׁמַּכְחִישִׁין פָּמַלְיָא שֶׁל מַעְלָה" רָצָה לוֹמַר, שֶׁרַק סִדּוּר כֹּחוֹת הַפָּמַלְיָא שֶׁל "הַכּוֹכָבִים וְהַמַּזָּלוֹת" קָבַע הַבּוֹרֵא יִתְבָּרֵךְ כֹּחַ בְּכֹחוֹת הַטֻּמְאָה שֶׁיִּהְיוּ יְכוֹלִין לְהָפְכָם, אֲבָל לֹא שֶׁיְּהֵא בְּכֹחָם לְשַׁנּוֹת חַס וְשָׁלוֹם מִסֵּדֶר הַפְּעֻלּוֹת הַקְּדוֹשִׁים שֶׁל כֹּחוֹת "הַמֶּרְכָּבָה קְדוֹשָׁה".

וְאַדְּרַבָּה, כְּשֶׁמַּשְׁבִּיעִין אוֹתָם בְּשֵׁמוֹת שֶׁל כֹּחוֹת הַקְּדֻשָּׁה, מִמֵּילָא כְּרֶגַע מִתְבַּטֵּל כָּל עִנְיְנֵי פְּעֻלָּתָם לִגְמְרֵי, וּכְמוֹ שֶׁכָּתוּב בְּתִקּוּן י"ח, אִלֵּין דְּיָדְעִין בִּקְלִפִּין, עָבְדִין אוֹמָאָה בִּשְׁמָהָן וּבַהֲוָיוֹת דְּקוּדְשָׁא בְּרִיךְ הוּא לְאִלֵּין קְלִפִּין, וּבַטְלִין גְּזֵרָה. [אֵלֶּה הַיּוֹדְעִים בַּקְּלִפּוֹת, עוֹשִׂים הַשְׁבָּעָה בַּשֵּׁמוֹת וּבַהֲוָיוֹת שֶׁל הַקָּדוֹשׁ בָּרוּךְ הוּא לְאֵלֶּה הַקְּלִפּוֹת, וּמְבַטְּלִים

הַגְּזֵרָה] וְעַיֵּן עֵץ חַיִּים בְּפֶרֶק הַנַּ"ל עַיֵּ"שׁ, כֵּיוָן שֶׁאֵין הַכֹּחַ שֶׁלָּהֶם מֵעַצְמָם חַס וְשָׁלוֹם, כִּי אֵין עוֹד מִלְּבַדּוֹ יִתְבָּרַךְ בַּעַל הַכֹּחוֹת כֻּלָּם, וְגַם שֶׁבֶּאֱמֶת הֲלֹא הַכֹּל מָלֵא רַק עַצְמוּת אַחְדּוּתוֹ הַפָּשׁוּט יִתְבָּרַךְ, וְאֵין עוֹד מִלְּבַדּוֹ שׁוּם מְצִיאוּת כֹּחַ כְּלָל, לֹא כֹּחוֹת הַטֻּמְאָה, וְלֹא שׁוּם כֹּחַ וְשׁוּם עוֹלָם וְנִבְרָא כְּלָל, זֶהוּ שֶׁאָמְרוּ "אֵין עוֹד מִלְּבַדּוֹ", אֲפִלּוּ כְּשָׁפִים.

וְזֶהוּ שֶׁמֵּבִיא שָׁם הַשַּׁ"ס עַל זֶה, עוּבְדָא דְּהַהִיא אִתְּתָא, דַּהֲוַת קָא מְהַדְרָא לְמִשְׁקַל עַפְרָא מִתּוּתָא כַּרְעֵיהּ דְּרַבִּי חֲנִינָא, אָמַר לָהּ, שְׁקוֹלִי, לָא מִסְתַּיְּעָא מִילְּתִיךְ, "אֵין עוֹד מִלְּבַדּוֹ" כְּתִיב, וּפָרִיךְ, וְהָאָמַר רַבִּי יוֹחָנָן, לָמָּה נִקְרָא שְׁמָן "כְּשָׁפִים", שֶׁמַּכְחִישִׁין פַּמַלְיָא שֶׁל מַעְלָה, שָׁאנֵי רַבִּי חֲנִינָא דִּנְפִישׁ זְכוּתֵיהּ. וַדַּאי שֶׁלֹּא הָיָה מַחֲזִיק עַצְמוֹ רַבִּי חֲנִינָא דִּנְפִישׁ זְכוּתֵיהּ כָּל כָּךְ מִתּוֹרָתוֹ וּמַעֲשָׂיו הַטּוֹבִים הַמְּרֻבִּים, עַד שֶׁבַּעֲבוּרָם הָיָה סָמוּךְ לִבּוֹ שֶׁלֹּא יִשְׁלֹט בּוֹ פְּעֻלַּת הַכְּשָׁפִים.

אֲבָל הָעִנְיָן כְּמוֹ שֶׁכָּתַבְתִּי לְעֵיל, כֵּיוָן שֶׁבֶּאֱמֶת אֵין בְּכֹחוֹת הַמֶּרְכָּבָה טְמֵאָה שׁוּם כֹּחַ מֵעַצְמָם חָלִילָה, אֶלָּא שֶׁהוּא יִתְבָּרַךְ קָבַע כֹּחָם לְמַעְלָה מִכֹּחוֹת טִבְעֵי הַכּוֹכָבִים וּמַזָּלוֹת, כְּדֵי שֶׁעַל יְדֵי זֶה יְהֵא בִּיכָלְתָּם לַעֲשׂוֹת פְּעֻלּוֹת, אַף גַּם לְשַׁנּוֹת סִדְרֵי טִבְעֵי הַמַּזָּלוֹת, וּבִלְתּוֹ יִתְבָּרַךְ הֵם אֶפֶס וָתֹהוּ.

וְלָכֵן גַּם רַבִּי חֲנִינָא, לֹא שֶׁבָּטַח עַל זְכוּת קְדֻשַּׁת תּוֹרָתוֹ וּמַעֲשָׂיו הַמְּרֻבִּים, רַק שֶׁיָּדַע וְשִׁעֵר בְּנַפְשׁוֹ, שֶׁזֹּאת הָאֱמוּנָה קְבוּעָה בְּלִבּוֹ לַאֲמִתָּהּ, שֶׁאֵין עוֹד מִלְּבַדּוֹ יִתְבָּרַךְ שׁוּם כֹּחַ כְּלָל, וְהִדְבִּיק עַצְמוֹ בִּקְדֻשַּׁת מַחְשַׁבְתּוֹ לְבַעַל הַכֹּחוֹת כֻּלָּם, אָדוֹן יָחִיד הַמָּלֵא כָּל עָלְמִין, וְאֵין כָּאן שׁוּם שְׁלִיטָה וּמְצִיאוּת כֹּחַ אַחֵר כְּלָל, לָכֵן הָיָה נָכוֹן לִבּוֹ בָּטוּחַ בָּזֶה, שֶׁלֹּא יִשְׁלְטוּ עָלָיו פְּעֻלּוֹת הַכְּשָׁפִים הַנִּמְשָׁכִים מִכֹּחוֹת הַמֶּרְכָּבָה טְמֵאָה, זֶה שֶׁאָמַר: לֹא מִסְתַּיְּעָא מִילְּתִיךְ, "אֵין עוֹד מִלְּבַדּוֹ" כְּתִיב.

וּבֶאֱמֶת הוּא עִנְיָן גָּדוֹל וּסְגֻלָּה נִפְלָאָה, לְהָסֵר וּלְבַטֵּל מֵעָלָיו כָּל דִּינִין וּרְצוֹנוֹת אֲחֵרִים, שֶׁלֹּא יוּכְלוּ לִשְׁלֹט בּוֹ וְלֹא יַעֲשׂוּ שׁוּם רֹשֶׁם כְּלָל, כְּשֶׁהָאָדָם קוֹבֵעַ בְּלִבּוֹ לֵאמֹר, הֲלֹא ה' הוּא הָאֱלֹקִים הָאֲמִתִּי, וְאֵין עוֹד מִלְּבַדּוֹ יִתְבָּרַךְ שׁוּם כֹּחַ בָּעוֹלָם וְכָל הָעוֹלָמוֹת כְּלָל, וְהַכֹּל מָלֵא רַק אַחְדּוּתוֹ הַפָּשׁוּט יִתְבָּרַךְ שְׁמוֹ, וּמְבַטֵּל בְּלִבּוֹ בִּטּוּל גָּמוּר, וְאֵינוֹ מַשְׁגִּיחַ כְּלָל עַל שׁוּם כֹּחַ וְרָצוֹן בָּעוֹלָם, וּמְשַׁעְבֵּד וּמְדַבֵּק טֹהַר מַחְשַׁבְתּוֹ רַק לְאָדוֹן יָחִיד בָּרוּךְ הוּא, כֵּן יַסְפִּיק הוּא יִתְבָּרַךְ בְּיָדוֹ, שֶׁמִּמֵּילָא יִתְבַּטְּלוּ מֵעָלָיו כָּל הַכֹּחוֹת וְהָרְצוֹנוֹת שֶׁבָּעוֹלָם, שֶׁלֹּא יוּכְלוּ לִפְעֹל לוֹ שׁוּם דָּבָר כְּלָל.

וְזֶה הָעִנְיָן הוּא גַּם כֵּן בִּכְלַל כַּוָּנַת הַזֹּהַר (בַּהַקְדָּמָה דַּף י"ב סוֹף ע"א), פִּקּוּדָא רְבִיעָאָה, לְמִנְדַּע דַּהֲוָיָ"ה הוּא הָאֱלֹקִים, כד"א "וְיָדַעְתָּ הַיּוֹם וגו' כִּי הֲוָיָ"ה הוּא הָאֱלֹקִים", וּלְאִתְכְּלָלָא שְׁמָא דֶּאֱלֹקִים בִּשְׁמָא דַּהֲוָיָ"ה. וְכַד יִנְדַּע בַּר נָשׁ דְּכֹלָּא חַד, וְלָא יְשַׁוֵּי פֵּרוּדָא, אֲפִילוּ הַהוּא ס"א יִסְתַּלֵּק מֵעַל עָלְמָא כוּ', [הַמִּצְוָה הָרְבִיעִית לָדַעַת כִּי הֲוָיָ"ה הוּא הָאֱלֹקִים, כְּמוֹ שֶׁנֶּאֱמַר וְיָדַעְתָּ הַיּוֹם וגו' כִּי הֲוָיָ"ה הוּא הָאֱלֹקִים. וְלִכְלֹל שֵׁם אֱלֹקִים בְּשֵׁם הֲוָיָ"ה וכו' וּכְשֶׁהָאָדָם יֵדַע שֶׁהַכֹּל אֶחָד וְלֹא יָשִׂים פֵּרוּד, אֲפִלּוּ הַסִּטְרָא אַחְרָא יִסְתַּלֵּק מִן הָעוֹלָם]. וְהָבֵן.

וְגַם יִגְזָר אֹמֶר וְיָקֻם לוֹ, לִפְעֹל עִנְיָנִים וְנִסִּים נִפְלָאִים הֵפֶךְ סִדּוּר כֹּחוֹת הַטִּבְעִיִּים, כֵּיוָן

שֶׁמְּשַׁעְבֵּד וּמְדַבֵּק טֹהַר אֱמוּנַת לִבּוֹ בֶּאֱמֶת בְּלִי תְּמוֹט רַק לוֹ יִתְבָּרַךְ לְבַד, וְאֶצְלוֹ יִתְבָּרַךְ הַכֹּל שָׁוֶה, כָּל רֶגַע, לִפְעֹל בְּסִדּוּר הַטֶּבַע שֶׁקָּבַע אוֹ הִפּוּךְ סִדּוּר הַטֶּבַע.

כְּמוֹ שֶׁמָּצִינוּ בְּרַבִּי חֲנִינָא בֶּן דּוֹסָא, שֶׁהָיָה גּוֹזֵר אֹמֶר, וּפוֹעֵל כְּפִי רְצוֹנוֹ כָּל עֵת, הִפּוּךְ סִדּוּר הַטֶּבַע, כְּאָמְרוֹ (תענית כה, א): "מִי שֶׁאָמַר לַשֶּׁמֶן וְיִדְלֹק יֹאמַר לַחֹמֶץ וְיִדְלֹק", רוֹצֶה לוֹמַר, הֲלֹא אֶצְלוֹ יִתְבָּרַךְ שָׁוֶה זֶה כְּמוֹ זֶה, כַּנַּ"ל, וְכֵן הִסְפִּיק הַבּוֹרֵא בָּרוּךְ הוּא בְּיָדוֹ. וְכָהֵנָּה רַבּוֹת אִתּוֹ, כַּמּוּבָא בַּשַּׁ"ס מִנִּפְלְאוֹת עִנְיָנָיו:

פֶּרֶק י"ג

וְזֶה הָיָה עִנְיַן עֲבוֹדַת הָאָבוֹת כָּל יְמֵיהֶם. כִּי הֵמָּה בְּנוֹרְאוֹת צִדְקָתָם וְטָהֳרַת קְדֻשַּׁת לִבָּם, הָיוּ מְדַבְּקִים מַחְשְׁבֹתָם לִרְצוֹנוֹ יִתְבָּרַךְ, כָּל יְמֵיהֶם בְּלִי הֶפְסֵק רֶגַע, וּבִטְּלוּ בִּרְצוֹנָם כָּל הַכֹּחוֹת שֶׁבָּעוֹלָם, וּלְאֶפֶס וָתֹהוּ נֶחְשְׁבוּ אֶצְלָם.

וְלָכֵן זָכוּ גַּם לְנִסִּים נִפְלָאִים בְּשִׁדּוּד הַמַּעֲרָכוֹת וּצְבָאֵיהֶם כַּנַּ"ל. וְלָכֵן נִתְיַחֵד שְׁמוֹ יִתְבָּרַךְ עֲלֵיהֶם לְהִקָּרֵא "אֱלֹהֵי אַבְרָהָם", "אֱלֹהֵי יִצְחָק" וכו', וּכְאָמְרוֹ יִתְבָּרַךְ בְּעַצְמוֹ (שמות ג, יג) "אֱלֹהֵי אֲבוֹתֵיכֶם", וְלָזֶה אָמְרוּ זִכְרוֹנָם לִבְרָכָה (ב"ר מז): "הָאָבוֹת הֵן הֵן הַמֶּרְכָּבָה".

אָמְנָם מַדְרֵגַת מֹשֶׁה רַבֵּנוּ עָלָיו הַשָּׁלוֹם הָיְתָה עוֹד יוֹתֵר גְּבוֹהָה, כְּמוֹ שֶׁהֵעִידָה הַתּוֹרָה (דברים לד, י) "וְלֹא קָם נָבִיא" וגו'. וְעֶצֶם חִלּוּק מַדְרֵגָתוֹ מִמַּדְרֵגָתָם בֵּאֵר הוּא יִתְבָּרַךְ בְּעַצְמוֹ, וְאָמַר "אֲנִי הֲוָיָ"ה וָאֵרָא אֶל אַבְרָהָם וכו' בְּאֵל שַׁדָּי וּשְׁמִי הֲוָיָ"ה לֹא נוֹדַעְתִּי לָהֶם". (שמות ו, ב–ג).

וְהָעִנְיָן, הוּא הוּא עֶצֶם הַחִלּוּק שֶׁנִּתְבָּאֵר לְמַעְלָה בֵּין הַשֵּׁם "אֱלֹהִים" לְשֵׁם "הֲוָיָ"ה" בָּרוּךְ הוּא. כִּי עַל הָרֹב, בְּעִנְיַן הַשָּׂגַת הָאָבוֹת, מָצִינוּ נֶאֱמַר הַשֵּׁם "אֱלֹקִים", "הָאֱלֹקִים אֲשֶׁר הִתְהַלְּכוּ אֲבֹתַי לְפָנָיו" (בראשית מח, טו) "הָאֱלֹקִים הָרֹעֶה אֹתִי מֵעוֹדִי" (שם), וְכֵן אֲנַחְנוּ קוֹרְאִים אוֹתוֹ יִתְבָּרַךְ "אֱלֹהֵי אַבְרָהָם" וכו'. כְּמוֹ שֶׁכָּתַבְתִּי לְעֵיל בְּעִנְיַן קְדֻשַּׁת מַדְרֵגָתָם, שֶׁלֹּא הִשְׁגִּיחוּ עַל שׁוּם כֹּחַ וְעִנְיָן בָּעוֹלָם כְּלָל.

אָמְנָם, הַשָּׂגַת נְבוּאָתָם לֹא הָיְתָה בְּבִטּוּל הַכֹּחוֹת מִמְּצִיאוּתָם לְגַמְרֵי, וְזֶהוּ שֶׁאָמַר הַכָּתוּב (שמות ו, ב.): "וָאֵרָא אֶל אַבְרָהָם וכו', בְּאֵל שַׁדָּי", שֶׁעִנְיָנוֹ גַּם כֵּן כְּעִנְיַן הַשֵּׁם אֱלֹהִים, וְרוֹצֶה לוֹמַר שֶׁאֲנִי בַּעַל הַכֹּחוֹת כֻּלָּם, וּבִרְצוֹתִי, כָּל רֶגַע, אֲנִי מְשַׁדֵּד מַעֲרֶכֶת כָּל הַכֹּחוֹת מֵאֲשֶׁר קָבַעְתִּי בָּהֶם בְּעֵת הַבְּרִיאָה, זֶהוּ "אֵל שַׁדָּי". אֲבָל בִּבְחִינַת עִנְיַן "שְׁמִי הֲוָיָ"ה" (כְּמוֹ שֶׁנִּתְבָּאֵר פֵּרוּשׁ עִנְיָנוֹ לְעֵיל פֶּרֶק י"א), "לֹא נוֹדַעְתִּי לָהֶם" בְּהַשָּׂגַת נְבוּאָתָם. אֲבָל מֹשֶׁה רַבֵּנוּ עָלָיו הַשָּׁלוֹם, הָיְתָה הַשָּׂגַת נְבוּאָתוֹ, בְּעִנְיַן בְּחִינַת הַשֵּׁם הָעֶצֶם הַמְיֻחָד, הֲוָיָ"ה בָּרוּךְ הוּא, וְלָכֵן לֹא הָיָה שׁוּם כֹּחַ חוֹצֵץ בִּפְנֵי אוֹר הַשָּׂגַת נְבוּאָתוֹ. וְכֵן עַל יְדֵי כָּל נִסֵּי ה' שֶׁנַּעֲשׂוּ עַל יָדוֹ, רָאוּ כֻּלָּם בִּטּוּל מְצִיאוּת כָּל הַכֹּחוֹת לְגַמְרֵי, וְאֵין עוֹד מִלְּבַדּוֹ יִתְבָּרַךְ לְגַמְרֵי כְּמַשְׁמָעוֹ, כְּמוֹ שֶׁאָמַר הַכָּתוּב: "אַתָּה הָרְאֵתָ לָדַעַת כִּי הֲוָיָ"ה הוּא הָאֱלֹקִים" וכו', וְהוּא עִנְיַן וּפֵרוּשׁ הַשֵּׁם הַמְיֻחָד הֲוָיָ"ה בָּרוּךְ הוּא כַּנַּ"ל.

זֶהוּ שֶׁכָּתוּב "וַיְדַבֵּר אֱלֹהִים אֶל מֹשֶׁה וַיֹּאמֶר אֵלָיו אֲנִי הֲוָיָ"ה", הוֹדִיעוֹ עֶצֶם בְּחִינַת

הַשָּׂגַת נְבוּאָתוֹ, שֶׁגַּם הַשֵּׁם "אֱלֹקִים" אֶצְלוֹ הַכֹּל בְּחִינַת "הֲוָיָ"ה" כְּעִנְיַן הַכָּתוּב "כִּי הֲוָיָ"ה הוּא הָאֱלֹהִים אֵין עוֹד מִלְּבַדּוֹ", וּמֵאָז וְאֵילָךְ לֹא נִזְכַּר אֶצְלוֹ אֶלָּא "וַיְדַבֵּר ה'" "וַיֹּאמֶר ה'". וְזֶהוּ (דברים לד, י) "וְלֹא קָם נָבִיא וכו' אֲשֶׁר יְדָעוֹ הֲוָיָ"ה פָּנִים אֶל פָּנִים".

וְזֶה שֶׁכָּתוּב בְּתִקּוּן כ"ו, וּלְגַבֵּי אַבְהָן לָא אִתְחַזְיָא אֶלָּא בְּמִנְעָלִים כו', אֲבָל לְגַבֵּי מֹשֶׁה בְּלָא כִּסּוּיָא כְּלָל, וְרָזָא דְּמִלָּה "וָאֵרָא אֶל אַבְרָהָם" וכו', עכ"ל: [וּלְגַבֵּי הָאָבוֹת לֹא הִתְרָאָה אֶלָּא בְּמִנְעָלִים וכו', אֲבָל לְגַבֵּי מֹשֶׁה בְּלֹא כִּסּוּי כְּלָל, וְסוֹד הַדָּבָר "וָאֵרָא אֶל אַבְרָהָם" וכו'.]

וְהוּא גַּם כֵּן עִנְיַן מַאֲמָרָם זִכְרוֹנָם לִבְרָכָה בְּסוֹף פֶּרֶק כִּסּוּי הַדָּם (חולין פט.): "גָּדוֹל שֶׁנֶּאֱמַר בְּמֹשֶׁה וְאַהֲרֹן יוֹתֵר מִמַּה שֶּׁנֶּאֱמַר בְּאַבְרָהָם, דְּאִלּוּ בְּאַבְרָהָם כְּתִיב (בראשית יח, כז) "וְאָנֹכִי עָפָר וָאֵפֶר", וְאִלּוּ בְּמֹשֶׁה וְאַהֲרֹן כְּתִיב (שמות טז, ז) "וְנַחְנוּ מָה".

כִּי "עָפָר וָאֵפֶר" עַל כָּל פָּנִים מִתְרָאֶה עֲדַיִן לִמְצִיאוּת עָפָר, אֲבָל מֹשֶׁה רַבֵּנוּ עָלָיו הַשָּׁלוֹם אָמַר "וְנַחְנוּ מָה", כְּאִלּוּ אֵין שׁוּם מְצִיאוּת בָּעוֹלָם כְּלָל לְגַמְרֵי (וְעִם כִּי גַּם אֶת אַהֲרֹן כָּלַל אִתּוֹ בְּזֹאת הַבְּחִינָה וּכְמַאֲמָרָם גָּדוֹל שֶׁנֶּאֱמַר בְּמֹשֶׁה וְאַהֲרֹן, לְפִי שֶׁתְּלוּנַּת יִשְׂרָאֵל הָיְתָה עַל שְׁנֵיהֶם, הֱשִׁיבָם בִּלְשׁוֹן רַבִּים, אֲבָל הָעִקָּר בְּזֹאת הַמַּדְרֵגָה הַנּוֹרָאָה הָיָה הוּא לְבַד).

וְזֶה שֶׁכָּתוּב בִּשְׁמוֹת רַבָּה פָּרָשָׁה י"א: "יִצְחָק אָמַר לְמֹשֶׁה אֲנִי גָּדוֹל מִמְּךָ שֶׁפָּשַׁטְתִּי צַוָּארִי כו' וְרָאִיתִי אֶת פְּנֵי הַשְּׁכִינָה, אָמַר לוֹ מֹשֶׁה אֲנִי נִתְעַלֵּיתִי יוֹתֵר מִמְּךָ, שֶׁאַתָּה רָאִיתָ פְּנֵי הַשְּׁכִינָה וְכָהוּ עֵינֶיךָ כו', אֲבָל אֲנִי הָיִיתִי מְדַבֵּר עִם הַשְּׁכִינָה פָּנִים בְּפָנִים וְלֹא כָהוּ עֵינַי". וּמְבֹאָר לַמֵּבִין. וְעַיֵּן מַה שֶּׁכָּתַב הרח"ו זִכְרוֹנוֹ לִבְרָכָה בְּסֵפֶר הַגִּלְגּוּלִים, בְּפֵרוּשׁ מַאֲמָרָם זִכְרוֹנָם לִבְרָכָה (שמו"ר ב) "אַבְרָהָם אַבְרָהָם, יַעֲקֹב יַעֲקֹב, פְּסִיק טַעְמָא, וּמֹשֶׁה מֹשֶׁה לֹא פְּסִיק טַעְמָא", שֶׁהוּא עַל עִנְיַן הֶפְסֵק וַחֲצִיצָה מְעֶטֶת מֵעִנְיַן הַגּוּף, עַיֵּן שָׁם:

פֶּרֶק י"ד

וְלָזֹאת, הָיָה מֹשֶׁה רַבֵּנוּ עָלָיו הַשָּׁלוֹם מוּכָן כָּל רֶגַע לִנְבוּאָה, כְּמוֹ שֶׁאָמַר (במדבר ט, ח) "עִמְדוּ וְאֶשְׁמְעָה מַה יְצַוֶּה ה' לָכֶם" וכו', וּכְמוֹ שֶׁאָמְרוּ רַבּוֹתֵינוּ זִכְרוֹנָם לִבְרָכָה , וְכֵן הָיָה מַשִּׂיג נְבוּאָתוֹ בְּכָל הַמְּקוֹמוֹת, בְּאֵיזֶה מָקוֹם שֶׁיִּהְיֶה, בְּהַשְׁוָאָה גְּמוּרָה בְּלֹא שׁוּם חִלּוּק כְּלָל, כְּמַאֲמָרָם זִכְרוֹנָם לִבְרָכָה בִּשְׁמוֹת רַבָּה פ"ב, וּבְבַמִּדְבַּר רַבָּה פָּרָשָׁה י"ב, וּבְחָזִית סִימָן ג' בְּפָסוּק (שה"ש) "עַמּוּדָיו עָשָׂה כֶסֶף" זֶה לְשׁוֹנָם: "לָמָּה דִּבֵּר הַקָּדוֹשׁ בָּרוּךְ הוּא עִם מֹשֶׁה מִתּוֹךְ הַסְּנֶה וכו', לְלַמֶּדְךָ שֶׁאֵין מָקוֹם פָּנוּי בָּאָרֶץ פָּנוּי מֵהַשְּׁכִינָה, שֶׁאֲפִלּוּ בְּתוֹךְ הַסְּנֶה הָיָה מְדַבֵּר עִמּוֹ". עַד כָּאן לְשׁוֹנָם. וְהוּא כְּפִי בְּחִינַת מַדְרֵגָתוֹ הַנּוֹרָאָה.

וְרַק אֲשֶׁר בִּקְּשָׁה נַפְשׁוֹ "הַרְאֵנִי נָא אֶת כְּבֹדֶךָ" (שמות לג, יח), לַעֲמֹד עַל מַהוּת זֶה הָעִנְיָן הַנּוֹרָא, וְלִרְאוֹת אֵיךְ הוּא יִתְבָּרַךְ שְׁמוֹ מְלֹא כָל הָאָרֶץ כְּבוֹדוֹ, וְלֵית אֲתַר פָּנוּי מִנֵּיהּ, זֶה לֹא נִתַּן לוֹ, וְהֱשִׁיבוֹ הוּא יִתְבָּרַךְ: "לֹא תוּכַל לִרְאוֹת וכו', כִּי לֹא יִרְאַנִי" וכו':

וְהָיָה הוֹלֵךְ וְגָדוֹל בְּזֹאת הַמַּדְרֵגָה כָּל עֵת, עַד שֶׁעָלָה בְּיָדוֹ, וְזָכָה אֵלֶיהָ קֹדֶם סִלּוּקוֹ

מִן הָעוֹלָם, בִּשְׁלֵמוּת הַיּוֹתֵר אֶפְשָׁרִי בְּכֹחַ הָאָדָם לִזְכּוֹת בְּעוֹדוֹ בְּזֶה הָעוֹלָם. כְּמוֹ שֶׁמָּצִינוּ בְּמִשְׁנֵה תּוֹרָה בְּפָרָשַׁת וְהָיָה אִם שָׁמוֹעַ, (דברים יא) שֶׁתְּחִלָּה אָמַר "לְאַהֲבָה אֶת ה' אֱלֹהֵיכֶם" וגו', וְתֵכֶף לוֹ בַּפָּסוּק שֶׁאַחֲרָיו אָמַר בִּלְשׁוֹן מְדַבֵּר בַּעֲדוֹ "וְנָתַתִּי מְטַר אַרְצְכֶם" כו', שֶׁהוּא הַנּוֹתֵן וְהַפּוֹעֵל, כִּי הִתְבַּטֵּל בְּעֵינֵי עַצְמוֹ מִמְּצִיאוּת כְּלָל, וְרַק הַשְּׁכִינָה לְבַד הַמְדַבֶּרֶת, לָכֵן אָמַר "וְנָתַתִּי". וְזֶה שֶׁאָמְרוּ זִכְרוֹנָם לִבְרָכָה (זוהר פנחס רלב): "שְׁכִינָה מְדַבֶּרֶת מִתּוֹךְ גְּרוֹנוֹ שֶׁל מֹשֶׁה", וּכְמוֹ שֶׁאָמַר הַכָּתוּב (שמות יב. ח): "פֶּה אֶל פֶּה אֲדַבֶּר בּוֹ", וְלֹא כְּתִיב "אֵלָיו", אֶלָּא "בּוֹ", בְּתוֹכוֹ מַמָּשׁ.

וּלְזֹאת הַמַּדְרֵגָה בִּשְׁלֵמוּת, עֲדַיִן לֹא זָכָה אֵלֶיהָ שׁוּם אָדָם זוּלָתוֹ, מֵעֵת חֵטְא אָדָם הָרִאשׁוֹן, וְגַם לֹא יִזְכֶּה אֵלֶיהָ שׁוּם אֱנָשׁ עַל יַבֶּשְׁתָּא, עַד בִּיאַת הַגּוֹאֵל בִּמְהֵרָה בְיָמֵינוּ, כְּמוֹ שֶׁהֵעִידָה הַתּוֹרָה הַקְּדוֹשָׁה (דברים לד, י) "וְלֹא קָם נָבִיא עוֹד בְּיִשְׂרָאֵל כְּמֹשֶׁה" כו'. (וְאַף שֶׁנֶּאֱמַר בִּלְשׁוֹן עָבָר, הַתּוֹרָה הִיא נִצְחִית, וְקָאֵי גַּם עַל זְמַן דּוֹרוֹת הַבָּאִים, שֶׁאַחַר עֲבֹר כָּל דּוֹר מֵהָעוֹלָם, נוּכַל לוֹמַר שֶׁלֹּא קָם בְּזֶה הַדּוֹר נָבִיא כְּמֹשֶׁה בְּזֹאת הַמַּדְרֵגָה).

וְלָכֵן אָמְרוּ בְּתָנָא דְּבֵי אֵלִיָּהוּ: (פֶּרֶק כ"ה) "חַיָּב אָדָם לוֹמַר מָתַי יַגִּיעוּ מַעֲשַׂי לְמַעֲשֵׂי אֲבוֹתַי אַבְרָהָם יִצְחָק וְיַעֲקֹב", וְלֹא אָמְרוּ לְמַעֲשֵׂי מֹשֶׁה רַבֵּנוּ עָלָיו הַשָּׁלוֹם.

אָמְנָם, עִם כָּל זֶה, רָאוּי לְכָל יְרֵא ה' אֲמִתִּי, שֶׁעַל כָּל פָּנִים בְּעֵת עָמְדוֹ לְהִתְפַּלֵּל, יְבַטֵּל בְּטֹהַר לְבָבוֹ כְּפִי יְכָלְתּוֹ וְהַשָּׂגָתוֹ, כָּל הַכֹּחוֹת שֶׁבָּעוֹלָם וְכָל כֹּחוֹתָיו, כְּאִלּוּ אֵין שׁוּם מְצִיאוּת בָּעוֹלָם כְּלָל, וּלְהִתְדַּבֵּק בְּלִבּוֹ רַק בּוֹ יִתְבָּרַךְ אָדוֹן יָחִיד בָּרוּךְ הוּא.

וְעַל כָּל פָּנִים, לִפְרָקִים, כִּי בֶּאֱמֶת לֹא כָּל הָעִתִּים שָׁווֹת בְּעִנְיַן טָהֳרַת הַלֵּב, וּבִפְרָט בַּדּוֹרוֹת הַלָּלוּ כִּמְעַט בִּלְתִּי אֶפְשָׁר לְהִתְפַּלֵּל בִּתְמִידוּת בְּזֹאת הַמַּדְרֵגָה הַגְּבוֹהָ. וּכְבָר אָמַר רַב שֵׁשֶׁת בְּשֵׁם רַב אֶלְעָזָר בֶּן עֲזַרְיָה (עירובין רפ"ג סה, ב): "יְכָלַנִי לִפְטֹר כָּל הָעוֹלָם מִדִּין תְּפִלָּה". אַף עַל פִּי כֵן, הָעוֹבֵד הַטָּהוֹר הָרוֹאֶה וּמִסְתַּכֵּל תָּמִיד בְּטָהֳרַת לְבָבוֹ עַל כָּל עִנְיָנָיו, שֶׁיִּהְיוּ לְרָצוֹן לִפְנֵי אָדוֹן כֹּל יִתְבָּרַךְ שְׁמוֹ, יוּכַל לְהַגִּיעַ שֶׁיִּתְפַּלֵּל עַל כָּל פָּנִים לִפְרָקִים, בְּזֹאת הַמַּדְרֵגָה.

וְעַתָּה מְבֹאָר כַּוָּנָתָם זִכְרוֹנָם לִבְרָכָה בְּמַאֲמָרָם (ברכות לא:) שֶׁהַמִּתְפַּלֵּל צָרִיךְ שֶׁיְּכַוֵּן אֶת לִבּוֹ לַ"מָּקוֹם", וְכֵן מַאֲמָרָם זִכְרוֹנָם לִבְרָכָה בְּאָבוֹת: "וּכְשֶׁאַתָּה מִתְפַּלֵּל אַל תַּעַשׂ וכו', אֶלָּא רַחֲמִים וְתַחֲנוּנִים לִפְנֵי הַ'מָּקוֹם' בָּרוּךְ הוּא" רָצָה לוֹמַר, שֶׁצָּרִיךְ לִיזָּהֵר בְּנַפְשׁוֹ מְאֹד, שֶׁלֹּא לְכַוֵּן וְלָשׂוּם מְגַמַּת לִבּוֹ בִּתְפִלָּתוֹ חַס וְשָׁלוֹם לְשׁוּם סְפִירָה, אֲפִלּוּ מֵהַנֶּאֱצָלִים.

וְלֹא זוֹ בִּלְבַד שֶׁלֹּא לְכַוֵּן לְשׁוּם סְפִירָה וְכֹחַ עֶלְיוֹן לְבַד, כִּי הוּא עֲבוֹדָה לְלֹא אֱלֹקֵי אֱמֶת וְקִצּוּץ נְטִיעוֹת חַס וְשָׁלוֹם, אֶלָּא שֶׁגַּם רָאוּי וְנָכוֹן, שֶׁיְּבַטֵּל בִּרְצוֹנוֹ בִּטּוּל גָּמוּר כָּל הַכֹּחוֹת עֶלְיוֹנִים וְתַחְתּוֹנִים, וְגַם כָּל כֹּחוֹתָיו, כְּאִלּוּ אֵינָם בִּמְצִיאוּת, (וְלֹא זוֹ בִּלְבַד בְּעִנְיַן הַתְּפִלָּה, אֶלָּא שֶׁגַּם הָעֵסֶק בַּתּוֹרָה שֶׁתִּתְקַיֵּם אֶצְלוֹ כָּרָאוּי, גַּם כֵּן צְרִיכָה שֶׁתִּהְיֶה עַל פִּי זֹאת הַמַּדְרֵגָה, כְּעִנְיַן מַאֲמָרָם זִכְרוֹנָם לִבְרָכָה (סוטה כ"א ע"ב): "אֵין דִּבְרֵי תוֹרָה מִתְקַיְּמִין

אֶלָּא בְּמִי שֶׁמֵּשִׂים עַצְמוֹ כְּמִי שֶׁאֵינוֹ"), וּלְכַוֵּן וּלְהַדְבִּיק טָהֳרַת לִבּוֹ בִּתְפִלָּתוֹ רַק לִמְקוֹמוֹ שֶׁל עוֹלָם, הוּא יְחִידוֹ שֶׁל עוֹלָם, אֵין סוֹף בָּרוּךְ הוּא, הַמְמַלֵּא כָּל הָעוֹלָם וְהָעוֹלָמוֹת כֻּלָּם, וְלֵית אֲתַר פָּנוּי מִנֵּיהּ.

וְעַיֵּן רוֹקֵחַ זִכְרוֹנוֹ לִבְרָכָה, סוֹף שֹׁרֶשׁ זְכִירַת הַשֵּׁם ז"ל: "וּכְשֶׁיֹּאמַר "בָּרוּךְ אַתָּה ה'", אַל יַחְשֹׁב עַל הַכָּבוֹד הַנִּרְאֶה בְּלֵב הַנְּבִיאִים, וּמַרְאֶה עַל הַכִּסֵּא, כִּי אִם עַל ה' הוּא הָאֱלֹקִים בַּשָּׁמַיִם וּבָאָרֶץ בָּאֲוִיר וּבַיָּם וּבְכָל הָעוֹלָם, שֶׁהוּא אֱלֹהֵי הָאָבוֹת". עַד כָּאן לְשׁוֹנוֹ. וְהָבֵן:

הַקְדָּמָה לְשַׁעַר ד'

פֶּרֶק א'

אַתָּה הַקּוֹרֵא נָעִים, הִנֵּה הִדְרַכְתִּיךָ בְּעֶזְרַת ה' בִּנְתִיבוֹת הָאֱמֶת, לְהוֹרוֹת לְפָנֶיךָ הַדֶּרֶךְ תֵּלֶךְ בָּהּ לָבֶטַח, וְתוּכַל לְחַנֵּךְ עַצְמְךָ לְאַט לְאַט בְּסֵדֶר הַמַּדְרֵגוֹת הַנַּ"ל, לְפִי טֹהַר לְבָבְךָ, וּלְפִי הַשָּׂגָתְךָ, יוֹתֵר מִמַּה שֶּׁעָרוּךְ לְפָנֶיךָ כָּאן, וְגַם לְפִי רֹב הַהֶרְגֵּל.

וּבְעֵינֶיךָ תִּרְאֶה, שֶׁכָּל אֲשֶׁר תַּרְגִּיל עַצְמְךָ יוֹתֵר בְּכָל מַדְרֵגָה מֵאֵלּוּ הַנַּ"ל, יִתְוַסֵּף בְּלִבְּךָ טָהֳרָה עַל טָהֳרָתְךָ, הֵן בְּעֵסֶק הַתּוֹרָה, וְהֵן בְּקִיּוּם הַמִּצְוֹת, וְיִרְאָתוֹ וְאַהֲבָתוֹ יִתְבָּרַךְ:

אָמְנָם הִשָּׁמֵר וְהִזָּהֵר מְאֹד, שֶׁלֹּא תָּזוּחַ דַּעְתְּךָ עָלֶיךָ וְתִתְנַשֵּׂא לְבָבְךָ, מֵאֲשֶׁר אַתָּה עוֹבֵד אֶת בּוֹרַאֲךָ בְּטָהֳרַת הַמַּחְשָׁבָה. וּבְהַשְׁקָפָה רִאשׁוֹנָה לֹא תַּרְגִּישׁ כָּל כָּךְ בְּהִתְנַשְּׂאוּת לִבְּךָ מִזֶּה, וְצָרִיךְ אַתָּה לְפַשְׁפֵּשׁ וּלְמַשְׁמֵשׁ בָּזֶה מְאֹד, וְכָתוּב מְפֹרָשׁ: "תּוֹעֲבַת ה' כָּל גְּבַהּ לֵב" (משלי ט"ז), שֶׁאַף אִם לֹא יִתְרָאֶה הַהִתְנַשְּׂאוּת לְעֵינֵי בְּנֵי אָדָם, רַק בְּמַחְשֶׁבֶת הַלֵּב לְבַד בְּעֵינֵי עַצְמוֹ, הִיא תּוֹעֵבָה מַמָּשׁ לְפָנָיו יִתְבָּרַךְ, כַּיָּדוּעַ שֶׁהִיא הַשֹּׁרֶשׁ וְהַשְּׂאוֹר שֶׁבָּעִסָּה לְכָל הַמִּדּוֹת רָעוֹת.

וְאָמְרוּ (סוטה דף ד':) שֶׁכָּל הַמִּתְיַהֵר כְּאִלּוּ בָּנָה בָּמָה, וּשְׁכִינָה מְיַלֶּלֶת עָלָיו, וּכְאִלּוּ דּוֹחֵק רַגְלָיו יִתְבָּרַךְ שְׁמוֹ, שֶׁקּוֹבֵל עָלָיו וְאוֹמֵר, אֵין אֲנִי וְהוּא יְכוֹלִין לָדוּר כְּאֶחָד (שם ה') וְקָצַר הַמַּצָּע מֵהִשְׂתָּרֵעַ, וְאוֹי לוֹ לַבֵּן הַמְגָרֵשׁ אֶת אָבִיו בִּזְרוֹעַ מִבֵּית פַּלְטִין שֶׁל אָבִיו. וְהִפְלִיגוּ בָּהּ זִכְרוֹנָם לִבְרָכָה מְאֹד, עַד שֶׁאָמְרוּ שָׁם, שֶׁהוּא כְּאִלּוּ עוֹבֵד עֲבוֹדָה זָרָה וְכָפַר בָּעִקָּר, וּכְאִלּוּ בָּא עַל כָּל הָעֲרָיוֹת. וְאָמְרוּ (פסחים ס"ו ע"ב): "כָּל הַמִּתְיַהֵר, אִם חָכָם הוּא חָכְמָתוֹ מִסְתַּלֶּקֶת הֵימֶנּוּ".

וְכָל אֲשֶׁר יִרְאַת ה' נָגַע בְּלִבּוֹ, תְּסַמֵּר שַׂעֲרוֹת רֹאשׁוֹ וְתִדְמַע עֵינוֹ בְּהַעֲלוֹתוֹ עַל לִבּוֹ מִמִּי לְמָדוּהוּ רַבּוֹתֵינוּ זִכְרוֹנָם לִבְרָכָה זֹאת, מֵהִלֵּל הַזָּקֵן, אֲשֶׁר יָדוּעַ וּמְפֻרְסָם בְּדִבְרֵיהֶם זִכְרוֹנָם לִבְרָכָה (עי' שבת לא, א) הַפְלָגַת עַנְוְתָנוּתוֹ וְשִׁפְלוּתוֹ הַנּוֹרָאָה, עִם כָּל זֶה, כַּאֲשֶׁר נִזְדַּמֵּן לְיָדוֹ פַּעַם אַחַת, קְצָת עִנְיָן, שֶׁהָיָה נִרְאֶה בְּהַשְׁקָפָה כְּהִתְנַשְּׂאוּת, לְפִי מַדְרֵגַת גֹּדֶל נְמִיכַת רוּחוֹ, תֵּכֶף נֶעֱנַשׁ עַל זֶה שֶׁנִּתְעַלְּמָה הֵימֶנּוּ הֲלָכָה (פסחים ס"ו ע"ב) מַה נֹּאמַר וּנְדַבֵּר אֲנַחְנוּ, אֵיךְ אָנוּ צְרִיכִים לְפַשְׁפֵּשׁ וּלְמַשְׁמֵשׁ עַל זֶה בְּכָל עֵת:

פֶּרֶק ב׳

גַּם תּוּכַל לִגְרֹם לָאָדָם הַהִתְנַשְּׂאוּת בַּלֵּב, מֵאֲשֶׁר הוּא עוֹבֵד אוֹתוֹ יִתְבָּרֵךְ בְּטָהֳרַת הַלֵּב, שֶׁיֵּקַל בְּעֵינָיו חַס וְשָׁלוֹם אִם יִרְאֶה מִי וָמִי שֶׁאֵין עִנְיְנֵי עֲבוֹדָתוֹ לוֹ יִתְבָּרֵךְ בְּמַחְשָׁבָה טְהוֹרָה, וּמְקַיֵּם כְּכָל הַכָּתוּב בְּתוֹרַת ה׳ בְּלֹא דְּבֵקוּת, וְכָל שֶׁכֵּן כְּשֶׁיִּרְאֶה אֵיזֶה אִישׁ עוֹסֵק בְּתוֹרַת ה׳, וְיִתְבּוֹנֵן עָלָיו שֶׁהוּא ״שֶׁלֹּא לִשְׁמָהּ״, יִתְבַּזֶּה בְּעֵינָיו מְאֹד חַס וְשָׁלוֹם, וְהוּא עָוֹן פְּלִילִי, הָרַחֲמָן יַצִּילֵנוּ.

כִּי בֶּאֱמֶת כָּל עִנְיַן הַטָּהֳרַת הַלֵּב בַּעֲבוֹדָתוֹ יִתְבָּרֵךְ, הוּא לְמִצְוָה, וְלֹא לְעִכּוּבָא, כְּמוֹ שֶׁכָּתַבְתִּי לְעֵיל סוֹף שַׁעַר א׳, וְיִתְבָּאֵר עוֹד לְהַלָּן אי״ה. וְכָל הַמְקַיֵּם מִצְוַת ה׳, כְּכָל אֲשֶׁר צִוָּנוּ בַּתּוֹרָה הַקְּדוֹשָׁה שֶׁבִּכְתָב וּבְעַל פֶּה, אַף בְּלֹא דְּבֵקוּת, נִקְרָא גַּם כֵּן עוֹבֵד אֱלֹהִים, וְאָהוּב לְפָנָיו יִתְבָּרֵךְ:

וְכֵן הָאָדָם הָעוֹסֵק בְּתוֹרַת ה׳ אֲפִלּוּ שֶׁלֹּא לִשְׁמָהּ, אִם כִּי וַדַּאי שֶׁעֲדַיִן אֵינוֹ בְּמַדְרֵגָה הַגְּבוֹהָה הָאֲמִתִּית, אָמְנָם חָלִילָה וְחָלִילָה לְבַזּוֹתוֹ אֲפִלּוּ בַּלֵּב. וְאַדְּרַבָּה, כָּל אִישׁ יִשְׂרָאֵל מְחֻיָּב גַּם לִנְהֹג בּוֹ כָּבוֹד, כְּמוֹ שֶׁכָּתוּב (משלי ג, טז): ״בִּשְׂמֹאלָהּ עֹשֶׁר וְכָבוֹד״ וְדָרְשׁוּ רַבּוֹתֵינוּ זִכְרוֹנָם לִבְרָכָה (שבת ס״ג) לַמַּשְׂמְאִילִים בָּהּ כו׳.

וּבַזֹּהַר וַיֵּשֶׁב קפ״ד ב׳: ״תּוֹרַת ה׳ תְּמִימָה״ כו׳, כַּמָּה אִית לוֹן לִבְנֵי נָשָׁא לְאִשְׁתַּדְּלָא בְּאוֹרַיְתָא, דְּכָל מַאן דְּאִשְׁתַּדֵּל בְּאוֹרַיְתָא לֶהֱוֵי לֵיהּ חַיִּים כו׳, וַאֲפִילוּ מַאן דְּאִשְׁתַּדֵּל בְּאוֹרַיְתָא וְלָא אִשְׁתַּדֵּל בָּהּ לִשְׁמָהּ כִּדְקָא יָאוּת, זָכֵי לַאֲגַר טַב בְּעָלְמָא דֵּין וְלָא דַּיְנִינָן לֵיהּ בְּהַהוּא עָלְמָא. וְתָא חֲזֵי, כְּתִיב ״אֹרֶךְ יָמִים בִּימִינָהּ בִּשְׂמֹאלָהּ עֹשֶׁר וְכָבוֹד״ כו׳ ״בִּשְׂמֹאלָהּ עֹשֶׁר וְכָבוֹד״, אֲגַר טַב וְשַׁלְוָה אִית לֵיהּ בְּהַאי עָלְמָא״. [תּוֹרַת ה׳ תְּמִימָה וגו׳ כַּמָּה יֵשׁ לָהֶם לִבְנֵי אָדָם לְהִשְׁתַּדֵּל בַּתּוֹרָה, כִּי כָּל מִי שֶׁמִּשְׁתַּדֵּל בַּתּוֹרָה יִהְיֶה לוֹ חַיִּים וכו׳ וַאֲפִילוּ מִי שֶׁמִּשְׁתַּדֵּל בַּתּוֹרָה וְאֵינוֹ מִשְׁתַּדֵּל בָּהּ לִשְׁמָהּ כָּרָאוּי, הוּא זוֹכֶה לְשָׂכָר טוֹב בָּעוֹלָם הַזֶּה וְאֵין דָּנִים אוֹתוֹ בָּעוֹלָם הָאֱמֶת, וּבוֹא וּרְאֵה כָּתוּב ״אֹרֶךְ יָמִים בִּימִינָהּ בִּשְׂמֹאלָהּ עֹשֶׁר וְכָבוֹד״, שָׂכָר טוֹב וְשַׁלְוָה יֵשׁ לוֹ בָּעוֹלָם הַזֶּה.]

הֲרֵי שֶׁאֲפִלּוּ הָאָדָם אֲשֶׁר עִסְקוֹ בְּתוֹרָתוֹ יִתְבָּרֵךְ שֶׁלֹּא לִשְׁמָהּ כָּרָאוּי, אֶלָּא בִּשְׁבִיל אֵיזֶה פְּנִיָּה לְגַרְמֵיהּ, רַק אִם אֵינוֹ לְקַנְטוּר חַס וְשָׁלוֹם, אֲשֶׁר עָלָיו אָמְרוּ רַבּוֹתֵינוּ זִכְרוֹנָם לִבְרָכָה (ירושלמי ברכות א, ב) ״נוֹחַ לוֹ שֶׁתֵּהָפֵךְ שִׁלְיָתוֹ עַל פָּנָיו״, וְכֵן אָמְרוּ (שם פ״ח:) שֶׁנַּעֲשֵׂית לוֹ סַם הַמָּוֶת חַס וְשָׁלוֹם, הַקָּדוֹשׁ בָּרוּךְ הוּא קוֹבֵעַ לוֹ שָׂכָר טוֹב, שֶׁמַּגִּיעַ לוֹ עֹשֶׁר וְכָבוֹד וְשַׁלְוָה בְּהַאי עָלְמָא, וְגַם לֹא דַּיְנִינָן לֵיהּ בְּהַהוּא עָלְמָא עַל אוֹתָהּ הַמַּחְשָׁבָה וְהַפְּנִיָּה שֶׁכִּוֵּן בָּהּ.

וְכָל שֶׁכֵּן אִם אֵינוֹ מְכַוֵּן כְּלָל לְשׁוּם פְּנִיָּה לְגַרְמֵיהּ, הֲגַם שֶׁאֵין כַּוָּנָתוֹ לִשְׁמָהּ דַּוְקָא, הַיְנוּ לְשֵׁם הַתּוֹרָה, כְּמוֹ שֶׁאֶכְתֹּב לְקַמָּן בְּפֶרֶק ג׳ מִשַּׁעַר ד׳ בְּשֵׁם הרא״ש זִכְרוֹנוֹ לִבְרָכָה, אֶלָּא עִקַּר עִסְקוֹ בָּהּ בִּסְתָמָא, אֲשֶׁר כִּ׳לִשְׁמָהּ׳ דָּמֵי, הֲרֵי עֵסֶק תּוֹרָתוֹ יָקָר מְאֹד בְּעֵינָיו יִתְבָּרֵךְ, יוֹתֵר מִכָּל הַמִּצְוֹת לִשְׁמָהּ בִּקְדֻשַּׁת וְטָהֳרַת הַמַּחְשָׁבָה כָּרָאוּי.

כַּמְבֹאָר וּמוּכָח לְהֶדְיָא מִגְּמָרָא דַּעֲרָכִין (ט״ז ע״ב): ״בְּעָא מִינֵּיהּ רַב יְהוּדָה בְּרֵיהּ דְּרַב

שִׁמְעוֹן בֶּן פָּזִי, תּוֹכָחָה לִשְׁמָהּ וַעֲנָוָה שֶׁלֹּא לִשְׁמָהּ, הֵי מִנַּיְהוּ עֲדִיפָא, וְאָמַר לֵיהּ, מִי לָא מוֹדֵית דַּעֲנָוָה לִשְׁמָהּ עֲדִיפָא, דְּאָמַר מַר, עֲנָוָה גְּדוֹלָה מִכֻּלָּן, שֶׁלֹּא לִשְׁמָהּ נָמֵי עֲדִיפָא, דְּאָמַר רַב יְהוּדָה אָמַר רַב, לְעוֹלָם יַעֲסֹק אָדָם בַּתּוֹרָה וּבְמִצְוֹת אֲפִלּוּ שֶׁלֹּא לִשְׁמָהּ, שֶׁמִּתּוֹךְ שֶׁלֹּא לִשְׁמָהּ בָּא לִשְׁמָהּ". וּמִמֵּילָא נִשְׁמַע, דִּכְוָתָהּ נָמֵי בְּעֵסֶק הַתּוֹרָה, מִי לָא מוֹדֵית דְּתוֹרָה לִשְׁמָהּ וַדַּאי דַּעֲדִיפָא מִמִּצְוֹת לִשְׁמָהּ, שֶׁהֲרֵי מִשְׁנָה שְׁלֵמָה שָׁנִינוּ (פאה א') "וְתַלְמוּד תּוֹרָה כְּנֶגֶד כֻּלָּם".

וְכֵן חִלְּקוּ רַבּוֹתֵינוּ זִכְרוֹנָם לִבְרָכָה (סוטה כ"א) בְּיִתְרוֹן עֵרֶךְ מַעֲלַת הַתּוֹרָה עַל הַמִּצְוֹת, שֶׁזְּכוּת וְאוֹר הַמִּצְוֹת בֵּין בְּעִדְּנָא דְּעָסִיק בָּהּ וּבֵין בְּעִדְּנָא דְּלָא עָסִיק בָּהּ, הִיא רַק מְגִנָּה מִן הַיִּסּוּרִין וְאֵינָהּ מַצֶּלֶת אֶת הָאָדָם שֶׁלֹּא יָבֹא לִידֵי חֵטְא, אֲבָל אוֹר הַתּוֹרָה, גַּם לְפִי הַמַּסְקָנָא שָׁם, עַל כָּל פָּנִים בְּעִדְּנָא דְּעָסִיק בָּהּ גַּם הִיא מַצֶּלֶת אוֹתוֹ מֵחֵטְא. וְאָמְרוּ בִּירוּשַׁלְמִי פֶּרֶק א' דְּפֵאָה שֶׁכָּל הַמִּצְוֹת אֵינָן שָׁוִין לְדָבָר אֶחָד מִן הַתּוֹרָה, וּכְמוֹ שֶׁיִּתְבָּאֵר לְהַלָּן אי"ה בְּשַׁעַר ד' בָּזֶה.

אִם כֵּן, גַּם עֵסֶק הַתּוֹרָה שֶׁלֹּא לִשְׁמָהּ נָמֵי עֲדִיפָא מִמִּצְוֹת לִשְׁמָהּ, מִזֶּה הַטַּעַם עַצְמוֹ, שֶׁמִּתּוֹךְ שֶׁלֹּא לִשְׁמָהּ בָּא לִשְׁמָהּ:

פֶּרֶק ג'

וְגַם כִּי בֶּאֱמֶת כִּמְעַט בִּלְתִּי אֶפְשָׁר לָבֹא תֵּכֶף בִּתְחִלַּת קְבִיעַת לִמּוּדוֹ לְמַדְרֵגַת לִשְׁמָהּ כָּרָאוּי, כִּי הָעֵסֶק בַּתּוֹרָה שֶׁלֹּא לִשְׁמָהּ, הוּא לְמַדְרֵגָה שֶׁמִּתּוֹךְ כָּךְ יוּכַל לָבֹא לְמַדְרֵגַת לִשְׁמָהּ, וְלָכֵן גַּם הוּא אָהוּב לְפָנָיו יִתְבָּרַךְ, כְּמוֹ שֶׁבִּלְתִּי אֶפְשָׁר לַעֲלוֹת מֵהָאָרֶץ לַעֲלִיָּה אִם לֹא דֶּרֶךְ מַדְרֵגוֹת הַסֻּלָּם.

וְלָזֶה אָמְרוּ (פסחים נ' ע"ב): "לְעוֹלָם יַעֲסֹק אָדָם בַּתּוֹרָה וּבְמִצְוֹת אֲפִלּוּ שֶׁלֹּא לִשְׁמָהּ". אָמְרָם "לְעוֹלָם" רוֹצֶה לוֹמַר, בִּקְבִיעוּת, הַיְנוּ שֶׁבִּתְחִלַּת לִמּוּדוֹ אֵינוֹ מְחֻיָּב רַק שֶׁיִּלְמַד בִּקְבִיעוּת תָּמִיד יוֹמָם וָלַיְלָה.

וְאַף אִם לִפְעָמִים וַדַּאי יִפֹּל בְּמַחְשַׁבְתּוֹ אֵיזֶה פְּנִיָּה לְגַרְמֵיהּ, לְשׁוּם גַּאֲוַת וְכָבוֹד וְכַיּוֹצֵא, עִם כָּל זֶה אַל יָשִׂים לֵב לִפְרֹשׁ אוֹ לְהִתְרַפּוֹת מִמֶּנָּה בַּעֲבוּר זֶה חַס וְשָׁלוֹם, אֶלָּא אַדְּרַבָּה, יִתְחַזֵּק מְאֹד בְּעֵסֶק הַתּוֹרָה, וִיהֵא נָכוֹן לִבּוֹ בָּטוּחַ שֶׁוַּדַּאי יָבֹא מִתּוֹךְ כָּךְ לְמַדְרֵגַת לִשְׁמָהּ. וְכֵן הוּא גַּם כֵּן בְּעִנְיַן הַמִּצְוֹת עַל דֶּרֶךְ זֶה.

וּמִי שֶׁיִּמְלָאוֹ לִבּוֹ לְבַזּוֹת וּלְהַשְׁפִּיל חַס וְשָׁלוֹם אֶת הָעוֹסֵק בַּתּוֹרָה וּמִצְוֹת אַף שֶׁלֹּא לִשְׁמָהּ, לֹא יִנָּקֶה רָע, וְעָתִיד לִיתֵּן אֶת הַדִּין חַס וְשָׁלוֹם: וְלֹא עוֹד אֶלָּא שֶׁנִּמְנֶה בְּדִבְרֵי רַבּוֹתֵינוּ זִכְרוֹנָם לִבְרָכָה (בברייתא ראש השנה יז, א) בֵּין אוֹתָם שֶׁאֵין לָהֶם חֵלֶק לָעוֹלָם הַבָּא לִגְמָרֵי חַס וְשָׁלוֹם, וְגֵיהִנֹּם כָּלֶה וְהֵם אֵינָם כָּלִין, וְהֵם הַמִּינִין וְהַמְּסוּרוֹת וְהָאֶפִּיקוֹרְסִין. וְכֵן בַּמִּשְׁנָה רֵישׁ פֶּרֶק חֵלֶק מָנוּ אֶת הָאֶפִּיקוֹרוֹס בִּכְלַל אוֹתָן שֶׁאֵין לָהֶם חֵלֶק לָעוֹלָם הַבָּא, וְאָמְרִינַן בַּגְּמָרָא שָׁם (צ"ט ב'): "רַב וְרַבִּי חֲנִינָא דְּאָמְרֵי תַּרְוַיְהוּ זֶה הַמְבַזֶּה תַּלְמִיד חָכָם, רַבִּי יוֹחָנָן וריב"ל אָמְרֵי שֶׁאֲפִילּוּ הַמְבַזֶּה חֲבֵרוֹ בִּפְנֵי תַּלְמִיד חָכָם נָמֵי אֶפִּיקוֹרוֹס הָוֵי", וְאַף

אִם אוֹמֵר, "מַאי אַהֲנֵי לָן רַבָּנָן, לְדִידְהוּ קָרוּ, לְדִידְהוּ תָּנוּ", הֲרֵי זֶה בִּכְלַל אֶפִּיקוֹרוֹס מְבַזֶּה תַּלְמִידֵי חֲכָמִים, וְגַם מְגַלֶּה פָּנִים בַּתּוֹרָה נָמֵי מִקְרֵי חַס וְשָׁלוֹם, וַהֲרֵי זֶה אִבֵּד חֶלְקוֹ בְּחַיֵּי עוֹלָם, הָרַחֲמָן יַצִּילֵנוּ.

וְכֵן הָרַבֵּינוּ יוֹנָה זִכְרוֹנוֹ לִבְרָכָה בְּשַׁעַר הַתְּשׁוּבָה, שֶׁמָּנָה סֵדֶר מַדְרֵגוֹת חֹמֶר הָעֳנָשִׁים, וּמַדְרֵגָה הָאַחֲרוֹנָה מָנָה אֶת הַכַּת שֶׁאָמְרוּ רַבּוֹתֵינוּ זִכְרוֹנָם לִבְרָכָה עֲלֵיהֶם שֶׁאֵין לָהֶם חֵלֶק לָעוֹלָם הַבָּא, וּמָנָה גַּם כֵּן שָׁם הַמְּבַזֶּה תַּלְמִיד חָכָם בִּכְלַל זֹאת הַכַּת. וְכֵן מָנָה אוֹתוֹ הרח"ו זִכְרוֹנוֹ לִבְרָכָה בְּשַׁעַר הַקְּדֻשָּׁה בִּכְלַל אוֹתָהּ הַכַּת. וְכָל חֹמֶר עָנְשׁוֹ הַנּוֹרָא הַזֶּה, הוּא מִטַּעַם עַל שֶׁהוּא בְּמוֹרִידֵי אוֹר מַעֲלַת הַתּוֹרָה הַקְּדוֹשָׁה, וְחָלִילָה חַס וְשָׁלוֹם, כְּמוֹ שֶׁהֶאֱרִיךְ בָּזֶה הָרַבֵּנוּ יוֹנָה זִכְרוֹנוֹ לִבְרָכָה שָׁם, עַיֵּן שָׁם דִּבְרֵי קָדוֹשׁ ה', (וְכָתַב הוּא ז"ל שָׁם, שֶׁגַּם עִקַּר הָעֹנֶשׁ שֶׁל כָּל הַמְּנוּיִים שָׁם בְּאוֹתָהּ הַכַּת, הוּא גַּם כֵּן רַק מִפְּנֵי חִלּוּל כְּבוֹד הַתּוֹרָה הַקְּדוֹשָׁה רַחֲמָנָא לִיצְּלַן).

כִּי כֵּיוָן שֶׁהוּא מַשְׁפִּיל וּמְבַזֶּה אֶת הָעוֹסֵק בַּתּוֹרָה שֶׁלֹּא לִשְׁמָהּ, הֲרֵי הוּא מְרַפֶּה אֶת יָדָיו מֵעֵסֶק הַתּוֹרָה, וְלֹא יוּכַל לָבֹא לְעוֹלָם לְמַדְרֵגַת לִשְׁמָהּ לִהְיוֹת תַּלְמִיד חָכָם גָּמוּר, וַהֲרֵי וַדַּאי מִקְרֵי בָּזֶה מְבַזֶּה תַּלְמִיד חָכָם, וְאֵין לְךָ חִלּוּל שְׁמוֹ יִתְבָּרַךְ וְתוֹרָתוֹ הַקְּדוֹשָׁה יוֹתֵר מִזֶּה. וּכְבָר הִשְׁפִּיל וְהוֹרִיד אֶת יְקַר תִּפְאַרְתָּהּ שֶׁל הַתּוֹרָה הַקְּדוֹשָׁה לָאָרֶץ יַגִּיעֶנָּה עַד עָפָר, וְהָרַס גַּם אֶת כָּל הָעֲבוֹדָה בִּכְלָלָהּ חַס וְשָׁלוֹם, כִּי אֵין עֲבוֹדָתוֹ יִתְבָּרַךְ מִתְקַיֶּמֶת כָּרָאוּי בַּעֲדַת יִשְׂרָאֵל בִּלְתִּי עַל יְדֵי הַתַּלְמִידֵי חֲכָמִים עוֹסְקֵי הַתּוֹרָה הַקְּדוֹשָׁה יוֹמָם וָלַיְלָה, כִּי עֵינֵי כָּל יִשְׂרָאֵל עֲלֵיהֶם לָדַעַת מַה יַּעֲשֶׂה בְּיִשְׂרָאֵל, לְהוֹרוֹת לָהֶם הַדֶּרֶךְ יֵלְכוּ בָהּ, וְאֶת הַמַּעֲשֶׂה אֲשֶׁר יַעֲשׂוּן. אִם כֵּן, הָאִישׁ אֲשֶׁר יָבֹא לִגְרֹם שֶׁלֹּא יִהְיוּ תַּלְמִידֵי חֲכָמִים מְצוּיִים בְּיִשְׂרָאֵל, הֲרֵי כְּבָר הָרַס גַּם כְּלַל עֲבוֹדָתוֹ יִתְבָּרַךְ לְגַמְרֵי, כִּי יִשָּׁאֲרוּ עֲדַת יִשְׂרָאֵל חַס וְשָׁלוֹם לְלֹא תּוֹרָה וּלְלֹא מוֹרֶה, וְלֹא יֵדְעוּ בַּמֶּה יִכָּשְׁלוּ חַס וְשָׁלוֹם. וּכְעֵין זֶה כָּתַב גַּם כֵּן רַבֵּנוּ יוֹנָה זִכְרוֹנוֹ לִבְרָכָה שָׁם, עַיֵּן שָׁם:

לָזֹאת, אַתָּה צָרִיךְ לִיזָּהֵר אַדְּרַבָּה, לְכַבֵּד וּלְהַגְבִּיהַּ כְּכָל אֲשֶׁר בְּכֹחֲךָ אֶת כָּל הָעוֹסֵק וּמַחֲזִיק בְּתוֹרַת ה', אֲפִלּוּ שֶׁלֹּא לִשְׁמָהּ, כְּדֵי שֶׁיֹּאחֵז צַדִּיק דַּרְכּוֹ בַּל יִתְרַפֶּה מִמֶּנָּה חַס וְשָׁלוֹם, כְּדֵי שֶׁיּוּכַל לָבֹא מִמֶּנָּה לְמַדְרֵגַת לִשְׁמָהּ:

וְגַם אִם נִרְאֶה, שֶׁכָּל יְמֵי חַיָּיו מִנְּעוּרָיו וְעַד זִקְנָה וְשֵׂיבָה הָיָה עִסְקוֹ בָּהּ שֶׁלֹּא לִשְׁמָהּ, גַּם כֵּן אַתָּה חַיָּב לִנְהֹג בּוֹ כָּבוֹד, וְכָל שֶׁכֵּן שֶׁלֹּא לְבַזּוֹתוֹ חַס וְשָׁלוֹם, שֶׁכֵּיוָן שֶׁעָסַק בְּתוֹרַת ה' בִּתְמִידוּת, בִּלְתִּי סָפֵק שֶׁהָיָה כַּוָּנָתוֹ פְּעָמִים רַבּוֹת גַּם לִשְׁמָהּ, כְּמוֹ שֶׁהִבְטִיחוּ רַבּוֹתֵינוּ זִכְרוֹנָם לִבְרָכָה (פסחים נ.) שֶׁמִּתּוֹךְ שֶׁלֹּא לִשְׁמָהּ בָּא לִשְׁמָהּ, כִּי אֵין הַפֵּרוּשׁ דַּוְקָא שֶׁיָּבֹא מִזֶּה לְלִשְׁמָהּ, עַד שֶׁאַחַר כָּךְ יַעֲסֹק בָּהּ תָּמִיד כָּל יָמָיו רַק לִשְׁמָהּ. אֶלָּא הַיְנוּ, שֶׁבְּכָל פַּעַם שֶׁהוּא לוֹמֵד בִּקְבִיעוּת זְמַן כַּמָּה שָׁעוֹת רְצוּפִים, אַף שֶׁדֶּרֶךְ כְּלָל הָיְתָה כַּוָּנָתוֹ שֶׁלֹּא לִשְׁמָהּ, עִם כָּל זֶה, בִּלְתִּי אֶפְשָׁר כְּלָל שֶׁלֹּא יִכָּנֵס בְּלִבּוֹ בְּאֶמְצַע הַלִּמּוּד עַל כָּל פָּנִים זְמַן מְעַט כַּוָּנָה רְצוּיָה לִשְׁמָהּ, וּמֵעַתָּה כָּל מַה שֶּׁלָּמַד עַד הֵנָּה שֶׁלֹּא לִשְׁמָהּ, נִתְקַדֵּשׁ וְנִטְהַר עַל יְדֵי אוֹתוֹ הָעֵת קָטָן שֶׁכִּוֵּן בּוֹ לִשְׁמָהּ:

פֶּרֶק ד'

וְכַמָּה זְהִירוּת יְתֵרָה צָרִיךְ הָאָדָם לְהִזָּהֵר בְּעִנְיָנִים כָּאֵלּוּ וְשֶׁכַּיּוֹצֵא בָּהֶם. וּכְבָר אָמְרוּ רַבּוֹתֵינוּ זִכְרוֹנָם לִבְרָכָה (סוכה נ"ב א'): "כָּל הַגָּדוֹל מֵחֲבֵרוֹ יִצְרוֹ גָּדוֹל הֵימֶנּוּ", כִּי הַיֵּצֶר מִתְהַפֵּךְ בְּתַחְבּוּלוֹתָיו לְכָל אָדָם, כְּפִי עִנְיָנוֹ וּמַדְרֵגָתוֹ בַּתּוֹרָה וַעֲבוֹדָה. שֶׁאִם הוּא רוֹאֶה, שֶׁכְּפִי גֹּבַהּ מַדְרֵגָתוֹ שֶׁל הָאָדָם, אִם יַשִּׁיאֵהוּ שֶׁיַּנִּיחַ מְקוֹמוֹ וּמַדְרֵגָתוֹ לַעֲשׂוֹת בְּפֹעַל אֵיזֶה עָוֹן וְחֵטְא חָמוּר אוֹ קַל, שֶׁלֹּא יֹאבֶה לוֹ, הוּא מִתְחַפֵּשׂ לְהִתְדַּמּוֹת אֶל הָאָדָם כְּיֵצֶר טוֹב, לְסַמּוֹת שִׂכְלוֹ, לְהָטִיל אֶרֶס, וּלְהַטְעוֹתוֹ בְּאוֹתוֹ הָאֹפֶן וְהַמַּדְרֵגָה עַצְמָהּ שֶׁהָאָדָם דָּבוּק בָּהּ, שֶׁמַּרְאֶה לוֹ בָּהּ אֵיזֶה דֶּרֶךְ, הַנִּרְאֶה לְהָאָדָם בְּהַשְׁקָפָה רִאשׁוֹנָה שֶׁהוּא עֲצַת יִצְרוֹ הַטּוֹב, לְהַדְרִיכוֹ בְּדֶרֶךְ יוֹתֵר גָּבוֹהַּ, כְּפִי שֶׁמַּרְאֶה לוֹ בָּהּ פָּנִים וְסִימָנֵי טָהֳרָה, וְהָאָדָם נוֹפֵל בְּרִשְׁתּוֹ כְּמַהֵר צִפּוֹר אֶל פַּח בְּלִי הִתְבּוֹנְנוּת רַב, וְלֹא יָדַע כִּי בְנַפְשׁוֹ הוּא וְרַגְלֶיהָ יוֹרְדוֹת מָוֶת חַס וְשָׁלוֹם:

לָזֹאת, הִזָּהֵר בְּנַפְשְׁךָ מְאֹד, שֶׁאַל יַשִּׁיאֲךָ יִצְרְךָ לֵאמֹר, שֶׁעִקַּר הַכֹּל תִּרְאֶה שֶׁתְּהֵא אַךְ עָסוּק כָּל יָמֶיךָ לְטַהֵר מַחְשַׁבְתְּךָ כָּרָאוּי, שֶׁתְּהֵא דְּבֵקוּת מַחְשַׁבְתְּךָ בְּבוֹרַאֲךָ בִּתְמִידוּת בַּל תִּמּוֹט, וְלֹא תָּשׁוּב מִפְּנֵי כֹּל לְהַנִּיחַ טֹהַר מַחְשַׁבְתְּךָ בְּשׁוּם עֵת כְּלָל, וְהַכֹּל לְשֵׁם שָׁמַיִם, בְּאָמְרוֹ לְךָ שֶׁכָּל עִקַּר תּוֹרָה וּמִצְוֹת הֵמָּה דַּוְקָא כְּשֶׁהֵם בְּכַוָּנָה עֲצוּמָה וּבִדְבֵקוּת אֲמִתִּי, וְכָל זְמַן שֶׁאֵין לֵב הָאָדָם מָלֵא לַעֲשׂוֹתָם בְּכַוָּנָה קְדוֹשָׁה וּבִדְבֵקוּת וְטָהֳרַת הַמַּחֲשָׁבָה, אֵינָהּ נֶחְשֶׁבֶת לְמִצְוָה וַעֲבוֹדָה כְּלָל, כַּאֲשֶׁר כְּבָר לִמֵּד הַמֶּלֶךְ זָקֵן וּכְסִיל, לְסַמּוֹת עֵינַיִם, וּלְהָבִיא רְאָיוֹתָיו מִמִּקְרָא וּמִשְׁנָה וְתַלְמוּד וּמִדְרָשִׁים וְסֵפֶר הַזֹּהַר, כְּעִנְיַן "רַחֲמָנָא לִבָּא בָּעֵי" (סנהדרין קו:) וְכָהֵנָּה רַבּוֹת עִמּוֹ חֲבִילוֹת רְאָיוֹת.

אָמְנָם אִם תִּזְכֶּה לְהַבְחִין בְּעֵינֵי שֵׂכֶל עַל פִּי הַתּוֹרָה, תָּבִין וְתִמְצָא, שֶׁזֶּה כָּל עִנְיָנוֹ, לְהַרְאוֹת לְהָאָדָם טְלָפָיו בְּסִימָנֵי טָהֳרָה, שֶׁדַּרְכּוֹ בַּקֹּדֶשׁ, וְרַגְלָיו יוֹרְדוֹת מָוֶת רַחֲמָנָא לִיצְלַן.

וְעַתָּה רְאֵה דְּרָכָיו וַחֲכַם גַּם בָּזֶה, אֵיךְ שֶׁהוּא חָכָם לְהָרַע מֵעֵין טוֹב, הַיּוֹם יֹאמַר לְךָ, שֶׁכָּל תּוֹרָה וּמִצְוָה שֶׁבְּלֹא דְּבֵקוּת אֵינָהּ כְּלוּם, וְצָרִיךְ אַתָּה לְהָכִין לֵב, וּלְהַגְבִּיהַּ עוּף מַחְשַׁבְתְּךָ, קֹדֶם עֲשִׂיַּת כָּל מִצְוָה אוֹ תְּפִלָּה, לְמַחֲשָׁבָה טְהוֹרָה שֶׁבִּטְהוֹרוֹת, וּכְמוֹ כֵן תְּהֵא מַחְשַׁבְתְּךָ טְרוּדָה בַּהֲכָנַת הַמִּצְוָה טֶרֶם עֲשׂוֹתָהּ, עַד שֶׁיַּעֲבֹר זְמַן הַמִּצְוָה אוֹ הַתְּפִלָּה. וְיַרְאֶה לְךָ פָּנִים, שֶׁכָּל תְּפִלָּה אוֹ מִצְוָה שֶׁנַּעֲשֵׂית בְּכַוָּנָה עֲצוּמָה בִּקְדֻשָּׁה וּבְטָהֳרָה אַף שֶׁלֹּא בִּזְמַנָּהּ, הֲרֵי הִיא יְקָרָה מִקִּיּוּם הַמִּצְוָה בִּזְמַנָּהּ וְשֶׁלֹּא בְּכַוָּנָה.

וּכְשֶׁיַּרְגִּילְךָ יִצְרְךָ שֶׁיִּקָּבַע בְּלִבְּךָ שֶׁלֹּא לָחוּשׁ כָּל כָּךְ לְשִׁנּוּי קְבִיעוּת זְמַן שֶׁל אֵיזֶה מִצְוָה אוֹ תְּפִלָּה, מֵחֲמַת קְבִיעוּת מַחְשַׁבְתְּךָ לְהִטָּהֵר וּלְפַנּוֹת הַלֵּב תְּחִלָּה, בְּהֶמְשֵׁךְ הַזְּמַן יַדְרִיכְךָ לְאַט לְאַט, בְּחֵלֶק שְׂפָתָיו, מִמַּדְרֵגָה לְמַדְרֵגָה, וְלֹא תַרְגִּישׁ כְּלָל, עַד שֶׁמִּמֵּילָא יְהֵא לְךָ כְּהֶתֵּר לְהַעֲבִיר מוֹעֵד הַתְּפִלָּה אוֹ הַמִּצְוֹת, אַף גַּם שֶׁתִּתְפַּנֶּה לִבְּךָ לְבַטָּלָה בִּדְבָרִים בְּטֵלִים, וְיַדִּיחֲךָ מִכֹּל, וְלֹא יִשָּׁאֵר לְךָ, לֹא מַעֲשֶׂה מִצְוָה בִּזְמַנָּהּ וְלֹא מַחֲשָׁבָה טוֹבָה.

וְגַם, הֲרֵי הוּא הֲרִיסַת כָּל הַתּוֹרָה בִּכְלָלָהּ רַחֲמָנָא לִיצְלַן, אִם חַס וְשָׁלוֹם נֹאבֶה לוֹ לְהַטּוֹת אֹזֶן לְחֵלֶק שְׂפָתָיו בְּדַרְכּוֹ זֶה. וְהַגַּע עַצְמְךָ, כְּגוֹן אִם יַטְרִיד אָדָם עַצְמוֹ לַיְלָה

הָרִאשׁוֹנָה שֶׁל פֶּסַח בְּכַוָּנַת אֲכִילַת כְּזַיִת מַצָּה, שֶׁתְּהֵא הָאֲכִילָה בִּקְדֻשָּׁה וְטָהֳרָה וּדְבֵקוּת, וְיַמְשִׁיךְ הַהֲכָנָה כָּל הַלַּיְלָה, עַד שֶׁיִּמְשֹׁךְ זְמַן הָאֲכִילָה עַד לְאַחַר שֶׁעָלָה הַשַּׁחַר, אוֹ לְאַחַר נֵץ הַחַמָּה, הֲרֵי כָּל טָהֳרַת מַחְשַׁבְתּוֹ פִּגּוּל הוּא לֹא יֵרָצֶה. וּמִי שֶׁאָכַל הַכְּזַיִת מַצָּה בִּזְמַנָּהּ אַף בְּלֹא קְדֻשָּׁה וְטָהֳרָה יְתֵרָה, הֲרֵי קִיֵּם מִצְוַת עֲשֵׂה הַכְּתוּבָה בַּתּוֹרָה, וְתָבֹא עָלָיו בְּרָכָה. וְכָהֵנָּה רַבּוֹת, אֲשֶׁר אִם לֹא נָכוֹן לִבֵּנוּ לָחוּשׁ לַעֲשׂוֹת כָּל הַמִּצְוֹת בְּמוֹעֲדָם וּבִזְמַנָּם, וְכִי מַאי נַפְקוּתָא בֵּין זֶה לְמִי שֶׁהָיָה תּוֹקֵעַ שׁוֹפָר בְּכַוָּנָה עֲצוּמָה בְּלֵיל רִאשׁוֹן שֶׁל פֶּסַח, בִּמְקוֹם מִצְוַת אֲכִילַת כְּזַיִת מַצָּה, וְאוֹכֵל הַכְּזַיִת מַצָּה בְּרֹאשׁ הַשָּׁנָה, וּמִתְעַנֶּה בְּעֶרֶב יוֹם הַכִּפּוּרִים, וּבְיוֹם הַכִּפּוּרִים נוֹטֵל לוּלָב בִּמְקוֹם מִצְוַת עִנּוּי, וְאַיֵּה מָקוֹם לַתּוֹרָה.

וְאַף גַּם זֹאת, אִם לֹא יַכְשִׁילְךָ בְּהַעֲבָרַת הַזְּמַן, יַטֶּה לִבְּךָ לִפְנוּתָהּ וּלְטַהֲרָהּ, עַד שֶׁיְּבִיאֲךָ שֶׁלֹּא יְהֵא לְךָ פְּנַאי לְדַקְדֵּק שֶׁתְּהֵא עֲשִׂיַּת הַמִּצְוָה בְּאָפְנֶיהָ כְּדִין בְּכָל פְּרָטֶיהָ, וְלִיזָּהֵר מִלַּעֲבֹר עַל דִּינִים מְפֹרָשִׁים בַּתַּלְמוּד וְרַבּוֹתֵינוּ הַגְּדוֹלִים זִכְרוֹנָם לִבְרָכָה. וְאַל יַבְטִיחֲךָ יִצְרְךָ, שֶׁלֹּא יוּכַל לִהְיוֹת שֶׁמֵּרֹב עֵסֶק טָהֳרַת הַמַּחְשָׁבָה יִגְרֹם בִּטּוּל פְּרָטֵי הַמַּעֲשֶׂה, כִּי תֵּדַע, שֶׁכָּל זְמַן שֶׁלִּבְּךָ יְהֵא מָשׁוּךְ לְדַעְתּוֹ לֵאמֹר, שֶׁכָּל עִקַּר תּוֹרַת הָאָדָם הוּא, שֶׁכָּל מִצְוָה אוֹ לִמּוּד שֶׁאֵינָהּ נְקִיָּה מִכָּל סִיג וּפְסֹלֶת כְּסֹלֶת נְקִיָּה, הֲרֵי הִיא בְּבַל יֵרָאֶה וּבַל יִמָּצֵא, הֲרֵי הוּא מְשַׁחֶדְךָ בָּזֶה וּמְעַוֵּר עֵינֶיךָ, שֶׁלֹּא תּוּכַל לְהַשְׁגִּיחַ עַל כָּל הַפְּרָטֵי מַעֲשִׂים וַהֲלָכוֹת וְדִינִים, שֶׁתַּעֲבֹר עֲלֵיהֶם חַס וְשָׁלוֹם וְלֹא תַּרְגִּישׁ בָּהֶם כְּלָל:

פֶּרֶק ה'

וְהִנֵּה גָּלוּי וּמְבֹאָר, שֶׁזֹּאת הַדֶּרֶךְ, אֵשׁ הִיא, עַד אֲבַדּוֹן תֹּאכֵל חַס וְשָׁלוֹם, וְהוֹרֶסֶת כַּמָּה יְסוֹדוֹת הַתּוֹרָה הַקְּדוֹשָׁה וְדָרְשׁוּ רַבּוֹתֵינוּ זִכְרוֹנָם לִבְרָכָה, וּכְבָר הִזְכַּרְנוּ לְעֵיל סוֹף שַׁעַר א', שֶׁהָעִקָּר בְּכָל הַמִּצְוֹת הוּא חֵלֶק הַמַּעֲשֶׂה, וְטָהֳרַת הַמַּחְשָׁבָה אֵינָהּ אֶלָּא מִצְטָרֶפֶת לַמַּעֲשֶׂה, וּלְמִצְוָה וְלֹא לְעִכּוּבָא, עַיֵּן שָׁם. וְכֵן מְבֹאָר לְכָל מַשְׂכִּיל יָשָׁר הוֹלֵךְ, שֶׁהֲרֵי קַיְמָא לָן (זבחים ב:) בְּעִנְיַן הַקְרָבַת הַקָּרְבָּנוֹת דִּסְתָמָן כְּלִשְׁמָן דָּמֵי, וְכֵן אָמְרוּ לְהֶדְיָא (נזיר כ"ג) בְּאוֹכֵל אֶת הַפֶּסַח לְשֵׁם אֲכִילָה גַסָּה, נְהִי דְּלָא קָא עָבֵיד מִצְוָה מִן הַמֻּבְחָר, פֶּסַח מִיהוּ קָעָבֵיד. וְאִם יַחְשֹׁב הָאָדָם בְּעֵת חִיּוּב הַקְרָבַת הַפֶּסַח וְעֵת חִיּוּב אֲכִילָתוֹ, כַּוָּנוֹת נוֹרָאוֹת שֶׁל עִנְיַן הַפֶּסַח בְּמַחְשָׁבָה גָּבֹהַּ שֶׁבִּגְבוֹהוֹת וּטְהוֹרָה שֶׁבִּטְהוֹרוֹת, וְחָדַל מֵעֲשׂוֹת הַפֶּסַח, וְנִכְרְתָה הַנֶּפֶשׁ הַהִיא, וְכֵן הוּא בְּכָל הַמִּצְוֹת:

וְלֹא זוֹ בִּלְבַד שֶׁבְּמִצְוֹת מַעֲשִׂיּוֹת הָעִקָּר בָּהֶם הוּא חֵלֶק הַמַּעֲשִׂי, אֶלָּא שֶׁגַּם בְּמִצְוַת הַתְּפִלָּה שֶׁנִּקְרֵאת עֲבוֹדָה שֶׁבַּלֵּב, וּלְמָדוּהוּ זִכְרוֹנָם לִבְרָכָה בְּרֵישׁ פֶּרֶק קַמָּא דְּתַעֲנִית מִכָּתוּב "וּלְעָבְדוֹ בְּכָל לְבַבְכֶם" (דברים יא, יג) עִם כָּל זֶה, הָעִקָּר, שֶׁצָּרִיךְ הָאָדָם לַחְתֹּךְ בִּשְׂפָתָיו דַּוְקָא כָּל תֵּבָה מִמַּטְבֵּעַ הַתְּפִלָּה, כְּמוֹ שֶׁאָמְרוּ רַבּוֹתֵינוּ זִכְרוֹנָם לִבְרָכָה (ברכות לא) בְּרֵישׁ פֶּרֶק אֵין עוֹמְדִין, מִקְרָאֵי דְּחַנָּה, דִּכְתִיב בָּהּ (שמו"א א, יג) "רַק שְׂפָתֶיהָ נָּעוֹת", מִכָּאן לַמִּתְפַּלֵּל צָרִיךְ שֶׁיַּחְתֹּךְ בִּשְׂפָתָיו. וְכֵן אִיתָא בְּשׁוֹחֵר טוֹב שְׁמוּאֵל פֶּרֶק ב': "יָכוֹל יְהֵא מְהַרְהֵר בַּלֵּב תַּלְמוּד לוֹמַר רַק שְׂפָתֶיהָ נָעוֹת כּוּ' הָא כֵּיצַד מְרַחִישׁ בִּשְׂפָתָיו".

וּבָרוּר הוּא, דְּלָאו לְעִנְיַן לְכַתְּחִלָּה וּלְמִצְוָה בְּעָלְמָא הוּא דְּאַגְמְרוּהוּ, אֶלָּא גַּם לְעִכּוּבָא דִּיעֲבַד, שֶׁאִם הִרְהֵר תֵּבוֹת הַתְּפִלָּה בַּלֵּב לְבַד, לֹא יָצָא יְדֵי חוֹבַת תְּפִלָּה כְּלָל, וְאִם עֲדַיִן לֹא עָבַר הַזְּמַן, צָרִיךְ לְהִתְפַּלֵּל פַּעַם אַחֶרֶת בְּחִתּוּךְ שְׂפָתַיִם כָּל תֵּבָה, וְאִם עָבְרָה זְמַנָּהּ, צָרִיךְ לְהִתְפַּלֵּל שְׁתַּיִם תְּפִלָּה שֶׁאַחֲרֶיהָ, כְּדִין מִי שֶׁלֹּא הִתְפַּלֵּל כָּל עִקָּר, כְּמוֹ שֶׁהֵעִיר עַל זֶה הַמָּגֵן אַבְרָהָם בסי' ק"א ס"ק ב' בִּרְאָיוֹת נְכוֹנוֹת, שֶׁהֵמָּה כְּדַאי לְהַכְרִיעַ בְּצֶדֶק, דִּבְהִרְהוּר הַתְּפִלָּה לְבַד לֹא יָצָא יְדֵי חוֹבָה.

וְיָדוּעַ בַּזֹּהַר וְכִתְבֵי הָאֲרִיזַ"ל, שֶׁעִנְיַן הַתְּפִלָּה הוּא תִּקּוּן הָעוֹלָמוֹת, וְהִתְעַלּוּת פְּנִימִיּוּתָם, כָּל בְּחִינוֹת נֶפֶשׁ רוּחַ נְשָׁמָה שֶׁבָּהֶם, מִמַּטָּה לְמַעְלָה, וְהוּא עַל יְדֵי הִתְדַּבְּקוּת וְהִתְקַשְּׁרוּת נֶפֶשׁ הָאָדָם בְּרוּחוֹ וְרוּחוֹ בְּנִשְׁמָתוֹ, כְּמוֹ שֶׁהִתְבָּאֵר בע"ה לְעֵיל סוֹף שַׁעַר ב', עַיֵּן שָׁם, וְהֵם נִקְשָׁרִים עַל יְדֵי עֲקִימַת וּתְנוּעַת שְׂפָתָיו בְּחִתּוּךְ תֵּבוֹת הַתְּפִלָּה, שֶׁהוּא בְּחִינַת הַמַּעֲשֶׂה שֶׁבְּדִבּוּר, כְּמוֹ שֶׁאָמְרוּ רַבּוֹתֵינוּ זִכְרוֹנָם לִבְרָכָה (סנהדרין סה): "עֲקִימַת שְׂפָתָיו הָוֵי מַעֲשֶׂה". וּבְפֶרֶק כָּל כִּתְבֵי (שבת קיט, ב) אָמְרוּ: "מִנַּיִן שֶׁהַדִּבּוּר כְּמַעֲשֶׂה שֶׁנֶּאֱמַר" כו', וְהוּא בְּחִינַת הַנֶּפֶשׁ שֶׁבַּדִּבּוּר. וְהַהֶבֶל וְהַקּוֹל שֶׁהוּא הַדִּבּוּר עַצְמוֹ, הוּא בְּחִינַת רוּחַ שֶׁבּוֹ. וְכַוָּנַת הַלֵּב בְּהַתֵּבוֹת בְּעֵת אֲמִירָתָם, הוּא בְּחִינַת הַנְּשָׁמָה שֶׁבַּדִּבּוּר.

לְזֹאת, לֹא יָצָא יְדֵי חוֹבַת עִנְיַן הַתְּפִלָּה בְּמַחֲשָׁבָה וְהִרְהוּר הַתֵּבוֹת בַּלֵּב לְבַד, כִּי אֵיךְ אֶפְשָׁר לְהַגִּיעַ לְהִתְקַשֵּׁר בִּבְחִינַת הַנְּשָׁמָה, אִם לֹא יֵלֵךְ בְּסֵדֶר הַמַּדְרֵגוֹת מִמַּטָּה לְמַעְלָה, שֶׁיִּתְקַשֵּׁר הַנֶּפֶשׁ שֶׁל הַדִּבּוּר שֶׁהוּא תְּנוּעַת הַשְּׂפָתַיִם, בָּרוּחַ שֶׁל הַדִּבּוּר שֶׁהוּא הַהֶבֶל וְהַקּוֹל, וְאַחַר כָּךְ יִתְקַשְּׁרוּ גַּם שְׁנֵיהֶם בַּנְּשָׁמָה, שֶׁהוּא הַמַּחֲשָׁבָה וְהַכַּוָּנָה שֶׁבַּלֵּב. וּכְשֶׁהִתְפַּלֵּל רַק בְּמַחֲשָׁבָה לְבַד, לֹא הוֹעִילָה תְּפִלָּתוֹ וְלֹא תִּקֵּן כְּלוּם. אָמְנָם כְּשֶׁהִתְפַּלֵּל בְּקוֹל וְחִתּוּךְ אוֹתִיּוֹת הַדִּבּוּר לְבַד, אַף עַל פִּי שֶׁלֹּא צֵרֵף הַמַּחֲשָׁבָה וְכַוָּנַת הַלֵּב אֵלֶיהָ, הֲגַם שֶׁוַּדַּאי אֵינָהּ בְּמַדְרֵגָה שְׁלֵמָה וּגְבוֹהָה כָּרָאוּי, וְאֵינָהּ יְכוֹלָה לַעֲלוֹת לְעוֹלַם הַמַּחֲשָׁבָה עוֹלַם הַנְּשָׁמָה, כֵּיוָן שֶׁחָסֵר מִמֶּנָּה בְּחִינַת מַחְשֶׁבֶת הָאָדָם, עִם כָּל זֶה אֵינָהּ לָרִיק חַס וְשָׁלוֹם, וְיוֹצֵא בָּהּ יְדֵי חוֹבָתוֹ, כִּי עַל כָּל פָּנִים הֲרֵי הֶעֱלָה וְקִשֵּׁר נַפְשׁוֹ בְּרוּחוֹ, וְעוֹלַם הַנֶּפֶשׁ בְּעוֹלַם הָרוּחַ.

וְעַיֵּן בַּזֹּהַר פְּקוּדֵי רס"ב ע"ב דְּאִצְטְרִיךְ צְלוֹתָא מִגּוֹ מַחֲשָׁבָה וּרְעוּתָא דְּלִבָּא, וְקָלָא, וּמִלָּה דְּשִׂפְוָן, לְמֶעְבַּד שְׁלִימוּ וְקִשּׁוּרָא וְיִחוּדָא לְעֵלָּא כְּגַוְנָא דְּאִיהוּ לְעֵלָּא כו', לְקַשְּׁרָא קִשְׁרָא כְּדְקָא יָאוּת כו', מַחֲשָׁבָה וּרְעוּתָא קָלָא וּמִלָּה אִלֵּין ד' מְקַשְּׁרִין קִשְׁרִין, לְבָתַר דְּקְשִׁירוּ קִשְׁרִין כֻּלָּא כַּחֲדָא, אִתְעֲבִידוּ כֻּלְּהוּ רְתִיכָא חֲדָא, לְאַשְׁרָאָה עֲלַיְהוּ שְׁכִינְתָּא כו', קָלָא דְּאִשְׁתְּמַע, סָלִיק לְקַשְּׁרָא קִשְׁרִין מִתַּתָּא לְעֵלָּא כו', [שֶׁצְּרִיכִים תְּפִלָּה מִתּוֹךְ מַחֲשָׁבָה וּרְצוֹן הַלֵּב וְקוֹל וּדְבַר שְׂפָתַיִם, לַעֲשׂוֹת שְׁלֵמוּת וְקֶשֶׁר וְיִחוּד לְמַעְלָה כְּמוֹ שֶׁהוּא לְמַעְלָה וכו' לִקְשֹׁר הַקֶּשֶׁר כָּרָאוּי וכו' מַחֲשָׁבָה רָצוֹן קוֹל וְדִבּוּר הֵם אַרְבָּעָה הַמְקַשְּׁרִים קְשָׁרִים, וְאַחַר שֶׁקָּשְׁרוּ כֻּלָּם יַחַד קְשָׁרִים נַעֲשׂוּ כֻּלָּם מֶרְכָּבָה אַחַת לִשְׁרוֹת עֲלֵיהֶם הַשְּׁכִינָה וכו' וְהַקּוֹל הַנִּשְׁמָע עוֹלֶה לִקְשֹׁר קְשָׁרִים מִמַּטָּה לְמַעְלָה וכו'] עַיֵּן שָׁם הֵיטֵב.

וּבְפָרָשַׁת בַּמִּדְבָּר ק"כ ע"ב, אָמְרוּ דֶּרֶךְ כְּלָל דְּעִקָּרָא דִּצְלוֹתָא תַּלְיָא בְּעוּבְדָא

בְּקַדְמִיתָא, וּלְבָתַר בְּמִלּוּלָא דְּפוּמָא דַּוְקָא, [עִקַּר הַתְּפִלָּה תְּלוּיָה בַּתְּחִלָּה בְּמַעֲשֶׂה וְאַחַר כַּךְ בְּדִבּוּר הַפֶּה דַּוְקָא] עַיֵּן שָׁם סִדְרָן.

וּבְאִדְּרָא זוּטָא רצ"ד ב', כָּל מַה דְּחָשִׁיב בַּר נָשׁ, וְכָל מַה דְּיִסְתַּכַּל בְּלִבֵּיהּ, לָא עָבִיד מִלָּה עַד דְּאַפִּיק לֵיהּ בְּשִׂפְוָתֵיהּ כוּ', וּבְגִין כָּךְ כָּל צְלוֹתָא וּבָעוּתָא כוּ', בָּעֵי לְאַפָּקָא מִלִּין בְּשִׂפְוָתֵיהּ, דְּאִי לָא אַפִּיק לוֹן, לָאו צְלוֹתֵיהּ צְלוֹתָא וְלָאו בָּעוּתֵיהּ בָּעוּתָא. וְכֵיוָן דְּמִלִּין נָפְקִין מִתְבַּקְעִין בַּאֲוִירָא וְסַלְקִין כוּ', וְנָטִיל לוֹן מַאן דְּנָטִיל וְאָחִיד לוֹן לְכִתְרָא קַדִּישָׁא כוּ'. [כָּל מַה שֶּׁחוֹשֵׁב הָאָדָם וְכָל מַה שֶּׁיִּסְתַּכֵּל בְּלִבּוֹ אֵינוֹ עוֹשֶׂה דָּבָר עַד שֶׁמּוֹצִיא בִּשְׂפָתָיו וכו' וּמִשּׁוּם זֶה כָּל תְּפִלָּה וּבַקָּשָׁה וכו' צָרִיךְ לְהוֹצִיא הַמִּלִּים בִּשְׂפָתָיו. שֶׁאִם אֵינוֹ מוֹצִיא אוֹתָן אֵין תְּפִלָּתוֹ תְּפִלָּה וְאֵין בַּקָּשָׁתוֹ בַּקָּשָׁה, וְכֵיוָן שֶׁהַמִּלִּים יוֹצְאוֹת מִתְבַּקְּעוֹת בָּאֲוִיר וְעוֹלוֹת וכו' וְלוֹקֵחַ אוֹתָן מִי שֶׁלּוֹקֵחַ וּמְאַחֵד אוֹתָן לַכֶּתֶר הַקָּדוֹשׁ.]

וְדֶרֶךְ כְּלָל אָמְרוּ בַּזֹּהַר אֱמוֹר ק"ה א', מַאן דְּאָמַר דְּלָא בָּעְיָא עוּבְדָא בְּכוֹלָא, אוֹ מִלֵּי לְאַפָּקָא לוֹן וּלְמֶעֱבַד קָלָא בְּהוּ, תִּפַּח רוּחֵיהּ [מִי שֶׁאוֹמֵר שֶׁאֵין צְרִיכִים מַעֲשֶׂה בַּכֹּל אוֹ מִלִּים לְהוֹצִיאָם וְלַעֲשׂוֹת קוֹל, תִּפַּח רוּחוֹ] רַחֲמָנָא לִיצְלַן. וְלֹא הִצְרִיכוּ רַבּוֹתֵינוּ זִכְרוֹנָם לִבְרָכָה עִנְיַן הַכַּוָּנָה לְעִכּוּבָא אֶלָּא בְּבִרְכַּת אָבוֹת לְבַד.

וּבְפָרָשַׁת וַיְחִי רמ"ג סוֹף ע"ב, מַאן דְּלִבֵּיהּ טָרִיד וּבָעֵי לְצַלָּאָה צְלוֹתֵיהּ, וְאִיהוּ בְּעָקוּ וְלָא יָכִיל לְסַדְּרָא שִׁבְחָא דְּמָארֵיהּ כִּדְקָא יָאוּת מַאי הוּא, אָמַר לֵיהּ אַף עַל גַּב דְּלָא יָכִיל לְכַוָּנָא לִבָּא וּרְעוּתָא, סִדּוּרָא וְשִׁבְחָא דְּמָארֵיהּ אַמַּאי גָּרַע, אֶלָּא יְסַדֵּר שִׁבְחָא דְמָארֵיהּ אַף עַל גַּב דְּלָא יָכִיל לְכַוָּנָא [מִי שֶׁלִּבּוֹ טָרוּד וְרוֹצֶה לְהִתְפַּלֵּל תְּפִלָּתוֹ אוֹ שֶׁהוּא בְּצָרָה וְאֵינוֹ יָכוֹל לְסַדֵּר שִׁבְחוֹ שֶׁל אֲדוֹנוֹ כְּמוֹ שֶׁצָּרִיךְ מַה הוּא, אָמַר לוֹ אַף עַל פִּי שֶׁאֵינוֹ יָכוֹל לְכַוֵּן אֶת הַלֵּב וְהָרָצוֹן, סֵדֶר שִׁבְחוֹ שֶׁל רִבּוֹנוֹ לָמָּה יִגְרַע, אֶלָּא סִידּוּר שִׁבְחוֹ שֶׁל רִבּוֹנוֹ אַף עַל פִּי שֶׁאֵינוֹ יָכוֹל לְכַוֵּן] כוּ':

פֶּרֶק ו'

וְהַגַּם שֶׁוַּדַּאי שֶׁמַּחְשֶׁבֶת הָאָדָם הִיא הָעוֹלָה לְמַעְלָה רֹאשׁ בִּשְׁמֵי רוּם בָּעוֹלָמוֹת הָעֶלְיוֹנִים, וְאִם יְצָרֵף הָאָדָם גַּם טֹהַר הַמַּחְשָׁבָה וְהַכַּוָּנָה בְּעֵת עֲשִׂיַּת הַמִּצְוֹת, יַגִּיעוּ מַעֲשָׂיו לִפְעֹל תִּקּוּנִים יוֹתֵר גְּדוֹלִים בָּעוֹלָמוֹת הַיּוֹתֵר עֶלְיוֹנִים, אָמְנָם לֹא הַמַּחְשָׁבָה הִיא הָעִקָּר אֶצְלֵנוּ, כְּמוֹ שֶׁנִּתְבָּאֵר.

וְעַיֵּן בַּזֹּהַר יִתְרוֹ צ"ג רֵישׁ ע"ב, וְאִי אִזְדַּמַּן לֵיהּ עוּבְדָא וִיכַוֵּין בֵּיהּ, זַכָּאָה אִיהוּ. וְאַף עַל גַּב דְּלָא מְכַוֵּין בֵּיהּ, זַכָּאָה אִיהוּ, דְּעָבִיד פִּקּוּדָא דְּמָארֵיהּ, אֲבָל לָא אִתְחֲשַׁב מַאן דְּעָבִיד רְעוּתָא לִשְׁמָהּ וִיכַוֵּין בָּהּ בִּרְעוּתָא כוּ', כְּמַאן דְּלָא יָדַע כוּ', דְּהָא בִּרְעוּתָא תַּלְיָא כוּ', וַאֲפִלּוּ הָכִי, אִי לָאו תַּמָּן רְעוּתָא דְּלִבָּא כוּ', עַל דָּא צַלֵּי דָּוִד וְאָמַר "וּמַעֲשֵׂה יָדֵינוּ כּוֹנְנָה עָלֵינוּ" כוּ', מַאי "כּוֹנְנָה עָלֵינוּ", "כּוֹנְנָה" וְאַתְקִין תִּקּוּנִין לְעֵלָּא כִּדְקָא יָאוּת, "עָלֵינוּ", אַף עַל גַּב דְּלֵית אֲנַן יַדְעִין לְשַׁוָּאָה רְעוּתָא, אֶלָּא עוּבְדָא בִּלְחוֹדוֹי, "מַעֲשֵׂה יָדֵינוּ כּוֹנְנֵהוּ", לְמַאן, לְהַהוּא דַּרְגָּא דְּאִצְטְרִיךְ לְאַתְקְנָא כוּ', [וְאִם יִזְדַּמֵּן לוֹ מַעֲשֶׂה וּמְכַוֵּן בָּהּ, זַכַּאי הוּא, וְאַף עַל פִּי

שֶׁאֵינוֹ מְכַוֵּן בָּהּ זַכַּאי הוּא (כֵּיוָן) שֶׁעוֹשֶׂה מִצְוַת רִבּוֹנוֹ אֲבָל אֵינוֹ נֶחְשָׁב לוֹ כְּמִי שֶׁעוֹשֶׂה רְצוֹנוֹ לִשְׁמָהּ וּמְכַוֵּן בָּהּ בִּרְצוֹן כו׳ כְּמִי שֶׁאֵינוֹ יוֹדֵעַ וכו׳ כִּי בָּרָצוֹן תָּלוּי וכו׳ וְעִם זֶה אִם אֵין שָׁם רְצוֹן הַלֵּב וכו׳ עַל זֶה הִתְפַּלֵּל דָּוִד וְאָמַר "וּמַעֲשֵׂה יָדֵינוּ כּוֹנְנָה עָלֵינוּ" וכו׳ מַהוּ "כּוֹנְנָה" עָלֵינוּ, "כּוֹנְנָה" וְהַתְקֵן תִּקּוּנִים לְמַעְלָה כָּרָאוּי, עָלֵינוּ, אַף עַל פִּי שֶׁאֵין אָנוּ יוֹדְעִים לָשִׂים הָרָצוֹן אֶלָּא מַעֲשֶׂה בִּלְבַד, מַעֲשֵׂה יָדֵינוּ כּוֹנְנֵהוּ, לְמִי, לַמַּדְרֵגָה הַהוּא שֶׁצְּרִיכִים לְתַקְּנָהּ וכו׳]. עַיֵּן שָׁם.

וְכֵן בְּעִנְיַן שֶׁנִּתְבָּאֵר לְמַעְלָה בְּשַׁעַר ג׳ (פ״ח) בְּעִנְיַן הַתְּפִלָּה, לְכַוֵּן אוֹתָהּ לִמְקוֹמוֹ שֶׁל עוֹלָם יִתְבָּרַךְ שְׁמוֹ, כְּפִי שֶׁנִּתְבָּאֵר שָׁם עִנְיַן "מְקוֹמוֹ שֶׁל עוֹלָם", עַיֵּן שָׁם. וְכֵן עִנְיַן כַּוָּנַת "אֶחָד" דְּפָסוּק רִאשׁוֹן דִּקְרִיאַת שְׁמַע שֶׁנִּתְבָּאֵר שָׁם בְּפֶרֶק י״א, עַיֵּן שָׁם הֵיטֵב, הַכֹּל הוּא רַק לְמִצְוָה וְלֹא לְעִכּוּבָא. שֶׁגַּם מִי שֶׁלֹּא יָדַע בָּזֶה כְּלָל, כִּי לֹא הֻרְגַּל בָּזֶה, אוֹ שֶׁמּוֹחֵיהּ לָא סָבִיל דָּא, שֶׁלֹּא יָרַד לְעָמְקוֹ, אוֹ שֶׁיָּרֵא לְנַפְשׁוֹ שֶׁלֹּא יִסְתַּכֵּן חַס וְשָׁלוֹם בַּהֲרִיסַת כַּמָּה יְסוֹדֵי הַתּוֹרָה, שֶׁיָּכוֹל לָבֹא מִזֶּה חַס וְשָׁלוֹם לְמִי שֶׁאֵין דַּעְתּוֹ יָפָה בָּזֶה כָּרָאוּי, כְּמוֹ שֶׁכָּתוּב שָׁם, עַיֵּן שָׁם, אֶלָּא שֶׁהוּא עוֹבֵד אוֹתוֹ יִתְבָּרַךְ, וּמְקַיֵּם כְּכָל הַכָּתוּב בְּתוֹרַת ה׳ שֶׁבִּכְתָב וּבְעַל פֶּה וְרַבּוֹתֵינוּ הַגְּדוֹלִים, וּמַאֲמִין וּמְכַוֵּן דֶּרֶךְ כְּלָל בְּפָסוּק רִאשׁוֹן דִּקְרִיאַת שְׁמַע, שֶׁהוּא יִתְבָּרַךְ הוּא אֶחָד, גַּם שֶׁאֵינוֹ יוֹדֵעַ עִנְיַן אַחְדּוּתוֹ יִתְבָּרַךְ, וּמְכַוֵּן תְּפִלָּתוֹ דֶּרֶךְ כְּלָל לוֹ יִתְבָּרַךְ בְּלֹא חֲקִירָה, גַּם כֵּן נִקְרָא "עוֹבֵד ה׳" (כְּעִנְיַן מ״ש בְּפַרְדֵּס שַׁעַר א׳ פֶּרֶק ט׳ בְּעִנְיַן הָאֱמוּנָה בִּמְצִיאוּת הַסְּפִירוֹת, עַיֵּן שָׁם), כִּי אֵין כָּל הַדְּבָרִים הָאֵלּוּ אֲמוּרִים אֶלָּא לְמִי שֶׁדַּעְתּוֹ יָפָה, וְכָל שֶׁכֵּן לְיִרְאֵי ה׳ וְחוֹשְׁבֵי שְׁמוֹ, אֲשֶׁר לָהֶם כֹּחַ לַעֲמֹד בָּזֶה:

לָזֹאת, חָלִילָה וְחָלִילָה לָנוּ לִדְחוֹת שׁוּם פְּרָט מִפְּרָטֵי הַמַּעֲשֶׂה, אַף דִּקְדּוּק אֶחָד מִדִּבְרֵי סוֹפְרִים, וְכָל שֶׁכֵּן לְשַׁנּוֹת זְמַנָּהּ חַס וְשָׁלוֹם, בִּשְׁבִיל מְנִיעַת טָהֳרַת הַמַּחְשָׁבָה, וְכָל הַמַּרְבֶּה לְדַקְדֵּק בְּמַעֲשָׂיו הֲרֵי זֶה מְשֻׁבָּח:

פֶּרֶק ז׳

עוֹד זֹאת יוּכַל יִצְרְךָ לְהִתְחַפֵּשׂ, בֶּאֱמוֹר לְךָ שֶׁכָּל עִקַּר הָעֲבוֹדָה הוּא שֶׁיִּהְיֶה רַק לְשֵׁם שָׁמַיִם, וְגַם עָוֹן וְחֵטְא לְמִצְוָה יֵחָשֵׁב אִם הוּא לְשֵׁם שָׁמַיִם לְתִקּוּן אֵיזֶה עִנְיָן, "וְרַחֲמָנָא לִבָּא בָּעֵי" (סנהדרין קו:), וּ"גְדוֹלָה עֲבֵרָה לִשְׁמָהּ" (נזיר כג: הוריות י:), וְכָהֵנָּה רַבּוֹת רְאָיוֹת.

גַּם יֵרָאֶה לְךָ פָּנִים לֵאמֹר, כִּי כֵן צֻוֵּיתָ, לֵילֵךְ בְּעִקְּבֵי אֲבוֹתֶיךָ הַקְּדוֹשִׁים וְכָל הַצַּדִּיקִים הָרִאשׁוֹנִים שֶׁהָיוּ קֹדֶם שֶׁנִּתְּנָה הַתּוֹרָה, שֶׁעִיקַּר דֶּרֶךְ עֲבוֹדָתָם לוֹ יִתְבָּרַךְ הָיְתָה, שֶׁכָּל מַעֲשֵׂיהֶם וְדִבּוּרָם וּמַחְשְׁבוֹתָם וְכָל עִנְיְנֵיהֶם בָּעוֹלָם הָיָה הַכֹּל בִּדְבֵקוּת וְטָהֳרַת מַחְשַׁבְתָּם לְשֵׁם שָׁמַיִם, וּפָנוּ לְמַעְלָה לְתִקּוּן וְהַעֲלָאַת וְיִחוּד הָעוֹלָמוֹת וְכֹחוֹת הָעֶלְיוֹנִים, בְּאֵיזֶה מַעֲשֶׂה שֶׁתִּהְיֶה וּבְאֵיזֶה אֹפֶן וּבְאֵיזֶה זְמַן שֶׁיִּהְיֶה, וְלֹא בְּמַעֲשִׂים וּמִצְוֹת קְבוּעִים וּסְדוּרִים שֶׁיִּהְיוּ חֹק וְלֹא יַעֲבֹר, כְּמוֹ יַעֲקֹב אָבִינוּ עָלָיו הַשָּׁלוֹם בְּעִנְיַן צֹאן לָבָן וְהַמַּקְלוֹת, וְכֵן אָמַר הַמַּגִּיד לְהַבֵּית יוֹסֵף בְּעִנְיַן חֲנוֹךְ שֶׁהָיָה תּוֹפֵר מִנְעָלִים וּבְכָל זִמְנָא דְּמָעֵיל מַחְטָא בְּסַנְדְּלָא הֲוָה מְשַׁבַּח לְקוּדְשָׁא בְּרִיךְ הוּא, עַיֵּן מַגִּיד מֵישָׁרִים פָּרָשַׁת מִקֵּץ.

וְאַף שֶׁאָמְרוּ רַבּוֹתֵינוּ זִכְרוֹנָם לִבְרָכָה "הָאָבוֹת קִיְּמוּ כָּל הַתּוֹרָה", וְכֵן אָמְרוּ בְּוַיִּקְרָא רַבָּה פ"ב: "מְלַמֵּד שֶׁלָּמַד נֹחַ תּוֹרָה", לֹא שֶׁהָיוּ מְצֻוִּים וְעוֹשִׂים וְהָיָה לָהֶם הַהֲלָכָה וְהַדִּין כָּךְ, אֶלָּא כְּמוֹ שֶׁכָּתַבְתִּי לְעֵיל סוֹף שַׁעַר א' (פֶּרֶק כ"א), שֶׁהֵמָּה קִיְּמוּ אֶת הַתּוֹרָה מֵחֲמַת שֶׁהִשִּׂיגוּ בְּנִפְלְאוֹת הַשָּׂגָתָם תִּקּוּנֵי הָעוֹלָמוֹת, וְסִדְרֵי הַכֹּחוֹת הָעֶלְיוֹנִים אֲשֶׁר יְתֻקְּנוּ בְּכָל מִצְוָה וּמִצְוָה, אֲבָל הָיָה גַּם כֵּן הָרְשׁוּת נְתוּנָה לָהֶם לְעָבְדוֹ גַּם בְּמַעֲשִׂים וְעִנְיָנִים אֲחֵרִים, לְבַד הַמִּצְוֹת, וְאַף גַּם לַעֲבֹר עַל אֵיזֶה מִצְוָה שֶׁלֹּא כַּתּוֹרָה, כְּפִי שֶׁרָאוּ וְהִשִּׂיגוּ, שֶׁזֶּה הָעִנְיָן וְהַמַּעֲשֶׂה הַפְּרָטִית הוּא נִצְרָךְ אָז לְתִקּוּן הָעוֹלָמוֹת. (וְעַיֵּן מִזֶּה בְּסוֹף סֵפֶר הָאֱמוּנוֹת לְרַבִּי שֵׁם טוֹב, וְכֵן הֵבִיא שָׁם כֵּן בְּשֵׁם רַבֵּינוּ חוּשִׁיאֵל גָּאוֹן זִכְרוֹנוֹ לִבְרָכָה, רַק שֶׁקִּצֵּר מְאֹד בָּעִנְיָן, כְּדַרְכָּם בַּקֹּדֶשׁ שֶׁל כָּל הָרִאשׁוֹנִים זִכְרוֹנָם לִבְרָכָה, שֶׁהֶעְלִימוּ וְהִסְתִּירוּ מְאֹד כָּל הָעִנְיָנִים).

וְאַתָּה תֶּחֱזֶה אִם עֵינֵי שֵׂכֶל לְךָ, שֶׁאֵין כָּאן לֹא רְאָיָה וְלֹא סֶמֶךְ כְּלָל, אַף לֹא מִשְׁעֶנֶת קָנֶה רָצוּץ, כִּי הָאֱמֶת הַבָּרוּר כְּמוֹ שֶׁנִּתְבָּאֵר לְעֵיל סוֹף שַׁעַר א'. שֶׁהָעֲבוֹדָה עַל זֶה הַדֶּרֶךְ לֹא הָיְתָה נוֹהֶגֶת אֶלָּא קֹדֶם מַתַּן תּוֹרָה לְבַד, אֲבָל מֵעֵת שֶׁבָּא מֹשֶׁה וְהוֹרִידָהּ לָאָרֶץ — לֹא בַשָּׁמַיִם הִיא. וְהוֹכַחְנוּ שָׁם בְּעֶזְרַת הַשֵּׁם מֵעִנְיַן חִזְקִיָּהוּ עִם יְשַׁעְיָהוּ, שֶׁאָסוּר לָנוּ לְשַׁנּוֹת חַס וְשָׁלוֹם מִשּׁוּם אַחַת מֵהֵנָּה מִמִּצְוֹת ה', אַף אִם תִּהְיֶה הַכַּוָּנָה לְשֵׁם שָׁמַיִם, וְאַף אִם יַשִּׂיג הָאָדָם שֶׁאִם יְקַיֵּם מִצְוָתוֹ הַמֻּטֶּלֶת עָלָיו, יוּכַל לְמֵיפַק מִנֵּיהּ חוּרְבָּא בְּאֵיזֶה עִנְיָן, וְאַף גַּם בְּשֵׁב וְאַל תַּעֲשֶׂה, עִם כָּל זֶה אֵין הַדָּבָר מָסוּר בְּיַד הָאָדָם לְהִמָּנַע מִמֶּנָּה חַס וְשָׁלוֹם, כִּי טַעֲמֵי מִצְוֹת לֹא נִתְגַּלּוּ, וְעַיֵּן שָׁם בְּאֹרֶךְ:

פֶּרֶק ח'

עוֹד אַחַת יוּכַל לְפַתּוֹתְךָ בַּחֲבִילוֹת רְאָיוֹת, שֶׁתַּכְלִית עֲבוֹדַת הָאָדָם הוּא רַק לְהַשִּׂיג יִרְאַת הָרוֹמְמוּת, וְרַק עַל זֶה יִהְיוּ עֵינָיו וְלִבּוֹ כָּל הַיָּמִים, וְשֶׁיִּרְאַת הָעֹנֶשׁ וּבוּשָׁה מִבְּנֵי אָדָם, הִיא מִדָּה גְּרוּעָה שֶׁבִּגְרוּעוֹת, וְהָרָאוּי לְשָׁרֵשׁ אוֹתָהּ מִלִּבְּךָ, וְיַנִּיחַ לְךָ יִצְרְךָ לְהוֹסִיף יִרְאָה עַל יִרְאָה בְּיִרְאַת הָרוֹמְמוּת, עַד שֶׁיִּקְבַּע בְּלִבְּךָ שֶׁיִּרְאַת הָעֹנֶשׁ וְהַבּוּשָׁה מִבְּנֵי אָדָם — הִיא עֲבֵרָה, וְתִהְיֶה בּוֹרֵחַ מִמֶּנָּה כְּבוֹרֵחַ מִן הָעֲבֵרָה, עַד שֶׁיּוּכַל לִהְיוֹת שֶׁתִּלָּכֵד בְּרִשְׁתּוֹ שֶׁלֹּא לְאַפְרוּשֵׁי מֵאִיסוּרָא, בִּזְמַן שֶׁאֵין לְךָ יִרְאַת הָרוֹמְמוּת כָּרָאוּי.

וְיָקֵל לְךָ כָּל דָּבָר, בַּאֲשֶׁר יַרְאֶה לְךָ פָּנִים מִפָּנִים שׁוֹנִים בָּזֶה. וְיוּכַל לְהִוָּלֵד מִזֶּה, שֶׁאִם יוֹכִיחֲךָ אָדָם, וְיֵרָאֶה לְךָ שֶׁאַתָּה עוֹבֵר עַל אֵיזֶה דִּין, יַשִּׁיאֲךָ לִבְּךָ שֶׁלֹּא לְאַפְרוּשֵׁי מִזֶּה כָּל זְמַן שֶׁיִּרְאַת הַמּוֹכִיחַ עַל פָּנֶיךָ, בְּאָמְרְךָ, שֶׁרַק אֵין יִרְאַת אֱלֹהִים בָּזֶה רַק יִרְאַת אָדָם, וְיִרְאָה חִיצוֹנִית.

וּכְבָר הוֹרוּנוּ חֲכָמֵינוּ זִכְרוֹנָם לִבְרָכָה בְּבִרְכַּת רַבִּי יוֹחָנָן בֶּן זַכַּאי לְתַלְמִידָיו (ברכות כח): "שֶׁתְּהֵא מוֹרָא שָׁמַיִם עֲלֵיכֶם כְּמוֹרָא בָּשָׂר וָדָם" וכו'. וּמִי לָנוּ גָּדוֹל וְחָסִיד מֵרַב עַמְרָם חֲסִידָא, וְעִם כָּל זֶה כְּשֶׁנִּזְדַּמֵּן לְיָדוֹ פַּעַם אַחַת דְּבַר עֲבֵרָה פִּתְאֹם רַחֲמָנָא לִיצְלָן, כַּמּוּבָא שִׁלְהֵי קִדּוּשִׁין (פא ע"א), נִלְחַם בְּתַחְבּוּלוֹת לְהִנָּצֵל מֵרֶשֶׁת יִצְרוֹ אַף מֵחֲמַת הַבּוּשָׁה מֵהַבְּרִיּוֹת, רַק שֶׁלֹּא לַעֲבֹר חַס וְשָׁלוֹם עַל מִצְוַת בּוֹרְאוֹ יִתְבָּרֵךְ שְׁמוֹ. וְנִרְאֶה הֲגַם שֶׁהַקָּדוֹשׁ

בָּרוּךְ הוּא חָס עַל כְּבוֹדָן שֶׁל צַדִּיקִים, עִם כָּל זֶה קְבָעוּהָ לְהַאי עוּבְדָא בַּתַּלְמוּד, לְהוֹרוֹת לָנוּ דַּרְכֵי ה' הַיְשָׁרִים:

וְעַתָּה הֶרְאֵיתִיךָ קְצוֹת דַּרְכֵי הַיֵּצֶר הַמִּתְחַפֵּשׂ בְּכָל מִינֵי תַּחְבּוּלוֹת, כְּמוֹ שֶׁאָמְרוּ רַבּוֹתֵינוּ זִכְרוֹנָם לִבְרָכָה (קדושין ל:): "אָמַר רַבִּי יִצְחָק יִצְרוֹ שֶׁל אָדָם מִתְחַדֵּשׁ עָלָיו בְּכָל יוֹם, שֶׁנֶּאֱמַר (בראשית ו, ה) "רַק רַע כָּל הַיּוֹם". שֶׁלֹּא דַּי לוֹ שֶׁמִּתְגַּבֵּר בְּתַחְבּוּלוֹתָיו שֶׁהִתְנַכֵּל עַל הָאָדָם מִתְּמוֹל שִׁלְשׁוֹם, אֶלָּא שֶׁעוֹד מִתְחַדֵּשׁ כָּל יוֹם בַּחֲדָשׁוֹת, וּכְאִלּוּ אֵינוֹ מְסִיתוֹ לְרַע כְּלָל, וְאַדְּרַבָּה, מַרְאֶה לָאָדָם שֶׁכָּל מַה שֶּׁלָּמַד תּוֹרָה אוֹ פָּעַל מִצְוֹת, עֲדַיִן לֹא הָיָה בָּהֶם שׁוּם טוֹב, וְהוּא רַק רַע כָּל הַיּוֹם. וּבָזֶה הוּא מִתְגַּבֵּר עַל הָאָדָם, כְּמוֹ שֶׁאָמְרוּ זִכְרוֹנָם לִבְרָכָה (סוכה נב, ב) עַל פָּסוּק "צוֹפֶה רָשָׁע לַצַּדִּיק וּמְבַקֵּשׁ לַהֲמִיתוֹ" וכו' (תהלים לז, לב) וְהוּא הַיֵּצֶר הָרַע, הוּא הַמַּלְאָךְ הַמָּוֶת מָלֵא עֵינַיִם, וְצוֹפֶה לִרְאוֹת הַנּוֹלָד בַּמֶּה לְהַכְשִׁיל (כִּי עִנְיַן "צְפִיָּה" הוּא עַל דָּבָר שֶׁעָתִיד לִהְיוֹת אַחַר כָּךְ), עַד אֲשֶׁר הָאָדָם לֹא יֵדַע לְהִזָּהֵר עוֹד:

וְאַתָּה הַקּוֹרֵא, אַל תְּדַמֶּה שֶׁמִּלִּבִּי הוֹצֵאתִי הַדְּבָרִים, כִּי אֶת כָּל זֹאת בָּחַנְתִּי וְנִסִּיתִי, כַּאֲשֶׁר נָתַתִּי לִבִּי לִדְרֹשׁ וְלָתוּר, וְעֵינַי רָאוּ רַבִּים אֲשֶׁר יַחְפְּצוּ קִרְבַת אֱלֹקִים, וְנִכְשָׁלִים בְּמוֹ אֵלֶּה הַדְּבָרִים הַנַּ"ל, אֲשֶׁר מִפִּיהֶם אֵלַי נֶאֶמְרוּ מִלִּבָּם. וּבְעֵינַי רָאִיתִי בְּמָקוֹם אֶחָד אֵיזֶה אֲנָשִׁים, שֶׁהֻרְגְּלוּ בָּזֶה זְמַן כַּבִּיר עַד שֶׁכִּמְעַט נִשְׁכַּח מֵהֶם זְמַן תְּפִלַּת הַמִּנְחָה שֶׁקָּבְעוּ לָנוּ רַבּוֹתֵינוּ זִכְרוֹנָם לִבְרָכָה. וְאַדְּרַבָּה, נִקְבַּע בְּלִבָּם מֵרֹב הַהֶרְגֵּל, כְּמוֹ דִּין וַהֲלָכָה, שֶׁתְּפִלַּת הַמִּנְחָה, עִקָּרָהּ אַחַר צֵאת הַכּוֹכָבִים. וּכְשֶׁאָדָם אוֹמֵר לַחֲבֵרוֹ נִתְפַּלֵּל תְּפִלַּת מִנְחָה, הוּא מְשִׁיבוֹ, נִרְאֶה וְנִעַיֵּן אִם כְּבָר נִרְאוּ הַכּוֹכָבִים בָּרָקִיעַ, וה' יִסְלַח לָהֶם, וִיכַפֵּר לְשׁוֹגֵג וּפֶתִי:

אֲבָל לִבְּךָ תָּשִׁית לָדַעַת חֲכָמִים בַּעֲלֵי תּוֹרָה, אֲשֶׁר כְּבָר הוֹרוּנוּ חז"ל, שֶׁהָעִקָּר הוּא עֲשִׂיַּת הַמִּצְוָה בִּזְמַנָּהּ בְּכָל פְּרָטֶיהָ וְדִקְדּוּקֶיהָ חֹק וְלֹא יַעֲבֹר, וְטָהֳרַת הַמַּחֲשָׁבָה טוֹבָה תִּצְטָרֵף לְמַעֲשֶׂה, אָז תֵּלֵךְ לָבֶטַח, וְזֶה וָזֶה יִתְקַיְּמוּ בְּיָדֶיךָ. וּמִשְׁנָה מְפֹרֶשֶׁת שָׁנוּ (אבות ג, יא) כָּל שֶׁמַּעֲשָׂיו מְרֻבִּים מֵחָכְמָתוֹ, אַף גַּם חָכְמָתוֹ מִתְקַיֶּמֶת בִּקְדֻשָּׁה וְטָהֳרָה וּדְבֵקוּת. וּמִי זוּטַר הוּא מַה שֶּׁהִמְשִׁילוּ חֲכָמֵינוּ זִכְרוֹנָם לִבְרָכָה (שם, כב) כָּל שֶׁמַּעֲשָׂיו מְרֻבִּים מֵחָכְמָתוֹ לְאִילָן שֶׁעֲנָפָיו מֻעָטִין וְשָׁרָשָׁיו מְרֻבִּין, שֶׁכָּל הָרוּחוֹת שֶׁבָּעוֹלָם אֵין מְזִיזִין אוֹתוֹ מִמְּקוֹמוֹ. וְהַשּׁוֹמֵעַ יִשְׁמַע:

שַׁעַר ד'

פֶּרֶק א'

עוֹד זֹאת אָמַרְתִּי, לָבֹא בִּמְגִלַּת סֵפֶר כָּתוּב, בְּגֹדֶל הַחִיּוּב שֶׁל עֵסֶק הַתּוֹרָה, עַל כָּל אִישׁ יִשְׂרָאֵל יוֹם וָלַיְלָה, וּלְהַרְחִיב מְעַט הַדִּבּוּר, בְּלָשׁוֹן מְדַבֶּרֶת גְּדוֹלוֹת, יְקַר תִּפְאַרְתָּהּ וּמַעֲלָתָהּ שֶׁל הַתּוֹרָה, וְהָאָדָם הַיָּשָׁר הָעוֹסֵק וְהוֹגֶה בָּהּ בְּתוֹרַת חֶסֶד עַל לְשׁוֹנוֹ, לַעֲשׂוֹת

נַחַת רוּחַ לְיוֹצְרוֹ וּבוֹרְאוֹ יִתְבָּרַךְ שְׁמוֹ, וְאִישׁ דַּעַת הַמְּאַמֵּץ כֹּחַ, לְתָמְכָהּ וּלְסַעֲדָהּ וּלְהַחֲזִיק בִּדְקֶיהָ.

אַחֲרֵי אֲשֶׁר זֶה יָמִים רַבִּים לְיִשְׂרָאֵל שֶׁהֻשְׁפַּל עֵסֶק תּוֹרָה הַקְּדוֹשָׁה בְּכָל דּוֹר וָדוֹר, וְהֵן עַתָּה בַּדּוֹרוֹת הַלָּלוּ בַּעֲווֹנוֹתֵינוּ הָרַבִּים, נָפְלָה מְאֹד מְאֹד, נְתוּנָה בְּסֵתֶר הַמַּדְרֵגָה הַתַּחְתּוֹנָה רַחֲמָנָא לִיצְּלָן, כַּאֲשֶׁר עֵינֵינוּ הָרוֹאוֹת עַתָּה בְּרֹבַּת בְּנֵי עַמֵּנוּ, מִגֹּדֶל סֵבֶל מַשָּׂא עֹל הַפַּרְנָסָה ה' יְרַחֵם.

וְגַם כַּמָּה מֵאוֹתָן אֲשֶׁר קִרְבַת אֱלֹקִים יֶחְפָּצוּן, הֵמָּה בָּחֲרוּ לְעַצְמָם לִקְבֹּעַ כָּל עִקַּר לִמּוּדָם בְּסִפְרֵי יִרְאָה וּמוּסָר כָּל הַיָּמִים, בְּלֹא קְבִיעוּת עִקַּר הָעֵסֶק בְּתוֹרָתֵנוּ הַקְּדוֹשָׁה, בְּמִקְרָאוֹת וַהֲלָכוֹת מְרֻבּוֹת, וַעֲדַיִן לֹא רָאוּ מְאוֹרוֹת מִימֵיהֶם, וְלֹא נָגַהּ עֲלֵיהֶם אוֹר הַתּוֹרָה, ה' יִסְלַח לָהֶם, כִּי כַּוָּנָתָם לַשָּׁמַיִם, אֲבָל לֹא זוֹ הַדֶּרֶךְ יִשְׁכֹּן בָּם אוֹר הַתּוֹרָה.

וְהָאֱמֶת, כִּי סִפְרֵי יִרְאָה, הִנָּם כְּכָל דַּרְכֵי ה' הַיְשָׁרִים, כִּי דּוֹרוֹת הָרִאשׁוֹנִים הָיוּ קְבוּעִים כָּל יְמֵיהֶם בְּעֵסֶק וְהֶגְיוֹן תּוֹרָתֵנוּ הַקְּדוֹשָׁה, תְּקוּעִים בְּאָהֳלֵי הַמִּדְרָשׁוֹת בְּגפ"ת, וְשַׁלְהֶבֶת אַהֲבַת תּוֹרָתֵנוּ הַקְּדוֹשָׁה הָיָה בּוֹעֵר בְּלִבָּם כְּאֵשׁ בּוֹעֶרֶת, בְּאַהֲבַת וְיִרְאַת ה' טְהוֹרָה, וְכָל חֶפְצָם לְהַגְדִּיל כְּבוֹדָהּ וּלְהַאְדִּירָהּ, וְהִרְחִיבוּ גְּבוּלָם בְּתַלְמִידִים רַבִּים הֲגוּנִים, לְמַעַן תִּמָּלֵא הָאָרֶץ דֵּעָה.

וְכַאֲשֶׁר אָרְכוּ הַיָּמִים, הִנֵּה כֵּן דַּרְכּוֹ שֶׁל הַיֵּצֶר מֵעוֹלָם, לְהִתְקַנֵּא בְּעַם ה' אֵלֶּה כַּאֲשֶׁר הֵמָּה דּוֹרְכִים בְּדֶרֶךְ ה' כָּרָאוּי, לְהָטִיל בָּהֶם אֶרֶס, עַד שֶׁכַּמָּה מֵהַתַּלְמִידִים שָׂמוּ כָּל קְבִיעוּתָם וְעִסְקָם רַק בְּפִלְפּוּלָהּ שֶׁל תּוֹרָה לְבַד, וְלֹא זוּלַת כְּלָל. וְשָׁנִינוּ בְּמִשְׁנָתֵנוּ (אבות ג, יז) "אִם אֵין יִרְאָה אֵין חָכְמָה", וְעוֹד הַרְבֵּה מַאַמְרֵי רַבּוֹתֵינוּ זִכְרוֹנָם לִבְרָכָה מִזֶּה, כְּמוֹ שֶׁיּוּבָא לְהַלָּן פֶּרֶק ד' אִם יִרְצֶה ה'.

לָזֹאת, הִתְעוֹרְרוּ עַצְמָם כַּמָּה מִגְּדוֹלֵיהֶם עֵינֵי הָעֵדָה, אֲשֶׁר דַּרְכָּם בַּקֹּדֶשׁ לִשְׁקֹד עַל תַּקָּנַת כְּלַל אַחֵינוּ בֵּית יִשְׂרָאֵל, לְיַשֵּׁר הַהֲדוּרִים וְלִגְדֹּר פִּרְצוֹתָם, לְהָרִים הַמִּכְשׁוֹל מִדֶּרֶךְ עַם ה', וּמִלְּאוּ אֶת יָדָם לָבוֹא בְּתוֹכָחוֹת בְּמוּסָרִים וּמִדּוֹת, וְחִבְּרוּ סִפְרֵי יִרְאָה לְהַיְשִׁיר לֵב הָעָם, לִהְיוֹתָם עוֹסְקִים בַּתּוֹרָה הַקְּדוֹשָׁה וּבַעֲבוֹדָה בְּיִרְאַת ה' טְהוֹרָה.

אָמְנָם כָּל אִישׁ תְּבוּנוֹת, אֲשֶׁר שִׂכְלוֹ יָשָׁר הוֹלֵךְ, יָבִין מִדַּעְתּוֹ, כִּי לֹא כִּוְּנוּ בָּהֶם לְהַזְנִיחַ חַס וְשָׁלוֹם הָעֵסֶק בְּגוּפֵי הַתּוֹרָה, וְלִהְיוֹת אַךְ עָסוּק כָּל הַיָּמִים בְּסִפְרֵי מוּסָרָם, אֶלָּא כַּוָּנָתָם רְצוּיָה הָיְתָה, שֶׁכָּל עִקַּר קְבִיעַת לִמּוּד עַם הַקֹּדֶשׁ, יִהְיֶה רַק בַּתּוֹרָה הַקְּדוֹשָׁה שֶׁבִּכְתָב וּבְעַל פֶּה, וַהֲלָכוֹת מְרֻבּוֹת, הֵן הֵן גּוּפֵי תּוֹרָה, וְגַם בְּיִרְאַת ה' טְהוֹרָה:

וְהֵן עַתָּה בַּדּוֹרוֹת הַלָּלוּ בַּעֲווֹנוֹתֵינוּ הָרַבִּים, נַהֲפוֹךְ הוּא, הַגָּבוֹהַּ הֻשְׁפַּל, שֶׁכַּמָּה וְכַמָּה שָׂמוּ כָּל עִקַּר קְבִיעַת לִמּוּדָם רֹב הַיָּמִים רַק בְּסִפְרֵי יִרְאָה וּמוּסָר, בְּאָמְרָם כִּי זֶה כָּל הָאָדָם בְּעוֹלָמוֹ לַעֲסֹק בָּהֶם תָּמִיד, כִּי הֵמָּה מַלְהִיבִים הַלְּבָבוֹת, אֲשֶׁר אָז יִכָּנַע לְבָבוֹ לְהַכְנִיעַ וּלְשַׁבֵּר הַיֵּצֶר מִתַּאֲווֹתָיו, וּלְהִתְיַשֵּׁר בְּמִדּוֹת טוֹבוֹת. וְכֶתֶר תּוֹרָה מֻנָּח בְּקֶרֶן זָוִית. וּבְעֵינַי רָאִיתִי בְּפֶלֶךְ אֶחָד, שֶׁכָּל כָּךְ הִתְפַּשֵּׁט אֶצְלָם זֹאת, עַד שֶׁבְּרֹב בָּתֵּי מִדְרָשָׁם אֵין בָּהֶם רַק סִפְרֵי מוּסָר לָרֹב, וַאֲפִלּוּ שַׁ"ס אֶחָד שָׁלֵם אֵין בּוֹ, וְטַח עֵינֵיהֶם מֵרְאוֹת, מֵהָבִין וְהַשְׂכִּיל

לִבּוֹתָם, אֲשֶׁר לֹא זוֹ הַדֶּרֶךְ בָּחַר בּוֹ ה', כִּי לֹא יִרְצֶה, וְעוֹד מְעַט בְּהֶמְשֵׁךְ הַזְּמַן יוּכְלוּ לִהְיוֹת חַס וְשָׁלוֹם לְלֹא כֹּהֵן מוֹרֶה, וְתוֹרָה מַה תְּהֵא עָלֶיהָ:

הֵן לָזֹאת, עָצַר בְּמִלִּין מִי יוּכַל, מִלְּהוֹדִיעַ בְּשִׁבְטֵי יִשְׂרָאֵל נֶאֱמָנָה, לְיִרְאֵי ה', וְחוֹשְׁבֵי שְׁמוֹ, אֶת הַדֶּרֶךְ יֵלְכוּ בָהּ לְאוֹרָהּ שֶׁל תּוֹרָה. אוֹי לָנוּ מִיּוֹם הַדִּין, אוֹי לָנוּ מִיּוֹם הַתּוֹכֵחָה עַל עֲוֹן בִּטּוּלָהּ שֶׁל תּוֹרָה, כַּאֲשֶׁר הוּא יִתְבָּרַךְ שְׁמוֹ יְקַנֵּא לָהּ לִתְבֹּעַ עֶלְבּוֹנָהּ:

וּתְחִלָּה אָשִׂים דִּבְרָתִי בְּעִנְיַן עֵסֶק הַתּוֹרָה לִשְׁמָהּ, מַהוּ עִנְיַן לְ"שְׁמָהּ". כִּי גַם זֶה פְּרִי חַטָּאת, לְכַמָּה הַמּוֹנְעִים עַצְמָן מֵעֵסֶק הַתּוֹרָה הַקְּדוֹשָׁה, בְּחָשְׁבָם כִּי עִנְיַן לִשְׁמָהּ פֵּרוּשׁוֹ, בִּדְבֵקוּת גָּדוֹל בְּלִי הֶפְסֵק.

וְגַם רָעָה חוֹלָה יוֹתֵר מִזֶּה, שֶׁסּוֹבְרִים בְּדַעְתָּם שֶׁעֵסֶק הַתּוֹרָה בְּלֹא דְּבֵיקוּת אֵין כְּלוּם, וּלְלֹא שׁוּם תּוֹעֶלֶת חַס וְשָׁלוֹם. לָזֹאת, כְּשֶׁרוֹאִין עַצְמָן שֶׁאֵין לִבָּם הוֹלֵךְ לְזֹאת הַמַּדְרֵגָה — שֶׁיְּהֵא לִמּוּדָם בִּדְבֵקוּת תְּמִידִי, לֹא יַתְחִילוּ כְּלָל לִלְמֹד, וְעַל כֵּן תָּפוּג תּוֹרָה חַס וְשָׁלוֹם.

וּמֵהֶמְשֵׁךְ הָעִנְיָנִים יִתְבָּאֵר אִם יִרְצֶה ה' מִמֵּילָא מַעֲלָתָהּ שֶׁל הַתּוֹרָה הַקְּדוֹשָׁה וְהָאָדָם הָעוֹסֵק בָּהּ כָּרָאוּי.

לָזֹאת, הֻכְרַח לְהָבִיא קְצָת מַאַמְרֵי רַבּוֹתֵינוּ זִכְרוֹנָם לִבְרָכָה בַּשַּׁ"ס וּמִדְרָשִׁים וְזֹהַר, אֲשֶׁר בָּם יְדֻבַּר נִפְלְאוֹת מַעֲלַת הַתּוֹרָה הַקְּדוֹשָׁה, וְהָעוֹסֵק בָּהּ, וְגֹדֶל שְׂכָרָהּ וְעָנְשָׁהּ ר"ל. הֲגַם שֶׁכָּל אֵלּוּ הַמַּאֲמָרִים יְדוּעִים וּמְפֻרְסָמִים, עִם כָּל זֶה קִבַּצְתִּים, לְהַלְהִיב לִבּוֹת הַחֲפֵצִים לְהִתְדַּבֵּק בְּאַהֲבַת תּוֹרָתוֹ יִתְבָּרַךְ, וּלְהִתְלוֹנֵן בְּצֵל הָעֶלְיוֹן נוֹרָא:

פֶּרֶק ב'

עִנְיַן עֵסֶק הַתּוֹרָה לִשְׁמָהּ, הָאֱמֶת הַבָּרוּר, כִּי "לִשְׁמָהּ" אֵין פֵּרוּשׁוֹ דְּבֵקוּת, כְּמוֹ שֶׁסּוֹבְרִים עַתָּה רֹב הָעוֹלָם, שֶׁהֲרֵי אָמְרוּ רַבּוֹתֵינוּ זִכְרוֹנָם לִבְרָכָה בַּמִּדְרָשׁ (שוח"ט תהלים א, א) שֶׁבִּקֵּשׁ דָּוִד הַמֶּלֶךְ עָלָיו הַשָּׁלוֹם מִלְּפָנָיו יִתְבָּרַךְ, שֶׁהָעוֹסֵק בִּתְהִלִּים יֵחָשֵׁב אֶצְלוֹ יִתְבָּרַךְ כְּאִלּוּ הָיָה עוֹסֵק בִּנְגָעִים וְאָהֳלוֹת, הֲרֵי שֶׁהָעֵסֶק בְּהִלְכוֹת הַשַּׁ"ס בְּעִיּוּן וִיגִיעָה, הוּא עִנְיָן יוֹתֵר נַעֲלֶה וְאָהוּב לְפָנָיו יִתְבָּרַךְ מֵאֲמִירַת תְּהִלִּים.

וְאִם נֹאמַר שֶׁ"לִשְׁמָהּ" פֵּרוּשׁוֹ דְּבֵקוּת דַּוְקָא, וְרַק בָּזֶה תָּלוּי כָּל עִקַּר עִנְיַן עֵסֶק הַתּוֹרָה, הֲלֹא אֵין דְּבֵקוּת יוֹתֵר נִפְלָא מֵאֲמִירַת תְּהִלִּים כָּרָאוּי כָּל הַיּוֹם.

וְגַם מִי יוֹדֵעַ אִם הִסְכִּים הַקָּדוֹשׁ בָּרוּךְ הוּא עַל יָדוֹ בָּזֶה, כִּי לֹא מָצִינוּ בְּדִבְרֵיהֶם זִכְרוֹנָם לִבְרָכָה מַה תְּשׁוּבָה הֵשִׁיבוֹ הוּא יִתְבָּרַךְ עַל שְׁאֵלָתוֹ (כְּמוֹ שֶׁמָּצִינוּ בְּבָבָא בַּתְרָא י"ז א', וְאִידָךְ, הַהוּא רַחֲמֵי הוּא דְּקָא בָּעֵי).

וְגַם כִּי הָיָה דַּי לְעִנְיַן הַדְּבֵקוּת, בְּמַסֶּכֶת אַחַת, אוֹ פֶּרֶק, אוֹ מִשְׁנָה אַחַת, שֶׁיַּעֲסֹק בָּהּ כָּל יָמָיו בִּדְבֵקוּת. וְלֹא כֵן מָצִינוּ לְ רַבּוֹתֵינוּ זִכְרוֹנָם לִבְרָכָה (סוכה כח, א) שֶׁאָמְרוּ עַל רַבִּי יוֹחָנָן בֶּן זַכַּאי שֶׁלֹּא הִנִּיחַ מִקְרָא מִשְׁנָה הֲלָכוֹת וְאַגָּדוֹת כו', וְהַיְנוּ כִּי מֵהַעֲלוֹתוֹ עַל לִבּוֹ תָּמִיד, כִּי עֲדַיִן לֹא יָצָא יְדֵי חוֹבַת עֵסֶק הַתּוֹרָה לִשְׁמָהּ בְּמַה שֶּׁלָּמַד עַד עַתָּה, לָזֹאת הָיָה שׁוֹקֵד כָּל יָמָיו לְהוֹסִיף לֶקַח תָּמִיד, מִיּוֹם לְיוֹם וּמִשָּׁעָה לְשָׁעָה.

וּבְמִשְׁלֵי רַבְּתָא פ"י: "אָמַר רַבִּי יִשְׁמָעֵאל בֹּא וּרְאֵה כַּמָּה קָשֶׁה יוֹם הַדִּין, שֶׁעָתִיד הַקָּדוֹשׁ בָּרוּךְ הוּא לָדוּן אֶת כָּל הָעוֹלָם כֻּלּוֹ כו', בָּא מִי שֶׁיֵּשׁ בְּיָדוֹ מִקְרָא וְאֵין בְּיָדוֹ מִשְׁנָה, הַקָּדוֹשׁ בָּרוּךְ הוּא הוֹפֵךְ אֶת פָּנָיו מִמֶּנּוּ וּמְצִירֵי גֵּיהִנֹּם מִתְגַּבְּרִין בּוֹ כו', וְהֵם נוֹטְלִין אוֹתוֹ וּמַשְׁלִיכִין אוֹתוֹ לְגֵיהִנֹּם. בָּא מִי שֶׁיֵּשׁ בְּיָדוֹ שְׁנֵי סְדָרִים אוֹ שְׁלֹשָׁה, הַקָּדוֹשׁ בָּרוּךְ הוּא אוֹמֵר לוֹ בְּנִי כָּל הַהֲלָכוֹת לָמָּה לֹא שָׁנִיתָ אוֹתָם כו'. בָּא מִי שֶׁיֵּשׁ בְּיָדוֹ הֲלָכוֹת, א"ל בְּנִי תּוֹרַת כֹּהֲנִים לָמָּה לֹא שָׁנִיתָ שֶׁיֵּשׁ בּוֹ כו'. בָּא מִי שֶׁיֵּשׁ בְּיָדוֹ תּוֹרַת כֹּהֲנִים, הַקָּדוֹשׁ בָּרוּךְ הוּא אוֹמֵר לוֹ בְּנִי חֲמִשָּׁה חֻמְּשֵׁי תּוֹרָה לָמָּה לֹא שָׁנִיתָ שֶׁיֵּשׁ בָּהֶם קְרִיאַת שְׁמַע תְּפִלִּין וּמְזוּזָה. בָּא מִי שֶׁיֵּשׁ בְּיָדוֹ חֲמִשָּׁה חֻמְּשֵׁי תּוֹרָה, אוֹמֵר לוֹ הַקָּדוֹשׁ בָּרוּךְ הוּא לָמָּה לֹא לָמַדְתָּ הַגָּדָה כו'. בָּא מִי שֶׁיֵּשׁ בְּיָדוֹ הַגָּדָה, הַקָּדוֹשׁ בָּרוּךְ הוּא אוֹמֵר לוֹ תַּלְמוּד לָמָּה לֹא לָמַדְתָּ כו'. בָּא מִי שֶׁיֵּשׁ בְּיָדוֹ תַּלְמוּד הַקָּדוֹשׁ בָּרוּךְ הוּא אוֹמֵר לוֹ בְּנִי הוֹאִיל וְנִתְעַסַּקְתָּ בְּתַלְמוּד צָפִיתָ בַּמֶּרְכָּבָה כו', כִּסֵּא כְבוֹדִי הֵאֵיךְ הוּא עוֹמֵד כו', חַשְׁמַל הֵאֵיךְ הוּא עוֹמֵד, וּבְכַמָּה פָּנִים הוּא מִתְהַפֵּךְ" כו' עַיֵּן שָׁם בְּאֹרֶךְ.

וּמִסְתַּבְּרָא נָמֵי הָכִי, שֶׁהֲרֵי כַּמָּה הֲלָכוֹת מְרֻבּוֹת יֵשׁ בַּשַּׁ"ס, שֶׁבְּעֵת אֲשֶׁר הָאָדָם עוֹסֵק בָּהֶם, הוּא צָרִיךְ לְעַיֵּן וּלְהַעֲמִיק מַחְשַׁבְתּוֹ וְשִׂכְלוֹ בְּעִנְיְנֵי הַגַּשְׁמִיּוּת שֶׁבָּהֶם, כְּגוֹן קִנִּין וּפִתְחֵי נִדָּה שֶׁהֵן הֵן גּוּפֵי הֲלָכוֹת, אוֹ הַמַּשָּׂא וּמַתָּן בַּשַּׁ"ס, וּכְלָלֵי דִּינֵי מִגּוֹ שֶׁל רַמָּאוּת שֶׁהָיָה הָרַמַּאי יָכוֹל לִטְעֹן, וְכִמְעַט בִּלְתִּי אֶפְשָׁר שֶׁיְּהֵא אֶצְלוֹ אָז גַּם הַדְּבֵקוּת בִּשְׁלֵמוּת כָּרָאוּי:

פֶּרֶק ג'

אֲבָל הָאֱמֶת כִּי עִנְיַן "לִשְׁמָהּ" פֵּרוּשׁ, לְשֵׁם הַתּוֹרָה, וְהָעִנְיָן כְּמוֹ שֶׁפֵּרֵשׁ הרא"ש ז"ל עַל מַאֲמַר רַבִּי אֶלְעָזָר בְּרַבִּי צָדוֹק (נדרים ס"ב) "עֲשֵׂה דְּבָרִים לְשֵׁם פָּעֳלָן" לִשְׁמוֹ שֶׁל הַקָּדוֹשׁ בָּרוּךְ הוּא שֶׁפָּעַל הַכֹּל לְמַעֲנֵהוּ, "וְדַבֵּר בָּהֶן לִשְׁמָן", כָּל דִּבּוּרְךָ וּמַשָּׂאֲךָ בְּדִבְרֵי תּוֹרָה יִהְיֶה לְשֵׁם הַתּוֹרָה, כְּגוֹן לֵידַע וּלְהָבִין, וּלְהוֹסִיף לֶקַח וּפִלְפּוּל, וְלֹא לְקַנְטֵר וּלְהִתְגָּאוֹת". עכ"ל.

דִּקְדֵּק לְבָאֵר שִׁנּוּי לְשׁוֹנוֹ דְּרַבִּי אֶלְעָזָר בְּרַבִּי צָדוֹק, שֶׁבָּעֲשִׂיָּה אָמַר "לְשֵׁם פָּעֳלָן", וּבַדִּבּוּר אָמַר "לִשְׁמָן", לָכֵן, בְּעִנְיַן הָעֲשִׂיָּה פֵּרֵשׁ לִשְׁמוֹ שֶׁל הַקָּדוֹשׁ בָּרוּךְ הוּא שֶׁפָּעַל הַכֹּל לְמַעֲנֵהוּ, וּבְעִנְיַן הַלִּמּוּד פֵּרֵשׁ, לְשֵׁם הַתּוֹרָה כו'.

וְכַוָּנָתוֹ זִכְרוֹנוֹ לִבְרָכָה מְבֹאָר, הַיְנוּ, כִּי עֲשִׂיַּת הַמִּצְוָה וַדַּאי שֶׁצְּרִיכָה לִהְיוֹת לְמִצְוָה מִן הַמֻּבְחָר, בִּדְבֵקוּת וּמַחֲשָׁבָה טְהוֹרָה שֶׁבַּטְּהוֹרוֹת כְּפִי שִׂכְלוֹ וְהַשָּׂגָתוֹ, כְּדֵי שֶׁיִּתְקַלֵּס עִלָּאָה, לִגְרֹם תִּקּוּנֵי הָעוֹלָמוֹת וְכֹחוֹת וּסְדָרִים הָעֶלְיוֹנִים, זֶהוּ "לְשֵׁם פָּעֳלָן", כִּי "כֹּל פָּעַל ה' לַמַּעֲנֵהוּ" (משלי טז, ד), וְאָמְרוּ רַבּוֹתֵינוּ זִכְרוֹנָם לִבְרָכָה — לְקִלּוּסוֹ (ילקוט שמעוני שם).

וְאִם כִּי וַדַּאי שֶׁגַּם בַּמִּצְוֹת, הָעִקָּר בָּהֶם לְעִכּוּבָא הוּא הָעֲשִׂיָּה בְּפֹעַל, וְהַכַּוָּנָה הַיְתֵרָה וְטֹהַר הַמַּחֲשָׁבָה אֵינָהּ מְעַכֶּבֶת כְּלָל, כְּמוֹ שֶׁנִּתְבָּאֵר לְעֵיל סוֹף שַׁעַר א' עַל נָכוֹן בעז"ה, עִם כָּל זֶה, מִצְטָרֵף קְדֻשַּׁת וְטֹהַר מַחֲשַׁבְתּוֹ לְעִקַּר הָעֲשִׂיָּה בְּפֹעַל, לְעוֹרֵר וְלִפְעֹל תִּקּוּנִים יוֹתֵר גְּדוֹלִים בְּהָעוֹלָמוֹת, מִשֶּׁאִם הָיְתָה הַמִּצְוָה נַעֲשֵׂית בְּלֹא דְּבֵקוּת וּקְדֻשַּׁת הַמַּחֲשָׁבָה.

אֲבָל עַל הַנְהָגַת הָאָדָם בִּשְׁעַת עֵסֶק הַתּוֹרָה בְּדִינֵי הַמִּצְוֹת וְהִלְכוֹתֵיהֶן, אָמַר "וְדַבֵּר

בָּהֶן", רָצָה לוֹמַר הַדִּבּוּר בְּעִנְיְנֵי הַמִּצְוֹת וְהִלְכוֹתֵיהֶן, יִהְיֶה "לִשְׁמָן", פֵּרוּשׁ, לְשֵׁם הַדִּבְרֵי תּוֹרָה, הַיְנוּ לֵידַע וּלְהָבִין וּלְהוֹסִיף לֶקַח וּפִלְפּוּל.

(וְרַשִׁ"י ז"ל גִּירְסָא אַחֶרֶת הָיְתָה לוֹ שָׁם, "וְדַבֵּר בָּהֶן לְשֵׁם שָׁמַיִם", לָכֵן פֵּרֵשׁ שֶׁתְּהֵא כָּל כַּוָּנָתְךָ לַשָּׁמַיִם. אָמְנָם עִנְיָן וּפֵרוּשׁ "לִשְׁמָהּ" שֶׁאָמְרוּ רַבּוֹתֵינוּ זִכְרוֹנָם לִבְרָכָה בְּכָל מָקוֹם, וַדַּאי שֶׁגַּם רַשִׁ"י ז"ל יְפָרֵשׁ כְּפֵרוּשׁ הרא"ש ז"ל כָּאן לְפִי גִּרְסָתוֹ, וְגַם רַשִׁ"י ז"ל כָּאן אֵין כַּוָּנָתוֹ דְּבֵקוּת, אֶלָּא דְּאָתֵי לַאֲפוּקֵי, שֶׁלֹּא יְהֵא לוֹמְדוֹ לְשֵׁם קִנְטוּר וְגֵיאוּת, כְּמוֹ שֶׁכָּתַב הרא"ש ז"ל, כִּדְמוּכָח מִסִּיּוּם דִּבְרֵי רַבִּי אֶלְעָזָר בְּרַבִּי צָדוֹק, "אַל תַּעֲשֵׂם עֲטָרָה לְהִתְגַּדֵּל בָּהֶם" כו').

וְזֶה שֶׁמְּסַיֵּם הַשַּׁ"ס גַּבֵּי רַבָּן יוֹחָנָן בֶּן זַכַּאי, שֶׁלֹּא הִנִּיחַ כו', לְקַיֵּם מַה שֶּׁנֶּאֱמַר (משלי ח, כא) "לְהַנְחִיל אוֹהֲבַי יֵשׁ" כו', שֶׁמְּבֹאָר הָעִנְיָן שָׁם בְּכָל אוֹתָהּ הַפָּרָשָׁה, שֶׁהוּא מַאֲמַר הַתּוֹרָה הַקְּדוֹשָׁה עַצְמָהּ, אֲשֶׁר בַּחוּץ תָּרֹנָּה, שֶׁיֵּשׁ לְאֵל יָדָהּ לְהַנְחִיל וְלִתֵּן שָׂכָר טוֹב, לְכָל הַהוֹגֶה וְעוֹסֵק בָּהּ מֵחֲמַת אַהֲבָתָהּ עַצְמָהּ מַמָּשׁ, הַיְנוּ לְהוֹסִיף בָּהּ לֶקַח וּפִלְפּוּל, וְזֶהוּ "אוֹהֲבַי":

פֶּרֶק ד'

אָמְנָם וַדַּאי דְּאִי אֶפְשָׁר לוֹמַר שֶׁאֵין צָרִיךְ לְעִנְיַן עֵסֶק הַתּוֹרָה שׁוּם טֹהַר הַמַּחְשָׁבָה וְיִרְאַת ה' חָלִילָה, שֶׁהֲרֵי מִשְׁנָה שְׁלֵמָה שָׁנִינוּ (אבות ג, יז) "אִם אֵין יִרְאָה אֵין חָכְמָה", וְאָמְרוּ (יומא עב, ב): מַאי דִּכְתִיב (משלי יז, טז) "לָמָּה זֶה מְחִיר בְּיַד כְּסִיל לִקְנוֹת חָכְמָה וְלֶב אָיִן", אוֹי לָהֶם לְתַלְמִידֵי חֲכָמִים שֶׁעוֹסְקִים בַּתּוֹרָה וְאֵין בָּהֶם יִרְאַת שָׁמַיִם" כו'. וּבִשְׁמוֹת רַבָּה פ"מ "כָּל מִי שֶׁהוּא יוֹדֵעַ וְאֵין בְּיָדוֹ יִרְאַת חֵטְא, אֵין בְּיָדוֹ כְּלוּם, שֶׁקִּפְלִיּוֹת שֶׁל תּוֹרָה בְּיִרְאַת חֵטְא".

וּבְהַקְדָּמַת הַזֹּהַר י"א ב' אָמַר רַבִּי שִׁמְעוֹן בֶּן יוֹחַאי, שֶׁהַיִּרְאָה אִיהִי תַּרְעָא לְאַעֲלָא לְגוֹ מְהֵימְנוּתָא, וְעַל פִּקּוּדָא דָּא אִתְקַיַּם כָּל עָלְמָא כו', וְדָא עִקָּרָא וִיסוֹדָא לְכָל שְׁאָר פִּקּוּדִין דְּאוֹרַיְתָא, מַאן דְּנָטִיר יִרְאָה נָטִיר כּוֹלָּא, לֹא נָטִיר יִרְאָה לֹא נָטִיר פִּקּוּדֵי אוֹרַיְתָא כו', [אָמַר רַבִּי שִׁמְעוֹן בֶּן יוֹחַאי שֶׁהַיִּרְאָה הִיא שַׁעַר לְהִכָּנֵס אֶל הָאֱמוּנָה, וְעַל מִצְוָה זוֹ מִתְקַיֵּם כָּל הָעוֹלָם וכו', וְזוֹ הִיא הַשֹּׁרֶשׁ וְהַיְסוֹד לְכָל שְׁאָר מִצְוֹת הַתּוֹרָה, מִי שֶׁשּׁוֹמֵר אֶת הַיִּרְאָה שׁוֹמֵר הַכֹּל, וּמִי שֶׁאֵינוֹ שׁוֹמֵר אֶת הַיִּרְאָה אֵינוֹ שׁוֹמֵר מִצְוֹת הַתּוֹרָה] עַיֵּן שָׁם.

וּבְפָרָשַׁת בְּהַר ק"ח א', מַאי עֹל מַלְכוּת שָׁמַיִם אֶלָּא כְּהַאי תּוֹרָא כו', הָכִי נָמֵי אִצְטְרִיךְ לֵיהּ לְבַר נַשׁ לְקַבָּלָא עֲלֵיהּ עוֹל בְּקַדְמֵיתָא, וּלְבָתַר דְּיִפְלַח לֵיהּ בְּכָל מַה דְּאִיצְטְרִיךְ, וְאִי לָא קַבִּיל עֲלֵיהּ הַאי בְּקַדְמֵיתָא, לָא יֵיכוּל לְמִפְלַח. הָדָא הוּא דִּכְתִיב "עִבְדוּ אֶת ה' בְּיִרְאָה", מַהוּ בְּיִרְאָה, כד"א "רֵאשִׁית חָכְמָה יִרְאַת ה'" כו', וְעַל דָּא הַאי בְּקַדְמֵיתָא הוּא דְּכֹלָּא כו', בְּגִין דִּבְהַאי עָיִיל לִשְׁאָר קְדוּשָׁה, וְאִי הַאי לָא אִשְׁתְּכַח לְגַבֵּיהּ, לָא שַׁרְיָא בֵּיהּ קְדוּשָּׁה דִּלְעֵילָּא כו' [מַהוּ עֹל מַלְכוּת שָׁמַיִם, אֶלָּא כְּאוֹתוֹ הַשּׁוֹר וכו', כָּךְ צָרִיךְ הָאָדָם לְקַבֵּל עָלָיו עֹל בִּתְחִלָּה, וְאַחַר כַּךְ יַעֲבֹד בּוֹ כָּל מַה שֶּׁצָּרִיךְ, וְאִם אֵינוֹ מְקַבֵּל עָלָיו זֶה בִּתְחִלָּה, אֵינוֹ יָכוֹל

לַעֲבֹד. וְזֶה שֶׁכָּתוּב "עִבְדוּ אֶת ה' בְּיִרְאָה", מַהוּ בְּיִרְאָה, כְּמוֹ שֶׁכָּתוּב "רֵאשִׁית חָכְמָה יִרְאַת ה'" וכו', וְעַל כֵּן זֶה הוּא תְּחִלַּת הַכֹּל וכו', מִשּׁוּם שֶׁבָּזֶה נִכְנָס לִשְׁאָר הַקְּדֻשָּׁה, וְאִם זוֹ אֵינוֹ נִמְצֵאת אֶצְלוֹ לֹא שׁוֹרָה בּוֹ קְדֻשָּׁה הָעֶלְיוֹנָה.]

וְאָמְרוּ עוֹד (אבות ג, יא): "כָּל שֶׁיִּרְאַת חֶטְאוֹ קוֹדֶמֶת לְחָכְמָתוֹ חָכְמָתוֹ מִתְקַיֶּמֶת", כִּי יִרְאַת ה' תְּחִלָּה, הִיא עִקַּר הַקִּיּוּם שֶׁל חָכְמַת הַתּוֹרָה.

וּכְמוֹ שֶׁאָמְרוּ רַבּוֹתֵינוּ זִכְרוֹנָם לִבְרָכָה (שבת לא, א): "אָמַר רֵישׁ לָקִישׁ, מַאי דִּכְתִיב (ישעיה לג, ו) "וְהָיָה אֱמוּנַת עִתֶּיךָ" כו', אֱמוּנַת, זֶה סֵדֶר זְרָעִים" כו', חָשִׁיב שָׁם בְּזֶה הַפָּסוּק כָּל הַשַּׁ"ס, וּמְסַיֵּם וַאֲפִלּוּ הָכִי "יִרְאַת ה' הִיא אוֹצָרוֹ", דִּמָּה הַכָּתוּב אֶת הַ"תּוֹרָה" — לְרֹב תְּבוּאוֹת, וְהַ"יִּרְאָה" — לְאוֹצָר הַמַּחֲזִיק בּוֹ הֲמוֹן תְּבוּאוֹת וּמִשְׁתַּמְּרִים בְּתוֹכוֹ, שֶׁיִּרְאַת ה' הִיא הָאוֹצָר לְחָכְמַת הַתּוֹרָה הַקְּדוֹשָׁה, שֶׁעַל יָדָהּ תִּתְקַיֵּם אֵצֶל הָאָדָם, וְאִם לֹא הֵכִין לוֹ הָאָדָם תְּחִלָּה אוֹצַר הַיִּרְאָה, הֲרֵי רֹב תְּבוּאוֹת הַתּוֹרָה כְּמֻנָּח עַל פְּנֵי הַשָּׂדֶה לְמִרְמַס רֶגֶל הַשּׁוֹר וְהַחֲמוֹר חַס וְשָׁלוֹם, שֶׁאֵינָהּ מִתְקַיֶּמֶת אֶצְלוֹ כְּלָל.

וְכֵן אָמְרוּ עַל זֶה הַכָּתוּב (בִּשְׁמוֹת רַבָּה פ"ל) "אַתָּה מוֹצֵא אָדָם שׁוֹנֶה מִדְרָשׁ הֲלָכוֹת וְאַגָּדוֹת, וְאִם אֵין בּוֹ יִרְאַת חֵטְא אֵין בְּיָדוֹ כְּלוּם, מָשָׁל לְאָדָם כו', יֵשׁ לִי אֶלֶף מִדּוֹת שֶׁל תְּבוּאָה, א"ל יֵשׁ לְךָ אַפּוֹתִיקָאוֹת לִתֵּן אוֹתָם בָּהֶם כו', שֶׁנֶּאֱמַר "וְהָיָה אֱמוּנַת עִתֶּךָ", עַיֵּן שָׁם:

פֶּרֶק ה'

וּלְפִי עֵרֶךְ גֹּדֶל אוֹצַר הַיִּרְאָה אֲשֶׁר הֵכִין לוֹ הָאָדָם, כֵּן עַל זֶה הָעֵרֶךְ, יוּכַל לִיכָּנֵס וּלְהִשְׁתַּמֵּר וּלְהִתְקַיֵּם בְּתוֹכוֹ תְּבוּאוֹת הַתּוֹרָה, כְּפִי אֲשֶׁר יַחְזִיק אוֹצָרוֹ.

כִּי הָאָב הַמְחַלֵּק תְּבוּאָה לְבָנָיו, הוּא מְחַלֵּק וְנוֹתֵן לְכָל אֶחָד מִדַּת הַתְּבוּאָה, כְּפִי אֲשֶׁר יַחְזִיק אוֹצָרוֹ שֶׁל הַבֵּן אֲשֶׁר הֵכִין עַל זֶה מִקֹּדֶם. שֶׁאַף אִם יִרְצֶה הָאָב, וְיָדוֹ פְּתוּחָה לִתֵּן לוֹ הַרְבֵּה, אָמְנָם כֵּיוָן שֶׁהַבֵּן אֵינוֹ יָכוֹל לְקַבֵּל יוֹתֵר, מֵחֲמַת שֶׁאֵין אוֹצָרוֹ גָּדוֹל כָּל כָּךְ, שֶׁיּוּכַל לְהַחְזִיק יוֹתֵר, גַּם הָאָב אִי אֶפְשָׁר לוֹ לִתֵּן לוֹ עַתָּה יוֹתֵר. וְאִם לֹא הֵכִין לוֹ הַבֵּן אַף אוֹצָר קָטָן, גַּם הָאָב לֹא יִתֵּן לוֹ כְּלָל, כֵּיוָן שֶׁאֵין לוֹ מָקוֹם מִשְׁמָר שֶׁתִּתְקַיֵּם אֶצְלוֹ.

כֵּן הוּא יִתְבָּרַךְ שְׁמוֹ, יָדוֹ פְּתוּחָה כִּבְיָכוֹל לְהַשְׁפִּיעַ תָּמִיד, לְכָל אִישׁ מֵעַם סְגֻלָּתוֹ, רֹב חָכְמָה וּבִינָה יְתֵרָה, וְשֶׁתִּתְקַיֵּם אֶצְלָם, וְיִקְשְׁרֵם עַל לוּחַ לִבָּם, לְהִשְׁתַּעְשֵׁעַ אִתָּם בְּבוֹאָם לָעוֹלָם הַמְּנוּחָה וְתַלְמוּדָם בְּיָדָם.

אָמְנָם הַדָּבָר תָּלוּי לְפִי אוֹצַר הַיִּרְאָה שֶׁתִּקְדַּם אֶל הָאָדָם, שֶׁאִם הֵכִין לוֹ הָאָדָם אוֹצָר גָּדוֹל שֶׁל יִרְאַת ה' טְהוֹרָה, כֵּן ה' יִתֵּן לוֹ חָכְמָה וּתְבוּנָה בְּרֹב שֶׁפַע כְּפִי שֶׁתַּחֲזִיק אוֹצָרוֹ, הַכֹּל לְפִי גֹּדֶל אוֹצָרוֹ.

וְאִם לֹא הֵכִין הָאָדָם אַף אוֹצָר קָטָן, שֶׁאֵין בּוֹ יִרְאָתוֹ יִתְבָּרַךְ כְּלָל חַס וְשָׁלוֹם, גַּם הוּא יִתְבָּרַךְ לֹא יַשְׁפִּיעַ לוֹ שׁוּם חָכְמָה כְּלָל, אַחַר שֶׁלֹּא תִּתְקַיֵּם אֶצְלוֹ, כִּי תּוֹרָתוֹ נִמְאֶסֶת חַס וְשָׁלוֹם, כְּמוֹ שֶׁאָמְרוּ רַבּוֹתֵינוּ זִכְרוֹנָם לִבְרָכָה.

וְעַל זֶה אָמַר הַכָּתוּב (תהלים קי״א): ״רֵאשִׁית חָכְמָה יִרְאַת ה׳״, וְכַמְבֹאָר בְּהַקְדָּמַת הַזֹּהַר ז׳ ב׳: ״ר״ח פָּתַח ״רֵאשִׁית חָכְמָה יִרְאַת ה׳״ כו׳, הַאי קְרָא הָכִי מִבָּעֵי לֵיהּ, סוֹף חָכְמָה כו׳, אֶלָּא אִיהִי רֵאשִׁית, לְאַעֲלָא לְגוֹ דַּרְגָּא דְחָכְמְתָא עִלָּאָה כו׳, תַּרְעָא קַדְמָאָה לְחָכְמָה עִלָּאָה יִרְאַת ה׳ אִיהִי״ כו׳, [ר״ח פָּתַח ״רֵאשִׁית חָכְמָה יִרְאַת ה׳״, מִקְרָא זֶה כָּךְ הָיָה צ״ל סוֹף חָכְמָה וכו׳, אֶלָּא הִיא רֵאשִׁית לְהִכָּנֵס לְתוֹךְ מַדְרֵגַת הַחָכְמָה הָעֶלְיוֹנָה וכו׳, הַשַּׁעַר הָרִאשׁוֹן לַחָכְמָה הָעֶלְיוֹנָה, הִיא יִרְאַת ה׳]. עַיֵּן שָׁם:

הֲרֵי מְבֹאָר, הֲגַם שֶׁהַיִּרְאָה הִיא מִצְוָה אַחַת, וְאָמְרוּ בִּירוּשַׁלְמִי (רֵישׁ פֵּאָה) שֶׁכָּל הַמִּצְוֹות אֵינָן שָׁווֹת לְדָבָר אֶחָד מִן הַתּוֹרָה, אָמְנָם מִצְוַת קְנִיַּת הַיִּרְאָה מִמֶּנּוּ יִתְבָּרַךְ, רַבָּה הִיא מְאֹד, מִצַּד שֶׁהִיא מֻכְרַחַת לְעִקַּר הַקִּיּוּם וְשִׁמּוּר הַתּוֹרָה הַקְּדוֹשָׁה, וּבִלְתָּהּ גַּם נִמְאֶסֶת חַס וְשָׁלוֹם בְּעֵינֵי הַבְּרִיּוֹת, לָכֵן צְרִיכָה שֶׁתִּקְדַּם אֵצֶל הָאָדָם קֹדֶם עֵסֶק הַתּוֹרָה:

פֶּרֶק ו׳

לְזֹאת הָאֱמֶת שֶׁזּוֹ הִיא הַדֶּרֶךְ הָאֲמִתִּי, אֲשֶׁר בָּזֶה בָּחַר הוּא יִתְבָּרַךְ שְׁמוֹ, שֶׁבְּכָל עֵת שֶׁיָּכִין הָאָדָם עַצְמוֹ לִלְמֹד, רָאוּי לוֹ לְהִתְיַשֵּׁב קֹדֶם שֶׁיַּתְחִיל, עַל כָּל פָּנִים זְמַן מְעַט, בְּיִרְאַת ה׳ טְהוֹרָה בְּטָהֳרַת הַלֵּב, לְהִתְוַדּוֹת עַל חַטֹּאתוֹ מֵעֻמְקָא דְלִבָּא, כְּדֵי שֶׁתְּהֵא תּוֹרָתוֹ קְדוֹשָׁה וּטְהוֹרָה.

וִיכַוֵּן לְהִתְדַּבֵּק בְּלִמּוּדוֹ — בּוֹ בַּתּוֹרָה, בּוֹ בְּהַקָּדוֹשׁ בָּרוּךְ הוּא, הַיְנוּ לְהִתְדַּבֵּק בְּכָל כֹּחוֹתָיו לְ״דְבַר ה׳״ — זוֹ הֲלָכָה״, וּבָזֶה הוּא דָּבוּק בּוֹ יִתְבָּרַךְ מַמָּשׁ כִּבְיָכוֹל, כִּי הוּא יִתְבָּרַךְ וּרְצוֹנוֹ חַד, כְּמוֹ שֶׁכָּתוּב בַּזֹּהַר, וְכָל דִּין וַהֲלָכָה מִתּוֹרָה הַקְּדוֹשָׁה, הוּא רְצוֹנוֹ יִתְבָּרַךְ, שֶׁכֵּן גָּזְרָה רְצוֹנוֹ שֶׁיְּהֵא כָּךְ הַדִּין, כָּשֵׁר אוֹ פָּסוּל, טָמֵא וְטָהוֹר, אָסוּר וּמוּתָּר, חַיָּב וְזַכַּאי.

וְגַם אִם הוּא עָסוּק בְּדִבְרֵי אַגָּדָה, שֶׁאֵין בָּהֶם נַפְקוּתָא לְשׁוּם דִּין, גַּם כֵּן הוּא דָּבוּק בְּדִבּוּרוֹ שֶׁל הַקָּדוֹשׁ בָּרוּךְ הוּא.

כִּי הַתּוֹרָה כֻּלָּהּ, בִּכְלָלֶיהָ וּפְרָטֶיהָ וְדִקְדּוּקֶיהָ, וַאֲפִלּוּ מַה שֶּׁהַתַּלְמִיד קָטָן שׁוֹאֵל מֵרַבּוֹ, הַכֹּל יָצָא מִפִּיו יִתְבָּרַךְ לְמֹשֶׁה בְּסִינַי, כְּמוֹ שֶׁאָמְרוּ רַבּוֹתֵינוּ זִכְרוֹנָם לִבְרָכָה סוֹף פֶּרֶק ב׳ דִּמְגִילָּה, וּבְפֶרֶק קַמָּא דִבְרָכוֹת ה׳ א׳, וּבְקֹהֶלֶת רַבָּה ס״א פי״א, וְשָׁם בְּסִימָן ה׳ פֶּרֶק ו׳, וּבִירוּשַׁלְמִי פֶּרֶק ב׳ דְּפֵאָה, וּבְוַיִּקְרָא רַבָּה פכ״ב, עַיֵּן שָׁם. וּבִשְׁמוֹת רַבָּה פ׳ מ״ג ״כְּתָב לְךָ אֶת הַדְּבָרִים הָאֵלֶּה״ (שמות לד, כז), בְּשָׁעָה שֶׁנִּגְלָה הַקָּדוֹשׁ בָּרוּךְ הוּא בְּסִינַי לִתֵּן תּוֹרָה לְיִשְׂרָאֵל, אָמַר לְמֹשֶׁה עַל הַסֵּדֶר מִקְרָא וּמִשְׁנָה הֲלָכוֹת וְאַגָּדוֹת, שֶׁנֶּאֱמַר (שמות כ, א) ״וַיְדַבֵּר אֱלֹהִים אֵת כָּל הַדְּבָרִים הָאֵלֶּה״, אֲפִלּוּ מַה שֶּׁהַתַּלְמִיד שׁוֹאֵל לָרַב, עַד כָּאן.

וְלֹא עוֹד, אֶלָּא כִּי גַּם בְּאוֹתוֹ הָעֵת שֶׁהָאָדָם עוֹסֵק בַּתּוֹרָה לְמַטָּה, כָּל תֵּבָה שֶׁמּוֹצִיא מִפִּיו, הֵן הֵן הַדְּבָרִים יוֹצְאִים כִּבְיָכוֹל גַּם מִפִּיו יִתְבָּרַךְ בְּאוֹתוֹ הָעֵת מַמָּשׁ, כִּדְאַשְׁכְּחַן בְּפֶרֶק קַמָּא דְּגִיטִּין (ו, ב), גַּבֵּי פִּלֶּגֶשׁ בַּגִּבְעָה ״וַתִּזְנֶה עָלָיו פִּילַגְשׁוֹ״, רַבִּי אֶבְיָתָר אָמַר זְבוּב מָצָא לָהּ, רַבִּי יוֹנָתָן אָמַר נִימָא כו׳, וְאַשְׁכְּחֵיהּ רַבִּי אֶבְיָתָר לְאֵלִיָּהוּ, אָמַר לֵיהּ, מַאי קָעָבִיד קוּדְשָׁא בְּרִיךְ הוּא, אָמַר לֵיהּ עָסִיק בְּפִלֶּגֶשׁ בַּגִּבְעָה, וּמַאי קָאָמַר, אֶבְיָתָר בְּנִי כָּךְ הוּא אוֹמֵר,

יוֹנָתָן בְּנִי כָּךְ הוּא אוֹמֵר. וְהַיְנוּ, מִפְּנֵי שֶׁרַבִּי אֶבְיָתָר וְרַבִּי יוֹנָתָן עָסְקוּ בֵּינֵיהֶם בְּעִנְיַן פִּלֶּגֶשׁ בַּגִּבְעָה, אָז בְּאוֹתוֹ עֵת, גַּם הוּא יִתְבָּרַךְ שָׁנָה דִּבְרֵיהֶם מַמָּשׁ.

וְהוּא יִתְבָּרַךְ שְׁמוֹ וְדִבּוּרוֹ חַד, וְכַמְפֹרָשׁ בַּתּוֹרָה הַקְּדוֹשָׁה בְּמִשְׁנֵה תּוֹרָה "לְאַהֲבָה אֶת ה' אֱלֹהֶיךָ" כו' (דברים ל, כ), וּפֵרְשׁוּהוּ רַבּוֹתֵינוּ זִכְרוֹנָם לִבְרָכָה בִּנְדָרִים בַּבָּרַיְתָא (ס"ב א'), דְּקָאֵי עַל עֵסֶק הַתּוֹרָה, עַיֵּן שָׁם, וְסֵיפֵיהּ דִּקְרָא "וּלְדָבְקָה בוֹ".

וְלָכֵן אָמַר דָּוִד הַמֶּלֶךְ עָלָיו הַשָּׁלוֹם (תהלים קיט, עב): "טוֹב לִי תוֹרַת פִּיךָ" וכו', אָמַר כִּי לִבִּי שָׂמֵחַ בַּעֲמָלִי בַּתּוֹרָה הַקְּדוֹשָׁה בְּרֹב עֹז, בְּהַעֲלוֹתִי עַל לִבִּי שֶׁהִיא תּוֹרַת "פִּיךָ", שֶׁכָּל תֵּבָה מַמָּשׁ מֵהַתּוֹרָה שֶׁאֲנִי עוֹסֵק בָּהּ כָּעֵת, הַכֹּל יָצָא וְגַם עַתָּה הִיא יוֹצֵאת מִפִּיךָ יִתְבָּרַךְ.

וְלָכֵן, כָּל הַתּוֹרָה, קְדֻשָּׁתָהּ שָׁוָה בְּלִי שׁוּם חִלּוּק וְשִׁנּוּי כְּלָל חַס וְשָׁלוֹם, כִּי הַכֹּל דִּבּוּר פִּיו יִתְבָּרַךְ שְׁמוֹ מַמָּשׁ, וְאִם חָסֵר בְּסֵפֶר תּוֹרָה אוֹת אַחַת מִפָּסוּק "אַלּוּף תִּמְנָע" (בראשית לו, מ), הִיא נִפְסֶלֶת כְּמוֹ אִם הָיָה נֶחְסַר אוֹת אֶחָד מֵעֲשֶׂרֶת הַדִּבְּרוֹת, אוֹ מִפָּסוּק שְׁמַע יִשְׂרָאֵל, וּכְמוֹ שֶׁכָּתַב גַּם הָרַמְבַּ"ם זִכְרוֹנוֹ לִבְרָכָה, וְהוּא מַתְנָא דְּבֵי אֵלִיָּהוּ סא"ז סוֹף פֶּרֶק ב':

פֶּרֶק ז'

וְלָזֹאת, רָאוּי לְהָאָדָם לְהָכִין עַצְמוֹ כָּל עֵת, קֹדֶם שֶׁיַּתְחִיל לִלְמֹד, לְהִתְחַשֵּׁב מְעַט עִם קוֹנוֹ יִתְבָּרַךְ שְׁמוֹ בְּטָהֳרַת הַלֵּב בְּיִרְאַת ה', וּלְהִטָּהֵר מֵעֲווֹנוֹתָיו בְּהִרְהוּרֵי תְּשׁוּבָה, כְּדֵי שֶׁיּוּכַל לְהִתְקַשֵּׁר וּלְהִתְדַּבֵּק בְּעֵת עָסְקוֹ בַּתּוֹרָה הַקְּדוֹשָׁה, בְּדִבּוּרוֹ וּרְצוֹנוֹ יִתְבָּרַךְ שְׁמוֹ.

וְגַם יְקַבֵּל עַל עַצְמוֹ, לַעֲשׂוֹת וּלְקַיֵּם כְּכָל הַכָּתוּב בַּתּוֹרָה שֶׁבִּכְתָב וּבְעַל פֶּה, וַאֲשֶׁר יִרְאֶה וְיָבִין דַּרְכּוֹ וְהַנְהָגָתוֹ מִתּוֹרָה הַקְּדוֹשָׁה.

וְכֵן כְּשֶׁרוֹצֶה לְעַיֵּן בִּדְבַר הֲלָכָה, רָאוּי לְהִתְפַּלֵּל שֶׁיְּזַכֵּהוּ יִתְבָּרַךְ לְאַסּוּקֵי שְׁמַעְתָּא אַלִּיבָּא דְּהִלְכְתָא, לְכַוֵּן לַאֲמִתָּהּ שֶׁל תּוֹרָה:

וְכֵן בְּאֶמְצַע הַלִּמּוּד, הָרְשׁוּת נְתוּנָה לְהָאָדָם לְהַפְסִיק זְמַן מֻעָט, טֶרֶם יִכְבֶּה מִלִּבּוֹ יִרְאָתוֹ יִתְבָּרַךְ שְׁמוֹ, שֶׁקִּבֵּל עָלָיו קֹדֶם הַתְחָלַת הַלִּמּוּד, לְהִתְבּוֹנֵן מֵחָדָשׁ עוֹד מְעַט בְּיִרְאַת ה'. כְּמוֹ שֶׁאָמְרוּ רַבּוֹתֵינוּ זִכְרוֹנָם לִבְרָכָה עוֹד (שבת לא, א) "מָשָׁל לְאָדָם שֶׁאָמַר לִשְׁלוּחוֹ הַעֲלֵה לִי כּוֹר שֶׁל חִטִּים לַעֲלִיָּה כו', אָמַר לוֹ עֵרַבְתָּ לִי בָּהֶן קַב חוֹמְטִין, אָמַר לוֹ לֹא, אָמַר לוֹ מוּטָב שֶׁלֹּא הֶעֱלִיתָ", וְקָאֵי עַל אֶמְצַע הָעֵסֶק בִּתְבוּאוֹת חָכְמַת הַתּוֹרָה, שֶׁרָאוּי גַּם כֵּן לְעָרֵב בְּתוֹכוֹ יִרְאָתוֹ יִתְבָּרַךְ, כְּדֵי שֶׁתִּתְקַיֵּם תַּלְמוּדוֹ בְּיָדוֹ.

וְלָכֵן סָמַךְ אֶצְלוֹ הַבָּרַיְתָא "תָּנֵי דְּבֵי ר"י, מְעָרֵב אָדָם קַב חוֹמְטִין בְּכוֹר שֶׁל תְּבוּאָה וְאֵינוֹ חוֹשֵׁשׁ", וְהוּא דִּין מִדִּינֵי גָּזֵל וְאוֹנָאָה, אֲשֶׁר מְקוֹמוֹ בְּסֵדֶר נְזִיקִין, וּמַאי שַׁיְּטֵיהּ הָכָא. אָמְנָם הוֹרוּנוּ בָּזֶה, שֶׁכְּמוֹ בְּמַשָּׂא וּמַתָּן, הֲגַם שֶׁנִּרְאֶה כְּגָזֵל וְאוֹנָאָה, אָמְנָם כֵּיוָן שֶׁהַקַּב עָפָר הוּא הַשִּׁמּוּר וְהַקִּיּוּם שֶׁל כָּל הַכּוֹר תְּבוּאָה, אֵינוֹ חוֹשֵׁשׁ מִשּׁוּם גָּזֵל, כֵּן רַשַּׁאי הָאָדָם לְהַפְסִיק וּלְבַטֵּל זְמַן מֻעָט מֵהַלִּמּוּד, לְהִתְבּוֹנֵן מְעַט בְּיִרְאַת ה', וְאֵינוֹ חוֹשֵׁשׁ בָּזֶה מִשּׁוּם בִּטּוּל תּוֹרָה, כֵּיוָן שֶׁהוּא הַגּוֹרֵם שֶׁתִּתְקַיֵּם אֶצְלוֹ חָכְמַת הַתּוֹרָה:

פֶּרֶק ח'

אָמְנָם דוּן מִינָהּ נַמִּי, מֵעִנְיַן שְׁנֵי הַמְּשָׁלִים שֶׁהִמְשִׁילוּ זִכְרוֹנָם לִבְרָכָה בְּעִנְיַן הַתּוֹרָה וְהַיִּרְאָה, הֵיפֶךְ מֵאֲשֶׁר שָׁגוּ בָּזֶה כַּמָּה מֵרַבַּת בְּנֵי עַמֵּנוּ, שֶׁקּוֹבְעִים כָּל עֵסֶק לִמּוּדָם בְּסִפְרֵי יִרְאָה וּמוּסָר לְבַד.

שֶׁכְּמוֹ בְּעִנְיַן קְדִימַת הָאוֹצָר לְהַתְּבוּאָה שֶׁבְּתוֹכוֹ, וְכִי יַעֲלֶה כְּלָל עַל לֵב אָדָם, כֵּיוָן שֶׁכָּל קִיּוּם וְשִׁמּוּר הַתְּבוּאָה הוּא הָאוֹצָר, יַעֲסֹק כָּל זְמַנּוֹ אוֹ רֻבּוֹ בְּבִנְיַן הָאוֹצָר לְבַד, וְלֹא יַכְנִיס בּוֹ תְּבוּאָה מֵעוֹלָם, כֵּן אֵיךְ יַעֲלֶה עַל לֵב אִישׁ לוֹמַר שֶׁזֶּה תַּכְלִית הָאָדָם מִיִּשְׂרָאֵל, שֶׁיָּשִׂים כָּל קְבִיעַת לִמּוּדוֹ בְּבִנְיַן הָאוֹצָר שֶׁל יִרְאַת שָׁמַיִם לְבַד, וְהוּא אוֹצָר רֵיק, וְלֹא עָלְתָה בְּיָדוֹ מִכָּל עֲמָלוֹ רַק מִצְוָה אַחַת שֶׁל "ה' אֱלֹהֶיךָ תִּירָא" (דברים ו, ג) וְגַם אֵין עָלֶיהָ שֵׁם אוֹצָר כְּלָל.

וְלֹא כִּוְּנוּ רַבּוֹתֵינוּ זִכְרוֹנָם לִבְרָכָה בְּמַאֲמָרָם הַנַּ"ל "אֵין לוֹ לְהַקָּדוֹשׁ בָּרוּךְ הוּא כוּ', אֶלָּא אוֹצָר שֶׁל יִרְאַת שָׁמַיִם בִּלְבַד", אֶלָּא עַל אוֹתָהּ הַיִּרְאָה, שֶׁבְּתוֹכָהּ מֻנָּחִים הָמוֹן תְּבוּאוֹת, מִקְרָא מִשְׁנָה וַהֲלָכוֹת וּשְׁאָרֵי עִנְיְנֵי הַתּוֹרָה, שֶׁהַיִּרְאָה הִיא אוֹצָרָם הַטּוֹב, וּמְשַׁמֶּרֶת שֶׁיִּתְקַיְּמוּ אֶצְלוֹ, עֲרוּכִים וּשְׁנוּנִים בְּפִיו, וַחֲרוּתִים עַל לוּחַ לִבּוֹ, כְּמוֹ שֶׁמּוּכָח וּמֻכְרָח מִמַּה שֶּׁאָמְרוּ עוֹד (ברכות ח, א) אֵין לוֹ לְהַקָּדוֹשׁ בָּרוּךְ בְּעוֹלָמוֹ אֶלָּא ד' אַמּוֹת שֶׁל הֲלָכָה בִּלְבָד.

(וְכַיָּדוּעַ בְּשֹׁרֶשׁ דָּבָר, עִנְיַן שְׁנֵי הַבְּחִינוֹת שֶׁל תּוֹרָה וְיִרְאַת ה' בַּמִּדּוֹת הָעֶלְיוֹנִים, שֶׁבְּחִינַת הַיִּרְאָה לֵית לָהּ מִגַּרְמָהּ כְּלוּם, כִּי הִיא נְקֵבָה בָּאָה, רַק שֶׁהִיא אוֹצָר בֵּית קִבּוּל הַשֶּׁפַע עֶלְיוֹן מִבְּחִינַת הַתּוֹרָה, וּכְמוֹ שֶׁכָּתוּב (חבקוק ב, כ) "וה' בְּהֵיכַל קָדְשׁוֹ", וְעַיֵּן בַּתִּקּוּנִים תִּקּוּן ב' וג').

וְזֶהוּ שֶׁאָמַר הַכָּתוּב (משלי טו, טז) "טוֹב מְעַט בְּיִרְאַת ה' מֵאוֹצָר רָב וּמְהוּמָה בוֹ":

פֶּרֶק ט'

וְכֵן בְּעִנְיַן הַהֶתֵּר לְהַפְסִיק בְּאֶמְצַע הַלִּמּוּד, לְהִתְבּוֹנֵן עוֹד מְעַט בְּיִרְאַת ה', שֶׁהִמְשִׁילוּהוּ זִכְרוֹנָם לִבְרָכָה, לְהֶתֵּר עֵרוּב הַקַּב חוֹמְטִין בְּכוֹר תְּבוּאָה, מִינָהּ נַמִּי, שֶׁכְּמוֹ שֶׁאִם עֵרֵב בְּכוֹר תְּבוּאָה יוֹתֵר מִקַּב חוֹמְטִין, אֲשֶׁר אֵינֶנּוּ צָרִיךְ לְקִיּוּם הַתְּבוּאָה, הֲרֵי הוּא גֶּזֶל וְאוֹנָאָה, כֵּן בְּעִנְיַן הַיִּרְאָה, אִם יַאֲרִיךְ בָּהּ הָאָדָם, זְמַן יָתֵר מִכְּדֵי מִדָּתָהּ הַנִּצְרָךְ לְקִיּוּם וְשִׁמּוּר רֹב תְּבוּאוֹת הַתּוֹרָה, הֲרֵי הוּא גוֹזֵל אוֹתוֹ הַזְּמַן הָעוֹדֵף, מֵהַתּוֹרָה שֶׁהָיָה צָרִיךְ לִלְמֹד בְּאוֹתוֹ הָעֵת, כִּי לֹא הֻרְשָׁה לַעֲסֹק בְּהִתְבּוֹנְנוּת וּקְנִיַּת הַיִּרְאָה, אֶלָּא כְּפִי אֲשֶׁר יִשְׁקֹל בְּשִׂכְלוֹ לְפִי טִבְעוֹ וְעִנְיָנוֹ, שֶׁזֶּה הָעֵת הוּא צֹרֶךְ וְהֶכְרֵחִי לוֹ לַעֲסֹק בִּקְנִיַּת הַיִּרְאָה וּמוּסָר, לְצֹרֶךְ הַשִּׁמּוּר וְהַקִּיּוּם שֶׁל תְּבוּאַת הַתּוֹרָה.

וּבֶאֱמֶת, כִּי הָאָדָם הַקָּבוּעַ בְּעֵסֶק הַתּוֹרָה לִשְׁמָהּ, כְּמוֹ שֶׁפֵּרַשְׁנוּ בְּפֶרֶק ג' עִנְיַן לִשְׁמָהּ, אֵינֶנּוּ צָרִיךְ לְרֹב עָמָל וִיגִיעָה וְאֹרֶךְ זְמַן הָעֵסֶק בְּסִפְרֵי יִרְאָה עַד שֶׁיִּקָּבַע בְּלִבּוֹ יִרְאָתוֹ יִתְבָּרַךְ, כְּאוֹתוֹ הָאָדָם אֲשֶׁר אֵינֶנּוּ קָבוּעַ בְּעֵסֶק הַתּוֹרָה.

כִּי הַתּוֹרָה הַקְּדוֹשָׁה מֵעַצְמָהּ תַּלְבִּישֵׁהוּ יִרְאַת ה' עַל פָּנָיו, בִּמְעַט זְמַן וִיגִיעָה מֻעֶטֶת

עַל זֶה, כִּי כָּךְ דַּרְכָּהּ וּסְגֻלָּתָהּ שֶׁל הַתּוֹרָה הַקְּדוֹשָׁה, כְּמוֹ שֶׁאָמְרוּ (אבות ו, א): "כָּל הָעוֹסֵק בַּתּוֹרָה לִשְׁמָהּ כו', וּמַלְבַּשְׁתּוֹ עֲנָוָה וְיִרְאָה".

וּבְמִשְׁלֵי רַבָּתָא פָּרָשָׁה א', חָכְמָה וּמוּסָר אֱוִילִים בָּזוּ (משלי א, ז), אִם מוּסָר, לָמָּה חָכְמָה, וְאִם חָכְמָה וכו', אֶלָּא אִם לָמַד אָדָם תּוֹרָה וְיוֹשֵׁב וּמִתְעַסֵּק בָּהּ כְּדֵי צָרְכּוֹ הֲרֵי בְּיָדוֹ חָכְמָה וּמוּסָר, וְאִם לָאו כו'.

וּבְתַנָּא דְּבֵי אֵלִיָּהוּ סֵדֶר אֵלִיָּהוּ רַבָּא (רֵישׁ פֶּרֶק יח) "וְעַל הַנַּחַל יַעֲלֶה עַל שְׂפָתוֹ, מִזֶּה וּמִזֶּה כָּל עֵץ מַאֲכָל" כו' (יחזקאל מז, יב), וּמַהוּ הָעֵץ אֲשֶׁר יַעֲלֶה בְּנַחַל זֶה, אֵלּוּ תַּלְמִידֵי חֲכָמִים, שֶׁיֵּשׁ בָּהֶם תּוֹרָה מִקְרָא וּמִשְׁנָה הֲלָכוֹת וְאַגָּדוֹת וּמַעֲשִׂים טוֹבִים וְשִׁמּוּשׁ תַּלְמִידֵי חֲכָמִים, כו'. מְשָׁלוֹ מָשָׁל, לְמָה הַדָּבָר דּוֹמֶה כו', כָּךְ תַּלְמִידֵי חֲכָמִים בָּעוֹלָם הַזֶּה בְּדִבְרֵי תוֹרָה, כֵּיוָן שֶׁקָּרְאוּ אֶת הַמִּקְרָא וְשָׁנוּ כו', וְדִבְרֵי תוֹרָה מָתוֹק עֲלֵיהֶם, הַקָּדוֹשׁ בָּרוּךְ הוּא מְרַחֵם עֲלֵיהֶם, וְנוֹתֵן בָּהֶם חָכְמָה וּבִינָה וְדֵעָה וְהַשְׂכֵּל לַעֲשׂוֹת מַעֲשִׂים טוֹבִים וְתַלְמוּד תּוֹרָה וְהַכֹּל מְתֻקָּן לִפְנֵיהֶם כו':

פֶּרֶק י'

וּבִשְׁעַת הָעֵסֶק וְהָעִיּוּן בַּתּוֹרָה, וַדַּאי שֶׁאֵין צָרִיךְ אָז לְעִנְיַן הַדְּבֵקוּת כְּלָל, כַּנַּ"ל [פ"ב], שֶׁבְּהָעֵסֶק וְעִיּוּן לְבַד, הוּא דָּבוּק בִּרְצוֹנוֹ וְדִבּוּרוֹ יִתְבָּרַךְ, וְהוּא יִתְבָּרַךְ וּרְצוֹנוֹ וְדִבּוּרוֹ חַד.

וְהוּא עִנְיַן מַאֲמָרָם זִכְרוֹנָם לִבְרָכָה בִּשְׁמוֹת רַבָּה פָּרָשָׁה ל"ג, אָדָם לוֹקֵחַ חֵפֶץ, שֶׁמָּא יָכוֹל לִקְנוֹת בְּעָלָיו, אֲבָל הַקָּדוֹשׁ בָּרוּךְ הוּא נָתַן תּוֹרָה לְיִשְׂרָאֵל, וְאוֹמֵר לָהֶם, כִּבְיָכוֹל לִי אַתֶּם לוֹקְחִים כו'.

וְזֶה שֶׁכָּתוּב בְּכַמָּה מְקוֹמוֹת בַּזֹּהַר דְּקוּדְשָׁא בְּרִיךְ הוּא וְאוֹרַיְתָא חַד. וּגְדוֹלָה מִזּוֹ בְּפָרָשַׁת בְּשַׁלַּח ס' ע"א, וְאוֹלִיפְנָא דְּקוּדְשָׁא בְּרִיךְ הוּא תּוֹרָה אִיקְרֵי כו', וְאֵין תּוֹרָה אֶלָּא קוּדְשָׁא בְּרִיךְ הוּא, [וְלָמַדְנוּ שֶׁהַקָּדוֹשׁ בָּרוּךְ הוּא נִקְרָא תּוֹרָה וכו' וְאֵין תּוֹרָה אֶלָּא הַקָּדוֹשׁ בָּרוּךְ הוּא.]

וְגַם כִּי שָׁרְשָׁהּ הָעֶלְיוֹן שֶׁל הַתּוֹרָה הַקְּדוֹשָׁה, הוּא בָּעֶלְיוֹן שֶׁבְּהָעוֹלָמוֹת הַנִּקְרָאִים עוֹלָמוֹת הָ"אֵין סוֹף", סוֹד הַמַּלְבּוּשׁ הַנֶּעְלָם, הַנִּזְכָּר בְּסִתְרֵי פְּלִיאוֹת חָכְמָה מִתּוֹרַת רַבֵּנוּ הָאֲרִיזַ"ל, שֶׁהוּא רֵאשִׁית סוֹד אוֹתִיּוֹת הַתּוֹרָה הַקְּדוֹשָׁה, וּכְמוֹ שֶׁכָּתוּב (משלי ח, כב) "ה' קָנָנִי רֵאשִׁית דַּרְכּוֹ קֶדֶם מִפְעָלָיו מֵאָז".

וְזֶה שֶׁאָמְרוּ זִכְרוֹנָם לִבְרָכָה (ב"ר א, ד) שֶׁקָּדְמָה לָעוֹלָם, הַיְנוּ גַּם מִכָּל הָעוֹלָמוֹת כֻּלָּם, שֶׁהֲרֵי אָמְרוּ בִּבְרֵאשִׁית רַבָּה פָּרָשָׁה א' שֶׁקָּדְמָה לְכִסֵּא הַכָּבוֹד, וְהָאֱמֶת שֶׁקָּדְמָה כִּבְיָכוֹל גַּם לְעוֹלָם הָאֲצִילוּת יִתְבָּרַךְ כַּנַּ"ל, אֶלָּא שֶׁהָאֲצִילוּת נִקְרָא "אַיִן", וּמִסּוֹד הַכִּסֵּא מַתְחִיל סוֹד הַשִּׁעוּר קוֹמָה כִּבְיָכוֹל, לָכֵן אָמְרוּ שֶׁקָּדְמָה לְכִסֵּא הַכָּבוֹד.

וְלָכֵן בָּהּ נֶאֶצְלוּ וְנִבְרְאוּ כָּל הָעוֹלָמוֹת עֶלְיוֹנִים וְתַחְתּוֹנִים, כְּמוֹ שֶׁכָּתוּב (משלי ח, ל) "וָאֶהְיֶה אֶצְלוֹ אָמוֹן", וְאָמְרוּ זִכְרוֹנָם לִבְרָכָה (תנחומא בראשית א) אַל תִּקְרֵי אָמוֹן אֶלָּא אוּמָן וכו'. וּבְמִשְׁלֵי רַבָּתָא רֵישׁ פָּרָשָׁה ט', חָכְמוֹת בָּנְתָה בֵיתָהּ (משלי ט, א), זוֹ הַתּוֹרָה שֶׁבָּנְתָה כָּל הָעוֹלָמוֹת.

וְהָעִנְיָן, כִּי הַתּוֹרָה הַקְּדוֹשָׁה הִיא דִּבּוּרוֹ יִתְבָּרַךְ, וּבְמַאֲמַר פִּיו יִתְבָּרַךְ בְּמַעֲשֵׂי בְּרֵאשִׁית נִבְרְאוּ הָעוֹלָמוֹת כֻּלָּם. שֶׁעַל יְדֵי סִדּוּר גִּלְגּוּל צֵרוּפֵי הָאוֹתִיּוֹת עַל פִּי סֵדֶר הרל"א שְׁעָרִים פָּנִים וְאָחוֹר שֶׁבְּמַאֲמַר "בְּרֵאשִׁית בָּרָא" וכו', נֶאֶצְלוּ וְנִבְרְאוּ הָעוֹלָמוֹת, עֶלְיוֹנֵי עֶלְיוֹנִים רִבֵּי רִבְוָן, בְּכָל סֵדֶר מַצָּבָם וּפְרָטֵי עִנְיְנֵיהֶם וְכָל הַנִּכְלָל בָּהֶם, וְכֵן בְּכָל מַאֲמָר וּמַאֲמָר שֶׁבּוֹ עַל דֶּרֶךְ הַנַּ"ל נִבְרְאוּ כָּל פְּרָטֵי הַמִּינִים וְהָעִנְיָנִים שֶׁבְּאוֹתוֹ הַסּוּג שֶׁעָלָיו נֶאֱמַר אוֹתוֹ הַמַּאֲמָר.

כְּמוֹ שֶׁכָּתוּב בַּזֹּהַר תְּרוּמָה קס"א א', דְּכַד בָּרָא קוּדְשָׁא בְּרִיךְ הוּא עָלְמָא, אִסְתַּכַּל בָּהּ בְּאוֹרַיְתָא וּבָרָא עָלְמָא, וּבְאוֹרַיְתָא אִתְבְּרֵי עָלְמָא, כְּמָה דְּאוֹקְמוּהָ, דִּכְתִיב "וָאֶהְיֶה אֶצְלוֹ אָמוֹן" כו', אוֹרַיְתָא צוֹוַחַת וָאֶהְיֶה אֶצְלוֹ אָמוֹן, בִּי בָּרָא קוּדְשָׁא בְּרִיךְ הוּא עָלְמָא, דְּעַד לָא אִתְבְּרֵי עָלְמָא אַקְדִּימַת אוֹרַיְתָא כו', וְכַד בְּעָא קוּדְשָׁא בְּרִיךְ הוּא לְמִבְרֵי עָלְמָא, הֲוָה מִסְתַּכֵּל בָּהּ בְּאוֹרַיְתָא בְּכָל מִלָּה וּמִלָּה, וְעָבִיד לְקִבְלָהּ אוּמָנוּתָא דְּעָלְמָא, בְּגִין דְּכָל מִלִּין וְעוֹבָדִין דְּכָל עָלְמִין בְּאוֹרַיְתָא אִנּוּן כו'. בְּאוֹרַיְתָא כְּתִיב בָּהּ "בְּרֵאשִׁית בָּרָא" וכו', אִסְתַּכַּל בְּהַאי מִלָּה וּבָרָא אֶת הַשָּׁמַיִם. כְּתִיב בָּהּ (בראשית א, ג) "וַיֹּאמֶר אֱלֹהִים יְהִי אוֹר", אִסְתַּכַּל בְּהַאי מִלָּה וּבָרָא אֶת הָאוֹר. וְכֵן בְּכָל מִלָּה וּמִלָּה דִּכְתִיב בָּהּ בְּאוֹרַיְתָא, אִסְתַּכַּל קוּדְשָׁא בְּרִיךְ הוּא, וַעֲבִיד הַהוּא מִלָּה. וְעַל דָּא כְּתִיב "וָאֶהְיֶה אֶצְלוֹ אָמוֹן", כְּגַוְנָא דָּא כָּל עָלְמָא אִתְבְּרֵי, [כְּשֶׁבָּרָא הַקָּדוֹשׁ בָּרוּךְ הוּא אֶת הָעוֹלָם, הִסְתַּכֵּל בָּהּ בַּתּוֹרָה וּבָרָא אֶת הָעוֹלָם. וּבַתּוֹרָה נִבְרָא הָעוֹלָם, כְּמוֹ שֶׁהֶעֱמִידוּהוּ שֶׁכָּתוּב וָאֶהְיֶה אֶצְלוֹ אָמוֹן וכו', הַתּוֹרָה צְוֹוחַת וָאֶהְיֶה אֶצְלוֹ אָמוֹן, בִּי בָּרָא הַקָּדוֹשׁ בָּרוּךְ הוּא אֶת הָעוֹלָם, דְּעַד שֶׁלֹּא נִבְרָא הָעוֹלָם קָדְמָה הַתּוֹרָה, וּכְשֶׁרָצָה הַקָּדוֹשׁ בָּרוּךְ הוּא לִבְרֹא הָעוֹלָם הָיָה מִסְתַּכֵּל בָּהּ — בַּתּוֹרָה בְּכָל מִלָּה וּמִלָּה וְעָשָׂה לְעֻמָּתָהּ אוּמָנוּת הָעוֹלָם, מִשּׁוּם שֶׁכָּל דִּבְרֵי וּמַעֲשֵׂי שֶׁל כָּל הָעוֹלָמוֹת כֻּלָּם הֵם בַּתּוֹרָה וכו', כָּתוּב בַּתּוֹרָה בְּרֵאשִׁית בָּרָא וכו' הִסְתַּכֵּל בְּמִלָּה זוֹ וּבָרָא אֶת הַשָּׁמַיִם, בַּתּוֹרָה כָּתוּב וַיֹּאמֶר אֱלוֹקִים יְהִי אוֹר הִסְתַּכֵּל בְּמִלָּה זוֹ וּבָרָא אֶת הָאוֹר, וְכֵן בְּכָל מִלָּה וּמִלָּה שֶׁכָּתוּב בַּתּוֹרָה הִסְתַּכֵּל הַקָּדוֹשׁ בָּרוּךְ הוּא וְעָשָׂה דָּבָר הַהוּא, וְעַל כֵּן כָּתוּב וָאֶהְיֶה אֶצְלוֹ אָמוֹן, בְּאוֹפֶן זֶה נִבְרָא כָּל הָעוֹלָם] ע"כ.

וְלָכֵן כָּל הַתּוֹרָה בִּכְלַל וְכָל הָעוֹלָמוֹת כְּלָלֵיהֶם וּפְרָטֵיהֶם וְסִדּוּרָם וְכָל עִנְיְנֵיהֶם, כֻּלָּם כְּלוּלִים וּרְמוּזִים בַּעֲשֶׂר הַמַּאֲמָרוֹת דְּמַעֲשֵׂה בְּרֵאשִׁית, וּכְמוֹ שֶׁכָּתַב רַבֵּינוּ הַגָּדוֹל הַגָּאוֹן הֶחָסִיד מוהר"א זצוק"ל בְּפֵרוּשׁוֹ עַל הַסִּפְרָא דִּצְנִיעוּתָא בְּפֶרֶק ה', וְעַיֵּן בָּזֶה בַּזֹּהַר בְּרֵאשִׁית מ"ז א':

וְלָכֵן אָמְרוּ בַּזֹּהַר, דְּאוֹרַיְתָא הִיא נְהִירוּ דְּכָל עָלְמִין, וְחִיּוּתָא וְקִיּוּמָא וְשָׁרְשָׁא דְּכֻלְּהוֹן.

וְהָעִנְיָן, כִּי הָעוֹלָמוֹת הוֹלְכִים עַל סֵדֶר הַהִשְׁתַּלְשְׁלוּת וְהַהַדְרָגָה, שֶׁכָּל עוֹלָם הַיּוֹתֵר עֶלְיוֹן וְגָבוֹהַּ, הוּא נִשְׁמָתוֹ וְחִיּוּתוֹ וְקִיּוּמוֹ וְאוֹרוֹ שֶׁל הָעוֹלָם שֶׁתַּחְתָּיו לְבַד. אָמְנָם יִתְרוֹן עוֹלַם הָאֲצִילוּת עַל הַג' עוֹלָמוֹת בְּרִיאָה יְצִירָה עֲשִׂיָּה, שֶׁהוּא מִתְפַּשֵּׁט וּמֵאִיר לְכָל הַג' עוֹלָמוֹת בְּרִיאָה יְצִירָה עֲשִׂיָּה שֶׁתַּחְתָּיו. עַיֵּן בְּעֵץ חַיִּים שַׁעַר פְּנִימִיּוּת וְחִיצוֹנִיּוּת דְּרוּשׁ ב', וְשָׁם רֵישׁ דְּרוּשׁ ח' וְרֵישׁ דְּרוּשׁ י', וּבְשַׁעַר דְּרוּשֵׁי אבי"ע פֶּרֶק ז', וּבְשַׁעַר הַשֵּׁמוֹת פֶּרֶק א', וּבְשַׁעַר קְלִפַּת נֹגַהּ פֶּרֶק א', שֶׁכֻּלּוֹ אֱלֹקוּת גָּמוּר, כְּמוֹ שֶׁכָּתוּב בְּהַקְדָּמַת הַתִּקּוּנִים: דְּעֶשֶׂר

סְפִירוֹת דַּאֲצִילוּת מַלְכָּא בְּהוֹן, אִיהוּ וְגַרְמֵיהּ חַד בְּהוֹן, אִיהוּ וְחַיּוֹהִי חַד בְּהוֹן, מַה דְּלָאו הָכִי בְּעֶשֶׂר סְפִירוֹת דִּבְרִיאָה, דְּלָאו אִנּוּן וְאִיהוּ חַד, לָאו אִנּוּן וְגַרְמֵיהוֹן חַד. [עֶשֶׂר סְפִירוֹת שֶׁאֲצִילוּת הַמֶּלֶךְ בָּם, הוּא וְעַצְמוּתוֹ אֶחָד בָּהֶם, הוּא וְחִיּוּתוֹ אֶחָד בָּהֶם, מַה שֶּׁאֵין כֵּן בְּעֶשֶׂר סְפִירוֹת שֶׁבַּבְּרִיאָה, שֶׁאֵין הוּא וְהֵם אֶחָד, וְאֵין הוּא וְעַצְמוּתָם אֶחָד.]

וְלָכֵן, הַתּוֹרָה הַקְּדוֹשָׁה, שֶׁשָּׁרְשָׁהּ הָעֶלְיוֹן הַנֶּעְלָם הוּא לְמַעְלָה מַעְלָה גַּם מֵאֲצִילוּת קָדְשׁוֹ יִתְבָּרַךְ כנ"ל, וְקוּדְשָׁא בְּרִיךְ הוּא וְאוֹרַיְתָא, כֻּלָּא חַד. הִיא הַנֶּפֶשׁ וְהַחִיּוּת וּנְהִירוּ וְשָׁרְשָׁא דְּעָלְמִין כֻּלְּהוּ.

שֶׁכְּמוֹ שֶׁבִּשְׁעַת הַבְּרִיאָה, בָּהּ נֶאֶצְלוּ וְנִבְרְאוּ כֻּלָּם, כֵּן מֵאָז, הִיא נִשְׁמָתָם וְחִיּוּתָם וְקִיּוּמָם עַל סֵדֶר מַצָּבָם, וּבִלְתִּי שִׁפְעַת אוֹרָהּ בָּהֶם, כָּל רֶגַע מַמָּשׁ לְהָאִירָם לְהַחֲיוֹתָם וּלְקַיְּמָם, הָיוּ חוֹזְרִים כֻּלָּם לְתֹהוּ וָבֹהוּ מַמָּשׁ:

פֶּרֶק י"א

וְלָזֹאת, עִקַּר חִיּוּתָם וְאוֹרָם וְקִיּוּמָם שֶׁל הָעוֹלָמוֹת כֻּלָּם עַל נָכוֹן, הוּא רַק כְּשֶׁאֲנַחְנוּ עוֹסְקִים בָּהּ כָּרָאוּי, כִּי קוּדְשָׁא בְּרִיךְ הוּא וְאוֹרַיְתָא וְיִשְׂרָאֵל כֻּלָּא חַד (עי' זהר פ' אחרי עג.), שֶׁכָּל אֶחָד מִיִּשְׂרָאֵל, שֹׁרֶשׁ נִשְׁמָתוֹ הָעֶלְיוֹנָה מְדֻבָּק וְנֶאֱחָז בְּאוֹת אַחַת מֵהַתּוֹרָה, וְהָיוּ לַאֲחָדִים מַמָּשׁ.

וּלְכָךְ אָמְרוּ בִּבְרֵאשִׁית רַבָּה פ"א, שֶׁמַּחְשַׁבְתָּן שֶׁל יִשְׂרָאֵל קָדְמָה לְכָל דָּבָר, וְלֹא בָּא לַחֲלֹק עַל מַה שֶּׁאָמְרוּ שֶׁהַתּוֹרָה קָדְמָה לְכָל דָּבָר, כִּי הַכֹּל אֶחָד בְּשָׁרְשָׁן, וְהִיא הִיא.

וז"ש "מַחְשַׁבְתָּן" שֶׁל יִשְׂרָאֵל. וּכְמוֹ שֶׁאָמְרוּ "יִשְׂרָאֵל עָלָה בְּמַחְשָׁבָה", רוֹצֶה לוֹמַר, רֵאשִׁית הַמַּחְשָׁבָה, סוֹד הָרְעוּתָא עִלָּאָה, כְּמוֹ שֶׁכָּתוּב בַּזֹּהַר וַיֵּרָא קי"ח ב', דְּהָא יִשְׂרָאֵל סָלִיק בִּרְעוּתָא דְּקוּדְשָׁא בְּרִיךְ הוּא עַד לָא יִבְרָא עָלְמָא. [כִּי יִשְׂרָאֵל עָלָה בִּרְצוֹן הַקָּדוֹשׁ בָּרוּךְ הוּא עַד שֶׁלֹּא נִבְרָא הָעוֹלָם.]

וְהָרְעוּתָא הִיא רֵאשִׁית הַכֹּל, אֱלָהוּת גָּמוּר כִּבְיָכוֹל, מֵעוֹלָמוֹת אֵין סוֹף, כַּנִּזְכָּר שָׁם בְּפָרָשַׁת נֹחַ ס"ה א', וּפְקוּדֵי רס"ח ב', אָמַר רַבִּי שִׁמְעוֹן אֲרֵימִית כו', דְּכַד רְעוּתָא עִלָּאָה כו', וְכָל אִנּוּן נְהוֹרִין מֵרָזָא דְּמַחֲשָׁבָה עִלָּאָה וּלְתַתָּא, כֻּלְּהוּ אִקְרוּן אֵין סוֹף. [אָמַר רַבִּי שִׁמְעוֹן הֲרִימוֹתִי וכו' שֶׁכַּאֲשֶׁר רָצוֹן הָעֶלְיוֹן וכו' וְכָל אֵלּוּ הָאוֹרוֹת מִסּוֹד הַמַּחְשָׁבָה הָעֶלְיוֹנָה וְהַתַּחְתּוֹנָה כֻּלָּם נִקְרָאִים אֵין סוֹף] עַיֵּן שָׁם הֵיטֵב, וּבְהַגָּהַת הרח"ו זִכְרוֹנוֹ לִבְרָכָה שָׁם, וּבְעֵץ חַיִּים שַׁעַר עִגּוּלִים וְיֹשֶׁר רֵישׁ עָנָף ד', וּבְשַׁעַר הִשְׁתַּלְשְׁלוּת הי' סְפִירוֹת רֵישׁ עָנָף ב'.

וְלָכֵן אָמְרוּ: "בְּרֵאשִׁית" – בִּשְׁבִיל הַתּוֹרָה שֶׁנִּקְרֵאת "רֵאשִׁית", וּבִשְׁבִיל יִשְׂרָאֵל שֶׁנִּקְרְאוּ "רֵאשִׁית".

(וְלָכֵן אָמְרוּ זִכְרוֹנָם לִבְרָכָה (מו"ק כה, א): "הָעוֹמֵד עַל הַמֵּת בִּשְׁעַת יְצִיאַת נְשָׁמָה חַיָּב לִקְרֹעַ, הָא לְמַה הַדָּבָר דּוֹמֶה, לְרוֹאֶה סֵפֶר תּוֹרָה שֶׁנִּשְׂרָף, שֶׁקְּדֻשַּׁת נִשְׁמַת כָּל אֶחָד מִיִּשְׂרָאֵל הִיא הִיא קְדֻשַּׁת סֵפֶר תּוֹרָה מַמָּשׁ").

וְלָכֵן, מֵעֵת הַבְּרִיאָה, שֶׁהָיְתָה הַתּוֹרָה גְּנוּזָה עֲדַיִן בִּמְקוֹר שָׁרְשָׁהּ הַנֶּעְלָם מִכָּל הָעוֹלָמוֹת עֶלְיוֹנִים, וּמֵרָחוֹק לְבַד הֵאִירָה לְכָל הָעוֹלָמוֹת לְהַחֲיוֹתָם וּלְקַיְּמָם, וְלֹא נִשְׁתַּלְשְׁלָה עַצְמוּתָהּ מַמָּשׁ לְמַטָּה לָזֶה הָעוֹלָם שֶׁיַּעַסְקוּ בָהּ קְבוּצֵי מַטָּה, עֲדַיִן הָיוּ הָעוֹלָמוֹת רוֹפְפִים וְרוֹתְתִים, וְלֹא הָיוּ עַל מְכוֹנָם הָאֲמִתִּי, וּקְרָאוּם רַבּוֹתֵינוּ זִכְרוֹנָם לִבְרָכָה (ע״ז ט, א) "שְׁנֵי אֲלָפִים תֹּהוּ".

וְהָיוּ תְּלוּיִים וְעוֹמְדִים עַד עֵת מַתַּן תּוֹרָה, כַּיָּדוּעַ מַאֲמָרָם זִכְרוֹנָם לִבְרָכָה (שבת פח, א) שֶׁהִתְנָה הַקָּדוֹשׁ בָּרוּךְ הוּא עִם מַעֲשֵׂי בְרֵאשִׁית, אִם מְקַבְּלִין יִשְׂרָאֵל וכו׳, וְאִם לָאו וכו׳. וְכֵן הוּא בִּשְׁמוֹת רַבָּה פמ״ז, וּדְבָרִים רַבָּה סוֹף פָּרָשָׁה ח׳, וּבְרֵישׁ הַתַּנְחוּמָא.

וּבְרַבָּה שִׁיר הַשִּׁירִים (א, ט) "דִּמִּיתִיךְ רַעְיָתִי", רַבָּנָן אָמְרֵי, רַעְיָתִי דְּעוֹלָמִי, שֶׁקִּבְּלוּ תּוֹרָתִי, שֶׁאִלּוּ לֹא קִבְּלוּ הָיִיתִי מַחֲזִיר אֶת עוֹלָמִי לְתֹהוּ וָבֹהוּ, דְּאָמַר ר״ח בְּשֵׁם ר״א, כְּתִיב (תהלים עה, ד) "נְמוֹגִים אֶרֶץ" כו׳, "אָנֹכִי תִכַּנְתִּי עַמּוּדֶיהָ סֶלָה", אִלּוּלֵי יִשְׂרָאֵל שֶׁעָמְדוּ עַל הַר סִינַי כו׳, וּמִי בִּסֵּס הָעוֹלָם, "אָנֹכִי" כו׳, בִּזְכוּת אָנֹכִי ה׳ אֱלֹהֶיךָ "תִּכַּנְתִּי עַמּוּדֶיהָ סֶלָה".

וּמֵאָז שֶׁנִּשְׁתַּלְשְׁלָה וְיָרְדָה כִּבְיָכוֹל מִמְּקוֹר שָׁרְשָׁהּ הַנֶּעְלָם לָזֶה הָעוֹלָם, כְּמַאֲמָרָם זִכְרוֹנָם לִבְרָכָה (בראשית רבה יט), בָּא מֹשֶׁה וְהוֹרִידָהּ לָאָרֶץ, כָּל חִיּוּתָם וְקִיּוּמָם שֶׁל כָּל הָעוֹלָמוֹת, הוּא רַק עַל יְדֵי הֶבֶל פִּינוּ וְהֶגְיוֹנֵינוּ בָּהּ.

וְהָאֱמֶת בִּלְתִּי שׁוּם סָפֵק כְּלָל, שֶׁאִם הָיָה הָעוֹלָם כֻּלּוֹ, מִקָּצֶה עַד קָצֵהוּ, פָּנוּי חַס וְשָׁלוֹם אַף רֶגַע אֶחָד מַמָּשׁ, מֵהָעֵסֶק וְהִתְבּוֹנְנוּת שֶׁלָּנוּ בַּתּוֹרָה, כְּרֶגַע הָיוּ נֶחֱרָבִים כָּל הָעוֹלָמוֹת, עֶלְיוֹנִים וְתַחְתּוֹנִים, וְהָיוּ לְאֶפֶס וָתֹהוּ חַס וְשָׁלוֹם. וְכֵן שִׁפְעַת אוֹרָם אוֹ מִעוּטוֹ חַס וְשָׁלוֹם, הַכֹּל רַק כְּפִי עִנְיַן וְרֹב עָסְקֵנוּ בָּהּ.

לָכֵן אָנוּ מְבָרְכִים עָלֶיהָ "וְחַיֵּי עוֹלָם נָטַע בְּתוֹכֵנוּ". כְּעִנְיַן הַנְּטִיעָה, שֶׁנְּטִיעָתָהּ כְּדֵי לַעֲשׂוֹת פְּרִי — לְהַרְבּוֹת טוֹבָה, כֵּן אִם אָנוּ מַחֲזִיקִים בַּתּוֹרָה הַקְּדוֹשָׁה בְּכָל כֹּחֵנוּ כָּרָאוּי, אָנוּ מַנְחִילִין חַיֵּי עַד, וּמַמְשִׁיכִים מִשָּׁרְשָׁהּ הַנֶּעְלָם לְמַעְלָה מִכָּל הָעוֹלָמוֹת, תּוֹסְפוֹת קְדֻשָּׁה וּבְרָכָה וְאוֹר גָּדוֹל בְּכָל הָעוֹלָמוֹת.

זֶה שֶׁאָמְרוּ בְּמִשְׁלֵי רַבְּתָא פָּרָשָׁה ב׳ "מִכָּל מִשְׁמָר נְצֹר לִבֶּךָ", שֶׁלֹּא תִּבְרַח מִדִּבְרֵי תוֹרָה, לָמָּה, "כִּי מִמֶּנּוּ תּוֹצְאוֹת חַיִּים", לְלַמֶּדְךָ שֶׁמִּדִּבְרֵי תוֹרָה יוֹצְאִין חַיִּים לָעוֹלָם.

וְגַם לִבְנוֹת הַנֶּהֱרָסוֹת בְּתִקּוּנִים גְּדוֹלִים, לְקַשֵּׁר וּלְיַחֵד וּלְהַשְׁלִים הָעֶלְיוֹנִים עִם הַתַּחְתּוֹנִים, וְכָל הָעָלְמִין שְׁקִילִין וּנְהִירִין כַּחֲדָא. כְּמַאֲמָרָם זִכְרוֹנָם לִבְרָכָה בְּפֶרֶק חֵלֶק (צט, ב): "אָמַר רַבִּי אֲלֶכְּסַנְדְּרִי, כָּל הָעוֹסֵק בַּתּוֹרָה לִשְׁמָהּ, כְּאִלּוּ עוֹשֶׂה שָׁלוֹם בְּפַמַּלְיָא שֶׁל מַעְלָה וּבְפַמַּלְיָא שֶׁל מַטָּה, שֶׁנֶּאֱמַר (ישעיה כז, ה) "אוֹ יַחֲזֵק בְּמָעֻזִּי יַעֲשֶׂה שָׁלוֹם לִי" כו׳, רַב אָמַר כְּאִלּוּ בָּנָה פַּלְטֵרִין שֶׁל מַעְלָה וּפַלְטֵרִין שֶׁל מַטָּה, שֶׁנֶּאֱמַר (ישעיה נא, טז) "וָאָשִׂים דְּבָרַי בְּפִיךָ וכו׳, לִנְטֹעַ שָׁמַיִם וְלִיסֹּד אָרֶץ".

וּבְחָזִית, "שׁוֹקָיו עַמּוּדֵי שֵׁשׁ" (שה״ש ה, טו) אֵלּוּ תַּלְמִידֵי חֲכָמִים, לָמָּה נִמְשְׁלוּ לְעַמּוּדִים, שֶׁהֵם עַמּוּדֵי עוֹלָם, שֶׁנֶּאֱמַר (ירמיה לג, כה) "אִם לֹא בְרִיתִי יוֹמָם וָלָיְלָה חֻקּוֹת שָׁמַיִם וָאָרֶץ לֹא שָׂמְתִּי" כו׳. וּבְמִשְׁלֵי רַבְּתָא (ט, א) "חָכְמוֹת בָּנְתָה בֵיתָהּ" כו׳, אָמַר

הַקָּדוֹשׁ בָּרוּךְ הוּא, אִם זָכָה אָדָם וְלָמַד תּוֹרָה וְחָכְמָה, חָשׁוּב לְפָנַי כְּמוֹ שֶׁבָּרָא שָׁמַיִם, וּכְאִלּוּ הֶעֱמִיד כָּל הָעוֹלָם כֻּלּוֹ. וְשָׁם (לא) בְּפֶרֶק אֵשֶׁת חַיִל אָמְרוּ: "אָמַר הַקָּדוֹשׁ בָּרוּךְ הוּא לְיִשְׂרָאֵל, בָּנַי הֱיוּ מִתְעַסְּקִין בַּתּוֹרָה בַּיּוֹם וּבַלַּיְלָה, וּמַעֲלֶה אֲנִי עֲלֵיכֶם כְּאִלּוּ אַתֶּם מַעֲמִידִים אֶת כָּל הָעוֹלָם".

וּבַזֹּהַר בְּרֵאשִׁית מ"ז א', כָּל מַאן דְּאִשְׁתַּדֵּל בְּאוֹרַיְתָא בְּכָל יוֹמָא, יִזְכֵּי לְמֶהֱוֵי לֵיהּ חוּלָקָא בְּעָלְמָא דְּאָתֵי, וְיִתְחַשִׁיב לֵיהּ כְּאִלּוּ בָּאנֵי עָלְמִין, דְּהָא בְּאוֹרַיְתָא אִתְבְּנֵי עָלְמָא וְאִשְׁתַּכְלַל, הֲדָא הוּא דִּכְתִּיב ה' בְּחָכְמָה יָסַד אֶרֶץ וגו', וּכְתִיב וָאֶהְיֶה אֶצְלוֹ אָמוֹן כו', וְכָל דְּאִשְׁתַּדֵּל בָּהּ שַׁכְלֵל עָלְמִין וְקַיֵּם לֵיהּ. וְתָא חֲזֵי, בְּרוּחָא עָבִיד קוּדְשָׁא בְּרִיךְ הוּא עָלְמָא, וּבְרוּחָא מִתְקַיְּמָא, דָּא רוּחָא דְּאִנּוּן דְּלָעָאן בְּאוֹרַיְתָא כו' [כָּל מִי שֶׁעוֹסֵק בַּתּוֹרָה בְּכָל יוֹם יִזְכֶּה שֶׁיִּהְיֶה לוֹ חֵלֶק בָּעוֹלָם הַבָּא, וְיִהְיֶה נֶחְשָׁב לוֹ כְּאִלּוּ בָּנָה עוֹלָמוֹת, שֶׁהֲרֵי בַּתּוֹרָה נִבְנָה הָעוֹלָם וְנִשְׁתַּכְלֵל, וְזֶה שֶׁכָּתוּב ה' בְּחָכְמָה יָסַד אֶרֶץ וגו' וְכֵן כָּתוּב וָאֶהְיֶה אֶצְלוֹ אָמוֹן וכו' וְכָל הָעוֹסֵק בָּהּ מְשַׁכְלֵל עוֹלָמוֹת וּמְקַיֵּם אוֹתָם, וּבֹא וּרְאֵה בְּרוּחַ עָשָׂה הַקָּדוֹשׁ בָּרוּךְ הוּא אֶת הָעוֹלָם וּבְרוּחַ מִתְקַיֵּם, זֶה רוּחַ שֶׁל אֵלּוּ הָעוֹסְקִים בַּתּוֹרָה.]

וְשָׁם בְּפָרָשַׁת וַיֵּשֶׁב, אַחַר שֶׁהֶאֱרִיךְ תְּחִלָּה בְּמַעֲלָתוֹ הַנּוֹרָאָה שֶׁל הָאָדָם הָעוֹסֵק בַּתּוֹרָה בָּעוֹלָם הַזֶּה וּבָעוֹלָם הַבָּא, וְעָנְשׁוֹ הַגָּדוֹל בִּשְׁנֵי הָעוֹלָמִים כְּשֶׁמִּתְרַפֶּה מִמֶּנָּה חַס וְשָׁלוֹם, סִיֵּם וְאָמַר "בְּגִין כָּךְ כֹּלָּא קַיְמָא עַל קִיּוּמָא דְּאוֹרַיְתָא, וְעָלְמָא לָא אִתְקַיַּם בְּקִיּוּמֵיהּ אֶלָּא בְּאוֹרַיְתָא, דְּאִיהוּ קִיּוּמָא דְּעָלְמִין עִלָּא וְתַתָּא, דִּכְתִיב "אִם לֹא בְרִיתִי יוֹמָם וָלָיְלָה" כו'. [מִשּׁוּם כָּךְ הַכֹּל עוֹמֵד עַל קִיּוּם הַתּוֹרָה וְהָעוֹלָם אֵינוֹ עוֹמֵד בְּקִיּוּמוֹ אֶלָּא בַּתּוֹרָה שֶׁהִיא הַקִּיּוּם שֶׁל עוֹלָמוֹת עֶלְיוֹן וְתַחְתּוֹן דִּכְתִיב וכו'.]

וּבְפָרָשַׁת תְּרוּמָה קס"א א', אַחַר שֶׁהֶאֱרִיךְ בָּעִנְיָן, לְבָאֵר אֵיךְ שֶׁבְּהַתּוֹרָה נִבְרְאוּ כָּל הָעוֹלָמוֹת, אָמַר אַחַר זֶה: "כֵּיוָן דְּאִתְבְּרֵי עָלְמָא, כָּל מִלָּה וּמִלָּה לָא הֲוָה מִתְקַיֵּם, עַד דְּסָלִיק בִּרְעוּתָא לְמִבְרֵי אָדָם דְּיֶהֱוֵי מִשְׁתַּדֵּל בְּאוֹרַיְתָא, וּבְגִינֵיהּ אִתְקַיַּם עָלְמָא. הַשְׁתָּא כָּל מַאן דְּאִסְתַּכַּל בָּהּ בְּאוֹרַיְתָא וְאִשְׁתַּדֵּל בָּהּ, כִּבְיָכוֹל הוּא מְקַיֵּם כָּל עָלְמָא. קוּדְשָׁא בְּרִיךְ הוּא אִסְתַּכַּל בְּאוֹרַיְתָא וּבָרָא עָלְמָא בַּר נָשׁ אִסְתַּכַּל בְּאוֹרַיְתָא וּמְקַיֵּם עָלְמָא, אִשְׁתַּכַּח דְּעוּבְדָא וְקִיּוּמָא דְּכָל עָלְמָא אוֹרַיְתָא אִיהִי. בְּגִין כָּךְ זַכָּאָה אִיהוּ בַּר נַשׁ דְּאִשְׁתַּדֵּל בְּאוֹרַיְתָא, דְּהַאי אִיהוּ מְקַיֵּם עָלְמָא. [כֵּיוָן שֶׁנִּבְרָא הָעוֹלָם, כָּל דָּבָר וְדָבָר לֹא הָיָה מִתְקַיֵּם, עַד שֶׁעָלָה בְּרָצוֹן לִבְרֹא אָדָם שֶׁיִּהְיֶה עוֹסֵק בַּתּוֹרָה, וּבִשְׁבִילוֹ יִתְקַיֵּם הָעוֹלָם, עַתָּה כָּל מִי שֶׁמִּסְתַּכֵּל בַּתּוֹרָה וְעוֹסֵק בָּהּ כִּבְיָכוֹל הוּא מְקַיֵּם כָּל הָעוֹלָם, הַקָּדוֹשׁ בָּרוּךְ הוּא הִסְתַּכֵּל בַּתּוֹרָה וּבָרָא עוֹלָם, אָדָם מִסְתַּכֵּל בַּתּוֹרָה וּמְקַיֵּם אֶת הָעוֹלָם, נִמְצָא שֶׁהַמַּעֲשֶׂה וְהַקִּיּוּם שֶׁל כָּל הָעוֹלָם הִיא הַתּוֹרָה, מִשּׁוּם זֶה אַשְׁרֵי הָאָדָם הָעוֹסֵק בַּתּוֹרָה כִּי הוּא מְקַיֵּם אֶת הָעוֹלָם.]

וּבְפָרָשַׁת וַיִּקְרָא י"א סוֹף ע"ב, "בְּגִין דְּעָלְמָא לָא אִתְבְּרֵי אֶלָּא בְּגִין אוֹרַיְתָא, וְכָל זִמְנָא דְּיִשְׂרָאֵל מִתְעַסְּקֵי בְּאוֹרַיְתָא עָלְמָא מִתְקַיְּמָא. וְכָל זִמְנָא דְּיִשְׂרָאֵל מִתְבַּטְּלֵי מֵאוֹרַיְתָא מַה כְּתִיב, "אִם לֹא בְרִיתִי יוֹמָם וָלָיְלָה" כו' [מִשּׁוּם שֶׁהָעוֹלָם לֹא נִבְרָא אֶלָּא בִּשְׁבִיל

הַתּוֹרָה, וְכָל זְמַן שֶׁיִּשְׂרָאֵל מִתְעַסְּקִים בַּתּוֹרָה הָעוֹלָם קַיָּם. וְכָל זְמַן שֶׁיִּשְׂרָאֵל מִתְבַּטְּלִים מִן הַתּוֹרָה מַה כָּתוּב אִם לֹא בְרִיתִי יוֹמָם וָלָיְלָה וכו'.]

וְלָכֵן אָמְרוּ בְּפֶרֶק מַעֲלוֹת הַתּוֹרָה (אבות ו, א), שֶׁכָּל הָעוֹסֵק בַּתּוֹרָה לִשְׁמָהּ נִקְרָא "רֵעַ", כִּי כִּבְיָכוֹל נַעֲשָׂה שֻׁתָּף לְיוֹצֵר בְּרֵאשִׁית יִתְבָּרַךְ שְׁמוֹ, כֵּיוָן שֶׁהוּא הַמְּקַיֵּם עַתָּה אֶת כָּל הָעוֹלָמוֹת בְּעֵסֶק תּוֹרָתוֹ, וּבִלְתִּי זֶה הָיוּ חוֹזְרִים כֻּלָּם לְתֹהוּ וָבֹהוּ, וּכְמוֹ שֶׁכָּתוּב בַּמִּדְרָשׁ הַנַּ"ל "דִּמִּיתִיךְ רַעְיָתִי", רַעְיָתִי דְּעוֹלָמִי, שֶׁקִּבְּלוּ תוֹרָתִי כו':

פֶּרֶק י"ב

וְכָל שֶׁכֵּן חִדּוּשִׁין אֲמִתִּיִּים דְּאוֹרַיְתָא הַמִּתְחַדְּשִׁין עַל יְדֵי הָאָדָם, אֵין עֲרֹךְ לְגֹדֶל נוֹרָאוֹת נִפְלְאוֹת עִנְיָנָם וּפְעֻלָּתָם לְמַעְלָה. שֶׁכָּל מִלָּה וּמִלָּה פְּרָטִית הַמִּתְחַדֶּשֶׁת מִפִּי הָאָדָם, קוּדְשָׁא בְּרִיךְ הוּא נָשִׁיק לָהּ וּמְעַטֵּר לָהּ, וְנִבְנָה מִמֶּנָּה עוֹלָם חָדָשׁ בִּפְנֵי עַצְמוֹ, וְהֵן הֵן "הַשָּׁמַיִם הַחֲדָשִׁים וְהָאָרֶץ הַחֲדָשָׁה" שֶׁאָמַר הַכָּתוּב (ישעי' סו, כב).

כְּמוֹ שֶׁכָּתוּב בְּהַקְדָּמַת הַזֹּהַר דַּף ד' ע"ב, רַבִּי שִׁמְעוֹן פָּתַח "וָאָשִׂים דְּבָרַי בְּפִיךָ" (ישעיה נא, טז), כַּמָּה אִית לֵיהּ לְבַר נַשׁ לְאִשְׁתַּדְּלָא בְּאוֹרַיְתָא יְמָמָא וְלֵילְיָא, בְּגִין דְּקוּדְשָׁא בְּרִיךְ הוּא צַיִּת לְקָלֵיהוֹן דְּאִנּוּן דְּמִתְעַסְקֵי בְּאוֹרַיְתָא, וּבְכָל מִלָּה דְּאִתְחַדֵּשׁ בְּאוֹרַיְתָא — עַל יְדָא דְּהַהוּא דְּאִשְׁתַּדֵּל בְּאוֹרַיְתָא — עָבִיד רְקִיעָא חֲדָא. תְּנַן בְּהַהוּא שַׁעֲתָא דְּמִלָּה דְּאוֹרַיְתָא אִתְחַדֵּשׁ מִפּוּמֵיהּ דְּבַר נַשׁ, הַהִיא מִלָּה סַלְקָא וְאִתְעַתְּדַת קַמֵּיהּ דְּקוּדְשָׁא בְּרִיךְ הוּא, וְקוּדְשָׁא בְּרִיךְ הוּא נָטִיל לְהַהוּא מִלָּה, וְנָשִׁיק לָהּ, וְעָטַר לָהּ בְּשִׁבְעִין עִטְרִין גְּלִיפִין וּמְחַקְקָן. וּמִלָּה דְּחָכְמְתָא דְּאִתְחַדְּשָׁא סַלְקָא וְיָתְבָא עַל רֵישָׁא כו', וְטָסָא מִתַּמָּן וְשָׁטְאַת בְּשִׁבְעִין אֶלֶף עָלְמִין, וּסְלִיקַת לְגַבֵּי עַתִּיק יוֹמִין כו', וְהַהִיא מִלָּה סְתִימָא דְּחָכְמְתָא דְּאִתְחַדְּשַׁת הָכָא, כַּד סַלְקָא, אִתְחַבְּרַת בְּאִנּוּן מִלִּין דְּעַתִּיק יוֹמִין, וְסַלְקָא וְנַחְתָּא בַּהֲדַיְהוּ, וְעָאלַת בְּתַמְנֵיסַר עָלְמִין גְּנִיזִין דְּעַיִן לֹא רָאָתָה כו', נַפְקִין מִתַּמָּן שָׁאטָן וְאַתְיָן מְלִיאָן וּשְׁלִימָן, וְאִתְעַתְּדוּ קַמֵּיהּ עַתִּיק יוֹמִין. בְּהַהִיא שַׁעֲתָא אֲרַח עַתִּיק יוֹמִין בְּהַהִיא מִלָּה, וְנִיחָא קַמֵּיהּ מִכֹּלָּא. נָטִיל לְהַהִיא מִלָּה וְאַעֲטַר לָהּ בש"ע אֶלֶף עִטְרִין. הַהִיא מִלָּה טָסַת וְסַלְקָא וְנַחְתָּא, וְאִתְעֲבִידַת רְקִיעָא חֲדָא. וְכֵן כָּל מִלָּה וּמִלָּה דְּחָכְמְתָא, אִתְעַבְדִין רְקִיעִין קַיָּמִין בְּקִיּוּמָא שְׁלִים קָמֵי עַתִּיק יוֹמִין, וְהוּא קָרֵי לוֹן "שָׁמַיִם חֲדָשִׁים" כו', סְתִימִין דְּרָזִין דְּחָכְמְתָא עִלָּאָה. וְכָל אִלֵּין שְׁאַר מִלִּין דְּאוֹרַיְתָא דְּמִתְחַדְּשִׁין, קַיְמִין קָמֵי קוּדְשָׁא בְּרִיךְ הוּא, וְסַלְקִין וְאִתְעֲבִידוּ "אַרְצוֹת הַחַיִּים", וְנַחְתִּין וּמִתְעַטְּרִין כו', וְאִתְחַדֵּשׁ וְאִתְעֲבִיד כֻּלָּא "אֶרֶץ חֲדָשָׁה" מֵהַהִיא מִלָּה דְּאִתְחַדֵּשׁ בְּאוֹרַיְתָא. וְעַל דָּא כְּתִיב "כִּי כַאֲשֶׁר הַשָּׁמַיִם הַחֲדָשִׁים וְהָאָרֶץ הַחֲדָשָׁה כו' אֲשֶׁר אֲנִי עוֹשֶׂה" כו' (ישעי' סו, כב). "עָשִׂיתִי" לֹא כְּתִיב, אֶלָּא "עוֹשֶׂה", דְּעָבִיד תָּדִיר, וְאִנּוּן חִידּוּשִׁין וְרָזִין דְּאוֹרַיְתָא. וְעַל דָּא כְּתִיב "וָאָשִׂים דְּבָרַי בְּפִיךָ כו' לִנְטֹעַ שָׁמַיִם וְלִיסֹד אָרֶץ" כו'. אָמַר ר"א מַהוּ "וּבְצֵל יָדִי כִּסִּיתִיךָ", אָמַר לֵיהּ כו', וְהַשְׁתָּא דְּהַאי מִלָּה סַלְקָא וְאִתְעַטְּרָא וְקַיְמָא קָמֵי קוּדְשָׁא בְּרִיךְ הוּא, אִיהוּ חָפֵי עַל הַהִיא מִלָּה, וְכַסֵּי עַל הַהוּא בַּר נַשׁ כו', עַד דְּאִתְעֲבִיד מֵהַהִיא מִלָּה שָׁמַיִם חֲדָשִׁים וְאֶרֶץ

חֲדָשָׁה כו'. "וְלֵאמֹר לְצִיּוֹן עַמִּי אָתָּה" כו', אַל תִּקְרָא "עַמִּי" אֶלָּא "עִמִּי", לְמֶהֱוֵי שׁוּתָּפָא עִמִּי, מַה אֲנָא בְּמִלּוּלָא דִּילִי עֲבְדִית שָׁמַיִם וָאָרֶץ כו', אוּף הָכִי אַתְּ, זַכָּאִין אִנּוּן דְּמִשְׁתַּדְּלִין בְּאוֹרַיְתָא.

[רַבִּי שִׁמְעוֹן פָּתַח וָאָשִׂים דְּבָרַי בְּפִיךָ, כַּמָּה יֵשׁ לוֹ לָאָדָם לַעֲמֹל בַּתּוֹרָה יוֹם וָלַיְלָה, כִּי הַקָּדוֹשׁ בָּרוּךְ הוּא מַקְשִׁיב לַקּוֹלוֹת שֶׁל הָעוֹסְקִים בַּתּוֹרָה, וּבְכָל מִלָּה שֶׁמִּתְחַדֶּשֶׁת בַּתּוֹרָה עַל יְדֵי אוֹתוֹ הָעוֹסֵק בַּתּוֹרָה – עוֹשֶׂה רָקִיעַ אֶחָד. לָמַדְנוּ שֶׁבְּאוֹתָהּ שָׁעָה שֶׁדְּבַר תּוֹרָה מִתְחַדֵּשׁ מִפִּי הָאָדָם, הַדִּבּוּר הַהוּא עוֹלֶה וּמִתְיַצֵּב לִפְנֵי הַקָּדוֹשׁ בָּרוּךְ הוּא, וְהַקָּדוֹשׁ בָּרוּךְ הוּא לוֹקֵחַ הַדִּבּוּר הַהוּא וּמְנַשֵּׁק אוֹתוֹ, וּמְעַטְּרוֹ בְּשִׁבְעִים עֲטָרוֹת מְפֻתָּחוֹת וּמְחֻקָּקוֹת, וּדְבַר הַחָכְמָה שֶׁנִּתְחַדֵּשׁ עוֹלֶה וְיוֹשֵׁב עַל רֹאשׁ וכו' וּמִשָּׁם עָף וְטָס בְּשִׁבְעִים אֶלֶף עוֹלָמוֹת וְעוֹלֶה לְעַתִּיק יוֹמִין וכו', וְאוֹתוֹ דְּבַר חָכְמָה הַסָּתוּם שֶׁנִּתְחַדֵּשׁ כָּאן, כְּשֶׁהוּא עוֹלֶה הוּא מִתְחַבֵּר בְּאֵלּוּ הַדְּבָרִים שֶׁל עַתִּיק יוֹמִין, וְעוֹלֶה וְיוֹרֵד עִמָּהֶם וְנִכְנָס בְּחַ"י עוֹלָמוֹת צְפוּנִים אֲשֶׁר עַיִן לֹא רָאֲתָה וכו' וְיוֹצְאִים מִשָּׁם וּמְשׁוֹטְטִים וּבָאִים מְלֵאִים וּשְׁלֵמִים וְנוֹעָדִים לִפְנֵי עַתִּיק יוֹמִין, בְּאוֹתָהּ הַשָּׁעָה עַתִּיק יוֹמִין מֵרִיחַ בְּאוֹתוֹ הַדִּבּוּר וְרָצוּי לְפָנָיו מִכֹּל, לוֹקֵחַ לְאוֹתוֹ הַדִּבּוּר וּמְעַטֵּר אוֹתוֹ שְׁלֹשׁ מֵאוֹת וְשִׁבְעִים אֶלֶף עֲטָרוֹת. וְהַדִּבּוּר הַהוּא מְשׁוֹטֵט וְעוֹלֶה וְיוֹרֵד וְנַעֲשֶׂה רָקִיעַ אֶחָד, וְכֵן כָּל דִּבּוּר וְדִבּוּר שֶׁל חָכְמָה נַעֲשִׂים רְקִיעִים עוֹמְדִים בְּקִיּוּם שָׁלֵם לִפְנֵי עַתִּיק יוֹמִין. וְהוּא קוֹרֵא אוֹתָן "הַשָּׁמַיִם הַחֲדָשִׁים" וכו'. סְתוּמוֹת שֶׁל סוֹדוֹת הַחָכְמָה הָעֶלְיוֹנָה, וְכָל שְׁאָר דִּבְרֵי תוֹרָה הַמִּתְחַדְּשִׁים עוֹמְדִים לִפְנֵי הַקָּדוֹשׁ בָּרוּךְ הוּא וְעוֹלִים וְנַעֲשִׂים "אַרְצוֹת הַחַיִּים" וְיוֹרְדִים וּמִתְעַטְּרִים וכו', וְנִתְחַדֵּשׁ וְנַעֲשָׂה הַכֹּל "אֶרֶץ חֲדָשָׁה" מֵאוֹתוֹ דָּבָר שֶׁנִּתְחַדֵּשׁ בַּתּוֹרָה, וְעַל זֶה כָּתוּב "כִּי כַאֲשֶׁר הַשָּׁמַיִם הַחֲדָשִׁים וְהָאָרֶץ הַחֲדָשָׁה אֲשֶׁר אֲנִי עוֹשֶׂה" וכו', "עָשִׂיתִי" לֹא כָּתוּב, אֶלָּא "עוֹשֶׂה", שֶׁעוֹשֶׂה תָּמִיד. וְאֵלּוּ הַחִדּוּשִׁים וְהַסּוֹדוֹת שֶׁל הַתּוֹרָה, וְעַל זֶה כָּתוּב וָאָשִׂים דְּבָרַי בְּפִיךָ וּבְצֵל יָדִי כִּסִּיתִיךָ לִנְטֹעַ שָׁמַיִם וְלִיסֹד אָרֶץ, אָמַר ר"א מַהוּ "וּבְצֵל יָדִי כִּסִּיתִיךָ" א"ל וכו'. וְעַתָּה שֶׁדִּבּוּר זֶה עוֹלֶה וּמִתְעַטֵּר לִפְנֵי הַקָּדוֹשׁ בָּרוּךְ הוּא, הוּא חוֹפֶה עַל הַדָּבָר הַהוּא וּמְכַסֶּה עַל אָדָם הַהוּא וכו', עַד שֶׁנַּעֲשָׂה מֵהַדִּבּוּר הַהוּא שָׁמַיִם חֲדָשִׁים וְאֶרֶץ חֲדָשָׁה וכו'. "וְלֵאמֹר לְצִיּוֹן עַמִּי אַתָּה" וכו' אַל תִּקְרָא "עַמִּי" אֶלָּא "עִמִּי", לִהְיוֹת שֻׁתָּף עִמִּי, מָה אֲנִי עָשִׂיתִי שָׁמַיִם וָאָרֶץ בִּדְבָרַי וכו' אַף אַתָּה כֵּן, אַשְׁרֵי הֵם הָעֲמֵלִים בַּתּוֹרָה.]

וּבְפָרָשַׁת וַיְחִי רמ"ג רֵישׁ ע"א, כְּתִיב (שה"ש ז, יד) "הַדּוּדָאִים נָתְנוּ רֵיחַ" כו', אִלֵּין אִנּוּן דְּאַשְׁכַּח רְאוּבֵן כו', "וְעַל פְּתָחֵינוּ כָּל מְגָדִים", אִנּוּן גָּרְמוּ לְמֶהֱוֵי עַל פִּתְחֵי בָּתֵּי כְּנֵסִיּוֹת וּבָתֵּי מִדְרָשׁוֹת כָּל מְגָדִים, "חֲדָשִׁים גַּם יְשָׁנִים", כַּמָּה מִלֵּי חַדְתָּאן וְעַתִּיקִין דְּאוֹרַיְתָא דְּאִתְגַּלְיָא עַל יְדַיְהוּ כו', "דּוֹדִי צָפַנְתִּי לָךְ" מֵהָכָא אוֹלִיפְנָא, כָּל מַאן דְּאִשְׁתַּדַּל בְּאוֹרַיְתָא כִּדְקָא יָאוּת, וְיָדַע לְמֶחֱדֵי מִלִּין וּלְחַדְתוּתֵי מִלִּין כִּדְקָא יָאוּת, אִנּוּן מִלִּין סַלְקִין עַד כָּרְסְיָא דְּמַלְכָּא, וּכְנֶסֶת יִשְׂרָאֵל פָּתַח לוֹן תַּרְעִין וְגָנִיז לוֹן, וּבְשַׁעְתָּא דְּעָאל קוּדְשָׁא בְּרִיךְ הוּא, לְאִשְׁתַּעְשְׁעָא עִם צַדִּיקַיָּא בְּגִנְתָא דְעֵדֶן, אַפִּיקַת לוֹן קַמֵּי', וּמִסְתַּכַּל בְּהוּ וְחָדֵי. כְּדֵין קוּדְשָׁא

בְּרִיךְ הוּא מִתְעַטֵּר בְּעִטְרִין עִלָּאִין וְחַדֵּי כוּ', וּמֵהַהִיא שַׁעֲתָא מִלּוּי כְּתִיבִין בְּסִפְרָא כוּ', זַכָּאָה חוּלְקֵיהּ מַאן דְּאִשְׁתַּדֵּל בְּאוֹרַיְתָא כִּדְקָא יָאוּת. זַכָּאָה הוּא בְּהַאי עָלְמָא, וְזַכָּאָה הוּא בְּעָלְמָא דְּאָתֵי.

[כָּתוּב "הַדּוּדָאִים נָתְנוּ רֵיחַ" וכו', אֵלּוּ הֵם שֶׁמָּצָא רְאוּבֵן וכו'. "וְעַל פְּתָחֵינוּ כָּל מְגָדִים", הֵם [הַדּוּדָאִים] גָּרְמוּ שֶׁיִּהְיֶה עַל פִּתְחֵי בָּתֵּי כְּנֵסִיּוֹת וּבָתֵּי מִדְרָשׁוֹת כָּל מְגָדִים. "חֲדָשִׁים גַּם יְשָׁנִים", כַּמָּה דִּבְרֵי תּוֹרָה חֲדָשִׁים וִישָׁנִים שֶׁמִּתְגַּלִּים עַל יְדֵיהֶם וכו'. "דּוֹדִי צָפַנְתִּי לָךְ", מִכָּאן לָמַדְנוּ שֶׁכָּל מִי שֶׁעוֹסֵק בַּתּוֹרָה כָּרָאוּי, וְיוֹדֵעַ לְשַׂמֵּחַ הַדְּבָרִים וּלְחַדֵּשׁ הַדְּבָרִים כָּרָאוּי, אֵלּוּ הַדְּבָרִים עוֹלִים עַד כִּסֵּא שֶׁל הַמֶּלֶךְ, וּכְנֶסֶת יִשְׂרָאֵל פּוֹתַחַת לָהֶם שְׁעָרִים וְגוֹנֶזֶת אוֹתָם, וּבְשָׁעָה שֶׁהַקָּדוֹשׁ בָּרוּךְ הוּא נִכְנָס לְגַן עֵדֶן לְהִשְׁתַּעְשֵׁעַ עִם הַצַּדִּיקִים, מוֹצִיאָה אוֹתָם לְפָנָיו וְהַקָּדוֹשׁ בָּרוּךְ הוּא מִסְתַּכֵּל בָּהֶם וְשָׂמֵחַ, אָז הַקָּדוֹשׁ בָּרוּךְ הוּא מִתְעַטֵּר בַּעֲטָרוֹת הָעֶלְיוֹנוֹת וְשָׂמֵחַ וכו' וּמֵאוֹתָהּ שָׁעָה דְּבָרָיו כְּתוּבִים בְּסֵפֶר וכו'. אַשְׁרֵי חֶלְקוֹ שֶׁל הָעוֹסֵק בַּתּוֹרָה כָּרָאוּי, אַשְׁרֵי הוּא בָּעוֹלָם הַזֶּה וְאַשְׁרֵי הוּא בָּעוֹלָם הַבָּא.]

וּבְתַנָּא דְּבֵי אֵלִיָּהוּ סֵדֶר אֵלִיָּהוּ רַבָּא פֶּרֶק י"ח, "וְעַל הַנַּחַל יַעֲלֶה עַל שְׂפָתוֹ מִזֶּה וּמִזֶּה כָּל עֵץ מַאֲכָל" (יחזקאל מז, יב), וּפֵרֵשׁ שָׁם כָּל זֶה הַכָּתוּב עַל דִּבְרֵי תּוֹרָה, וְאוֹמֵר שָׁם, מַהוּ "לָחֳדָשָׁיו יְבַכֵּר", לִמְחַדְּשֵׁי תּוֹרָה שֶׁמְּחַדְּשִׁין אֶת הַתּוֹרָה בְּכָל יוֹם תָּמִיד. לְבֵן שֶׁהוּא בְּכוֹר לְאָבִיו וּלְאִמּוֹ, שֶׁמְּחַדֵּשׁ דִּבְרֵי תוֹרָה שֶׁהַכֹּל שְׂמֵחִין בּוֹ כוּ', שִׂמְחָה מִתְחַדֵּשׁ לוֹ לְאָבִיו בְּכָל יוֹם כוּ'. וּבְכָל מָקוֹם שֶׁמְּחַדְּשִׁין תּוֹרָה שֶׁבִּישִׁיבַת בֵּית הַכְּנֶסֶת וּבִישִׁיבַת בֵּית הַמִּדְרָשׁ, שִׂמְחָה מִתְחַדֵּשׁ לְהַקָּדוֹשׁ בָּרוּךְ הוּא בְּכָל יוֹם תָּמִיד כוּ', עַיֵּן שָׁם.

פֶּרֶק י"ג

וְעַל יְדֵי עֵסֶק הַתּוֹרָה הַקְּדוֹשָׁה, נִשְׁלָם כַּוָּנָתוֹ יִתְבָּרַךְ בַּבְּרִיאָה, שֶׁהָיָה רַק בִּשְׁבִיל הַתּוֹרָה שֶׁיַּעַסְקוּ בָהּ יִשְׂרָאֵל, כְּמַאֲמָרָם זִכְרוֹנָם לִבְרָכָה, "בְּרֵאשִׁית", בִּשְׁבִיל הַתּוֹרָה כוּ', וּבִשְׁבִיל יִשְׂרָאֵל כוּ', וּבִשְׁבִיל מֹשֶׁה כוּ', שֶׁהוּא הַסַּרְסוּר בְּקַבָּלַת הַתּוֹרָה, וְכִבְיָכוֹל הוּא יִתְבָּרַךְ שָׂמֵחַ בְּמַעֲשָׂיו בְּעוֹלָמוֹ וּבְרִיּוֹתָיו, שֶׁמַּעֲלִים חֵן לְפָנָיו יִתְבָּרַךְ כְּשָׁעָה רִאשׁוֹנָה בְּעֵת הַבְּרִיאָה, כְּמוֹ שֶׁקִּנָּה הוּא יִתְבָּרַךְ בְּעַצְמוֹ כִּבְיָכוֹל.

כְּמוֹ שֶׁכָּתוּב בְּרַבָּה בְּרֵאשִׁית פ"ט, לְמֶלֶךְ שֶׁבָּנָה פַּלְטֵרִין, רָאָה אוֹתָהּ וְעָרְבָה לוֹ, אָמַר, פַּלְטִין פַּלְטִין, הַלְוַאי תְּהֵא מַעֲלָה חֵן כוּ'. כָּךְ אָמַר הַקָּדוֹשׁ בָּרוּךְ הוּא לְעוֹלָמוֹ, עוֹלָמִי עוֹלָמִי, הַלְוַאי תְּהֵא מַעֲלַת חֵן לְפָנַי בְּכָל עֵת, כְּשֵׁם שֶׁהֶעֱלֵית חֵן לְפָנַי בְּשָׁעָה זוֹ. וְכֵן נֶאֱמַר (משלי ה, יט) בְּשֶׁבַח הַתּוֹרָה "אַיֶּלֶת אֲהָבִים וְיַעֲלַת חֵן".

וּבַזֹּהַר צַו ל"ה א', פָּתַח רַבִּי אֶלְעָזָר וְאָמַר "וָאָשִׂים דְּבָרַי בְּפִיךָ" כוּ' (ישעיה נא, טז), תָּנִינָן, כָּל בַּר נָשׁ דְּאִשְׁתַּדֵּל בְּמִלֵּי דְּאוֹרַיְתָא, וְשִׂפְוָתֵיהּ מְרַחֲשָׁן אוֹרַיְתָא כוּ', וְלֹא עוֹד אֶלָּא דְּהוּא מְקַיֵּם עָלְמָא, וְקוּדְשָׁא בְּרִיךְ הוּא חַדֵּי עִמֵּיהּ, כְּאִלּוּ הַהוּא יוֹמָא נָטַע שְׁמַיָּא וְאַרְעָא, הֲדָא הוּא דִּכְתִיב (שם) "לִנְטֹעַ שָׁמַיִם וְלִיסֹד אָרֶץ" [פָּתַח רַבִּי אֶלְעָזָר וְאָמַר "וָאָשִׂים דְּבָרַי בְּפִיךָ" וכו' לָמַדְנוּ כָּל אָדָם הָעוֹסֵק בַּתּוֹרָה וְשִׂפְתוֹתָיו דּוֹבְבוֹת תּוֹרָה וכו' וְלֹא עוֹד שֶׁהוּא

מְקַיֵּם אֶת הָעוֹלָם וְהַקָּדוֹשׁ בָּרוּךְ הוּא שָׂמֵחַ עִמּוֹ כְּאִלּוּ בַּיּוֹם הַהוּא נוֹטֵעַ שָׁמַיִם וָאָרֶץ וְזֶהוּ שֶׁכָּתוּב "לִנְטֹעַ שָׁמַיִם וְלִיסֹד אָרֶץ".]

וּבְפָרָשַׁת תְּרוּמָה קנ"ה ב', פָּתַח רַבִּי חִיָּא וְאָמַר "עֵת לַעֲשׂוֹת לַה' הֵפֵרוּ תּוֹרָתֶךָ" (תהלים קיט, קכו) בְּכָל זִמְנָא דְּאוֹרַיְתָא מִתְקַיְּמָא בְּעָלְמָא, וּבְנֵי נָשָׁא מִשְׁתַּדְּלִין בָּהּ, כִּבְיָכוֹל קוּדְשָׁא בְּרִיךְ הוּא חָדֵי בְּעוֹבָדוֹי יְדוֹי, וְחָדֵי בְּעָלְמִין כּוּלְּהוּ, וּשְׁמַיָּא וְאַרְעָא קַיְמֵי בְּקִיּוּמַיְהוּ, וְלֹא עוֹד, אֶלָּא קוּדְשָׁא בְּרִיךְ הוּא כָּנִישׁ כָּל פַּמַּלְיָא דִּילֵיהּ וְאָמַר לוֹן, חָמוּ עַמָּא קַדִּישָׁא דְּאִית לִי בְּאַרְעָא, דְּאוֹרַיְתָא מִתְעַטְּרָא בְּגִינֵיהוֹן כו', וְאִנּוּן כַּד חָמוּ חֶדְוָא דְּמָארֵיהוֹן בְּעַמֵּיהּ, מִיַּד פַּתְחֵי וְאַמְרֵי, "וּמִי כְּעַמְּךָ יִשְׂרָאֵל גּוֹי אֶחָד בָּאָרֶץ" (שמו"ב ז, כג). [פָּתַח רַבִּי חִיָּא וְאָמַר "עֵת לַעֲשׂוֹת לַה' הֵפֵרוּ תּוֹרָתֶךָ" וכו', בְּכָל זְמַן שֶׁהַתּוֹרָה מִתְקַיֶּמֶת בָּעוֹלָם, וּבְנֵי אָדָם עוֹסְקִים בָּהּ כִּבְיָכוֹל הַקָּדוֹשׁ בָּרוּךְ הוּא שָׂמֵחַ בְּמַעֲשֵׂי יָדָיו, וְשָׂמֵחַ בָּעוֹלָמוֹת כֻּלָּם, וְשָׁמַיִם וָאָרֶץ עוֹמְדִים בְּקִיּוּמָם, וְלֹא עוֹד אֶלָּא שֶׁהַקָּדוֹשׁ בָּרוּךְ הוּא מַקְהִיל כָּל הַפָּמַלְיָא שֶׁלּוֹ וְאוֹמֵר לָהֶם, רְאוּ הָעָם הַקָּדוֹשׁ שֶׁיֵּשׁ לִי בָּאָרֶץ, שֶׁהַתּוֹרָה מִתְעַטֶּרֶת בִּשְׁבִילָם וכו', וְהֵם כְּשֶׁרוֹאִים שִׂמְחַת אֲדוֹנָם בְּעַמּוֹ מִיָּד פּוֹתְחִים וְאוֹמְרִים "וּמִי כְּעַמְּךָ יִשְׂרָאֵל" וגו'.]

וּבְרֵישׁ פָּרָשַׁת שְׁמִינִי (לה:), זַכָּאִין אִנּוּן יִשְׂרָאֵל, דְּקוּדְשָׁא בְּרִיךְ הוּא יְהַב לוֹן אוֹרַיְתָא קַדִּישָׁא, חֶדְוָתָא דְּכֹלָּא, חֶדְוָתָא דְּקוּדְשָׁא בְּרִיךְ הוּא, וַאֲטַיְלוּתָא דִּילֵיהּ, דִּכְתִיב (משלי ח, ל) "וָאֶהְיֶה שַׁעֲשׁוּעִים יוֹם יוֹם" כו' [אַשְׁרֵיהֶם יִשְׂרָאֵל, שֶׁהַקָּדוֹשׁ בָּרוּךְ הוּא נָתַן לָהֶם הַתּוֹרָה הַקְּדוֹשָׁה, שֶׁהִיא שִׂמְחַת הַכֹּל, שִׂמְחַת הַקָּדוֹשׁ בָּרוּךְ הוּא, וּמְקוֹם טִיּוּל שֶׁלּוֹ, שֶׁכָּתוּב וָאֶהְיֶה שַׁעֲשׁוּעִים יוֹם יוֹם.]

פֶּרֶק י"ד

וְגַם הָעוֹלָמוֹת וְהַבְּרִיּוֹת כֻּלָּם הֵם אָז בְּחֶדְוָתָא יַתִּירְתָא, וּנְהִירִין מִזִּיו הָאוֹר הָעֶלְיוֹן, הַשּׁוֹפֵעַ עֲלֵיהֶם מִמְּקוֹם שֹׁרֶשׁ עֶלְיוֹן שֶׁל הַתּוֹרָה, כְּמוֹ שֶׁאָמְרוּ בְּפֶרֶק מַעֲלוֹת הַתּוֹרָה (אבות ו, א), מְשַׂמֵּחַ אֶת הַמָּקוֹם מְשַׂמֵּחַ אֶת הַבְּרִיּוֹת. וְכֵן אָמְרָה הַתּוֹרָה (משלי ח, ל) "וָאֶהְיֶה שַׁעֲשׁוּעִים יוֹם יוֹם".

וּבַזֹּהַר וַיַּקְהֵל ר"ז א', פָּתַח וְאָמַר "אָז נִדְבְּרוּ יִרְאֵי ה'" (מלאכי ג, טז) כו', "אָז דִּבְּרוּ" מִבָּעֵי לֵיהּ, מַאי "נִדְבְּרוּ", אֶלָּא נִדְבְּרוּ לְעֵלָּא מִכָּל אִינוּן רְתִיכִין קַדִּישִׁין, וְכָל אִנּוּן חַיָּלִין קַדִּישִׁין, בְּגִין דְּאִנּוּן מִלִּין קַדִּישִׁין סַלְקִין לְעֵילָּא, וְכַמָּה אִנּוּן דְּמַקְדְּמֵי וְנַטְלֵי לוֹן קָמֵי מַלְכָּא קַדִּישָׁא, וּמִתְעַטְּרִין בְּכַמָּה עִטְרִין בְּאִנּוּן נְהוֹרִין עִלָּאִין, וְכוּלְּהוּ נִדְבְּרוּ מִקָּמֵי מַלְכָּא עִלָּאָה, מַאן חָמֵי חֶדְוָן, מַאן חָמֵי תּוּשְׁבְּחָן דְּסַלְקִין בְּכָל אִנּוּן רְקִיעִין קָמֵי מַלְכָּא קַדִּישָׁא, וּמַלְכָּא קַדִּישָׁא מִסְתַּכֵּל בְּהוּ וְאִתְעֲטַר בְּהוּ, וְאִנּוּן סַלְקִין עַל רֵישֵׁיהּ וַהֲווּ עִטְרָא וְנַחְתִּין וְיַתְבִין עַל חֵיקֵיהּ לְגוֹ בְּתוּקְפֵיהּ וּמִתַּמָּן סַלְקִין עַל רֵישֵׁיהּ, וְעַל דָּא אָמְרָה אוֹרַיְתָא "וָאֶהְיֶה שַׁעֲשׁוּעִים יוֹם יוֹם", "וְהָיִיתִי" לָא כְתִיב, אֶלָּא "וָאֶהְיֶה", בְּכָל זְמַן וּבְכָל עִידָן דְּמִלִּין עִלָּאִין סַלְקִין קָמֵיהּ, ע"כ [פָּתַח וְאָמַר אָז נִדְבְּרוּ וגו' "אָז דִּבְּרוּ" הָיָה צָרִיךְ לוֹמַר, מַהוּ "נִדְבְּרוּ". אֶלָּא נִדְבְּרוּ לְמַעְלָה מִכָּל אֵלּוּ הַמֶּרְכָּבוֹת הַקְּדוֹשׁוֹת וְכָל אֵלּוּ צְבָאוֹת קְדוֹשִׁים, מִשּׁוּם שֶׁאֵלּוּ מִלִּים

הַקְּדוֹשׁוֹת עוֹלוֹת לְמַעְלָה, וְכַמָּה מֵהֶם שֶׁמַּקְדִּימִים וְנוֹשְׂאִים אוֹתָם לִפְנֵי הַמֶּלֶךְ הַקָּדוֹשׁ, וּמִתְעַטְּרִים בְּכַמָּה עֲטָרוֹת בְּאֵלּוּ אוֹרוֹת עֶלְיוֹנִים, וְכֻלָּם נִדְבָּרִים מִלִּפְנֵי מֶלֶךְ הָעֶלְיוֹן, מִי רָאָה שְׂמָחוֹת וּמִי רָאָה תִּשְׁבָּחוֹת הָעוֹלוֹת בְּכָל אֵלּוּ הָרְקִיעִים לִפְנֵי הַמֶּלֶךְ הַקָּדוֹשׁ, וְהַמֶּלֶךְ הַקָּדוֹשׁ מִסְתַּכֵּל בָּהֶם, וּמִתְעַטֵּר בָּהֶם וְהֵן עוֹלוֹת עַל רֹאשׁוֹ וְנַעֲשׂוּ עֲטָרָה וְיוֹרְדִים וְיוֹשְׁבִים בְּחֵיקוֹ בִּפְנִים בְּתָקְפּוֹ, וּמִשָּׁם עוֹלוֹת עַל רֹאשׁוֹ, וְעַל זֶה אָמְרָה הַתּוֹרָה "וָאֶהְיֶה שַׁעֲשׁוּעִים יוֹם יוֹם", "וְהָיִיתִי" לֹא כָּתוּב, אֶלָּא "וָאֶהְיֶה", הַיְינוּ בְּכָל זְמַן וּבְכָל עֵת שֶׁהַדִּבּוּרִים הָעֶלְיוֹנִים עוֹלִים לְפָנָיו.]

וּבְכָל עֵת שֶׁהָאָדָם עוֹסֵק וּמִתְדַּבֵּק בָּהּ כָּרָאוּי, הַדְּבָרִים שְׂמֵחִים כִּנְתִינָתָן מִסִּינַי, כְּמוֹ שֶׁכָּתוּב בַּזֹּהַר רֵישׁ פָּרָשַׁת חֻקַּת, ר"י פָּתַח "זֹאת הַתּוֹרָה" כו', תָּא חֲזֵי, מִלִּין דְּאוֹרַיְתָא קַדִּישִׁין אִנּוּן, עִלָּאִין אִנּוּן, מְתִיקִין אִנּוּן, כְּמָה דִּכְתִיב "הַנֶּחֱמָדִים מִזָּהָב" כו'. מַאן דְּאִשְׁתַּדַּל בְּאוֹרַיְתָא, כְּאִלּוּ קָאִים כָּל יוֹמָא עַל טוּרָא דְּסִינַי לְקַבֵּל אוֹרַיְתָא, הה"ד (דברים כז, ט) "הַיּוֹם הַזֶּה נִהְיֵיתָ לְעָם". [ר"י פָּתַח, "זֹאת הַתּוֹרָה" וכו', בֹּא וּרְאֵה, דִּבְרֵי תּוֹרָה קְדוֹשִׁים הֵם, עֶלְיוֹנִים הֵם, מְתוּקִים הֵם, כְּמוֹ שֶׁכָּתוּב "הַנֶּחֱמָדִים מִזָּהָב" וכו', מִי שֶׁעוֹסֵק בַּתּוֹרָה הוּא כְּאִלּוּ עוֹמֵד כָּל יוֹם עַל הַר סִינַי לְקַבֵּל הַתּוֹרָה, זֶה שֶׁכָּתוּב "הַיּוֹם הַזֶּה נִהְיֵיתָ לְעָם".]

וּבְפָרָשַׁת אַחֲרֵי ס"ט א' דְּתָאנָא כָּל מַאן דְּאָצִית לְמִלּוֹי דְּאוֹרַיְתָא, זַכָּאָה הוּא בְּהַאי עָלְמָא, וּכְאִלּוּ קַבִּיל תּוֹרָה מִסִּינַי. וַאֲפִילּוּ מִכָּל בַּר נָשׁ נָמֵי בָּעֵי לְמִשְׁמַע מִלּוֹי דְּאוֹרַיְתָא, וּמַאן דְּאַרְכִין אוּדְנֵיהּ לְקַבְלֵיהּ, יָהִיב יְקָרָא לְמַלְכָּא קַדִּישָׁא, וְיָהִיב יְקָרָא לְאוֹרַיְתָא, עֲלֵיהּ כְּתִיב "הַיּוֹם הַזֶּה נִהְיֵיתָ לְעָם" כו' [כִּי לָמַדְנוּ כָּל מִי שֶׁמַּקְשִׁיב לְדִבְרֵי תּוֹרָה אַשְׁרָיו בָּעוֹלָם הַזֶּה, וּכְאִלּוּ קִבֵּל תּוֹרָה מִסִּינַי, וַאֲפִילּוּ מִכָּל אָדָם צְרִיכִים לִשְׁמֹעַ דִּבְרֵי תּוֹרָה, וּמִי שֶׁמַּטֶּה אָזְנוֹ לְקַבְּלָם נוֹתֵן כָּבוֹד לַמֶּלֶךְ הַקָּדוֹשׁ וְנוֹתֵן כָּבוֹד לַתּוֹרָה עָלָיו כָּתוּב "הַיּוֹם הַזֶּה נִהְיֵיתָ לְעָם".]

וְהַטַּעַם, שֶׁכְּמוֹ שֶׁבְּעֵת הַמַּעֲמָד הַמְקֻדָּשׁ נִתְדַּבְּקוּ כִּבְיָכוֹל בְּדִבּוּרוֹ יִתְבָּרֵךְ, כֵּן גַּם עַתָּה, בְּכָל עֵת מַמָּשׁ שֶׁהָאָדָם עוֹסֵק וְהוֹגֶה בָּהּ, הוּא דָּבוּק עַל יָדָהּ בְּדִבּוּרוֹ יִתְבָּרֵךְ מַמָּשׁ, מֵחֲמַת שֶׁהַכֹּל מַאֲמַר פִּיו יִתְבָּרֵךְ לְמֹשֶׁה בְּסִינַי, וַאֲפִילּוּ מַה שֶּׁתַּלְמִיד קָטָן שׁוֹאֵל מֵרַבּוֹ, כַּנַּ"ל פֶּרֶק ו'.

וְגַם עַתָּה בְּעֵת שֶׁהָאָדָם עוֹסֵק בָּהּ, בְּכָל תֵּבָה, אוֹתָהּ הַתֵּבָה מַמָּשׁ נֶחְצֶבֶת אָז לַהֶבֶת אֵשׁ מִפִּיו יִתְבָּרֵךְ כִּבְיָכוֹל כמש"ש. וְנֶחְשָׁב כְּאִלּוּ עַתָּה מְקַבְּלָהּ בְּסִינַי מִפִּיו יִתְבָּרֵךְ שְׁמוֹ, לָכֵן אָמְרוּ רַבּוֹתֵינוּ זִכְרוֹנָם לִבְרָכָה כַּמָּה פְּעָמִים "וְהָיוּ הַדְּבָרִים שְׂמֵחִים כִּנְתִינָתָן מִסִּינַי":

וְאָז מִשְׁתַּלְשֵׁל וְנִמְשָׁךְ שִׁפְעַת אוֹר וּבְרָכָה, מִמְּקוֹר שָׁרְשָׁהּ הָעֶלְיוֹן, עַל כָּל הָעוֹלָמוֹת, וְגַם הָאָרֶץ הֵאִירָה מִכְּבוֹדָהּ וּמִתְבָּרֶכֶת, וּמֵבִיא הַרְבֵּה טוֹבָה וְשִׁפְעַת בְּרָכָה לָעוֹלָם.

וּבְתַנָּא דְּבֵי אֵלִיָּהוּ סֵדֶר אֵלִיָּהוּ רַבָּא פֶּרֶק י"ח אָמַר, כֵּיוָן שֶׁלּוֹמֵד אֶת הַתּוֹרָה, הֲרֵי זֶה מֵבִיא טוֹבָה לָעוֹלָם, וְיָכוֹל הוּא לְבַקֵּשׁ רַחֲמִים וּלְהִתְפַּלֵּל לִפְנֵי הַקָּדוֹשׁ בָּרוּךְ הוּא, וִיפַקְפֵּק אֶת הָרָקִיעַ, וְיָבִיא מָטָר לָעוֹלָם כו'.

וְאָמַר שָׁם עוֹד, כָּל זְמַן שֶׁיִּשְׂרָאֵל עוֹסְקִין בַּתּוֹרָה וְעוֹשִׂין רְצוֹן אֲבִיהֶם שֶׁבַּשָּׁמַיִם,

הַקָּדוֹשׁ בָּרוּךְ הוּא בְּעַצְמוֹ נִפְנָה אֲלֵיהֶם לִבְרָכָה, שֶׁנֶּאֱמַר (תהלים פה, יב) "אֱמֶת מֵאֶרֶץ תִּצְמָח וְצֶדֶק מִשָּׁמַיִם נִשְׁקָף", וְאֵין "הַשְׁקָפָה" אֶלָּא לִבְרָכָה, שֶׁנֶּאֱמַר (דברים כו, טו) "הַשְׁקִיפָה כו' וּבָרֵךְ אֶת עַמְּךָ" כו':

פֶּרֶק ט"ו

וְהִנֵּה, הַמְבָרֵךְ מִתְבָּרֵךְ, וּמִבִּרְכָתָם שֶׁל הָעוֹלָמוֹת יְבֹרַךְ גַּם הָאָדָם, הָעוֹסֵק בָּהּ כָּרָאוּי לַאֲמִתָּהּ, הַגּוֹרֵם לְכָל זֶה, וּכְבוֹד ה' חוֹפֵף עָלָיו כָּל הַיּוֹם, וּמַשִּׂיג לִנְשָׁמָה אֲצוּלָה מִמָּקוֹם קָדוֹשׁ, לְפִי עֵרֶךְ גֹּדֶל עִסְקוֹ וְדִבּוּקוֹ בָּהּ, כְּמוֹ שֶׁאָמְרוּ (יומא לט): "אָדָם מְקַדֵּשׁ עַצְמוֹ מִלְּמַטָּה, מְקַדְּשִׁין אוֹתוֹ מִלְּמַעְלָה, מְעַט, מְקַדְּשִׁין אוֹתוֹ הַרְבֵּה".

וּבְהַקְדָּמַת הַזֹּהַר י"ב ב', פִּקּוּדָא חֲמִישָׁאָה כו', בְּהַאי קְרָא אִית תְּלַת פִּקּוּדִין וכו', וְחַד לְמִלְעֵי בְּאוֹרַיְתָא, לְאִשְׁתַּדְּלָא בָּהּ, וּלְאַפָּשָׁא לָהּ בְּכָל יוֹמָא, לְתַקָּנָא נַפְשֵׁיהּ וְרוּחֵיהּ, דְּכֵיוָן דְּבַר נַשׁ אִתְעֲסַק בְּאוֹרַיְתָא, אִתְתַּקַּן בְּנִשְׁמְתָא אָחֳרָא קַדִּישָׁא, דִּכְתִיב "שֶׁרֶץ נֶפֶשׁ חַיָּה", נֶפֶשׁ דְּהַהִיא חַיָּה קַדִּישָׁא כו', וְכַד אִשְׁתַּדֵּל בְּאוֹרַיְתָא, בְּהַהוּא רְחִישׁוּ דְּרָחִישׁ בָּהּ זָכֵי לְהַהִיא נֶפֶשׁ חַיָּה, וּלְמֶהֱדַר כְּמַלְאָכִין קַדִּישִׁין כו', דָּא אוֹרַיְתָא דְּאִקְרֵי מַיִם, יִשְׁרְצוּן, וְיִפְקוּן רִיחֲשָׁא דְּנֶפֶשׁ חַיָּה מֵאֲתַר דְּהַהִיא חַיָּה, וּמַשְׁכִין לָהּ לְתַתָּא, כְּמָא דְּאִתְּמַר. וְעַל דָּא אָמַר דָּוִד (תהלים נא, יב) "לֵב טָהוֹר בְּרָא לִי אֱלֹקִים", לְמִלְעֵי בְּאוֹרַיְתָא, וּכְדֵין "וְרוּחַ נָכוֹן חַדֵּשׁ בְּקִרְבִּי":

[הַמִּצְוָה הַחֲמִישִׁית וכו' בַּמִּקְרָא הַזֶּה יֵשׁ ג' מִצְווֹת וכו', וְאַחַת לַעֲסֹק בַּתּוֹרָה וּלְהַרְבּוֹת בָּהּ בְּכָל יוֹם לְתַקֵּן נַפְשׁוֹ וְרוּחוֹ, מִכֵּיוָן שֶׁהָאָדָם עוֹסֵק בַּתּוֹרָה הוּא מִתְתַּקֵּן בִּנְשָׁמָה אַחֶרֶת קְדוֹשָׁה, שֶׁכָּתוּב "שֶׁרֶץ נֶפֶשׁ חַיָּה". נֶפֶשׁ מֵחַיָּה הַהִיא הַקְּדוֹשָׁה וכו'. וּכְשֶׁהוּא עוֹסֵק בַּתּוֹרָה, בְּאוֹתוֹ הָרַחַשׁ שֶׁדּוֹבֵב בָּהּ זוֹכֶה לְנֶפֶשׁ חַיָּה הַהִיא וְלִהְיוֹת כְּמַלְאָכִים הַקְּדוֹשִׁים וכו' זוֹ הַתּוֹרָה שֶׁנִּקְרֵאת "מַיִם", "יִשְׁרְצוּ" וְיוֹצִיאוּ רַחַשׁ שֶׁל "נֶפֶשׁ חַיָּה", מִמְּקוֹמָהּ שֶׁל חַיָּה הַהִיא וּמוֹשְׁכִין אוֹתָהּ לְמַטָּה, כְּמוֹ שֶׁלָּמַדְנוּ. וע"ז אָמַר דָּוִד "לֵב טָהוֹר בְּרָא לִי אֱלֹקִים" לַעֲסֹק בַּתּוֹרָה, וְאָז "וְרוּחַ נָכוֹן חַדֵּשׁ בְּקִרְבִּי".]

וְהוּא הָרוֹדֶה וּמוֹשֵׁל בַּכֹּל. וְכָל הַדִּינִין בִּישִׁין מִסְתַּלְּקִין מֵעָלָיו, וְאֵין לָהֶם עָלָיו שׁוּם שְׁלִיטָה חַס וְשָׁלוֹם, בֵּין בְּעוֹדוֹ בְּזֶה הָעוֹלָם, כְּמוֹ שֶׁכָּתוּב בְּפֶרֶק קַמָּא דִּבְרָכוֹת (ה, א) "אָמַר רַבִּי שִׁמְעוֹן בֶּן לָקִישׁ כָּל הָעוֹסֵק בַּתּוֹרָה יִסּוּרִין בְּדֵלִין הֵימֶנּוּ". וּבְפֶרֶק כֵּיצַד מְעַבְּרִין (עירובין נד, א) "חָשׁ בְּרֹאשׁוֹ יַעֲסֹק בַּתּוֹרָה שֶׁנֶּאֱמַר כו', חָשׁ בִּגְרוֹנוֹ יַעֲסֹק בַּתּוֹרָה שֶׁנֶּאֱמַר כו', חָשׁ בְּמֵעָיו כו', חָשׁ בְּכָל גּוּפוֹ יַעֲסֹק בַּתּוֹרָה, שֶׁנֶּאֱמַר (משלי ד, כב) "וּלְכָל בְּשָׂרוֹ מַרְפֵּא". וּכְעֵין סִגְנוֹן זֶה אָמְרוּ בְּוַיִּקְרָא רַבָּה פָּרָשָׁה י"ב, וּבְתַנְחוּמָא פָּרָשַׁת יִתְרוֹ, וּבְמִדְרַשׁ תְּהִלִּים מִזְמוֹר ק"ט, עַיֵּן שָׁם.

וּבְתָנָא דְּבֵי אֵלִיָּהוּ סֵדֶר אֵלִיָּהוּ רַבָּא רֵישׁ פֶּרֶק ה', "מְקִימִי מֵעָפָר דָּל" כו' (תהלים קיג, ז), אָדָם שֶׁעָבַר עֲבֵרוֹת הַרְבֵּה, וְקָנַס עָלָיו מִיתָה כו', וְחָזַר וְעָשָׂה תְּשׁוּבָה, וְקוֹרֵא תּוֹרָה נְבִיאִים וּכְתוּבִים, וְשָׁנָה מִשְׁנָה מִדְרָשׁ הֲלָכוֹת וְהַגָּדוֹת, וְשִׁמֵּשׁ חֲכָמִים, אֲפִלּוּ נִגְזְרוּ עָלָיו מֵאָה גְּזֵרוֹת, הַקָּדוֹשׁ בָּרוּךְ הוּא מַעֲבִירָן מִמֶּנּוּ כו'.

וְשָׁם רֵישׁ פֶּרֶק ו׳ ״הֱבִיאַנִי הַמֶּלֶךְ חֲדָרָיו״ (שה״ש א, ג) כְּשֵׁם שֶׁיֵּשׁ לְהַקָּדוֹשׁ בָּרוּךְ הוּא חַדְרֵי חֲדָרִים בְּתוֹרָתוֹ, כָּךְ יֵשׁ לָהֶם לְתַלְמִידֵי חֲכָמִים לְכָל אֶחָד וְאֶחָד חַדְרֵי חֲדָרִים בְּתוֹרָתוֹ, וְאִם רָאִיתָ שֶׁהַיִּסּוּרִין מְמַשְׁמְשִׁין וּבָאִין עָלֶיךָ, רוּץ לְחַדְרֵי תּוֹרָה, וּמִיָּד הַיִּסּוּרִין בּוֹרְחִין מִמְּךָ, שֶׁנֶּאֱמַר (ישעיה כו, כ) ״לֵךְ עַמִּי בֹּא בַחֲדָרֶיךָ״ וגו׳, לְכָךְ נֶאֱמַר ״הֱבִיאַנִי הַמֶּלֶךְ חֲדָרָיו״. ״נָגִילָה וְנִשְׂמְחָה בָּךְ״, בְּמָה שֶׁגִּדַּלְתָּנוּ וְרוֹמַמְתָּנוּ, וְקָשַׁרְתָּ לָנוּ כֶּתֶר גָּדוֹל בְּדִבְרֵי תוֹרָה מִסּוֹף הָעוֹלָם וְעַד סוֹפוֹ.

וְשָׁם בְּפֶרֶק ה׳ ״וַיְהִי הֵמָּה הוֹלְכִים הָלוֹךְ וְדַבֵּר״ (מלכים ב. ב, יא) וְאֵין ״דַּבֵּר״ אֶלָּא דִּבְרֵי תוֹרָה כו׳, וּכְשֶׁנִּשְׁתַּלַּח מַלְאָךְ כו׳, וּבָא וּמְצָאָן שֶׁהָיוּ עוֹסְקִין בְּדִבְרֵי תוֹרָה, וְלֹא הָיָה יָכוֹל לִשְׁלֹט בָּהֶם כו׳, מִכָּאן אָמְרוּ שְׁנֵי בְּנֵי אָדָם שֶׁהוֹלְכִין בַּדֶּרֶךְ וְעוֹסְקִין בַּתּוֹרָה, אֵין דָּבָר רַע יָכוֹל לִשְׁלֹט בָּהֶן כו׳, עַיֵּן שָׁם.

וּבַזֹּהַר וַיְחִי רמ״ב סוֹף ע״א, ״יִשָּׂשכָר חֲמוֹר גָּרֶם״ כו׳, פָּתַח וְאָמַר ״לְדָוִד ה׳ אוֹרִי״ (תהלים כז, א) כו׳, כַּמָּה חֲבִיבִין אִנּוּן מִלִּין דְּאוֹרַיְתָא, כַּמָּה חֲבִיבִין אִנּוּן דְּמִשְׁתַּדְּלֵי בְּאוֹרַיְתָא, קָמֵי קוּדְשָׁא בְּרִיךְ הוּא, דְּכָל מַאן דְּאִשְׁתַּדַּל בְּאוֹרַיְתָא לָא דָּחִיל מִפְּגָעֵי עָלְמָא, נָטִיר הוּא לְעֵלָּא, נָטִיר הוּא לְתַתָּא, וְלֹא עוֹד אֶלָּא כָּפֵי לְכָל פְּגִיעֵי דְּעָלְמָא, וְאַחִית לוֹן לְעוּמְקָא דִּתְהוֹם רַבָּה. תָּא חֲזִי, בְּשַׁעְתָּא דְּעָאל לֵילְיָא כו׳, כַּד אִתְעַר רוּחַ צָפוֹן וְאִתְפְּלִיג לֵילְיָא, אִתְעֲרוּתָא קַדִּישָׁא אִתְעַר בְּעָלְמָא כו׳, זַכָּאָה חוּלָקֵיהּ דְּהַהוּא בַּר נַשׁ, דְּאִיהוּ קָאִים בְּהַהִיא שַׁעְתָּא וְאִשְׁתַּדַּל בְּאוֹרַיְתָא, כֵּיוָן דְּאִיהוּ פָּתַח בְּאוֹרַיְתָא, כָּל אִנּוּן זִינִין בִּישִׁין, אָעִיל לוֹן בְּנוּקְבָא דִּתְהוֹם רַבָּא כו׳. בְּגִין כָּךְ יִשָּׂשכָר דְּאִשְׁתַּדְּלוּתֵיהּ בְּאוֹרַיְתָא, כָּפִית לֵיהּ לַחֲמוֹר וְנָחִית לֵיהּ כו׳, דְּאִיהוּ סָלִיק לְנִזְקָא עָלְמָא, וְשַׁוִּי מְדוֹרֵיהּ ״בֵּין הַמִּשְׁפְּתָיִם״ כו׳.

[יִשָּׂשכָר חֲמוֹר גָּרֶם וכו׳ פָּתַח וְאָמַר ״לְדָוִד ה׳ אוֹרִי״ וכו׳ כַּמָּה חֲבִיבִים הֵם דִּבְרֵי תוֹרָה, כַּמָּה חֲבִיבִים הֵם אוֹתָם שֶׁעוֹסְקִים בַּתּוֹרָה לִפְנֵי הַקָּדוֹשׁ בָּרוּךְ הוּא, כִּי כָּל מִי שֶׁעוֹסֵק בַּתּוֹרָה אֵינוֹ מְפַחֵד מִמַּזִּיקֵי הָעוֹלָם. נִשְׁמָר הוּא לְמַעְלָה, נִשְׁמָר הוּא לְמַטָּה, וְלֹא עוֹד אֶלָּא שֶׁמַּכְנִיעַ כָּל הַמַּזִּיקִים שֶׁבָּעוֹלָם וּמוֹרִידָם לְעִמְקֵי תְּהוֹם רַבָּה. בֹּא וּרְאֵה, בְּשָׁעָה שֶׁבָּא הַלַּיְלָה וכו׳ כְּשֶׁנִּתְעוֹרֵר רוּחַ צָפוֹן וְנֶחְלַק הַלַּיְלָה, הִתְעוֹרְרוּת קְדֻשָּׁה מִתְעוֹרֶרֶת בָּעוֹלָם וכו׳. אַשְׁרֵי חֶלְקוֹ שֶׁל אוֹתוֹ אָדָם שֶׁקָּם בְּאוֹתָהּ שָׁעָה וְעוֹסֵק בַּתּוֹרָה. כֵּיוָן שֶׁהוּא פּוֹתֵחַ בַּתּוֹרָה, כָּל אֵלּוּ מִינֵי מַזִּיקִים הָרָעִים מַכְנִיס אוֹתָם בְּנִקְבֵי תְּהוֹם הַגָּדוֹל וכו׳ מִשּׁוּם זֶה יִשָּׂשכָר שֶׁעִסְקוֹ בַּתּוֹרָה מַכְנִיעַ הַחֲמוֹר וּמוֹרִידוֹ וכו׳, שֶׁעוֹלֶה לְהַזִּיק לָעוֹלָם, וּמֵשִׂים מְדוֹרוֹ ״בֵּין הַמִּשְׁפְּתָיִם״ וכו׳.]

וְכֵן אָמְרוּ זִכְרוֹנָם לִבְרָכָה בְּפֶרֶק ג׳ דְּסוֹטָה (כא, א) דְּהַתּוֹרָה אַגּוּנֵי מַגְּנֵי מִן הַיִּסּוּרִין בֵּין בְּעִדָּנָא דְּעָסִיק בָּהּ בֵּין בְּעִדָּנָא דְּלָא עָסִיק בָּהּ, ע״ש. כִּי הִיא ״גְּמָלַתְהוּ (רַק) טוֹב וְלֹא רָע כֹּל יְמֵי חַיֶּיהָ״ (משלי לא, יב), הַיְנוּ אֲפִלּוּ בְּעִדָּנָא דְּלֹא עָסִיק בָּהּ, כָּל זְמַן שֶׁהוּא דָּבוּק וְלֹא פֵּרֵשׁ חַס וְשָׁלוֹם מֵחַיֵּי עוֹלָם שֶׁלָּהּ, וְדַעְתּוֹ עָלֶיהָ תָּמִיד לַחֲזֹר וְלַהֲגוֹת בָּהּ:

פֶּרֶק ט״ז

וְגַם מַעֲבִירִין וּמְסַלְּקִין מֵעָלָיו כָּל הַטְּרָדוֹת וְהָעִנְיָנִים מֵעֹל דֶּרֶךְ אֶרֶץ וכו', וְכָל שְׁאָר עִנְיָנֵי זֶה הָעוֹלָם הַמּוֹנְעוֹת תְּמִידוּת הָעֵסֶק בַּתּוֹרָה הַקְּדוֹשָׁה, כְּמוֹ שֶׁאָמְרוּ (אבות ג, ו): "כָּל הַמְקַבֵּל עָלָיו עֹל תּוֹרָה, מַעֲבִירִין מִמֶּנּוּ עֹל מַלְכוּת וְעֹל דֶּרֶךְ אֶרֶץ". וְאָמְרוּ בְּבַמִּדְבַּר רַבָּה, וּבְתַנְחוּמָא פָּרָשַׁת חֻקַּת (אות כא), שֶׁמִּזֶּה הַטַּעַם נִתְּנָה הַתּוֹרָה בַּמִּדְבָּר, כְּשֵׁם שֶׁמִּדְבָּר אֵינוֹ נִזְרָע וְאֵינוֹ נֶעֱבָד, כָּךְ הַמְקַבֵּל עָלָיו עֹל תּוֹרָה, פּוֹרְקִין מִמֶּנּוּ עֹל [גָּלוּת וְעֹל דֶּרֶךְ אֶרֶץ], וּכְשֵׁם שֶׁמִּדְבָּר אֵינוֹ מַעֲלֶה אַרְנוֹן (רָצָה לוֹמַר מַס), כָּךְ בְּנֵי תּוֹרָה בְּנֵי חוֹרִין [בָּעוֹלָם הַזֶּה] כו'.

וּבַזֹּהַר וַיְחִי רמ"ב ב', דְּכָל מַאן דְּיָדַע לְאִשְׁתַּדְּלָא בְּאוֹרַיְתָא וְלָא אִשְׁתַּדַּל, אִתְחַיַּב בְּנַפְשֵׁיהּ. וְלָא עוֹד, אֶלָּא דְיַהֲבִין עֲלֵיהּ עוּלָא דְּאַרְעָא וְשִׁעְבּוּדָא בִישָׁא, דִּכְתִיב בְּיִשָּׂשכָר "וַיֵּט שִׁכְמוֹ לִסְבֹּל" (בראשית מט, טו) כו', מַאן דְּסָטָא אָרְחֵיהּ וְגַרְמֵיהּ דְּלָא לְמִסְבַּל עוּלָא דְאוֹרַיְתָא, מִיָּד, "וַיְהִי לְמַס עוֹבֵד", [כָּל מִי שֶׁיּוֹדֵעַ לַעֲסֹק בַּתּוֹרָה, וְאֵינוֹ עוֹסֵק, מִתְחַיֵּב בְּנַפְשׁוֹ, וְלֹא עוֹד, אֶלָּא שֶׁנּוֹתְנִים עָלָיו עֹל דֶּרֶךְ אֶרֶץ וְשִׁעְבּוּד רַע, שֶׁכָּתוּב בְּיִשָּׂשכָר "וַיֵּט שִׁכְמוֹ לִסְבֹּל" מִי שֶׁמַּטֶּה דַּרְכּוֹ וְעַצְמוֹ שֶׁלֹּא לִסְבֹּל עֹל תּוֹרָה מִיָּד "וַיְהִי לְמַס עוֹבֵד"]. וְכֵן לְהֶפֶךְ כו'.

וְכָךְ הַדִּין הֲלָכָה פְּסוּקָה בַּשַּׁ"ס, שֶׁתַּלְמִידֵי חֲכָמִים פְּטוּרִין מִמִּסִּים, כְּמוֹ שֶׁאָמְרוּ (נדרים ס"ב ב' ב"ב ח' ע"א) שָׁארֵי לֵיהּ לְצוּרְבָא מֵרַבָּנַן לְמֵימַר לָא יָהִיבְנָא כַּרְגָא, דִּכְתִיב (עזרא ז, כד) מִנְדָּה בְלוֹ וַהֲלָךְ לָא שַׁלִּיט לְמִרְמֵא עֲלֵיהֹם.

וְשָׁם, רַב הוּנָא בַּר רַב חִסְדָּא שָׁדָא כַּרְגָא אַרַבָּנַן, אָמַר לֵיהּ רַב נַחְמָן בַּר יִצְחָק עֲבַרְתְּ אַדְּאוֹרַיְתָא, אַדִּנְבִיאִים, אַדִּכְתוּבִים, דִּכְתִיב כו', כְּמוֹ שֶׁאָמְרוּ שָׁם, דְּרַבָּנַן לָא צְרִיכֵי נְטִירוּתָא.

וּבְתָנָא דְּבֵי אֵלִיָּהוּ סֵדֶר אֵלִיָּהוּ רַבָּא פֶּרֶק ד', כָּל תַּלְמִיד חָכָם שֶׁעוֹסֵק בַּתּוֹרָה בְּכָל יוֹם תָּמִיד, בִּשְׁבִיל לְהַרְבּוֹת כְּבוֹד שָׁמַיִם, אֵינוֹ צָרִיךְ לֹא חֶרֶב וְלֹא חֲנִית וְלֹא כָּל דָּבָר שֶׁיִּהְיֶה לוֹ שׁוֹמֵר, אֶלָּא הַקָּדוֹשׁ בָּרוּךְ הוּא מְשַׁמְּרוֹ בְּעַצְמוֹ כו'. וְשָׁם בְּפֶרֶק י"ח, אִם יֵשׁ בּוֹ בָּאָדָם דֶּרֶךְ אֶרֶץ וּמִקְרָא לְבַד, מוֹסְרִין לוֹ מַלְאָךְ אֶחָד לְשָׁמְרוֹ, שֶׁנֶּאֱמַר כו'. קָרָא אָדָם תּוֹרָה נְבִיאִים וּכְתוּבִים, מוֹסְרִים לוֹ שְׁנֵי מַלְאָכִים, שֶׁנֶּאֱמַר כִּי מַלְאָכָיו יְצַוֶּה לָּךְ לִשְׁמָרְךָ כו'. אֲבָל קָרָא אָדָם תּוֹרָה נְבִיאִים וּכְתוּבִים, וְשָׁנָה מִשְׁנָה וּמִדְרַשׁ הֲלָכוֹת וְאַגָּדוֹת, וְשִׁמֵּשׁ תַּלְמִידֵי חֲכָמִים, הַקָּדוֹשׁ בָּרוּךְ הוּא מְשַׁמְּרוֹ בְּעַצְמוֹ כו', שֶׁנֶּאֱמַר (תהלים קל) "ה' שֹׁמְרֶךָ" כו'.

וּכְפִי עֵרֶךְ הַקִּבּוּל אֲשֶׁר יְקַבֵּל עָלָיו עֹל תּוֹרָה בֶּאֱמֶת וּבְכָל כֹּחוֹ, כֵּן לְפִי זֶה הָעֵרֶךְ יָסִירוּ וְיַעֲבִירוּ מִמֶּנּוּ טִרְדּוֹת עִנְיְנֵי זֶה הָעוֹלָם, וְהַשְּׁמִירָה עֶלְיוֹנָה חוֹפֶפֶת עָלָיו, וְהוּא כְּבֵן הַמִּתְחַטֵּא עַל אָבִיו, וְאָבִיו עוֹשֶׂה לוֹ רְצוֹנוֹ וּמַשְׁלִים לוֹ כָּל חֶפְצוֹ, כְּמוֹ שֶׁאָמְרוּ רַבּוֹתֵינוּ זִכְרוֹנָם לִבְרָכָה (ע"ז יט, א): "כָּל הָעוֹסֵק בַּתּוֹרָה, הַקָּדוֹשׁ בָּרוּךְ הוּא עוֹשֶׂה לוֹ חֶפְצוֹ". וְכֵן אִיתָא בְּמִדְרַשׁ תְּהִלִּים מִזְמוֹר א'. וְאָמְרוּ עוֹד שָׁם, שֶׁכָּתוּב בַּתּוֹרָה וְשָׁנוּי בַּנְּבִיאִים וּמְשֻׁלָּשׁ בַּכְּתוּבִים, שֶׁכָּל הָעוֹסֵק בַּתּוֹרָה נְכָסָיו מַצְלִיחִין.

וּבְמִשְׁלֵי רַבְּתָא סוֹף פָּרָשָׁה ח' "וַיָּפֶק רָצוֹן מֵה'", כָּל מִי שֶׁהוּא מֵפִיק בְּדִבְרֵי תוֹרָה

וּמְלַמְּדוֹ בָּרַבִּים, אַף אֲנִי בְּעֵת רָצוֹן מֵפִיק לוֹ רָצוֹן כו׳. וּמְזוֹנוֹתָיו מוּכָנִים לוֹ תָּמִיד, בְּלֹא שׁוּם עָמָל וִיגִיעָה מְעַט עֲלֵיהֶם. כְּמוֹ שֶׁאָמְרוּ שָׁם בְּפֶרֶק אֵשֶׁת חַיִל, כָּל זְמַן שֶׁתַּלְמִיד חָכָם יוֹשֵׁב וְעוֹסֵק בַּתּוֹרָה כו׳, וְלֹא עוֹד אֶלָּא שֶׁהַקָּדוֹשׁ בָּרוּךְ הוּא מַמְצִיא לוֹ מְזוֹנוֹתָיו בְּכָל יוֹם וָיוֹם, שֶׁנֶּאֱמַר "וַתִּתֵּן טֶרֶף לְבֵיתָהּ".

וּבְתַנָּא דְּבֵי אֵלִיָּהוּ סֵדֶר אֵלִיָּהוּ רַבָּא פֶּרֶק י״ח, בָּרוּךְ הַמָּקוֹם בָּרוּךְ הוּא שֶׁבָּחַר בַּחֲכָמִים וּבְתַלְמִידֵיהֶם כו׳, כְּשֵׁם שֶׁהֵם יוֹשְׁבִין בְּבָתֵּי כְּנֵסִיּוֹת וּבְבָתֵּי מִדְרָשׁוֹת, וּבְכָל מָקוֹם שֶׁהוּא פָּנוּי לָהֶם, וְקוֹרִין וְשׁוֹנִין לְשֵׁם שָׁמַיִם, וְיִרְאָה בִּלְבָבָם, וּמַחֲזִיקִים דִּבְרֵי תוֹרָה בְּפִיהֶם, וּמְקַיְּמִין עֲלֵיהֶם הַפָּסוּק "טוֹב לַגֶּבֶר כִּי יִשָּׂא עֹל בִּנְעוּרָיו" (איכה ג, כז) כָּךְ כִּבְיָכוֹל אֲפִלּוּ הֵם יִשְׁאֲלוּ אֶת כָּל הָעוֹלָם כֻּלּוֹ בְּשָׁעָה אַחַת, הוּא נוֹתֵן לָהֶם מִיָּד כו׳.

וְיָתֵר עַל כֵּן, אֶלָּא הֲגַם שֶׁהוּא עַצְמוֹ וַדַּאי בּוֹרֵחַ מֵהַכָּבוֹד וּגְדֻלָּה, כִּי בְּלֹא זֶה בִּלְתִּי אֶפְשָׁר בָּעוֹלָם כְּלָל לִהְיוֹת עוֹסֵק בַּתּוֹרָה לִשְׁמָהּ, וְלֹא תִתְקַיֵּם אֶצְלוֹ כְּלָל, כְּמוֹ שֶׁאָמְרוּ זִכְרוֹנָם לִבְרָכָה בְּפֶרֶק מַעֲלוֹת הַתּוֹרָה (אבות ו, ה), "אַל תְּבַקֵּשׁ גְּדֻלָּה לְעַצְמְךָ, וְאַל תַּחְמֹד כָּבוֹד", כִּי הָאָדָם אָסוּר לוֹ לְפַנּוֹת דַּעְתּוֹ לָזֶה כְּלָל.

אָמְנָם גָּדוֹל הָעֵצָה יִתְבָּרַךְ שְׁמוֹ, נוֹתֵן לוֹ שִׂמְחָה וּגְדֻלָּה בְּעַל כָּרְחוֹ, כְּמוֹ שֶׁכָּתוּב בְּתַנָּא דְּבֵי אֵלִיָּהוּ שָׁם, בָּרוּךְ הַמָּקוֹם בָּרוּךְ הוּא, שֶׁבָּחַר בַּחֲכָמִים וּבְתַלְמִידֵיהֶם כו׳, כְּמוֹ שֶׁהֵם יוֹשְׁבִין בְּבָתֵּי כְּנֵסִיּוֹת וּבְבָתֵּי מִדְרָשׁוֹת בְּכָל יוֹם, וְקוֹרִין וְשׁוֹנִין לְשֵׁם שָׁמַיִם, וְיִרְאַת שָׁמַיִם בִּלְבָבָם, וּמַחֲזִיקִים דִּבְרֵי תוֹרָה עַל פִּיהֶם, וּמְקַבְּלִין עֲלֵיהֶם בְּשִׂמְחָה עַל מַלְכוּת שָׁמַיִם, כָּךְ כִּבְיָכוֹל הַקָּדוֹשׁ בָּרוּךְ הוּא נוֹתֵן לָהֶם שִׂמְחָה לַצַּדִּיקִים בְּעַל כָּרְחָם שֶׁלֹּא בְּטוֹבָתָם כו׳, עַד כָּאן.

וּכְמַאֲמַר הַכָּתוּב (תהלים כג, ו) "אַךְ טוֹב וָחֶסֶד יִרְדְּפוּנִי כָּל יְמֵי חַיָּי", רוֹצֶה לוֹמַר, הֲגַם שֶׁאֲנִי בּוֹרֵחַ מֵהֶם, הֵמָּה רוֹדְפִים אַחֲרַי בְּעַל כָּרְחִי:

פֶּרֶק י״ז

בֵּין אַחַר פְּטִירָתוֹ מִזֶּה הָעוֹלָם, אָמְרוּ רַבּוֹתֵינוּ זִכְרוֹנָם לִבְרָכָה (חגיגה כז, א) תַּלְמִידֵי חֲכָמִים אֵין אוּר שֶׁל גֵּיהִנֹּם שׁוֹלֵט בָּהֶם כו׳. וְכֵן אָמְרוּ שָׁם (טו, ב) תַּלְמִיד חָכָם שֶׁסָּרַח אֵין תּוֹרָתוֹ נִמְאֶסֶת. וּבְמִשְׁלֵי רַבְּתָא בַּפָּסוּק "לְהָבִין מָשָׁל וּמְלִיצָה" כו׳ (משלי א), זוֹ הַתּוֹרָה עַצְמָהּ, וְלָמָּה נִקְרֵאת שְׁמָהּ מְלִיצָה, שֶׁהִיא מַצֶּלֶת עוֹסְקֶיהָ מִדִּינָהּ שֶׁל גֵּיהִנֹּם.

וְשָׁם רֵישׁ פָּרָשָׁה ב׳ "בְּנִי אִם תִּקַּח אֲמָרַי" כו׳, אָמַר הַקָּדוֹשׁ בָּרוּךְ הוּא לְיִשְׂרָאֵל עַל הַר סִינַי, אִם זְכִיתֶם לְהַצְפִּין וּלְקַבֵּל תּוֹרָתִי וְלַעֲשׂוֹתָהּ, אֲנִי מַצִּיל אֶתְכֶם מִשָּׁלֹשׁ פּוּרְעָנִיּוֹת: מִמִּלְחֶמֶת גּוֹג וּמָגוֹג, מֵחֶבְלוֹ שֶׁל מָשִׁיחַ, מִדִּינָהּ שֶׁל גֵּיהִנֹּם. "וּמִצְוֹתַי תִּצְפֹּן אִתָּךְ", אִם זְכִיתֶם לְהַצְפִּין תּוֹרָתִי, אֲנִי מַשְׂבִּיעַ אֶתְכֶם מִטּוּב הַצָּפוּן לֶעָתִיד לָבֹא, שֶׁנֶּאֱמַר (תהלים לא, כ) "מָה רַב טוּבְךָ אֲשֶׁר צָפַנְתָּ" כו׳.

וְשָׁם בְּפָרָשָׁה י׳, אָמַר רַבִּי חֲנִינָא בֶּן דּוֹסָא, אֵין לְךָ צְדָקָה שֶׁמַּצֶּלֶת אֶת הָאָדָם מִדִּינָהּ שֶׁל גֵּיהִנֹּם אֶלָּא תּוֹרָה בִּלְבַד כו׳, שֶׁיֵּשׁ בָּהּ כֹּחַ לְהַצִּיל אוֹתוֹ מִיּוֹם הַדִּין, וַאֲפִלּוּ נִתְחַיֵּב אָדָם

בִּדְבַר עֲבֵרָה, יְכוֹלָה לְהַצִּיל אוֹתוֹ מִיּוֹם הַדִּין כו', הֲרֵי מִכָּאן לְתַלְמִיד חָכָם שֶׁעָבַר בִּדְבַר עֲבֵרָה שֶׁהִיא מַצֶּלֶת אוֹתוֹ.

וּבְמִדְרַשׁ תְּהִלִּים מִזְמוֹר י"ט "וּתְקוּפָתוֹ כו', וְאֵין נִסְתָּר מֵחַמָּתוֹ" כו', רַבִּי יַנַּאי וְרַבִּי שִׁמְעוֹן בֶּן לָקִישׁ אַמְרֵי תַּרְוַיְהוּ, אֵין גֵּיהִנֹּם לֶעָתִיד לָבֹא, אֶלָּא הַשֶּׁמֶשׁ הַזּוֹ הִיא מְלַהֶטֶת אֶת הָרְשָׁעִים, שֶׁנֶּאֱמַר (מלאכי ג, יט) "הִנֵּה הַיּוֹם בָּא בֹּעֵר כַּתַּנּוּר וְהָיוּ כָל זֵדִים כו', וְלִהַט אוֹתָם" כו', אֲבָל לֶעָתִיד לָבֹא, מִי נִסְתָּר מֵחַמָּתוֹ, מִי שֶׁהוּא עוֹסֵק בַּתּוֹרָה, מַה כְּתִיב אַחֲרָיו "תּוֹרַת ה' תְּמִימָה" כו', וְכֵן הוּא אוֹמֵר "אֵין חֹשֶׁךְ וְאֵין צַלְמָוֶת לְהִסָּתֶר שָׁם פֹּעֲלֵי אָוֶן" (איוב לד, כב) וּמִי נִסְתָּר, מִי שֶׁהוּא עוֹסֵק בַּתּוֹרָה כו', עַיֵּן שָׁם.

וְקַל וָחֹמֶר מֵאֱלִישָׁע אַחֵר, שֶׁאָמְרוּ (חגיגה טו, ב): "לָא מֵידָן נְדַיְנֵיהּ מִשּׁוּם דְּגָמִיר אוֹרַיְתָא". וְכֵן אָמְרוּ בִּירוּשַׁלְמִי שָׁם, וּבְקֹהֶלֶת רַבָּה סִימָן ז', בְּפָסוּק "טוֹב אַחֲרִית דָּבָר" כו', וְלֹא כֵן תְּנֵינַן, מַצִּילִין תִּיק הַסֵּפֶר עִם הַסֵּפֶר כו', מַצִּילִין לֶאֱלִישָׁע בִּזְכוּת תּוֹרָתוֹ.

וּבַזֹּהַר יִתְרוֹ פ"ג ב', אָמַר רַבִּי יִצְחָק אַמַּאי אִתְיְהִיב אוֹרַיְתָא בְּאֶשָּׁא וַחֲשׁוֹכָא כו', דְּכָל מַאן דְּיִשְׁתַּדֵּל בְּאוֹרַיְתָא, אִשְׁתְּזִיב מֵאֶשָּׁא אָחֳרָא בְּגֵיהִנָּם, וּמֵחֲשׁוֹכָא דְּמַחְשְׁכִין כָּל שְׁאָר עַמִּין לְיִשְׂרָאֵל כו', [אָמַר רַבִּי יִצְחָק, לָמָּה נִתְּנָה תּוֹרָה בְּאֵשׁ וְחֹשֶׁךְ וכו', שֶׁכָּל מִי שֶׁעוֹסֵק בַּתּוֹרָה, נִצָּל מֵאֵשׁ אַחֶרֶת שֶׁל גֵּיהִנּוֹם, וּמֵהַחֹשֶׁךְ שֶׁמַּחְשִׁיכִים כָּל שְׁאָר הָאֻמּוֹת לְיִשְׂרָאֵל] עַיֵּן שָׁם.

וּבְרַעְיָא מְהֵימְנָא תְּרוּמָה קל"ד ב', פִּקּוּדָא לִלְמֹד תּוֹרָה בְּכָל יוֹמָא, דְּאִיהוּ רָזָא דִּמְהֵימְנוּתָא עִלָּאָה, לְמִנְדַּע אָרְחֵיהּ דְּקוּדְשָׁא בְּרִיךְ הוּא, דְּכָל מַאן דְּאִשְׁתַּדֵּל בְּאוֹרַיְתָא, זָכֵי בְּהַאי עָלְמָא וְזָכֵי בְּעָלְמָא דְּאָתֵי, וְאִשְׁתְּזִיב מִכָּל קִטְרוּגִין בִּישִׁין, בְּגִין דְּאוֹרַיְתָא רָזָא דִּמְהֵימְנוּתָא אִיהִי, דְּמַאן דְּיִתְעַסֵּק בָּהּ אִתְעֲסַק בִּמְהֵימְנוּתָא עִלָּאָה, אַשְׁרֵי שְׁכִינְתָּא בְּגַוֵּיהּ דְּלָא תַּעְדֵי מִינֵּיהּ כו', [מִצְוָה לִלְמֹד תּוֹרָה בְּכָל יוֹם, שֶׁהוּא סוֹד הָאֱמוּנָה הָעֶלְיוֹנָה, לֵידַע דְּרָכָיו שֶׁל הַקָּדוֹשׁ בָּרוּךְ הוּא, שֶׁכָּל מִי שֶׁעוֹסֵק בַּתּוֹרָה זוֹכֶה בָּעוֹלָם הַזֶּה, וְזוֹכֶה בָּעוֹלָם הַבָּא, וְנִצָּל מִכָּל קִטְרוּגִים רָעִים, מִשּׁוּם שֶׁהַתּוֹרָה סוֹד הָאֱמוּנָה הִיא, וּמִי שֶׁעוֹסֵק בָּהּ עוֹסֵק בָּאֱמוּנָה הָעֶלְיוֹנָה הַקָּדוֹשׁ בָּרוּךְ הוּא מַשְׁרֶה שְׁכִינָתוֹ בְּתוֹכוֹ שֶׁלֹּא תָּסוּר מִמֶּנּוּ.]

וּכְמַאֲמָרָם זִכְרוֹנָם לִבְרָכָה (שבת סג, א) עַל פָּסוּק "אֹרֶךְ יָמִים בִּימִינָהּ" כו' (משלי ג, טז) לַמַּיְמִינִים בָּהּ אֹרֶךְ יָמִים, וְכָל שֶׁכֵּן עֹשֶׁר וְכָבוֹד, וְהוּא בִּשְׁנֵי הָעוֹלָמִים, "עֹשֶׁר וְכָבוֹד" בָּעוֹלָם הַזֶּה, "וְאֹרֶךְ יָמִים" לָעוֹלָם הַבָּא, שֶׁעִקַּר הָאֹרֶךְ יָמִים, הַכַּוָּנָה לָעוֹלָם שֶׁכֻּלּוֹ אָרֹךְ, כְּמוֹ שֶׁאָמְרוּ רַבּוֹתֵינוּ זִכְרוֹנָם לִבְרָכָה בְּכַמָּה דּוּכְתֵּי, (קדושין לט, ב) וּבַזֹּהַר וַיֵּשֶׁב קפ"צ רֵישׁ ע"א, עַיֵּן שָׁם.

וְשָׁם בְּפָרָשַׁת חַיֵּי קל"א ב', רַבִּי אֶלְעָזָר פָּתַח וְאָמַר "גַּל עֵינַי וְאַבִּיטָה נִפְלָאוֹת מִתּוֹרָתֶךָ" (תהלים קיט, יח), כַּמָּה אִנּוּן בְּנֵי נָשָׁא טִפְּשִׁין, דְּלָא יָדְעִין וְלָא מִסְתַּכְּלִין לְאִשְׁתַּדְּלָא בְּאוֹרַיְתָא, בְּגִין דְּאוֹרַיְתָא כָּל חַיִּין, וְכָל חֵירוּ, וְכָל טוּב, בְּעָלְמָא דֵּין וּבְעָלְמָא דְּאָתֵי, אִיהוּ חֵירוּ דְּעָלְמָא דֵּין וּדְעָלְמָא דְּאָתֵי אִיהִי, חַיִּין אִנּוּן בְּעָלְמָא דֵּין, דְּיִזְכּוּן לְיוֹמִין שְׁלֵימִין בְּהַאי עָלְמָא, כד"א כו', וּלְיוֹמִין אֲרִיכִין בְּעָלְמָא דְּאָתֵי, בְּגִין דְּאִנּוּן חַיִּין שְׁלֵמִין

אִנּוּן, חַיִּין דְּחֵירוּ, חַיִּין בְּלָא עַצִיבוּ, חַיִּין דְּאִנּוּן חַיִּין, חֵירוּ בְּעָלְמָא דֵּין חֵירוּ דְּכֹלָּא, דְּכָל מַאן דְּאִשְׁתַּדַּל בְּאוֹרַיְתָא, לָא יַכְלִין לְשַׁלְטָאָה עֲלוֹי כָּל עַמִּין דְּעָלְמָא כו׳, וְעַל דָּא, כָּל מַאן דְּיִשְׁתַּדַּל בְּאוֹרַיְתָא, חֵירוּ אִית לֵיהּ מִכֹּלָּא, בְּעָלְמָא דֵין — מִשִּׁעְבּוּדָא דִשְׁאָר עַמִּין, חֵירוּ בְּעָלְמָא דְאָתֵי — בְּגִין דְּלָא יִתְבְּעוּן מִנֵּיהּ דִּינָא בְּהַהוּא עָלְמָא כְּלָל כו׳.

[רַבִּי אֶלְעָזָר פָּתַח "גַּל עֵינַי וְאַבִּיטָה נִפְלָאוֹת מִתּוֹרָתֶךָ", כַּמָּה הֵם שׁוֹטִים בְּנֵי אָדָם, שֶׁאֵינָם יוֹדְעִים וְלֹא מִסְתַּכְּלִים לַעֲסֹק בַּתּוֹרָה, שֶׁהֲרֵי הַתּוֹרָה הִיא כָּל הַחַיִּים, וְכָל הַחֵרוּת וְכָל הַטּוֹב בָּעוֹלָם הַזֶּה וּבָעוֹלָם הַבָּא, שֶׁהִיא חֵרוּת בָּעוֹלָם הַזֶּה וּבָעוֹלָם הַבָּא הִיא, חַיִּים הִיא בָּעוֹלָם הַזֶּה — שֶׁיִּזְכּוּ לְיָמִים שְׁלֵמִים בָּעוֹלָם הַזֶּה וכו׳. וּלְיָמִים אֲרֻכִּים בָּעוֹלָם הַבָּא. בִּשְׁבִיל שֶׁהֵם חַיִּים שְׁלֵמִים הֵם, חַיִּים שֶׁל חֵרוּת, חַיִּים בְּלֹא עַצְבוּת, חַיִּים שֶׁהֵם חַיִּים, חֵרוּת בָּעוֹלָם הַזֶּה, חֵרוּת מִכֹּל, כִּי כָּל מִי שֶׁעוֹסֵק בַּתּוֹרָה לֹא יוּכְלוּ לִשְׁלֹט עָלָיו כָּל עַמֵּי הָעוֹלָם וכו׳. וְעַל כֵּן כָּל מִי שֶׁעוֹסֵק בַּתּוֹרָה יֵשׁ לוֹ חֵרוּת מִכֹּל, בָּעוֹלָם הַזֶּה — מִשִּׁעְבּוּד אֻמּוֹת הָעוֹלָם, וְחֵרוּת בָּעוֹלָם הַבָּא — כִּי לֹא יִדְרְשׁוּ מִמֶּנּוּ דִּין בָּעוֹלָם הַבָּא כְּלָל]. עַיֵּן שָׁם.

וּבְתַנָּא דְּבֵי אֵלִיָּהוּ סֵדֶר אֵלִיָּהוּ רַבָּא פֶּרֶק י״ח, בַּפָּסוּק (יחזקאל מז, יב) "וְעַל הַנַּחַל יַעֲלֶה עַל שְׂפָתוֹ מִזֶּה וּמִזֶּה כָּל עֵץ מַאֲכָל" וכו׳, מַאי "וְלֹא יִרְאֶה כִּי יָבֹא חֹם", לוֹמַר לְךָ, כָּל הָעוֹסֵק בַּתּוֹרָה אֵינוֹ רוֹאֶה מִדַּת פּוּרְעָנִיּוֹת, בֵּין בָּעוֹלָם הַזֶּה בֵּין לִימוֹת בֶּן דָּוִד וּבֵין לָעוֹלָם הַבָּא. וּכְמוֹ שֶׁפֵּרְשׁוּ זִכְרוֹנָם לִבְרָכָה (סוטה כא, א) "בְּהִתְהַלֶּכְךָ תַּנְחֶה אוֹתָךְ" (משלי ו, כב) — בָּעוֹלָם הַזֶּה, "בְּשָׁכְבְּךָ תִּשְׁמֹר עָלֶיךָ" — בַּקֶּבֶר, "וַהֲקִיצוֹתָ הִיא תְשִׂיחֶךָ" — לָעוֹלָם הַבָּא.

וּבַזֹּהַר פָּרָשַׁת וַיֵּשֶׁב קפ״ד ב׳, וקפ״ה א׳, רַבִּי יְהוּדָה פָּתַח וְאָמַר "תּוֹרַת ה׳ תְּמִימָה" (תהלים יט) כו׳, כַּמָּה אִית לוֹן לִבְנֵי נָשָׁא לְאִשְׁתַּדְּלָא בְּאוֹרַיְתָא, דְּכָל מַאן דְּאִשְׁתַּדַּל בְּאוֹרַיְתָא, לֶהֱוֵי לֵיהּ חַיִּים בְּעָלְמָא דֵין וּבְעָלְמָא דְאָתֵי, וְזָכֵי בִּתְרֵין עָלְמִין. וַאֲפִילוּ מַאן דְּאִשְׁתַּדַּל בְּאוֹרַיְתָא, וְלָא אִשְׁתַּדַּל בָּהּ לִשְׁמָהּ כִּדְקָא יָאוּת, זָכֵי לַאֲגַר טַב בְּעָלְמָא דֵין, וְלָא דַיְנִין לֵיהּ בְּהַהוּא עָלְמָא. וְתָא חֲזֵי כְּתִיב "אֹרֶךְ יָמִים בִּימִינָהּ" כו׳, "אֹרֶךְ יָמִים" בְּהַהוּא דְאִשְׁתַּדַּל בְּאוֹרַיְתָא לִשְׁמָהּ, דְּאִית לֵיהּ "אֹרֶךְ יָמִים" בְּהַהוּא עָלְמָא דְבֵיהּ אוּרְכָא דְיוֹמִין כו׳, "בִּשְׂמֹאלָהּ עֹשֶׁר וְכָבוֹד", אֲגַר טוֹב וְשַׁלְוָה אִית לֵיהּ בְּהַאי עָלְמָא. וְכָל מַאן דְּיִשְׁתַּדַּל בְּאוֹרַיְתָא לִשְׁמָהּ, כַּד נָפִיק מֵהַאי עָלְמָא, אוֹרַיְתָא אַזְלָא קָמֵיהּ, וְאַכְרְזַת קָמֵיהּ, וַאֲגִינַת עֲלֵיהּ, דְּלָא יִקְרְבוּן בַּהֲדֵיהּ מָארֵיהוֹן דְּדִינָא, כַּד שָׁכִיב גּוּפָא בְּקִבְרָא הִיא נַטְרַת לֵיהּ, כַּד נִשְׁמָתָא אַזְלַת לְאִסְתַּלְּקָא לְמֵיתַב לְאַתְרָהּ, אִיהִי אַזְלַת קָמָהּ דְּהַהִיא נִשְׁמָתָא, וְכַמָּה תַּרְעִין אִתְבְּרוּ מִקַּמָּהּ דְּאוֹרַיְתָא עַד דְּעָאלַת לְדוּכְתָּא, וְקַיְמָא עֲלֵיהּ דְּבַר נַשׁ, עַד דְּיִתְעַר בְּזִמְנָא דִּיקוּמוּן מֵתַיָּא דְעָלְמָא, וְאִיהִי סַנֵּיגוֹרָא עֲלֵיהּ, הֲדָא הוּא דִכְתִיב "בְּהִתְהַלֶּכְךָ תַּנְחֶה אוֹתָךְ בְּשָׁכְבְּךָ תִּשְׁמֹר עָלֶיךָ" כו׳, "בְּהִתְהַלֶּכְךָ תַּנְחֶה אוֹתָךְ" — כְּמָה דְּאִתְּמַר, "בְּשָׁכְבְּךָ תִּשְׁמֹר עָלֶיךָ" — בְּשַׁעְתָּא דְשָׁכִיב גּוּפָא בְּקִבְרָא, דְּהָא כְּדֵין בְּהַהוּא זִמְנָא אִתְדַּן גּוּפָא בְּקִבְרָא, וּכְדֵין אוֹרַיְתָא אֲגִינַת עֲלֵיהּ, "וַהֲקִיצוֹתָ הִיא תְשִׂיחֶךָ" — כְּמָה דְּאִתְּמַר, בְּזִמְנָא דְיִתְעֲרוּן מֵתֵי עָלְמָא מִן עַפְרָא, "הִיא תְשִׂיחֶךָ" — לְמֶהֱוֵי סַנֵּיגוֹרָא עֲלָךְ כו׳.

[כַּמָּה יֵשׁ לָהֶם לִבְנֵי אָדָם לְהִשְׁתַּדֵּל בַּתּוֹרָה, כִּי כָּל מִי שֶׁמִּשְׁתַּדֵּל בַּתּוֹרָה, יִהְיֶה לוֹ חַיִּים בָּעוֹלָם הַזֶּה וּבָעוֹלָם הַבָּא, וְהוּא זוֹכֶה בִּשְׁנֵי עוֹלָמוֹת. וַאֲפִילוּ מִי שֶׁמִּשְׁתַּדֵּל בַּתּוֹרָה וְאֵינוֹ מִשְׁתַּדֵּל בָּהּ לִשְׁמָהּ כָּרָאוּי, הוּא זוֹכֶה לִשְׂכַר טוֹב בָּעוֹלָם הַזֶּה, וְאֵין דָּנִים אוֹתוֹ בְּעוֹלַם הָאֱמֶת. בֹּא וּרְאֵה, כָּתוּב "אֹרֶךְ יָמִים בִּימִינָהּ" וגו', "אֹרֶךְ יָמִים" — הוּא לְאוֹתוֹ הַמִּשְׁתַּדֵּל בַּתּוֹרָה לִשְׁמָהּ, שֶׁיֵּשׁ לוֹ אֹרֶךְ יָמִים בְּאוֹתוֹ הָעוֹלָם שֶׁבּוֹ אֲרִיכוּת יָמִים וכו'. "בִּשְׂמֹאלָהּ עֹשֶׁר וְכָבוֹד", שְׂכַר טוֹב וְשַׁלְוָה יֵשׁ לוֹ בָּעוֹלָם הַזֶּה. וְכָל מִי שֶׁעוֹסֵק בַּתּוֹרָה לִשְׁמָהּ, בְּעֵת שֶׁיּוֹצֵא מִן הָעוֹלָם הַזֶּה, הַתּוֹרָה הוֹלֶכֶת לְפָנָיו, וּמַכְרֶזֶת לְפָנָיו וּמְגִנַּת עָלָיו, שֶׁלֹּא יִתְקָרְבוּ אֵלָיו בַּעֲלֵי דִּין. כְּשֶׁהַגּוּף שׁוֹכֵב בַּקֶּבֶר הִיא מִשְׁמַרְתּוֹ, כְּשֶׁהַנְּשָׁמָה הוֹלֶכֶת לְהִסְתַּלֵּק וְלָשׁוּב לִמְקוֹמָהּ, הִיא הוֹלֶכֶת לִפְנֵי הַנְּשָׁמָה, וְהַרְבֵּה שְׁעָרִים נִשְׁבָּרִים מִלִּפְנֵי הַתּוֹרָה עַד שֶׁבָּאָה לִמְקוֹמָהּ, וְעוֹמֶדֶת עַל הָאָדָם עַד שֶׁיִּתְעוֹרֵר בְּשָׁעָה שֶׁיָּקוּמוּ הַמֵּתִים שֶׁל הָעוֹלָם, וְהִיא מְלַמֶּדֶת זְכוּת עָלָיו, זֶה שֶׁכָּתוּב "בְּהִתְהַלֶּכְךָ תַּנְחֶה אוֹתָךְ" וגו'. "בְּהִתְהַלֶּכְךָ תַּנְחֶה אוֹתָךְ" — הוּא כְּמוֹ שֶׁאָמַרְנוּ, "בְּשָׁכְבְּךָ תִּשְׁמֹר עָלֶיךָ" — הוּא בְּשָׁעָה שֶׁהַגּוּף שׁוֹכֵב בַּקֶּבֶר, כִּי אָז בִּזְמַן הַהוּא נִדּוֹן הַגּוּף בַּקֶּבֶר, וְהַתּוֹרָה מְגִנַּת עָלָיו. "וַהֲקִיצוֹתָ הִיא תְשִׂיחֶךָ" — הוּא כְּמוֹ שֶׁאָמַרְנוּ לְעֵיל, שֶׁהוּא בִּזְמַן שֶׁיָּקִיצוּ מֵתֵי עוֹלָם מִן הֶעָפָר, "הִיא תְשִׂיחֶךָ" לְלַמֵּד עָלֶיךָ זְכוּת.]

וְכֵן אָמְרוּ רַבּוֹתֵינוּ זִכְרוֹנָם לִבְרָכָה בְּפֶרֶק חֵלֶק (צט, ב) בַּפָּסוּק (משלי טז, כו) "נֶפֶשׁ עָמֵל עָמְלָה לּוֹ" כו', הוּא עָמֵל בְּמָקוֹם זֶה וְהַתּוֹרָה עוֹמֶלֶת לוֹ בְּמָקוֹם אַחֵר. וּבְמִשְׁלֵי רַבְּתָא פָּרָשָׁה י"ד "חַכְמוֹת נָשִׁים בָּנְתָה בֵיתָהּ" (משלי יד, א), כָּל מִי שֶׁקָּנָה לוֹ חָכְמָה בָּעוֹלָם הַזֶּה, יְהֵא מֻבְטָח שֶׁהִיא בָּנְתָה לוֹ בַּיִת לָעוֹלָם הַבָּא, "וְאִוֶּלֶת בְּיָדֶיהָ תֶהֶרְסֶנּוּ" (שם) כָּל מִי שֶׁלֹּא קָנָה לוֹ חָכְמָה, יְהֵא מֻבְטָח שֶׁקָּנָה לוֹ גֵּיהִנֹּם לֶעָתִיד לָבֹא.

וּבְסִתְרֵי תּוֹרָה לֶךְ לְךָ (זוה"ק בראשית פח, א), "אַחַר הַדְּבָרִים הָאֵלֶּה", דָּא פִּתְגָּמֵי אוֹרַיְתָא כו', הֲדָא הוּא דִכְתִיב (בראשית טו, א) "אַל תִּירָא אַבְרָם אָנֹכִי מָגֵן לָךְ", מִכָּל זִינֵי בִּישִׁין דְּגֵיהִנֹּם, "שְׂכָרְךָ הַרְבֵּה מְאֹד", בְּגִין דְּכָל מַאן דְּאִשְׁתַּדֵּל בְּאוֹרַיְתָא בְּהַאי עָלְמָא, זָכֵי וְאַחְסִין יְרוּתַת אַחְסַנְתֵּיהּ לְעָלְמָא דְּאָתֵי כו', ["אַחַר הַדְּבָרִים הָאֵלֶּה", הֵם דִּבְרֵי תּוֹרָה וכו', וְזֶה שֶׁכָּתוּב "אַל תִּירָא אַבְרָהָם אָנֹכִי מָגֵן לָךְ" — מִכָּל בְּחִינוֹת הָרָעוֹת שֶׁבַּגֵּיהִנּוֹם, "שְׂכָרְךָ הַרְבֵּה מְאֹד" מִשּׁוּם שֶׁכָּל מִי שֶׁעוֹסֵק בַּתּוֹרָה בָּעוֹלָם הַזֶּה, זוֹכֶה וְיוֹרֵשׁ יְרֻשַּׁת נַחֲלָה בָּעוֹלָם הַבָּא וכו'] עַיֵּן שָׁם.

וּבְזֹהַר וַיַּקְהֵל ר' ע"א, בְּגִין דְּכַד בַּר נַשׁ עָסִיק בְּאוֹרַיְתָא, קוּדְשָׁא בְּרִיךְ הוּא קָאִים תַּמָּן כו', וְאִשְׁתְּזֵיב בַּר נַשׁ מִתְּלַת דִּינִין: מִדִּינָא דְּהַאי עָלְמָא, וּמִדִּינָא דְּמַלְאַךְ הַמָּוֶת דְּלָא יָכִיל לְשַׁלְטָאָה עָלֵיהּ, וּמִדִּינָא דְּגֵיהִנֹּם [מִשּׁוּם שֶׁכְּשֶׁהָאָדָם עוֹסֵק בַּתּוֹרָה, הַקָּדוֹשׁ בָּרוּךְ הוּא עוֹמֵד שָׁם וכו' וְנִצּוֹל הָאָדָם מִשָּׁלֹשׁ דִּינִים: מִדִּין שֶׁבָּעוֹלָם הַזֶּה, וּמִדִּין שֶׁל מַלְאַךְ הַמָּוֶת שֶׁאֵינוֹ יָכוֹל לִשְׁלֹט עָלָיו, וּמִדִּין שֶׁל גֵּהִנּוֹם.]

וּכְמוֹ שֶׁאָמְרוּ רַבּוֹתֵינוּ זִכְרוֹנָם לִבְרָכָה בְּפֶרֶק מַעֲלַת הַתּוֹרָה (אבות ו, ב), וּבְבַמִּדְבָּר רַבָּה פָּרָשָׁה ט"ז, וּבְחָזִית בַּפָּסוּק מִי זֹאת עוֹלָה כו'. וּבְתַנְחוּמָא פָּרָשַׁת עֵקֶב, אַל תִּקְרֵי "חָרוּת" אֶלָּא חֵרוּת, שֶׁאֵין לְךָ בֶּן חוֹרִין אֶלָּא מִי שֶׁעוֹסֵק בְּתַלְמוּד תּוֹרָה, וּפֵרְשׁוּ זִכְרוֹנָם

לִבְרָכָה, חֵרוּת, מִמַּלְאַךְ הַמָּוֶת. וְכֵן אָמְרוּ בְּפֶרֶק ב׳ דְּמַכּוֹת (י׳ ע״א) שֶׁדִּבְרֵי תּוֹרָה קוֹלְטִין מִמַּלְאַךְ הַמָּוֶת.

וּבַזֹּהַר פָּרָשַׁת חַיֵּי בַּדַּף הַנַּ״ל (קלא, ב), חֵירוּ בְּעָלְמָא דֵּין, חֵירוּ דִּכְלָא כוּ׳, חֵירוּ דְּמַלְאַךְ הַמָּוֶת, דְּלָא יָכוֹל לְשָׁלְטָאָה עֲלוֹי, וְהָכִי הוּא וַדַּאי, דְּאִי אָדָם הֲוָה אִתְדְּבִיק בְּאִילָנָא דְּחַיֵּי, דְּאִיהוּ אוֹרַיְתָא, לָא גָּרִים מוֹתָא לֵיהּ וּלְכָל עָלְמָא, וּבְגִין כָּךְ, כַּד יָהִיב קוּדְשָׁא בְּרִיךְ הוּא אוֹרַיְתָא לְיִשְׂרָאֵל, מַה כְּתִיב בָּהּ (שמות לב, טז), "חָרוּת עַל הַלּוּחוֹת" כוּ׳, וְקוּדְשָׁא בְּרִיךְ הוּא אָמַר (תהלים פב, ו) "אֲנִי אָמַרְתִּי אֱלֹקִים אַתֶּם" כוּ׳. וְעַל דָּא, כָּל מַאן דְּאִשְׁתַּדַּל בְּאוֹרַיְתָא, לָא יָכִיל לְשָׁלְטָאָה עֲלוֹי הַהוּא חִוְיָא בִּישָׁא דְּאַחְשִׁיךְ עָלְמָא. [חֵרוּת בָּעוֹלָם הַזֶּה, חֵרוּת מִכֹּל וכו׳, חֵרוּת מִמַּלְאַךְ הַמָּוֶת שֶׁאֵינוֹ יָכוֹל לִשְׁלֹט עָלָיו, וְכֵן הוּא בְּוַדַּאי שֶׁהֲרֵי אִם אָדָם הָיָה מִתְדַּבֵּק בְּעֵץ הַחַיִּים שֶׁהוּא הַתּוֹרָה לֹא הָיָה גּוֹרֵם מָוֶת לוֹ וּלְכָל הָעוֹלָם. וּמִשּׁוּם זֶה, כְּשֶׁנָּתַן הַקָּדוֹשׁ בָּרוּךְ הוּא הַתּוֹרָה לְיִשְׂרָאֵל, מַה כָּתוּב בָּהּ, "חָרוּת עַל הַלֻּחֹת" וכו׳, וְהַקָּדוֹשׁ בָּרוּךְ הוּא אָמַר "אֲנִי אָמַרְתִּי אֱלֹקִים אַתֶּם" וכו׳, וְעַל כֵּן כָּל מִי שֶׁעוֹסֵק בַּתּוֹרָה, אֵינוֹ יָכוֹל לִשְׁלֹט עָלָיו אוֹתוֹ נָחָשׁ רַע שֶׁהֶחְשִׁיךְ הָעוֹלָם.]

פֶּרֶק י״ח

וְלָזֹאת, הָאָדָם הַמְקַבֵּל עַל עַצְמוֹ עֹל הַתּוֹרָה הַקְּדוֹשָׁה לִשְׁמָהּ לַאֲמִתָּהּ, כְּמוֹ שֶׁהִתְבָּאֵר לְעֵיל (פ״ב) פֵּרוּשׁ "לִשְׁמָהּ" — הוּא נַעֲלֶה מֵעַל כָּל עִנְיְנֵי זֶה הָעוֹלָם, וּמֻשְׁגָּח מֵאִתּוֹ יִתְבָּרַךְ הַשְׁגָּחָה פְּרָטִית, לְמַעְלָה מֵהוֹרָאַת כֹּחוֹת הַטְּבָעִים וְהַמַּזָּלוֹת כֻּלָּם. כֵּיוָן שֶׁהוּא דָּבוּק בַּתּוֹרָה וּבְהַקָּדוֹשׁ בָּרוּךְ הוּא מַמָּשׁ כִּבְיָכוֹל, וּמִתְקַדֵּשׁ בִּקְדֻשָּׁה הָעֶלְיוֹנָה שֶׁל הַתּוֹרָה הַקְּדוֹשָׁה, שֶׁהִיא לְמַעְלָה לְאֵין עֲרֹךְ מִכָּל הָעוֹלָמוֹת, וְהִיא הַנּוֹתֶנֶת הַחִיּוּת וְהַקִּיּוּם לְכֻלָּם וּלְכָל הַכֹּחוֹת הַטִּבְעִיִּים, הֲרֵי הָאָדָם הָעוֹסֵק בָּהּ — מְחַיֶּה וּמְקַיֵּם אֶת כֻּלָּם וּלְמַעְלָה מִכֻּלָּם, וְאֵיךְ אֶפְשָׁר שֶׁתְּהֵא הַנְהָגָתוֹ מֵאִתּוֹ יִתְבָּרַךְ עַל יְדֵי הַכֹּחוֹת הַטִּבְעִיִּים.

וְזֶה שֶׁאָמְרוּ רַבּוֹתֵינוּ זִכְרוֹנָם לִבְרָכָה: כְּתִיב "עַד שָׁמַיִם חַסְדֶּךָ" (תהלים קח, ה) וּכְתִיב "מֵעַל שָׁמַיִם חַסְדֶּךָ", לָא קַשְׁיָא, כָּאן בְּעוֹסְקִים לִשְׁמָהּ, כָּאן בְּעוֹסְקִים שֶׁלֹּא לִשְׁמָהּ" (פסחים נ׳ ע״ב).

הַיְנוּ, שֶׁהָעוֹסֵק בַּתּוֹרָה שֶׁלֹּא לִשְׁמָהּ, אִם כִּי וַדַּאי שֶׁגַּם הוּא מְרֻצֶּה לְפָנָיו יִתְבָּרַךְ, אַף אִם כַּוָּנָתוֹ לְשֵׁם אֵיזֶה פְּנִיָּה שֶׁתִּהְיֶה, רַק אִם אֵינוֹ לְקַנְטוּר חַס וְשָׁלוֹם, וְכָל שֶׁכֵּן אִם אֵינוֹ מְכַוֵּן לְשׁוּם פְּנִיָּה, רַק לְפִי שֶׁהֻרְגַּל בְּכָךְ, כִּי מִתּוֹכָהּ יָבֹא לְמַדְרֵגָה לִשְׁמָהּ כַּיָּדוּעַ מִמַּאֲמָרָם זִכְרוֹנָם לִבְרָכָה, עִם כָּל זֶה, עֲדַיִן לֹא נִתְקַדֵּשׁ וְנִתְעַלָּה, שֶׁיִּהְיֶה הַנְהָגָתוֹ יִתְבָּרַךְ אִתּוֹ בְּכָל עִנְיָנָיו לְמַעְלָה מִכֹּחוֹת הַטִּבְעִיִּים, לָכֵן כְּתִיב בֵּיהּ רַק "עַד שָׁמַיִם", הַיְנוּ עַד הַכֹּחוֹת הַטִּבְעִיִּים הַקְּבוּעִים בַּשָּׁמַיִם, וְלֹא לְמַעְלָה מֵהֶם.

אֲבָל עַל הָעוֹסֵק בָּהּ לִשְׁמָהּ, אָמַר "מֵעַל שָׁמַיִם", רוֹצֶה לוֹמַר, שֶׁכָּל הַנְהָגוֹתָיו יִתְבָּרַךְ עִמּוֹ רַק לְמַעְלָה מֵהוֹרָאַת כֹּחוֹת הַטִּבְעִיִּים.

וְזֶה שֶׁכָּתוּב בְּרַעְיָא מְהֵימְנָא פִּנְחָס רי״ו ב׳, תָּא חֲזִי, כָּל בִּרְיָין דְּעָלְמָא, קוֹדֶם דְּאִתְיְהִיבַת

אוֹרַיְתָא לְיִשְׂרָאֵל הֲווּ תַּלְיָן בְּמַזָּלָא כו׳, אֲבָל בָּתַר דְּאִתְיְהִיבַת אוֹרַיְתָא לְיִשְׂרָאֵל, אַפִּיק לוֹן מֵחִיּוּבָא דְּכָכְבֵי וּמַזָּלֵי כו׳, וּבְגִין דָּא, כָּל הַמִּשְׁתַּדֵּל בְּאוֹרַיְתָא, בָּטִיל מִנֵּיהּ חִיּוּבָא דְּכָכְבַיָּא וּמַזָּלֵי, אִי אוֹלִיף לָהּ כְּדֵי לְקַיְּמָא פִּקּוּדָהָא. וְאִי לָאו, כְּאִלּוּ לָא אִשְׁתַּדֵּל בָּהּ, וְלָא בָּטִיל מִנֵּיהּ חִיּוּבָא דְּכָכְבַיָּא וּמַזָּלֵי. [בֹּא וּרְאֵה, כָּל בְּרִיּוֹת הָעוֹלָם, קֹדֶם שֶׁנִּתְּנָה הַתּוֹרָה לְיִשְׂרָאֵל הָיוּ תְּלוּיִים בְּמַזָּל וכו׳, אֲבָל אַחַר שֶׁנִּתְּנָה תּוֹרָה לְיִשְׂרָאֵל, הוֹצִיאָם מִגְּזֵירָתָם שֶׁל כּוֹכָבִים וּמַזָּלוֹת, וכו׳ וּמִשּׁוּם זֶה כָּל הָעוֹסֵק בַּתּוֹרָה בָּטֵל מִמֶּנּוּ גְּזֵירָתָם שֶׁל כּוֹכָבִים וּמַזָּלוֹת, אִם לוֹמֵד הַתּוֹרָה כְּדֵי לְקַיֵּם מִצְוֹתֶיהָ. וְאִם לֹא, הֲרֵי הוּא כְּמִי שֶׁלֹּא עָסַק בַּתּוֹרָה, וְלֹא מִתְבַּטֵּל מִמֶּנּוּ גְּזֵירָתָם שֶׁל כּוֹכָבִים וּמַזָּלוֹת.]

וְאַדְּרַבָּה הַכֹּחוֹת הַטִּבְעִיִּים מְסוּרִים אֵלָיו כַּאֲשֶׁר יִגְזֹר אֹמֶר עֲלֵיהֶם, וּלְכָל אֲשֶׁר יַחְפֹּץ יַטֵּם, וְאֵימָתוֹ מֻטֶּלֶת עַל כֻּלָּם, כְּמוֹ שֶׁאָמְרוּ בְּפֶרֶק הַתּוֹרָה (אבות ו, א) "וְנוֹתֶנֶת לוֹ מַלְכוּת וּמֶמְשָׁלָה". כִּי נֵזֶר אֱלֹקָיו, אוֹר הַתּוֹרָה, מְאִירָה וּמַבְהֶקֶת עַל רֹאשׁוֹ, וְחוֹסֶה כִּבְיָכוֹל בְּצֵל כַּנְפֵי הַשְּׁכִינָה.

כְּמוֹ שֶׁאָמְרוּ בַּזֹּהַר צַו ל״ה א׳, פָּתַח רַבִּי אֶלְעָזָר וְאָמַר "וָאָשִׂים דְּבָרַי בְּפִיךָ וּבְצֵל יָדִי כִּסִּיתִיךָ" (ישעיה נא, טז) כו׳, תַּנְיָנָן, כָּל בַּר נַשׁ דְּאִשְׁתַּדֵּל בְּמִלֵּי דְּאוֹרַיְתָא, וְשִׂפְוָתֵיהּ מְרַחֲשָׁן אוֹרַיְתָא, קוּדְשָׁא בְּרִיךְ הוּא חָפֵי עֲלֵיהּ, וּשְׁכִינְתָּא פַּרְשָׂא עֲלֵיהּ גַּדְפָהָא, הֲדָא הוּא דִּכְתִיב "וָאָשִׂים דְּבָרַי בְּפִיךָ וּבְצֵל יָדִי כִּסִּיתִיךָ" כו׳ [פָּתַח רַבִּי אֶלְעָזָר וְאָמַר, "וָאָשִׂים דְּבָרַי בְּפִיךָ" וגו׳, לָמַדְנוּ כָּל אָדָם הָעוֹסֵק בְּדִבְרֵי תּוֹרָה, וְשִׂפְתוֹתָיו דּוֹבְבוֹת תּוֹרָה, הַקָּדוֹשׁ בָּרוּךְ הוּא מְכַסֶּה עָלָיו, וְהַשְּׁכִינָה פּוֹרֶשֶׂת עָלָיו כְּנָפֶיהָ, זֶהוּ שֶׁאָמַר "וָאָשִׂים דְּבָרַי בְּפִיךָ וּבְצֵל יָדִי כִּסִּיתִיךָ" וכו׳.]

וּבְהַקְדָּמַת הַזֹּהַר י״א א, וְכֵן הוּא בְּאוֹתוֹ הַלָּשׁוֹן בְּפָרָשַׁת וָאֶתְחַנַּן ר״ס ע״א, תָּא חֲזֵי, כַּמָּה הוּא חֵילָא תַּקִּיפָא דְּאוֹרַיְתָא, וְכַמָּה הוּא עִלָּאָה עַל כֹּלָּא, דְּכָל מַאן דְּאִשְׁתַּדֵּל בְּאוֹרַיְתָא, לָא דָּחִיל מֵעִלָּאֵי וְתַתָּאֵי, וְלָא דָּחִיל מֵעַרְעוּרִין בִּישִׁין דְּעָלְמָא, בְּגִין דְּאִיהוּ אָחִיד בְּאִילָנָא דְּחַיֵּי, וְאָכִיל מִנֵּיהּ בְּכָל יוֹמָא, דְּהָא אוֹרַיְתָא אוֹלִיף לֵיהּ לְבַר נַשׁ בְּאֹרַח קְשׁוֹט, אוֹלִיף לֵיהּ עֵיטָא כו׳ [בֹּא וּרְאֵה, כַּמָּה חָזָק כֹּחַ הַתּוֹרָה, וְכַמָּה הִיא עֶלְיוֹנָה עַל הַכֹּל, כִּי כָּל מִי שֶׁעוֹסֵק בַּתּוֹרָה אֵינוֹ יָרֵא מֵעֶלְיוֹנִים וּמִתַּחְתּוֹנִים, וְאֵינוֹ יָרֵא מֵחֳלָיִים רָעִים שֶׁבָּעוֹלָם, מִפְּנֵי שֶׁהוּא אָחוּז בְּעֵץ הַחַיִּים וְאוֹכֵל מִמֶּנּוּ כָּל יוֹם, כִּי הַתּוֹרָה מְלַמֶּדֶת אֶת הָאָדָם לָלֶכֶת בְּדֶרֶךְ אֱמֶת מְלַמֶּדֶת לוֹ עֵצָה וכו׳.]

וּבְפָרָשַׁת בְּשַׁלַּח מ״ו א׳, ר״י פָּתַח כו׳, כַּמָּה חֲבִיבָא אוֹרַיְתָא קַמֵּיהּ דְּקוּדְשָׁא בְּרִיךְ הוּא, דְּכָל מַאן דְּיִשְׁתַּדֵּל בְּאוֹרַיְתָא, רָחִים הוּא לְעֵלָּא, רָחִים הוּא לְתַתָּא, קוּדְשָׁא בְּרִיךְ הוּא אָצִית לֵיהּ לְמִלּוֹלֵי, לָא שָׁבִיק לֵיהּ בְּהַאי עָלְמָא, וְלָא שָׁבִיק לֵיהּ בְּעָלְמָא דְּאָתֵי כו׳, [ר״י פָּתַח וְאָמַר כַּמָּה חֲבִיבָה הַתּוֹרָה לִפְנֵי הַקָּדוֹשׁ בָּרוּךְ הוּא, שֶׁכָּל מִי שֶׁעוֹסֵק בַּתּוֹרָה אָהוּב הוּא לְמַעְלָה, אָהוּב הוּא לְמַטָּה, וְהַקָּדוֹשׁ בָּרוּךְ הוּא מַקְשִׁיב לְדִבּוּרָיו, וְאֵינוֹ עוֹזֵב אוֹתוֹ בָּעוֹלָם הַזֶּה, וְאֵינוֹ עוֹזֵב אוֹתוֹ לָעוֹלָם הַבָּא וכו׳] עַיֵּן שָׁם.

וּבְפָרָשַׁת מְצֹרָע נ״ב ב׳, וְכַד אִיהוּ אִשְׁתַּדַּל בְּפוּלְחָנָא דְּמָארֵיהּ, וְלָעֵי בְּאוֹרַיְתָא, כַּמָּה

נְטוּרִין זְמִינִין לְקַבְּלֵיהּ לְנַטְרָא לֵיהּ, וּשְׁכִינְתָּא שַׁרְיָא עֲלֵיהּ, וְכֻלָּא מַכְרְזֵי קַמֵּיהּ וְאַמְרֵי, הָבוּ יְקָרָא לְדְיוּקְנָא דְּמַלְכָּא, אִתְנְטִיר הוּא בְּעָלְמָא דֵּין, וּבְעָלְמָא דְּאָתֵי, זַכָּאָה חוּלְקֵיהּ [וּכְשֶׁהוּא מִשְׁתַּדֵּל בַּעֲבוֹדַת אֲדוֹנוֹ, וְעוֹסֵק בַּתּוֹרָה, כַּמָּה שׁוֹמְרִים מוּכָנִים לְקָרָתוֹ לְשָׁמְרוֹ, וְהַשְּׁכִינָה שׁוֹרָה עָלָיו, וְכֻלָּם מַכְרִיזִים לְפָנָיו וְאוֹמְרִים תְּנוּ כָּבוֹד לְצוּרַת הַמֶּלֶךְ, שָׁמוּר הוּא בָּעוֹלָם הַזֶּה וּבָעוֹלָם הַבָּא, אַשְׁרֵי חֶלְקוֹ.]

פֶּרֶק י״ט

וְשֵׁם ה׳ נִקְרָא עָלָיו, כִּי הַתּוֹרָה כֻּלָּהּ שְׁמוֹתָיו שֶׁל הַקָּדוֹשׁ בָּרוּךְ הוּא, כְּמַאֲמָרָם זִכְרוֹנָם לִבְרָכָה: ״מִנַּיִן לְבִרְכַּת הַתּוֹרָה לְפָנֶיהָ מִן הַתּוֹרָה, שֶׁנֶּאֱמַר (דברים לב, ג) ״כִּי שֵׁם ה׳ אֶקְרָא״ וגו׳ (ברכות כא, א). וְכֵן לָמְדוּ (שם ו, א), שֶׁהָעוֹסֵק בַּתּוֹרָה שְׁכִינָה שְׁרוּיָה עִמּוֹ, דִּכְתִיב (שמות כ, כא) ״בְּכָל הַמָּקוֹם אֲשֶׁר אַזְכִּיר אֶת שְׁמִי אָבוֹא אֵלֶיךָ וּבֵרַכְתִּיךָ״ כו׳.

וּבַזֹּהַר בַּמִּדְבָּר קי״ח א׳, כַּמָּה חֲבִיבָא אוֹרַיְתָא קַמֵּיהּ קוּדְשָׁא בְּרִיךְ הוּא, דְּהָא בְּכָל אֲתַר דְּמִלֵּי דְּאוֹרַיְתָא אִשְׁתְּמָעוּ, קוּדְשָׁא בְּרִיךְ הוּא וְכָל חַיָּלִין דִּילֵיהּ כֻּלְּהוּ צַיְתִין לְמִלּוּלֵיהּ, וְקוּדְשָׁא בְּרִיךְ הוּא אָתֵי לְדַיְּרָא עִמֵּיהּ, הֲדָא הוּא דִכְתִיב ״בְּכָל הַמָּקוֹם אֲשֶׁר אַזְכִּיר אֶת שְׁמִי״ וגו׳ [כַּמָּה חֲבִיבָה הַתּוֹרָה לִפְנֵי הַקָּדוֹשׁ בָּרוּךְ הוּא, כִּי בְּכָל מָקוֹם שֶׁדִּבְרֵי תּוֹרָה נִשְׁמָעִים, הַקָּדוֹשׁ בָּרוּךְ הוּא וְכָל צְבָאוֹתָיו כֻּלָּם מַקְשִׁיבִים לִדְבָרָיו, וְהַקָּדוֹשׁ בָּרוּךְ הוּא בָּא לָדוּר עִמּוֹ, זֶה שֶׁכָּתוּב ״בְּכָל מָקוֹם אֲשֶׁר אַזְכִּיר אֶת שְׁמִי״ וגו׳.]

וּבְפָרָשַׁת מִשְׁפָּטִים קכ״ד א׳, דְּכָל מַאן דְּיִנְטַר אָרְחֵי דְּאוֹרַיְתָא וְאִשְׁתַּדֵּל בָּהּ, כְּמַאן דְּאִשְׁתַּדֵּל בִּשְׁמָא קַדִּישָׁא, דְּתַנְיָנָן, אוֹרַיְתָא כֻּלָּא שְׁמָא דְקוּדְשָׁא בְּרִיךְ הוּא, וּמַאן דְּמִשְׁתַּדֵּל בָּהּ כְּמַאן דְּמִשְׁתַּדֵּל בִּשְׁמָא קַדִּישָׁא, בְּגִין דְּאוֹרַיְתָא כֻּלָּא שְׁמָא חַד קַדִּישָׁא אִיהִי, שְׁמָא עִלָּאָה, שְׁמָא דִּכְלִיל כָּל שְׁמָהָן, וּמַאן דְּגָרַע אָת חַד מִנָּהּ, כְּאִלּוּ עָבִיד פְּגִימוּתָא בִּשְׁמָא קַדִּישָׁא. [כָּל מִי שֶׁשּׁוֹמֵר דַּרְכֵי הַתּוֹרָה וְעוֹסֵק בָּהּ, כְּמִי שֶׁעוֹסֵק בַּשֵּׁם הַקָּדוֹשׁ, שֶׁלָּמַדְנוּ שֶׁהַתּוֹרָה כֻּלָּהּ הִיא הַשֵּׁם שֶׁל הַקָּדוֹשׁ בָּרוּךְ הוּא, וּמִי שֶׁמִּתְעַסֵּק בָּהּ כְּאִלּוּ עוֹסֵק בַּשֵּׁם הַקָּדוֹשׁ, מִשּׁוּם שֶׁהַתּוֹרָה כֻּלָּהּ הִיא שֵׁם קָדוֹשׁ אֶחָד, שֵׁם עֶלְיוֹן, שֵׁם שֶׁכּוֹלֵל כָּל הַשֵּׁמוֹת, וּמִי שֶׁגּוֹרֵעַ אוֹת אַחַת מִמֶּנָּה כְּאִלּוּ עָשָׂה פְּגַם בַּשֵּׁם הַקָּדוֹשׁ.]

וּבְפָרָשַׁת וַיִּקְרָא י״ג ב׳, רַבִּי אַבָּא פָּתַח, ״כָּל זֹאת בָּאַתְנוּ וְלֹא שְׁכַחֲנוּךָ״ כו׳ (תהלים מד, יח), וְלָא אַנְשִׁינָן מִלּוּלֵי אוֹרַיְתָךְ, מִכָּאן אוֹלִיפְנָא, כָּל מַאן דְּאַנְשֵׁי מִלּוּלֵי אוֹרַיְתָא וְלָא בָּעֵי לְמִלְעֵי בָהּ, כְּאִלּוּ אַנְשֵׁי לְקוּדְשָׁא בְּרִיךְ הוּא, דְּהָא אוֹרַיְתָא כֻּלָּא שְׁמָא דְקוּדְשָׁא בְּרִיךְ הוּא הֲוֵי. [רַבִּי אַבָּא פָּתַח, ״כָּל זֹאת בָּאַתְנוּ וְלֹא שְׁכַחֲנוּךָ״ וגו׳, וְלֹא שָׁכַחְנוּ דִּבְרֵי תּוֹרָתֶךָ. מִכָּאן לָמַדְנוּ, כָּל מִי שֶׁשּׁוֹכֵחַ דִּבְרֵי תּוֹרָה וְאֵינוֹ רוֹצֶה לַעֲסֹק בָּהּ, כְּאִלּוּ שָׁכַח אֶת הַקָּדוֹשׁ בָּרוּךְ הוּא, כִּי הַתּוֹרָה כֻּלָּהּ הִיא שְׁמוֹ שֶׁל הַקָּדוֹשׁ בָּרוּךְ הוּא.]

וְשָׁם דַּף י״ט סוֹף ע״א, דְּהָא אוֹרַיְתָא, מַאן דְּיִשְׁתַּדֵּל בָּהּ מִתְעַטֵּר בְּעִטְרוֹי דִּשְׁמָא קַדִּישָׁא, דְּהָא אוֹרַיְתָא שְׁמָא קַדִּישָׁא הוּא, וּמַאן דְּיִשְׁתַּדֵּל בָּהּ, אִתְרְשִׁים וְאִתְעַטַּר בִּשְׁמָא קַדִּישָׁא, וּכְדֵין יָדַע אָרְחִין סְתִימִין וְרָזִין עֲמִיקִין כו׳. [כִּי הַתּוֹרָה, כָּל הָעוֹסֵק בָּהּ מִתְעַטֵּר

בְּעִטְרוֹת שְׁמוֹ הַקָּדוֹשׁ, כִּי הַתּוֹרָה הִיא שֵׁם הַקָּדוֹשׁ, וּמִי שֶׁעוֹסֵק בָּהּ נִרְשָׁם וּמִתְעַטֵּר בְּשֵׁם הַקָּדוֹשׁ, וְאָז יוֹדֵעַ דְּרָכִים הַסְּתוּמִים וְסוֹדוֹת הָעֲמֻקִּים.]

וְכֵן אִיתָא בְּרֵישׁ פָּרָשַׁת שְׁמִינִי, וּבְפָרָשַׁת אַחֲרֵי ע״א: וע״ב סוֹף ע״א, וע״ג א׳, וע״ה א׳, וּבְפָרָשַׁת אֱמוֹר פ״ט ב׳, וּבְרֵישׁ פָּרָשַׁת קֹרַח, עַיֵּין שָׁם.

וְלָכֵן, גַּם מִזֶּה הַטַּעַם אָמְרוּ, ד״קוּדְשָׁא בְּרִיךְ הוּא וְאוֹרַיְתָא חַד״, כִּי הוּא וּשְׁמֵיהּ חַד הוּא, וּכְמוֹ שֶׁאָמְרוּ בַּזֹּהַר יִתְרוֹ צ׳ ע״ב, וְאוֹרַיְתָא כֻּלָּא שְׁמָא חַד הֲוֵי, שְׁמָא קַדִּישָׁא דְּקוּדְשָׁא בְּרִיךְ הוּא מַמָּשׁ, זַכָּאָה חוּלָקֵיהּ דְּמַאן דְּזָכֵי בָּהּ, מַאן דְּזָכֵי בְּאוֹרַיְתָא זָכֵי בִּשְׁמָא קַדִּישָׁא דְּקוּדְשָׁא בְּרִיךְ הוּא מַמָּשׁ. רַבִּי יוֹסִי אוֹמֵר בְּקוּדְשָׁא בְּרִיךְ הוּא מַמָּשׁ זָכֵי, דְּהָא הוּא וּשְׁמֵיהּ חַד הוּא. [וְהַתּוֹרָה כֻּלָּהּ הִיא שֵׁם אֶחָד, שֵׁם הַקָּדוֹשׁ שֶׁל הַקָּדוֹשׁ בָּרוּךְ הוּא מַמָּשׁ, אַשְׁרֵי חֶלְקוֹ שֶׁל מִי שֶׁזָּכָה בָּהּ, שֶׁמִּי שֶׁזָּכָה בַּתּוֹרָה זָכָה בִּשְׁמוֹ הַקָּדוֹשׁ מַמָּשׁ. רַבִּי יוֹסִי אָמַר בְּהַקָּדוֹשׁ בָּרוּךְ הוּא מַמָּשׁ זָכָה, כִּי הוּא וּשְׁמוֹ אֶחָד הוּא.]

וְלָכֵן אָמַר בְּתַנָּא דְּבֵי אֵלִיָּהוּ, (רבה, פי״ח ד״ה ד״א לא תלך) שֶׁכָּל מִי שֶׁעוֹשֶׂה מְרִיבָה עַל תַּלְמִיד חָכָם, כְּאִלּוּ עוֹשֶׂה מְרִיבָה עַל מִי שֶׁאָמַר וְהָיָה עוֹלָם, שֶׁנֶּאֱמַר (במדבר כו, ט): ״הוּא דָתָן וַאֲבִירָם כו׳ בְּהַצֹּתָם עַל ה׳״.

לָכֵן, כַּאֲשֶׁר הָאָדָם בָּא בְּשֵׁם ה׳, הַכֹּל יְרֵאִים וּמִזְדַּעְזְעִים מִמֶּנּוּ, כְּמוֹ שֶׁכָּתוּב (דברים כח, י) ״וְרָאוּ כָּל עַמֵּי הָאָרֶץ כִּי שֵׁם ה׳ נִקְרָא עָלֶיךָ וְיָרְאוּ מִמֶּךָּ״, וּכְמוֹ שֶׁכָּתוּב (תהלים צא, יד) ״כִּי בִי חָשַׁק וַאֲפַלְּטֵהוּ אֲשַׂגְּבֵהוּ כִּי יָדַע שְׁמִי״. כִּי ״בִּי״ חָשַׁק, בּוֹ יִתְבָּרֵךְ מַמָּשׁ כִּבְיָכוֹל, כַּנַּ״ל.

וּבְפָרָשַׁת בָּלָק ר״ב א׳, תָּא חֲזֵי כַּמָּה חֲבִיבִין אִינּוּן דְּמִשְׁתַּדְּלֵי בְּאוֹרַיְתָא קָמֵי קוּדְשָׁא בְּרִיךְ הוּא, דַּאֲפִלּוּ בִּזְמְנָא דְּדִינָא תַּלְיָא בְּעָלְמָא, וְאִתְיְהִיב רְשׁוּ לִמְחַבְּלָא לְחַבָּלָא, קוּדְשָׁא בְּרִיךְ הוּא פָּקִיד לֵיהּ עָלַיְיהוּ עַל אִנּוּן דְּקָא מִשְׁתַּדְּלֵי בְּאוֹרַיְתָא, וְהָכִי אָמַר לֵיהּ קוּדְשָׁא בְּרִיךְ הוּא ״כִּי תָצוּר אֶל עִיר״ (דברים כ, יט) בְּגִין חוֹבֵיהוֹן סַגִּיאִין כו׳, תָּא וְאַפְקִיד לָךְ עַל בְּנֵי בֵיתִי, ״לֹא תַשְׁחִית אֶת עֵצָהּ״, דָּא תַּלְמִיד חָכָם דְּאִיהוּ בְּמָתָא, דְּאִיהוּ אִילָנָא דְּחַיֵּי, אִילָנָא דְּיָהִיב אִבִּין. ״אֶת עֵצָהּ״, הַהוּא דְּיָהִיב עֵיטָא לְמָתָא כו׳, וְאוֹלִיף לוֹן אוֹרְחָא דִּיהָכוּן בַּהּ, וְעַל דָּא ״לֹא תַשְׁחִית אֶת עֵצָהּ לִנְדֹּחַ עָלָיו גַּרְזֶן״, לְנַדְחָא עָלֵיהּ דִּינָא, וְלָא לְאוֹשְׁטָא עָלֵיהּ חַרְבָּא מְלַהֲטָא כו׳, ״כִּי הָאָדָם עֵץ הַשָּׂדֶה״, דָּא אִקְרֵי אָדָם, דְּאִשְׁתְּמוֹדַע עֵלָּא וְתַתָּא כו׳, וְכָל דָּא, פָּקִיד קוּדְשָׁא בְּרִיךְ הוּא עַל אִנּוּן דְּמִשְׁתַּדְּלֵי בְּאוֹרַיְתָא כו׳.

[בֹּא וּרְאֵה, כַּמָּה חֲבִיבִים הֵם אוֹתָם הָעוֹסְקִים בַּתּוֹרָה לִפְנֵי הַקָּדוֹשׁ בָּרוּךְ הוּא, שֶׁאֲפִלּוּ בִּזְמַן שֶׁהַדִּין תָּלוּי בָּעוֹלָם, וְנִתַּן רְשׁוּת לַמַּשְׁחִית לְהַשְׁחִית, הַקָּדוֹשׁ בָּרוּךְ הוּא מְצַוֶּה אוֹתוֹ עַל אֵלּוּ הָעוֹסְקִים בַּתּוֹרָה, וְכָךְ אָמַר לוֹ הַקָּדוֹשׁ בָּרוּךְ הוּא, ״כִּי תָצוּר עַל עִיר״ — בִּגְלַל עֲוֹנוֹתֵיהֶם הָרַבִּים וכו׳, בֹּא וַאֲצַוֶּה לְךָ עַל בְּנֵי בֵיתִי, ״לֹא תַשְׁחִית אֶת עֵצָהּ״ — זֶה תַּלְמִיד חָכָם שֶׁהוּא בָּעִיר, שֶׁהוּא ״עֵץ הַחַיִּים״ עֵץ הַנּוֹתֵן פֵּרוֹת. [דָּבָר אַחֵר[, ״אֶת עֵצָהּ״ — הַיְינוּ אוֹתוֹ שֶׁנּוֹתֵן עֵצָה לִבְנֵי הָעִיר וכו׳, וּמְלַמֵּד לָהֶם הַדֶּרֶךְ שֶׁיֵּלְכוּ בוֹ, וְעַל כֵּן ״לֹא תַשְׁחִית אֶת עֵצָהּ לִנְדֹּחַ עָלָיו גַּרְזֶן״, דְּהַיְינוּ לִנְדֹּחַ עָלָיו דִּין, וְלֹא לְהוֹשִׁיט עָלָיו חֶרֶב לוֹהֶטֶת וכו׳, ״כִּי

הָאָדָם עֵץ הַשָּׂדֶה", זֶה נִקְרָא אָדָם הַנּוֹדָע לְמַעְלָה וּלְמַטָּה וכו', וְכָל זֶה מְצַוֶּה הַקָּדוֹשׁ בָּרוּךְ הוּא בִּשְׁבִיל אֵלּוּ הַמִּשְׁתַּדְּלִים בַּתּוֹרָה]. עַיֵּן שָׁם בְּאֹרֶךְ:

פֶּרֶק כ'

וְהוּא הַבֵּן יַקִּיר, מִבְּנֵי פַּלְטְרִין דְּמַלְכָּא, מִבְּנֵי הֵיכָלָא דְּמַלְכָּא, אֲשֶׁר לוֹ לְבַדּוֹ הָרְשׁוּת נְתוּנָה, בְּכָל עֵת, לְחַפֵּשׂ בְּגִנְזֵי דְּמַלְכָּא קַדִּישָׁא, וְכָל הַשְּׁעָרִים עֶלְיוֹנִים פְּתוּחִים לְפָנָיו, כְּמַאֲמָרָם זִכְרוֹנָם לִבְרָכָה (סוטה מ"ט א'): "כָּל הָעוֹסֵק בַּתּוֹרָה מִתּוֹךְ דֹּחַק כו', רַבִּי אַחָא בַּר חֲנִינָא אוֹמֵר, אַף אֵין הַפַּרְגּוֹד נִנְעָל בְּפָנָיו, שֶׁנֶּאֱמַר (ישעיה ל, כ) "וְלֹא יִכָּנֵף עוֹד מוֹרֶיךָ".

וְנִכְנָס בְּשַׁעֲרֵי הַתּוֹרָה הַקְּדוֹשָׁה, לְהַשִּׂיג וּלְהִסְתַּכֵּל בְּאוֹר הַפְּנִימִי, בְּעִמְקֵי רָזִין עִלָּאִין דִּילָהּ, וּכְמוֹ שֶׁאָמְרוּ בְּפֶרֶק הַתּוֹרָה (אבות ו, א) "וּמְגַלִּין לוֹ רָזֵי תוֹרָה". וְכֵן אָמְרוּ (ע"ז ל"ה ב'): "וְלֹא עוֹד אֶלָּא שֶׁדְּבָרִים הַמְכֻסִּין מִבְּנֵי אָדָם מִתְגַּלִּין לוֹ".

וּבְמִדְרַשׁ תְּהִלִּים (מִזְמוֹר יט) אָמְרוּ עַל שְׁמוּאֵל, שֶׁאָמַר, מַכִּיר אֲנִי חוּצוֹת הָרָקִיעַ [כְּשֵׁם שֶׁאֲנִי מַכִּיר חוּצוֹת נְהַרְדְּעָא] כו', (וּבַשַּׁ"ס (ברכות נח, ב) הַגִּרְסָא נְהִירִין לִי שְׁבִילֵי דִרְקִיעָא כו'), וְכִי שְׁמוּאֵל עָלָה לָרָקִיעַ, אֶלָּא עַל יְדֵי שֶׁיָּגַע בְּחָכְמָתָהּ שֶׁל תּוֹרָה, לָמַד מִתּוֹכָהּ מַה שֶּׁיֵּשׁ בַּשְּׁחָקִים. וּבְמִשְׁלֵי רַבְּתָא (פָּרָשָׁה ח'), "וּמִפְתַּח שְׂפָתַי מֵישָׁרִים" (משלי ח, ו) דְּבָרִים שֶׁהֵם פּוֹתְחִין לָכֶם חַדְרֵי חֲדָרִים שֶׁבַּמָּרוֹם.

וּבְתַנָּא דְּבֵי אֵלִיָּהוּ (סֵדֶר אֵלִיָּה רַבָּא פֶּרֶק כז), בָּרוּךְ הַמָּקוֹם שֶׁבָּחַר בְּדִבְרֵי חֲכָמִים וּבְתַלְמִידֵיהֶם כו', כְּשֵׁם שֶׁהֵם יוֹשְׁבִים בְּבָתֵּי כְּנֵסִיּוֹת וּבְבָתֵּי מִדְרָשׁוֹת וּבְכָל מָקוֹם שֶׁפָּנוּי לָהֶם, וְקוֹרִין וְשׁוֹנִין לְשֵׁם שָׁמַיִם, וְיִרְאָה בְּלִבָּם, וּמַחֲזִיקִין דִּבְרֵי תוֹרָה עַל פִּיהֶם, כְּמוֹ כֵן הַקָּדוֹשׁ בָּרוּךְ הוּא יוֹשֵׁב כְּנֶגְדָּם, וּמְגַלֶּה לָהֶם סוֹדוֹת הַתּוֹרָה בְּפִיהֶם וּבְלִבָּבָם כו'.

וְרוּחַ קָדְשׁוֹ יִתְבָּרֵךְ יִשְׁכֹּן לָבֶטַח עָלָיו תָּמִיד, כְּמוֹ שֶׁכָּתוּב בַּזֹּהַר שְׁמוֹת ו' ב', חַכִּימֵי עֲדִיפֵי מִנְּבִיאֵי בְּכֹלָּא, דְּהָא לִנְבִיאֵי – לְזִמְנִין שָׁרַת עֲלֵיהוֹן רוּחַ קוּדְשָׁא, וּלְזִמְנִין לָא, וְחַכִּימִין – לָא אַעֲדֵי מִנְּהוֹן רוּחַ קוּדְשָׁא אֲפִילוּ רִגְעָא חֲדָא זְעֵיר, דְּיַדְעִין מַה דִּי לְעֵלָּא וְתַתָּא, וְלָא בָעוּ לְגַלָּאָה. [חֲכָמִים עֲדִיפִים מִנְּבִיאִים בַּכֹּל, כִּי נְבִיאִים – פְּעָמִים שׁוֹרָה עֲלֵיהֶם רוּחַ הַקּוֹדֶשׁ וּפְעָמִים לֹא, וַחֲכָמִים – לֹא הוּסַר מֵהֶם רוּחַ הַקּוֹדֶשׁ אַף רֶגַע אֶחָד קָטָן, וְהֵם יוֹדְעִים מַה לְּמַעְלָה וּמַה לְּמַטָּה, וְאֵינָם חֲפֵצִים לְגַלּוֹת.]

וּבְתַנָּא דְּבֵי אֵלִיָּהוּ (סֵדֶר אֵלִיָּהוּ זוּטָא פֶּרֶק א), וְכֵיוָן שֶׁקָּרָא אָדָם תּוֹרָה נְבִיאִים וּכְתוּבִים, וְשָׁנָה מִשְׁנָה מִדְרַשׁ הֲלָכוֹת וְהַגָּדוֹת, וְשָׁנָה הַגְּמָרָא, וְשָׁנָה הַפִּלְפּוּל לִשְׁמָהּ, מִיָּד רוּחַ הַקֹּדֶשׁ שׁוֹרָה עָלָיו, שֶׁנֶּאֱמַר (שמואל ב, כג, ב) "רוּחַ ה' דִּבֶּר בִּי" כו'.

וְדֶרֶךְ כְּלָל אָמְרוּ בְּפֶרֶק הַתּוֹרָה (אבות ו, ב), שֶׁכָּל הָעוֹסֵק בְּתַלְמוּד תּוֹרָה הֲרֵי זֶה מִתְעַלֶּה כו'. וְכֵן אִיתָא (בְּסוֹף פֶּרֶק הָרוֹאֶה ברכות סג, ב), "אִם נָבַלְתָּ בְהִתְנַשֵּׂא" (משלי ל, לב), כָּל הַמְנַבֵּל עַצְמוֹ עַל דִּבְרֵי תוֹרָה מִתְנַשֵּׂא. עַד שֶׁאָמְרוּ זִכְרוֹנָם לִבְרָכָה, שֶׁמַּדְרֵגָתָם

לְמַעְלָה מִמַּדְרֵגַת הַנְּבִיאִים, כְּמוֹ שֶׁכָּתוּב (בבא בתרא יב, א) חָכָם עָדִיף מִנָּבִיא. וּכְמוֹ שֶׁכָּתוּב בַּזֹּהַר שְׁמוֹת הַנַּ"ל.

וְיוֹתֵר מְבֹאָר הָעִנְיָן בְּפָרָשַׁת צַו ל"ה א', תָּא חֲזִי, מַה בֵּין אִינוּן דְּמִשְׁתַּדְּלֵי בְּאוֹרַיְתָא לִנְבִיאֵי מְהֵימְנֵי, דְּאִנּוּן דְּמִשְׁתַּדְּלֵי בְּאוֹרַיְתָא עֲדִיפֵי מִנְּבִיאֵי בְּכָל זִמְנָא, מַאי טַעֲמָא, דְּאִנּוּן קַיְמֵי בְּדַרְגָּא עִלָּאָה יַתִּיר מִנְּבִיאֵי, אִנּוּן דְּמִשְׁתַּדְּלֵי בְּאוֹרַיְתָא קַיְמֵי לְעֵלָּא – בְּאַתְרָא דְּאִקְרֵי "תּוֹרָה", דְּהוּא קִיּוּמָא דְּכָל מְהֵימְנוּתָא, וּנְבִיאֵי קַיְמֵי לְתַתָּא – בַּאֲתַר דְּאִקְרֵי "נֶצַח וָהוֹד", עַל דָּא אִנּוּן דְּמִשְׁתַּדְּלֵי בְּאוֹרַיְתָא עֲדִיפֵי מִנְּבִיאֵי, וְעִלָּאִין מִנְּהוֹן יַתִּיר, דְּאִלֵּין קַיְמִין לְעֵלָּא, וְאִלֵּין קַיְמִין לְתַתָּא כו', וְעַל דָּא זַכָּאִין אִנּוּן דְּמִשְׁתַּדְּלֵי בְּאוֹרַיְתָא, דְּאִנּוּן בְּדַרְגָּא עִלָּאָה יַתִּיר עַל כֹּולָּא.

[בֹּא וּרְאֵה, מַה בֵּין אֵלּוּ הָעוֹסְקִים בַּתּוֹרָה לַנְּבִיאִים הַנֶּאֱמָנִים, שֶׁאֵלּוּ הָעוֹסְקִים בַּתּוֹרָה חֲשׁוּבִים בְּכָל זְמַן מֵהַנְּבִיאִים, מַהוּ הַטַּעַם, מִשּׁוּם שֶׁהֵם עוֹמְדִים בְּדַרְגָּה עֶלְיוֹנָה יוֹתֵר מֵהַנְּבִיאִים, כִּי אֵלּוּ הָעוֹסְקִים בַּתּוֹרָה עוֹמְדִים לְמַעְלָה – בְּמָקוֹם הַנִּקְרָא "תּוֹרָה" שֶׁהוּא קִיּוּם כָּל הָאֱמוּנָה, וְהַנְּבִיאִים עוֹמְדִים לְמַטָּה – בְּמָקוֹם שֶׁנִּקְרָא "נֶצַח וְהוֹד", וְעַל כֵּן אֵלּוּ הָעוֹסְקִים בַּתּוֹרָה חֲשׁוּבִים מִנְּבִיאִים וְעֶלְיוֹנִים מֵהֶם יוֹתֵר, שֶׁאֵלּוּ עוֹמְדִים לְמַעְלָה וְאֵלּוּ עוֹמְדִים לְמַטָּה וכו'. וְעַל כֵּן אַשְׁרֵי אֵלּוּ שֶׁעוֹסְקִים בַּתּוֹרָה, שֶׁהֵם בְּדַרְגָּה עֶלְיוֹנָה יְתֵרָה עַל כֻּלָּם]. כו':

פֶּרֶק כ"א

וְאִם כָּל כָּךְ נִפְלָאָה מַדְרֵגָתָם שֶׁל עוֹמְלֵי תּוֹרָה, גַּם בְּעוֹדָם בָּזֶה הָעוֹלָם הֶחָשׁוּךְ, לְהַשִּׂיג וּלְהִסְתַּכֵּל בְּרוּחַ קָדְשָׁם בְּאוֹר הָעֶלְיוֹן, גְּדוֹלִים צַדִּיקִים בְּמִיתָתָן יוֹתֵר מִבְּחַיֵּיהֶם (חולין ז, ב) לְאֵין עֲרֹךְ, אַחַר אֲשֶׁר נִשְׁמָתוֹ הַטְּהוֹרָה רַבַּת שָׂבְעָה לָהּ תּוֹרָה וּמִצְוֹת, וְהִיא שָׁבָה אֶל בֵּית אָבִיהָ מְקֻדֶּשֶׁת וּמְטֹהָרָה כַּאֲשֶׁר נִתְּנָה, וּבְיִתְרוֹן אוֹר הַתּוֹרָה הַקְּדוֹשָׁה תַּלְמוּדוֹ בְּיָדוֹ, כָּל הַשְּׁעָרִים נִפְתָּחִים לְפָנָיו, וְסָלִיק וּבָקַע רְקִיעִין כו', וְצָרוּר בִּצְרוֹר הַחַיִּים אֶת ה' אֱלֹהָיו יִתְבָּרַךְ שְׁמוֹ.

וּבְתַנָּא דְּבֵי אֵלִיָּהוּ (סֵדֶר אֵלִיָּהוּ רַבָּא פֶּרֶק ד) אָמַר: וְשֶׁמָּא תֹּאמַר הוֹאִיל וְנִכְנַס מֹשֶׁה לְבֵית עוֹלָמוֹ, שֶׁמָּא בָּטֵל מִמֶּנּוּ אוֹתוֹ הַכֶּתֶר שֶׁל מְאוֹר פָּנִים, תַּלְמוּד לוֹמַר (דברים לד, י) "וְלֹא קָם נָבִיא עוֹד בְּיִשְׂרָאֵל כְּמֹשֶׁה אֲשֶׁר יְדָעוֹ ה', פָּנִים אֶל פָּנִים", מַה אוֹר פָּנִים שֶׁלְּמַעְלָה קַיָּם לְעוֹלָם וּלְעוֹלְמֵי עוֹלָמִים, כָּךְ מְאוֹר פָּנָיו שֶׁל מֹשֶׁה נִכְנַס עִמּוֹ לְבֵית עוֹלָמוֹ כו'. וְלֹא מֹשֶׁה בִּלְבַד, אֶלָּא כָּל תַּלְמִיד חָכָם שֶׁעוֹסֵק בַּתּוֹרָה מִקַּטְנוּתוֹ וְעַד זִקְנוּתוֹ, וּמֵת, בֶּאֱמֶת לֹא מֵת, אֶלָּא הוּא עֲדַיִן בַּחַיִּים לְעוֹלָם וּלְעוֹלְמֵי עוֹלָמִים, שֶׁנֶּאֱמַר (שמו"א כה, כט) "וְהָיְתָה נֶפֶשׁ אֲדֹנִי צְרוּרָה בִּצְרוֹר הַחַיִּים אֵת ה' אֱלֹהֶיךָ", מַקִּישׁ הַתַּלְמִיד חָכָם הַצַּדִּיק אֶל אֱלֹקִים, מָה אֱלֹקִים – יְהֵא שְׁמוֹ הַגָּדוֹל מְבֹרָךְ – חַי וְקַיָּם כו', כָּךְ תַּלְמִיד חָכָם שֶׁעָסַק בַּתּוֹרָה כָּל יָמָיו, וּמֵת, הֲרֵי הוּא בַּחַיִּים, וַעֲדַיִן לֹא מֵת, וְהוּא חַי לְעוֹלָם כו', וְהֵיכָן הוּא נִשְׁמָתוֹ, תַּחַת כִּסֵּא הַכָּבוֹד, עַד כָּאן.

וְנַפְשׁוֹ תִּשְׂבַּע בְּצַחְצָחוֹת הָאוֹר עֶלְיוֹן הַגָּנוּז, כְּמַאֲמָרָם זִכְרוֹנָם לִבְרָכָה: "כָּל תַּלְמִיד חָכָם הָעוֹסֵק בַּתּוֹרָה מִתּוֹךְ הַדְּחַק כו', רַבִּי אֲבָהוּ אוֹמֵר, אַף מַשְׂבִּיעִין אוֹתוֹ מִזִּיו שְׁכִינָה, שֶׁנֶּאֱמַר (ישעיה ל, כ) "וְהָיוּ עֵינֶיךָ רוֹאוֹת אֶת מוֹרֶיךָ" (סוֹטָה מט, א).

וּבְפֶרֶק קַמָּא דְּבַתְרָא (י, א): מַאי "אֶשְׂבְּעָה בְהָקִיץ תְּמוּנָתֶךָ" (תהלים יז, טו), אֵלּוּ תַּלְמִידֵי חֲכָמִים שֶׁמְּנַדְּדִין שֵׁנָה מֵעֵינֵיהֶם בָּעוֹלָם הַזֶּה, הַקָּדוֹשׁ בָּרוּךְ הוּא מַשְׂבִּיעָן מִזִּיו הַשְּׁכִינָה לָעוֹלָם הַבָּא. וּבְפֶרֶק חֵלֶק (ק, א): דָּרֵישׁ רַבִּי יְהוּדָה בְּרַבִּי סִימוֹן, כָּל הַמַּשְׁחִיר פָּנָיו עַל דִּבְרֵי תוֹרָה בָּעוֹלָם הַזֶּה, הַקָּדוֹשׁ בָּרוּךְ הוּא מַבְהִיק זִיווֹ לָעוֹלָם הַבָּא.

וְהַכֹּל לְפִי עֵרֶךְ רֹב עִסְקוֹ וְנִפְלְאוֹת דְּבֵקוּתוֹ בַּתּוֹרָה הַקְּדוֹשָׁה, כְּמוֹ שֶׁכָּתוּב בְּתַנָּא דְּבֵי אֵלִיָּהוּ (סֵדֶר אֵלִיָּהוּ זוּטָא פֶּרֶק יב): אֵצֶל הַצַּדִּיקִים מַה נֶּאֱמַר בָּהֶם "וְאֹהֲבָיו כְּצֵאת הַשֶּׁמֶשׁ בִּגְבֻרָתוֹ" (שופטים ה, לא), מַה שֶּׁאֵין כֵּן בְּמַלְאֲכֵי הַשָּׁרֵת, מַה יָּפֶה כֹּחוֹ שֶׁל בַּעַל הַבַּיִת, שֶׁהוּא מְיַפֶּה כֶּתֶר עֲבָדָיו כְּמוֹ כִּתְרוֹ. וְאִם תֹּאמַר, מִי שֶׁקָּרָא הַרְבֵּה וְשָׁנָה הַרְבֵּה, וּמִי שֶׁקָּרָא וְשָׁנָה קִמְעָא, יִהְיֶה מְאוֹר פְּנֵיהֶם שָׁוִין כְּאֶחָד בִּמְאוֹר פָּנִים לָעוֹלָם הַבָּא, אֵינוֹ כֵּן, בָּרוּךְ הַמָּקוֹם בָּרוּךְ הוּא, שֶׁאֵין לְפָנָיו מַשּׂוֹא פָנִים כו', נֶאֱמַר בְּמָקוֹם אַחֵר (משלי יב, כו), יָתֵר מֵרֵעֵהוּ צַדִּיק" כו', אֶלָּא כָּל אֶחָד וְאֶחָד לְפִי דְּרָכָיו כו'.

וְהוּא הוּא סוֹד הָאוֹר שֶׁנִּבְרָא בְּיוֹם רִאשׁוֹן, שֶׁגְּנָזוֹ הַקָּדוֹשׁ בָּרוּךְ הוּא לַצַּדִּיקִים (חגיגה יב, א).

וְכֵן אִיתָא בַּזֹּהַר בְּרֵאשִׁית מ"ז א', רַבִּי אֶלְעָזָר פָּתַח, "מָה רַב טוּבְךָ אֲשֶׁר צָפַנְתָּ" כו' (תהלים לא, כ). תָּא חֲזֵי, קוּדְשָׁא בְּרִיךְ הוּא בָּרָא לְבַר נָשׁ בְּעָלְמָא, וְאַתְקִין לֵיהּ לְמֶהֱוֵי שְׁלִים בְּפוּלְחָנָא, וּלְאַתְקְנָא אָרְחוֹי, בְּגִין דְּיִזְכֵּי לִנְהוֹרָא עִלָּאָה דִּגְנִיז קוּדְשָׁא בְּרִיךְ הוּא לְצַדִּיקַיָּא, כד"א (ישעיה סד, ג) "עַיִן לֹא רָאָתָה כו' יַעֲשֶׂה לִמְחַכֵּה לוֹ". וּבְמָה זָכֵה בַּר נָשׁ לְהַהוּא נְהוֹרָא, בְּאוֹרַיְתָא [רַבִּי אֶלְעָזָר פָּתַח, "מָה רַב טוּבְךָ אֲשֶׁר צָפַנְתָּ" וכו', בֹּא וּרְאֵה, הַקָּדוֹשׁ בָּרוּךְ הוּא בָּרָא אֶת הָאָדָם בָּעוֹלָם, וְתִקֵּן אוֹתוֹ שֶׁיִּהְיֶה שָׁלֵם בַּעֲבוֹדָתוֹ, וְשֶׁיְּתַקֵּן דְּרָכָיו, כְּדֵי שֶׁיִּזְכֶּה לָאוֹר הָעֶלְיוֹן שֶׁגָּנַז הַקָּדוֹשׁ בָּרוּךְ הוּא לַצַּדִּיקִים, כְּמוֹ שֶׁכָּתוּב "עַיִן לֹא רָאָתָה וגו' יַעֲשֶׂה לִמְחַכֵּה לוֹ", וּבַמֶּה יִזְכֶּה הָאָדָם לְאוֹתוֹ אוֹר? בַּתּוֹרָה]. כו'.

וְאָמְרוּ רַבּוֹתֵינוּ זִכְרוֹנָם לִבְרָכָה (חגיגה יד, א) "אֲשֶׁר קֻמְּטוּ וְלֹא עֵת נָהָר יוּצַק יְסוֹדָם" (איוב כב, טז), אֵלּוּ תַּלְמִידֵי חֲכָמִים, שֶׁמְּקַמְּטִין שֵׁנָה מֵעֵינֵיהֶם בָּעוֹלָם הַזֶּה, הַקָּדוֹשׁ בָּרוּךְ הוּא מְגַלֶּה לָהֶם סוֹד לָעוֹלָם הַבָּא, שֶׁנֶּאֱמַר "נָהָר יוּצַק יְסוֹדָם". וְהֵם הַטַּעֲמֵי תוֹרָה הַגְּנוּזִים, שֶׁהֵם הָאוֹר הָעֶלְיוֹן הַגָּנוּז.

וְלָכֵן אָמַר בְּפֶרֶק הַתּוֹרָה (אבות ו, א) "כָּל הָעוֹסֵק בַּתּוֹרָה לִשְׁמָהּ, זוֹכֶה לִדְבָרִים הַרְבֵּה", סָתַם וְלֹא פֵּרֵשׁ מַה הֵם אוֹתָן הַדְּבָרִים. וְאִי אֶפְשָׁר לוֹמַר שֶׁהֵם הַדְּבָרִים שֶׁפֵּרֵט שָׁם אַחַר זֶה, שֶׁהֲרֵי אָמַר אַחַר זֶה "וְלֹא עוֹד" כו', מַשְׁמַע שֶׁהוּא מִלְּתָא בְּאַפֵּי נַפְשָׁא.

אָמְנָם רֶמֶז לְהָעִדּוּן וְצִחְצוּחַ הַנֶּפֶשׁ בָּאוֹר הַגָּנוּז, אֲשֶׁר גַּם כָּל מַלְאֲכֵי מַעְלָה וְחַיּוֹת וְשַׂרְפֵי קֹדֶשׁ וְשׁוּם נָבִיא וְחוֹזֶה — לֹא הִשִּׂיגוּהוּ כְּלָל עֶצֶם עִנְיָנוֹ.

וּכְמַאֲמָרָם ז"ל (ברכות לד, ב) "כָּל הַנְּבִיאִים כֻּלָּן לֹא נִתְנַבְּאוּ אֶלָּא כו', אֲבָל תַּלְמִידֵי

חֲכָמִים עַצְמָן "עַיִן לֹא רָאָתָה" כו', וְהוּא הָ"עֵדֶן" וְהַ"יַּיִן הַמְּשֻׁמָּר בַּעֲנָבָיו", שֶׁאָמְרוּ שָׁם מַאי "עַיִן לֹא רָאָתָה" וכו', וְהַכֹּל אֶחָד, סוֹד הַטַּעֲמֵי תּוֹרָה הַגְּנוּזִים שֶׁלֹּא נִתְגַּלּוּ עֲדַיִן, לָכֵן אָמַר סְתָם "לִדְבָרִים הַרְבֵּה", שֶׁאֵינוֹ דָּבָר הַמֻּשָּׂג לְאָמְרוֹ וּלְבָאֲרוֹ.

וּבְתַנָּא דְּבֵי אֵלִיָּהוּ (סֵדֶר אֵלִיָּהוּ רַבָּה פֶּרֶק כז) אָמַר, אַשְׁרֵי אָדָם שֶׁיֵּשׁ בּוֹ דִּבְרֵי תּוֹרָה, וְהוּא יוֹשֵׁב וְקוֹרֵא וְשׁוֹנֶה בְּמָקוֹם צָנוּעַ וְסֵתֶר, אֵצֶל מִי מְלִינִין אוֹתוֹ, הֱוֵי אוֹמֵר אֵצֶל הַקָּדוֹשׁ בָּרוּךְ הוּא, שֶׁנֶּאֱמַר (תהלים צא, א) "יוֹשֵׁב בְּסֵתֶר עֶלְיוֹן בְּצֵל שַׁדַּי יִתְלוֹנָן", כְּשֵׁם שֶׁהֵם מְשִׂימִין עַצְמָן יְחִידִים בָּעוֹלָם הַזֶּה וְאֵין עִמָּהֶם זָר, כְּמוֹ כֵן הֵם בָּעוֹלָם הַבָּא, הֵם יוֹשְׁבִין אֵצֶל הַקָּדוֹשׁ בָּרוּךְ הוּא לְבַדּוֹ כו':

פֶּרֶק כ"ב

וְאִם חַס וְשָׁלוֹם אֲנַחְנוּ עוֹסְקִים בָּהּ בְּרִפְיוֹן, כִּבְיָכוֹל מִתְמַעֵט שֶׁפַע הָאוֹר עֶלְיוֹן בְּכָל הָעוֹלָמוֹת, כָּל אֶחָד לְפִי עֶרְכּוֹ. וּבְמִסְתָּרִים תִּבְכֶּה נַפְשׁוֹ יִתְבָּרֵךְ כִּבְיָכוֹל, כְּמוֹ שֶׁאָמְרוּ רַבּוֹתֵינוּ זִכְרוֹנָם לִבְרָכָה (חגיגה ה' ב') שְׁלֹשָׁה הַקָּדוֹשׁ בָּרוּךְ הוּא בּוֹכֶה עֲלֵיהֶם, וְחָשִׁיב חַד מִנְּהוֹן עַל מִי שֶׁאֶפְשָׁר לוֹ לַעֲסֹק בַּתּוֹרָה וְאֵינוֹ עוֹסֵק. וְכֵן אָמְרוּ שָׁם שְׁלֹשָׁה דְּמָעוֹת הַלָּלוּ לָמָּה כו', וְאִיכָּא דְּאָמְרֵי אַחַת עַל בִּטּוּל תּוֹרָה. וְאוֹי לוֹ לַבֵּן הַמּוֹרִיד דִּמְעוֹת אָבִיו בְּכָל יוֹם. וְעִנְיַן זֹאת הַבְּכִיָּה, הוּא הִתְגַּבְּרוּת הַדִּין, בְּהִתְמַעֲטוּת הָאוֹר עֶלְיוֹן – שֶׁהֵם הָרַחֲמִים הַגְּדוֹלִים בָּעוֹלָמוֹת הַנִּסְתָּרִים.

וְהָאָדָם אֲשֶׁר עֲדַיִן לֹא רָאָה אוֹר הַתּוֹרָה מִיָּמָיו, וְלֹא עָסַק בָּהּ מֵעוֹלָם, אֵינוֹ זוֹכֶה כְּלָל שֶׁתִּשְׁרֶה עָלָיו קְדֻשָּׁה הָעֶלְיוֹנָה, וְאֵינוֹ זוֹכֶה לְנֶפֶשׁ טְהוֹרָה. כְּמוֹ שֶׁכָּתוּב בְּהַקְדָּמַת הַזֹּהַר י"ב ב', פִּקּוּדָא חֲמִישָׁאָה כו' בְּהַאי קְרָא אִית בֵּיהּ תְּלַת פִּקּוּדִין, חַד לְמִלְעֵי בְּאוֹרַיְתָא כו', דְּכַד בַּר נָשׁ לָא אִתְעַסַּק בְּאוֹרַיְתָא, לֵית לֵיהּ נַפְשָׁא קַדִּישָׁא, קְדוּשָּׁה דִּלְעֵלָּא לָא שַׁרְיָא עֲלוֹי [הַמִּצְוָה הַחֲמִישִׁית כו' בַּמִּקְרָא הַזֶּה יֵשׁ שְׁלֹשָׁה מִצְוֹת, א' לַעֲסֹק בַּתּוֹרָה וכו', כִּי כְּשֶׁהָאָדָם אֵינוֹ עוֹסֵק בַּתּוֹרָה אֵין לוֹ נֶפֶשׁ קְדוֹשָׁה, הַקְּדֻשָּׁה הָעֶלְיוֹנָה לֹא שׁוֹרָה עָלָיו]. כו'.

וְגַם הוּא מְשֻׁלָּח וְנֶעֱזָב חַס וְשָׁלוֹם לְכֹחוֹת הַדִּין שֶׁל הַסִּטְרָא אַחְרָא שֶׁיִּהְיוּ יְכוֹלִין לִשְׁלֹט עָלָיו, כְּמוֹ שֶׁאָמְרוּ רַבּוֹתֵינוּ זִכְרוֹנָם לִבְרָכָה בְּפֶרֶק קַמָּא דִּבְרָכוֹת (ה, א) שֶׁכָּל מִי שֶׁאֶפְשָׁר לוֹ לַעֲסֹק בַּתּוֹרָה וְאֵינוֹ עוֹסֵק, הַקָּדוֹשׁ בָּרוּךְ הוּא מֵבִיא עָלָיו יִסּוּרִין מְכֹעָרִין וְעוֹכְרִין אוֹתוֹ, שֶׁנֶּאֱמַר (תהלים לט, ג) "הֶחֱשֵׁיתִי מִטּוֹב וּכְאֵבִי נֶעְכָּר".

וּמְאַבֵּד טוֹבָה הַרְבֵּה, מִמֶּנּוּ וּמִכָּל הָעוֹלָם, כִּי הִכְרִיעַ חַס וְשָׁלוֹם אֶת עַצְמוֹ וְאֶת כָּל הָעוֹלָם לְכַף חוֹב, כְּמַאֲמָרָם זִכְרוֹנָם לִבְרָכָה בִּדְבָרִים רַבָּה רֵישׁ פָּרָשָׁה ד' "שִׁמְעוּ וְאַל תִּגְבָּהוּ" (ירמיה יג, טו) שִׁמְעוּ לְדִבְרֵי תּוֹרָה כו', "וְאַל תִּגְבָּהוּ", אַל תַּגְבִּיהוּ אֶת הַטּוֹבָה מִלָּבֹא לָעוֹלָם. וְכֵן אָמְרוּ בְּפֶרֶק קַמָּא דְּבָתְרָא (ח' ע"א) שֶׁאֵין פּוּרְעָנוּת בָּאָה לָעוֹלָם אֶלָּא בִּשְׁבִיל עַמֵּי הָאָרֶץ.

וְאִם חַס וְשָׁלוֹם יָבֹא פּוּרְעָנוּת עַל אֵיזֶה אָדָם אוֹ מְדִינָה, אֲפִלּוּ בִּקְצֵה הָעוֹלָם, דַּיְן גְּרָמָא דִּילֵיהּ חַס וְשָׁלוֹם. הָרַחֲמָן יִתְבָּרֵךְ שְׁמוֹ יַצִּילֵנוּ:

וְאִם כְּבָר עָסַק בָּהּ וּפֵרֵשׁ הֵימֶנָּה חַס וְשָׁלוֹם, הוּא מַתִּישׁ חַס וְשָׁלוֹם כֹּחַ פָּמַלְיָא שֶׁל מַעְלָה, וּמְתַקַלְקְלִים וּמִתְבַּלְבְּלִים סִדְרֵי הָעוֹלָמוֹת וְהַמֶּרְכָּבָה הַקְּדוֹשָׁה, וְגָבְרָה יַד הַסִּטְרָא אַחֲרָא רַחֲמָנָא לִיצְּלָן, וְכִבְיָכוֹל מַחְלִישׁ וּמַחְשִׁיךְ כֹּחַ הַקְּדֻשָּׁה הָעֶלְיוֹנָה שְׁכִינַת עֻזֵּנוּ אֱמוּנַת יִשְׂרָאֵל, הַשּׁוֹכֶנֶת בְּתוֹכֵנוּ תָּמִיד עַל יְדֵי עֵסֶק הַתּוֹרָה כָּרָאוּי.

כְּמוֹ שֶׁכָּתוּב בַּזֹּהַר תְּרוּמָה קנ"ה ב', פָּתַח רַבִּי חִיָּא וְאָמַר "עֵת לַעֲשׂוֹת לה' הֵפֵרוּ תּוֹרָתֶךָ" (תהלים קיט), בְּכָל זִמְנָא דְאוֹרַיְתָא מִתְקַיְּמָא בְּעָלְמָא, וּבְנֵי נָשָׁא מִשְׁתַּדְּלִין בָּהּ, כִּבְיָכוֹל קוּדְשָׁא בְּרִיךְ הוּא חָדֵי בְּעוֹבָדֵי יְדוֹי, וְחָדֵי בְּעָלְמִין כֻּלְּהוּ, וּשְׁמַיָּא וְאַרְעָא קַיְמֵי בְּקִיוּמַיְהוּ כו', וּבְשַׁעֲתָא דְיִשְׂרָאֵל מִתְבַּטְּלִין מֵאוֹרַיְתָא, כִּבְיָכוֹל תָּשַׁשׁ חֵילֵיהּ, וּכְדֵין "עֵת לַעֲשׂוֹת לה'", אִנּוּן בְּנֵי עָלְמָא צַדִּיקַיָּא דְאִשְׁתָּאֲרוּן, אִית לוֹן לְחַגְרָא חַרְצִין וּלְמֶעְבַּד עוֹבָדִין דְּכַשְׁרָאן, בְּגִין דְּקוּדְשָׁא בְּרִיךְ הוּא יִתְתְּקַף בְּהוּ בְּצַדִּיקַיָּא כו', מַאי טַעְמָא, בְּגִין דְ"הֵפֵרוּ תּוֹרָתֶךָ", וְלָא מִשְׁתַּדְּלֵי בַּהּ בְּנֵי עָלְמָא כִּדְקָא יָאוּת כו', וְהָכִי בְּזִמְנָא דְיִשְׂרָאֵל מִשְׁתַּדְּלָן בְּאוֹרַיְתָא, הַהוּא עֵת, רָזָא מְהֵימְנוּתָא קַדִּישָׁא מִתְתַּקְּנָא בְּתִקּוּנָהָא, וּמִתְקַשְּׁטָא בִּשְׁלֵימוּתָא כִּדְקָא יָאוּת, וּבְזִמְנָא דְיִשְׂרָאֵל מִתְבַּטְּלֵי מֵאוֹרַיְתָא, הַהוּא עֵת לָאו אִיהִי בְּתִקּוּנָהָא, וְלָא אִשְׁתַּכְּחָא בִּשְׁלִימוּ וְלָא בִנְהוֹרָא, הָא דִכְתִיב "עֵת לַעֲשׂוֹת לה'" מַאי "לַעֲשׂוֹת" כו', אוּף הָכִי "עֵת לַעֲשׂוֹת", אִשְׁתָּאַר בְּלָא תִּקּוּנָא וּבְלָא שְׁלִימוּ, מַאי טַעְמָא, מִשּׁוּם דְ"הֵפֵרוּ תּוֹרָתֶךָ", בְּגִין דְּאִתְבַּטְּלוּ יִשְׂרָאֵל לְתַתָּא מִפִּתְגָּמֵי אוֹרַיְתָא, בְּגִין דְּהַהוּא עֵת הָכִי קַיְמָא, אוֹ סַלְקָא אוֹ נַחֲתָא בְּגִינְהוֹן דְּיִשְׂרָאֵל.

[פָּתַח רַבִּי חִיָּא וְאָמַר, "עֵת לַעֲשׂוֹת לה' הֵפֵרוּ תּוֹרָתֶךָ", בְּכָל זְמַן שֶׁהַתּוֹרָה מִתְקַיֶּמֶת בָּעוֹלָם וּבְנֵי אָדָם עוֹסְקִים בָּהּ, כִּבְיָכוֹל הַקָּדוֹשׁ בָּרוּךְ הוּא שָׂמֵחַ בְּמַעֲשֵׂי יָדָיו, וְשָׂמֵחַ בָּעוֹלָמוֹת כֻּלָּם, וְשָׁמַיִם וָאָרֶץ עוֹמְדִים בְּקִיּוּמָם וכו'. וּבְשָׁעָה שֶׁיִּשְׂרָאֵל מִתְבַּטְּלִים מֵהַתּוֹרָה, כִּבְיָכוֹל תָּשׁ כֹּחוֹ, וְאָז "עֵת לַעֲשׂוֹת לה'", שֶׁאֵלּוּ בְּנֵי הָעוֹלָם צַדִּיקִים שֶׁנִּשְׁאֲרוּ יֵשׁ לָהֶם לֶאֱזֹר מָתְנַיִם וְלַעֲשׂוֹת מַעֲשִׂים טוֹבִים כְּדֵי שֶׁהַקָּדוֹשׁ בָּרוּךְ הוּא יִתְחַזֵּק בָּהֶם בַּצַּדִּיקִים וכו'. מַהוּ הַטַּעַם, מִשּׁוּם "שֶׁהֵפֵרוּ תּוֹרָתֶךָ", וְלֹא עוֹסְקִים בָּהּ בְּנֵי הָעוֹלָם כָּרָאוּי וכו'. וְכֵן בִּזְמַן שֶׁיִּשְׂרָאֵל עוֹסְקִים בַּתּוֹרָה, בָּעֵת הַהוּא הָאֱמוּנָה מְתֻקֶּנֶת בְּתִקּוּנֶיהָ וּמִתְקַשֶּׁטֶת בִּשְׁלֵמוּת כָּרָאוּי, וּבִזְמַן שֶׁיִּשְׂרָאֵל מִתְבַּטְּלִים מֵהַתּוֹרָה, בָּעֵת הַהוּא אֵינָהּ בְּתִקּוּנֶיהָ וְאֵינָהּ נִמְצֵאת בִּשְׁלֵמוּת וְלֹא בְּאוֹר. זֶה שֶׁכָּתוּב "עֵת לַעֲשׂוֹת לה'", מַהוּ לַעֲשׂוֹת וכו', אַף כָּאן "עֵת לַעֲשׂוֹת", נִשְׁאֲרָה בְּלֹא תִּקּוּן וּבְלֹא שְׁלֵמוּת, מַה טַּעַם, מִשּׁוּם "דְּהֵפֵרוּ תּוֹרָתֶךָ", מִשּׁוּם שֶׁנִּתְבַּטְּלוּ יִשְׂרָאֵל לְמַטָּה מִדִּבְרֵי תּוֹרָה, כִּי עֵת הַהוּא נִמְצֵאת כָּךְ אוֹ שֶׁמִּתְעַלֵּית אוֹ שֶׁיּוֹרֶדֶת בִּשְׁבִיל יִשְׂרָאֵל.]

וְכִבְיָכוֹל הוּא מִתְרַחֵק מִמֶּנּוּ יִתְבָּרַךְ. כְּמוֹ שֶׁכָּתוּב בַּזֹּהַר וַיִּקְרָא כ"א א', כַּד בַּר נָשׁ אִתְרַחִיק מֵאוֹרַיְתָא, רָחִיק הוּא מִקּוּדְשָׁא בְּרִיךְ הוּא, [כְּשֶׁאָדָם מִתְרַחֵק מִן הַתּוֹרָה רָחוֹק הוּא מֵהַקָּדוֹשׁ בָּרוּךְ הוּא] כִּי קוּדְשָׁא בְּרִיךְ הוּא וְאוֹרַיְתָא חַד, כַּנַּ"ל.

וְהַשְּׁמִירָה הָעֶלְיוֹנָה שֶׁל הַקְּדֻשָּׁה סַר מֵעָלָיו, וְאִשְׁתְּמוֹדַע וְנִכָּר לְכֹחוֹת הַדִּין אֲשֶׁר הִגְבִּיר בְּעַצְמוֹ, שֶׁיּוּכְלוּ לִשְׁלֹט עָלָיו, בֵּין בְּחַיָּיו, כְּמוֹ שֶׁאָמְרוּ רַבּוֹתֵינוּ זִכְרוֹנָם לִבְרָכָה בְּפֶרֶק

קַמָּא דִּבְרָכוֹת (ה, א) הַמּוּבָא לְעֵיל, וְכֵן אִיתָא שָׁם (סג, א), וּבְמִשְׁלֵי רַבְּתָא רֵישׁ פָּרָשָׁה כ"ה, אָמַר רַבִּי טוֹבִי בּ"ר אֲשִׁיָּה, כָּל הַמְּרַפֶּה עַצְמוֹ מִדִּבְרֵי תּוֹרָה אֵינוֹ יָכוֹל לַעֲמֹד בְּיוֹם צָרָה, שֶׁנֶּאֱמַר "הִתְרַפִּיתָ בְּיוֹם צָרָה צַר כֹּחֶכָה" (משלי כד, י).

וּבְפֶרֶק שְׁתֵּי הַלֶּחֶם (מנחות צט, ב) כָּל הַמְּשַׁמֵּר אֶת הַתּוֹרָה נִשְׁמָתוֹ מִשְׁתַּמֶּרֶת, וְכָל שֶׁאֵינוֹ מְשַׁמֵּר אֶת הַתּוֹרָה כוּ'. וְאָמְרוּ בְּמִדְרַשׁ תְּהִלִּים מִזְמוֹר י"ז: "אָמַר הַקָּדוֹשׁ בָּרוּךְ הוּא לְיִשְׂרָאֵל, אִם שָׁמַרְתָּ אֶת הַתּוֹרָה אֲנִי אֶשְׁמֹר אוֹתְךָ, שֶׁנֶּאֱמַר (דברים יא, כב) "אִם שָׁמוֹר תִּשְׁמְרוּן" כוּ'.

וְכַיָּדוּעַ גַּם כֵּן מַאֲמָרָם זִכְרוֹנָם לִבְרָכָה בִּבְרֵאשִׁית רַבָּה פָּרָשָׁה ס"ה, בִּזְמַן שֶׁהַקּוֹל קוֹל יַעֲקֹב בְּבָתֵּי כְנֵסִיּוֹת וּבְבָתֵּי מִדְרָשׁוֹת אֵין יְדֵי עֵשָׂו שׁוֹלְטוֹת, הַקֹּל קוֹל יַעֲקֹב, אָז יָדָיו שׁוֹלְטוֹת רַחֲמָנָא לִיצְּלַן.

וְאָמְרוּ בְּוַיִּקְרָא רַבָּה פָּרָשָׁה ל"ה, וּדְבָרִים רַבָּה רֵישׁ פָּרָשָׁה ד', הַסַּיִף וְהַסֵּפֶר נִתְּנוּ מְכֹרָכִין כוּ', אָמַר הַקָּדוֹשׁ בָּרוּךְ הוּא, אִם שְׁמַרְתֶּם מַה שֶּׁכָּתוּב בַּסֵּפֶר, אַתֶּם נִצּוֹלִים מִן הַסַּיִף, וְאִם לָאו כוּ'.

וּבִפְתִיחְתָא אֵיכָה (אות ב), וּבְתַנָּא דְּבֵי אֵלִיָּהוּ (סֵדֶר אֵלִיָּהוּ רַבָּא פֶּרֶק יח), אֵימָתַי הַמַּלְכוּת גּוֹזֶרֶת גְּזֵירָה וּגְזֵרָתָהּ מַצְלַחַת, בְּשָׁעָה שֶׁיִּשְׂרָאֵל מַשְׁלִיכִין דִּבְרֵי תּוֹרָה לָאָרֶץ, הֲדָא הוּא דִּכְתִיב (דניאל ח, יב) "וְצָבָא תִּנָּתֵן עַל הַתָּמִיד בְּפָשַׁע", אֵין "צָבָא", אֶלָּא מַלְכִיּוֹת כוּ', "בְּפָשַׁע", בִּפְשִׁיעָה שֶׁל תּוֹרָה, כָּל זְמַן שֶׁיִּשְׂרָאֵל מַשְׁלִיכִין דִּבְרֵי תּוֹרָה לָאָרֶץ, הַמַּלְכוּת הִיא גּוֹזֶרֶת וּמַצְלַחַת, שֶׁנֶּאֱמַר (שם) "וְתַשְׁלֵךְ אֱמֶת אַרְצָה וְעָשְׂתָה וְהִצְלִיחָה" וגו', אֵין "אֱמֶת" אֶלָּא תּוֹרָה כוּ', אִם הִשְׁלַכְתָּ דִּבְרֵי תּוֹרָה לָאָרֶץ מִיַּד הִצְלִיחָה הַמַּלְכוּת הֲדָא הוּא דִּכְתִיב (שם) "וְעָשְׂתָה וְהִצְלִיחָה".

וְאָמְרוּ שָׁם (בפתיחתא איכה) עוֹד, מָצִינוּ שֶׁוִּתֵּר הַקָּדוֹשׁ בָּרוּךְ הוּא עַל עֲבוֹדָה זָרָה וְגִלּוּי עֲרָיוֹת וּשְׁפִיכוּת דָּמִים, וְלֹא וִתֵּר עַל מָאֳסָהּ שֶׁל תּוֹרָה, שֶׁנֶּאֱמַר (ירמיה ט, יא) "עַל מָה אָבְדָה הָאָרֶץ", "עַל עֲבוֹדַת כּוֹכָבִים וְגִלּוּי עֲרָיוֹת וּשְׁפִיכוּת דָּמִים" אֵין כְּתִיב כָּאן, אֶלָּא "וַיֹּאמֶר ה' עַל עָזְבָם אֶת תּוֹרָתִי".

וּבְתַנָּא דְּבֵי אֵלִיָּהוּ שָׁם, בֹּא וּרְאֵה כַּמָּה גָּדוֹל כֹּחַ פְּשִׁיעָה שֶׁל תּוֹרָה, שֶׁלֹּא חָרְבָה יְרוּשָׁלַיִם וְלֹא חָרַב בֵּית הַמִּקְדָּשׁ אֶלָּא בִּפְשִׁיעָה שֶׁל תּוֹרָה, שֶׁנֶּאֱמַר כוּ'.

וּבְתַנְחוּמָא בְּשַׁלַּח (אות כה), כְּשֵׁם שֶׁאִי אֶפְשָׁר וכו', כָּךְ אִי אֶפְשָׁר לְיִשְׂרָאֵל לִחְיוֹת אֶלָּא אִם כֵּן מִתְעַסְּקִין בְּדִבְרֵי תּוֹרָה, וּלְפִי שֶׁפֵּרְשׁוּ יִשְׂרָאֵל מִדִּבְרֵי תּוֹרָה לְפִיכָךְ הַשּׂוֹנֵא בָּא עֲלֵיהֶם כוּ', וְכֵן אַתְּ מוֹצֵא, שֶׁאֵין הַשּׂוֹנֵא בָּא אֶלָּא עַל יְדֵי רִפְיוֹן יָדַיִם מִן הַתּוֹרָה כוּ', עַיֵּן שָׁם:

פֶּרֶק כ"ג

וְכֵן אַחַר פְּטִירָתוֹ מִזֶּה הָעוֹלָם, אָמְרוּ (בבא בתרא עט, א): כָּל הַמְּרַפֶּה עַצְמוֹ מִדִּבְרֵי תּוֹרָה נוֹפֵל בַּגֵּיהִנֹּם כוּ'. וְאָמְרוּ שָׁם עוֹד, כָּל הַפּוֹרֵשׁ עַצְמוֹ מִדִּבְרֵי תּוֹרָה, וְעוֹסֵק בְּדִבְרֵי שִׂיחָה, אֵשׁ אוֹכַלְתּוֹ כוּ'.

וּבְמִשְׁלֵי רַבָּתִי פָּרָשָׁה י' "וְעוֹזֵב תּוֹכַחַת מַתְעֶה" (משלי י, יז), אָמַר ר"א, כָּל תַּלְמִיד חָכָם שֶׁהוּא עוֹזֵב דִּבְרֵי תּוֹרָה, מַעֲלִין עָלָיו כְּאִלּוּ מִתְעַתֵּעַ בְּמִי שֶׁאָמַר וְהָיָה הָעוֹלָם, וְלֹא עוֹד, אֶלָּא כֵּיוָן שֶׁעָזַב דִּבְרֵי תּוֹרָה בָּעוֹלָם הַזֶּה, הַקָּדוֹשׁ בָּרוּךְ הוּא עוֹזְבוֹ לָעוֹלָם הַבָּא כו'.

וּבַזֹּהַר וַיִּקְרָא כ"ה ב', אָמַר רַבִּי שִׁמְעוֹן, זַכָּאִין אִנּוּן מָארֵי דְּנִשְׁמָתָא, מָארֵי דְּאוֹרַיְתָא, בְּנֵי פּוּלְחָנָא דְּמַלְכָּא קַדִּישָׁא, וַי לְאִנּוּן חַיָּבִין דְּלָא זַכָּאָן לְאִתְדַּבְּקָא בְּמָארֵיהוֹן, וְלָא זַכָּאָן בְּאוֹרַיְתָא, דְּכָל מַאן דְּלָא זָכֵי בְּאוֹרַיְתָא, לָא זָכֵי לָא בְּרוּחַ וְלָא בְּנִשְׁמָה, וְאִתְדַּבְּקוּתָא דִּדְהוֹן בְּהַהוּא סִטְרָא דְּזִינִין בִּישִׁין, וְהַאי לֵית לֵיהּ חוּלָקָא דְּקְדוּשָּׁה, וַי לֵיהּ כַּד יִפּוֹק מֵהַאי עָלְמָא, דְּהָא אִשְׁתְּמוֹדַע הוּא לְגַבֵּי אִנּוּן זִינִין בִּישִׁין, מָארֵי חֲצִיפוּתָא, תַּקִּיפֵי כְּכַלְבֵּי, שְׁלוּחֵי דְּנוּרָא דְּגֵיהִנָּם, דְּלָא מְרַחֲמָא עֲלַיְהוּ. [אָמַר רַבִּי שִׁמְעוֹן, אַשְׁרֵי בַּעֲלֵי נְשָׁמָה, בַּעֲלֵי תּוֹרָה, בְּנֵי עֲבוֹדַת הַמֶּלֶךְ הַקָּדוֹשׁ, אוֹי לְאוֹתָם הָרְשָׁעִים שֶׁלֹּא זָכוּ לְהִתְדַּבֵּק בַּאֲדוֹנָם, וְלֹא זָכוּ בַּתּוֹרָה. שֶׁכָּל מִי שֶׁלֹּא זָכָה בַּתּוֹרָה אֵינוֹ זוֹכֶה לֹא בְּרוּחַ וְלֹא בִּנְשָׁמָה, וְהַדְּבֵקוּת שֶׁלָּהֶם הִיא בְּאוֹתוֹ הַצַּד שֶׁל הַמִּינִים הָרָעִים, וְזֶה אֵין לוֹ חֵלֶק בַּקְּדֻשָּׁה, אוֹי לוֹ כְּשֶׁיֵּצֵא מֵהָעוֹלָם הַזֶּה, כִּי נוֹדָע הוּא אֵצֶל אֵלּוּ הַמִּינִים הָרָעִים, בַּעֲלֵי חֻצְפָּה קָשִׁים כַּכְּלָבִים, שְׁלִיחֵי אֵשׁ הַגֵּיהִנֹּם, שֶׁאֵינָם מְרַחֲמִים עֲלֵיהֶם] כו'.

וּבְפָרָשַׁת וַיֵּשֶׁב קפ"ה א', אַחַר שֶׁהֶאֱרִיךְ שָׁם בְּגֹדֶל שִׁבְחוֹ וּמַדְרֵגָתוֹ שֶׁל הָעוֹסֵק בַּתּוֹרָה, בָּעוֹלָם הַזֶּה וְעוֹלָם הַבָּא, אָמַר אַחַר זֶה, תָּא חֲזֵי, הַהוּא בַּר נָשׁ דְּלָא זָכֵי לְאִשְׁתַּדְּלָא בְּהַאי עָלְמָא בְּאוֹרַיְתָא, וְאִיהוּ אָזִיל בַּחֲשׁוֹכָא, כַּד נָפֵק מֵהַאי עָלְמָא, נַטְלִין לֵיהּ, וְאַעֲלִין לֵיהּ לְגֵיהִנָּם, אֲתַר תַּתָּאָה, דְּלָא יְהֵא מְרַחֵם עָלֵיהּ, דְּאִקְרֵי "בּוֹר שָׁאוֹן טִיט הַיָּוֵן" כד"א (תהלים מ, ג) "וַיַּעֲלֵנִי מִבּוֹר שָׁאוֹן מִטִּיט הַיָּוֵן" כו'. וּבְגִין כָּךְ, הַהוּא דְּלָא אִשְׁתַּדֵּל בְּאוֹרַיְתָא בְּהַאי עָלְמָא וְאִתְטְנַף בְּטִנּוּפֵי עָלְמָא, מַה כְּתִיב (בראשית לז, כד) "וַיִּקָּחֻהוּ וַיַּשְׁלִכוּ אֹתוֹ הַבֹּרָה", דָּא הוּא גֵּיהִנָּם, אֲתַר דְּדַיְנִין לְהוּ לְאִנּוּן דְּלָא אִשְׁתַּדְּלוּ בְּאוֹרַיְתָא, "וְהַבּוֹר רֵק", כְּמָה דְּאִיהוּ הֲוָה רֵיק, מַאי טַעֲמָא, בְּגִין דְּלָא הֲוָה בֵּיהּ מַיִם, וְתָא חֲזֵי כַּמָּה הוּא עוֹנְשָׁא דְּאוֹרַיְתָא, דְּהָא לָא אִתְגְּלוּ יִשְׂרָאֵל מֵאַרְעָא קַדִּישָׁא אֶלָּא בְּגִין דְּאִסְתַּלְּקוּ מֵאוֹרַיְתָא וְאִשְׁתַּבְקוּ מִנָּהּ, הֲדָא הוּא דִכְתִיב (ירמיה ט, יא) מִי הָאִישׁ הֶחָכָם וְיָבֵן כו' עַל מָה אָבְדָה הָאָרֶץ וַיֹּאמֶר ה' עַל עָזְבָם אֶת תּוֹרָתִי.

[בּוֹא וּרְאֵה, הָאָדָם שֶׁלֹּא זָכָה לַעֲסֹק בַּתּוֹרָה בָּעוֹלָם הַזֶּה, וְהוּא הוֹלֵךְ בַּחֹשֶׁךְ, כְּשֶׁיּוֹצֵא מִזֶּה הָעוֹלָם, לוֹקְחִים אוֹתוֹ, וּמַכְנִיסִים אוֹתוֹ לַגֵּיהִנֹּם, בְּמָקוֹם תַּחְתּוֹן, שֶׁלֹּא יְהֵא מְרַחֵם עָלָיו, שֶׁנִּקְרָא "בּוֹר שָׁאוֹן טִיט הַיָּוֵן" כְּמוֹ שֶׁכָּתוּב "וַיַּעֲלֵנִי מִבּוֹר שָׁאוֹן מִטִּיט הַיָּוֵן" וכו'. וּמִשּׁוּם כָּךְ אוֹתוֹ שֶׁלֹּא מִשְׁתַּדֵּל בַּתּוֹרָה בָּעוֹלָם הַזֶּה וְנִטְנַף בְּטִנּוּפֵי עוֹלָם הַזֶּה, מַה כָּתוּב עָלָיו, "וַיִּקָּחוּהוּ וַיַּשְׁלִיכוּ אוֹתוֹ הַבּוֹרָה", זֶהוּ הַגֵּהִנֹּם, מָקוֹם שֶׁדָּנִים שָׁם לְאוֹתָם שֶׁלֹּא עָסְקוּ בַּתּוֹרָה, וְהַבּוֹר רֵיק כְּמוֹ שֶׁהוּא הָיָה רֵיק, מַה טַּעַם, מִשּׁוּם שֶׁלֹּא הָיָה שָׁם מַיִם. וּבוֹא וּרְאֵה כַּמָּה עָנְשָׁהּ שֶׁל תּוֹרָה, שֶׁהֲרֵי לֹא גָּלוּ יִשְׂרָאֵל מֵאֶרֶץ הַקֹּדֶשׁ אֶלָּא מִשּׁוּם שֶׁנִּסְתַּלְּקוּ מֵהַתּוֹרָה וְנֶעֶזְבוּ מִמֶּנָּה. וְזֶה שֶׁכָּתוּב "מִי הָאִישׁ הֶחָכָם וְיָבֵן וגו' עַל מָה אָבְדָה הָאָרֶץ וַיֹּאמֶר ה' עַל עָזְבָם אֶת תּוֹרָתִי" וכו']. כו'.

וְלֹא עוֹד, אֶלָּא שֶׁתְּחִלַּת דִּינוֹ שֶׁל אָדָם, בְּבֹאוֹ לַמִּשְׁפָּט לְפָנָיו יִתְבָּרַךְ, הוּא עַל דִּבְרֵי תּוֹרָה, כְּמוֹ שֶׁכָּתוּב בְּסוֹף פֶּרֶק קַמָּא דְּקִדּוּשִׁין (מ, ב), וּבְפֶרֶק קַמָּא דְּסַנְהֶדְרִין (ז' א'), אָמַר רַב הַמְנוּנָא, אֵין תְּחִלַּת דִּינוֹ שֶׁל אָדָם, אֶלָּא עַל דִּבְרֵי תּוֹרָה, שֶׁנֶּאֱמַר (משלי יז, יד) "פּוֹטֵר מַיִם רֵאשִׁית מָדוֹן" כו':

וְאָמְרוּ (אבות ו, ב): "בְּכָל יוֹם וָיוֹם, בַּת קוֹל יוֹצֵאת מֵהַר חוֹרֵב, וּמַכְרֶזֶת כו', אוֹי לָהֶם לַבְּרִיּוֹת מֵעֶלְבּוֹנָהּ שֶׁל תּוֹרָה שֶׁכָּל מִי שֶׁאֵינוֹ עוֹסֵק בַּתּוֹרָה נִקְרָא נָזוּף" כו'. כִּי כֵן מִשְׁפָּטוֹ, מִפְּרִי מַעֲלָלָיו יַשְׂבִּיעוּהוּ, כֵּיוָן שֶׁלֹּא רָצָה לִבְחוֹר בַּחַיִּים וּבַטּוֹב הָאֲמִתִּי, לוֹ וּלְכָל הַבְּרִיּוֹת וְהָעוֹלָמוֹת כֻּלָּם, וּלְהִתְדַּבֵּק עַצְמוֹ בּוֹ יִתְבָּרַךְ, וְהִמְעִיט שִׁפְעַת אוֹרָם שֶׁל הָעוֹלָמוֹת, וְקִלְקֵל וּבִלְבֵּל סִדְרֵי הַמֶּרְכָּבָה הַקְּדוֹשָׁה, וְהֶחְשִׁיכָם, וְגָרַם רָעָה לְעַצְמוֹ, שֶׁפָּשַׁט בִּגְדֵי הַקֹּדֶשׁ, וְלָבַשׁ תַּחְתָּם בְּגָדִים צוֹאִים וּמְטֻנָּפִים, הַנַּעֲשִׂים מֵעִסְקֵי תַּאֲוֹת זֶה הָעוֹלָם וְתַעֲנוּגוֹת עִנְיָנָיו, וְהוּא מְטַמֵּא וּמְטַנֵּף מֵהֶם, וַדַּאי שֶׁלֹּא יַנִּיחוּהוּ וְלֹא יוּכַל לִיכָּנֵס, (כמ"ש שו"ע יו"ד בדין הנזוף) וְכָל הַחֲיָלִין קַדִּישִׁין הַשּׁוֹמְרִים אוֹתוֹ, מִתְרַחֲקִים מֵאִתּוֹ, בְּלֹא יוּכְלוּ יִגְּעוּ בִּלְבוּשָׁיו הַמְטֻנָּפִים, וְאָזִיל וּמְשׁוֹטֵט בָּעוֹלָם, וְ"טָמֵא טָמֵא" יִקְרָא, שֶׁמִּתְדַּבֵּק בְּמִינוֹ, בַּחֲיָלִין טְמֵאִים שֶׁל כֹּחוֹת הַטֻּמְאָה אֲשֶׁר הִגְבִּירָם עַל עַצְמוֹ.

כְּמוֹ שֶׁכָּתוּב בַּזֹּהַר רֵישׁ פָּרָשַׁת מְצֹרָע (נג, ב), רַבִּי אַבָּא פָּתַח כו', כַּמָּה אִית לוֹן לִבְנֵי נָשָׁא לְאִסְתַּמְּרָא אָרְחַיְהוּ, וּלְדַחֲלָא מִקַּמֵּי קוּדְשָׁא בְּרִיךְ הוּא, דְּלָא יִסְטֵי מֵאָרְחָא דְּכַשְׁרָא, וְלָא יַעֲבוֹר עַל פִּתְגָּמֵי אוֹרַיְתָא, וְלָא יִתְנְשֵׁי מִנַּהּ. דְּכָל מַאן דְּלָא לָעֵי בְּאוֹרַיְתָא, וְלָא יִשְׁתַּדֵּל בַּהּ, נְזִיפָא אִיהוּ מִקּוּדְשָׁא בְּרִיךְ הוּא, רְחִיקָא הוּא מִנֵּיהּ, לָא שַׁרְיָא שְׁכִינְתָּא עִמֵּיהּ, וְאִנּוּן נְטוּרִין דְּאָזְלִין עִמֵּיהּ אִסְתַּלְּקוּ מִנֵּיהּ, וְלָא עוֹד, אֶלָּא דְּמַכְרְזֵי קָמֵיהּ וְאַמְרֵי, אִסְתַּלְּקוּ מִסּוּחְרָנֵיהּ דִּפְלָנְיָא דְּלָא חָשׁ עַל יְקָרָא דְּמָארֵיהּ, וַי לֵיהּ, דְּהָא שְׁבָקוּהוּ עִלָּאִין וְתַתָּאִין, לֵית לֵיהּ חוּלְקָא בְּאָרְחָא דְּחַיֵּי. וְכַד אִיהוּ אִשְׁתַּדַּל כו', וְלָעֵי בְּאוֹרַיְתָא, כַּמָּה נְטוּרִין זְמִינִין לְקִבְלֵיהּ, לְנַטְרָא לֵיהּ, וּשְׁכִינְתָּא שַׁרְיָא עֲלֵיהּ, וְכוּלְּהוּ מַכְרְזֵי קָמֵיהּ וְאַמְרֵי, הָבוּ יְקָרָא לְדִיוֹקְנָא דְּמַלְכָּא, הָבוּ יְקָרָא לִבְרֵיהּ דְּמַלְכָּא, אִתְנְטִיר הוּא בְּעָלְמָא דֵּין, וּבְעָלְמָא דְּאָתֵי, זַכָּאָה חוּלְקֵיהּ.

[רַבִּי אַבָּא פָּתַח וְאָמַר, כַּמָּה יֵשׁ לָהֶם לִבְנֵי אָדָם לִשְׁמֹר אָרְחוֹתָם וְלִירֹא מִפְּנֵי הַקָּדוֹשׁ בָּרוּךְ הוּא, שֶׁלֹּא יִסְטוּ מִדֶּרֶךְ הַיָּשָׁר, וְלֹא יַעַבְרוּ עַל דִּבְרֵי תּוֹרָה, וְלֹא יָמִישׁוּ מִמֶּנָּה. כִּי כָּל מִי שֶׁאֵינוֹ עוֹסֵק בַּתּוֹרָה, וְאֵינוֹ מִשְׁתַּדֵּל בָּהּ, נָזוּף הוּא מֵהַקָּדוֹשׁ בָּרוּךְ הוּא, רָחוֹק הוּא מִמֶּנּוּ, הַשְּׁכִינָה אֵינָהּ שׁוֹרָה עִמּוֹ, וְאֵלּוּ הַשּׁוֹמְרִים הַהוֹלְכִים עִמּוֹ מִסְתַּלְּקִים מִמֶּנּוּ, וְלֹא עוֹד, אֶלָּא שֶׁמַּכְרִיזִים לְפָנָיו וְאוֹמְרִים, הִסְתַּלְּקוּ מִסָּבִיב לִפְלוֹנִי שֶׁאֵינוֹ דּוֹאֵג לִכְבוֹד אֲדוֹנָיו. אוֹי לוֹ שֶׁעֲזָבוּהוּ הָעֶלְיוֹנִים וְהַתַּחְתּוֹנִים, אֵין לוֹ חֵלֶק בְּדֶרֶךְ הַחַיִּים. וּכְשֶׁהוּא מִשְׁתַּדֵּל וכו' וְעוֹסֵק בַּתּוֹרָה, כַּמָּה שׁוֹמְרִים מוּכָנִים לִקְרָאתוֹ לְשָׁמְרוֹ, וְהַשְּׁכִינָה שׁוֹרָה עָלָיו, וְכֻלָּם מַכְרִיזִים לְפָנָיו וְאוֹמְרִים תְּנוּ כָּבוֹד לְצוּרַת הַמֶּלֶךְ, תְּנוּ כָּבוֹד לְבֶן מֶלֶךְ. שָׁמוּר הוּא בָּעוֹלָם הַזֶּה וּבָעוֹלָם הַבָּא, אַשְׁרֵי חֶלְקוֹ.]

וְאָמְרוּ בַּמִּשְׁנָה פֶּרֶק קַמָּא דַּחֲגִיגָה (ט' א'): "מְעֻוָּת לֹא יוּכַל לִתְקֹן" (קהלת א, טו), רַבִּי

שִׁמְעוֹן בֶּן יוֹחַאי אוֹמֵר, אֵין קוֹרִין "מְעֻוָּת" אֶלָּא לְמִי שֶׁהָיָה מְתֻקָּן בַּתְּחִלָּה וְנִתְעַוֵּת, וְאֵי זֶה, זֶה תַּלְמִיד חָכָם הַפּוֹרֵשׁ מִן הַתּוֹרָה". וְאוֹי לָהֶם לַבְּרִיּוֹת שֶׁרוֹאוֹת וְאֵינָן יוֹדְעוֹת מָה רוֹאוֹת, אוֹי לָנוּ מֵעֶלְבּוֹנָהּ שֶׁל תּוֹרָה.

וְכַמָּה צָרִיךְ הָאָדָם לְהִתְבּוֹנֵן עַל זֶה תָּמִיד, וְלָשִׁית דַּעְתּוֹ וְכִלְיוֹתָיו יִשְׁתּוֹנָן, בַּל יֵלֶךְ חוֹשֶׁךְ חַס וְשָׁלוֹם כָּל יְמֵי הֶבְלוֹ, מִסְפַּר יָמָיו אֲשֶׁר נִקְצְבוּ לוֹ בְּרַחֲמָיו וַחֲסָדָיו יִתְבָּרַךְ שְׁמוֹ, בְּאַוַּת נַפְשׁוֹ מְשֻׁלָּח חָפְשִׁי מִן הַתּוֹרָה, כִּי בְנַפְשׁוֹ הוּא. כִּי יַגִּיעַ עֵת פְּקוּדָתוֹ, וְיָשׁוּב הֶעָפָר עַל הָאָרֶץ, וְהָרוּחַ לֹא תָשׁוּב אֶל הָאֱלֹקִים לְהִצָּרֵר בִּצְרוֹר הַחַיִּים הָעֶלְיוֹנִים, כִּי תְקֻלַּל חֶלְקָתוֹ לְהִתְקַלֵּעַ, וְלֹא תַרְגִּיעַ, כִּי נִדָּחָה קָרְאוּ לָהּ, נָזִיף לְעֵלָּא נָזִיף לְתַתָּא, אוֹי לָהּ לְאוֹתָהּ בּוּשָׁה כו'. הָרַחֲמָן יִתְבָּרַךְ שְׁמוֹ יַצִּילֵנוּ:

פֶּרֶק כ"ד

וְכָל כָּךְ הִפְלִיגוּ רַבּוֹתֵינוּ זִכְרוֹנָם לִבְרָכָה, בְּחֹמֶר עָנְשׁוֹ שֶׁל הָאָדָם שֶׁאֶפְשָׁר לוֹ לַעֲסֹק בַּתּוֹרָה וְאֵינוֹ עוֹסֵק, אוֹ שָׁנָה וּפֵרֵשׁ חַס וְשָׁלוֹם, עַד שֶׁכְּרָתוּהוּ בְּרוּחַ קָדְשָׁם מֵעוֹלָם הַבָּא לְגַמְרֵי, רַחֲמָנָא לִיצְּלָן. כְּמוֹ שֶׁכָּתוּב בְּפֶרֶק חֵלֶק (צט, א): "כִּי דְבַר ה' בָּזָה" כו' (במדבר טו, לא), רַבִּי נָתָן אוֹמֵר כָּל שֶׁאֵינוֹ מַשְׁגִּיחַ עַל הַמִּשְׁנָה, רַבִּי נְהוֹרַאי אוֹמֵר כָּל שֶׁאֶפְשָׁר לוֹ לַעֲסֹק בַּתּוֹרָה וְאֵינוֹ עוֹסֵק. וְסֵיפֵיהּ דְּהַאי קְרָא "הִכָּרֵת תִּכָּרֵת הַנֶּפֶשׁ הַהִיא", וּפֵרְשׁוּ זִכְרוֹנָם לִבְרָכָה שָׁם לְעֵיל מִינֵּהּ "הִכָּרֵת" – בָּעוֹלָם הַזֶּה "תִּכָּרֵת" – לָעוֹלָם הַבָּא.

הִשְׁמִיעָנוּ הַכָּתוּב חֹמֶר זֶה הַכָּרֵת, שֶׁאֵינוֹ כִּשְׁאָר הַכְּרִיתוּת הָאֲמוּרוֹת בַּתּוֹרָה עַל שְׁאָר עֲוֹנוֹת, אֲשֶׁר אַף אִם דִּינוֹ חָרוּץ שֶׁהוּא נִכְרָת חַס וְשָׁלוֹם, עִם כָּל זֶה לֹא אִבֵּד חֶלְקוֹ בְּחַיֵּי עוֹלָם הַבָּא, שֶׁרַק אוֹתוֹ הַנִּצּוֹץ הַקָּטָן שֶׁל הַנֶּפֶשׁ, שֶׁעָשָׂה בּוֹ אֶת הֶעָוֹן, הוּא הַנִּכְרָת מִקִּשּׁוּר וְדִבּוּק הַחֶבֶל הַנִּמְרָץ, שֶׁהָיָה מְקֻשָּׁר וְדָבוּק עַד עַתָּה עַד שֹׁרֶשׁ נִשְׁמָתוֹ בְּקוּדְשָׁא בְּרִיךְ הוּא, כְּמוֹ שֶׁנִּתְבָּאֵר לְעֵיל בְּשַׁעַר א' בְּאֹרֶךְ. אָמְנָם כָּאן אָמַר "הִכָּרֵת תִּכָּרֵת", הַיְנוּ, שֶׁכָּל חֵלֶק "בְּחִינַת נַפְשׁוֹ" אִבְּדָה חֶלְקָהּ בְּחַיֵּי עוֹלָם לְגַמְרֵי חַס וְשָׁלוֹם, וְאֵין לָהּ חֵלֶק לָעוֹלָם הַבָּא כְּלָל.

וְכֵן פָּסַק הָרַמְבַּ"ם זִכְרוֹנוֹ לִבְרָכָה לַהֲלָכָה, בְּהִלְכוֹת תַּלְמוּד תּוֹרָה (פֶּרֶק ג' הֲלָכָה י"ג), וְקָבַע כֵּן הַבֵּית יוֹסֵף בְּשֻׁלְחָן עָרוּךְ שָׁם (סי' רמ"ו סעיף כ"ה) לַהֲלָכָה.

וְכֵן הָרַבֵּינוּ יוֹנָה זִכְרוֹנוֹ לִבְרָכָה בְּשַׁעַר הַתְּשׁוּבָה (שער השלישי), מָנָה עֶשֶׂר מַדְרֵגוֹת בְּחֹמֶר עָנְשֵׁי הָעֲוֹנוֹת, וְהַמַּדְרֵגָה הָאַחֲרוֹנָה מוֹנֶה אוֹתָם הַכַּת, שֶׁאָמְרוּ רַבּוֹתֵינוּ זִכְרוֹנָם לִבְרָכָה עֲלֵיהֶם שֶׁאֵין לָהֶם חֵלֶק לָעוֹלָם הַבָּא, וּמָנָה שָׁם (ש"ג, קנג) בִּכְלָל זֶה גַּם מִי שֶׁאֶפְשָׁר לוֹ לַעֲסֹק בַּתּוֹרָה וְאֵינוֹ עוֹסֵק.

וְכֵן הרח"ו זִכְרוֹנוֹ לִבְרָכָה בְּשַׁעֲרֵי קְדֻשָּׁה שַׁעַר ח' חֵלֶק ב', מָנָה אוֹתוֹ גַּם כֵּן בִּכְלַל אוֹתָם שֶׁאֵין לָהֶם חֵלֶק לָעוֹלָם הַבָּא, וּבְחַדָּא מַחְתָּא מַחְתִּינְהוּ שָׁם, שֶׁדִּינוֹ שָׁוֶה עִם אוֹתָן שֶׁאָמְרוּ זִכְרוֹנָם לִבְרָכָה עֲלֵיהֶם בְּפֶרֶק קַמָּא דְּרֹאשׁ הַשָּׁנָה (יז, א), שֶׁגֵּיהִנֹּם כָּלֶה וְהֵם אֵינָם כָּלִים, רַחֲמָנָא לִיצְּלָן.

וְכָתַב הָרַמְבַּ"ם זִכְרוֹנוֹ לִבְרָכָה, וְהַבֵּית יוֹסֵף זִכְרוֹנוֹ לִבְרָכָה שָׁם, שֶׁמִּי שֶׁקָּרָא וְשָׁנָה, וּפֵרַשׁ לְהַבְלֵי עוֹלָם, וְהִנִּיחַ תַּלְמוּדוֹ וּזְנָחוֹ, גַּם כֵּן דִּינוֹ אֶחָד עִם מִי שֶׁאֶפְשָׁר לוֹ לַעֲסֹק בַּתּוֹרָה וְאֵינוֹ עוֹסֵק.

וְכֵן בַּדִּין, מַעֲשָׂיו אֲשֶׁר לֹא טוֹבִים הֵמָּה יַרְחִקוּהוּ, וְחַטָּאתוֹ מָנְעוּ הַטּוֹב מֵאִתּוֹ, אַחַר שֶׁהָיָה אֶפְשָׁר לוֹ וְסִפֵּק בְּיָדוֹ לַעֲסֹק בַּתּוֹרָה, וּבִזְדוֹן לֵב וּשְׁאָט נֶפֶשׁ, בָּחַר וְלָקַח מֵקַח רַע לְעַצְמוֹ וְלַאֲחֵרִים וְהָעוֹלָמוֹת כֻּלָּם, וּמָאַס בְּחַיֵּי עוֹלָם שֶׁל הַתּוֹרָה הַקְּדוֹשָׁה, חִיּוּתָא וּנְהִירוּ דְּכָל עָלְמִין, אֲשֶׁר עַל יָדָהּ הָיָה מִתְדַּבֵּק כִּבְיָכוֹל בְּקוּדְשָׁא בְּרִיךְ הוּא יִתְבָּרַךְ שְׁמוֹ, הַמְּחַיֶּה אֶת כֻּלָּם, וְשָׁלַח יָדוֹ לַהֲרֹס פַּלְטִין שֶׁל מֶלֶךְ, וְהִמְעִיט וְהֶחֱשִׁיךְ וְכִבָּה שִׁפְעַת אוֹרָם שֶׁל הָעוֹלָמוֹת, וְגַם שֶׁל נַפְשׁוֹ, לָמָּה לוֹ חַיִּים אֲמִתִּים, כִּי הֲלֹא תֶּחְשַׁכְנָה עֵינָיו מֵרְאוֹת וְהַבֵּט בְּאוֹר הַחַיִּים הַנִּצְחִים, וְלֹא יוּכַל לִסְבּוֹל גֹּדֶל עֹצֶם הָאוֹר עֶלְיוֹן, כִּי לֹא נִסָּה בָּזֶה מֵעוֹדוֹ בְּזֶה הָעוֹלָם, וְהוּא מְגֹרָשׁ וְנִכְרָת מֵאֵלָיו מֵעֵדֶן גַּן אֱלֹקִים יִתְבָּרַךְ שְׁמוֹ, מִלְּהִצָּרֵר בִּצְרוֹר הַחַיִּים אֶת ה' אֱלֹקָיו יִתְבָּרַךְ שְׁמוֹ, וּמֵרָעָה אֶל רָעָה הוּא יוֹצֵא חַס וְשָׁלוֹם, אוֹי לְאוֹתָהּ בּוּשָׁה כוּ':

וְכֵן פָּסְקוּ וְחָתְכוּ זִכְרוֹנָם לִבְרָכָה דִּינוֹ, שֶׁנִּגְזְרָה אָבְדָה תִּקְוָתוֹ לְדוֹר דּוֹרִים חַס וְשָׁלוֹם, שֶׁגַּם עַד נֶצַח לֹא יִרְאֶה אוֹר, בַּל יְחִי עוֹד לָנֶצַח בְּעֵת קֵץ הַיָּמִין, אֲשֶׁר יְשֵׁנֵי אַדְמַת עָפָר יָקִיצוּ לְחַיֵּי עוֹלָם, כְּמַאֲמָרָם זִכְרוֹנָם לִבְרָכָה (בסוף כתובות קיא, ב): "[הָקִיצוּ וְרַנְּנוּ שֹׁכְנֵי עָפָר] כִּי טַל אוֹרוֹת טַלֶּךָ" (ישעיה כו, יט) "כָּל הַמִּשְׁתַּמֵּשׁ בְּאוֹר תּוֹרָה אוֹר תּוֹרָה מְחַיֵּהוּ, וְכָל שֶׁאֵין מִשְׁתַּמֵּשׁ בְּאוֹר תּוֹרָה אֵין אוֹר תּוֹרָה מְחַיֵּהוּ".

וְלֹא מָצְאוּ שָׁם רַבּוֹתֵינוּ זִכְרוֹנָם לִבְרָכָה תַּקָּנָה לְעַמֵּי הָאָרֶץ – שֶׁיָּקוּמוּ לְעֵת הַתְּחִיָּה, אֶלָּא בְּהַחֲזִיקָם וְתוֹמְכִים עַל כָּל פָּנִים בְּעֵץ הַחַיִּים, תָּמְכֵי דְּאוֹרַיְתָא, לְהָנוֹת תַּלְמִידֵי חֲכָמִים מִנִּכְסֵיהֶם. כְּמוֹ שֶׁאָמְרוּ (שָׁם), אָמַר לוֹ, רַבִּי מָצָאתִי לָהֶם תְּרוּפָה [תַּקָּנָה] מִן הַתּוֹרָה "וְאַתֶּם הַדְּבֵקִים בַּה' אֱלֹהֵיכֶם חַיִּים כֻּלְּכֶם הַיּוֹם" (דברים ה, ד) וְכִי אֶפְשָׁר לִדְבוּקֵי בַּשְּׁכִינָה כוּ', אֶלָּא כָּל הַמַּשִּׂיא בִּתּוֹ לְתַלְמִיד חָכָם, וְהָעוֹשֶׂה פְּרַקְמַטְיָא לְתַלְמִיד חָכָם, וְהַמְּהַנֶּה תַּלְמִיד חָכָם מִנְּכָסָיו, מַעֲלֶה עָלָיו הַכָּתוּב כְּאִלּוּ מְדַבֵּק בַּשְּׁכִינָה.

וּבְתַנָּא דְּבֵי אֵלִיָּהוּ (סֵדֶר אֵלִיָּהוּ רַבָּה פֶּרֶק ה): "הָקִיצוּ וְרַנְּנוּ שׁוֹכְנֵי עָפָר" (ישעיהו שם) מִכָּאן אָמַר דָּוִד הַמֶּלֶךְ עָלָיו הַשָּׁלוֹם, יְהֵא חֶלְקִי עִם אֵלּוּ שֶׁהֵם מְמִיתִין אֶת עַצְמָן עַל דִּבְרֵי תּוֹרָה כוּ', "הָקִיצוּ וְרַנְּנוּ שׁוֹכְנֵי עָפָר", מִכָּאן אָמְרוּ, כָּל הַנַּעֲשֶׂה שָׁכֵן לֶעָפָר בְּחַיָּיו עֲפָרוֹ נִנְעָר לִתְחִיַּת הַמֵּתִים, וְכָל שֶׁאֵין נַעֲשֶׂה שָׁכֵן לֶעָפָר בְּחַיָּיו, אֵין עֲפָרוֹ נִנְעָר לִתְחִיַּת הַמֵּתִים כוּ', אֵלּוּ בְּנֵי אָדָם שֶׁמַּשְׁכִּינִים עַצְמָם עַל הֶעָפָר לִלְמֹד תּוֹרָה, הַקָּדוֹשׁ בָּרוּךְ הוּא מֵבִיא עֲלֵיהֶם טַל אוֹרוֹת שֶׁל תּוֹרָה כוּ', וּמְבִיאָן לְחַיֵּי עוֹלָם הַבָּא, שֶׁנֶּאֱמַר (ישעיה כו, יט) "כִּי טַל אוֹרוֹת טַלֶּךָ".

וְלָזֹאת קָרְאוּ זִכְרוֹנָם לִבְרָכָה הַמִּקְרָא "מְעֻוָּת לֹא יוּכַל לִתְקֹן" (קהלת א, טו), עַל תַּלְמִיד חָכָם הַפּוֹרֵשׁ מִן הַתּוֹרָה (משנה חגיגה ט, א), שֶׁחַס וְשָׁלוֹם אֵין לוֹ תַּקָּנָה עוֹלָמִית. הָרַחֲמָן יִתְבָּרַךְ שְׁמוֹ יַצִּילֵנוּ מִזֶּה וְכָל כַּיּוֹצֵא בּוֹ:

פֶּרֶק כ"ה

וְכָל זֶה, כְּשֶׁעֲדַיִן יֵשׁ אֲנָשִׁים מִיִּשְׂרָאֵל, שֶׁדְּבֵקִים בּוֹ יִתְבָּרֵךְ וּבְתוֹרָתוֹ בְּעִיּוּן וּשְׁקִידָה וִיגִיעָה גְּדוֹלָה לִשְׁמָהּ, וְרַק בְּתוֹרַת יְיָ חֶפְצָם כָּל הַיָּמִים, וְאָז הָאֲנָשִׁים שֶׁבְּטֵלִים לְגַמְרֵי מֵעֵסֶק הַתּוֹרָה מֵרֹעַ בְּחִירָתָם, הֵמָּה יֵרְדוּ שְׁאוֹל חַיִּים, וּמְגֹרָשִׁים מֵהִסְתַּפֵּחַ בְּנַחֲלַת עַבְדֵי ה' הַדְּבוּקִים בּוֹ יִתְבָּרֵךְ וּבְתוֹרָתוֹ, וּמֵאֶרֶץ חַיִּים יִכָּרְתוּ חַס וְשָׁלוֹם, וְעַל כָּל פָּנִים, הָעוֹלָם, גַּם כָּל הָעוֹלָמוֹת, הֲגַם כִּי נִתְמַעֲטוּ וְיָרְדוּ מִקְּדֻשָּׁתָם וְאוֹרָם, בְּסִבַּת הַחֲטָאִים הָאֵלֶּה בְּנַפְשׁוֹתָם, וְכִמְעַט שֶׁנָּטָיוּ רַגְלָם לֵיחָרֵב חַס וְשָׁלוֹם, כְּמוֹ שֶׁכָּתוּב בְּתַנָּא דְּבֵי אֵלִיָּהוּ (סֵדֶר אֵלִיָּהוּ רַבָּה פֶּרֶק ב), אָמְרוּ חֲכָמִים, כָּל זְמַן שֶׁבְּנֵי אָדָם מְבַטְּלִין מִן הַתּוֹרָה מְבַקֵּשׁ הַקָּדוֹשׁ בָּרוּךְ הוּא לְהַחֲרִיב אֶת הָעוֹלָם כו'.

וְשָׁם בְּסֵדֶר אֵלִיָּהוּ זוּטָא (פֶּרֶק ה) "כִּי לַה' מְצֻקֵי אֶרֶץ וַיָּשֶׁת עֲלֵיהֶם תֵּבֵל" (שמו"א ב, ח), וְאֵין מְצוּקִים אֶלָּא תַּלְמִידֵי חֲכָמִים כו'. בְּכָל יוֹם יוֹצְאִים מַלְאֲכֵי חַבָּלָה מִלִּפְנֵי הַקָּדוֹשׁ בָּרוּךְ הוּא לְחַבֵּל אֶת כָּל הָעוֹלָם כֻּלּוֹ, וְאִלְמָלֵא בָּתֵּי כְּנֵסִיּוֹת וּבָתֵּי מִדְרָשׁוֹת, שֶׁתַּלְמִידֵי חֲכָמִים יוֹשְׁבִין בָּהֶם וְעוֹסְקִים בְּדִבְרֵי תּוֹרָה, הָיוּ מְחַבְּלִין אֶת כָּל הָעוֹלָם כֻּלּוֹ מִיָּד כו', עַיֵּן שָׁם.

עִם כָּל זֶה, עֲדַיִן יוּכְלוּ לְהִתְקַיֵּם עַל יְדֵי הַשְּׂרִידִים אֲשֶׁר ה' קוֹרֵא, הָעוֹסְקִים בַּתּוֹרָה הַקְּדוֹשָׁה יוֹמָם וָלַיְלָה, שֶׁלֹּא יִתְבַּטְּלוּ לְגַמְרֵי לַחֲזֹר לְתֹהוּ וָבֹהוּ חַס וְשָׁלוֹם.

אֲבָל אִם הָיָה חַס וְשָׁלוֹם הָעוֹלָם פָּנוּי לְגַמְרֵי, אֲפִלּוּ רֶגַע אֶחָד מַמָּשׁ, מֵעֵסֶק וְהִתְבּוֹנְנוּת עַם סְגֻלָּה בַּתּוֹרָה הַקְּדוֹשָׁה, תֵּכֶף כְּרֶגַע הָיוּ כָּל הָעוֹלָמוֹת נֶחֱרָבִים וּבְטֵלִים מִמְּצִיאוּת לְגַמְרֵי חַס וְשָׁלוֹם.

וְאַף גַּם אִישׁ אֶחָד מִיִּשְׂרָאֵל לְבַד, רַב כֹּחוֹ, שֶׁבְּיָדוֹ לְהַעֲמִיד וּלְקַיֵּם אֶת כָּל הָעוֹלָמוֹת וְהַבְּרִיאָה בִּכְלָלָהּ, עַל יְדֵי עִסְקוֹ וְהִתְבּוֹנְנוּתוֹ בַּתּוֹרָה הַקְּדוֹשָׁה לִשְׁמָהּ. כְּמוֹ שֶׁכָּתוּב בְּחֵלֶק (צט, ב): "כָּל הָעוֹסֵק בַּתּוֹרָה לִשְׁמָהּ כו', רַבִּי יוֹחָנָן אוֹמֵר אַף מֵגֵן עַל כָּל הָעוֹלָם כֻּלּוֹ". וְכֵן אִיתָא בְּפֶרֶק הַתּוֹרָה (אבות ו, א), "כָּל הָעוֹסֵק בַּתּוֹרָה לִשְׁמָהּ כו', וְלֹא עוֹד אֶלָּא שֶׁכָּל הָעוֹלָם כֻּלּוֹ כְּדַאי הוּא לוֹ".

וְאֵיךְ לֹא יִתְלַהֵב לֵב הָאָדָם, בְּהַעֲלוֹתוֹ עַל לִבּוֹ וּמִתְבּוֹנֵן בְּזֶה הָעִנְיָן הַנּוֹרָא, וְתִפֹּל עָלָיו אֵימָתָה וָפַחַד, לְבַל יִתְרַפֶּה חַס וְשָׁלוֹם מֵעֵסֶק הַתּוֹרָה הַקְּדוֹשָׁה תָּמִיד, כַּאֲשֶׁר יַחְשֹׁב בִּלְבָבוֹ, אוּלַי חַס וְשָׁלוֹם לְעֵת כָּזֹאת, הָעוֹלָם כֻּלּוֹ מִקָּצֶה וְעַד קָצֵהוּ, פָּנוּי לְגַמְרֵי מֵעֵסֶק הַתּוֹרָה הַקְּדוֹשָׁה, וּבִלְתִּי עִסְקוֹ וְהֶגְיוֹן לִבּוֹ עַתָּה בְּזֶה הָעֵת בַּתּוֹרָה, הָיוּ נֶחֱרָבִים כָּל הָעוֹלָמוֹת, וּכְרֶגַע סָפוּ תַּמּוּ חַס וְשָׁלוֹם.

זוֹ תּוֹרָה וְזוֹ שְׂכָרָהּ מְרֻבֶּה מְאֹד, אֵין לְהַעֲרִיךְ, שֶׁהוּא הַנּוֹטֵל שְׂכַר כֻּלָּם, אַחַר שֶׁהוּא אֲשֶׁר קִיֵּם וְהֶעֱמִיד בְּרֹב כֹּחוֹ אֶת כָּל הָעוֹלָמוֹת עַתָּה.

וְעַל כְּגוֹן זֶה אָמְרוּ רַבּוֹתֵינוּ זִכְרוֹנָם לִבְרָכָה בַּמִּשְׁנָה (סנהדרין לז, א) שֶׁכָּל אֶחָד מִיִּשְׂרָאֵל חַיָּב לוֹמַר בִּשְׁבִילִי נִבְרָא הָעוֹלָם.

וְאַף שֶׁבִּשְׁאָר עֲוֹנוֹת, יֵשׁ אַלְפֵי רִבּוֹאוֹת עוֹלָמוֹת קְדוֹשִׁים עֶלְיוֹנִים, שֶׁאֵין שׁוּם חֵטְא וְעָוֹן הַתַּחְתּוֹנִים מַגִּיעַ עֲדֵיהֶם כְּלָל, לִפְגֹּם חַס וְשָׁלוֹם, וְתָמִיד עֹז וְחֶדְוָה בִּמְקוֹם כְּבוֹדָם,

וַעֲלֵיהֶם נֶאֱמַר (תהלים ה, ה) "לֹא יְגֻרְךָ רָע", אָמְנָם עֲוֹן בִּטּוּל תּוֹרָה, הִיא הָעוֹלָה עַל כֻּלָּם, שֶׁהוּא נוֹגֵעַ לְקִיּוּם כָּל הָעוֹלָמוֹת:

פֶּרֶק כ"ו

וְטַעְמוֹ שֶׁל דָּבָר, כְּמוֹ שֶׁנִּתְבָּאֵר לְעֵיל (פֶּרֶק י), שֶׁמְּקוֹר שָׁרְשָׁהּ הָעֶלְיוֹן הַנֶּעְלָם שֶׁל הַתּוֹרָה הַקְּדוֹשָׁה, מְאֹד נַעֲלָה מֵעַל כָּל הָעוֹלָמוֹת, רֵאשִׁית וְשֹׁרֶשׁ אֲצִילוּת קָדְשׁוֹ יִתְבָּרַךְ, סוֹד הַמַּלְבּוּשׁ הָעֶלְיוֹן, כְּמוֹ שֶׁכָּתַב רַבֵּנוּ אִישׁ הָאֱלֹקִים נוֹרָא הָאֲרִ"י זַ"ל. רַק שֶׁנִּשְׁתַּלְשְׁלָה וְיָרְדָה כִּבְיָכוֹל, עַד לָאָרֶץ אֲשֶׁר הֵאִירָה מִכְּבוֹדָהּ, וּמְסָרָהּ וּנְטָעָהּ הוּא יִתְבָּרַךְ בְּתוֹכֵנוּ, שֶׁנִּהְיֶה אֲנַחְנוּ הַמַּחֲזִיקִים וְתוֹמְכִים בְּעֵץ הַחַיִּים.

לָזֹאת, מֵאָז, כָּל חִיּוּתָם וְקִיּוּמָם שֶׁל הָעוֹלָמוֹת כֻּלָּם, תָּלוּי וְעוֹמֵד רַק כְּפִי עִנְיַן וְרֹב עֵסֶקֵנוּ וְהֶגְיוֹנֵנוּ בָּהּ. שֶׁאִם אֲנַחְנוּ עוֹסְקִים בָּהּ וּמַחֲזִיקִים וְתוֹמְכִים אוֹתָהּ כָּרָאוּי, בְּלִי רִפְיוֹן כְּלָל, אָנוּ מְעוֹרְרִים מְקוֹר שָׁרְשָׁהּ הָעֶלְיוֹן, מְקוֹר הַקְּדֻשּׁוֹת וְהַבְּרָכוֹת, לְהַמְשִׁיךְ וּלְהָרִיק תּוֹסֶפֶת בְּרָכָה, וְחַיֵּי עוֹלָם, וּקְדֻשָּׁה נוֹרָאָה עַל כָּל הָעוֹלָמוֹת, כָּל עוֹלָם לְפִי עֵרֶךְ קְדֻשָּׁתוֹ, שֶׁיּוּכַל לְקַבֵּל וְלִסְבֹּל.

וְאִם חַס וְשָׁלוֹם עֵסֶקֵנוּ בָּהּ בְּרִפְיוֹן, מִתְקַמֵּט וּמִתְמַעֵט הַקְּדֻשָּׁה וְאוֹר הָעֶלְיוֹן שֶׁל הַתּוֹרָה מִכָּל הָעוֹלָמוֹת, כָּל אֶחָד לְפִי עֶרְכּוֹ הוֹלֵךְ וְחָסֵר, רוֹתְתִים וּרְפוּיִים חַס וְשָׁלוֹם. וְאִם חַס וְשָׁלוֹם הָיִינוּ כֻּלָּנוּ מַנִּיחִים וּמַזְנִיחִים אוֹתָהּ מִלְּהִתְעַסֵּק בָּהּ מִכֹּל וָכֹל, גַּם הָעוֹלָמוֹת כֻּלָּם כְּרֶגַע הָיוּ מִתְבַּטְּלִים מִכֹּל וָכֹל חַס וְשָׁלוֹם.

מַה שֶּׁאֵין כֵּן בְּכָל הַמִּצְוֹת, וַאֲפִלּוּ מִצְוַת הַתְּפִלָּה, שֶׁגַּם אִם הָיוּ חַס וְשָׁלוֹם כָּל יִשְׂרָאֵל מַנִּיחִים וְעוֹזְבִים מִלְּהִתְפַּלֵּל לוֹ יִתְבָּרַךְ, לֹא הָיוּ חוֹזְרִים הָעוֹלָמוֹת עֲבוּר זֶה לְתֹהוּ וָבֹהוּ.

וְלָכֵן הַתְּפִלָּה נִקְרֵאת בְּדִבְרֵי רַבּוֹתֵינוּ זִכְרוֹנָם לִבְרָכָה "חַיֵּי שָׁעָה", וְהַתּוֹרָה נִקְרֵאת "חַיֵּי עוֹלָם", כְּמַאֲמָרָם זִכְרוֹנָם לִבְרָכָה בְּפֶרֶק קַמָּא דְּשַׁבָּת (י, א) "רָבָא חַזְיֵיהּ לְרַב הַמְנוּנָא דְּקָא מַאֲרִיךְ בִּצְלוֹתָא, אָמַר, מַנִּיחִין חַיֵּי עוֹלָם וְעוֹסְקִין בְּחַיֵּי שָׁעָה". שֶׁעִנְיַן הַתְּפִלָּה הוּא, "הוֹסָפוֹת" תִּקּוּן בְּהָעוֹלָמוֹת, בְּתוֹסֶפֶת קְדֻשָּׁה וּבְרָכָה, בְּאוֹתוֹ עֵת הַקָּבוּעַ לָהֶם, וְלָכֵן, אִם עָבְרָה הַשָּׁעָה, שׁוּב לֹא תּוֹעִיל כְּלָל לְהוֹסִיף תֵּת בְּהָעוֹלָמוֹת הַתּוֹסֶפֶת קְדֻשָּׁה וּבְרָכָה.

אָמְנָם עִנְיַן הָעֵסֶק בַּתּוֹרָה הַקְּדוֹשָׁה, הוּא נוֹגֵעַ לְ'עֶצֶם הַחִיּוּת' וְקִיּוּם עֲמִידַת הָעוֹלָמוֹת בַּל יֵהָרְסוּ לְגַמְרֵי, לָכֵן, הָאָדָם חַיָּב לַעֲסֹק וְלַהֲגוֹת בָּהּ בְּכָל עֵת תָּמִיד, כְּדֵי לְהַעֲמִיד וּלְקַיֵּם כָּל הָעוֹלָמוֹת כָּל רֶגַע:

וְלֹא עוֹד, אֶלָּא שֶׁגַּם כָּל עִקַּר עִנְיַן הַתְּפִלָּה, אֵינָהּ תְּלוּיָה רַק בְּעֵסֶק הַתּוֹרָה הַקְּדוֹשָׁה, וּבִלְתָּהּ אֵינָהּ נִשְׁמַעַת חַס וְשָׁלוֹם, כְּמוֹ שֶׁאָמַר הַכָּתוּב (משלי כח, ט) "מֵסִיר אָזְנוֹ מִשְּׁמֹעַ תּוֹרָה גַּם תְּפִלָּתוֹ תּוֹעֵבָה", וּכְמוֹ שֶׁאָמְרוּ רַבּוֹתֵינוּ זִכְרוֹנָם לִבְרָכָה בְּשַׁבָּת שָׁם, וּבְמִשְׁלֵי רַבָּתָא פָּרָשָׁה כ"ח.

וְאָמְרוּ (בסוף סוטה מט, א): "כָּל הָעוֹסֵק בַּתּוֹרָה מִתּוֹךְ דֹּחַק, תְּפִלָּתוֹ נִשְׁמַעַת, וְאֵין הַפַּרְגּוֹד נִנְעָל בְּפָנָיו". וּבַזֹּהַר מִקֵּץ ר"ב ב' "וְעֵץ חַיִּים תַּאֲוָה בָאָה" (משלי יג, יב), תָּנִינָן,

מַאן דְּבָעֵי דְּקוּדְשָׁא בְּרִיךְ הוּא יְקַבֵּל צְלוֹתֵיהּ, יִשְׁתַּדֵּל בְּאוֹרַיְתָא, דְּאִיהִי עֵץ חַיִּים ["עֵץ חַיִּים תַּאֲוָה בָאָה", לָמַדְנוּ, מִי שֶׁרוֹצֶה שֶׁהַקָּדוֹשׁ בָּרוּךְ הוּא יְקַבֵּל תְּפִלָּתוֹ, יַעֲסֹק בַּתּוֹרָה שֶׁהִיא עֵץ חַיִּים וכו'.]

לָכֵן הַדִּין פָּסוּק בַּשַּׁ"ס (מגילה כז, א) "בֵּית הַכְּנֶסֶת מוּתָּר לַעֲשׂוֹתוֹ בֵּית הַמִּדְרָשׁ", מִשּׁוּם דְּעִלּוּיֵי קָא מַעֲלֵי לֵיהּ לִקְדֻשָּׁה יוֹתֵר חֲמוּרָה, שֶׁרַק הִיא הַנּוֹתֶנֶת הַשֶּׁפַע חִיּוּת וּקְדֻשָּׁה וְאוֹר לְכָל הָעוֹלָמוֹת, מִטַּעַם שֶׁהִיא לְמַעְלָה מִכֻּלָּם:

פֶּרֶק כ"ז

וְעוֹד זֹאת, יִתְרָה עֵרֶךְ וְיִתְרוֹן קְדֻשָּׁתָהּ הַנּוֹרָאָה מֵהָעוֹלָמוֹת, כִּי הָעֶלְיוֹנִים, אַף שֶׁקְּדֻשָּׁתָם רַבָּה מְאֹד, אָמְנָם כַּאֲשֶׁר נִשְׁתַּלְשְׁלוּ וְיָרְדוּ דֶּרֶךְ הִשְׁתַּלְשְׁלוּת וְהַדְרָגוֹת עֲצוּמוֹת, הֲגַם שֶׁבְּכָל עוֹלָם נִצְטַיֵּר וְנֶחְתַּם בּוֹ כָּל סִדְרֵי הָעוֹלָם שֶׁמֵּעָלָיו, בִּדְמוּתוֹ כְּצַלְמוֹ מַמָּשׁ כַּיָּדוּעַ, וּכְמוֹ שֶׁכָּתוּב בַּזֹּהַר יִתְרוֹ פ"ב ב', תָּאנָא, כְּגַוְנָא דִּלְעֵילָּא אִית לְתַתָּא מִינַּיְיהוּ, וְכֵן בְּכֻלְּהוּ עָלְמִין, כֻּלְּהוּ אֲחִידָן, דָּא בְּדָא, וְדָא בְּדָא. [לָמַדְנוּ, כְּעֵין שֶׁיֵּשׁ לְמַעְלָה כֵּן יֵשׁ לְמַטָּה מֵהֶן, וְכֵן בְּכָל הָעוֹלָמוֹת כֻּלָּם אֲחוּזִים זֶה בָּזֶה וְזֶה בָּזֶה]. וּכְמוֹ שֶׁכָּתוּב בְּעֵץ חַיִּים בְּעִנְיַן הָאַרְבַּע עוֹלָמוֹת אבי"ע, עַיֵּן שָׁם בְּשַׁעַר דְּרוּשֵׁי אבי"ע פֶּרֶק א', וּבְפֶרֶק ד' שָׁם, וּבְשַׁעַר הַשֵּׁמוֹת רֵישׁ פֶּרֶק א', עִם כָּל זֶה אֵינוֹ שָׁוֶה וְדוֹמֶה כְּלָל, עֵרֶךְ קְדֻשָּׁתוֹ וְאוֹרוֹ לְהָעוֹלָם שֶׁמֵּעָלָיו, עַד שֶׁכָּל כָּךְ נִתְעַבּוּ, וְנִתְמַעֲטוּ מִקְּדֻשָּׁתָם וְאוֹרָם דֶּרֶךְ הִשְׁתַּלְשְׁלוּת וְהַדְרָגוֹת עֲצוּמוֹת, עַד שֶׁבְּזֶה הָעוֹלָם נַעֲשׂוּ חוּלִין, שֶׁאָנוּ נוֹהֲגִין בָּהֶן מִנְהָג חוֹל.

אָמְנָם הַתּוֹרָה הַקְּדוֹשָׁה, אַף שֶׁגַּם הִיא נִשְׁתַּלְשְׁלָה וְיָרְדָה מִמְּקוֹר שָׁרְשָׁהּ הָעֶלְיוֹן בַּקֹּדֶשׁ, מַדְרֵגוֹת אֵין שִׁעוּר, מֵעוֹלָם לְעוֹלָם, וּמִמַּדְרֵגָה לְמַדְרֵגָה, עִם כָּל זֶה, קְדֻשָּׁתָהּ הָרִאשׁוֹנָה, כְּמוֹ שֶׁהוּא בִּמְקוֹר שָׁרְשָׁהּ, רֵאשִׁית דַּרְכָּהּ בַּקֹּדֶשׁ, כִּדְקָאֵי קָאֵי גַּם בְּזֶה הָעוֹלָם, שֶׁכֻּלָּהּ קֹדֶשׁ, וְאָסוּר לִנְהֹג בָּהּ מִנְהַג חוֹל חַס וְשָׁלוֹם, שֶׁגַּם הַהִרְהוּר בְּדִבְרֵי תּוֹרָה אָסוּר בִּמְקוֹמוֹת הַמְּטֻנָּפִים.

וְלָזֹאת, הֶחְמִירוּ וְהִפְלִיגוּ רַבּוֹתֵינוּ זִכְרוֹנָם לִבְרָכָה בְּעָנְשׁוֹ, וְאָמְרוּ (ברכות כד ע"ב) שֶׁגַּם הוּא בִּכְלָל "כִּי דְבַר ה' בָּזָה" (במדבר טו, לא). וְסֵיפֵיהּ דְּהַאי קְרָא "הִכָּרֵת תִּכָּרֵת", וּפֵרְשׁוּ רַבּוֹתֵינוּ זִכְרוֹנָם לִבְרָכָה "הִכָּרֵת" — בָּעוֹלָם הַזֶּה, "תִּכָּרֵת" — לָעוֹלָם הַבָּא.

וְאָמְרוּ (מגילה לב, א) הָאוֹחֵז סֵפֶר תּוֹרָה עָרוֹם, נִקְבָּר עָרוֹם מֵאוֹתָהּ מִצְוָה. גַּם אָסְרוּ לְטַלְטְלָהּ מִמָּקוֹם לְמָקוֹם, וְאַף מִבֵּי כְּנִישְׁתָּא לְבֵי כְּנִשְׁתָּא אָסְרוּ בַּזֹּהַר פָּרָשַׁת אַחֲרֵי (ע"א ב) לְטַלְטְלָהּ, עַיֵּן שָׁם, מִטַּעַם שֶׁהִיא לְעוֹלָם בִּקְדֻשָּׁתָהּ הָרִאשׁוֹנָה עוֹמֶדֶת.

(וְכֵן אֲפִלּוּ הָאָדָם, שֶׁשֹּׁרֶשׁ נִשְׁמָתוֹ הִיא מֵעוֹלָם עֶלְיוֹן וְגָבוֹהַּ מְאֹד, מֵהָעוֹלָמוֹת הָעֶלְיוֹנִים, וְיִקַּח לוֹ בְּשִׂכְלוֹ מַחֲשָׁבָה נְכוֹנָה, לְהִתְדַּבֵּק לְטָהֳרַת אֵיזֶה מִדָּה נְכוֹנָה, הוּא רַשַּׁאי לֵילֵךְ בְּזֹאת הַמַּחֲשָׁבָה גַּם בִּמְקוֹמוֹת הַמְּטֻנָּפִים, וְאִלּוּ הַהִרְהוּר דִּבְרֵי תּוֹרָה בְּדִינֵי נְגָעִים וְאֳהָלוֹת, אוֹ שְׁאָרֵי דִּינִים וְאֵיזֶה דִּבְרֵי תּוֹרָה שֶׁתִּהְיֶה, אָסוּר בִּמְקוֹמוֹת הַמְּטֻנָּפִים):

וְהוּא גַּם כֵּן עִנְיַן מַאֲמָרָם זִכְרוֹנָם לִבְרָכָה בַּזֹּהַר, דְּקוּדְשָׁא בְּרִיךְ הוּא וְאוֹרַיְתָא חַד. וְהוּא,

שֶׁאַף עַל פִּי שֶׁהָעוֹלָמוֹת הוֹלְכִים כֻּלָּם דֶּרֶךְ הַדְרָגָה וְהִשְׁתַּלְשְׁלוּת וְשִׁנּוּיִים רַבִּים בְּעֵרֶךְ קְדֻשָּׁתָם, כָּל זֶה הוּא רַק מִצִּדֵּנוּ, אֲבָל מִצִּדּוֹ יִתְבָּרֵךְ – אֵין שׁוּם חִלּוּק וְשִׁנּוּי מְקוֹמוֹת כְּלָל חַס וְשָׁלוֹם, וּכְמוֹ שֶׁכָּתוּב (מלאכי ג, ו): "אֲנִי ה' לֹא שָׁנִיתִי", וְלֹא נִשְׁתַּנָּה הַקְּדֻשָּׁה, כְּמוֹ שֶׁכָּתוּב בָּאֹרֶךְ לְמַעְלָה בְּשַׁעַר ג' (פ"ג וכו'), עַיֵּן שָׁם.

כֵּן הַתּוֹרָה הַקְּדוֹשָׁה, אַף כִּי יָרְדָה וְנִשְׁתַּלְשְׁלָה דֶּרֶךְ הַדְּרָגוֹת רַבּוֹת עֲצוּמוֹת, עִם כָּל זֶה, הִיא לֹא נִשְׁתַּנְּתָה מִקְּדֻשָּׁתָהּ כְּלָל, וּבִקְדֻשָּׁתָהּ הָרִאשׁוֹנָה עוֹמֶדֶת גַּם בְּזֶה הָעוֹלָם הַתַּחְתּוֹן, כַּאֲשֶׁר הָיְתָה בְּאָמְנָה אִתּוֹ יִתְבָּרֵךְ בִּמְקוֹר שָׁרְשָׁהּ, בְּלֹא שׁוּם חִלּוּק וְשִׁנּוּי מָקוֹם כְּלָל.

אָמְנָם, אַף עַל פִּי שֶׁמִּצִּדּוֹ יִתְבָּרֵךְ – כָּל הַמְּקוֹמוֹת שָׁוִים, בְּלִי שׁוּם שִׁנּוּי כְּלָל, שֶׁאֵין מְקוֹמוֹת הַמְּטֻנָּפִים חוֹצְצִים לְאַחְדּוּתוֹ וְעֶצֶם קְדֻשָּׁתוֹ יִתְבָּרַךְ, וְכֵן הוּא בְּעִנְיַן עֶצֶם קְדֻשַּׁת הַתּוֹרָה הַקְּדוֹשָׁה, עִם כָּל זֶה, אֲנַחְנוּ נֶאֱסַרְנוּ לְדַבֵּר, גַּם לְהַרְהֵר בָּהּ, בַּמְּבוֹאוֹת הַמְּטֻנָּפוֹת, כִּי מִצִּדֵּנוּ וַדַּאי יֵשׁ חִלּוּק וְשִׁנּוּי מְקוֹמוֹת, כְּמוֹ שֶׁנִּתְבָּאֵר שָׁם בָּאֹרֶךְ.

אֲבָל הַתּוֹרָה הַקְּדוֹשָׁה בְּעַצְמוּתָהּ, לֹא נִשְׁתַּנְּתָה בְּסִבַּת יְרִידָתָהּ מִקְּדֻשָּׁתָהּ וְאוֹרָהּ הָעֶלְיוֹן, רַק שֶׁטֶּחַ עֵינֵינוּ מֵרְאוֹת בְּעֶצֶם קְדֻשָּׁתָהּ וְאוֹרָהּ הַפְּנִימִי. וְלָכֵן אָמַר דָּוִד הַמֶּלֶךְ עָלָיו הַשָּׁלוֹם "גַּל עֵינַי וְאַבִּיטָה נִפְלָאוֹת מִתּוֹרָתֶךָ" (תהלים קיט, יח), כִּי בֶּאֱמֶת קְדֻשַּׁת וְאוֹר הַתּוֹרָה הַקְּדוֹשָׁה, הֵם פְּנִימִיּוּת סְתָרֶיהָ, הֵמָּה מְפֹרָשִׁים וְנִגְלִים, וּמְאִירִים בִּקְדֻשַּׁת אוֹרָם הָעֶלְיוֹן כַּאֲשֶׁר הוּא, רַק שֶׁעֵינֵינוּ אֵין יְכוֹלוֹת לִסְבֹּל עֶצֶם קְדֻשָּׁתָהּ וְאוֹרָהּ כַּאֲשֶׁר הוּא:

פֶּרֶק כ"ח

וְלָזֹאת אַף הִיא, דֶּרֶךְ יְרִידָתָהּ וְהִשְׁתַּלְשְׁלוּתָהּ מִמַּדְרֵגָה לְמַדְרֵגָה וּמֵעוֹלָם לְעוֹלָם, צִמְצְמָה עַצְמָהּ, לְהִתְלַבֵּשׁ בְּכָל עוֹלָם לְדַבֵּר בְּעִנְיְנֵי אוֹתוֹ הָעוֹלָם, כְּפִי עִנְיַן וְעֵרֶךְ אוֹתוֹ הָעוֹלָם, כְּדֵי שֶׁיּוּכַל לִסְבֹּל קְדֻשָּׁתָהּ וְאוֹרָהּ, עַד שֶׁבִּרְדִתָהּ לָבֹא לְזֶה הָעוֹלָם, נִתְלַבְּשָׁה גַּם כֵּן לְדַבֵּר בְּעֶרְכֵּי וְעִנְיְנֵי זֶה הָעוֹלָם, וְסִפּוּרִין דְּהַאי עָלְמָא, כְּדֵי שֶׁיּוּכַל זֶה הָעוֹלָם לִסְבֹּל קְדֻשַּׁת אוֹרָהּ. אָמְנָם, אִם שֶׁהִיא מְדַבֶּרֶת בַּתַּחְתּוֹנִים, רוֹמֶזֶת הִיא בָּהֶם גּוּפֵי תּוֹרָה, וְעִנְיָנִים פְּנִימִיִּים, וּפְנִימִיִּים לִפְנִימִיִּים, גָּבוֹהַּ מֵעַל גָּבוֹהַּ עַד אֵין תַּכְלִית.

וְעַיֵּן בַּזֹּהַר בְּהַעֲלֹתְךָ קנ"ב א', רַבִּי שִׁמְעוֹן אוֹמֵר כו', וּבְפָרָשַׁת תּוֹלְדוֹת קמ"ה ב', אָמַר רַבִּי יוֹסֵי, וַדַּאי כָּל מַה דְּעָבִיד קוּדְשָׁא בְּרִיךְ הוּא בְּאַרְעָא, כֹּלָּא הֲוָה בְּרָזָא דְּחָכְמְתָא [אָמַר רַבִּי יוֹסֵי, וַדַּאי כָּל מַה שֶּׁהַקָּדוֹשׁ בָּרוּךְ הוּא עוֹשֶׂה בָּאָרֶץ, הַכֹּל הוּא בְּסוֹד הַחָכְמָה, וכו']. וּבְפָרָשַׁת בָּלָק ר"ב א' תּוּ פָּתַח וְאָמַר כו' כַּמָּה טָבִין אִינוּן אָרְחִין וּשְׁבִילִין דְּאוֹרַיְתָא [עוֹד פָּתַח וְאָמַר וכו', כַּמָּה טוֹבִים הֵם אוֹרָחוֹת וּשְׁבִילִים שֶׁל הַתּוֹרָה, וכו']. וּבְפָרָשַׁת בְּשַׁלַּח נ"ה סוֹף ע"ב, רַבִּי אַבָּא פָּתַח כו', כַּמָּה אִית לָן לְאִסְתַּכְּלָא בְּפִתְגָּמֵי אוֹרַיְתָא [רַבִּי אַבָּא פָּתַח, כַּמָּה יֵשׁ לָנוּ לְהִסְתַּכֵּל בְּדִבְרֵי תּוֹרָה וכו']. וּבְפָרָשַׁת תּוֹלְדוֹת קל"ד סוֹף ע"ב, בְּאוֹרַיְתָא אִנּוּן כָּל רָזִין עִלָּאִין חֲתִימִין [בַּתּוֹרָה הֵם כָּל סוֹדוֹת הָעֶלְיוֹנִים חֲתוּמִים וכו']. וְהֵם פְּרָטוּת עִנְיְנֵי כָּל הָרִבֵּי רִבּוֹאוֹת הָעוֹלָמוֹת וְהַמַּדְרֵגוֹת, שֶׁנִּתְלַבְּשָׁה בָּהֶם דֶּרֶךְ יְרִידָתָהּ.

וְלָכֵן שְׁגוּרָה בְּפִי הַזֹּהַר, דְּאוֹרַיְתָא כֻּלָּהּ אִיהִי "סָתִים וְגַלְיָא", שֶׁהוּא מְבֹאָר לְכָל מֵבִין

שֶׁפֵּרוּשׁוֹ הוּא, שֶׁהוּא הַדֶּרֶךְ הַ"נִּסְתָּר" מֵהַתּוֹרָה הַקְּדוֹשָׁה, שֶׁאֵינוֹ כָּתוּב מְפֹרָשׁ וּמְבֹאָר בָּהּ, אֶלָּא שֶׁנִּסְתָּר וְנִטְמָן הָעִנְיָנִים אֵלּוּ בְּרֶמֶז בִּדְבָרֶיהָ, וְדֶרֶךְ הַ"נִּגְלֶה" שֶׁבָּהּ הוּא הַפְּשׁוּטוֹ שֶׁל מִקְרָא, שֶׁהוּא כָּתוּב מְפֹרָשׁ וּמְבֹאָר בָּהּ.

(וְלֹא כְּמוֹ שֶׁרָאִיתִי בְּסֵפֶר כָּתוּב, מֵאֶחָד שֶׁחָקַר עַל הָעִנְיָן, מִפְּנֵי מָה קוֹרְאִים לְחָכְמַת הַקַּבָּלָה בְּשֵׁם "נִסְתָּר", הֲלֹא מִי שֶׁמֵּבִין בָּהֶם אֶצְלוֹ הֵם נִגְלִים, וְלַאֲנָשִׁים שֶׁאֵינָם יוֹדְעִים וּמְבִינִים הֲלֹא יֵשׁ שֶׁגַּם פְּשׁוּטוֹ שֶׁל מִקְרָא אֵינָם יוֹדְעִים לְפָרֵשׁ, וְאֶצְלָם גַּם הַפְּשׁוּטוֹ שֶׁל מִקְרָא דַּרְכּוֹ נִסְתָּרָה מֵהֶם, וְתֵרֵץ שָׁם מָה שֶׁתֵּרֵץ).

וְעַיֵּן זֹהַר בְּהַעֲלוֹתְךָ קמ"ט א' וב', כַּמָּה חֲבִיבִין מִלֵּי דְּאוֹרַיְתָא, דִּבְכָל מִלָּה וּמִלָּה אִית רָזִין עִלָּאִין [כַּמָּה חֲבִיבִין הֵם דִּבְרֵי תּוֹרָה, שֶׁבְּכָל מִלָּה וּמִלָּה יֵשׁ סוֹדוֹת עֶלְיוֹנִים] כו', עַיֵּן שָׁם. וְכָל אֶחָד מִסְתַּכֵּל בְּסִתְרֵי עֹמֶק פְּנִימִיּוּתָם, כְּפִי רֹב חָכְמָתוֹ וְזֹךְ שִׂכְלוֹ, וּקְדֻשַּׁת טָהֳרַת לְבָבוֹ, וְרֹב עִסְקוֹ וְהֶגְיוֹנוֹ בָּהּ.

אָמְנָם, עִקַּר הַטַּעֲמֵי תּוֹרָה, סוֹד נִשְׁמָתָא לְנִשְׁמָתָא דִּילָהּ, סִתְרֵי סְתָרֶיהָ, הֵמָּה דְּבָרִים שֶׁכִּסָּה עַתִּיק יוֹמִין, וְהֶעְתִּיקָן מִבְּרִיּוֹתָיו, וְאִישׁ לֹא יְדָעָם עֲדַיִן, רַק אָבִינוּ הָרִאשׁוֹן, הוּא אֲשֶׁר הִשִּׂיג בִּבְחִינַת נִשְׁמָתָא לְנִשְׁמָתָא דִּילֵיהּ, שֶׁבָּהּ הָיָה מִסְתַּכֵּל בְּזִיהֲרָא עִלָּאָה, נִשְׁמָתָא לְנִשְׁמָתָא שֶׁל הַתּוֹרָה הַקְּדוֹשָׁה, וְהַחָכְמוֹת הָעֶלְיוֹנוֹת הָיוּ גְּלוּיוֹת לְפָנָיו בְּשֹׁרֶשׁ שָׁרְשָׁם הָעֶלְיוֹן.

וּמֵעֵת אֲשֶׁר חָטָא, וְאִסְתַּלֵּק מִנֵּיהּ הַזִּיהֲרָא עִלָּאָה, וְנִתְבַּלְבְּלוּ וְנִתְעַרְבְּבוּ הַסְּדָרִים הָעֶלְיוֹנִים, נִסְתְּמוּ גַּם הַנְּתִיבוֹת וּשְׁבִילִין עֶלְיוֹנִים דְּחָכְמְתָא דְּאוֹרַיְתָא, סוֹד הַנִּשְׁמָתָא לְנִשְׁמָתָא דִּילָהּ.

וְגַם בְּמַעֲמָד הַקָּדוֹשׁ בְּעֵת קַבָּלַת הַתּוֹרָה הַקְּדוֹשָׁה, אַף דְּאִתְבַּסַּם עָלְמָא, עַד שֶׁאָמְרוּ זִכְרוֹנָם לִבְרָכָה (שבת קמו, א) "יִשְׂרָאֵל שֶׁעָמְדוּ עַל הַר סִינַי פָּסְקָה זֻהֲמָתָן", עִם כָּל זֶה, לֹא זָכוּ לְהַשִּׂיג רַק עֹמֶק פְּנִימִיּוּת הַנִּשְׁמָתָא דְּאוֹרַיְתָא, אֲבָל לֹא בְּחִינַת הַנִּשְׁמָתָא לְנִשְׁמָתָא. עַד אֲשֶׁר יֵעָרֶה רוּחַ מִמָּרוֹם, וְיִשְׁפֹּךְ הוּא יִתְבָּרַךְ אֶת רוּחוֹ עַל כָּל בָּשָׂר, אָז יִתְגַּלּוּ מַבּוּעִין דְּחָכְמְתָא, נְתִיבוֹת פְּלִיאוֹת הַחָכְמָה הָעֶלְיוֹנָה, נִשְׁמָתָא לְנִשְׁמָתָא דִּילָהּ.

כְּמוֹ שֶׁכָּתוּב בַּזֹּהַר בְּהַעֲלוֹתְךָ קנ"ב א', אוֹרַיְתָא אִית לָהּ גּוּפָא כו', טִפְּשִׁין דְּעָלְמָא לָא מִסְתַּכְּלֵי אֶלָּא בְּהַהוּא לְבוּשָׁא כו'. אִנּוּן דְּיַדְעִין יַתִּיר – לָא מִסְתַּכְּלָן בִּלְבוּשָׁא אֶלָּא בְּגוּפָא, דְּאִיהוּ תְּחוֹת הַהוּא לְבוּשָׁא. חַכִּימִין עַבְדֵי דְּמַלְכָּא עִלָּאָה, אִנּוּן דְּקָיְמוּ בְּטוּרָא דְּסִינַי – לָא אִסְתַּכְּלֵי אֶלָּא בְּנִשְׁמָתָא, דְּאִיהִי עִקָּרָא דְּכֹלָּא אוֹרַיְתָא מַמָּשׁ. וּלְעָלְמָא דְּאָתֵי – זְמִינִין לְאִסְתַּכָּלָא בְּנִשְׁמָתָא דְּנִשְׁמָתָא דְּאוֹרַיְתָא. [הַתּוֹרָה יֵשׁ לָהּ גּוּף וכו' הַטִּפְּשִׁים שֶׁבָּעוֹלָם – אֵינָם מִסְתַּכְּלִים אֶלָּא בַּלְּבוּשׁ הַהוּא וכו'. אֵלּוּ שֶׁיּוֹדְעִים יוֹתֵר – אֵינָם מִסְתַּכְּלִים בַּלְּבוּשׁ, אֶלָּא בַּגּוּף, שֶׁהוּא תַּחַת הַלְּבוּשׁ הַהוּא. הַחֲכָמִים עַבְדֵי הַמֶּלֶךְ הָעֶלְיוֹן, אוֹתָם שֶׁעָמְדוּ בְּהַר סִינַי – אֵינָם מִסְתַּכְּלִים אֶלָּא בַּנְּשָׁמָה, שֶׁהִיא עִקַּר הַכֹּל תּוֹרָה מַמָּשׁ. וְלֶעָתִיד לָבוֹא – עֲתִידִים לְהִסְתַּכֵּל בַּנְּשָׁמָה שֶׁל נְשָׁמָה שֶׁל הַתּוֹרָה]. וּכְמוֹ שֶׁכָּתוּב (ישעיה ל, כ) "וְהָיוּ עֵינֶיךָ רוֹאוֹת אֶת מוֹרֶיךָ וְלֹא יִכָּנֵף עוֹד מוֹרֶיךָ".

וְהוּא עִנְיַן הָאוֹר שֶׁל יוֹם רִאשׁוֹן, שֶׁגְּנָזוֹ לַצַּדִּיקִים לֶעָתִיד לָבֹא (חגיגה יב, א). וְזֶהוּ שֶׁאָמְרוּ רַבּוֹתֵינוּ זִכְרוֹנָם לִבְרָכָה (נדרים ח, ב) "לֶעָתִיד לָבֹא, הַקָּדוֹשׁ בָּרוּךְ הוּא מוֹצִיא חַמָּה מִנַּרְתִּיקָהּ" כו', וְהוּא סוֹד הָ"עֵדֶן" כַּיָּדוּעַ, שֶׁהוּא הַבְּחִינַת נִשְׁמְתָא דְּנִשְׁמְתָא.

וְאָדָם הָרִאשׁוֹן קֹדֶם חֶטְאוֹ הָיָה דָּר בַּ"גַּן", וּמִתּוֹכוֹ הָיָה מִסְתַּכֵּל בָּ"עֵדֶן" הַנַּ"ל, וּבְחֶטְאוֹ אֲשֶׁר מֵאָז נִסְתַּלְּקָה מִמֶּנּוּ זֹאת הַבְּחִינָה הָעֶלְיוֹנָה, לָכֵן גֹּרַשׁ אָז מִגַּן עֵדֶן. וְהוּא סוֹד הַצֵּרוּפֵי אוֹתִיּוֹת דִּילָהּ, כַּאֲשֶׁר הִיא כְּתוּבָה בַּמָּרוֹם, כְּמוֹ שֶׁנִּתְבָּאֵר לְעֵיל סוֹף שַׁעַר ב' (סוֹף פֶּרֶק יז).

וְעַל זֶה אָמְרוּ בְּמִדְרַשׁ תְּהִלִּים רֵישׁ מִזְמוֹר ג', "לֹא יָדַע אֱנוֹשׁ עֶרְכָּהּ" כו' (איוב כח, יג), לֹא נִתְּנוּ פָּרְשִׁיּוֹתֶיהָ שֶׁל תּוֹרָה עַל הַסֵּדֶר, שֶׁאִלְמָלֵא נִתְּנוּ עַל הַסֵּדֶר, כָּל מִי שֶׁהוּא קוֹרֵא בָּהֶן, מִיָּד הָיָה יָכוֹל לִבְרֹאת עוֹלָם וּלְהַחֲיוֹת מֵתִים [וְלַעֲשׂוֹת מוֹפְתִים, לְפִיכָךְ נִתְעַלֵּם סִידוּרָהּ שֶׁל תּוֹרָה.]

וְנָשׁוּב לְבָאֵר קְצָת עִנְיַן הַהֶפְרֵשׁ וְיִתְרוֹן אוֹר קְדֻשַּׁת הַתּוֹרָה הַקְּדוֹשָׁה עַל הַמִּצְוֹת:

פֶּרֶק כ"ט

הִנֵּה רַבּוֹתֵינוּ זִכְרוֹנָם לִבְרָכָה אָמְרוּ (סוטה כ"א א') דָּרַשׁ רַבִּי מְנַחֵם בַּר יוֹסֵי "כִּי נֵר מִצְוָה וְתוֹרָה אוֹר" (משלי ו, כג), תָּלָה הַכָּתוּב אֶת הַמִּצְוָה – בְּנֵר, וְאֶת הַתּוֹרָה – בְּאוֹר, לוֹמַר לְךָ, מַה נֵּר אֵינוֹ מֵאִיר אֶלָּא לְפִי שָׁעָה, אַף מִצְוָה אֵינָהּ מְגִנָּה אֶלָּא לְפִי שָׁעָה, וּמָה אוֹר מֵאִיר לְעוֹלָם, אַף תּוֹרָה מְגִינָה לְעוֹלָם, וּמַסִּיק, דְּתוֹרָה, בְּעִידְנָא דְּעָסִיק בָּהּ מְגִינָּה וּמַצְּלָה, בְּעִדְנָא דְּלָא עָסִיק בָּהּ אֲגוּנֵי מַגְנֵי, אֲצוּלֵי לָא מַצְלָה, מִצְוָה, בֵּין בְּעִדְנָא דְּעָסִיק בָּהּ בֵּין בְּעִדְנָא דְּלָא עָסִיק בַּהּ, אֲגוּנֵי מַגְנֵי, אֲצוּלֵי לָא מַצְּלָה. וְכֵן אָמְרוּ שָׁם: עֲבֵרָה מְכַבָּה מִצְוָה, וְאֵין עֲבֵרָה מְכַבָּה תּוֹרָה.

וְכֵן יָדוּעַ בַּזֹּהַר, שֶׁהַתַּרְיַ"ג מִצְוֹת הֵם מְכֻוָּנִים נֶגֶד הַתַּרְיַ"ג אֵיבָרִים וְגִידִים שֶׁבָּאָדָם, וּבַעֲשׂוֹת הָאָדָם אַחַת מִמִּצְוֹת ה' כָּרָאוּי, מִתְקַדֵּשׁ עַל יָדָהּ אוֹתוֹ הָאֵבֶר הַמְכֻוָּן נֶגְדָּהּ, וּמְחַיָּה אוֹתוֹ. אוֹ אִם בָּא וְנִזְדַּמֵּן לְיָדוֹ אַחַת מִמִּצְוֹת ה' אֲשֶׁר לֹא תֵעָשֶׂנָה וְנִמְנַע וּפֵרַשׁ וְלֹא עֲשָׂאָהּ, אֲשֶׁר עָלָיו אָמְרוּ רַבּוֹתֵינוּ זִכְרוֹנָם לִבְרָכָה (קִדּוּשִׁין לט, ב): "יָשַׁב אָדָם וְלֹא עָבַר עֲבֵירָה, נוֹתְנִין לוֹ שָׂכָר כְּעוֹשֶׂה מִצְוָה", נִטְהַר וְנִתְקַדֵּשׁ גַּם כֵּן אוֹתוֹ הַגִּיד הַפְּרָטִי הַמְכֻוָּן נֶגְדָּהּ, וּמְחַיָּה אוֹתוֹ, כְּמוֹ שֶׁאָמַר הַכָּתוּב (ויקרא יח, ה) "אֵלֶּה הַמִּצְוֹת אֲשֶׁר יַעֲשֶׂה אוֹתָם הָאָדָם, וָחַי בָּהֶם" שֶׁאָז הוּא נִקְרָא "אִישׁ חַי".

אָמְנָם כְּשֶׁהָאָדָם עוֹסֵק בַּתּוֹרָה, כְּתִיב בָּהּ "וּלְכָל בְּשָׂרוֹ מַרְפֵּא" (משלי ד, כב), וּכְמוֹ שֶׁאָמְרוּ (עירובין נ"ד א'): "חָשׁ בְּרֹאשׁוֹ יַעֲסֹק בַּתּוֹרָה, שֶׁנֶּאֱמַר "כִּי לִוְיַת חֵן הֵם לְרֹאשֶׁךָ", חָשׁ בִּגְרוֹנוֹ יַעֲסֹק בַּתּוֹרָה, שֶׁנֶּאֱמַר כו', חָשׁ בִּבְנֵי מֵעָיו יַעֲסֹק בַּתּוֹרָה כו', חָשׁ בְּכָל גּוּפוֹ יַעֲסֹק בַּתּוֹרָה שֶׁנֶּאֱמַר "וּלְכָל בְּשָׂרוֹ מַרְפֵּא". וְכֵן הוּא בְּוַיִּקְרָא רַבָּה פָּרָשָׁה י"ב, וּבְתַנְחוּמָא יִתְרוֹ, וּבְמִדְרַשׁ תְּהִלִּים מִזְמוֹר י"ט, שֶׁעַל יְדֵי עֵסֶק הַתּוֹרָה, מִתְקַדְּשִׁים וּמִזְדַּכְּכִים כָּל אֵבָרָיו וְגִידָיו וְכֹחוֹתָיו כֻּלָּם. וְלָכֵן אָמְרוּ (פאה, א) "וְתַלְמוּד תּוֹרָה כְּנֶגֶד כֻּלָּם".

וְכֵן לְהֵפוּךְ חַס וְשָׁלוֹם, עֲוֹן בִּטּוּל תּוֹרָה הוּא גַּם כֵּן כְּנֶגֶד כֻּלָּם, כִּי בְּעָבְרוֹ עַל אַחַת מִמִּצְוֹת ה', נִפְגָּם רַק אוֹתוֹ הָאֵבֶר אוֹ הַגִּיד לְבַד הַמְּכֻוָּן נֶגְדָּהּ, שֶׁהַחִיּוּת שֶׁל הַקְּדֻשָּׁה וְאוֹר הָעֶלְיוֹן, סוֹד שֵׁם הֲוָיָ"ה יִתְבָּרַךְ הַשּׁוֹרֶה עַל כָּל אֵבֶר, מִסְתַּלֶּקֶת הֵימֶנּוּ חַס וְשָׁלוֹם, וּמוֹתָא דְּסִטְרָא אַחֲרָא שַׁרְיָא בֵּיהּ רַחֲמָנָא לִיצְלָן, וְנַעֲשָׂה בַּעַל מוּם, חָסֵר מֵאוֹתוֹ אֵבֶר.

אֲבָל בַּעֲוֹן בִּטּוּל תּוֹרָה חַס וְשָׁלוֹם, הוּא פּוֹגֵם אֶת כָּל אֵבָרָיו וְגִידָיו, וְכָל כֹּחוֹתָיו כֻּלָּם, וְחִיּוּת הַקְּדֻשָּׁה שֶׁל כָּל גּוּפוֹ מִסְתַּלֶּקֶת, וְהוּא נַעֲשֶׂה תֵּכֶף כְּמֵת מַמָּשׁ, שֶׁאֵין לוֹ שׁוּם חִיּוּת חַס וְשָׁלוֹם, כְּמוֹ שֶׁכָּתוּב (דברים ל, כ) "כִּי הוּא חַיֶּיךָ" וכו'.

וּכְמוֹ שֶׁאָמְרוּ רַבּוֹתֵינוּ זִכְרוֹנָם לִבְרָכָה (ע"ז ג, ב): "מַאי דִּכְתִיב (חבקוק א, יד), "וַתַּעֲשֶׂה אָדָם כִּדְגֵי הַיָּם", לָמָּה נִמְשְׁלוּ בְּנֵי אָדָם לִדְגֵי הַיָּם, לוֹמַר לְךָ, מָה דָּגִים שֶׁבַּיָּם כֵּיוָן שֶׁפּוֹרְשִׁין מִן הַמַּיִם מִיָּד מֵתִים, כָּךְ בְּנֵי אָדָם כֵּיוָן שֶׁפּוֹרְשִׁין מִן הַתּוֹרָה מִיָּד מֵתִים. (כָּךְ הִיא גִּרְסַת הַיַּלְקוּט חֲבַקּוּק רֶמֶז תקס"ב עַל פָּסוּק הַנַּ"ל). וּבְרַעְיָא מְהֵימְנָא סוֹף פָּרָשַׁת שְׁמִינִי, מַה נּוּנֵי יַמָּא חִיּוּתָן בְּמַיָּא, אוּף תַּלְמִידֵי חֲכָמִים מָארֵי מַתְנִיתִין חִיּוּתַיְהוּ בְּאוֹרַיְתָא, וְאִי אִתְפָּרְשׁוּ מִנָּהּ מִיָּד מֵתִים, [מַה דְּגֵי הַיָּם חִיּוּתָן בַּמַּיִם, אַף תַּלְמִידֵי חֲכָמִים בַּעֲלֵי מִשְׁנָה חִיּוּתָם בַּתּוֹרָה, וְאִם נִפְרָדִים מִן הַתּוֹרָה מִיָּד מֵתִים.]

וְזֶהוּ שֶׁאָמְרוּ רַבּוֹתֵינוּ זִכְרוֹנָם לִבְרָכָה (ברכות ה, א): "אִם רוֹאֶה אָדָם שֶׁיִּסּוּרִים בָּאִים עָלָיו יְפַשְׁפֵּשׁ בְּמַעֲשָׂיו, פִּשְׁפֵּשׁ וְלֹא מָצָא יִתְלֶה בְּבִטּוּל תּוֹרָה". וְלִכְאוֹרָה יִפָּלֵא, כֵּיוָן שֶׁיֵּשׁ בְּיָדוֹ עֲוֹן בִּטּוּל תּוֹרָה חַס וְשָׁלוֹם, הֲלֹא אֵין לְךָ "מָצָא" יוֹתֵר מִזֶּה, וְאֵיךְ אָמַר "וְלֹא מָצָא". אָמְנָם כְּבָר נִזְהַר רַשִׁ"י זִכְרוֹנוֹ לִבְרָכָה מִזֶּה, בְּמַה שֶּׁפֵּרֵשׁ שָׁם, שֶׁלֹּא מָצָא עָוֹן שֶׁיִּהְיוּ רְאוּיִין הַיִּסּוּרִין הַלָּלוּ לָבֹא עָלָיו.

וְהוּא, כִּי מִדָּתוֹ יִתְבָּרַךְ, שֶׁ"פֹּעַל אָדָם יְשַׁלֵּם" מִדָּה כְּנֶגֶד מִדָּה, שֶׁאוֹתוֹ הָאֵבֶר שֶׁקִּלְקֵל וּפָגַם בְּחֶטְאוֹ, עַל אוֹתוֹ הָאֵבֶר עַצְמוֹ מֵבִיא עָלָיו יִסּוּרִין, וְתַכְלִית כַּוָּנָתוֹ יִתְבָּרַךְ בָּזֶה, כְּדֵי שֶׁמִּתּוֹךְ הַיִּסּוּרִין יָבִין הָאָדָם וְיֵדַע עַל אֵיזֶה חֵטְא בָּאוּ, וְיָשִׁיב אֶל לִבּוֹ לִהְיוֹת מוֹדֶה וְעוֹזֵב, וָשָׁב וְרָפָא לוֹ.

זֶהוּ שֶׁאָמְרוּ, שֶׁאִם רוֹאֶה אָדָם שֶׁיִּסּוּרִין בָּאִים עָלָיו יְפַשְׁפֵּשׁ בְּמַעֲשָׂיו, וְיָבִין דַּרְכּוֹ מִתּוֹךְ הַיִּסּוּרִין. וְאִם פִּשְׁפֵּשׁ, וְלֹא מָצָא בְּיָדוֹ עָוֹן אֲשֶׁר חֵטְא, בְּאוֹתוֹ אֵבֶר וּבְאוֹתוֹ אֹפֶן, שֶׁיִּהְיוּ רְאוּיִין הַיִּסּוּרִין הַלָּלוּ דַּוְקָא לָבֹא עָלָיו, מִדָּה כְּנֶגֶד מִדָּה, יִתְלֶה בְּבִטּוּל תּוֹרָה, כִּי בַּעֲוֹן בִּטּוּל תּוֹרָה לֹא שַׁיָּךְ מִדָּה כְּנֶגֶד מִדָּה, כִּי בִּטּוּלָהּ חַס וְשָׁלוֹם הוּא נוֹגֵעַ לְכָל גּוּפוֹ, אֵיזֶה מָקוֹם וְאֵיזֶה אֵבֶר שֶׁיִּהְיֶה, כַּנַּ"ל.

וְטַעְמוֹ שֶׁל דָּבָר, הוּא כְּמוֹ שֶׁכָּתַבְתִּי לְעֵיל בְּשַׁעַר א' פֶּרֶק ו', שֶׁמְּקוֹר שָׁרְשָׁם הָעֶלְיוֹן שֶׁל הַמִּצְוֹת, תְּלוּיוֹת וּקְשׁוּרוֹת בְּסוֹד הַשִּׁעוּר קוֹמָה, וּפִרְקֵי הַמֶּרְכָּבָה סוֹד הָאָדָם הָעֶלְיוֹן כִּבְיָכוֹל, שֶׁכָּל מִצְוָה פְּרָטִית, שָׁרְשָׁהּ הָעֶלְיוֹן קָשׁוּר וְנֶאֱחָז בְּעוֹלָם וְכֹחַ אֶחָד מֵהַשִּׁעוּר קוֹמָה. וְכֵן זֶה כָּל הָאָדָם, שֶׁהוּא גַּם כֵּן מְתֻקָּן וּמְסֻדָּר, בְּכָל אֵבָרָיו וְגִידָיו וּפְרָקָיו וְכָל פְּרָטֵי כֹּחוֹתָיו, בְּתַבְנִית דְּמוּת הַמֶּרְכָּבָה וְשִׁעוּר קוֹמָה.

וְלָזֹאת, כָּל מִצְוָה מְכֻוֶּנֶת נֶגֶד אֵבֶר אוֹ גִּיד אֶחָד פְּרָטִי שֶׁבָּאָדָם, אָמְנָם הַתּוֹרָה הַקְּדוֹשָׁה

הִיא כּוֹלֶלֶת הָעוֹלָמוֹת כֻּלָּן כַּנַּ"ל, לָכֵן הִיא שְׁקוּלָה נֶגֶד כָּל הַמִּצְוֹת, וְלָכֵן הִיא גַּם כֵּן "לְכָל בְּשָׂרוֹ מַרְפֵּא":

פֶּרֶק ל'

וְעוֹד זֹאת יְתֵרָה הַתּוֹרָה הַקְּדוֹשָׁה, בְּיִתְרוֹן אוֹר וְתוֹסֶפֶת קְדֻשָּׁה, גַּם עַל כָּל הַמִּצְוֹת כֻּלָּן בְּיַחַד, שֶׁגַּם אִם קִיֵּם הָאָדָם כָּל הַתַּרְיַ"ג מִצְוֹת כֻּלָּן, בִּשְׁלֵמוּת הָאֲמִתִּי כָּרָאוּי, בְּכָל פְּרָטֵיהֶם וְדִקְדּוּקֵיהֶם, וּבְכַוָּנָה וְטָהֳרָה וּקְדֻשָּׁה, אֲשֶׁר אָז נַעֲשָׂה הָאָדָם כֻּלּוֹ, בְּכָל אֵבָרָיו וּפְרָקָיו וְכָל כֹּחוֹתָיו, "מֶרְכָּבָה גְּמוּרָה", שֶׁתִּשְׁרֶה עֲלֵיהֶם הַקְּדֻשָּׁה עֶלְיוֹנָה שֶׁל הַמִּצְוֹת כֻּלָּן, עִם כָּל זֶה, אֵין עֵרֶךְ וְדִמְיוֹן כְּלָל קְדֻשַּׁת וְאוֹר הַמִּצְוֹת, לְגֹדֶל עֹצֶם קְדֻשַּׁת וְאוֹר הַתּוֹרָה הַקְּדוֹשָׁה, אֲשֶׁר תּוֹפִיעַ נֹהֲרָהּ עַל הָאָדָם הָעוֹסֵק וְהוֹגֶה בָּהּ כָּרָאוּי.

כִּי רֵאשִׁית דַּרְכָּהּ בַּקֹּדֶשׁ, הוּא הַגְבֵּהַּ לְמַעְלָה מַעְלָה מִשֹּׁרֶשׁ הַקְּדֻשָּׁה וְאוֹר הָעֶלְיוֹן שֶׁל הַמִּצְוֹת כֻּלָּן יַחַד כַּנַּ"ל. וְזֶהוּ שֶׁאָמְרוּ בְּפֶרֶק הַתּוֹרָה (אבות ו, א) "וּמְגַדַּלְתּוֹ וּמְרוֹמַמְתּוֹ עַל כָּל הַמַּעֲשִׂים", הַיְנוּ עַל כָּל מַעֲשֵׂי הַמִּצְוֹת כֻּלָּן. וְכֵן אָמְרוּ בִּירוּשַׁלְמִי פֶּרֶק א' דְּפֵאָה, שֶׁכָּל הַמִּצְוֹת כֻּלָּן אֵינָן שָׁווֹת לְדָבָר אֶחָד מִן הַתּוֹרָה:

וְגַם, כִּי קְדֻשַּׁת וְאוֹר הַמִּצְוָה, אֲשֶׁר תַּשְׁכִּין אוֹרָהּ עַל אוֹתוֹ הַדָּבָר וְהַחֵפֶץ, אֲשֶׁר בּוֹ וְעַל יָדוֹ תֵּעָשֶׂה הַמִּצְוָה, אֵינוֹ שׁוֹרֶה עֲלֵיהֶם רַק לְפִי שַׁעְתּוֹ, בְּעֵת שֶׁהַמִּצְוָה נַעֲשֵׂית בָּהֶם, אֲבָל אַחַר שֶׁנַּעֲשָׂה בָּהֶן מִצְוָתָן, הַקְּדוּשָׁה וְהָאוֹר מִתְעַלֶּה וּמִסְתַּלֵּק מֵהֶם תֵּכֶף, וְנִשְׁאָר כְּבָרִאשׁוֹנָה.

אֲבָל הַתּוֹרָה הַקְּדוֹשָׁה, כָּל מָקוֹם שֶׁתַּזְרִיחַ וְתוֹפִיעַ אוֹרָהּ וּקְדֻשָּׁתָהּ פַּעַם אַחַת, קְדֻשַּׁת עוֹלָם תִּהְיֶה לוֹ, וְנִשְׁאָר תָּמִיד בִּקְדֻשָּׁתוֹ, כְּמוֹ שֶׁשָּׁנִינוּ בְּבָרַיְתָא (מגילה כ"ו ב') שֶׁתַּשְׁמִישֵׁי מִצְוָה נִזְרָקִין לְאַחַר שֶׁנַּעֲשָׂה מִצְוָתָן, וְתַשְׁמִישֵׁי קְדֻשָּׁה נִגְנָזִין. וְלָכֵן מָנוּ שָׁם תַּשְׁמִישֵׁי תְּפִלִּין וּמְזוּזוֹת בִּכְלַל תַּשְׁמִישֵׁי קְדֻשָּׁה, מֵחֲמַת פַּרְשִׁיּוֹת הַתּוֹרָה שֶׁהָיוּ מֻנָּחִים בְּתוֹכָם פַּעַם אַחַת.

וְלֵית לָךְ מִידֵי בְּדִבְרֵיהֶם זִכְרוֹנָם לִבְרָכָה דְּלָא רְמִיזָא בִּקְרָא, וְיֵשׁ לְכַוֵּן הַכָּתוּב (משלי ו, כג) "כִּי נֵר מִצְוָה וְתוֹרָה אוֹר" גַּם עַל זֶה הָעִנְיָן הַנִּזְכָּר, עַל פִּי פֵּרוּשָׁם זִכְרוֹנָם לִבְרָכָה הַנַּ"ל בְּסוֹטָה שָׁם (כא, א), מַה "נֵר" אֵינוֹ מֵאִיר אֶלָּא לְפִי שָׁעָה, וּמַה "אוֹר" מֵאִיר לְעוֹלָם. וְהֵם זִכְרוֹנָם לִבְרָכָה עָשׂוּ הַהֶפְרֵשׁ בֵּינֵיהֶם לְעִנְיַן הַהֲגָנָה וְהַהַצָּלָה לְהָאָדָם. וְאֶפְשָׁר לְפָרְשׁוֹ גַּם כֵּן, שֶׁיִּרְמֹז הַכָּתוּב גַּם לְעִנְיַן הַהֶפְרֵשׁ וְהַהֶבְדֵּל, בֵּין הַתּוֹרָה הַקְּדוֹשָׁה וְהַמִּצְוֹת, הַמְבֹאָר בְּבָרַיְתָא דִּמְגִילָּה הַנַּ"ל:

וְלֹא עוֹד, אֶלָּא שֶׁגַּם אוֹתָהּ הַקְּדֻשָּׁה, וְחִיּוּתָן וְאוֹרָן שֶׁל הַמִּצְוֹת, שֶׁמְּקַדְּשִׁים וּמְחַיִּים לְהָאָדָם הַמְקַיְּמָם, הוּא נִלְקָח וְנִשְׁפָּע רַק מִקְּדֻשָּׁתָהּ וְאוֹרָהּ שֶׁל הַתּוֹרָה הַקְּדוֹשָׁה, כִּי הַמִּצְוָה לֵית לָהּ מִגַּרְמָהּ שׁוּם חִיּוּת וּקְדֻשָּׁה וְאוֹר כְּלָל, רַק מִצַּד קְדֻשַּׁת אוֹתִיּוֹת הַתּוֹרָה הַכְּתוּבוֹת בְּעִנְיַן אוֹתָהּ הַמִּצְוָה.

וְיֵשׁ לְכַוֵּן גַּם זֶה הָעִנְיָן בַּכָּתוּב "כִּי נֵר מִצְוָה וְתוֹרָה אוֹר", כְּעִנְיַן הַנֵּר שֶׁאֵין לָהּ בְּעַצְמָהּ שׁוּם אוֹר כְּלָל, רַק מֵהָאוֹר הַמֵּאִיר בָּהּ.

וַדַּאי שֶׁגַּם הָעֵסֶק בַּתּוֹרָה לְבַד, בְּלִי קִיּוּם הַמִּצְוֹת כְּלָל חַס וְשָׁלוֹם, גַּם כֵּן אֵין כְּלוּם, כְּמוֹ שֶׁאָמְרוּ רַבּוֹתֵינוּ זִכְרוֹנָם לִבְרָכָה (יבמות קט): "כָּל הָאוֹמֵר אֵין לוֹ אֶלָּא תּוֹרָה, אַף תּוֹרָה אֵין לוֹ". וּבְפֶרֶק ב' דִּבְרָכוֹת (י"ז א') מַרְגְּלָא בְּפוּמֵיהּ דְּרָבָא, תַּכְלִית חָכְמָה, תְּשׁוּבָה וּמַעֲשִׂים טוֹבִים, שֶׁלֹּא יְהֵא אָדָם קוֹרֵא וְשׁוֹנֶה, וּבוֹעֵט בְּאָבִיו וּבְרַבּוֹ כו', "לְלוֹמְדֵיהֶם" לֹא נֶאֱמַר, אֶלָּא "לְעוֹשֵׂיהֶם".

וּבִשְׁמוֹת רַבָּה פָּרָשָׁה מ', כָּל מִי שֶׁהוּא יוֹדֵעַ תּוֹרָה וְאֵינוֹ עוֹשֶׂה, מוּטָב לוֹ שֶׁלֹּא יָצָא לָעוֹלָם, אֶלָּא נֶהֶפְכָה הַשִּׁלְיָא עַל פָּנָיו. וְכֵן הוּא בְּוַיִּקְרָא רַבָּה פָּרָשָׁה ל"ה, וּבְתַנְחוּמָא פָּרָשַׁת עֵקֶב.

וּבַזֹּהַר שְׁמוֹת ה' רֵישׁ ע"ב, דְּאָמַר רַבִּי יְהוּדָה, כָּל מַאן דְּאִשְׁתַּדֵּל בְּאוֹרַיְתָא בְּהַאי עָלְמָא, וּמְסַגֵּל עוֹבָדִין טָבִין, יָרִית עָלְמָא שְׁלֵימָא, וְכָל מַאן דְּאִשְׁתַּדֵּל בְּאוֹרַיְתָא בְּהַאי עָלְמָא, וְלָא עָבִיד עוֹבָדִין טָבִין, לָא יָרִית לָא הַאי וְלָא הַאי כו', אמר רַבִּי יִצְחָק, לָא תְּנָן אֶלָּא מַאן דְּלֵית לֵיהּ עוֹבָדִין טָבִין כְּלָל, [כִּי אָמַר רַבִּי יְהוּדָה, כָּל מִי שֶׁעוֹסֵק בַּתּוֹרָה בָּעוֹלָם הַזֶּה, וְרוֹכֵשׁ מַעֲשִׂים טוֹבִים, יוֹרֵשׁ עוֹלָם שָׁלֵם, וְכָל מִי שֶׁעוֹסֵק בַּתּוֹרָה בָּעוֹלָם הַזֶּה, וְאֵינוֹ עוֹשֶׂה מַעֲשִׂים טוֹבִים, אֵינוֹ יוֹרֵשׁ לֹא זֶה וְלֹא זֶה וכו'. אמר רַבִּי יִצְחָק, לֹא לָמַדְנוּ אֶלָּא מִי שֶׁאֵין לוֹ מַעֲשִׂים טוֹבִים כְּלָל.]

עַד שֶׁאָמְרוּ בְּפֶרֶק קַמָּא דַּעֲבוֹדָה זָרָה (יז, ב): "כָּל הָעוֹסֵק בַּתּוֹרָה לְבַד, דּוֹמֶה כְּמִי שֶׁאֵין לוֹ אֱלוֹהַּ", כִּי בִּלְתִּי קִיּוּם הַמִּצְוֹת חַס וְשָׁלוֹם, אֵין דָּבָר בַּמֶּה לְהִתְאַחֵז וּלְהִתְקַשֵּׁר בּוֹ אוֹר הַתּוֹרָה, לִשְׁרוֹת עָלָיו וּלְהִתְקַיֵּם בּוֹ, כְּדִמְיוֹן הָאוֹר בְּלֹא פְּתִילָה. אָמְנָם, עַצְמוּת הָאוֹר מְקַבֶּלֶת הַמִּצְוָה מֵאוֹתִיּוֹת הַתּוֹרָה הַכְּתוּבוֹת בְּעִנְיָנָהּ.

וְזֶהוּ שֶׁאָמְרוּ בְּפֶרֶק הַתּוֹרָה (אבות ו, ז) "גְּדוֹלָה תּוֹרָה שֶׁהִיא נוֹתֶנֶת חַיִּים לְעוֹשֶׂיהָ", וְלֹא אָמַר לְלוֹמְדֶיהָ אוֹ לְעוֹסְקֶיהָ, אֶלָּא "לְעוֹשֶׂיהָ", וְרוֹצֶה לוֹמַר, שֶׁהַתּוֹרָה הִיא הַנּוֹתֶנֶת חַיֵּי עַד וּקְדֻשָּׁה, גַּם לְעוֹשֵׂי הַמִּצְוֹת הַכְּתוּבוֹת בְּתוֹכָהּ.

וְלָכֵן אָמְרוּ בְּתַנְחוּמָא בְּחֻקֹּתַי (אות ה), שֶׁאַף אִם הוּא צַדִּיק, וְאֵינוֹ עוֹסֵק בַּתּוֹרָה, אֵין בְּיָדוֹ כְּלוּם חַס וְשָׁלוֹם:

וְהַטַּעַם בָּזֶה, גַּם כֵּן כְּמוֹ שֶׁנִּתְבָּאֵר לְעֵיל, (שער א' פֶּרֶק ו') שֶׁהַמִּצְוֹת בִּמְקוֹר שָׁרְשָׁן, קְשׁוּרוֹת וּתְלוּיוֹת בְּסִדּוּר פִּרְקֵי הַמֶּרְכָּבָה הָעוֹלָמוֹת וְכֹחוֹת הָעֶלְיוֹנִים, וּמְקוֹר שֹׁרֶשׁ הָעֶלְיוֹן שֶׁל הַתּוֹרָה הַקְּדוֹשָׁה הִיא מְאֹד נַעֲלָה, מֵעַל כָּל הָעוֹלָמוֹת וְהַכֹּחוֹת כֻּלָּם, וְהִיא הַמִּתְפַּשֶּׁטֶת בִּפְנִימִיּוּת כֻּלָּם, וּמְקַבְּלִים מִמֶּנָּה עֶצֶם חִיּוּתָם וְשִׁפְעַת קְדֻשָּׁתָם, לָכֵן הִיא הַנּוֹתֶנֶת וּמַשְׁפַּעַת הַחִיּוּת וְהַקְּדֻשָּׁה וְהָאוֹר לְהַמִּצְוֹת כֻּלָּן:

פֶּרֶק ל"א

וּמִזֶּה הַטַּעַם גַּם כֵּן, עֵסֶק הַתּוֹרָה הִיא מְכַפֶּרֶת עַל כָּל הָעֲוֹנוֹת שֶׁל הַנֶּפֶשׁ הַחוֹטֵאת, כְּמַאֲמָרָם זִכְרוֹנָם לִבְרָכָה (סוֹף מְנָחוֹת דף קי) מַאי דִּכְתִיב (ויקרא ז, לז) "זֹאת הַתּוֹרָה לָעֹלָה לַמִּנְחָה וְלַחַטָּאת" כו', וּמַסִּיק, שֶׁכָּל הָעוֹסֵק בַּתּוֹרָה, אֵין צָרִיךְ לֹא עוֹלָה וְלֹא מִנְחָה

וְלֹא חַטָּאת וְלֹא אָשָׁם. וְכֵן הוּא בְּתַנְחוּמָא פָּרָשַׁת צַו (יד), וּבִשְׁמוֹת רַבָּה פָּרָשָׁה ל"ח, "קְחוּ עִמָּכֶם דְּבָרִים וְשׁוּבוּ אֶל ה'", לְפִי שֶׁיִּשְׂרָאֵל אוֹמְרִים כו', עֲנִיִּים אָנוּ וְאֵין לָנוּ לְהָבִיא קָרְבָּנוֹת, אָמַר לָהֶם הַקָּדוֹשׁ בָּרוּךְ הוּא, דְּבָרִים אֲנִי מְבַקֵּשׁ כו', וַאֲנִי מוֹחֵל לָכֶם עַל כָּל עֲוֹנוֹתֵיכֶם, וְאֵין "דְּבָרִים" אֶלָּא דִּבְרֵי תוֹרָה כו'.

וּבְתַנְחוּמָא וַיַּקְהֵל (אות ז) בְּעִנְיַן הָאָרוֹן אָמְרוּ, שֶׁהוּא נוֹשֵׂא עֲוֹנוֹתֵיהֶם שֶׁל יִשְׂרָאֵל, שֶׁהַתּוֹרָה שֶׁבּוֹ נוֹשֵׂא עֲוֹנוֹתֵיהֶם שֶׁל יִשְׂרָאֵל.

וּבְתָנָּא דְּבֵי אֵלִיָּהוּ סֵדֶר אֵלִיָּהוּ רַבָּה פֶּרֶק ה', אָדָם שֶׁעָבַר עֲבֵרוֹת הַרְבֵּה וְקָנְסוּ עָלָיו מִיתָה כו', וְחָזַר וְעָשָׂה תְּשׁוּבָה, וְקוֹרֵא תּוֹרָה נְבִיאִים וּכְתוּבִים, וְשָׁנָה מִשְׁנָה מִדְרָשׁ הֲלָכוֹת וְהַגָּדוֹת, וְשִׁמֵּשׁ חֲכָמִים, אֲפִלּוּ נִגְזְרוּ עָלָיו מֵאָה גְּזֵרוֹת, הַקָּדוֹשׁ בָּרוּךְ הוּא מַעֲבִירָן מִמֶּנּוּ כו'.

וּבַזֹּהַר שְׁלַח קנ"ט א', רַבִּי יְהוּדָה פָּתַח כו', כַּמָּה אִית לְהוּ לִבְנֵי נָשָׁא לְאִסְתַּכָּלָא בְּפוּלְחָנָא דְּקוּדְשָׁא בְּרִיךְ הוּא, כַּמָּה אִית לְהוּ לְאִסְתַּכָּלָא בְּמִלֵּי דְּאוֹרַיְתָא, דְּכָל מַאן דְּאִשְׁתַּדֵּל בְּאוֹרַיְתָא, כְּאִלּוּ מַקְרִיב כָּל קוּרְבָּנִין דְּעָלְמָא לְקָמֵיהּ קוּדְשָׁא בְּרִיךְ הוּא, וְלָא עוֹד, אֶלָּא דְּקוּדְשָׁא בְּרִיךְ הוּא מְכַפֵּר לֵיהּ עַל כָּל חוֹבוֹי, וּמְתַקְּנִין לֵיהּ כַּמָּה כּוּרְסָוָן לְעָלְמָא דְּאָתֵי. [רַבִּי יְהוּדָה פָּתַח וכו', כַּמָּה יֵשׁ לָהֶם לִבְנֵי אָדָם לְהִסְתַּכֵּל בַּעֲבוֹדַת הַקָּדוֹשׁ בָּרוּךְ הוּא, כַּמָּה יֵשׁ לָהֶם לְהִסְתַּכֵּל בְּדִבְרֵי תוֹרָה, שֶׁכָּל מִי שֶׁעוֹסֵק בַּתּוֹרָה כְּאִלּוּ מַקְרִיב כָּל הַקָּרְבָּנוֹת שֶׁבָּעוֹלָם לִפְנֵי הַקָּדוֹשׁ בָּרוּךְ הוּא, וְלֹא עוֹד אֶלָּא שֶׁהַקָּדוֹשׁ בָּרוּךְ הוּא מְכַפֵּר לוֹ עַל כָּל עֲווֹנוֹתָיו וּמְתַקְּנִים לוֹ כַּמָּה כִּסְאוֹת לָעוֹלָם הַבָּא.]

וְגַם עַל אוֹתָן הָעֲוֹנוֹת חֲמוּרִים, שֶׁאֵין הַקָּרְבָּנוֹת מְכַפְּרִים, עֵסֶק הַתּוֹרָה מְכַפֶּרֶת, כְּמוֹ שֶׁאָמְרוּ רַבּוֹתֵינוּ זִכְרוֹנָם לִבְרָכָה בִּבְנֵי עֵלִי (ר"ה יח, א): "בְּזֶבַח וּבְמִנְחָה הוּא דְּאֵינוֹ מִתְכַּפֵּר, אֲבָל מִתְכַּפֵּר הוּא בְּדִבְרֵי תוֹרָה". וְכֵן אָמְרוּ (מגילה ג' ע"ב): "גָּדוֹל תַּלְמוּד תּוֹרָה יוֹתֵר מֵהַקְרָבַת תְּמִידִין".

וּבַזֹּהַר צַו ל"ה א', תָּא חֲזֵי כו', וְעַל דָּא, מַאן דְּלָעֵי בְּאוֹרַיְתָא, לָא אִצְטְרִיךְ לָא לְקָרְבָּנִין וְלָא לַעֲלָוָן, דְּהָא אוֹרַיְתָא עָדִיף מִכֹּלָּא, וְקִשּׁוּרָא דִּמְהֵימְנוּתָא דְּכֹלָּא, וְעַל דָּא כְּתִיב (משלי ג, יז) "דְּרָכֶיהָ דַּרְכֵי נֹעַם וְכָל נְתִיבוֹתֶיהָ שָׁלוֹם" וכו', וּכְתִיב (תהלים קיט, קסה) "שָׁלוֹם רָב לְאֹהֲבֵי תוֹרָתֶךָ וְאֵין לָמוֹ מִכְשׁוֹל". [בּוֹא וּרְאֵה וכו', וְעַל כֵּן מִי שֶׁעוֹסֵק בַּתּוֹרָה אֵינוֹ צָרִיךְ לֹא לְקָרְבָּנוֹת וְלֹא לְעוֹלוֹת, כִּי הַתּוֹרָה יוֹתֵר טוֹבָה מִכֹּל, וְהִיא קֶשֶׁר הָאֱמוּנָה שֶׁל הַכֹּל. וְעַל כֵּן כָּתוּב "דְּרָכֶיהָ דַּרְכֵי נֹעַם וְכָל נְתִיבוֹתֶיהָ שָׁלוֹם".]

וּבְפָרָשַׁת קְדוֹשִׁים פ' ע"ב, "בְּזֶבַח וּבְמִנְחָה" כו', אֲבָל מִתְכַּפֵּר הוּא בְּדִבְרֵי תוֹרָה, אַמַּאי, בְּגִין דְּדִבְרֵי תוֹרָה סַלְקִין עַל כָּל קָרְבָּנִין דְּעָלְמָא, כְּמָה דְּאוּקְמוּהָ, דִּכְתִיב "זֹאת הַתּוֹרָה לָעֹלָה לַמִּנְחָה וְלַחַטָּאת" כו', שְׁקִיל אוֹרַיְתָא לָקֳבֵיל כָּל קָרְבָּנִין דְּעָלְמָא. אָמַר לֵיהּ הָכִי הוּא וַדַּאי, דְּכָל מַאן דְּאִשְׁתַּדֵּל בְּאוֹרַיְתָא, אַף עַל גַּב דְּאִתְגְּזַר עָלֵיהּ עוֹנְשָׁא מִלְּעֵלָּא, נִיחָא לֵיהּ מִכָּל קָרְבָּנִין וַעֲלָוָן, וְהַהוּא עוֹנְשָׁא אִתְקְרַע. וְתָא חֲזֵי, לָא אִתְדְּכֵי בַּר נַשׁ לְעָלְמִין אֶלָּא בְּמִלִּין דְּאוֹרַיְתָא כו'. וְאוֹרַיְתָא קְדוּשָּׁה אִתְקְרֵי, דִּכְתִיב (ויקרא כ. כו) "כִּי קָדוֹשׁ אֲנִי ה'", וְדָא אוֹרַיְתָא, דְּהִיא שְׁמָא קַדִּישָׁא עִלָּאָה, וְעַל דָּא, מַאן דְּאִשְׁתַּדֵּל בַּהּ אִתְדְּכֵי, וּלְבָתַר

אִתְקַדַּשׁ כו', תָּאנָא, קְדוּשָּׁה דְּאוֹרַיְתָא, קְדוּשָּׁה דְּסַלְּקַת עַל כָּל קְדוּשִּׁין כו', ["בְּזֶבַח וּבְמִנְחָה" וכו', אֲבָל מִתְכַּפֵּר הוּא בְּדִבְרֵי תּוֹרָה. לָמָּה? מִשּׁוּם שֶׁדִּבְרֵי תּוֹרָה עוֹלִים עַל כָּל קָרְבָּנוֹת שֶׁבָּעוֹלָם, כְּמוֹ שֶׁהֶעֱמִידוּ מַה שֶּׁכָּתוּב "זֹאת הַתּוֹרָה לָעֹלָה לַמִּנְחָה וְלַחַטָּאת" וכו', שֶׁשְּׁקוּלָה הַתּוֹרָה כְּנֶגֶד כָּל הַקָּרְבָּנוֹת שֶׁבָּעוֹלָם, אָמַר לֵיהּ כָּךְ הוּא וַדַּאי, שֶׁכָּל מִי שֶׁעוֹסֵק בַּתּוֹרָה אַף עַל פִּי שֶׁנִּגְזַר עָלָיו עֹנֶשׁ מִלְמַעְלָה, טוֹב לוֹ מִכָּל הַקָּרְבָּנוֹת וְהָעוֹלוֹת, וְהָעֹנֶשׁ הַהוּא נִקְרָע. בֹּא וּרְאֵה, אֵין הָאָדָם נִטְהָר לְעוֹלָם אֶלָּא בְּדִבְרֵי תּוֹרָה וכו', וְהַתּוֹרָה נִקְרֵאת קְדוֹשָׁה, שֶׁכָּתוּב "כִּי קָדוֹשׁ אֲנִי ה'", וְזוֹ הִיא הַתּוֹרָה שֶׁהִיא שֵׁם הַקָּדוֹשׁ הָעֶלְיוֹן, וְעַל כֵּן מִי שֶׁעוֹסֵק בָּהּ נִטְהָר, וְאַחַר כָּךְ מִתְקַדֵּשׁ וכו', לָמַדְנוּ קְדֻשַּׁת הַתּוֹרָה הִיא קְדֻשָּׁה עֶלְיוֹנָה הָעוֹלָה עַל כָּל הַקְּדֻשּׁוֹת וכו'], עַיֵּן שָׁם.

וּבְמִדְרַשׁ הַנֶּעְלָם וַיֵּרָא ק' ע"א אָמְרוּ, בָּטְלוּ הַקָּרְבָּנוֹת לֹא בָּטְלָה הַתּוֹרָה. הַאי דְּלָא אִיעֲסַק בְּקָרְבָּנוֹת לִיעֲסַק בַּתּוֹרָה, וְיִתְהַנֵּי לֵיהּ יַתִּיר, דְּאָמַר רַבִּי יוֹחָנָן כו', אָמַר לֵיהּ, יַעַסְקוּ בַּתּוֹרָה, וַאֲנִי מוֹחֵל לָהֶם בִּשְׁבִילָהּ יוֹתֵר מִכָּל הַקָּרְבָּנוֹת שֶׁבָּעוֹלָם, שֶׁנֶּאֱמַר (ויקרא ז, לז) "זֹאת הַתּוֹרָה לָעֹלָה לַמִּנְחָה" כו', זֹאת הַתּוֹרָה בִּשְׁבִיל עוֹלָה, בִּשְׁבִיל מִנְחָה כו'. אָמַר רַבִּי כְּרוּסְפְּדָאֵי, הַאי מַאן דְּמַדְכַּר בְּפוּמֵיהּ בְּבָתֵּי כְּנֵסִיּוֹת וּבְבָתֵּי מִדְרָשׁוֹת בב"כ ובמ"ד עִנְיָנָא דְּקָרְבְּנַיָּא כו', בְּרִית כְּרוּתָה הוּא, דְּאִנּוּן מַלְאֲכַיָּא דְּמַדְכְּרָן חוֹבֵיהּ לְאַבְאָשָׁא לֵיהּ, דְּלָא יָכְלִין לְמֶעֱבַד לֵיהּ אֶלָּא טִיבוּ [בָּטְלוּ הַקָּרְבָּנוֹת לֹא בָּטְלָה הַתּוֹרָה, זֶה שֶׁלֹּא עוֹסֵק בַּקָּרְבָּנוֹת יַעֲסֹק בַּתּוֹרָה, וְיוֹעִיל לוֹ עוֹד יוֹתֵר מִקָּרְבָּנוֹת וכו', אָמַר רַבִּי כְּרוּסְפְּדָאֵי כָּל מִי שֶׁמַּזְכִּיר בְּפִיו בְּבָתֵּי כְּנֵסִיּוֹת וּבְבָתֵּי מִדְרָשׁוֹת עִנְיְנֵי הַקָּרְבָּנוֹת וכו', בְּרִית כְּרוּתָה הוּא שֶׁאוֹתָן הַמַּלְאָכִים הַמַּזְכִּירִים עֲווֹנוֹתָיו לְהָרַע לוֹ, אֵינָם יְכוֹלִים לַעֲשׂוֹת לוֹ רַק טוֹב.]

וְאָמְרוּ עוֹד בְּפֶרֶק שֵׁנִי דִּבְרָכוֹת (טז, א), וּבְתַנָּא דְּבֵי אֵלִיָּהוּ סֵדֶר אֵלִיָּה רַבָּה פֶּרֶק כ"ה, לָמָּה נִסְמְכוּ אֳהָלִים לִנְחָלִים, דִּכְתִיב (במדבר כד, ו) "כִּנְחָלִים נִטָּיוּ וכו' כַּאֲהָלִים נָטַע ה'" כו', לוֹמַר לְךָ, מַה נְּחָלִים מַעֲלִין אֶת הָאָדָם מִטֻּמְאָה לְטָהֳרָה, אַף אֹהָלִים מַעֲלִים אֶת הָאָדָם מִכַּף חוֹבָה לְכַף זְכוּת. וּבְפֶרֶק י"ח שָׁם "שִׁפְכִי כַמַּיִם לִבֵּךְ" כו', מַה מַּיִם הַלָּלוּ מִקְוֶה טָהֳרָה הֵן לְיִשְׂרָאֵל, וּלְכָל אֲשֶׁר נִבְרָא בָּעוֹלָם כו', כָּךְ דִּבְרֵי תּוֹרָה, מִקְוֶה טָהֳרָה הֵן לְיִשְׂרָאֵל בְּכָל מְקוֹמוֹת מוֹשְׁבוֹתֵיהֶם. בֹּא וּרְאֵה כַּמָּה גְּדוֹלָה כֹּחָהּ שֶׁל תּוֹרָה, שֶׁמְּטַהֶרֶת אֶת פּוֹשְׁעֵי יִשְׂרָאֵל, בִּזְמַן שֶׁעוֹשִׂין תְּשׁוּבָה, אֲפִלּוּ מֵעֲבוֹדָה זָרָה שֶׁבְּיָדָם, שֶׁנֶּאֱמַר (יחזקאל לו, כה) "וְזָרַקְתִּי עֲלֵיכֶם מַיִם טְהוֹרִים וּטְהַרְתֶּם" כו', עַיֵּן שָׁם.

כִּי עִקַּר הַתְּשׁוּבָה שְׁלֵמָה הָאֲמִתִּית שֶׁהִיא מֵאַהֲבָה, הוּא רַק עַל יְדֵי עֵסֶק הַתּוֹרָה כָּרָאוּי, כְּמוֹ שֶׁכָּתוּב בְּמַעֲלוֹת הַתּוֹרָה (אבות ו, א) "אוֹהֵב אֶת הַמָּקוֹם", וּכְמוֹ שֶׁכָּתוּב "הֲשִׁיבֵנוּ אָבִינוּ לְתוֹרָתֶךָ" כו' "וְהַחֲזִירֵנוּ בִּתְשׁוּבָה שְׁלֵמָה לְפָנֶיךָ".

וּבַזֹּהַר וַיִּקְרָא כ"א א', כַּד בַּר נַשׁ אִתְרְחִיק מֵאוֹרַיְתָא, רָחִיק הוּא מִקּוּדְשָׁא בְּרִיךְ הוּא, וּמַאן דְּקָרִיב לְאוֹרַיְתָא, קָרִיב לֵיהּ קוּדְשָׁא בְּרִיךְ הוּא בַּהֲדֵיהּ, [כְּשֶׁהָאָדָם מִתְרַחֵק מִן הַתּוֹרָה, הוּא רָחוֹק מֵהַקָּדוֹשׁ בָּרוּךְ הוּא וּמִי שֶׁקָּרוֹב לַתּוֹרָה, הַקָּדוֹשׁ בָּרוּךְ הוּא מְקָרֵב אוֹתוֹ עִמּוֹ.]

כִּי עַל כָּל פְּשָׁעִים תְּכַסֶּה אַהֲבַת הַתּוֹרָה, כְּמוֹ שֶׁכָּתוּב בְּתַנָּא דְּבֵי אֵלִיָּהוּ (סֵדֶר אֵלִיָּהוּ רַבָּה פֶּרֶק ג) עַל זֶה הַפָּסוּק (משלי י, יב), וְכֵן אָמְרוּ (פתיחתא איכה): "הַמָּאוֹר שֶׁבָּהּ מַחֲזִירוֹ לְמוּטָב", וּבְפֶרֶק הֶחָלִיל (סוכה נ"ב ב') "אִם פָּגַע בְּךָ מְנֻוָּל זֶה מָשְׁכֵהוּ לְבֵית הַמִּדְרָשׁ, אִם אֶבֶן הוּא נִמּוֹחַ" וכו'. וּכְעֵין זֶה אָמְרוּ בְּתַנְחוּמָא פָּרָשַׁת הַאֲזִינוּ, עַיֵּן שָׁם. וּבִבְרֵאשִׁית רַבָּה פָּרָשָׁה כ"ב "אִם בָּא יִצְרְךָ לְהַשְׂחִיקְךָ, שַׂמְּחֵהוּ בְּדִבְרֵי תוֹרָה", וּבְמִדְרַשׁ תְּהִלִּים סוֹף מִזְמוֹר ל"ד "אִם עָמַד עָלֶיךָ יֵצֶר הָרַע, הַאֲכִילֵהוּ לַחְמָהּ שֶׁל תּוֹרָה" כו'.

וּבַזֹּהַר וַיֵּשֶׁב ק"צ ע"א, אָמַר רַבִּי יוֹסִי, כַּד חָמֵי בַּר נַשׁ דְּהִרְהוּרִין בִּישִׁין אַתְיָן לְגַבֵּיהּ יִתְעֲסַק בְּאוֹרַיְתָא, וּכְדֵין יִתְעַבְרוּן מִנֵּיהּ. אָמַר רַבִּי אֶלְעָזָר, כַּד הַהוּא סִטְרָא בִּישָׁא אָתֵי לְמִפְתֵּי לֵיהּ לְבַר נַשׁ, יְהֵא מָשִׁיךְ לֵיהּ לְגַבֵּי אוֹרַיְתָא, וְיִתְפְּרַשׁ מִנֵּיהּ [אָמַר רַבִּי יוֹסִי כְּשֶׁהָאָדָם רוֹאֶה שֶׁהִרְהוּרִים רָעִים בָּאִים אֵלָיו, יַעֲסֹק בַּתּוֹרָה, וְאָז יַעַבְרוּ מִמֶּנּוּ. אָמַר רַבִּי אֶלְעָזָר, כְּשֶׁאוֹתוֹ צַד הָרַע בָּא לְפַתּוֹת אֶת הָאָדָם, יַמְשִׁיךְ אוֹתוֹ אֶל הַתּוֹרָה וְיִפָּרֵד מִמֶּנּוּ.]

וְזֶה שֶׁכָּתוּב בְּפֶרֶק הַתּוֹרָה (אבות ו, א) "וְנַעֲשֶׂה כְּמַעְיָן הַמִּתְגַּבֵּר וְהוֹלֵךְ". וְיֵשׁ מָקוֹם לְפָרְשׁוֹ גַּם עַל זֶה הָעִנְיָן הַנַּ"ל, שֶׁכְּמוֹ הַמַּעְיָן הַנּוֹבֵעַ וּבוֹקֵעַ, אַף שֶׁלִּפְעָמִים נִרְפָּשׁ וְנִשְׁחַת בְּהַרְבֵּה רֶפֶשׁ וָטִיט, עִם כָּל זֶה, הוּא נוֹבֵעַ וּבוֹקֵעַ, וּמִתְגַּבֵּר וְהוֹלֵךְ מְעַט מְעַט, עַד שֶׁבְּרְבוֹת הַיָּמִים יִתְגַּבֵּר וְיִתְגַּלֶּה לְגַמְרֵי, וְיִתְפַּשֵּׁט כְּמֵאָז, כֵּן הָעוֹסֵק בַּתּוֹרָה לִשְׁמָהּ, אַף אִם נִתְלַכְלֵךְ תְּחִלָּה בַּעֲווֹנוֹת וַחֲטָאִים עֲצוּמִים, וְנִטְבַּע מְאֹד בְּרֶפֶשׁ וָטִיט מְצוּלוֹת הָרַע חַס וְשָׁלוֹם, עִם כָּל זֶה, עַל יְדֵי עֵסֶק הַתּוֹרָה, יְהֵא נָכוֹן לִבּוֹ בָּטוּחַ, שֶׁוַּדַּאי הַמָּאוֹר שֶׁבָּהּ יַחֲזִירוֹ לְמוּטָב, וְהַטּוֹב מִתְגַּבֵּר וְהוֹלֵךְ עַל הָרַע שֶׁבּוֹ מְעַט מְעַט, עַד שֶׁלְּבַסּוֹף בְּהֶכְרֵחַ יִתְגַּבֵּר הַטּוֹב, וְיִתְפַּשֵּׁט בְּכֻלּוֹ לְגַמְרֵי, וְהוּא מִתְקַדֵּשׁ מִטֻּמְאָתוֹ, וּפָרְחָה טָהֳרָה בְּכֻלּוֹ.

וְכֵן אָמַר שָׁם "וּמַכְשַׁרְתּוֹ לִהְיוֹת צַדִּיק חָסִיד" כו', לְשׁוֹן הֶכְשֵׁר וְהַגְעָלָה וְלִבּוּן מִפִּגּוּל גְּעוּלֵי הָרַע שֶׁהָיָה בּוֹ תְּחִלָּה, וּכְמוֹ שֶׁכָּתוּב (ירמיה כ"ג כט) "הֲלֹא כֹה דְבָרִי כָּאֵשׁ" וכו', שֶׁהִיא מְלַבַּנְתּוֹ וּמַכְשַׁרְתּוֹ כו', וְכֵן אִיתָא בְּתַנְחוּמָא וַיַּקְהֵל (סי' י"ג), שֶׁהַתּוֹרָה מְטַהֶרֶת לִבָּן וְכִלְיוֹתָן שֶׁל תַּלְמִידֵי חֲכָמִים:

פֶּרֶק ל"ב

וְהַכֹּל מִטַּעַם הַנַּ"ל, שֶׁשָּׁרְשָׁהּ הָעֶלְיוֹן שֶׁל הַתּוֹרָה הַקְּדוֹשָׁה הִיא מֵעַל כָּל הָעוֹלָמוֹת כֻּלָּם.

וְהָעִנְיָן הוּא, כְּמוֹ שֶׁכָּתַבְתִּי לְעֵיל (בְּשַׁעַר א' פֶּרֶק כ'), טַעַם מַאֲמָרָם זִכְרוֹנָם לִבְרָכָה (שבת קיט, ב) שֶׁכָּל הָעוֹנֶה אָמֵן יְהֵא שְׁמֵיהּ רַבָּה – בְּכָל כֹּחוֹ, מוֹחֲלִין לוֹ עַל כָּל עֲוֹנוֹתָיו, עַיֵּן שָׁם.

כֵּן הָעִנְיָן, שֶׁעַל יְדֵי עֵסֶק הַתּוֹרָה כָּרָאוּי, הוּא מְעוֹרֵר שָׁרְשָׁהּ הָעֶלְיוֹן, לְהַאֲצִיל וּלְהַשְׁפִּיעַ שִׁפְעַת אוֹר עֶלְיוֹן וּקְדֻשָּׁה עַל הָעוֹלָמוֹת כֻּלָּם, וּרְשָׁפֶיהָ רִשְׁפֵּי אֵשׁ שַׁלְהֶבֶת נוֹרָא, לְגָרֵשׁ וּלְכַלּוֹת כָּל הַטֻּמְאוֹת וְהַזֻּהֲמוֹת שֶׁגָּרַם בְּמַעֲשָׂיו בְּכָל הָעוֹלָמוֹת, לְהִתְקַדֵּשׁ וּלְהָאִיר עוֹד בִּקְדֻשָּׁה הָעֶלְיוֹנָה, לְהִתְקַשֵּׁר יַחַד אֶחָד בַּחֲבֵרוֹ, וְכָל הַפְּגָמִים מִתְמַלְּאִים, וְכָל הַקִּלְקוּלִים

נִתְקָנִים, וְכָל הַהֲרִיסוֹת מִתְבַּנִּים, וְהַשִּׂמְחָה וְחֶדְוָתָא יְתֵרְתָא וְאוֹר הָעֶלְיוֹן מִתְרַבֶּה בְּכָל הָעוֹלָמוֹת.

וְגַם כִּי יָדוּעַ שֶׁכָּל דָּבָר אֵינוֹ נִתְקָן אֶלָּא בְּשָׁרְשׁוֹ הָעֶלְיוֹן, וְכָל אֶחָד מִיִּשְׂרָאֵל שֹׁרֶשׁ הָעֶלְיוֹן שֶׁל נִשְׁמָתוֹ הוּא מֵאוֹת אַחַת מֵהַתּוֹרָה הַקְּדוֹשָׁה, לָכֵן, כָּל פְּגָמֵי הַנֶּפֶשׁ הַחוֹטֵאת, נִתְקָנִים וְנִמְתָּקִים בְּשָׁרְשָׁם בַּתּוֹרָה הַקְּדוֹשָׁה, עַל יְדֵי הָעֵסֶק בָּהּ כָּרָאוּי.

וּכְמוֹ שֶׁאָמַר הַכָּתוּב (תהלים יט, ח) "תּוֹרַת ה' תְּמִימָה מְשִׁיבַת נָפֶשׁ", שֶׁאַף אִם כְּבָר נִכְרְתָה הַנֶּפֶשׁ מִשָּׁרְשָׁהּ חַס וְשָׁלוֹם, וַתֵּרֶד פְּלָאִים בְּעִמְקֵי מְצוּלוֹת הָרַע חַס וְשָׁלוֹם, הַתּוֹרָה הַקְּדוֹשָׁה שֶׁעוֹסֵק בָּהּ הִיא מְקִימָהּ וּמוֹצִיאָהּ מִמַּסְגְּרִים, וּמְשִׁיבָה אוֹתָהּ לְהִתְקַשֵּׁר כְּבַתְּחִלָּה, וּבְיִתְרוֹן אוֹר הַתּוֹרָה הַקְּדוֹשָׁה.

וְזֶהוּ שֶׁאָמְרוּ בְּפֶרֶק קַמָּא דְּתַעֲנִית (ז, א): "תַּנְיָא רַבִּי בְּנָאָה אוֹמֵר, כָּל הָעוֹסֵק בַּתּוֹרָה לִשְׁמָהּ, תּוֹרָתוֹ נַעֲשֵׂית לוֹ סַם חַיִּים, שֶׁנֶּאֱמַר (משלי ג, יח) "עֵץ חַיִּים הִיא" כו', וְאוֹמֵר (שם ח, לה) "כִּי מוֹצְאִי מָצָא חַיִּים" כו'. וְאָמְרוּ בִּמְכִילְתָא: "מַה תַּלְמוּד לוֹמַר "כִּי אֲנִי ה' רוֹפְאֶךָ" (שמות טו, כו) אָמַר לוֹ הַקָּדוֹשׁ בָּרוּךְ הוּא לְמֹשֶׁה, אֱמוֹר לָהֶם לְיִשְׂרָאֵל, תּוֹרָה שֶׁנָּתַתִּי לָכֶם, רְפוּאָה הִיא לָכֶם, חַיִּים הִיא לָכֶם, שֶׁנֶּאֱמַר (שם ד, כב) "כִּי חַיִּים הֵם לְמוֹצְאֵיהֶם".

וְלָכֵן תִּקְּנוּ הָרִאשׁוֹנִים זִכְרוֹנָם לִבְרָכָה נוֹסַח הַוִּדּוּי עַל פִּי סֵדֶר הכ"ב אוֹתִיּוֹת, כְּדֵי לְעוֹרֵר שֹׁרֶשׁ הָעֶלְיוֹן שֶׁל נַפְשׁוֹ, אֲשֶׁר הִיא מְקֻשֶּׁרֶת וְנֶאֱחֶזֶת בַּתּוֹרָה הַקְּדוֹשָׁה, לְטַהֲרָהּ וּלְקַדְּשָׁהּ:

וְכָל עוֹד שֶׁהָאָדָם קָשׁוּר וְדָבוּק בְּתוֹרָתוֹ יִתְבָּרַךְ, וּבְאַהֲבָתָהּ יִשְׁגֶּה תָּמִיד, אַף הִיא תָּאִיר אֵלָיו, וּמְשַׁמַּרְתּוֹ בְּכָל דְּרָכָיו וְעִנְיָנָיו, שֶׁלֹּא יִפֹּל בְּרֶשֶׁת הַיֵּצֶר חַס וְשָׁלוֹם, כְּמוֹ שֶׁכָּתוּב בִּשְׁמוֹת רַבָּה פָּרָשָׁה ל"ו, עַיֵּן שָׁם.

וּבְמִדְרַשׁ תְּהִלִּים בְּמִזְמוֹר תְּמַנְיָא אַפֵּי (קיט, יא) "בְּלִבִּי צָפַנְתִּי אִמְרָתֶךָ לְמַעַן לֹא אֶחֱטָא לָךְ", אֵין יֵצֶר הָרַע שׁוֹלֵט אֶל הַתּוֹרָה, וּמִי שֶׁהַתּוֹרָה בְּלִבּוֹ אֵין יֵצֶר הָרַע שׁוֹלֵט בּוֹ, וְלֹא נוֹגֵעַ בּוֹ.

וּבְתָנָּא דְּבֵי אֵלִיָּהוּ סֵדֶר אֵלִיָּהוּ זוּטָא רֵישׁ פֶּרֶק ט"ז, וּבְאָבוֹת דְּרַבִּי נָתָן, אָמַר רַבִּי שִׁמְעוֹן בֶּן יוֹחַאי, כָּל הַנּוֹתֵן דִּבְרֵי תּוֹרָה עַל לִבּוֹ, מַעֲבִירִין מִמֶּנּוּ עֲשָׂרָה דְּבָרִים קָשִׁים, הִרְהוּרֵי עֲבֵרָה, הִרְהוּרֵי חֶרֶב, הִרְהוּרֵי מַלְכוּת, הִרְהוּרֵי שְׁטוּת, הִרְהוּרֵי יֵצֶר הָרַע, הִרְהוּרֵי זְנוּת, הִרְהוּרֵי אִשָּׁה רָעָה, הִרְהוּרֵי עֲבוֹדָה זָרָה, הִרְהוּרֵי עַל בָּשָׂר וָדָם, הִרְהוּרֵי דְּבָרִים בְּטֵלִים,

וּמַלְבַּשְׁתּוֹ עֲנָוָה וְיִרְאַת ה' עַל פָּנָיו וְכָל מִדָּה נְכוֹנָה, וְאֵינוֹ מִתְיָרֵא מִפִּתּוּיֵי יִצְרוֹ בְּעִנְיְנֵי הֲנָאוֹת הָעוֹלָם וְתַעֲנוּגוֹתָיו, כִּי יִצְרוֹ מָסוּר בְּיָדוֹ, לְכָל אֲשֶׁר יַחְפֹּץ יַטֶּנּוּ, וּבַעֲצָתָהּ תַּנְחֵהוּ, וְתַעֲמִידֵהוּ בְּקֶרֶן אוֹרָה, וְעַל כָּל דְּרָכָיו נָגַהּ אוֹר הַתּוֹרָה, עַד שֶׁגַּם כָּל עִנְיְנֵי זֶה הָעוֹלָם הֵם אֶצְלוֹ בְּעִנְיָן טוֹב, בְּמִדָּה וּבְמִשְׁקָל כָּרָאוּי.

כְּמַאֲמָרָם זִכְרוֹנָם לִבְרָכָה (קדושין ל, ב) עַל הַכָּתוּב "וְשַׂמְתֶּם" (דברים יא) סַם תָּם, נִמְשְׁלָה תּוֹרָה כְּסַם חַיִּים, מָשָׁל לְאָדָם שֶׁהִכָּה אֶת בְּנוֹ מַכָּה גְּדוֹלָה, וְהִנִּיחַ לוֹ רְטִיָּה עַל

מַכָּתוֹ, וְאָמַר לוֹ, בְּנִי, כָּל זְמַן שֶׁרְטִיָּה זוֹ עַל מַכָּתְךָ, אֱכֹל מַה שֶּׁהֲנָאָתְךָ וּשְׁתֵה מַה שֶּׁהֲנָאָתְךָ, וְאֵין אַתָּה מִתְיָרֵא, וְאִם אַתָּה מַעֲבִירָהּ, הֲרֵי הִיא מַעֲלָה נוֹמִי, כָּךְ אָמַר הַקָּדוֹשׁ בָּרוּךְ הוּא, בָּנַי, בָּרָאתִי יֵצֶר הָרַע בָּרָאתִי לוֹ תּוֹרָה תַּבְלִין, אִם אַתֶּם עוֹסְקִין בַּתּוֹרָה אֵין אַתֶּם נִמְסָרִים בְּיָדוֹ, שֶׁנֶּאֱמַר (בראשית ד, ז) "הֲלֹא אִם תֵּיטִיב שְׂאֵת", וְאִם אֵין אַתֶּם עוֹסְקִין בַּתּוֹרָה אַתֶּם נִמְסָרִים בְּיָדוֹ, שֶׁנֶּאֱמַר "לַפֶּתַח חַטָּאת רוֹבֵץ".

וּכְמוֹ שֶׁפֵּרְשׁוּ זִכְרוֹנָם לִבְרָכָה (סוטה כא, א) "בְּהִתְהַלֶּכְךָ תַּנְחֶה אוֹתָךְ", בָּעוֹלָם הַזֶּה. וּבְמִשְׁלֵי רַבְּתָא, אַשְׁרֵי אָדָם שֶׁקָּנָה לוֹ תּוֹרָה, לָמָּה, שֶׁהִיא מְשַׁמְּרָה אוֹתוֹ מִדֶּרֶךְ רָעָה, דִּכְתִיב (משלי ו, כב) "בְּהִתְהַלֶּכְךָ" כו'. וְכֵן הוּא בְּוַיִּקְרָא רַבָּה פָּרָשָׁה ל"ה, כִּי הִיא מְיַשֶּׁרֶת וּמְכַוֶּנֶת אֶת לִבּוֹ, עַד אֲשֶׁר יְהֵא לְבָבוֹ שָׁלֵם עִם אֱלֹקָיו, וְנֶאֱמָנָה אֶת אֵל רוּחוֹ, לְעָבְדוֹ יִתְבָּרַךְ בְּכָל לְבָבוֹ בִּשְׁנֵי יְצָרָיו. (ברכות נד.) כְּמוֹ שֶׁאָמְרוּ בְּפֶרֶק קַמָּא דַּחֲגִיגָה (ג' ב'): "דִּבְרֵי חֲכָמִים כַּדָּרְבֹנוֹת" (קהלת יב, יא), לָמָּה נִמְשְׁלוּ דִּבְרֵי תוֹרָה לְדָרְבָן, מַה דָּרְבָן זֶה מְכַוֵּן אֶת הַפָּרָה לְתַלְמֶיהָ לְהָבִיא חַיִּים לָעוֹלָם, אַף דִּבְרֵי תוֹרָה מְכַוְּנִין לֵב לוֹמְדֵיהֶן מִדַּרְכֵי מִיתָה לְדַרְכֵי חַיִּים. וְכֵן אָמְרוּ בְּבַמִּדְבָּר רַבָּה פָּרָשָׁה י"ה, וּבְתַנְחוּמָא פָּרָשַׁת בְּהַעֲלוֹתְךָ, וּבְרֵישׁ פָּרָשַׁת וַיֵּלֶךְ שָׁם.

כִּי אֵין תְּרוּפָה וְתַקָּנָה אַחֶרֶת בָּעוֹלָם כְּלָל, לְהִנָּצֵל מֵרֶשֶׁת יִצְרוֹ אֲשֶׁר פּוֹרֵשׂ לְרַגְלָיו תָּמִיד, לְלָכְדוֹ וּלְהַפִּילוֹ עַד שְׁאוֹל תַּחְתִּית, לַהֲמִיתוֹ מִיתַת עוֹלָם חַס וְשָׁלוֹם, אֶלָּא עַל יְדֵי הָעֵסֶק בַּתּוֹרָה הַקְּדוֹשָׁה, אֲשֶׁר אָז נִקְרָא "אִישׁ חַי", שֶׁהוּא דָּבוּק עַל יָדָהּ בְּחֶלְקוֹ בְּחַיֵּי עוֹלָם הָאֲמִתִּיִּים, כְּמוֹ שֶׁכָּתוּב "כִּי הִיא חַיֶּיךָ" כו' (דברים ל, כ).

וְאָמְרוּ רַבּוֹתֵינוּ זִכְרוֹנָם לִבְרָכָה (ע"ז ג, ב): "מַאי דִּכְתִיב "וַתַּעֲשֶׂה אָדָם כִּדְגֵי הַיָּם" כו' (חבקוק א, יד), מַה דָּגִים שֶׁבַּיָּם כֵּיוָן שֶׁפּוֹרְשִׁים מִן הַמַּיִם מִיָּד מֵתִים, אַף בְּנֵי אָדָם כֵּיוָן שֶׁפּוֹרְשִׁים מִן הַתּוֹרָה מִיָּד מֵתִים". וְכֵן הֵשִׁיבוֹ רַבִּי עֲקִיבָא לְפַפּוּס "וּמַה בִּמְקוֹם חִיּוּתֵנוּ כָּךְ" כו' (ברכות ס"א ב'). וּבְרַעְיָא מְהֵימְנָא סוֹף פָּרָשַׁת שְׁמִינִי, מַה נוּנֵי יַמָּא — חִיּוּתָן בְּמַיָּא, אוּף תַּלְמִידֵי חֲכָמִים, מָארֵי מַתְנִיתִין — חֵיוּתֵיהוֹ בְּאוֹרַיְתָא, וְאִי אִתְפָּרְשָׁן מִנַּהּ מִיָּד מֵתִים. [מַה דְּגֵי הַיָּם חִיּוּתָן בַּמַּיִם אַף תַּלְמִידֵי חֲכָמִים בַּעֲלֵי הַמִּשְׁנָה חִיּוּתָם בַּתּוֹרָה וְאִם נִפְרָדִים מִן הַתּוֹרָה מִיָּד מֵתִים]. וּבְתַנְחוּמָא פָּרָשַׁת עֵקֶב "כִּי חַיִּים הֵם לְמוֹצְאֵיהֶם" (משלי ד, כב), כָּל מִי שֶׁמּוֹצֵא דִּבְרֵי תוֹרָה, חַיִּים הוּא מוֹצֵא כו', לָכֵן נֶאֱמַר "כִּי חַיִּים הֵם לְמוֹצְאֵיהֶם".

וּבַזֹּהַר לֶךְ לְךָ צ"ב א', זַכָּאָה חוּלָקֵיהוֹן דְּיִשְׂרָאֵל, דְּאוֹרַיְתָא אוֹלִיף לְהוּ אוֹרְחוֹי דְּקוּדְשָׁא בְּרִיךְ הוּא כו', וַדַּאי, כְּתִיב (תהלים יט, ח)" תּוֹרַת ה' תְּמִימָה" וגו', זַכָּאָה חוּלָקֵיהּ מַאן דְּאִשְׁתַּדַּל בְּאוֹרַיְתָא וְלָא יִתְפְּרַשׁ מִנַּהּ, דְּכָל מַאן דְּיִתְפְּרַשׁ מֵאוֹרַיְתָא, אֲפִילוּ שַׁעֲתָא חֲדָא, כְּמָה דְּאִתְפְּרַשׁ מֵחַיֵּי דְּעָלְמָא, דִּכְתִיב (דברים ל, כ) "כִּי הִיא חַיֶּיךָ" וגו', וּכְתִיב (משלי ג, ב) "אֹרֶךְ יָמִים וּשְׁנוֹת חַיִּים וְשָׁלוֹם יוֹסִיפוּ לָךְ" [אַשְׁרֵי חֶלְקָם שֶׁל יִשְׂרָאֵל, שֶׁהַתּוֹרָה מְלַמֶּדֶת אוֹתָם דְּרָכָיו שֶׁל הַקָּדוֹשׁ בָּרוּךְ הוּא וכו', וַדַּאי. כָּתוּב תּוֹרַת ה' תְּמִימָה וגו', אַשְׁרֵי חֶלְקוֹ שֶׁל מִי שֶׁעוֹסֵק בַּתּוֹרָה וְאֵינוֹ נִפְרָד מִמֶּנָּה, כִּי כָּל מִי שֶׁנִּפְרָד מִתּוֹרָה אֲפִילוּ שָׁעָה אַחַת, הוּא כְּמוֹ

שֶׁנִּפְרָד מֵחַיֵּי הָעוֹלָם, שֶׁכָּתוּב כִּי הוּא חַיֶּיךָ וגו', וְכָתוּב אֹרֶךְ יָמִים וּשְׁנוֹת חַיִּים וגו'.]

וּבְרֵישׁ פָּרָשַׁת בְּהַעֲלוֹתְךָ, זַכָּאָה חוּלָקֵיהוֹן דְּיִשְׂרָאֵל, דְּקוּדְשָׁא בְּרִיךְ הוּא אִתְרְעֵי בְּהוֹן, וִיהַב לְהוֹן אוֹרַיְתָא דִּקְשׁוֹט, אִילָנָא דְחַיֵּי, דְּבֵיהּ אָחִיד בַּר נָשׁ, וְיָרִית חַיִּין לְהַאי עָלְמָא וְחַיִּין לְעָלְמָא דְּאָתֵי, דְּכָל מַאן דְּאִשְׁתַּדֵּל בְּאוֹרַיְתָא וְאָחִיד בַּהּ, אִית לֵיהּ חַיִּין וְאָחִיד בְּחַיִּין, וְכָל מַאן דְּשָׁבִיק מִלֵּי דְּאוֹרַיְתָא וְאִתְפְּרַשׁ מֵאוֹרַיְתָא, כְּאִלּוּ מִתְפְּרַשׁ מֵחַיִּין, בְּגִין דְּהִיא חַיִּין, וְכָל מִלּוֹי חַיִּין, הֲדָא הוּא דִכְתִיב "כִּי חַיִּים הֵם" וגו' (שם ד, כב) וּכְתִיב ")שם ג, ח) "רִפְאוּת תְּהִי לְשָׁרֶךָ" וגו' [אַשְׁרֵי חֶלְקָם שֶׁל יִשְׂרָאֵל, שֶׁהַקָּדוֹשׁ בָּרוּךְ הוּא רָצָה בָּהֶם וְנָתַן לָהֶם תּוֹרַת אֱמֶת, עֵץ הַחַיִּים, שֶׁבּוֹ אוֹחֵז הָאָדָם וְיוֹרֵשׁ חַיִּים לָעוֹלָם הַזֶּה וְחַיִּים לָעוֹלָם הַבָּא. שֶׁכָּל מִי שֶׁמִּשְׁתַּדֵּל בַּתּוֹרָה וְאוֹחֵז בָּהּ יֵשׁ לוֹ חַיִּים וְאוֹחֵז בַּחַיִּים, וְכָל מִי שֶׁעוֹזֵב דִּבְרֵי תּוֹרָה וְנִפְרָד מֵהַתּוֹרָה, הוּא כְּאִלּוּ נִפְרָד מֵהַחַיִּים. מִשּׁוּם שֶׁהִיא חַיִּים וְכָל דְּבָרֶיהָ חַיִּים, זֶה שֶׁכָּתוּב כִּי חַיִּים הֵם וגו'.]

פֶּרֶק ל"ג

וְלָזֹאת נִצְטַוֵּינוּ בְּאַזְהָרָה נוֹרָאָה מִפִּיו יִתְבָּרַךְ, "לֹא יָמוּשׁ סֵפֶר הַתּוֹרָה הַזֶּה מִפִּיךָ וְהָגִיתָ בּוֹ יוֹמָם וָלַיְלָה" (יהושע א, ח). וּכְמוֹ שֶׁכָּתוּב בְּהַקְדָּמַת הַזֹּהַר (יא, א), תָּא חֲזֵי כַּמָּה הוּא חֵילָא תַּקִּיפָא דְּאוֹרַיְתָא, וְכַמָּה הוּא עִלָּאָה עַל כֹּלָּא כו', וּבְגִין כָּךְ בָּעֵי לֵיהּ לְבַר נָשׁ לְאִשְׁתַּדְּלָא בְּאוֹרַיְתָא יְמָמָא וְלֵילְיָא, וְלָא יִתְעֲדֵי מִנַּהּ, הֲדָא הוּא דִכְתִיב "וְהָגִיתָ בּוֹ יוֹמָם וָלַיְלָה", וְאִי אִתְעֲדֵי אוֹ אִתְפְּרַשׁ מִנַּהּ, כְּאִלּוּ אִתְפְּרַשׁ מֵאִילָנָא דְחַיֵּי. [בֹּא וּרְאֵה כַּמָּה חָזָק כֹּחַ הַתּוֹרָה, וְכַמָּה הִיא עֶלְיוֹנָה עַל הַכֹּל וכו', וּמִשּׁוּם זֶה צָרִיךְ הָאָדָם לַעֲסֹק בַּתּוֹרָה יוֹמָם וָלַיְלָה וְלֹא יָסוּר מִמֶּנָּה, זֶה שֶׁכָּתוּב "וְהָגִיתָ בּוֹ יוֹמָם וָלַיְלָה", וְאִם הוּא סָר אוֹ נִפְרָד מִמֶּנָּה, הוּא כְּאִלּוּ נִפְרָד מֵעֵץ הַחַיִּים.]

וּבְתַנָּא דְּבֵי אֵלִיָּהוּ סֵדֶר אֵלִיָּהוּ זוּטָא פֶּרֶק י"ג אָמַר, וְיִשְׁתַּדֵּל אָדָם בְּעַצְמוֹ בְּדִבְרֵי תּוֹרָה, שֶׁדִּבְרֵי תּוֹרָה הֵן מְשׁוּלִים בְּלֶחֶם וּבְמַיִם כו', לְלַמֶּדְךָ, שֶׁכְּשֵׁם שֶׁאִי אֶפְשָׁר לוֹ לָאָדָם לַעֲמֹד בְּלֹא לֶחֶם וּבְלֹא מַיִם, כָּךְ אִי אֶפְשָׁר לוֹ לָאָדָם לַעֲמֹד בְּלֹא תּוֹרָה, שֶׁנֶּאֱמַר "לֹא יָמוּשׁ סֵפֶר הַתּוֹרָה הַזֶּה מִפִּיךָ" וגו'. וְכֵן אָמְרוּ בְּתַנְחוּמָא פָּרָשַׁת תָּבֹא, בְּפָסוּק "וְהָיָה אִם שָׁמוֹעַ", וּבְפָרָשַׁת הַאֲזִינוּ, וּבְמִדְרַשׁ תְּהִלִּים מִזְמוֹר א'.

וְאָמַר הַכָּתוּב (משלי ג, יח) "עֵץ חַיִּים הִיא לַמַּחֲזִיקִים בָּהּ" וגו', כִּי צָרִיךְ הָאָדָם לִקְבֹּעַ בְּלִבּוֹ, וִידַמֶּה בְּדַעְתּוֹ, כִּי אִלּוּ הָיָה טוֹבֵעַ בְּנַחַל שׁוֹטֵף, וְרוֹאֶה לְפָנָיו בַּנָּהָר אִילָן חָזָק, וַדַּאי יְאַמֵּץ כֹּחַ לְהִתְאַחֵז וּלְהִתְדַּבֵּק עַצְמוֹ בּוֹ בְּכָל כֹּחוֹ, וְלֹא יַרְפֶּה יָדָיו הֵימֶנּוּ אֲפִלּוּ רֶגַע אֶחָד, אַחַר שֶׁרַק בָּזֶה תָּלוּי עַתָּה כָּל חִיּוּתוֹ, מִי פֶּתִי וְלֹא יָבִין, שֶׁאִם יִתְעַצֵּל חַס וְשָׁלוֹם אַף רֶגַע אֶחָד, וְיַרְפֶּה יָדָיו מֵהִתְאַחֵז בּוֹ, יִטָּבַע תֵּכֶף.

כֵּן הַתּוֹרָה הַקְּדוֹשָׁה נִקְרֵאת "עֵץ חַיִּים", אִילָנָא דְחַיֵּי, שֶׁרַק אוֹתוֹ הָעֵת שֶׁהָאָדָם אָחוּז בְּאַהֲבָתָהּ, וְעוֹסֵק וּמְהַגֶּה בָּהּ בִּקְבִיעוּת, אָז הוּא חַי הַחַיִּים הָאֲמִתִּים הָעֶלְיוֹנִים, קָשׁוּר וְדָבוּק כִּבְיָכוֹל בְּחֵי הָעוֹלָמִים יִתְבָּרַךְ שְׁמוֹ, דְּקוּדְשָׁא בְּרִיךְ הוּא וְאוֹרַיְתָא חַד. וְאִם חַס

וְשָׁלוֹם יַזְנִיחַ תַּלְמוּדוֹ, וּפוֹרֵשׁ מִקְּבִיעוּת הָעֵסֶק בָּהּ, לַעֲסֹק בְּהַבְלֵי הָעוֹלָם וַהֲנָאוֹתָיו, הוּא נִפְסָק וְנִכְרָת מֵהַחַיִּים הָעֶלְיוֹנִים, וְטוֹבֵעַ עַצְמוֹ בַּמַּיִם הַזֵּדוֹנִים, רַחֲמָנָא לִיצְּלָן.

וּבַזֹּהַר וַיֵּצֵא קנ"ב ב', זַכָּאִין אִנּוּן יִשְׂרָאֵל, דְּקוּדְשָׁא בְּרִיךְ הוּא יָהַב לוֹן אוֹרַיְתָא דִּקְשׁוֹט, לְאִשְׁתַּדְּלָא בַּהּ יְמָמָא וְלֵילְיָא. דְּהָא כָּל מַאן דְּאִשְׁתַּדֵּל בְּאוֹרַיְתָא, אִית לֵיהּ חֵירוּ מִכֹּלָּא, חֵירוּ מִן מוֹתָא דְּלָא יָכְלָא לְשַׁלְטָאָה עָלֵיהּ כו', בְּגִין דְּכָל מַאן דְּאִשְׁתַּדֵּל בְּאוֹרַיְתָא, וְאִתְאֲחִיד בַּהּ, אִתְאֲחִיד בְּאִילָנָא דְּחַיֵּי, וְאִי אַרְפֵּי גַּרְמֵיהּ מֵאִילָנָא דְּחַיֵּי, הָא אִילָנָא דְּמוֹתָא שַׁרְיָא עָלוֹי, וְאִתְאֲחִיד בֵּיהּ, הֲדָא הוּא דִכְתִיב (משלי כד, י) "הִתְרַפִּיתָ בְּיוֹם צָרָה צַר כֹּחֶכָה" כו', עַיֵּן שָׁם. [אַשְׁרֵי הֵם יִשְׂרָאֵל, שֶׁהַקָּדוֹשׁ בָּרוּךְ הוּא נָתַן לָהֶם תּוֹרַת אֱמֶת לַעֲסֹק בָּהּ יוֹם וָלַיְלָה, כִּי כָּל מִי שֶׁעוֹסֵק בַּתּוֹרָה יֵשׁ לוֹ חֵרוּת מִכָּל דָּבָר, חֵרוּת מִן הַמָּוֶת, שֶׁאֵינוֹ יָכוֹל לִשְׁלֹט עָלָיו וכו', כִּי כָּל מִי שֶׁעוֹסֵק בַּתּוֹרָה וְנִתְאָחֵז נִתְאָחֵז בָּהּ בְּעֵץ הַחַיִּים, וְאִם מַרְפֶּה אֶת עַצְמוֹ מֵעֵץ הַחַיִּים הֲרֵי עֵץ הַמָּוֶת שׁוֹרֶה עָלָיו וְאוֹחֵז בּוֹ, וְזֶה שֶׁכָּתוּב "הִתְרַפִּיתָ" וכו' עי"ש.]

וְכַמָּה צָרִיךְ הָאָדָם, לִתְקֹעַ וְלִקְבֹּעַ זֶה הָעִנְיָן הַנּוֹרָא בְּמַחְשְׁבוֹת לִבּוֹ, בַּל תִּמּוֹט, שֶׁכָּל הָאָדָם וְחַיָּיו הוּא רַק אוֹתוֹ הָעֵת שֶׁהוּא דָּבוּק בַּתּוֹרָה הַקְּדוֹשָׁה, וּכְשֶׁמְּסַלֵּק וּפוֹרֵשׁ עַצְמוֹ הֵימֶנָּה, לַעֲסֹק בְּנוֹיוֹ שֶׁל זֶה הָעוֹלָם הַחָשׁוּךְ, הֲרֵי הוּא מָסוּר בְּיַד יִצְרוֹ, וְלָמָּה לוֹ חַיִּים, כִּי כְּבָר נִטְבַּע בַּמַּיִם הַזֵּדוֹנִים רַחֲמָנָא לִיצְּלָן, וְנִשְׁקַע בְּעִמְקֵי מְצוּלוֹת הָרַע, וְנֶחְשַׁב כְּמֵת מַמָּשׁ גַּם בְּעוֹדוֹ בְּזֶה הָעוֹלָם, הוֹלֵךְ מִדְּחִי אֶל דְּחִי, צַלְמָוֶת וְלֹא סְדָרִים, וְלֹא יֵדַע כִּי בְנַפְשׁוֹ הוּא.

וְלָזֹאת, הַתּוֹרָה עַצְמָהּ אֲמָרֶיהָ תֹּאמַר "וְחוֹטְאִי חוֹמֵס נַפְשׁוֹ" (משלי ח, לו) וּכְמוֹ שֶׁכָּתוּב (דברים ד, ט) "הִשָּׁמֶר לְךָ וּשְׁמֹר נַפְשְׁךָ מְאֹד פֶּן תִּשְׁכַּח אֶת הַדְּבָרִים" כו'. וּכְמַאֲמָרָם זִכְרוֹנָם לִבְרָכָה עַל זֶה (מנחות צ"ט ב') "מָשָׁל לְאָדָם שֶׁמָּסַר צִפּוֹר דְּרוֹר לְעַבְדּוֹ, אָמַר לוֹ, כִּמְדֻמֶּה אַתָּה שֶׁאִם אַתָּה מְאַבְּדָהּ אִיסָּר אֲנִי נוֹטֵל מִמְּךָ, נִשְׁמָתְךָ אֲנִי נוֹטֵל מִמְּךָ".

וְכַיָּדוּעַ מַאֲמָרָם זִכְרוֹנָם לִבְרָכָה עַל זֶה בִּדְבָרִים רַבָּה רֵישׁ פָּרָשָׁה ד', שֶׁאָמַר הַקָּדוֹשׁ בָּרוּךְ הוּא לָאָדָם, נֵרִי בְּיָדְךָ, וְנֵרְךָ בְּיָדִי, אִם שָׁמַרְתָּ אֶת נֵרִי, אֲנִי מְשַׁמֵּר אֶת נֵרְךָ, וְאִם לֹא שָׁמַרְתָּ אֶת נֵרִי כו', עַיֵּן שָׁם. וְכֵן הוּא בְּתַנְחוּמָא פָּרָשַׁת תִּשָּׂא, וּבְמִדְרַשׁ תְּהִלִּים מִזְמוֹר ז', עַיֵּן שָׁם:

פֶּרֶק ל"ד

וּמֵעֵת חָרְבַּן בֵּית קָדְשֵׁנוּ, וְגָלוּ הַבָּנִים מֵעַל שֻׁלְחַן אֲבִיהֶם, שְׁכִינַת כְּבוֹדוֹ יִתְבָּרַךְ אַזְלָא וּמִתְרַכְּא כִּבְיָכוֹל וְלֹא תַּרְגִּיעַ, וְאֵין שִׁיּוּר רַק הַתּוֹרָה הַזֹּאת, כְּשֶׁיִּשְׂרָאֵל עַם הַקֹּדֶשׁ מְצַפְצְפִים וּמְהַגִּים בָּהּ כָּרָאוּי, הֵן הֵמָּה לָהּ לְמִקְדָּשׁ מְעַט, לְהָכִין אוֹתָהּ וּלְסַעֲדָהּ, וְשׁוֹרָה עִמָּהֶם, וּפוֹרֶשֶׂת כְּנָפֶיהָ עֲלֵיהֶם כִּבְיָכוֹל, וּבֵין כָּךְ אִית נַיְחָא מְעַט כו'. כְּמַאֲמָרָם זִכְרוֹנָם לִבְרָכָה בְּפֶרֶק קַמָּא דִּבְרָכוֹת (ח, א): "מִיּוֹם שֶׁחָרַב בֵּית הַמִּקְדָּשׁ אֵין לוֹ לְהַקָּדוֹשׁ בָּרוּךְ הוּא בְּעוֹלָמוֹ אֶלָּא אַרְבַּע אַמּוֹת שֶׁל הֲלָכָה בִּלְבַד".

וְאָמְרוּ שָׁם (ברכות ו, א) עוֹד, מִנַּיִן שֶׁאֲפִלּוּ אֶחָד שֶׁיּוֹשֵׁב וְעוֹסֵק בַּתּוֹרָה, שֶׁשְּׁכִינָה

שְׁרוּיָה עִמּוֹ, שֶׁנֶּאֱמַר (שמות כ, כא) "בְּכָל הַמָּקוֹם אֲשֶׁר אַזְכִּיר" וכו'. וּבְמִשְׁלֵי רַבְּתָא סוֹף פָּרָשָׁה ח' "כִּי מוֹצְאִי מָצָא חַיִּים", אָמַר הַקָּדוֹשׁ בָּרוּךְ הוּא, כָּל מִי שֶׁהוּא מָצוּי בְּדִבְרֵי תוֹרָה, אַף אֲנִי מָצוּי לוֹ בְּכָל מָקוֹם, לְכָךְ נֶאֱמַר "כִּי מוֹצְאִי מָצָא חַיִּים".

וּבַזֹּהַר בָּלָק ר"ב א', פָּתַח וְאָמַר "כִּי תָצוּר אֶל עִיר כו', לֹא תַשְׁחִית אֶת עֵצָהּ" (דברים כ, יט), דָּא תַּלְמִיד חָכָם, דְּאִיהוּ אִילָנָא דְּחַיֵּי כו', "כִּי מִמֶּנּוּ תֹאכֵל", וְכִי הַהוּא מְחַבְּלָא אָכִיל מִנֵּיהּ, לָא, אֶלָּא "כִּי מִמֶּנּוּ תֹאכֵל", הַהוּא טִינָרָא תַּקִּיפָא, הַהִיא דְּכָל רוּחִין תַּקִּיפִין קַדִּישִׁין נַפְקִין מִנָּהּ, דְּלֵית הֲנָאָה וְתֵיאוּבְתָּא לְרוּחַ קוּדְשָׁא בְּהַאי עָלְמָא אֶלָּא אוֹרַיְתָא, דְּהַהוּא זַכָּאָה כִּבְיָכוֹל אִיהוּ מְפַרְנֵס לָהּ, וְיָהִיב לָהּ מְזוֹנָא בְּהַאי עָלְמָא, יַתִּיר מִכָּל קָרְבָּנִין דְּעַלְמָא כו', וּמִיּוֹמָא דְּאִתְחָרִיב בֵּית מַקְדְּשָׁא, וּבָטְלוּ קָרְבָּנִין, לֵית לֵיהּ לְקוּדְשָׁא בְּרִיךְ הוּא אֶלָּא אִנּוּן מִלִּין דְּאוֹרַיְתָא, וְאוֹרַיְתָא דְּאִתְחַדְּשַׁת בְּפוּמֵיהּ. בְּגִין כָּךְ "כִּי מִמֶּנּוּ תֹאכֵל", וְלֵית מְזוֹנָא בְּהַאי עָלְמָא אֶלָּא מִמֶּנּוּ, וְאִנּוּן דִּכְוָתֵיהּ כו', "כִּי הָאָדָם עֵץ הַשָּׂדֶה", דָּא אִקְרֵי אָדָם דְּאִשְׁתְּמוֹדַע עֵלָּא וְתַתָּא, "עֵץ הַשָּׂדֶה", אִילָנָא רַבְרְבָא וְתַקִּיף, דְּהַהִיא שָׂדֶה אֲשֶׁר בֵּרְכוֹ ה', דְּסָמִיךְ עֲלֵיהּ, אִילָן דְּאִשְׁתְּמוֹדַע לְהַהוּא שָׂדֶה תָּדִיר.

[פָּתַח וְאָמַר, "כִּי תָצוּר עַל עִיר וכו' לֹא תַשְׁחִית אֶת עֵצָהּ", זֶה תַּלְמִיד חָכָם שֶׁהוּא עֵץ הַחַיִּים. "כִּי מִמֶּנּוּ תֹאכֵל", וְכִי אוֹתוֹ מְחַבֵּל אוֹכֵל מִמֶּנּוּ, אֶלָּא "כִּי מִמֶּנּוּ תֹאכֵל", אוֹתוֹ הַסֶּלַע הַקָּשֶׁה, אוֹתָהּ שֶׁכָּל הָרוּחוֹת הַתַּקִּיפִים הַקְּדוֹשִׁים יוֹצְאִים מִמֶּנָּה, כִּי אֵין הֲנָאָה וּתְשׁוּקָה לְרוּחַ הַקֹּדֶשׁ בָּעוֹלָם הַזֶּה, אֶלָּא הַתּוֹרָה שֶׁל אוֹתוֹ צַדִּיק כִּבְיָכוֹל, הוּא מְפַרְנֵס אוֹתָהּ וְנוֹתֵן לָהּ מְזוֹנוֹת בָּעוֹלָם הַזֶּה יוֹתֵר מִכָּל הַקָּרְבָּנוֹת שֶׁבָּעוֹלָם, וּמִיּוֹם שֶׁחָרַב בֵּית הַמִּקְדָּשׁ וּבָטְלוּ הַקָּרְבָּנוֹת אֵין לוֹ לְהַקָּדוֹשׁ בָּרוּךְ הוּא אֶלָּא דִּבְרֵי תוֹרָה וְהַתּוֹרָה הַמִּתְחַדֶּשֶׁת בְּפִיו, מִשּׁוּם זֶה "כִּי מִמֶּנּוּ תֹאכֵל", וְאֵין לָהּ מָזוֹן בָּעוֹלָם הַזֶּה אֶלָּא מִמֶּנּוּ וּמֵאֵלּוּ שֶׁכָּמוֹהוּ וכו'. "כִּי הָאָדָם עֵץ הַשָּׂדֶה", זֶה נִקְרָא אָדָם הַנּוֹדָע לְמַעְלָה וּלְמַטָּה, "עֵץ הַשָּׂדֶה" אִילָן גָּדוֹל וְחָזָק שֶׁל אוֹתוֹ "שָׂדֶה אֲשֶׁר בֵּרְכוֹ ה'" שֶׁהִיא סְמוּכָה עָלָיו, שֶׁהוּא עֵץ הַנּוֹדָע לַשָּׂדֶה הַהוּא תָּמִיד.]

וְזֶהוּ גַּם כֵּן הַמְכֻוָּן הַפְּנִימִי בְּמַאֲמָרָם זִכְרוֹנָם לִבְרָכָה בְּפֶרֶק קַמָּא דְּתַעֲנִית (ז, א), מַאי דִּכְתִיב "כִּי הָאָדָם עֵץ הַשָּׂדֶה כו', כִּי מִמֶּנּוּ תֹאכֵל" כו', (שם) אִם תַּלְמִיד חָכָם הָגוּן הוּא "מִמֶּנּוּ תֹאכֵל" כו', וְאִם לָאו כו'.

וּבַזֹּהַר וַיִּשְׁלַח קע"ד ב', וְהֵיךְ יִתְתַּקֵּף בַּר נַשׁ בֵּיהּ בְּקוּדְשָׁא בְּרִיךְ הוּא, יִתְקִיף בְּאוֹרַיְתָא, דְּכָל מַאן דְּאִתְתְּקַף בְּאוֹרַיְתָא אִתְתְּקַף בְּאִילָנָא דְּחַיֵּי, וְכִבְיָכוֹל יָהִיב תּוּקְפָּא לִכְנֶסֶת יִשְׂרָאֵל לְאִתְתַּקְּפָא, וְאִי הוּא יִתְרַפֵּי, מַה כְּתִיב (משלי כד, י) "הִתְרַפִּיתָ", אִי אִיהוּ אִתְרַפֵּי מִן אוֹרַיְתָא "בְּיוֹם צָרָה צַר כֹּחֶכָה", בְּיוֹמָא דְּיֵיתֵי לֵיהּ עָקוּ, כִּבְיָכוֹל דָּחִיק לָהּ לִשְׁכִינְתָּא, דְּאִיהִי חֵילָא דְּעַלְמָא. [וְאֵיךְ יִתְגַּבֵּר הָאָדָם בְּקוּדְשָׁא בְּרִיךְ הוּא, שֶׁיִּתְגַּבֵּר בַּתּוֹרָה, כִּי כָּל מִי שֶׁיִּתְגַּבֵּר בַּתּוֹרָה הוּא מִתְגַּבֵּר בְּעֵץ הַחַיִּים, וְכִבְיָכוֹל הוּא נוֹתֵן כֹּחַ לִכְנֶסֶת יִשְׂרָאֵל לְהִתְחַזֵּק, וְאִם הוּא מִתְרַפֶּה מִתּוֹרָה מַה כָּתוּב, "הִתְרַפִּיתָ" — אִם הוּא מִתְרַפֶּה מִתּוֹרָה, "בְּיוֹם צָרָה צַר כֹּחֶכָה" — בְּיוֹם שֶׁתָּבוֹא לוֹ צָרָה כִּבְיָכוֹל הוּא דּוֹחֵק אֶת הַשְּׁכִינָה שֶׁהִיא כֹּחוֹ שֶׁל הָעוֹלָם.]

וּבְעֵסֶק הַתּוֹרָה הוּא עוֹשֶׂה כִּבְיָכוֹל דִּירָה לוֹ יִתְבָּרֵךְ בַּתַּחְתּוֹנִים, לְשַׁכֵּן כָּבוֹד בָּאָרֶץ יִתְבָּרֵךְ שְׁמוֹ. כְּמַאֲמָרָם זִכְרוֹנָם לִבְרָכָה בִּשְׁמוֹת רַבָּה פָּרָשָׁה ל"ג, עַד שֶׁלֹּא נִתְּנָה תּוֹרָה לְיִשְׂרָאֵל, "וּמֹשֶׁה עָלָה אֶל הָאֱלֹקִים", מִשֶּׁנִּתְּנָה תּוֹרָה, אָמַר הַקָּדוֹשׁ בָּרוּךְ הוּא "וְעָשׂוּ לִי מִקְדָּשׁ וְשָׁכַנְתִּי בְּתוֹכָם".

וְדַי בְּדְבָרֵינוּ אֵלֶּה לַמַּשְׂכִּיל, אֲשֶׁר מִתּוֹכָם יִרְאֶה וְיָבִין דַּרְכּוֹ בַּקֹּדֶשׁ, וְיֹאחֵז צֶדֶק דַּרְכּוֹ, לַעֲמֹד עַל מִשְׁמֶרֶת הָעֵסֶק בַּתּוֹרָה הַקְּדוֹשָׁה, כָּל הַיָּמִים אֲשֶׁר הוּא חַי, וְלִהְיוֹת מָאוֹס בָּרַע וּבָחוֹר בַּטּוֹב, לוֹ וּלְכָל הַבְּרִיּוֹת וְהָעוֹלָמוֹת כֻּלָּם, לַעֲשׂוֹת נַחַת רוּחַ לְיוֹצְרוֹ וּבוֹרְאוֹ יִתְבָּרֵךְ:

וִיהִי רָצוֹן מִלְּפָנָיו יִתְבָּרֵךְ שְׁמוֹ, שֶׁיִּפְתַּח לִבֵּנוּ בְּתוֹרָתוֹ, וְיָשֵׂם בְּלִבֵּנוּ אַהֲבָתוֹ וְיִרְאָתוֹ, וִישַׁלֵּם כַּוָּנָתוֹ בִּבְרִיאַת עוֹלָמוֹ, שֶׁיְּתֻקַּן עוֹלָם בְּמַלְכוּת שַׁדַּי, וְיֵדַע כָּל פָּעוּל כוּ', וִיקַבְּלוּ כֻּלָּם עַל מַלְכוּתוֹ יִתְבָּרֵךְ, כְּפִי הָרָצוֹן הָעֶלְיוֹן יִתְבָּרֵךְ, וְיִהְיֶה ה' אֶחָד וּשְׁמוֹ אֶחָד:

אָמֵן כֵּן יְהִי רָצוֹן:

תַּם וְנִשְׁלָם

בכי טוב ג' לסדר והי' האיש אשר יבחר ה', כ"ו סיון

"עיני בנאמני ארץ" לפרט. (תקפ"ד)

בנל"ך. ברוך אתה ה' למדני חקיך:

גַּל עֵינַי וְאַבִּיטָה נִפְלָאוֹת מִתּוֹרָתֶךָ.